Italy and the Middle East

Italy and the Middle East

Geopolitics, Dialogue and Power during the Cold War

Edited by
Luciano Monzali and Paolo Soave

Foreword by
Antonio Varsori

I.B. TAURIS
LONDON • NEW YORK • OXFORD • NEW DELHI • SYDNEY

I.B. TAURIS
Bloomsbury Publishing Plc
50 Bedford Square, London, WC1B 3DP, UK
1385 Broadway, New York, NY 10018, USA
29 Earlsfort Terrace, Dublin 2, Ireland

BLOOMSBURY, I.B. TAURIS and the I.B. Tauris logo are trademarks of
Bloomsbury Publishing Plc

First published in Great Britain 2021
This paperback edition published in 2022

Copyright © Luciano Monzali, Paolo Soave and Contributors, 2021

Luciano Monzali and Paolo Soave have asserted their right under the Copyright, Designs and Patents Act, 1988, to be identified as Editors of this work.

Copyright Individual Chapters © 2021 Luciano Monzali, Paolo Soave, Joseph A. Bongiorno, Matteo Gerlini, Federico Imperato, Silvio Labbate, Roberta La Fortezza, Azzedine Layachi, Arturo Marzano, Lorenzo Medici, Rosario Milano, Bruno Pierri, Luca Riccardi, Giuseppe Spagnulo, Antonio Varsori

Series cover design: Adriana Brioso
Cover image © [top] Bettino Craxi, Felipe Gonzalez and Giulio Andreotti (© Alberto Roveri/Mondadori/Getty Images); [bottom] Hafez al Assad, Muammar al-Qaddafi and Yasser Arafat (© Henri Bureau/Corbis/VCG/Getty Images)

All rights reserved. No part of this publication may be reproduced or transmitted in any form or by any means, electronic or mechanical, including photocopying, recording, or any information storage or retrieval system, without prior permission in writing from the publishers.

Bloomsbury Publishing Plc does not have any control over, or responsibility for, any third-party websites referred to or in this book. All internet addresses given in this book were correct at the time of going to press. The author and publisher regret any inconvenience caused if addresses have changed or sites have ceased to exist, but can accept no responsibility for any such changes.

A catalogue record for this book is available from the British Library.

A catalog record for this book is available from the Library of Congress.

ISBN: HB: 978-1-8386-0693-0
PB: 978-0-7556-3659-4
ePDF: 978-1-8386-0696-1
eBook: 978-1-8386-0695-4

Typeset by Newgen KnowledgeWorks Pvt. Ltd., Chennai, India

To find out more about our authors and books visit www.bloomsbury.com and sign up for our newsletters.

Contents

List of Contributors	vii
Foreword *Antonio Varsori*	xi
List of Archives, Archival Collections, Collections of Documents and Abbreviations	xvi
Introduction: The foreign policy of a middle power at the geopolitical crossroads *Luciano Monzali and Paolo Soave*	1
Part 1 The Middle East in a period of change	7
1 Footholds in the sand – the Middle East and the Cold War, 1973–93: An introductory chapter and review *Joseph A. Bongiorno*	9
2 The Middle East beyond the Cold War: The case of the Israeli–Palestinian conflict, 1989–93 *Arturo Marzano*	25
Part 2 A bridge towards the Arab world: Italian regionalism between the Atlantic Alliance and Europe	41
3 The Middle East in Italian foreign policy: A historical perspective *Luciano Monzali*	43
4 Italy's foreign policy and the Palestinian question *Luca Riccardi*	93
5 Cultural diplomacy in the Middle East: The Italian contribution *Lorenzo Medici*	109
6 The EU, Italy and the Middle East: The Euro-Arab dialogue *Silvio Labbate*	123
7 Italy and the Lebanese 'civil' war *Roberta La Fortezza*	139
8 The Sigonella crisis: The Middle East and the Atlantic alliance *Matteo Gerlini*	153

9 Gaddafi and the troubled relations with Italy *Paolo Soave* 169

10 Italy and Algeria: A resilient connection *Azzedine Layachi* 187

Part 3 Italy and the greater Middle East 201

11 Italy and Turkey: Between Europe and the Middle East (1969–93) *Federico Imperato* 203

12 Partners in rivalry: Britain, ENI and the Tehran oil agreements of 1971 *Bruno Pierri* 219

13 Italy and the Iranian Revolution *Rosario Milano* 235

14 Italy, King Zahir and the Soviet occupation of Afghanistan, 1979–89 *Luciano Monzali* 249

15 Italy and Pakistan, 1971–91 *Giuseppe Spagnulo* 265

Bibliography 291
Index 295

Contributors

Joseph A. Bongiorno is Associate Professor of History at St John's University (NY-USA). His academic and research interests include Italian history, Austrian history, diplomatic history and international law and organization. He is also a practicing attorney. He resides with his family in Connecticut (USA).

Matteo Gerlini is Guest Lecturer of History and Policy of Scientific Research at the University of Rome La Sapienza. He is an expert of the Independent Scientific Evaluation Group in the NATO Science for Peace and Security Program. As a diplomatic historian, he wrote *Il dirottamento dell'Achille Lauro e i suoi inattesi e sorprendenti risvolti* (2016) and *Sansone e la Guerra Fredda: La capacita nucleare israeliana tra le due superpotenze* (2010).

Federico Imperato (PhD) obtained the National Scientific Qualification as Associate Professor in History of International Relations. He participates in the teaching and research activities of the chair of History of International Relations at the Political Sciences Department in the University of Bari 'Aldo Moro'. His research interests concern the history of Italian foreign relations during the Liberal and Republican periods. He is author of the following monographs: *Aldo Moro e la pace nella sicurezza. La politica estera del centro-sinistra (1963–1968)* (2011) and *Aldo Moro, l'Italia e la diplomazia multilaterale. Momenti e problemi* (2013).

Silvio Labbate is Adjunct Professor of Contemporary History at the Department of History, Social Science and Human Studies (University of Salento). He has a PhD in History of International Relations (University of Rome 'Sapienza'). He has written the book *Illusioni mediterranee: Il dialogo euro-arabo* (2016) and *Il governo dell'energia: L'Italia dal petrolio al nucleare,1945–1975* (2016). He has written many articles for various international journals (*Clio, Ventunesimo Secolo, Nuova Rivista Storica, Italia Contemporanea, European Review of History* and *Journal of European Integration History*).

Roberta La Fortezza earned a PhD in Science of Human Relationships from the University of Bari 'Aldo Moro'. Her research interests are centred on Middle East history and geopolitical dynamics, with particular attention to Lebanon. Currently, she works as an analyst for the MENA (Middle East and North Africa) region at a private consulting society.

Azzedine Layachi is Professor in the Department of Government and Politics at St John's University in New York City and Rome. He teaches courses on several topics, including migration, the Middle East, Africa and international law. He received a PhD and master's degree in Political Science from New York University, and a bachelor's degree from the Institut des Etudes Politiques (IEP) of the University of Algiers, Algeria. He is the author of several books, journal articles and book chapters on North Africa, the Middle East and US foreign policy. He is Senior Fellow at the Vincentian Institute for Social Action, New York, and is a member of the Advisory Board of the Maghreb Center, Washington, DC.

Arturo Marzano is Associate Professor at the Department of Civilization and Forms of Knowledge, University of Pisa. His research mainly deals with history of Judaism, Zionism, the Israeli–Palestinian conflict and the relationship between Italy and the Middle East in the twentieth century. Among his main publications, there are the volumes *Una terra per rinascere. Gli ebrei italiani e l'immigrazione in Palestina prima della guerra (1920–1940)* [A Land to Be Born Again: The Italian Jews and Their Migration to Palestine before the War (1920–1940)] (2003) and *Onde fasciste. La propaganda araba di Radio Bari (1934–43)* [Fascist Waves: Radio Bari's Arab Propaganda (1934–43)] (2015).

Lorenzo Medici is Associate Professor of History of International Relations at the University of Perugia. Among his main publications is *Dalla propaganda alla cooperazione: Le origini della diplomazia culturale italiana nel secondo dopoguerra* [From Propaganda to Cooperation: The Origins of Italian Cultural Diplomacy after the Second World War] (2009). His current research focuses on the role of culture in international relations.

Rosario Milano is an Associate Professor in History of International Relations, Societies and Institutions according to the National Scientific Qualification and collaborates with the chair of History of International Relations at the University of Bari 'Aldo Moro'. His main scientific interests are focused on the history of Iran's international relations in the nineteenth century, especially in the field of hydrocarbons and with particular reference to the relationship with the Italian Republic, and the history of relations between Italy and the Western Balkan countries.

Luciano Monzali is Full Professor of History of International Relations at the University of Bari 'Aldo Moro'. He is author of many books and studies on Italian foreign policy in the nineteenth and in the twentieth centuries.

Bruno Pierri, PhD in History, Institutions and International Relations of Extra-European Countries at the University of Pisa, former research fellow at the University of Salento, gained the US State Department *Exchange Visitor Program* scholarship in 2007. He has written numerous essays and articles, a few of which are in English. He has written the monographs *Giganti petroliferi e grandi consumatori* (2015) and *Guerra fredda e illusioni imperiali* (2007). He has taught the English language at the University of Salento and is now Adjunct Professor of History of Italian Foreign Policy at the University of Parma, as well as an English language teacher at I.S.S. 'Racchetti-Da Vinci' of Crema. Most of his research interests are oriented to American and British policy towards the Middle East and Southern Africa, but he is also working on the post-Cold War scenario in the Euro-Asian area.

Luca Riccardi is Full Professor of History of International Relations at University of Cassino (Italy). He has written many books and essays about Italian foreign policy in the nineteenth and twentieth centuries.

Paolo Soave, PhD, is Associate Professor in History of International Relations at the Alma Mater Studiorum-University of Bologna, Forlì Campus. His main research interests are focused on the history of Italian foreign policy and Italian colonialism, US foreign policy, the Cold War and the history of the Mediterranean. Among his recent publications are *Una vittoria mutilata? L'Italia e la Conferenza della Pace di Parigi* (2020); 'Power vs. Diplomacy, Globalism vs. Regionalism: United States and Italy Facing International Terrorism. The Sidra Crisis, 1986', *Nuova Rivista Storica* I (2017), 161–79; *Fra Reagan e Gheddafi. La politica estera italiana e l'escalation libico-americana degli anni '80* (2017); and *La democrazia allo specchio. L'Italia e il regime militare ellenico (1967–1974)* (2014).

Giuseppe Spagnulo, PhD, is a scholar in History of International Relations and Contemporary History at the Political Sciences Department of the University of Bari. His main scientific and research interests are focused on the history of Southern Italy, diplomatic history and Italian foreign policy towards the Middle East and the Indian subcontinent.

Antonio Varsori is Full Professor of History of International Relations at the University of Padua. He is the president of the Italian Society of International History, member of the Committee for the Publication of the Italian Diplomatic Documents at the Italian Foreign Ministry and editor of the journal *Ventunesimo Secolo*. Among his recent publications are *Mogadiscio 1948 un eccidio di italiani fra decolonizzazione e guerra fredda*, with A. Urbano (2019); *Le relazioni internazionali dopo la guerra fredda 1989–2017* (2018); *Italy in the International System from Détente to the End of the Cold War*, ed. with B. Zaccaria (2018); and *Storia internazionale dal 1919 a oggi* (2015).

Foreword

Antonio Varsori

Since national unification, Italy's rulers have pursued a high international profile, trying to make Italy become a new great power. Such a goal was a fundamental part of the Risorgimento's ideals: if a new nation had to be created through a hard and bloody struggle against Austrian domination and reactionary kings, such a struggle and its ensuing sacrifices had to lead to the rebirth of Italy's past glory, from the Roman Empire to the centre of Christianity to the greatness of the Renaissance. But such an ambitious goal contrasted with the reality of a weak and backward nation, which during its early life had to struggle in order to survive and, until 1882, when Italy became a part of the Triple Alliance as a junior partner of both the German and Austro-Hungarian empires, the new nation had been isolated in a largely hostile international system.[1]

In spite of all of its weaknesses, Italy's struggle to be recognized as a great power implied an expansionist and aggressive foreign policy, especially as far as the Mediterranean and the African continent were concerned. It is well known that Italy's early ambitions had focused on Tunisia, although they were quickly frustrated by the French decision to impose Paris's protectorate over this territory. During the following decades, Italy tried to join the most powerful European powers in the 'scramble for Africa', with contrasting fortunes: although the Italian state was able to create its first colonies in Eritrea and in Somaliland, its attempts at an expansion towards the Abyssinian Empire were frustrated as a consequence of the military defeats at Dogali and at Adwa.[2] During the first decade of the twentieth century, however, the Italian state experienced a period of industrial take-off, economic growth, social transformation and a partial stabilization of its political system. From the diplomatic viewpoint, while maintaining its role in the Triple Alliance, Italian diplomats were able to work out some agreements with France, Britain and Russia in order to achieve recognition of Italy's interest in a future expansion towards the last vestige of the Ottoman Empire in North Africa.[3] In October 1911 Italy declared war on the Ottoman Porte and, although the military campaign was more difficult than had been hoped, was able to impose its rule over Libya and to maintain control of the Dodecanese islands, thereby enlarging its African empire and strengthening its position in the Mediterranean Sea.[4]

In summer 1914, with the outbreak of the First World War, the Italian government, led by Antonio Salandra, chose neutrality, but in May 1915, after signing the London Treaty with the Entente powers, Rome joined the Allies in their war against the Central Empires.[5] Although Italy pursued a sort of autonomous war against

Austria-Hungary – only in 1916 did Italy declare war on Germany – and its war aims mainly focused on the annexation – 'liberation' – of some areas along its northern and eastern borders (Trentino, South Tyrol, the Istrian peninsula and the Dalmatian Coast), the Italian authorities aimed at complete control of the Adriatic Sea, owing to an influence over Albania; and in the London Treaty there were references to an influence in the Anatolian peninsula to the detriment of the Ottoman Empire, thus strengthening Italy's position in the Eastern Mediterranean, a sort of early move towards the Near East. In the immediate post-war period, however, Italy's ambitions had to be reassessed: the birth of Turkish nationalism, led by Kemal Ataturk, convinced the Italians to give up their influence in the Anatolian peninsula, although in the following years Italian control of the Dodecanese islands would be confirmed, and Italian troops left Albania, although during the 1920s the new Balkan state was compelled to resort to Italy's patronage.[6]

During the Fascist period, especially in the mid-1930s, Italy renewed its expansionist policy on the African continent, which led to the war against Ethiopia and its annexation to the Italian Empire.[7] But Mussolini pointed out Italy's ambition to create a new 'Mare nostrum' in the Mediterranean, and he focused his ambitions on the Middle East in the hope of destroying Britain's 'informal empire'. Such a policy was mainly based on propaganda initiatives, such as the broadcasts in Arab from an 'ad hoc' radio station, 'Radio Bari', and the support of various anti-British nationalist movements, from Egypt to Palestine, Iraq to Yemen.[8]

The alliance with Germany, the involvement in the Second World War and the military defeats suffered as early as autumn 1940 revealed that Italy's aspiration to become a great power had been a tragic bluff that led to total defeat,[9] its military occupation and a punitive peace treaty, the consequence of which was the loss of some border areas (e.g. the Istrian peninsula, Fiume, Zara, etc.), as well as of its African empire with the exception of Somaliland which, in 1948, owing to the decision by the United Nations, became a ten-year Italian trusteeship under the supervision of the UN.[10] In spite of everything, most of the decision makers in Republican Italy (both leading politicians and diplomats) thought that the new democratic nation had to aim at being recognized as a middle-rank power that could exert some influence in both Europe and an enlarged Mediterranean, which would include some part of the Middle East and the African continent. Obviously, such aims were tied to political and economic interests. In fact, Italy hoped that its policy could profit from two contemporary historical dynamics: on the one hand, the Cold War, which would lead to Italy becoming an actor in the Western system under the American hegemony and, on the other, the fast-paced crisis of the British and French empires, which offered room for manoeuvre to the Italians, especially in the Arab world. Actually, during the late 1940s and the first half of the 1950s, Prime Minister Alcide De Gasperi and his foreign minister, Count Carlo Sforza, focused their attention and energies mainly in imposing Italy as a relevant actor in the new American-led Western system, and in strengthening the nation's position in the emerging European integration process.[11] Even in these difficult years, when Italy had to reconstruct both its role and its image in the international system, Italian diplomats carefully analysed the development in the Arab world as they hoped that in the near future Italy would have a chance to become a relevant player in this area.¹² The mid-1950s, especially the final crisis of the French and British empires, marked a turning point in Italy's Mediterranean and Middle East policy, which became an important aspect of its international role, as most chapters of this volume demonstrate.¹³ The volume moreover argues that economy and policy were the two major interests/issues in Italy's initiatives towards this area, a part of the world which, after the Suez crisis and the Six-Day War, became more and more an issue at stake in the 'global Cold War' between the United States and the Soviet Union. As is pointed out in this volume, it was not an easy task for the Italian authorities to reconcile Italy's loyalty to the Western alliance and its aspirations at creating friendly relations with most Arab countries, especially from an economic viewpoint, when most nations of the Middle East were influenced by strong anti-Western, nationalist and anti-Israeli feelings. The 1969 nationalist revolution in Libya was a further reason for concern to Italian politicians and diplomats, although the expulsion of Italian citizens from the North African nation did not impede the concluding of advantageous economic agreements between the Tripoli regime and important Italian firms.¹⁴

The Yom Kippur War and the first 'oil shock' that severely hit the Italian economy were further serious problems, but also opportunities for strengthening Italy's interest in the Arab world, whose oil Italy desperately needed for its economy, not to forget the Western powers' increasing concern about the stronger Russian naval presence in the Mediterranean.¹⁵

As several chapters in the volume clearly demonstrate, Italian authorities tried to reconcile their position in the Western alliance while maintaining close dialogue with the Arab world. In this connection, Italy showed some understanding towards Arab claims, especially as far as the Palestinian question was concerned, and aimed at favouring diplomatic compromise solutions and developing strong relations with some moderate Arab countries, especially Egypt. In the background there was the vital interest in maintaining, in some cases in strengthening, closer economic relations, even with some uneasy partners such as Libya and Iraq.

During the 1980s, the Mediterranean and the Arab world were deeply involved in the 'new' Cold War, owing to the policies pursued by the Reagan administration, while some local crises became even more serious (Lebanon, Palestinian terrorism, Iraq-Iran war, etc.). In this decade, after coping with the crises of the 1970s, Italy appeared able to develop a more active and consistent foreign policy, from NATO to the European Community, to the Arab world, as was demonstrated by Italy's participation in the multinational peace-keeping force in Lebanon and its leaders' good relationship with the PLO, especially Yasser Arafat. Last but not least, in spite of the military confrontation between the United States and the Libyan regime, Italy was able to maintain fruitful economic relations with Tripoli.¹⁶

The end of the Cold War and the ensuing institutional and economic crisis that characterized Italy during the first half of the 1990s marked a turning point in Italy's policy towards the Arab world.¹⁷ Although Italy has aimed, with some results, at maintaining good relations with this part of the world, its foreign policy has been more and more involved in the European Union context, whereby now it is difficult to separate foreign policy from domestic issues and, especially in most recent times, the southern shore of the Mediterranean and the Middle East are perceived as sources of serious destabilization from the terrorist threat to the migration issue. So, although Italy needs to develop an active role in both the Mediterranean and the Middle East, it is difficult to determine clear-cut points of reference in Italy's most recent foreign policy, although such uneasiness is characteristic not only of Italy's position, but also of the whole European Union, whose policies towards the Mediterranean's southern shore and the Middle East often appear very uncertain.[18]

The present volume, which presents contributions by several Italian scholars of international history, largely based on first-hand sources from various Italian and foreign archives, offers a thoughtful historical analysis of a foreign policy not well known to non-Italian readers, but which is a fundamental point of reference to understand the relationship between Italy and the Arab world from the post-war period up until today.

Notes

1 Federico Chabod, *Storia della politica estera italiana dal 1870 al 1896: Le premesse* (Bari: Laterza, 1951); and Emilio Gentile, *La Grande Italia. Il mito della nazione nel XX secolo* (Rome: Laterza, 2009).
2 In general on Italy's colonial policy, see Nicola Labanca, *Oltremare. Storia dell'espansione coloniale italiana* (Bologna: Il Mulino, 2002). See also Luciano Monzali, *Il colonialismo nella politica estera italiana 1878–1949: Momenti e protagonisti* (Rome: Società Dante Alighieri, 2017).
3 Richard Webster, *L'imperialismo industriale italiano 1908–1915. Studio sul prefascismo* (Turin: Einaudi, 1975); R. J. B. Bosworth, *Italy the Least of the Great Powers: Italian Foreign Policy before the First World War* (London: Cambridge University Press, 1979).
4 Luca Micheletta and Andrea Ungari (eds), *L'Italia e la guerra di Libia cent'ani dopo* (Rome: Studium, 2013).
5 Antonio Varsori, *Radioso maggio. Come l'Italia entrò in guerra* (Bologna: Il Mulino, 2015).
6 On Albania, see Pietro Pastorelli, *L'Albania nella politica estera italiana 1914–1920* (Naples: Jovene, 1970); and Pastorelli, *Italia e Albania 1924–1927. Origini diplomatiche del trattato di Roma del 22 novembre 1927* (Florence: Rivista di studi politici internazionali, 1967). On Italy's policy towards Turkey, see Fiorella Perrone, *La politica estera italiana e la dissoluzione dell'impero ottomano (1914–1923)* (Lecce: i libri di Icaro, 2010).
7 John F. Coverdale, *I fascisti italiani alla guerra di Spagna* (Rome: Laterza, 1977).
8 Nir Arieli, *Fascist Italy and the Middle East, 1933–1940* (Basingstoke: Palgrave, 2010); Arturo Marzano, *Onde fasciste. La propaganda araba di Radio Bari (1934–1943)* (Rome: Carocci, 2015).
9 Among the numerous works on Italy during the Second World War and its defeat, see, for example, Renzo De Felice, *Mussolini l'alleato (1940–1945), L'Italia in Guerra 1940–1943*, 2 vols (Turin: Einaudi, 1990); Elena Aga Rossi, *L'Italia nella sconfitta: Politica interna e situazione internazionale durante la seconda Guerra mondiale* (Naples: ESI, 1985); Aga Rossi, *Una nazione allo sbando. L'armistizio italiano del settembre 1943* (Bologna: Il Mulino, 1993).

10 For a synthesis, see Sara Lorenzini, *L'Italia e il trattato di pace del 1947* (Bologna: Il Mulino, 2007).
11 Antonio Varsori, 'La dimensione internazionale della transizione postbellica in Italia (1943–1949)', *Il Politico* LXXXII, no. 3 (September/December 2018), 124–59.
12 Matteo Pizzigallo (ed.), *L'Italia e il Mediterraneo orientale (1946–1950)* (Milan: Franco Angeli, 2004); Matteo Pizzigallo, *La diplomazia italiana e i paesi arabi del'Oriente mediterraneo (1946–1952)* (Milan: Franco Angeli, 2008).
13 See also Elena Calandri, *Il Mediterraneo e la difesa dell'Occidente 1947–1956: Eredità imperiali e logiche di guerra fredda* (Florence: Il Maestrale, 1997); Bruna Bagnato, *Petrolio e politica: Mattei in Marocco* (Florence: Polistampa, 2004); Bagnato, *L'Italia e la guerra d'Algeria 1954–1962* (Soveria Mannelli: Rubbettino, 2012).
14 On the relations between Italy and Libya, see also Arturo Varvelli, *L'Italia e l'ascesa di Gheddafi. La cacciata degli italiani, le armi e il petrolio (1969–1974)* (Milan: Baldini Castoldi Dalai, 2009); Federico Cresti and Massimiliano Cricco, *Storia della Libia contemporanea* (Rome: Carocci, 2015); Paolo Soave, *Fra Reagan e Gheddafi. La politica estera italiana e l'escalation libico-americana degli anni '80* (Soveria Mannelli: Rubbettino, 2017).
15 Daniele Caviglia and Massimiliano Cricco, *La diplomazia italiana e gli equilibri mediterranei. La politica mediorientale dell'Italia dalla guerra dei sei giorni al conflitto dello Yom Kippur (1967–1973)* (Soveria Mannelli: Rubbettino, 2006).
16 See, in particular, Luca Riccardi, *L'ultima politica estera. L'italia e il Medio Oriente alla fine della prima Repubblica* (Soveria Mannelli: Rubbettino, 2014).
17 Antonio Varsori, *L'Italia e la fine della guerra fredda. La politica estera dei governi Andreotti 1989–1992* (Bologna: Il Mulino, 2013).
18 Rory Miller, *Inglorious Disarray: Europe, Israel and the Palestinians since 1967* (London: Hurst, 2011).

Archives, Archival Collections, Collections of Documents and Abbreviations

AAD	Access to Archival Databases
ACDA	Arms Control and Disarmament Agency
ACS	Archivio Centrale dello Stato, Rome
ADAP	Akten zur Deutschen Auswärtigen Politik 1918–45, Göttingen, 1950–95
Agip	Agenzia generale italiana petroli
AM	Carte Aldo Moro
ANSA	Agenzia Nazionale Stampa Associata
AP	Atti Parlamentari
ASENI	Archivio Storico Ente Nazionale Idrocarburi, Pomezia, Italy
ASMAE	Archivio Storico-Diplomatico del Ministero degli Affari Esteri e della Cooperazione Internazionale, Rome
ASPR	Archivio Storico Presidenza della Repubblica, Rome
ASSR	Archivio Storico del Senato della Repubblica, Rome
BD	British documents on the origins of the War 1898–1914, HMSO, London
BP	British Petroleum
CD	Camera dei Deputati
CENTO	Central Treaty Organization, or Baghdad Pact
CFPF	Cental Foreign Policy Files
CGG	Carte Giovanni Giolitti
COCOM	Coordinating Committee for Multilateral Export Controls
COREU	Correspondance Européenne
Cons.Dipl.	Consigliere Diplomatico
CPLGC	Carte personali Luigi Guidobono Cavalchini
DC	Democrazia Cristiana
DDF	Documents diplomatiques français, Imprimèrie Nationale, Paris
DDI	I Documenti Diplomatici Italiani, Istituto Poligrafico e Zecca dello Stato, Rome
DE	Direzione Estero file
DGAE	Direzione Generale Affari Esteri
DGAP	Direzione Generale Affari Politici
DGFP	Documents on German Foreign Policy 1918–45, HMSO, London 1949-
DGP	Direzione Generale del Personale
DGRC	Direzione Generale delle Relazioni Culturali
EAD	Euro-Arab Dialogue
EC	European Community
ECC	European Communities

EE	Eni Estero file
EEC	European Economic Community
EM	Edoardo Martino Archival Collections
EN	Emile Noël Archival Collections
ENI	Ente Nazionale Idrocarburi
EPC	European Political Co-operation
EU	European Union
FCA	Foreign and Commonwealth Affairs
FCO	Foreign and Commonwealth Office
FDM	Francesco De Martino File
FO	Foreign Office
FOIA	Freedom of Information Act
FRUS	The Foreign Relations of the United States, United States Department of State, Government Printing Office, Washington
GA	Carte Giulio Andreotti
GC	General Committee, Euro-Arab Dialogue
GM	Carte Gaetano Martino
GP	Die Grosse Politik der Europäischen Kabinette, Deutsche Verlagsgesellschaft für Politik und Geschichte, Berlin
GRDS	General Records of the Department of State
GRF-0314	Memoranda of Conversations (Nixon and Ford Administrations) 1973–7
GS	Giovanni Spadolini File
GSP	Generalised Scheme of Preferences
HAEU	Historical Archives of the European Union, European University Institute, Badia Fiesolana, Italy
IBRD	International Bank for Reconstruction and Development
IDF	Israel Defense Forces
ILS	Istituto Luigi Sturzo, Rome
IMF	International Monetary Fund
Iminoco	Iranian Marine International Oil Company
IRP	Islamic Republican Party
ITALAIR	Italian Air Task Force, United Nations Interim Force in Lebanon
ITALCON	Italian Contingent, Multinational Force in Lebanon
KM	Klaus Meyer File, Historical Archives of the European Union
LAS	League of Arab States
MAE	Ministero Affari Esteri Italiano
ME	Middle East
MemCons	Memoranda of Face to Face Conversation
MFO	Multinational Force & Observers, Sinai
MNF	Multinational Force in Lebanon
NARA	National Archives and Records Administration, College Park, MD
NATO	North Atlantic Treaty Organization
NENAD	Near East and North African Department
NIAF	National Italian American Foundation
NIE	National Intelligence Estimate

NIOC	National Iranian Oil Company
NPMP	Nixon Presidential Materials Project
NSC	National Security Council
NSDD	National Security Directive Decisions
NSF	National Security Files
NSPP	National Security Policy Papers
OAPEC	Organization of Arab Petroleum Exporting Countries
OPEC	Organization of Petroleum Exporting Countries
OECD	Organization for Economic Co-operation and Development
OEU	Österreich-Ungarns Aussenpolitik von der Bosnischen Krise 1908 bis zum Kriegsausbruch 1914
PCI	Partito Comunista Italiano
PCM	Presidenza del Consiglio dei Ministri
PEC	Presidency of the European Council
PLO	Palestine Liberation Organization
PPP	Pakistan Peoples Party
PRI	Partito Repubblicano Italiano
PSI	Partito Socialista Italiano
RAU	Repubblica Araba Unita
RF	Reagan Files
RG 59	Record Group 59
RRL	Ronald Reagan Library
RRPL	Ronald Reagan Presidential Papers
S	Senato della Repubblica
SDI	Strategic Defence Initiative
SecState	Secretary of State
Sga	Secrétaire Général Adjont
Sirip	Iran-Italian Petroleum Company
Sovmedron	Soviet Mediterranean Squadron
TNA	The National Archive, Kew
UNEF II	Second United Nations Emergency Force
UNESCO	United Nations Educational, Scientific and Cultural Organization
UNIFIL	United Nations Interim Force in Lebanon
USDSVRR	US Department of State Virtual Reading Room

Abbreviations used in archival sources

b.	box
doc.	document
docs	documents
ET	Electronic Telegrams
et sqq.	and following
f.	file
n.	number

nn.	numbers
s.	series
n.d.	no date
Tel.	telegram
vol.	volume
vols	volumes

Introduction: The foreign policy of a middle power at the geopolitical crossroads

Luciano Monzali and Paolo Soave

Avoiding any kind of determinism, a simple glance at geography can easily point out the complexity of the Italian geopolitical condition. On the one hand, as a continental country, Italy has always tried to stay linked to European political and economic processes, dealing with the most influential Western powers. After the Second World War, no longer being a great military power, the general objective of this north-western direction of Italian foreign policy was to take part in the emerging community of the most advanced countries, the Euro-Atlantic world, in order to safeguard national security and contribute to a common, integrated political and economic development. On the other hand, most parts of the country, the peninsula, largely represents a Mediterranean area, deeply affected by relevant social and economic differences and open to extra-European cultures. Far from being only a factor of weakness, the Italian articulated identity inspires a south-eastern foreign policy aimed at encouraging peace, multilateralism, and economic cooperation in the Middle East, especially for providing energy supplies and preserving the rights of Italian communities in the area. Moreover, because of its political instability, after the Second World War Italy always tried to widen the area of coalition governments pursuing international autonomy from the Atlantic Alliance, especially with Arab countries. This kind of foreign policy was shared by the socialists and communists, as well as by cultural and social forces, granting a larger consensus. However, for a middle power, this kind of double foreign policy was quite difficult to carry out, particularly in case of international tensions, as frequently occurred during the Cold War.

The strong relationship which Italy kept with the Middle East throughout the Cold War largely contributed to relaunching the country as a Mediterranean power, revealing the unique nature of Italian foreign policy. While the UK and France were able to preserve a recognizable international role beyond any geographical identity leading their post-colonial transition, Italy was forced to distance itself from its past and define a new credibility starting from its geopolitical condition. Moreover, resources for an effective regional policy were, in the Italian case, considerably less than in the French and the British cases. No longer a military power after the Second World War, with its national security through NATO taken for granted, Italy turned its weakness into new relevance, focusing on political dialogue and economic cooperation with the Islamic countries. Its preference for that part, after an initial sympathy for Israel, was the evidence of its being a Mediterranean, 'unarmed prophet', aiming at regional peace and common prosperity according to its roots. As Prof. Varsori clearly outlines in his preface, the peculiarity of the Italian role in the Middle East was not only the consequence of a general inferiority and of its oil addiction but also a historical heritage in strong continuity with the past. As France pursued its political autonomy, and the UK acted in compliance with the Western alliance, both of them showing an interest in the Mediterranean as a way to gain greater international influence, Italy played the role of bridge across the basin to preserve the regional identity of the Middle East and to help the Western bloc to maintain its influence in the face of Soviet initiatives.

Following on from these premises, this volume focuses on Italy's peculiar relationship with the Middle East in a crucial era of long-term transition, from the 1970s to the early 1990s. While those decades were shaped by so-called globalization following the Cold War, as Westad described, which eventually culminated in the end of bipolarity, the Middle East was deeply affected by the connection between regional tensions and superpowers' interferences. Some important dynamics emerged after the Yom Kippur War, a turning point in the Middle East's contemporary history. While Sadat's political and military effectiveness and the Soviet loss of influence paved the way to the first historical step of the peace process, the oil producers shared a common struggle in the oil market against the Western powers. To the surprise of Western diplomats and politicians, the local governments used oil for the first time as a political weapon, putting Europe in disarray, especially Italy, and the United States.

The Yom Kippur War had a strong impact on Italian foreign policy. As the prominent diplomat Robert Gaja noted, the Middle East crisis of 1973 showed that while the Atlantic alliance could fully guarantee Italy's military security, it did not manage to safeguard Italy's manufacturing capacity and its economic security. This stimulated a new Italian diplomatic activism in the 1970s and in the 1980s, which ascertained the ineffectiveness of collective European initiatives as the Euro-Arab dialogue, devoted to setting friendly bilateral relations and intense economic cooperation with such oil producers as Libya, Algeria, Iran and Saudi Arabia. The search for energy supplies and markets was a pivotal element of Italian policy in the Mediterranean area in those years. Even the strong engagement in supporting multilateral peace initiatives in Palestine was spurred not only by interest of Italian public opinion in this issue but also to sustain the cooperation between oil producers and Western states.

Another important aspect of Italian policies in the Middle East was the search for political stability and order. Disorder and war in the Mediterranean meant additional troubles for Italy. The ambition to play a role of mediator between Western powers and the Middle East states was not just a mere search for prestige (the so-called 'politica di presenza', according to a quite ironic American definition) but an answer to a serious Italian political and economic interest in a safer and more stable Mediterranean region. For Italian diplomats and politicians, the best guarantee for peace and stability was the balance of power, not the destruction or humiliation of some local political actors. This attitude provoked some tensions with the United States and Israel, strictly tied in an alliance pursuing strategic superiority over the Arab countries sustained by the USSR.

The Yom Kippur War clearly frustrated the Soviet search for regional influence, especially through the partnership with Egypt, changing forever the local balance of power. However, the harshest consequence of the war was the oil retaliation imposed by the producers on Western consumers. In the late 1970s the regional expressions of the so-called Second Cold War, especially the Iranian revolution, deeply affected the Middle East. As the region experienced the birth of political terror, eventually exported to Western countries, the international community promoted multilateral peace interventions in order to provide political stability, as in the Lebanese case.

As a regional power particularly devoted to multilateralism, all during the Cold War Italian diplomacy tried to promote, as credible international partners, Arafat and Gaddafi, leaders much criticized by the Americans. In some circumstances, performing as a diplomatic bridge forced Italy to face tough opposition from its allies, especially the United States. At the same time Italy tried to get the European Community engaged in Middle East affairs in order to enforce its diplomatic initiatives. As the bipolar era came to an end, even the meaning of some basic political terms like autonomy and democracy had to be defined again and applied to different contexts, as the Algerian post-electoral case clearly demonstrated in the early 1990s. The transition to the post-Cold War world confirmed the political characters and the complexity of the Middle East. In the early 1990s, Italy experienced a serious political crisis that eventually culminated in the end of the so-called 'Prima Repubblica' and of its main political parties. The crisis largely affected the course of Italian foreign policy starting from the first Gulf War. The end of the confrontation between the Soviet Union and the United States and the beginning of American hegemony in the Middle East cancelled opportunities and space for an Italian diplomatic role in the Mediterranean. The multilateral military intervention against Iraq frustrated any effort oriented to promote a diplomatic solution, and eventually Italy lost a large part of its regional relevance, even though it remained the most Mediterranean of the European powers.

The present volume demonstrates the huge political, economic, diplomatic and strategic effort practiced in the decades from the 1970s to the early 1990s in order to promote a regional policy, basically focused on multilateralism, cooperation, respect and understanding for all local countries, an inclusive approach to some extent opposing the divisive policies of the superpowers which for so long exploited the local tensions to gain some influence.

Although this effort was too ambitious for a middle power, to some extent Italy was successful in searching for regional credibility. The volume gives evidence of the whole, impressive range of Italian interests in the Middle East in a period of profound local change and global transition to the post-Cold War scenario. Regional stability, peace and free access to energy supplies were always in strict connection with Italian national security, leading to many cooperation initiatives. As diplomacy was the main source of this ambitious approach, promoting a regional, inclusive view was the most important special characteristic of the Italian role in the Middle East. Moreover, the Italian proposal was largely appreciated by many Middle East countries, especially in periods of crisis. The volume is also aimed at stimulating the multidisciplinary research field based on the concept of regionalism applied to many dimensions – diplomacy, politics, economic relations – of Middle East studies. As international history is moving towards an impressive development through the so-called *Global Turn*, which occurred in historiography after the end of the Cold War, regionalism is a concrete perspective for further studies, a deeper alternative, even more respectful of local factors and identities, than a Cold War approach.

The contributions collected in the volume are arranged according to three main general issues: the Middle East in a period of change from the 1970s to the first post-Cold War (Part One); the Italian role in promoting a regional view, even trying in some cases to balance Cold War influences and local tensions (Part Two); the progressive broadening of the Italian initiatives to a greater Middle East (Part Three). Since relations with the Arab states played a pivotal role in Italian foreign policy towards the Middle East, the book pays particular attention to it.

In Part One, Joseph A. Bongiorno introduces the general terms of the critical interaction between Middle East patterns, especially the Arab–Israeli conflict, and the influence of the most relevant Cold War actors, which exploited the pre-existing divisions. Those basic factors, clearly pointed out by Bongiorno, deeply affected Italy as a regional power, stressing both the national security issue, largely dependent on NATO integrity, and the geostrategic interest for a safe and stable region, based on peace and multilateral cooperation. In the early 1990s, as the Cold War dissolved, new chances for regional peace and cooperation appeared, but Italian expectations regarding a safer and more cooperative Middle East were once again frustrated by the emerging of old and local factors of fragmentation between Israel and Palestine, as well as among the Arabs, as Arturo Marzano clearly shows in his contribution. Although indirectly, the outcomes of Cold War deeply impacted the Middle East, as Marzano sharply outlines. While Israel was getting stronger along with its strategic relations with the emerging American global leadership, the Arab countries were even weaker, both for the loss of Soviet cooperation and because of a general political fragmentation. The first Gulf War in the early 1990s was a turning point for a Middle East divided along the inter-Arab tensions. Those contradictions deeply affected the Oslo treaty.

In Part Two, Luciano Monzali draws the complex historical course of Italian foreign policy and its relations with the Middle East. Soon after Italian national unification in 1861, that region started playing a relevant role as Italy was a latecomer searching for a Mediterranean influence. In the age of colonial empires, Italy had to fight for some geopolitical space in the Mediterranean basin in order to avoid any kind of blocking and encirclement by the main powers, the UK and France. Historically, that weakness forced Italy to carry on bilateral relations and alliances with both continental and Mediterranean powers. In some historical circumstances this huge diplomatic effort was badly appraised by the main European powers, but it was really consistent with the complexity of Italy's national geopolitical interests. Monzali points out these historical continuities and the skillfulness of Italian diplomacy in facing frequent tensions with the allies, until the second post-war period. Luca Riccardi clearly outlines the importance of the Arab–Israeli dispute in the course of post-Second World War Italian foreign policy, a main issue for the national debate among political parties, the cultural world and the society. There was a progressive shift from the first pro-Israeli attitude to an emerging pro-Arab engagement, inspired by the search for regional stability, in opposition to the strong American support for Israel, and securing the energy supplies for national economic development. Lorenzo Medici points out the relevance of cultural diplomacy as an Italian way of promoting dialogue and cooperation in the Middle East. On one hand, the Cold War reduced the international influence of Italy, while on the other hand, Rome was stimulated to exploit its cultural sensitivity in a global approach which, to some extent, went beyond the Cold War walls opening to many countries. Silvio Labbate examines the Italian support for a Euro-Arab dialogue in order to remove the reasons for tension. Italy continuously encouraged the common effort, especially trying to stimulate the European partners to launch a serious multilateralism. The case of the Lebanese civil war, examined by Roberta La Fortezza, was a historical turning point in Italian foreign policy because of the first participation in a multinational peacekeeping intervention promoted by the United Nations in order to stabilize that country. Matteo Gerlini explores the Sigonella crisis, the most critical point in US–Italy Cold War relations: the Italian regional approach to the Middle East, based on dialogue with the Arabs and aimed at promoting international legitimization for the Palestine Liberation Organization (PLO), was harshly counteracted by the divisive American attitude, inspired by the Cold War confrontation and with strong support for Israel. The same issue is dealt with by Paolo Soave, focusing on the building of the special relationship between Italy and Libya in the years of Gaddafi's regime, so unpredictable and causing some troubles in the bilateral relations between Italy and the United States. Azzedine Layachi deals with the Algerian case, particularly relevant for Italian investments in the energy field. However, from the 1990s, the main issue in dealing with this country was the emergence of the Islamic forces through the general elections. The Western countries reacted with deep concern to this first case of electoral radicalization, as Algeria fell into civil war. The Sant'Egidio community led a meaningful effort in so-called 'parallel diplomacy' in order to favour a political stabilization in Algeria.

In Part Three Federico Imperato outlines the relations between Italy and Turkey, which Rome tried to upgrade in the Cold War era to a new strategic partnership for the Western system, even if a never-ending transition occurred between Europe and Ankara. The oil trade is the main issue of Bruno Pierri's contribution on the Tehran agreement of 1971, a case of international competition for energy supplies which led ENI to oppose the British initiatives. Rosario Milano examines the case of the Iranian revolution, a dramatic change in the political scenario of the Middle East, as well as a new factor in the Cold War because of the consequences for the relations between Tehran and Washington. While the superpowers had some difficulties in understanding the complexity of the Iranian change, Italy tried to secure closer relations with Tehran by means of its diplomatic skills. The Soviet invasion of Afghanistan was another step in the so-called Second Cold War, as Luciano Monzali outlines. Italian diplomacy always gave evidence of some interest towards Afghanistan, a country open to many international influences but at the same time so difficult to control. Italian interest in a greater Middle East in the light of the Muslim issue was extended even to Pakistan, as proved by Giuseppe Spagnulo, whose contribution confirms the cultural attitude of Italian diplomacy to think in terms of the global balance of power.

Part One

The Middle East in a period of change

1

Footholds in the sand – the Middle East and the Cold War, 1973–93: An introductory chapter and review

Joseph A. Bongiorno

Introduction

During the 1956 American presidential campaign, the Democratic Party's presidential candidate, Adlai E. Stevenson, criticized American foreign policy towards the Middle East under the incumbent presidential administration of Dwight D. Eisenhower. Reacting to the latter's foreign policy decisions at the height of both the Suez Crisis in the Middle East and the presidential campaign, Stevenson declared that administration foreign policy officials

> have given the Soviet Union two great victories – a *foothold* in the Middle East and the breakdown of the Western Alliance; the Soviets' 'supreme objective' since World War II. … As a result, the United States found itself arrayed in the United Nations with Soviet Russia and the dictator of Egypt against the democracies of Britain, France and Israel. 'A foreign policy which has brought about these results … is a foreign policy which has failed'.[1]

The statement and events that surrounded it are representative of the Cold War and its impact on the Middle East during the post-war years. Decades marked by a multitude of attempts to establish footholds by various powers such as the United States and the Soviet Union left imprints in a region marred by contesting ideologies, competing national interests and violence. Like all footprints in the sand, they slowly disappeared with the passage of time only to be replaced with new ones.

The general understanding of the origins and reasons for the Cold War differs among various historians. For some, the Cold War was perhaps about an exaggerated ideological struggle over the incompatibility of communism with American ideals.[2] Others saw it as a natural consequence of geopolitical expansions of two nation states with specific national interests and the quest for geopolitical/strategic parity over a period of time.[3] Others still see it as a confrontation that had its origins as the result of the First World War and the burgeoning Soviet state as an unwanted member of the post-war international community.[4] Whatever its origins, the Cold War left no continent of the world unaffected or immune. A series of networks of alliances or treaty arrangements developed between 1945 and 1991 that in one way or another were linked to either the United States or the Soviet Union. Hence, as in many other regions of the world, the Middle East and its post-Second World War creation of independent nation states became part of those various networks, leaving the infamous footprints created by the consequences of the Cold War and its rival superpowers.

The geopolitical importance of the Middle East cannot be underestimated. Contiguous to many major oceans and straits and including the Suez Canal, the Middle East is a lynchpin in terms of mastery of the seas and East–West trade routes. Combined with such trade is the necessity of naval control, essential to former powers such as the Persian, Roman and British empires. This still serves as an essential subject of the lessons regarding sea power and survival of the nation state.[5] Likewise, the land mass stretching from north-eastern Africa to the Arabian Peninsula, Iran and Afghanistan is vital for international commerce, military movement and access to important natural resources such as petroleum, river systems and water. In addition, the region's demography would also play a role for the world's superpowers in the Cold War struggle. Thus, the internal conditions of the various Middle Eastern nation states and their respective diasporas would have an impact on the formulation of foreign and national security policies for the United States, the Soviet Union and their respective allies.[6]

Hence, it is understandable that the Middle East would play a pivotal role in Cold War politics. During the time frame and scope of this book, the Middle East was an essential part of the calculation of a geopolitical strategy for both the United States and the Soviet Union. Simultaneously, the Cold War had an impact upon the positions and foreign policy strategies of the Middle East nation states, taking into account what role the superpowers could play in regard to the advancement of their own national interests. Since the end of the Second World War, issues such as the founding of the State of Israel, the question of Palestine and the continued evolution of the Arab states and Iran have been catalysts in both the former Cold War as well as the emerging 'new' Cold War in the contemporary Middle East.[7] The interrelationship between the historic Cold War and the Middle East region in terms of the search for peace was probably best summed up by Henry Kissinger in a speech delivered at the opening of one of the many peace conferences, held in Geneva in 1973:

> In all efforts for peace the overriding problem is to relate the sense of individual justice to the common good. The great tragedies of history occur not when right confronts wrong but when two rights face each other.
>
> The problems of the Middle East today have such a character. There is justice on all sides, but there is a greater justice still in finding a truth which merges all aspirations in the realization of a common humanity. It was a Jewish sage who, speaking for all mankind, expressed this problem well: 'If I am not for myself, who is for me, but if I am for myself alone, who am I?'[8]

The United States, the Cold War and the Middle East

The American relationship with the Middle East region is a long and complicated one, going as far back as the presidency of Thomas Jefferson and the issues regarding the Barbary and Tripoli wars.[9] During the Second World War era, America's evolving relationship with the emerging Arab states[10] and the founding of the State of Israel[11] deepened its involvement in the region. For obvious geopolitical reasons, the Cold War period forced the United States into creating its own footholds spanning from the shores of the eastern Mediterranean to Iran. During both the Truman and Eisenhower presidencies, separate American 'doctrines' or foreign policy exhortations were made regarding the eastern Mediterranean and Middle Eastern regions in response to the Greek civil war and the Lebanon Crisis of 1958 in relationship to the containment policy.[12] Thus, the American experience serves to throw a spotlight on the history of the period under examination.

The American relationship with the Middle East, notwithstanding the perceived necessity of containment, was (and still is) marred with frustration with several persistent and aggravating problems. Foremost, of course, is the continued search for Middle East peace and a solution to the Arab–Israeli conflict over the geographical territory of Palestine. Second is the accommodation of the various Arab states and their own particular national interests beyond the parameters of the Arab–Israeli conflict and within the framework of the containment policy. Third is the continued political and military access to the region and its natural resources. Fourth is the maintenance of an alliance system within the containment policy framework, known formerly as the Baghdad Pact or Central Treaty Organization (CENTO), which would prevent Soviet expansion into the Middle Eastern region. CENTO was understood as a logical extension of the North Atlantic Treaty Organization (NATO), stretching across the Middle East region from Turkey to Pakistan, exclusive of Israel. However, unlike NATO, there is no unified command. CENTO is also hampered by changing internal political circumstances and conditions as well as exterior issues such as the various Indo-Pakistani wars. The alliance, by the 1970s, had become a formality. With the Islamic republican revolution in Iran in 1979, CENTO was formally disbanded.[13]

The historical period from the 1970s to 1990s has been a continuation of the American experience in the Middle East region since the Second World War. These experiences were intertwined with various political challenges within the containment policy. For example, during the 1950s and 1960s, the United States was confronted with the opposing interests of the Egyptian government under President Gamal Abdel Nasser. While trying to foster more stable relationships with the various Arab states contiguous to Israel, the United States ensured the protection of Israeli interests with bilateral arrangements that were adverse to those same Arab states. Simultaneously, the United States attempted to extract concessions from Israel to achieve a framework for peace as well as diplomatic recognition for the latter by its immediate neighbours.

All of this required a delicate balancing act on the part of successive American administrations and their foreign policy advisors. The Arab–Israeli wars of 1956[14] and 1967 demonstrated the difficulty of maintaining such a policy, at times forsaking traditional relationships with American allies in order to prevent or limit the ability of the Soviet Union from penetrating into or meddling in the region. The administration of John F. Kennedy suffered several setbacks in its Middle Eastern policies, for example, in attempting to be 'even-handed' to accommodate both Israeli and Arab interests, only to remain 'empty-handed' at the end.[15] The Johnson administration had similar experiences, complicated further by the Arab–Israeli War of 1967 and the threat of superpower military confrontation in the area.[16] The Arab–Israeli War of 1973 was a reminder of the spectre of a possible confrontation between the United States and the Soviet Union fostered by irreconcilable differences among the Israelis and Arabs. Despite United Nations Security Council resolutions 242 (1967) and 338 (1973),[17] no solution seemed in sight for the settlement of the major issues, much less Israeli withdrawal to the *de facto* pre-1967 borders. During the Nixon and Ford administrations, American foreign policy was guided by Henry Kissinger, initially appointed as National Security Advisor, later to become Secretary of State. Supported by the Nixon Doctrine of 1969,[18] Kissinger embarked upon several aggressive diplomatic initiatives during and after the 1973 Arab–Israeli War in order to accomplish three main objectives: (1) maintain a stable truce among the warring Parties; (2) continue the search for some permanent solution to the Arab–Israeli conflict; and (3) either prevent or limit Soviet participation in a future Middle East peace settlement. In what became known as the famous 'shuttle diplomacy' on the 'Yo-Yo Express', Kissinger travelled to and from the Israeli and Arab capitals, framing a permanent truce with the perhaps reluctant use of United Nations peacekeeping mechanisms and troops while attempting to lay a basis for some sort of peace settlement. As Kissinger later wrote in his voluminous memoirs:

> My November (1973) trip marked the real end of the Middle East war. It stabilized the ceasefire; it settled the immediate postwar lines. ... We had been instrumental in all these negotiations. We were gradually getting into a position where our support was essential for progress while the Soviet capacity for mischief was being systematically reduced. We could now focus on the next step – to assemble the Geneva Conference[19] and to chart the road toward peace.[20]

However, one has to note that the international political conditions had changed since 1967 with détente between the United States and the Soviet Union. This, of course, was also pushed at that time by the unexpected rapprochement between China and the United States during 1971 and 1972, along with the apparent Sino–Soviet rift with its own particular origins stemming back to 1961. More immediate was the change in political leadership in Cairo in 1970 with the death of President Nasser and the succession to power of Anwar Sadat. This change was significant in that it would eventually reverse the ties between Moscow and Cairo while seeming to make Egyptian policy more amenable to American ideas for further peace proposals.[21]

The Nixon and Ford administrations also learned the invaluable lesson about the importance of the search for Middle East peace for American economic interests. During the 1973 Arab–Israeli War, when the United States had assisted Israel with the use of NATO military bases, the Arab world angrily reacted with an oil embargo. This embargo had a profound negative impact on those nations, including the United States, which had assisted or supported Israel during the war. The embargo had thus signalled a changed response by the Arab world with the means to change the status quo.[22] The short-term effectiveness of the oil embargo was also supplemented by the rise of the Palestine Liberation Organization (PLO), founded in 1964, the initial goal of which was 'to mobilize the Palestinian people to recover their usurped homeland'.[23] Hence, evolving methods such as terrorist activities in the form of hijackings or bombings would be wielded against those who were responsible for supporting Israel or her allies counter to this mission. By the 1970s, the PLO, led by Yasir Arafat, received support at the United Nations, where it was granted observer status in the UN system, signalling a change in the voting majority regarding Middle East peace issues such as the question of Palestine.[24] Both the Arab states and the PLO were successful sponsors of a UN General Assembly resolution equating Zionism as a form of racism,[25] and critical of continued Israeli military occupation of the pre-1967 border territories of the Sinai, Gaza, West Bank and Golan Heights.

The Carter administration continued the search for a Middle East peace settlement. Although the prior Kissinger policies were successful in containing Soviet diplomacy to discussions in the halls and chambers of the United Nations in Geneva and New York, they accomplished little else. The stalemate for Middle East peace continued. President Carter was advised by two major figures in his administration, Cyrus Vance as Secretary of State and Zbigniew Brzezinski as National Security Advisor. Carter considered the latter to be his teacher or mentor regarding foreign policy. Both Vance and Brzezinski were at opposite ends regarding treatment of the Soviets. The former was generally disposed to negotiation while the latter saw the world as a bipolar one, every crisis interpreted as a deliberate Soviet challenge to American power. The arbiter was a president with relatively no foreign policy experience.[26]

These attitudes, or differing policy directions, would have another impact upon American foreign policy toward the Middle East. Thus far, the United Nations mandates regarding the search for peace was a 'comprehensive' one, meaning that it was understood that all issues would be resolved simultaneously, ranging from Israeli withdrawal to the de facto pre-1967 border areas, defining the final status of Jerusalem and the establishment of a Palestinian state. However, the lack of accomplishment of these goals led to a series of frustrations in many Middle Eastern capitals such as Cairo.

In the particular case of Egypt, President Anwar Sadat sought an alternative solution to Middle East peace, due to dissatisfaction with his nation's relationship with the USSR and a series of inconclusive wars with Israel. President Sadat's decision to alter his posture towards the United States and venture into direct peace negotiations with Israel culminated with his historic visit to Jerusalem in 1977. With this initiative began the arduous road to Israeli–Egyptian peace negotiations under American political and financial (and later military) sponsorship, which led to the Camp David Accords in 1978 and the Israeli–Egyptian Peace Treaty of 1979.

Accounts of the Camp David Accords and the ensuing Israeli–Egyptian Peace Treaty have been well reported and discussed over the years.[27] The Camp David Accords provided a framework of principles for achieving peace in the Middle East, including a plan for Palestinian self-determination and a process for achieving peace between Israel and their Arab neighbours. However, what was eventually concluded was a peace treaty between Israel and Egypt, with additional appendices or references to the other aforementioned matters. Hence, the Israeli–Egyptian Peace Treaty accomplished but one part of the 1978 Camp David Accords, including phased and complete Israeli military withdrawal from the Sinai Peninsula. Included were also provisions for continued military peacekeeping mechanisms under the auspices of the United Nations. The treaty was signed at the White House in Washington, DC, in March 1979, without the apparent participation or presence of America's European allies and friends, much less the other Arab states, PLO and the USSR.[28]

The agreements first met with scepticism, then with outright hostility from various quarters of the international community. The Arab states, with the signing of the peace treaty, undertook measures to ostracize and condemn Egypt for its 'separate peace deal' with Israel. The PLO rejected the provisions of both documents, stating that such arrangements regarding Palestinian territory and self-determination could not be acceptable without the direct participation of the Palestinians. The Soviets also rejected the peace accords, reaffirming Arab and Palestinian reasoning but also pointing out that the accords abandoned the comprehensive nature of Middle East negotiations, envisaged by the Geneva Peace Conference sessions under the co-chairmanship of both themselves and the Americans. With Soviet opposition came the warning that no UN mechanisms could be used or permitted to support the treaty arrangements, meaning the eventual end of UNEF II peacekeeping operations in the Sinai by the end of July 1979.[29] Therefore, there would be no peacekeeping support from the United Nations to augment and guarantee the Israeli military withdrawal provisions from the Egyptian Sinai.[30]

On its face, notwithstanding the purported nature of the agreements, the United States successfully prevented the Soviet Union from participating in Middle East peace negotiations. The Soviet threat to veto further UN peacekeeping actions in the Sinai, on the one hand, was a response to the seemed abandonment and promises of the Geneva Conference peace process on the part of the United States while further isolating the Soviet Union from Middle East deliberations. On the other hand, the Soviet action forced the United States to seek an unprecedented and risky solution – namely, to find a peacekeeping mechanism outside the United Nations framework. Hence, the United States would now have to create its own peacekeeping force even with its own military personnel in order to separate the Egyptians and Israelis. This would invite the Soviets or others potentially to do the same in the region for any reason or excuse, abrogating therefore an important principle that no troops of the major powers and/or their allies should be introduced into the area unless they were placed under only the colours of the UN flag.[31]

The last two years of the Carter administration were complicated by the Islamic republican revolution in Iran, led by Ayatollah Ruhollah Khomeini.[32] Shah Reza Pahlavi and his government were overthrown and, with them, the foundations of American foreign policy in the Middle East. The revolution was followed by a diplomatic hostage crisis in Tehran – which lasted until the first day of the presidential administration of Ronald Reagan in January 1981 – and the Carter administration was thereby weakened in terms of its foreign policy efforts in the region. Simultaneously, in 1979, the Soviets invaded Afghanistan, attempting to salvage the Marxist government recently installed there. Hence, American foreign policy in the Middle East suffered a major setback, if not a complete failure.[33]

During the Reagan presidency of the 1980s, American diplomatic efforts were marked by continued efforts to contain the Soviet Union in the Middle East and extract them from Afghanistan. The Lebanese civil war, which began during the mid-1970s, became ever more complicated with the entry of Israel into southern Lebanon in 1978. Notwithstanding the placement of UN peacekeeping troops in southern Lebanon, a second Israeli invasion occurred during 1981–2, further complicating the internal politics of the Lebanese people and the PLO. The Reagan administration decided to deploy troops in the area to fill the void of a prior Israeli withdrawal while attempting to protect its Lebanese Christian allies in Beirut. This effort was met with opposition and resulted in a devastating bombing of the American embassy in Beirut in 1982. The aftermath of this confusing political and military episode was an American military withdrawal from the area, replaced by a temporary multinational peacekeeping force (MNF) in Beirut and the surrounding areas.[34] Reminiscent of the events of 1958 during the Eisenhower years, the Lebanese experience presented the Reagan presidential administration with the continued frustration of creating footholds at great expense and loss in the region. Later, the American bombing of Libya during the Gulf of Sidra Crisis of 1986 also added another significant twist and complication to overall Middle East politics.[35] In that air raid, which threatened the life of Muammar Ghaddafi, the Americans responded to the perceived challenge of state-sponsored terrorism while bolstering their military/political presence in the Mediterranean region.[36]

However, American foreign policy in the Middle East would remain at another standstill. Notwithstanding changes in Soviet leadership during the 1980s, including Soviet head of state Mikhail Gorbachev's burgeoning policies of *glasnost* and *perestroika*, which would have an impact on Soviet foreign policy with the United States and Western Europe during that decade, the Middle East initially seemed untouched by those same significant changes. However, the *rapprochement* between the USSR and the West would, in due course, have a positive impact on issues such as those in the Middle East and Afghanistan over the short term. With *détente*, the Middle East benefited from the potential of a new round of negotiations among Israel, the various Arab states and Palestinians. The 1978 Camp David Accords were slowly accepted by a greater number of nations within the international community, and the continued but difficult path to Middle East peace through the Oslo Accords of 1993 was finally under way.[37] The significance, of course, now was that the United States was either viewed as the only viable mediator for any future Middle East peace deal by both Israelis and their Arab counterparts, either with caution or by default, due to the demise of the USSR in 1991 and the presumed end of the Cold War. With the balance of power changed, the footholds imprinted upon the proverbial sands did so as well.

The Soviet Union, the Cold War and the Middle East, 1973–93

The Soviet Union's role in the Middle East can be traced back to the nineteenth century during the period of czarist Russia. Russia had sought the title of 'protector' of the Orthodox Christians in Jerusalem at the time of the Ottoman Empire. Along with Western European opposition to this Russian initiative, the historical premises of the Soviet influence over the Middle East can be found in its role of 'protector' of the Orthodox in Jerusalem and in its ambitions with respect to Ottoman Empire, which eventually led to the Crimean War of 1856 against Turks and the main Western powers.[38] Of course, Russian initiatives in the eastern Mediterranean area and Middle East went beyond religious questions. These initiatives were a manifestation of the Russian national interest in the search for a balance of power or geopolitical parity vis-à-vis Great Britain and France.[39]

Like the United States, the Soviet Union saw the Middle East region as an important geopolitical lynchpin to its own defence and political/naval expansion. Hence, the Cold War witnessed consistent Soviet efforts to undermine American influence in that area by courting many of the Arab states, particularly Egypt. The Arab–Israeli conflicts served as opportunities to rival the influence of the United States and its Israeli ally at the perceived expense of the Arabs and Arab Palestinians. In the process, the Soviets would place their own footholds or imprints in the sand.

The USSR initiated its foreign and military objectives in the Middle East during the 1940s at the same time as demanding Libya become a Soviet UN trusteeship, and also simultaneous with the Iran Crisis of 1946, the founding of the State of Israel and the ensuing Arab–Israeli conflicts. The Suez Crisis of 1956 was another example of a Soviet attempt to exploit the Arab–Israeli conflict to establish a political and military presence in the area. At the same time, the US decision not to assist Egypt and its president, Gamel Abdel Nasser, allowed the Soviets to fill the void left by the Americans, especially on the question of the construction of the famous Aswan Dam. The hope was that Egypt would become a grateful ally and provide the USSR with much-needed eastern Mediterranean military/naval bases to counter those of the nearby NATO bases in Italian and Greek waters.[40]

However, the USSR's relationship with Egypt was a problematic one. Notwithstanding Nikita Khrushchev's praise for the Egyptian president and his willingness to listen to the former's suggestions and policy recommendations, the Russians had seemed to question Egyptian motives and policies, both economic and political, vis-à-vis the 1967 decision to go to war against Israel. The Arab–Israeli conflict, which had given the USSR a way into the Middle East, also divided the Soviets from their Arab allies. The Arab losses against Israel added frustration to the relationship.[41]

As in Egypt, the USSR pursed similar policies in currying favour with other Arab nations such as Iraq and Syria. With the Arab–Israeli conflict and geopolitical parity central to their motives, the USSR and its allies positioned themselves as champions of the Arab and Palestinian causes. In addition, their vocal support was usually accompanied with significant military and economic assistance, rivalled only by that of the United States. As Leonid Brezhnev, chairman of the Supreme Soviet, neatly summarized in a foreign policy speech:

> We [the USSR] have broad, many-sided relations with a number of Arab countries. The entire course of events has shown that friendship with the Soviet Union ensures the progressive Arab States the necessary support and aid in their most difficult hour. This is well-known in Egypt, Syria, Iraq and the Yemen. We have treaties of friendship with Egypt and Iraq and shall develop our relations. ... We

are firmly resolved to strengthen friendly ties with Syria, Algeria and other Arab countries, too.

The present international situation is such that all who desire to consolidate world peace should multiply their efforts for extinguishing the hotbed of war in the Middle East and overcoming the consequences of the Israeli aggression against the Arab States. ... Israel would be compelled to agree to a peaceful settlement, to recognize the legitimate rights of the Arab peoples. As for the Soviet Union, our readiness to contribute to this is well known.[42]

The height of Soviet success in the Middle East may have in fact come in 1972, with the conclusion of the Soviet–Egyptian Friendship Treaty. Yet, after the death of Nasser in 1970 and the apparent political purge of Ali Sabra and the 'Russian group' by President Anwar Sadat, the relationship between the two nations had been destined to change, even more so after the Arab–Israeli War of 1973. With Sadat's later decision to seek a new policy with the United States, coupled with the final expulsion of Soviet advisors from Egypt by 1974, the Soviet Union had seemed to lose its only stable foothold in the Middle East.[43]

From 1973 until 1991, the Soviet Union continued to oppose American policy in the Middle East, although, by the end of the 1980s, one can argue that the Middle East was no longer a viable objective of Soviet foreign policy given well-known intervening circumstances and priority changes. The USSR remained a 'co-chairperson' of the Geneva Peace Conference; in theory, it still held shared responsibility with the United States and United Nations for finding a comprehensive solution to Middle East peace. However, that particular diplomatic venue became relatively useless with the conclusion of the 1978 Camp David Accords and 1979 Israeli–Egyptian Peace Treaty. The USSR opposed the signing of the treaty and, as a permanent member of the UN Security Council, threatened to veto any resolution extending the UNEF II mandate to supervise the new peace treaty arrangements. Yet, despite that action, the reality was that the USSR was relegated to the position of a defeated opponent, unable to counter a growing American political and military presence in and around the Middle East. Notwithstanding earlier Soviet–American understanding regarding the joint search for a Middle East comprehensive peace settlement, the USSR was now left out in the diplomatic cold. Despite the claims of 'steadfastness', the Soviet footholds began to disappear in the winds of the desert.[44]

In a joint press conference with President François Mitterrand of France in October 1985, Mikhail Gorbachev, in response to a journalist's question, signalled a change in Soviet foreign policy regarding the Middle East. While still opposing American initiatives in the region, the USSR seemed ready to make some concessions on certain issues such as the future of the State of Israel:

Everything taking place in the Middle East worries us. We have never been aloof from a search for ways to settle the situation in the Middle East on a just basis. This means that troops must be withdrawn from occupied territories, that the Palestinian problem must be resolved on the basis of self-determination and that the indivisibility of Lebanon and its peaceful development and the legitimate rights of the Israeli people, the Israeli State, must be ensured. ... I think that other approaches – by separate deals and circumventing maneuvers – can lead only to some temporary settlement, but will not produce a solution to the problem so that a lasting peace in the Middle East can be created. ... And as to what the Americans think to be a sphere of their "vital interests' as you say, it is they who think so. The Americans claim 'vital interests' now here, now there. Let the Americans think about that formula.[45]

It is apparent in hindsight that Mikhail Gorbachev was presiding over the final demise of the USSR. In 1991, after a military coup,[46] Gorbachev was removed as leader and the USSR transformed its former Soviet republics into independent nation states, including the Russian Federation. With the end of the USSR came the finality of Soviet policy in the Middle East. Yet the Russian Federation would eventually continue from where the czars and commissars had left, creating new footholds in the deserts of the Middle East such as Syria with the building of new naval bases such as Lataika (Laodicea ad Mare) on the eastern Mediterranean and geopolitical strategic alliances under the presidency of Vladimir Putin.

Conclusion

The Cold War in the Middle East was fought by two main protagonists, the Soviet Union and the United States. As discussed in this chapter, the Cold War had an impact upon the Middle East as a region and on the various nation states. The Middle East, of course, had a significant political and economic impact upon the international community. The United States and its allies and their Soviet/socialist counterparts invested politically and financially in the region, hoping these efforts would bear positive results and long-standing spheres of influence as a partial step to winning the Cold War.

The struggle, of course, was neither constant nor consistent. International law and organizations such as the United Nations provided mechanisms to avoid any type of superpower conflicts in the region, to avoid the feared nuclear or conventional Armageddon. International law and organization indeed played a role in the Cold War struggle, whether in the form of binding resolutions, recommendations, peacekeeping forces or humanitarian assistance.[47] Although unfortunately beyond the scope of this chapter, the United Nations, the League of Arab States and various specialized agencies intervened in the many crises, defusing situations which may have otherwise resulted in another world war.[48] As has been amply discussed elsewhere in historical works, official documents and academic circles, this history deserves at least one chapter in any book regarding the Middle East. One of the few positive consequences of the Cold War was the development of international law and the practices of collective security within the United Nations framework. On the other hand, the world has witnessed the dangers of mirrored efforts conducted outside that framework to supposedly achieve the same, but in fact has heightened risks of great-power rivalry and possible direct conflicts in areas of the Middle East such as Iraq or Syria. These principles or rules no longer seem to have any relevant application or place in the contemporary Middle East.

Many historians seemed to be obsessed with the question as to who had won the Cold War in the Middle East, much less who won the Cold War itself. Most scholars would conclude that, at least during the present period under review, the United States had engineered a diplomatic strategy which had successfully isolated the former USSR from having any significant impact upon the resolution of Middle Eastern questions or issues stemming from the Arab–Israeli conflict. The USSR, moreover, had isolated itself from its own Arab allies and client states due to misunderstandings, miscalculations or the inability to compete with the United States in the spheres of military or financial assistance. In the end, as demonstrated by the signings of the Camp David and Oslo Accords, the United States seemed to gain the upper hand over its Soviet, and later Russian, counterparts by 1995. Yet, since then, given current circumstances, only time and history will continue to determine as to whose footholds or imprints have remained deeper and more pronounced as the winds of change and time continue in the capitals and deserts of the Middle East.

Notes

1. John Bartlow Martin, *Adlai Stevenson and the World* (New York: Anchor/Doubleday Press, 1978), 387.
2. Thomas G. Paterson, *Meeting the Communist Threat: Truman to Reagan* (London: Oxford University Press, 1988), vii–xii.
3. Walter LaFeber, *America, Russia and the Cold War, 1945–1990* (New York: McGraw-Hill, 1991), 1–3.
4. Carole K. Fink, *Cold War: An International History* (Boulder, CO: Westview Press, 2017), 5.
5. See Alfred Thayer Mahan, *The Influence of Sea Power Upon History* (New York: Dover, 1987). For a more contemporary examination of the impact of the Arab–Israeli wars upon naval policy and strategy, see Alberto Santoni, *Da Lissa alle Falkland: Storia e politica navale dell'eta contemporanea* (Milan: Mursia Editore, 1987), 320–30.
6. For a good introduction on the subject, see Ewan W. Anderson, *Middle East: Geography and Geopolitics* (London: Routledge Press, 2000).
7. See Mohammed Ayoob, 'The New Cold War in the Middle East', in the *National Interest* at http://nationalinterest.org/commentary/the-new-cold-war-the-middle-east-7974 (Brookings Institution Paper). The present conflicts in Syria and Yemen, the emerging rivalry between Saudi Arabia and Iran, Russian and American military involvement in the Middle East region, the transfer of the American embassy from Tel Aviv to Jerusalem are all examples of former Cold War patterns and footprints, although, as Foreign Minister Sergei Lavrov of the Russian Confederation commented, without the formerly understood rules, see Associated Press, 'What You Need to Know about Russia's Sergei Lavrov', *Moscow Times*, 25 April 2017, at https://themoscowtimes.com/news/the-man-behind-the-title-what-you-need-to-know-about-lavrov-57818.
8. Henry A. Kissinger, *American Foreign Policy* (New York: W. W. Norton, 1974), 290.
9. See Thomas A. Bailey, *A Diplomatic History of the American People* (Englewood Cliffs, NJ: Prentice-Hall, 1980), 64–5; and Merrill D. Peterson, *Thomas Jefferson and the New Nation* (London: Oxford University Press, 1970), 798–9.

10 See Bailey, *Diplomatic History*, 793–4: 'needing oil and bases in the Middle East to curb Soviet Russia', which of course would play a role on the containment policy.
11 Much has been written on the question of the American decision to recognize the state of Israel in 1948 and the developing relationship thereafter. Such an analysis would be beyond the scope of this chapter. However, from President Truman's perspective, see Harry S. Truman, *Memoirs by Harry S. Truman, Volume 2: Years of Trial and Hope* (Garden City, NY: Doubleday, 1956), 164–9, by which support was proclaimed on 'humanitarianism' grounds, notwithstanding the simultaneous events of the 1948 American presidential election and the role of the domestic Jewish electorate; see also Joseph P. Lash, *Eleanor: The Years Alone* (New York: W. W. Norton, 1972), 133–5. Eleanor Roosevelt, as a United Nations representative, noted on the American policy towards the recognition of Israel within the United Nations, 'Evidently at last we mean to follow through on a policy of aid to the Jewish State. The British role seems to me quite stupid, no more greedy and self-interested than ours has been but at last we seem to be doing better.' Henry Kissinger writes later about the reasoning behind realpolitik, in which Israel was part of an emerging policy of containment: 'In the end, America was drawn into the Middle East by the containment theory, which required opposition to Soviet expansion in every region'; see Henry Kissinger, *Diplomacy* (New York: Simon and Schuster, 1994), 525. For a brief documentary history on the creation of the State of Israel at the United Nations and General Assembly resolution 181 (II), see Roslyn Higgins, *United Nations Peacekeeping, 1946–1967* (London: Oxford University Press, 1969), 1–10.
12 On the question and origins of the containment policy, see George F. Kennan, 'The Sources of Soviet Conduct', in *Foreign Affairs* XXV (July 1947), 566–82. For a brief background on the Truman and Eisenhower Doctrines, see LaFeber, *America, Russia and the Cold War*, 48–58 and 191–2, respectively; and Fink, *Cold War*, 62–4 and 104, respectively. Interestingly enough, see also the writings of Walter Lippmann, suggesting, on the one hand, that the Cold War is not about ideological confrontation but, rather, the understanding of traditional Russian national interests, and, on the other, that Americans would have to shoulder the responsibility of the free world and the new environment that accompanied that of the Cold War; see Walter Lippmann, *The Cold War: A Study in U.S. Foreign Policy* (New York: Torchbook, 1973); and Clinton Rossiter and James Lare (eds), *The Essential Lippmann* (New York: Vintage, 1965), 70–4.
13 See, for example, Kevin W. Martin, 'Baghdad Pact', in Ruud Van Dijk and William Glenn Gray (eds), *Encyclopedia of the Cold War* (New York: Routledge Press, 2008), 57.
14 For an account of the 1956 Arab–Israeli or Suez Canal War from the United Nations perspective, see Brian Urquhart, *Hammarskjold* (New York: Alfred A. Knopf, 1972), 159–95; from the American perspective, which demonstrated the dilemmas of the crisis, see Dwight D. Eisenhower, *Waging Peace: The White House Years, a Personal Account, 1956–1961* (New York: Doubleday, 1965), 58–103; as President Eisenhower wrote, 'Some critics have said that the United States should have sided with the British and French in the Middle East, that it was fatuous to lean so heavily on the United Nations. If we had taken this advice, where would it have led us? Would we now be, with them, an occupying Power in a seething Arab world? If so, I am sure we would regret it. During the campaign, some political figures kept talking of our failure to "back Israel". If the administration had been incapable of withstanding this kind of

advice in an election year, could the United Nations thereafter have retained any influence whatsoever? This, I definitely doubt.'

15 See Douglas Little, 'From Even-Handed to Empty Handed: Seeking Order in the Middle East', in Thomas G. Paterson (ed.), *Kennedy's Quest for Victory, American Foreign Policy, 1961–1963* (New York: Oxford University Press, 1989), 156–78.

16 See, for example, Lyndon Baines Johnson, *The Vantage Point: Perspectives of the Presidency, 1963–1969* (New York: Holt, Rinehart and Winston, 1971), 287–304; and Dean Rusk, *As I Saw It* (New York: Norton and Norton, 1990), 384–90. Interestingly, Rusk writes regarding the consequences of the 1967 Arab–Israeli War: 'For twenty years, since the creation of Israel, the United States had tried to persuade the Arabs that they needn't fear Israeli territorial expansion. Throughout the 1960s the Arabs talked continuously about their fear of Israeli expansion. With the full knowledge of successive governments in Israel, we did our utmost to persuade the Arabs that their anxieties were illusory. And then following the Six-Day War, Israel decided to keep the Golan Heights, the West Bank, the Gaza Strip and the Sinai, despite the fact that Israeli Prime Minister Levi Eshkol on the first day of the war went on Israeli radio and said that Israel had no territorial ambitions. Later in the summer I reminded Abba Eban of this, and he simply shrugged his shoulders and said, 'We've changed our minds'.

17 For the text of UN Security Council Resolution 242 (1967), see https://unispal.un.org/DPA/DPR/unispal.nsf/0/7D35E1F729DF491C85256EE700686136; for the text of UN Security Council resolution 338 (1973), see https://unispal.un.org/DPA/DPR/unispal.nsf/0/7FB7C26FCBE80A31852560C50065F878; see also historical background of both resolutions provided by United Nations publications at https://www.un.org/Depts/dpi/palestine/ch3.pdf.

18 The Nixon Doctrine was a policy formulated by President Richard Nixon in 1969 during his first year in office. Targeted to Asia and Vietnamese issues, according to the president, that the doctrine 'provided the only sound basis for America's staying in [Asia] and continuing to play a responsible role in helping the non-Communist nations and neutrals as well as our Asian allies to defend their independence'. The principles of doctrine were of course applied to the Middle East region and helped armed American allies such as Iran and Israel. See Richard Nixon, *The Memoirs of Richard Nixon* (New York: Grosset and Dunlap, 1978), 394–5; and LaFeber, *America, Russia and the Cold War*, 262–5.

19 For an interesting but revealing account on the logistics and purpose of the Geneva Conference, see Brian Urquhart, *A Life in Peace and War* (New York: Norton and Norton, 1987), 243–6.

20 Henry Kissinger, *Years of Upheaval* (Boston: Little, Brown, 1982), 666.

21 The change was a curious one given the chronology. Sadat had removed or purged from Egyptian leadership known as the 'pro-Soviet group' including Ali Sabri whom many had thought would have succeeded to the Egyptian presidency. Notwithstanding this development in 1971, Sadat signed a new Soviet-Egyptian treaty that same year only to have Soviet technicians and advisors expelled one year later. See Mohammed Heikal, *The Sphinx and the Commissar* (New York: Harper and Row, 1978), 228–42.

22 See Office of the Historian, Bureau of Public Affairs, *Oil Embargo, 1973–1974* (United States Department of State) at https://history.state.gov/milestones/1969-1976/oil-embargo. Note that a similar oil embargo was maintained in 1979 against the United

States for its Middle East policies, in particular for its sponsorship of the 1978 Camp David Accords and Israeli–Egyptian Peace Treaty of 1979.
23 See 'Arabs Create Organization for Recovery of Palestine', *New York Times*, 29 May 1964, 1.
24 For a brief history and enabling resolutions regarding the relationship between the Palestine Liberation Organization and the United Nations, see 'Question of Palestine' at http://www.un.org/en/ga/62/plenary/palestine/bkg.shtml.
25 For an account of the adoption of this General Assembly resolution, which was, in effect, a defeat for America's Middle East diplomacy and Israel at the United Nations, see *A Dangerous Place* (Boston: Atlantic-Little Brown, 1978), 169–99. For the text of General Assembly resolution 3379 (resolution 3379 10 November 1975), see https://web.archive.org/web/20121206052903/http://unispal.un.org/UNISPAL.NSF/0/761C1063530766A7052566A2005B74D1; for the voting record, see https://digitallibrary.un.org/record/650324?ln=en. The resolution was later revoked by the UN General Assembly in 1991.
26 See Zbigniew Brzezinski, *Power and Principle: Memoirs of the National Security Adviser, 1977–1981* (New York: Farrar, Strauss and Giroux, 1983); and Cyrus Vance, *Hard Choices: Critical Years in America's Foreign Policy* (New York: Simon and Schuster, 1983).
27 See Joseph A. Bongiorno, 'The European Reaction to the Camp David Accords and the Israeli-Egyptian Peace Treaty (1979–1982)', in Gianvito Galasso et al. (eds), *Europa e Medio Oriente (1973–1993)* (Bari: Cacucci Editore, 2018), 171–81. See also the same author's additional paper, 'Canadian Reaction to the Camp David Accords and the Multinational Observer Force in the Sinai, 1978–1986', delivered at the 23rd Biennial Conference of the Association of Canadian Studies in the United States (ACSUS), Las Vegas, USA, 14–17 October 2015; available at http://www.acsus.org/conf/23rd-biennial-conference-las-vegas-oct-14-17-2015.
28 See FRUS, 1977–1980, vol. VIII, Arab-Israeli Dispute, January 1977–August 1978, and FRUS, 1977–1980, vol. IX, Arab-Israeli Dispute, August 1978–December 1980.
29 See Urquhart, *A Life in Peace and War*, 300–1; as UN Under-Secretary-General Brian Urquhart wrote in his memoirs, 'As the Soviets and Arabs were dead against this [the use of UNEF II forces to support the aforementioned treaties], there was no possibility of the Security Council agreeing to it. ... Another substitute would have to be primarily from the United States, thereby introducing a sizable American force into the region, something the Soviet Union didn't want. I tried this impeccable piece of logic on the Soviet [UN] Ambassador, Oleg Troyanovsky, but he only smiled politely. Thus we set about dismantling UNEF II, the force which had played such an important role in the 1973 crisis and ever since.'
30 For a history of UNEF II, see Department of Public Information, *The Blue Helmets: A Review of United Nations Peacekeeping* (New York: United Nations, 1990), 79–98.
31 See Bongiorno, 'The European Reaction to the Camp David Accords and the Israeli-Egyptian Peace Treaty (1979–1982)'. The placement of American and allied troops in Iraq in 2003 and Russian troops in the Syrian civil war as of this writing are examples of this consequence.
32 See, for example, Michael Axworthy, *Revolutionary Iran: A History of the Islamic Republic* (London: Oxford University Press, 2016).
33 For a description of the crisis by the incumbent president, see Jimmy Carter, *Keeping Faith: Memoirs of a President* (New York: Bantam, 1982), 431–597.

34 See George Shultz, *Turmoil and Triumph: My Years as Secretary of State* (New York: Charles Scribner's Sons, 1993), 43–61. See also Gino Nebiolo, *Gli Italiani a Beirut* (Milan: Bompiani Editore, 1984).
35 See Paolo Soave, *Fra Reagan e Gheddafi, la politica estera italiana e l'escalation libico-americana degli anni '80* (Catanzaro: Rubbettino Editore, 2017).
36 Stephen Howarth, *To Shining Sea: A History of the United States Navy* (Norman: University of Oklahoma Press, 1991), 546.
37 See Chris Hedges, 'Mideast Accord: The Overview; Rabin and Arafat Sign Accord Ending Israel's 27-Year Hold on Jericho and the Gaza Strip', *New York Times*, 5 May 1994, 1; available at https://www.nytimes.com/1994/05/05/world/mideast-accord-overview-rabin-arafat-sign-accord-ending-israel-s-27-year-hold.html?pagewanted=all.
38 See Hugh Seton-Watson, *The Russian Empire, 1801–1917* (London: Clarendon Press, 1967), 317–18. See also Firuz Kazemzadeh, 'Russia and the Middle East', in Ivo J. Lederer (ed.), *Russian Foreign Policy: Essays in Historical Perspective* (New Haven, CT: Yale University Press, 1962), 489–531.
39 The search for a balance of power was to secure warm water ports for Russian naval ships in the pursuit of protecting the Russian Empire's 'southern flank' extending from the eastern Mediterranean to Persia and Afghanistan. The policies of the former czars and commissars were in fact quite similarly laced with the unforgotten lessons of the Crimean War of 1856. See, for example, Donald W. Mitchell, *A History of Russian and Soviet Naval Power* (New York: Macmillan, 1974), 135–82.
40 Note that the USSR had lost its important naval bases in Albania after the diplomatic break with that nation's government then led by Enver Hoxha in 1961. Thus, Soviet prospects or designs in the Middle East gained a more important geopolitical significance in terms of naval strategy and parity in the Eastern Mediterranean to counter both the United States and NATO interests. See Mitchell, *A History of Russian and Soviet Naval Power*, 486.
41 See Edward Crankshaw (ed.) and Nikita Khrushchev, *Khrushchev Remembers* (New York: Bantam Books, 1971), 474–500.
42 Leonid Brezhnev, *On the Policy of the Soviet Union and the International Situation* (New York: Doubleday, 1973), 222.
43 Although a full examination of Soviet–Egyptian and Soviet–Arab relations would be beyond the scope of this chapter, the reader may wish to consult the following: Mohammed Heikal, *The Sphinx and the Commissar* (New York: Harper and Row, 1978); see also an informative paper written at Princeton University concerning Soviet affairs in the Middle East with a useful bibliography by Sean Paul Ashley, 'Cold War Politics in the Middle East' 30 August 2012; available at http://www.e-ir.info/2012/08/30/cold-war-politics-in-the-middle-east/.
44 See Nikolai Lebedev, *The USSR in World Politics* (Moscow: Progress, 1980), 290. The results would be contrary to what Lebedev had foretold: 'The far-seeing Soviet policy in regard to the Middle East conflict ruined Washington's calculations aimed at alienating the Arab countries from the Soviet Union. ... With the recurring outbreaks of conflicts and the rising tension in the Middle East, the steadfastness and constructive nature of the Soviet stance serves as a guarantee that political realism will eventually prevail here too.'
45 Mikhail Gorbachev, *A Time for Peace* (New York: Richardson and Steierman, 1985), 297.

46 Mikhail Gorbachev, *The August Coup: The Truth and the Lessons* (New York: HarperCollins, 1991).

47 In 2003, the United Nations Security Council examined the agenda item of the question of justice and the rule of law, along with the role of the United Nations in areas of the world such as the Middle East. The author, who served as a political and legal advisor to the Permanent Mission of the Republic of San Marino, co-authored a statement delivered by San Marino's ambassador, Gian Nicola Balestra. Reflecting on the historical importance of the roles of both international law and the United Nations, Ambassador Balestra said, 'One need only consider its many activities. In the political, social and humanitarian fields, the United Nations has striven for such a definition of justice, whether it has to do with improving the social and economic lives of millions through cooperation, food programmes or financial assistance, or with sending civil and military personnel as peacekeeping operatives for the purpose of preserving life and security in troubled lands.' See UNSC, S/PV.4385, Tuesday, 30 September 2003, New York, 21; available at http://www.un.org/en/ga/search/view_doc.asp?symbol=S/PV.4835.

48 On the League of Arab States, see Robert W. MacDonald, *The League of Arab States* (Princeton, NJ: Princeton University Press, 1965); on the United Nations in the period between 1973 and 1993, one may refer to, among many sources, Urquhart, *A Life In Peace and War*, 209–370; Kurt Waldheim, *In the Eye of the Storm* (Bethesda, MD: Adler and Adler, 1985); Kurt Waldheim, *The Challenge of Peace* (New York: Rawson, Wade, 1980); Javier Perez de Cuellar, *Pilgrimage for Peace* (New York: St. Martin's Press, 1997); Boutros Boutros-Ghali, *Unvanquished: A U.S. U.N. Saga* (New York: Random House, 1999), 3–114; Office of Public Information, *The Blue Helmets: A Review of United Nations Peacekeeping* (New York: United Nations, 1990).

2

The Middle East beyond the Cold War: The case of the Israeli–Palestinian conflict, 1989–93

Arturo Marzano

Introduction

In this chapter, I will concentrate on the years 1989–93 in order to enquire about the main consequences that the end of the Cold War brought to the Middle East. In particular, I will focus on the way in which the Israeli–Palestinian conflict, in its internal, regional and international dimensions, was affected by the collapse of the communist bloc and the end of bipolarity. More specifically, I intend to investigate the impact of these events on the two main actors in the conflict, that is, the Palestine Liberation Organization (PLO) and Israel: How did the end in the Cold War and the Gulf War affect the PLO and the Israeli government? Were they weakened or strengthened by these events? To what extent did these happenings influence the PLO and Israel in the two crucial years that passed between the Madrid Conference in October–November 1991 and the signature of the Declaration of Principles in September 1993?

By drawing on a vast bibliography existing on the history of the Israeli–Palestinian conflict, I intend to demonstrate that, on one hand, the post-1989 new international and regional order was a main catalyst for the peace process; yet, on the other hand, it had negative outcomes, such as exacerbating the imbalance of power between Israel and the PLO. Such an imbalance would negatively affect the way in which the Oslo agreements were conceived, thus preparing the way for their failure.

Israel and the PLO at the end of the Cold War

It is clear that in this chapter I can neither comprehensively deal with the several causes that have led to the Israeli–Palestinian conflict, nor summarize its history.[1] However, it is worth highlighting that it is not possible to understand the complexity of the conflict if three different dimensions are not analysed and studied. The first one is 'internal', that is the conflict between Israelis and Palestinians, who represent the core actors of the conflict. The second one is 'regional', that is, the way in which the various Middle Eastern States have played a major or minor role in the several phases of the conflict. Finally, there is an 'international' dimension, showing the interference that the world powers have brought into the conflict by supporting either one of the two actors.[2]

If the British Empire was certainly playing a major role in the first half of the twentieth century,[3] starting from the late 1950s to the early 1960s, it was the Cold War that represented the framework within which the Israeli–Palestinian conflict developed and evolved until the end of the 1980s. According to Yair Evron, the two superpowers practised 'controlled competition' in the Middle East, since they developed an 'intense competition that was moderated by the shared desire of both superpowers to avoid direct escalations between them'.[4] The consequence of the USSR and the US involvement[5] – as Salim Yaqoub has correctly stated – is that 'from the late 1960s on, Cold War rivalries were increasingly mapped onto the Arab-Israeli conflict'.[6] The same applies to the opposite: the Israeli–Palestinian conflict highly intertwined with the Cold War and both the Israeli government and the PLO depended on the United States and the USSR, respectively. In terms of political and economic support that the United States provided to Israel, we should take into account that the American economic assistance to Israel between 1949 and 1991 amounted to more than US$17 billion, while the military assistance in the same years totalled more than US$32 billion.[7] At the same time, the PLO used the USSR and the communist bloc to advance its own strategy and depended on them for its economic and military strength.[8] As to the Israeli–Palestinian clashes, just to give an example, the Israeli invasion of Lebanon and the siege of Beirut could not be understood without a green light by the American administration of Ronald Reagan.[9]

Given the relevance of the Cold War to the Israeli–Palestinian conflict, the collapse of the communist bloc in 1989 could not but have crucial consequences. The most relevant, to use the words of Israeli political scientist Shlomo Avineri, was the 'de-globalization of the Arab-Israeli conflict'.[10] As stated, since the 1950s, the Soviet Union and the United States had progressively been drawn into in the Middle East and in the Arab–Israeli conflict. At the end of the 1980s, this conflict stopped being part of the 'global Cold War,'[11] and the role played by the internal actors, at least during the 1990s, increased. At the same time, the end of the Cold War had an extremely relevant impact on the two main actors, Israel and the PLO.

As for Israel, the end of the communist bloc influenced negatively the primacy of Israel in the network of US alliances in the Middle East: the Jewish state remained an essential ally, but issues at stake were far more negotiable compared to what had happened in the previous decades. Once the Cold War was over, even if the financial support did not decline, there was no more need of Israel as anti-communist buffer. For almost thirty years, the special relationship between Israel and the United States had been based on US support to Israel in exchange for the role of the latter in guarding the interests of the former in the Middle East. During those years, Washington had tried to indulge the Israeli government's wishes, given the advantages the United States was getting in return. After 1989, the relationship changed, as Israel's role had become less relevant. As a consequence, Washington would be able to use 'the stick' in addition to the 'carrot', as actually happened in 1991, when President George Bush forced the Israeli Prime Minister Yitzhak Shamir to participate in the Madrid Conference.

As for the PLO, the consequences were more severe. The support that the Palestinians had received from the communist bloc in the previous thirty years cannot be overestimated. Both the Soviet Union and other socialist countries, from the Eastern European states to Cuba, had politically and financially supported the PLO and provided it with military equipment. At the same time, these countries had hosted many Palestinians in their universities, thus giving birth to a qualified middle class composed of engineers, doctors and teachers who were coming back to the Occupied Palestinian Territories, thus enriching the Palestinian civil society. Starting from 1968-9, Moscow decided to support the PLO and, during the second half of the 1970s, due to the USSR dissatisfaction over the increasingly close ties between Egypt and the United States, Soviet-PLO relations blossomed. After a cooling in the early 1980s, when Moscow sided with Syria in the increasing Syrian-PLO tensions in Lebanon, the Soviet-PLO relationship improved again so that 'by 1989, the PLO and the Soviet Union had recaptured the earlier warmth of their relationship'.[12] With its collapse in 1991, the support by the Soviet Union and the other communist countries ended, leaving the PLO without political and – even worse – economic support, and at the same time depriving Palestinian society of reliable friends.[13] Therefore, by the beginning of the 1990s the PLO had entered a severe crisis that would deteriorate even further in the following months due to the events related to the Gulf War.

The Gulf War and its consequences

This chapter is not the place suitable to deal with an incredibly complex issue such as the reasons that led to the Iraqi invasion of Kuwait.[14] At the same time, it would be impossible to concentrate on the wider consequences that the Gulf War had on the Middle East.[15] It is enough to recall that the Gulf War demonstrated once again how strategic, yet unstable, was the Middle East for the international order and how its stability was crucial for the Western – and in particular American – interests. As a brief example, while the end of the Cold War had reduced Turkey's importance to the West, since it was not a barrier to Soviet ambitions in the Middle East any more, the Gulf War reminded the West that Turkey was still in one of the most strategic locations of the world, and her cooperation was essential for the protection of Western interests in the Middle East.[16] At the same time, the Gulf War strengthened even more the relevance of 'sovereignty as the basis of the regional order', as exemplified by the Damascus Declaration of March 1991. The main value of this pan-Arab security arrangement among the participants (the Gulf States, Syria and Egypt) was 'recognition of the legitimacy of the Arab states' borders, the right of each state to arrange its own security, and the exclusive claim to its resources'.[17]

In the next pages, I will mainly analyse the consequences of the Gulf War on the Israeli-Palestinian conflict. As is well known, Iraqi troops invaded Kuwait on 2 August 1990. The following day, during the Arab League meeting of foreign ministers in Cairo, Iraq was condemned for its aggression, and a final resolution – which 'asked Iraq for the immediate and unconditional withdrawal of the Iraqi forces' – was approved by participants with fourteen votes in favour and six abstentions and rejections, among them Palestine, that is, the PLO.[18] A week later, on 10 August, the Arab Summit Conference adopted a resolution in line with the condemnation of Iraq that had been foreseen by the UN resolutions nos. 660, 661 and 662: twelve countries voted in favour; two abstained (Algeria and Yemen), three voted against (Libya, Iraq and Palestine), three expressed reservations (among them Jordan) and Tunisia was not present.

Why did the PLO decide to support Iraq? First of all, the Palestinian leadership highly appreciated Saddam Hussein's decision to negotiate Iraq's withdrawal from Kuwait in exchange for Israel's withdrawal from the occupied Palestinian territories. On 12 August, in a message broadcast by Baghdad radio and television, Saddam Hussein openly confirmed such a connection: 'I propose that all issues of occupation, or the issues that have been depicted as occupation in the entire region, be resolved in accordance with the same bases, principles, and premises to be set by the UN Security Council.' Therefore, according to him, Iraq would withdraw from Kuwait on conditions that other withdrawals would happen at the same time, starting with 'the immediate and unconditional withdrawal of Israel from the occupied Arab territories in Palestine, Syria, and Lebanon'.[19]

At the same time, the PLO leaders acknowledged the extensive support that Saddam Hussein enjoyed in the occupied Palestinian territories. At the end of 1990, there was a widespread feeling of frustration in the West Bank and Gaza. Many Palestinians were highly disappointed with the course of the Intifada.[20] Nothing had really changed: the Intifada's mainly non-violent tactics and the political change in the PLO attitude towards Israel that had concretized in the 15 November 1988 'Declaration of Independence'[21] had done almost nothing to advance the Palestinian request to end the occupation and give birth to an independent state. Saddam Hussein's strategy of linking the occupation of Kuwait with that of the Palestinian Territories seemed an opportunity for Palestinian public opinion. As Gideon Gera recalls, Saddam Hussein 'was assaulting the hated status quo' and promised to 'redeem the Palestinians with his wondrous military might'. Despite the relevance of the Palestinian community in Kuwait and the country's strong support for the PLO, the Palestinians chose Saddam Hussein: 'passions warred with interests and passions won'.[22] The reaction of the Palestinian public opinion to Saddam's position should be understood – to use the Palestinian journalist Hanna Siniora's words – as that of 'a drowning man [who] sees land disappear slowly in front of him, and suddenly a man throws him a rope, he will not ask who that man is'.[23]

In the meantime, PLO Chairman Yasser Arafat believed that he could play a role as negotiator, thus enhancing the PLO's political and diplomatic roles in the Arab world and, more important, in US perception.[24]

The consequences of the PLO decision to side with Saddam Hussein were various and severe. First, it led to the increasing Palestinian isolation. Regionally, the Gulf War completed the trend that had started with the Camp David Accords of 1979, when Egypt was removed from the bloc of Arab countries that might counterbalance Israeli military power in the Middle East. The Gulf War removed Iraq and Syria: the first because its military power was destroyed; and the second because it entered the anti-Iraq coalition and therefore the American orbit. As to the international dimension – apart from the already mentioned collapse of the communist bloc – the main consequence of the PLO decision to stand by Saddam Hussein was a cooling down of the West European countries' support, after two decades of increasing backing.[25]

Second, the Gulf War jeopardized the PLO relationship with Saudi Arabia and Kuwait, among the most important and generous donors that the PLO had. Both Arab countries stopped financing the PLO and, in addition to that, Kuwait also expelled about four hundred thousand Palestinians who had been living there for several years. These (the Palestinians who had been living in Saudi Arabia and in Kuwait) were a very cohesive and successful community, which basically constituted the core of the civil administration and private sector in Kuwait and had highly contributed to the economic and political transformation of that country. At the same time, they had played a crucial role in supporting the Palestinians living in the occupied territories.[26] The economic consequences were massive, in addition to the already mentioned end of financial support from the communist countries. If we think that Saudi Arabia and Kuwait started financing the Islamist organization Hamas,[27] which was already at that time the main rival of the PLO, the political blow was even more dramatic. Actually, the currency transfer from the Gulf countries to the occupied Palestinian territories was not the only transfer to stop. In fact, Israel shut the borders between the Territories and Israel between mid-January and the end of February, thus cutting off a large percentage of Palestinians from their livelihood in Israel. According to some estimates, before 1990 there were 120,000 Palestinian workers – more than 40 per cent of the total workforce in Gaza and a third of that of the West Bank – whose living was earned from employment in Israel. By the Spring of 1991, Palestinians were permitted to go back to work in Israel, but the total number of permits that the Palestinians needed in order to cross the Green Line was highly reduced.[28]

Of course, the Gulf War had consequences on Israel as well. As to the international spectrum, the war damaged the Israeli-American relationship. If during the Cold War, and in particular the Reagan Presidency, Israel was embodying the bastion of Western-style democracies against the threat of a Soviet-backed communist invasion, with the Gulf War it was perceived as a liability for US interests. As Avi Shlaim correctly states, the Gulf War 'was a conflict which threatened America's most vital interests in the region and the best service that Israel could render to her senior partner was to refrain from doing anything. Far from being a strategic asset, Israel was widely perceived as an embarrassment and a liability.'[29] This does not mean that Israel did not have any leverage that could be used with Washington. For the American administration, it was crucial for Israel not to take part in the military coalition against Saddam Hussein. Had it actively participated, several Arab countries would have felt disconcerted and might have withdrawn their support to the operation. This allowed Israel to ask concessions from Washington in exchange for its decision not to react against the Iraqi attacks. But the American perception of Israel as a 'liability' had certainly a negative impact on the relationship between Washington and Jerusalem.

As to the regional dimension, contrary to what happened to the PLO, the Gulf War impact also included positive outcomes. For the first time Israel was on the same side of several Arab countries: not only Egypt, with which Jerusalem signed a peace agreement in 1979 and not only Saudi Arabia and Kuwait, which had been strong allies of the US during the Cold War and therefore shared a common friendship with Washington, but also Syria, which had long-lasting rivalry with Iraq and agreed to support the coalition. The fact that some Arab countries and Israel were on the same side made the Jewish state a 'normal' Middle Eastern country. As a consequence, many Arab states started changing their approach towards the Israeli–Palestinian conflict, transforming it 'from an ideological into an interstate contest', and some of them even got to the point of indicating their willingness to reconcile – if not recognize – Israel.[30]

As to the internal situation in Israel, the Gulf War had a double-edged impact on the so-called 'peace camp'. On one hand, the war negatively affected the pacifist groups, by splitting them. Two among the most famous and committed doves, Yossi Sarid of the Labour Party and Dedi Zucker of the left-wing *Ratz* party, backed the war, after being disappointed with the Palestinians' support of Saddam Hussein. A division took place even within the association *Yesh Gvul* [There is a limit/border], whose members refused to serve in the Occupied Territories: some of them opposed the war; others supported it as they perceived Saddam Hussein as a security threat that had to be militarily defeated.[31] On the other hand, the war had a positive effect. Pacifists could openly state that the occupied Palestinian territories were not that relevant in enhancing the security of the Jewish state. Controlling the West Bank had not prevented Saddam Hussein from launching thirty-nine missiles against Israel, hitting the country as had not happened since the 1948 war. Even though some sectors of the right-wing parties reaffirmed that the West Bank was crucial in protecting the coast – where 75 per cent of the Israeli population was living in the early 1990s – from neighbouring Arab countries' attacks, the lesson that the left-wing camp presented to the public opinion was that 'Israel has discovered that the addition of territory does not necessarily increase its deterrent capability'.[32] In addition to that, as Max Abrahms states, the defeat of Saddam Hussein 'dramatically changed Israel's strategic environment'. The fact that a major threat had disappeared, since Iraq's arsenal of missiles and non-conventional weapons had been destroyed, led several left-wing Israeli politicians, including Yitzhak Rabin, to think that 'Israel could run unprecedented risks in pursuit of peace'.[33]

The Madrid Conference

The decision to hold a peace conference in which all actors involved in the Israeli–Palestinian conflict would participate was a direct consequence of the Gulf War. As Galia Golan explains well, it was a 'sequential linkage', and therefore different from the 'direct linkage' that Saddam Hussein was willing to establish between the occupation of Kuwait and that of the occupied Palestinian territories. This 'sequential linkage' was promised by the United States to Syria and Russia in exchange for their agreement to create an anti-Iraq coalition.[34] The results of such an agreement was clear in the addresses that Mikhail Gorbachev and George Bush delivered in Helsinki on 9 September 1990. On that occasion, the American president was asked whether 'the conflict in the Gulf gives the opportunity to solve the Palestinian problem through an international peace conference for the Middle East'. While recalling that the invasion of Kuwait was 'separate' from the other questions, Bush also stated, 'I strongly support … that under certain circumstances the consideration of a conference of that nature would be acceptable indeed, it's been a part of our policy from time to time'.[35]

At the end of operation Desert Storm, Washington was ready to push for a peace agreement. As Bush stated to Congress on 6 March 1991, 'the time has come to put an end to [the] Arab-Israeli conflict'.[36] The diplomatic initiative that led to the convening of the Madrid Conference on 30 October 1990 was launched on that occasion. But it took eight months of shuttle diplomacy before Secretary of State James Baker could bridge the differences between the Israeli government and the Arab states.[37] Despite the fact that Syria and Jordan had agreed to participate in the conference in July, the tensions between the United States and Israel were overcome only on 20 October, when the Israeli cabinet voted to go to Madrid.[38] It was only due to the 'immense pressure' applied by the American administration that Yitzhak Shamir agreed to participate in the Madrid Conference.[39]

The main leverage that Washington used with Jerusalem concerned the issue of the Soviet Jews, for whose settlement in Israel Shamir needed American political and – more important – financial support. The two countries had reached an agreement on a first loan in Autumn 1990. As the Israeli Minister of Foreign Affairs David Levy wrote in a letter sent to the American Secretary of State James Baker on 2 October 1990, the Israeli government had committed 'not to direct or settle Soviet Jews beyond the green line'[40] in exchange for the decision of the United States to release US$400 million in housing loan guarantees for the settlement of Soviet Jews. Yet, as Levy clarified two weeks later in another letter, the Israeli decision contained 'no commitment – either direct or indirect – to avoid building in Jerusalem, nor to limit construction in Jerusalem or anywhere else, including Judaea, Samaria, and Gaza'. The Israeli government was quite clear in stating that it would not 'change [its] "credo" … as a result of this loan', since it considered Judea, Samaria and Gaza as integral part of Israel and 'the question of Israeli sovereignty over Jerusalem' was not to be discussed.[41]

Another more relevant loan was negotiated the following year, and Washington conditioned it to the Israeli participation in the conference. On 12 September 1991, Bush went as far as to threaten the Congress to veto the latter's decision of allowing a loan of US$10 billion had Jerusalem not agreed to participate in the conference. Then, Shamir realised that should he not agree to go to Madrid, he would risk jeopardizing his relationship with Bush. For this reason, he decided not only to be part of the conference, but also to head the delegation himself.[42] It was an excellent decision. On one hand, he showed Bush his willingness to compromise, thus saving the status of the relationship between Israel and the United States. On the other hand, he was totally aware that the conference would lead nowhere, as he had already decided to make it fail. In his opening speech, Shamir clearly stated that he had no intention to withdraw from the territories: to him, the aim of Madrid was 'to reach an agreement on interim self-government arrangements with the Palestinian Arabs', without any retreat, as 'the issue is not territory, but our existence'.[43] A declaration that better clarifies what the Israeli prime minister had in mind in 1991 was given by Shamir the following year:

I know how to display the tactics of moderation, but without conceding anything on the goal – the integrity of the Land of Israel. I would have carried on autonomy talks for ten years and meanwhile we would have reached half a million [Jewish] people in Judea and Samaria.[44]

As for the PLO, it was not invited to participate in the conference. As Martin Indyk recalls, in 1991, Egypt, Syria and the Gulf states did not make any reference to the PLO in their joint communiqués. After almost two decades in which the Arab states were insisting on the PLO involvement in the peace process, such a change was certainly a real breakthrough.[45] While no Arab state welcomed the PLO, Israel had been very clear in opposing its participation. In exchange for accepting to go to Madrid, Shamir was reassured by Bush on two crucial issues. First of all, the PLO would not be present: only Palestinians from the West Bank and Gaza, excluding Jerusalem, would be part of the so-called Jordanian delegation. In fact, the Palestinian team, which was part of a joint Palestinian–Jordanian delegation, consisted only of Palestinians from the West Bank and Gaza. The head of the delegation was Haidar Abdel-Shafi, a Palestinian physician living in Gaza, who did not have a formal mandate from the PLO, yet was in constant contact with the Tunis-based PLO leadership. Second, the United States would not support the creation of a Palestinian state.

As Shamir was hoping, the three-day Madrid Conference (30 October–1 November 1991) did not have any immediate positive outcome. Gideon Gera's comment concerning the Middle East events during the entire year – 'no decisive turning point occurred in the Middle East in 1991' – applies well to the peace conference. Yet, it led to relevant changes, 'whose realisation or abandonment would be determined in the future'.[46]

From Madrid to Washington

In order to understand the events that led to the Declaration of Principles of 13 September 1993 – when Yasser Arafat and Yitzhak Rabin shook their hands in front of the White House, thus formally 'recogniz[ing] their mutual legitimate and political rights' and 'establish[ing] a Palestinian Interim Self-Government Authority … for the Palestinian people in the West Bank and the Gaza Strip'[47] – it is crucial to highlight the political relevance that the Palestinians living in the Occupied Territories had acquired in the late 1980s. The Israeli political scientist Hillel Frisch quotes the Egyptian historian Wahid 'Abd al-Majid, who identifies three different phases as to the role played by the Palestinians in the Arab–Israeli conflict. After a first phase in which Palestinians had 'put their faith in the Arab states' with the idea that the latter would defeat Israel, and a second phase in which the PLO led the fight 'mobilizing militarily through guerrilla action', starting from the invasion of Lebanon in 1982 and going through the Intifada 'the local Palestinians began to take their fate into their own hands'.[48]

The relevance of the so-called 'Insiders', that is the Palestinians living in the Occupied Territories who composed the Palestinian team at the Madrid Conference, led to increasing tensions between them and the PLO leadership. Mahdi Abdul Hadi, founder and president of the Palestinian Academic Society for the Study of International

Affairs, was quite aware of the problems that the separation between the 'Insiders' and the 'Outsiders' could represent. During a roundtable held in February 1991, which was published the following April, he highlighted the existence of problematic relationships between the 'Inside' and the 'Outside'. Abdul Hadi stressed that 'the outside leadership comes under pressure' of the inside leadership, as this one 'may consider itself more informed of the conditions and their particulars, and consequently more capable of evaluating the immediate or future results'.[49]

These tensions would emerge clearly in 1992–3. In the eight negotiation rounds that followed the Madrid Conference between November 1991 and December 1992, the Palestinian delegation, composed of 'Insiders', rejected the Israeli proposals as these were not addressing the Palestinian request of an independent state.[50] Despite the political earthquake of 23 June 1992, when the Labour Party led by Yitzhak Rabin defeated the Likud in the Israeli political elections, thus opening the path to a left-wing government, the position of the Israeli delegation at the bilateral negotiations did not change. As Emma Murphy recalls, in those negotiations, 'Rabin was virtually as uncompromising as the former Israeli prime minister, Yitzhak Shamir, had been before him, and concentrated on using the bilaterals as a route to agreement with Syria and Jordan'.[51] While the Palestinian delegation remained stuck in its opposition to an agreement that did not include recognition by Israel of a Palestinian state, the PLO started to be more willing to make significant compromises, thus increasing the tensions with the 'insiders'. The frictions between the PLO and the Palestinian delegation – who was becoming less keen to defer to Tunis – were not the only ones at that time. In the occupied Palestinian territories, the PLO was highly challenged by the Hamas-led rejectionist front, that also included the left-wing organizations, including the Popular Front.

It was at that moment that the Israeli government decided to negotiate with the PLO, as it clearly realised that the latter would be a more compromising partner. After almost four years of Intifada, the newly elected prime minister realized that the only way to call a halt to the Intifada was through negotiations.[52] But, as stated, the Palestinian delegation showed no intention to give up the issue of an independent state. The Israeli government was also aware that the occupied Palestinian territories were coming more and more under the influence of rejectionist groups, in particular Hamas. As Avi Shalim highlights, the 'assessment of the IDF director of military intelligence that Arafat's dire situation, and possibly imminent collapse, made him the most convenient interlocutor for Israel at that particular juncture'.[53]

At the end of 1992, two contemporary negotiations took place at the same time. While talking with the 'Insiders', the Israeli Deputy Foreign Minister Yossi Beilin, with the permission of the Foreign Minister Shimon Peres, opened a secret dialogue with the PLO, without the Palestinians from the West Bank and Gaza being even informed. Thanks to the commitment of the Norwegian Foreign Minister Johan Jorgen Holst, two 'unofficial' Israeli representatives – Professor Yair Hirschfeld and Dr. Ron Pundak of Haifa University – started negotiating with the PLO representative, Abu Ala'a, the PLO minister of finance. These discussions took place in Oslo.

As Galia Golan states, Arafat wanted the Oslo talks to succeed because he wanted to gain a physical foothold in the Palestinian Territories and at the same time assert his leadership over the 'Insiders', who were too independent.[54] What Golan does not say is that, in exchange for reaching an agreement and therefore being able to achieve those aims, Arafat decided to compromise on crucial issues. Basically, the PLO could not really choose whether to make a deal with Israel or not. As Israel's former Mossad chief Efraim Halevi has stated, 'If they didn't we would overrun them entirely.'[55]

The PLO leadership was much weaker than the 'Insiders'. As stated in the previous pages, the former had lost the political and economic backing of the USSR and of the communist bloc because of the end of the Cold War. It had not condemned Saddam Hussein's behaviour in the 1990–1 Gulf crisis, and therefore it had lost the financial support of the Gulf States, mainly Kuwait and Saudi Arabia. Finally, it was far away from the occupied Palestinian territories, and it was at risk of losing its control of the Palestinian population living under the Israeli occupation. An effective synthesis of the PLO's weakened position in 1993 is offered by Shamir Hassan:

> The first Intifada had been launched at the initiative of Palestinians in the West Bank and Gaza, and not the PLO leadership based at Tunis. This in turn signalled a weakening of the PLO within Palestinian politics, which was now being shaped by local Palestinians and especially Hamas. The PLO lost further in the eyes of the local Palestinians when it entered into negotiations with the US at the end of 1988. On the other hand, the PLO's diplomatic and financial position weakened when Arafat supported Saddam Hussein in the Gulf War of 1991, in line with the strong public support in Palestine for Saddam. This support to Saddam alienated the US and Arafat's so-called 'moderate' Arab allies. With the end of the cold war and the collapse of the Soviet Union soon after, the PLO had no serious alternative source of support left internationally. Against this background, the PLO had a clear interest in entering into negotiations.[56]

Given these premises, it was quite obvious that the PLO would be a weaker and a softer negotiator compared with the Palestinians from West Bank and Gaza. This is exactly what happened. With the Oslo agreements, the PLO ended up by relinquishing at least two fundamental demands: the Israeli recognition of the existence of a Palestinian state, and the interruption of the construction of new Israeli settlements in the occupied Palestinian territories. In exchange for such a renunciation, the PLO leadership was allowed to go back to the West Bank and Gaza, and it was given a relevant economic and political power that it would have never been able to get otherwise.

The entire negotiation was destined to fail, as the Palestinians from the West Bank had understood from the very beginning, because what the PLO got – in exchange for the recognition of the State of Israel – was only temporary autonomy. It did not get what the Palestinians had been asking for, that is to say an independent state or a formal commitment to that.[57] The many agreements signed during the years 1993–2000 would not challenge the basic assumption Oslo was built on. The fundamental issues – that is, settlements, borders of the Palestinian state, Jerusalem, refugees – were never part of the negotiation, until the Camp David summit of July 2000.[58]

The well-known Palestinian intellectual Edward Said stigmatized the PLO decision to sign the agreement with Israel in a very harsh way. According to him, 'all secret deals between a very strong and a very weak partner necessarily involve concessions hidden in embarrassment by the latter'.[59] The PLO had made too many concessions to the Israeli government with the aim of signing the agreement, and these concessions would make the Oslo agreements destined to fail.

Conclusion

It is not possible in this chapter to deal with the Oslo agreements, their contents, their development and their failure.[60] Certainly, one of the main issues concerning its negotiation is that the Labour party decided to recognize the Palestinian right to self-government but not to an independent state in the West Bank and Gaza. Yitzhak Rabin did not dare to follow the suggestion of a Likud politician, who had openly spoken in favour of the creation of a Palestinian state. While Eli Landau, the mayor of Herzliya, had called in 1990 for direct negotiations between Israel and the PLO, the mayor of Tel Aviv, former IDF General Shlomo Lahat, had moved further, stating that 'the Palestinians are the Jews of the Arab world' and that the Palestinians deserved 'a state of their own in the West Bank and Gaza!'[61] It was certainly not a surprise. Rabin had been very clear on that during a debate with Yitzhak Shamir that was broadcast on the Israeli TV a few days before the elections.[62] On that occasion, Rabin stated that he was 'not in favour of a state', but of 'a certain form of self-government', in line with the position of the doves of the Labour party, such as Yael Dayan, daughter of Moshe Dayan, the Ministry of Defence during the Six-Day War, and the already mentioned Yossi Beilin, both of whom had campaigned in favour of an evacuation from the Occupied Territories.[63]

In the aftermath of the Cold War and the Gulf War, the Israeli government managed to reach an agreement with the PLO from a position of strength. There was an obvious asymmetry of power between Israel and the PLO,[64] as Israel held 'all cards', to use the words of Valerie Yorke. According to her, 'negotiations within the context of this asymmetrical relationship have served to strengthen Israel and to put the PLO at a clearer disadvantage'.[65] That agreement, that is, the Declaration of Principles that would be the basis for the Oslo season, failed to deliver what the Palestinians had been – and still are – dreaming of, the birth of a Palestinian state on the West Bank, the Gaza Strip and East Jerusalem. As Oren Barak states, 'the Palestinian National Authority, while indeed representing a first autonomous Palestinian foothold in the Territories and having certain attributes of a state, was nevertheless *not* a state, although it was encouraged to *perform* as a state'.[66] As Edward Said wrote, the Declaration of Principles implied 'redeployment rather than withdrawal of the Israeli army' from parts of the occupied Palestinian territories.[67] The main consequence was that the Israeli occupation did not end, but was simply reframed in a different way.

It was certainly a lost chance. The end of the Cold War did not have those effects that could be expected. In fact, even though the two former enemy superpowers were on the same side and were supporting negotiations between the PLO and Israel, these two did not reach a peace agreement that took into consideration their mutual requests. The end of the Cold War and the events of the Gulf War, as stated in this chapter, made the PLO much weaker than it had been a few years earlier. It negotiated with Israel from a position of weakness, thus accepting an agreement that was very far from its main aim, the creation of a Palestinian state. As some intellectuals anticipated, the Oslo agreements could not deliver a real peace, and the Israeli–Palestinian conflict remained unsolved, with the on-going pain and additional casualties.

Notes

1. The best overview of the conflict is Benny Morris, *Righteous Victims: A History of the Zionist-Arab Conflict, 1881–2001* (New York: Vintage Books, 2001). See also James L. Gelvin, *The Israel-Palestine Conflict: One Hundred Years of War* (Cambridge: Cambridge University Press, 2007).
2. These three dimensions are highlighted in Beverley Milton-Edwards, *The Israeli-Palestinian Conflict: A People's War* (London: Routledge, 2009), in particular chapter 8.
3. On the topic, among others, see Lorenzo Kamel, *Imperial Perceptions of Palestine. British Influence and Power in Late Ottoman Times* (London: I.B. Tauris, 2015).
4. Yair Evron, 'The International System and the Middle East Regional System: Interactions during the Transition from Bipolarity to Unipolarity', in Lorenz M. Lüthu (ed.), *The Regional Cold Wars in Europe, East Asia, and the Middle East: Crucial Periods and Turning Points* (Washington, DC: Woodrow Wilson Center Press, 2015), 338–57 (esp. 342).
5. See George W. Breslauer (ed.), *Soviet Strategy in the Middle East* (Boston: Unwin Hyman, 1990); Joel S. Migdal, *Shifting Sands: The United States in the Middle East* (New York: Columbia University Press, 2014).
6. Salim Yaqub, 'The Cold War and the Middle East', in Robert J. McMahon (ed.), *The Cold War in the Third World* (Oxford: Oxford University Press, 2013), 11–26 (esp. 12).
7. Bernard Reich, *Securing the Covenant: United States–Israel Relations after the Cold War* (Westport, CT: Greenwood Press, 1995), 7–8.
8. See Paul T. Chamberlin, *The Global Offensive: The United States, the Palestine Liberation Organization, and the Making of the Post-Cold War Order* (Oxford: Oxford University Press, 2012).
9. Ze'ev Schiff and Ehud Ya'ari, *Israel's Lebanon War* (New York: Simon & Schuster, 1984), 31–2.
10. Shlomo Avineri, 'Israel and the End of the Cold War: The Shadow Has Faded', *Brookings Review*, 11/2 (1993), 26–31.
11. See Odd Arne Westad, *The Global Cold War: Third World Interventions and the Making of Our Times* (Cambridge: Cambridge University Press, 2005).
12. Roland Dannreuther, *The Soviet Union and the PLO* (New York: St. Martin's Press, 1998), 144.
13. Yezid Sayigh, 'The Palestinians', in Yezid Sayigh and Avi Shlaim (eds), *The Cold War and the Middle East* (Oxford: Oxford University Press, 2003), 125–55.
14. On that, see Musallam Ali Musallam, *The Iraqi Invasion of Kuwait: Saddam Hussein, His State and International Power Politics* (London: British Academy Press, 1996).

15 On the consequences of the 1990–1 events on Iran, see Trita Parsi, *Treacherous Alliance: The Secret Dealings of Israel, Iran, and the United States* (New Haven, CT: Yale University Press, 2007), esp. 139–47.
16 See Mustafa Aydin, 'Turkish Foreign Policy during the Gulf War of 1990–1991', *Cairo Papers in Social Sciences* 21/1 (1998), 1–85.
17 Michael N. Barnett, 'Regional Security after the Gulf War', *Political Science Quarterly* 111/4 (1996), 597–618 (esp. 602).
18 'Arab League Ministerial Council, Resolution on the Gulf Crisis, Cairo, 3 August 1990', Documents and Source Material, *Journal of Palestine Studies* 20/2 (1991), 177–8.
19 'Saddam Hussein's Initiative Linking the Solution of the Gulf Crisis to Settlement of Other Middle East Disputes', Baghdad, 12 August 1990, Documents and Source Material, *Journal of Palestine Studies* 20/2 (1991), 179–80.
20 See Robert O. Freedman (ed.), *The Intifada: Its Impact on Israel, the Arab World, and the Superpowers* (Miami: Florida International University Press, 1991).
21 The PLO implied acceptance of the 'two-state solution', thus implicitly recognising the existence of Israel. The text in English is available here: https://unispal.un.org/DPA/DPR/unispal.nsf/0/6EB54A389E2DA6C6852560DE0070E392 (accessed 31 July 2018).
22 Gideon Gera, 'The Middle East in 1990: A Year of Crisis', in Ami Ayalon (ed.), *Middle East Contemporary Survey* XIV (1990), 5–15 (esp. 12).
23 Emma C. Murphy, 'The Arab-Israeli Conflict in the New World Order', in Haifaa A. Jawad (ed.), *The Middle East in the New World Order* (London: Macmillan Press, 1997), 110–40 (esp. 118).
24 Yezid Sayigh, *Armed Struggle and the Search for State: The Palestinian National Movement, 1949–1953* (Washington, DC: Institute for Palestine Studies, 1999), 641–3.
25 See Lamis Andoni, 'The PLO at the Crossroads', *Journal of Palestine Studies* 21/1 (1991), 54–65.
26 See George T. Abed, 'The Palestinians and the Gulf Crisis', *Journal of Palestine Studies* 20/2 (1991), 29–42.
27 See Baconi Tareq, *Hamas Contained: The Rise and Pacification of Palestinian Resistance* (Stanford, CA: Stanford University Press, 2018), 26–8.
28 See Don Peretz, 'The Impact of the Gulf War on Israeli and Palestinian Political Attitudes', *Journal of Palestine Studies*, 21/1 (1991), 17–35.
29 Avi Shlaim, 'Israel and the Conflict', in Alex Danchev and Dan Keohane (eds), *International Perspectives on the Gulf Conflict 1990–91* (London: Palgrave Macmillan, 1994), 59–79 (esp. 77).
30 Barnett, *Regional Security after the Gulf War*, 603. See also Ibrahim Karawan, 'Arab Dilemmas in the 1990s: Breaking Taboos and Searching for Signposts', *Middle East Journal*, 48/3 (1994), 433–54.
31 Peretz, 'The Impact of the Gulf War', 22–23.
32 Ze'ev Schiff, 'Israel after the War', *Foreign Affairs* 70/2 (1991), 19–33 (esp. 29).
33 Max Abrahms, 'A Window of Opportunity for Israel?', *Middle East Quarterly* 10/3 (2003), https://www.meforum.org/articles/other/a-window-of-opportunity-for-israel (accessed 31 July 2018).
34 Galia Golan, *Israeli Peacemaking since 1967: Factors behind the Breakthroughs and Failures* (London: Routledge, 2015), 119.
35 Bush-Gorbachev News Conference, Helsinki, 9 September 1990, Documents and Source Material, *Journal of Palestine Studies* 20/2 (1991), 160–201 (esp. 161).
36 In Martin Indyk, 'Peace without the PLO', *Foreign Policy*, 83 (1991), 30–8 (esp. 30).

37 Daniel C. Kurtzer et al., *The Peace Puzzle: America's Quest for Arab-Israeli Peace, 1989-2011* (Ithaca, NY: Cornell University Press, 2013), 15-18.
38 William B. Quandt, *Peace Process: American Diplomacy and the Arab-Israeli Conflict since 1967* (Berkeley: University of California Press, 2005), 308-10.
39 Murphy, 'The Arab-Israeli Conflict', 119.
40 'Foreign Minister David Levy, Letter to U.S. Secretary of State Baker on Assurances Concerning the Settlement of Soviet Jews', Washington, DC, 2 October 1990, Documents and Source Material, *Journal of Palestine Studies* 20/2 (1991), 190.
41 'Foreign Minister David Levy, Letter to U.S. Secretary of State Baker Clarifying the Israeli Assurances, Jerusalem, 18 October 1990', Documents and Source Material, *Journal of Palestine Studies* 20/2 (1991), 191-2.
42 Martin Indyk, 'Watershed in the Middle East', *Foreign Affairs* 71/1 (1991/1992), 70-93.
43 'Opening Addresses in Madrid: Head of the Israeli Delegation, Prime Minister Yitzhak Shamir, 31 October 1991 (excerpts), The Madrid Peace Conference', *Journal of Palestine Studies* 21/2 (1992), 130-1.
44 Golan, *Israeli Peacemaking since 1967*, 120.
45 Indyk, 'Peace without the PLO', 36-38.
46 Gideon Gera, 'The Middle East in 1991: A Year of Promises Unfulfilled', in Ami Ayalon (ed.), *Middle East Contemporary Survey*, xv (1991), 5-15 (esp. 15).
47 In http://www.mfa.gov.il/mfa/foreignpolicy/peace/guide/pages/declaration%20of%20 principles.aspx (accessed 31 July 2018).
48 Hillel Frisch, 'The Death of the PLO', *Middle Eastern Studies* 45/2 (2009), 243-61 (esp. 244).
49 Mahdi Abdul Hadi, 'Post Gulf-War Assessment: A Palestinian Perspective', in *Palestinian Assessments of the Gulf War and Its Aftermath* (East Jerusalem: PASSIA, 1991), 121-71 (esp. 165).
50 Camille Mansour, 'The Palestinian-Israeli Peace Negotiations: An Overview and Assessment', *Journal of Palestine Studies* 22/3 (1993), 5-31.
51 Murphy, 'The Arab-Israeli Conflict', 121.
52 The relevance of the Intifada in pushing the new Israeli government led by Rabin to negotiate with the PLO is highlighted by a vast majority of authors. See Avi Shlaim, *The Iron Wall: Israel and the Arab World* (London: Penguin Books, 2014), esp. 465-9. See also Joe Stork and Beshara Doumani, 'After Oslo: The Shape of Palestine to Come', *Middle East Report* 186 (1994), 2-26.
53 Avi Shlaim, 'The Rise and Fall of the Oslo Peace Process', in Louise Fawcett (ed.), *International Relations of the Middle East* (Oxford: Oxford University Press, 2016), 285-303 (esp. 288).
54 Golan, *Israeli Peacemaking since 1967*, 121.
55 Parsi, *Treacherous Alliance*, 160.
56 Shamir Hassan, 'Oslo Accords: The Genesis and Consequences for Palestine', *Social Scientist* 39/7-8 (2011), 65-72 (esp. 66).
57 The already mentioned Haidar Abdel-Shafi was among those who opposed the Oslo Agreements for these reasons. See 'The Oslo Agreement: An Interview with Haydar 'Abd al-Shafi', *Journal of Palestine Studies* 23/1 (1993), 14-19.
58 Sara Roy, 'Why Peace Failed: An Oslo Autopsy', *Current History* 101/651 (2002), 8-16.
59 Edward Said, *Peace and Its Discontents: Gaza-Jericho, 1993-1995* (London: Vintage, 1995), 2.
60 Among the many volumes, see those who present the opinion of the main characters of those events: David Makovsky, *Making Peace with the PLO: The Rabin Government's*

Road to the Oslo Accord (Boulder, CO: Westview Press, 1996); Uri Savir, *The Process: 1,100 Days that Changed the Middle East* (New York: Random House, 1998); Yossi Beilin, *The Path to Geneva: The Quest for a Permanent Solution, 1996–2004* (New York: RDV Books, 2004).

61 Peretz, 'The Impact of the Gulf War', 25.
62 For the video of that debate in Hebrew, see https://www.youtube.com/watch?v=uvwc6ULGes4 (accessed 31 May 2018).
63 Peretz, 'The Impact of the Gulf War', 27.
64 Giorgio Gallo and Arturo Marzano, 'The Dynamics of Asymmetric Conflicts: The Israeli-Palestinian Case', *Journal of Conflict Studies* 29 (2009), https://journals.lib.unb.ca/index.php/jcs/article/view/15231/19943.
65 Valerie Yorke, 'The Middle East's Slow March towards Peace', *The World Today* 50/5 (1994), 86–92 (esp. 88).
66 Oren Barak, 'The Failure of the Israeli-Palestinian Peace Process, 1993–2000', *Journal of Peace Research* 42/6 (2005), 719–36 (esp. 728).
67 Edward W. Said, *The End of the Peace Process: Oslo and After* (New York: Vintage Books, 2000), xvi.

Part Two

A bridge towards the Arab world

*Italian regionalism between the Atlantic
Alliance and Europe*

3

The Middle East in Italian foreign policy: A historical perspective

Luciano Monzali

1861: The troubled emergence of a Mediterranean power

The birth of a united and independent Italian state in 1861, ruled by the Savoy monarchy, was a major change in the European and Mediterranean balance of power. The Great Powers system which dominated the European continental policy was obliged to accept the emerging of a new state whose legitimacy came from the principles of national self-determination and soon aimed at acquiring an autonomous political role in world politics.

The new Italian state nurtured its national identity celebrating the past glories of Ancient Rome, the Italian Middle Ages and the Renaissance civilization, which had had a strong impact on European and Mediterranean life for centuries. In the perspective of foreign politicians and diplomats, it was quite obvious that sooner or later the new Italian state would search to gain political and economic influence in the Eastern Mediterranean regions, most of them ruled by the Ottoman Empire and where, for centuries, Italian states like Genoa, Pisa and Venice had played an important role. As Habsburg Foreign Minister Rechberg, trying to convince the English government to support Austrian attempts to defend its own possessions in Italy, said to British diplomats in 1860 and 1861, the new Italy was the political heir of the Republic of Venice and renunciation of the Veneto by the Habsburgs would have given further encouragement to the expansionistic designs of the Savoy state, eager to obtain control on other lands inhabited by Italians or previously ruled by the Venetians. In the view of the Austrian minister, the government in Turin had plans of conquest that were aimed at creating a large Italian empire including the whole Adriatic coast as far as Cattaro and the Alpine territories to the Brenner Pass, which would undermine the status quo in the Balkans and the Mediterranean, strengthen France and bring about grave damage to British interests.[1]

In fact, in the early years of its existence, Liberal Italy had no plans to play a meaningful active role in the Eastern Mediterranean and the Middle East. The Piedmont's and then Italy's prime minister, Camillo Benso of Cavour, well aware of the dangers that the proliferation of maximalist territorial claims might create to the Italian cause, and conscious of the hostility of many German states towards Savoy ambition on Trento and Trieste, as well as of Russian and British suspicion of the Italian plan of conquest of the former Venetian possessions in the Adriatic and Mediterranean, imposed a prudent behaviour on the Italian policy in the Adriatic and in the Mediterranean. In Cavour's view, Italy wished to pursue a friendly foreign policy towards France and Great Britain and had only commercial and economic interests in the Mediterranean area.[2]

Basically, this meant a conservative and peaceful attitude towards the Ottoman Empire. In the 1860s and 1870s the survival of the Ottomans was regarded by Italian diplomacy as extremely useful, especially for the role of the Turkish rule in preventing – in the Balkans, Egypt and North Africa – more dangerous and uncontrollable expansionism by the Russians, Hapsburgs, British or French.[3] In addition, the status quo would allow Italy to develop its own commercial and cultural influence in those regions.[4]

This peaceful and passive political attitude became hardly sustainable, beginning in the summer of 1875, with the outbreak of bloody revolts against the Turks first in Herzegovina and then in Bulgaria. As the Balkan crisis was a great chance for Austria-Hungary and Russia to induce the collapse of the Ottoman Empire, the Italian government was deeply concerned.[5] As Italian Foreign Minister Emilio Visconti Venosta wrote in March 1875 to Italy's ambassador in Vienna, Carlo di Robilant:

> Our situation today, in this state of affairs, is extremely delicate. Our interests in the East, as you know, are fairly conservative. And we have a positive interest in making sure that, if the debacle is inevitable, it does not happen now and is put off until a time when Italy has a greater freedom of action and can protect itself better. The *status quo* is for the moment the best that we can desire.[6]

Despite the conservative action in the Balkans led by the Minghetti government, especially in improving the conditions of the Christian populations under Ottoman sovereignty, very little was achieved. The Italian desire for peace came into collision with Austria-Hungary's and Russia's plans of expansion and the territorial ambitions of Serbia and Montenegro.

The emerging of the Liberal Left in Italy in 1876 as a new ruling political force did not bring a radical change in Italian foreign policy, as both Right and Left had their roots in the same Liberal national ideology. However, the leaders of the Left wanted Italy to play an active and dynamic role in international politics, especially in the Mediterranean and the Balkans. Many members of the Liberal Left had once been followers of Mazzini: they still clung to their former mentor's vision of Italy as a great European and Mediterranean power and considered Austria and the Ottoman Empire the embodiment of values and interests that were inevitably opposing the Italian ones.

The changes in European and Mediterranean politics produced by the Balkan crisis,[7] forced the Italian government to react to the initiatives of the other European powers. After the policy of maintenance of the status quo in the Balkans that had been pursued by Visconti Venosta, the new Italian foreign minister, Melegari, and Tornielli, the secretary general of Italian Ministry of Foreign Affairs, tried from October to December 1876 to convince the other powers that any change in the Balkan situation favourable to Austria-Hungary would disrupt the European balance of power and damage Italian interests.[8] In doing so Italian diplomacy started to hope for some territorial compensations, the Trentino or the region of the Isonzo, by Austria-Hungary in case of its strengthening in the Balkans.

Encountering Austrian hostility and German, English and Russian indifference, the Italian attempts were a complete failure. The more general causes of the failure of Italian diplomacy lay in an inability to rapidly grasp the dynamics of European politics and to react to them pragmatically: for a long time it nursed the illusion of a possible Italo-Russian and Italo-British collaboration in the maintenance of the status quo in the Balkans and in countering Austrian ambitions, without realizing that the Russians and British also harboured plans of expansion and were ready to go along with certain Habsburg designs if they were compatible with their own political aims.[9] At the same time there was no clear understanding of the shift in Austro-German relations and no awareness of the emergence of ever closer political cooperation between Vienna and Berlin.[10] The failure of Agostino Depretis, leader of the government, and Melegari's attempts to block Habsburg expansionism or obtain territorial concessions in Trentino led in March 1878 to the formation of the first Benedetto Cairoli government, with the assumption of the office of foreign minister by Luigi Corti, minister plenipotentiary in Constantinople.[11]

Corti and Cairoli, aware of Italy's international isolation, abandoned the previous basically anti-Austrian strategy of Depretis and Melegari, which had its instigator in Tornielli, and chose to make a wholesale retreat, ceasing to obstruct Austro-Hungarian policy and avoiding engagement in independent initiatives in the Balkans and the Mediterranean.

However, this passivity on Italy's part came at the same time as a series of Russian, Habsburg and British political initiatives, which led to the disruption of the setup in the Balkans in 1878, with a reduction in the size of the Ottoman Empire and the establishment of the hegemony of Vienna and St. Petersburg in the region. Austria-Hungary and Russia not only achieved direct control of important Balkan territories (Bosnia-Herzegovina, the sanjak of Novi Pazar, southern Bessarabia) but, thanks to the Treaty of Berlin and its long and difficult application, were also able to assert their political and economic influence over the various more or less independent Balkan states.

The weakening of the Ottoman Empire ensuing from events in the Balkans and the Treaty of Berlin provided the opportunity for a change in the political setup in North Africa over the following years: Ottoman powerlessness facilitated French and British actions in Tunisia and Egypt, that is, in territories nominally part of the Turkish empire. Even in Mediterranean politics Italy's isolation translated into impotence. Its attempts to counter French influence in Tunisia took the government in Rome to the brink of conflict with Paris when the French government decided to impose its protectorate on the Tunisian bey in May 1881, a possibility that the country preferred to avoid, given the lack of any international support for Italian positions. As for the Egyptian question, after having tried to preserve the autonomy of the khedivate of Egypt in the face of British and French interference,[12] Italy attempted to assert its own influence in Egypt, alongside the French and British, but then avoided a possible military intervention in support of Great

Britain when the British armies invaded that region in 1882. Any such intervention would have been dangerous, owing to the deterioration in the domestic situation, the difficult relations with France and the Austro-German refusal to back the Italian initiative.

The loss of influence and political role, and the weakening of the country's strategic position in the Adriatic and Mediterranean, forced the Italian leaders to a general review of foreign policy. It became definitely clear that the policy of 'independence' towards the European great powers pursued by Italian governments since the fall of Napoleon III was quite ineffective. A latecomer like Italy needed to enter into political and military alliance to protect its own interests internationally. In May 1882 Italy entered the Triple Alliance with Germany and Austria-Hungary, its worst enemy.[13] The decision to conclude this alliance met various general requirements of Italian foreign and domestic policy, such as the need to emerge from a dangerous international isolation, the need to improve relations with the Habsburg empire and to give them new content and character, the necessity to guarantee the internal and external security of the state and the desire to exercise more influence on the course of European and Mediterranean politics.

A decisive part in this reappraisal of foreign policy was played by Pasquale Stanislao Mancini, a member of parliament and jurist from Campania, who was foreign minister in the fourth Depretis cabinet from 1881 to 1885.[14] He saw the creation of an alliance with the Austro-German powers as a crucial factor if Italy were to exercise effective international action; the alliance between Italy and the Germanic states was now possible since there had been a 'complete cessation of the age-old hatred and rancor between the Italian and German peoples, after the latter, with Italy restored to the complete independence to which she is entitled, had forever crossed back over the Alps'.[15] This relationship of alliance, established at the same time as a marked political rapprochement with Great Britain, the major naval power in the Mediterranean, would permit the Savoy kingdom to increase its international weight and conduct a dynamic and effective foreign policy.

The various articles of the treaty of the Triple Alliance signed in 1882, to a great extent conceived and inspired by Italy, created the conditions for Italo-Austrian negotiations in the event of war between Austria-Hungary and Russia or of conflict in the Balkans, on the basis of the hypothesis of Italian aid to Vienna in exchange for territory. The *casus foederis* provided for automatic Italian military intervention only in the event of an attack on Germany by France (article II) or on the contracting states by two or more great powers (article III). The 'benevolent neutrality' in the event of a conflict stemming from the initiative of a member of the alliance (for instance a war provoked by Vienna against Turkey, Serbia or Russia) allowed Italy to negotiate intervention in exchange for concessions. So, the Triple Alliance was deemed a useful tool to support expansionist aims not only in Europe but also in the Near East: it gave Italy the chance to participate in a future partition of the Ottoman Empire.[16]

In the 1880s Italian foreign policy started to abandon its former support for maintaining the territorial integrity of the Ottoman Empire and elaborated a colonial expansionism in the Mediterranean and in the Horn of Africa. Mancini tried to exploit the rising colonial rivalry between Paris and London after the British occupation of

Egypt – and the English hostility towards Russian imperialism in the Middle East – to forge close Italian-British cooperation. Friendship with Italy meant for Great Britain the weakening of French positions and influence in the Mediterranean and forging a connection with the Triple Alliance.[17] Thanks to British diplomatic support Italy was able to take control of Massawa in 1885 and to enlarge its presence in the Horn of Africa. In the Mediterranean the Depretis-Mancini government began to think about a future Italian occupation of the Ottoman vilayets of Tripolitania and Cyrenaica. It should be reminded that the French occupation of Tunisia sparked among the European great powers appetites of conquest towards Northern Africa. Yet unsatisfied, France wished the future control of Morocco and of Tripolitania. According to French Foreign Minister Barthélemy Saint-Hilaire, Tripolitania was the main Mediterranean outlet of the trade routes of Central Africa, and it was necessary to avoid Italy or other powers taking control there; if Italy wished to conquer African territories it could annex Cyrenaica.[18]

In the light of the diplomatic action of the Depretis-Mancini government between 1881 and 1885, it is evident that during the negotiations for the first renewal of the Triple Alliance, Robilant, Mancini's successor at the Foreign Ministry from 1885 to 1887, was limited to continuing the policy outlined by his predecessor. Robilant continued with Mancini's scheme of offering Italy's cooperation with Austria and Germany to facilitate further expansion of their possessions and asking for territorial rewards in exchange. He made this clear in a letter written to Nigra, ambassador in Vienna, in March 1886:

> Obviously the moment has not yet come to speak of this, but if the circumstances were such that Austria were to seriously consider altering the situation in the Balkan peninsula to its advantage, not a minute should be lost in putting our cards on the table. ... The line of the Isonzo and Tyrol *feraient une affaire*, and with this, and on condition of taking Tripolitania from Turkey, I would have no difficulty in letting Austria go as far as Salonika.[19]

On 20 February 1887, a new series of accords was signed by the Triple Alliance. It comprised three treaties, one common to the three Powers, ratifying the renewal of the alliance, one between Italy and Germany and one between Austria-Hungary and Italy.[20] The agreement with Germany, as well as committing both states to act against any change in the territorial status quo in the East that would damage one of them, guaranteed German military and political assistance to Italy in the event of a war between Italy and France over North Africa. The Italo-Austrian treaty is highly significant. At its heart was article I (which would be denominated article VII on the occasion of the treaty's renewal in 1891), committing the two powers to coordinate their policies should it prove impossible to maintain the status quo in the Balkans and the Ottoman territories in the Adriatic and Aegean, and to reach an agreement in advance on what to do in the case of a temporary or permanent occupation of some territory in the area. Such an agreement was to be founded on the principle of reciprocal compensation for any 'territorial or other' advantage that one of the contracting parties should obtain with respect to the existing status quo.

Italian plans and attempts to provoke the partition of the Ottoman Empire and the conquest of Tripolitania and Cyrenaica

Francesco Crispi, one of the protagonists of Giuseppe Garibaldi's expedition to Sicily in 1860 and a prominent exponent of the Liberal Left for over two decades, reentered government in April 1887, as minister of internal affairs in the Depretis cabinet, after many years of political isolation.[21] He now appeared to be the only leader of the Liberal Left capable of taking on the mantle of Depretis, an ailing man who could no longer handle the government by himself, and of continuing to pursue the same domestic and foreign policies.

When Crispi assumed the leadership of the government and the post of foreign minister at Depretis's death in July 1887,[22] he committed himself to essentially following the lines of international policy laid down by Mancini and Depretis, with the consent of King Umberto I, and continued by Robilant. Crispi proclaimed himself a keen supporter of the Triple Alliance, which he regarded as a means of strengthening Italy's international influence, and devoted all his energies to giving this alliance real cohesion and internal solidity, elements that had in fact been lacking until 1887, and making it of greater utility to Italy.

Crispi's efforts to forge concrete political cooperation with Berlin were an undeniable success. The German diplomatic corps and Bismarck showed that they appreciated the seriousness of intentions and the energy of the ex-Mazzinian and, at the end of the 1980s, cordial relations were established between Berlin and Rome. These found public expression in the meetings between Bismarck and Crispi in Germany[23] and the Italo-German military accords of 1888.

Crispi's attempts to establish close political collaboration and solidarity with Austria-Hungary proved less successful. The government in Rome tried to exploit the Bulgarian crisis and the resurgence of Austro-Russian rivalry in the Balkans to carry out an action of decided support for the Habsburg policy in favour of Ferdinand of Saxe-Coburg, prince of Bulgaria.[24] At the same time, it used the bugbear of the threat of Russian expansionism to try to form an Italo-Austro-British alliance in defense of the territorial integrity of the Ottoman Empire and the independent Balkan states: Austrian acceptance of the Italo-British exchange of notes in February 1887, the Austro-Italo-British understanding of 12 December 1887, and the Italian adherence to the Austro-Romanian alliance in 1888 were the results of this intense diplomatic action on Crispi's part.

For the Italians particular importance had the Austro-Italo-British understanding of December 1887. The agreement foresaw the maintenance of peace and the status quo within the Ottoman Empire, its independence and freedom of transit in the Dardanelles and Bosporus Straits. It assumed the duty to protect the Ottoman Empire from possible foreign attacks or threats. In case the Ottomans were not able to resist foreign invasion, Italy, Great Britain and Austria-Hungary had the right to temporarily occupy some parts of the empire to re-establish the balance of power.[25] Crispi hoped that the Entente of December 1887 could be the diplomatic and juridical basis to justify Italian participation in the partition of Ottoman Turkey, which the Sicilian politician thought was about to happen. With the breaking out of the Armenian crisis within the Ottoman state, the European powers started debating again about the eventual partition of the Turkish territories. Great Britain, Austria-Hungary and Germany were hostile to any Russian expansion drive towards the Mediterranean and suspected that Saint Petersburg incited the Armenian nationalists in order to have a pretext of intervening in the internal affairs of the Ottoman Empire. In summer 1895 the British Prime Minister Salisbury let the German ambassador in London understand that Great Britain was getting prepared for the possibility of the breaking up of the Ottoman Empire and that in such a case it would be ready to give to Italy the control of Tripolitania and Albania.[26] In those months Crispi and the Italian foreign minister, Blanc, hoped for future implementation of the exchange of notes of December 1887 by a common policy in the Near East and by a naval expedition against Russia to create the chance to occupy Tripolitania.[27] In November 1895 an Italian naval expedition was sent to Thessaloniki to take part in a military demonstration by several great powers, and Crispi ordered the Italian commanders to be ready to occupy Tripoli in case of the partition of the Ottoman Empire.[28] Despite Italian hopes, in the following months the political crisis provoked by the massacres of Armenians diminished in intensity, and Austria-Hungary and Great Britain preferred to maintain a conservative and moderate approach to the Near East question, refusing an aggressive and dynamic interpretation of the Entente of December 1887 as proposed by the Italians.[29]

Between 1887 and 1896, notwithstanding Crispi's efforts, it proved impossible for Italian diplomacy to persuade Vienna to conclude a secret bilateral understanding that would cover the eventuality of the Ottoman Empire's collapse. Nor were there any Italo-Austrian accords of military and naval cooperation against the Russians and French: although greatly desired by Crispi,[30] they were not drawn up because of suspicions on the part of the Habsburg government. The goal of Italy's pro-Austrian and anti-Russian Balkan policy was, apart from the ritual declarations of defense of the status quo, to create the juridical and political conditions for a future application of the article of the Triple Alliance on compensation: Austria's eastward drive, the possible Habsburg conquest of Ottoman territories and a Russian-Austrian war were situations that could have forced Vienna to seek Italy's military backing, and thus allowed the government in Rome to demand territories in exchange, some regions of Austria inhabited by Italians, and likewise some of the Ottoman Empire such as Tripolitania. The Austrian, German and British reluctance to strengthen political cooperation with Italy emptied Crispi's policy and provoked growing dissatisfaction on the part of the Sicilian politician with the alliance with Vienna and Berlin over the course of 1895 and the beginning of 1896. Crispi and Blanc harshly criticized Great Britain, Austria and Germany for their lack of support of Italy's colonial policy.[31] They went on attempting to create room for maneuver by trying to revitalize the British-Italo-Austrian understanding of December 1887, which had remained purely theoretical.[32] The Sicilian politician's aim was to render the obligations and purposes of this understanding more precise in order to be ready for an eventual carve-up of the Ottoman Empire: 'It is our desire', Crispi told Nigra in January 1896, 'for the territorial status quo in the Balkan peninsula to remain the same. But if it were to change, if an apportionment of the Turkish empire were to take place, we want Italy to have its share.'³³

Crispi's plan came to nothing, encountering a lack of interest on the British part in bringing the Mediterranean accords of 1887 to life and in negotiating the future setup of the Ottoman territories with Italy and Austria.³⁴ While Crispi and Blanc were trying to forge an alliance with the Austrians and British in the Mediterranean, the events of the Italo-Ethiopian war carried the government in Rome towards military catastrophe.³⁵ The defeat inflicted on the Italian army by the Ethiopian forces at Adwa on March 1 brought an end to the political career of Francesco Crispi, who resigned as premier a few days later and was succeeded by Rudinì.

The defeat at Adwa and Crispi's political downfall thwarted his plan of imposing modifications on the alliance with Vienna and Berlin. His successor, Antonio di Rudinì – at the head of a government that brought together all the currents opposed to Crispi, with Onorato Caetani and then Emilio Visconti Venosta as foreign minister – had to face a difficult political situation. For several months the principal aim of Rudinì's foreign policy was to bring the war with Ethiopia to an end, a goal that was not achieved until October 1896, with the Treaty of Addis Ababa.³⁶ Another great question that confronted Rudinì was of course the renewal of the Triple Alliance. In a dangerous international situation, Rudinì decided to abandon the plans of modification conceived by his predecessor and limited himself to declaring his readiness to renew the treaty as it stood, but asked for the reintroduction of the declaration that had been made with respect to Great Britain on the occasion of the first treaty of alliance:³⁷ the so-called Mancini declaration, which had laid down the condition that no stipulation of the treaty of the Triple Alliance was to be considered leveled against Great Britain but which had been left out in the first renewal. The Italian request was rejected both by Berlin and Vienna.³⁸ Rudinì had tried unsuccessfully to assert his point of view and sent a new note to Berlin and Vienna that was not legally binding and required no answer, but underlined the Italian vision of the scope of the alliance: the note declared that the Triple Alliance could have no anti-British purpose and that Italy, owing to its geographical position, was unable to take part in a conflict with the two strongest naval powers in the world.³⁹

The negotiations for the renewal of the Triple Alliance confirmed that an improvement in the relations with the two great Mediterranean powers, France and Great Britain, was an important plank of Rudinì's foreign policy. The period of Crispi's government had painfully demonstrated the untenability of a political and economic conflict with France: better relations with Paris were indispensable to strengthening the Italian position in the Mediterranean and Africa, and to making the country less dependent on Berlin and Vienna.⁴⁰ The rapprochement with France was even more urgent in view of the fruitlessness of the so-called Italo-British friendship:⁴¹ Great Britain had frowned on Crispi's attempts to create a major colonial empire in East Africa and was suspicious of Italy's desire to increase its influence in the Mediterranean, where the government in London was defending a highly favourable status quo. The first signs of a change in the relations between Rome and Paris emerged in 1896.⁴² In September several agreements were reached on Tunisia, as Italy recognized the French protectorate in exchange for the concession of certain legal and cultural privileges for the Italian community in Tunisia. The peace treaty with Ethiopia was rapidly concluded thanks to the cooperation of French agents in Addis Ababa, who gave the Italian negotiator, Cesare Nerazzini, considerable help over the course of the talks.[43]

The governments headed by Pelloux (1898–1900), with first Felice Canevaro and then Emilio Visconti Venosta as foreign minister, and by Giuseppe Saracco (1900–1), with Visconti in the same post, essentially continued to follow the direction imparted to Italian foreign policy by Rudinì, that is, a marked improvement in relations with France and Great Britain and maintenance of the Triple Alliance. This showed that the pro-Western shift in Italian foreign policy after 1896 found broad support across the whole Liberal alignment in Italy.[44] Even Pelloux, a military man and member of parliament with ties to royal court circles,[45] realized the need to give Italian diplomatic action a free hand, going beyond Crispi's reliance on the Triple Alliance.

So it was no coincidence that it was the Pelloux government which reached a trade agreement with France in November 1898.[46] The Pelloux and Saracco governments attempted, with mixed results, to exploit the improvement in relations with Paris to promote a more effective and ambitious Italian colonial policy: they succeeded in obtaining an expression of no French interest on Tripolitania with the Barrère-Visconti Venosta exchange of notes dated 14–16 December 1900,[47] and in taking advantage of Franco-British benevolence to impose the treaties of July 1900 on Ethiopia; but they failed miserably in their attempts to set up an Italian colony in China.

The resurgence of national and religious conflicts in Ottoman Turkey since the middle of the 1890s (Armenian uprisings, Greek revolt on Crete, Bulgarian and Macedonian guerrilla warfare in Macedonia)[48] suggested a progressive decline in the solidity of the Ottoman Empire and rendered an imminent carve-up of the Turkish territories among the European powers a not unlikely prospect.[49]

In such a context the maintenance of the Triple Alliance constituted an indispensable instrument of Italian policy towards the Near East, a vital weapon for the protection of Italy's political and economic interests.

To prepare for the partition of the Ottoman Empire, on the one hand, Italian governments tried to develop a policy of economic and cultural penetration in some parts of the Ottoman state by opening schools, banks, consulates and postal offices and by obtaining trade and economic concessions. On the other, they tried to obtain diplomatic recognition from the other European powers of their special rights on Tripolitania and Cyrenaica. These territories were deemed important for Italian strategic interests as an instrument to guarantee balance of power in the Mediterranean against the stronger presence of France and Great Britain.

It would be the Zanardelli-Prinetti government, which came into office in February 1901, to obtain important diplomatic agreements which guaranteed British, Austrian and French recognition of the future Italian rights to control those parts of the Ottoman Empire.

The objective of the Zanardelli-Prinetti government was the conquest of new political and economic spaces in the Balkans and the Mediterranean: to this aim it set out to consolidate relations with Paris and improve relations with Russia, which had been very stand-offish since the 1880s as a consequence of Italian participation in the Triple Alliance. At the same time, however, Prinetti and Zanardelli wanted to preserve the Triple Alliance, making it better suited to their own aims, without renouncing a determined and fierce defense of Italian interests, even at the expense of those of their allies. Hence Prinetti's policy was not opposed to the Triple Alliance: he did not want to abandon it, but to turn it into a more flexible instrument that would be of more advantage to the Italian state.[50]

Playing on the still-existing Franco-British rivalry, Prinetti was able to obtain from London formal recognition of the Italian right to a future conquest of Tripolitania and Cyrenaica (11 March 1902).[51] The Lombard politician also showed great skill in his dealings with France. Taking advantage of French ignorance of the exact text of the Triple Alliance, with the Prinetti-Barrère exchange of notes (concluded in June 1902) he won major concessions in return for an Italian commitment to neutrality in the event of a Franco-German war provoked by Berlin, a promise perfectly compatible with the Triple Alliance: an unconditional French green light for attempts to conquer Tripolitania and Cyrenaica and France's promise to remain neutral in the event of an Italo-Habsburg war.

The results achieved by the Zanardelli-Prinetti government in the area of relations with the powers of the Triple Alliance and Russia were much less satisfactory. The pursuit of greater influence in the Balkans very quickly led to a marked deterioration in the political relationship between Rome and Vienna. The consolidation of Italian influence in Montenegro and Ottoman Albania, thanks to intense efforts of economic, political and cultural penetration, rang alarm bells in Vienna over Italian aims.[52] The dissension between Italy and Austria was also worsened by the fact that Italy demanded to be recognized by the Habsburg government as a primary interlocutor in Balkan policy, on equal terms with Russia.[53] But Habsburg diplomacy refused any recognition of Italy as a Balkan great power equal to Austria-Hungary and Russia.

During the negotiations for the renewal of the treaty of the Triple Alliance in spring 1902, which was renewed without changes on 30 June 1902, if Prinetti failed to get new guarantees for Italy in case of partition of the Balkans,[54] he at least obtained from Austria-Hungary a declaration of a lack of interest in Tripolitania, a further step in the diplomatic preparations for the Italian conquest of the African region.

When Giovanni Giolitti[55] became prime minister in November 1903, he had to face a difficult international situation. The improvement in Italo-French relations, the attempts at rapprochement with Russia and the rise of anti-Austrian irredentism had worsened relations within the Triple Alliance, obliging the government in Rome to deal with Austrian hostility and German irritation.

Giolitti worked forcefully for an improvement in the relations with Vienna. He considered the tough and brazen style that Prinetti had imparted to Italian international action as dangerous, since behind this aggressiveness lay a serious military weakness, due to economic and technological backwardness and the fragility of the defenses on the border with Austria. Giolitti's international strategy had the support of the new foreign minister, Tommaso Tittoni, and, most importantly, of Vittorio Emanuele III. In the following years Giolitti and Tittoni tried to impose on Vienna and St. Petersburg the participation of all the European great powers in the policy of reforms in Macedonia, but ran up against the Russian and Habsburg determination to keep a dominant and preponderant role with regard to reforms within the Ottoman Empire and thereby guarantee the survival of the understanding of 1897 and the Mürzsteg Pact.[56] At the same time, it stepped up a policy of Italian cultural and economic penetration of Ottoman territories, aimed at creating concrete ties between the indigenous populations and Italy and countering the action of the same type carried out by the other great powers.[57] Particularly intense was the Italian action in the Ottoman vilayets of Tripolitania and Cyrenaica. Elements of this economic and political penetration were the opening of Italian post offices and schools, the winning of mining, railroad and industrial concessions and the creation of cultural institutions.

The international crisis triggered by the annexation of Bosnia in October 1908, and brought to an end in March 1909 when Germany forced Russia to accept the *fait accompli*, and Serbia recognized Habsburg sovereignty over that territory,[58] gave Italy the chance to improve relations with Russia and to complete the diplomatic preparation of the conquest of Tripolitania. The Bosnian crisis also resulted in a sharp deterioration in Germany's and Austria-Hungary's relations with St. Petersburg. The growing political cooperation of Russia, Great Britain and France meant that the maintenance of Italian benevolence and the preservation of the Triple Alliance were no longer marginal factors in Berlin's foreign policy. Thus, after the Bosnian crisis, Italy's international position was considerably reinforced. The conclusion of the Italo-Russian agreement at Racconigi (24 October 1909)[59] and the Italo-Austrian exchange of notes on the sanjak of Novi Pazar (19 December 1909)[60] provided confirmation of the growing international clout of the Italian state and set the seal on its role as a Balkan and Mediterranean great power. For Italy, particularly relevant was the content of the Racconigi agreement; Italy and Russia engaged to maintain status quo in the Balkans and in case of unavoidable changes to support the development of the Balkan Christian states according to the principle of nationality. In exchange for a benevolent Italian attitude towards Russian interests on the Turkish Straits, St, Petersburg recognized the Italian rights of influence in Tripolitania and Cyrenaica.

During the first decade of the twentieth century, Italian hopes of a peaceful economic penetration in the Libyan territories slowly faded away, clashing against Ottoman hostility to any greater Italian influence in those regions. The brief reopening of the Moroccan question, following the Franco-German diplomatic crisis caused by the landing of the German gunboat *Panther* at Agadir in July 1911 – a crisis that was resolved some months later with a colonial treaty of 4 November 1911 between France and Germany – gave Italy the opportunity to act in Tripolitania and Cyrenaica.[61] The Italian government expressed full support for the French positions during the diplomatic crisis with Berlin, refusing to support demands of its German ally and adopting benevolent neutrality towards France.[62] At the same time, since July 1911, the Roman government announced to Great Britain and Austria-Hungary that Italy, if provoked by Ottoman hostility, could be forced to wage war to protect its own rights in Tripolitania.[63]

The reopening of the Moroccan question and the rapid moves made towards its peaceful solution thanks to the negotiations between France and Germany over the course of 1911 obliged the Italian government to think carefully about what it should do in Tripolitania. The government in Rome was fully aware of the possible consequences in Europe and the Balkans of a military venture in Tripolitania and Cyrenaica.[64] Rather than the possibility of an action by the Balkan states against the Ottoman Empire, what the Italian diplomatic corps feared was that Austria-Hungary, taking Italy's initiative as a pretext, would carry out a *coup de main* in the sanjak of Novi Pazar, Albania or Macedonia.[65]

The decision to go to war in Northern Africa without consulting or warning its allies stemmed from the Italian desire to confront Austria-Hungary, Germany and the other great powers with a *fait accompli*, in order not to be obstructed in the conquest of Tripolitania and Cyrenaica and above all to avert the possibility of a Habsburg initiative in the Balkans. Considering that the 1900 and 1902 treaties had already settled the issue of French recognition of Italian claims on Tripolitania and Cyrenaica, the Italian government chose also not to inform Paris, neither directly nor in advance of its intention to resolve the Libyan question by force, nor to ask France for permission regarding its activities. It should be pointed out that if the French government assumed a friendly attitude towards the Italian plans, some French diplomats stressed that a war against the Ottoman Empire threatened to provoke a general military conflict, and that the Italian conquest of Libyan territories would radically change the political and military balance of power in the Mediterranean to the benefit of the Triple Alliance.[66]

After the first diplomatic note on 23 September, by which Italian Foreign Minister San Giuliano denounced the alleged threats against the Italians in Tripolitania, on 27 September the Italian government sent an ultimatum to the Ottoman Empire, threatening war if this were not accepted.[67] Faced with the Ottoman refusal, Italy declared war on the Constantinople government and launched the invasion of Tripolitania and Cyrenaica.[68]

The major European powers took an attitude of passive acquiescence against Italian aggression, which was legitimized on past treaties signed by Italy with various European states, recognizing the rights of Italy to take control of Tripolitania and Cyrenaica. France refused to be involved in any possible mediation request by the Ottomans to the great power signatories of the Paris and Berlin treaties of 1856 and 1878, and was charged by Constantinople to have given, with the invasion of Fez, the way to the European action of dispossession and conquest of Islamic Africa, and to have provided moral support for the Italian aggression.[69] In the following weeks French benevolence towards the Italian aggression manifested itself especially in its reluctance to participate in any mediation efforts between Italy and the Ottoman Empire that were seen negatively by Rome. Paris did not participate in Austrian and German attempts to persuade Constantinople to accept a 'Bosnian' solution to the Libyan question, that is letting the Italians occupy and rule the Libyan territories while preserving Ottoman sovereignty,[70] nor did France support an Ottoman demand to call an international conference to resolve the conflict between Rome and Constantinople.[71]

Italian reaction to the 'Bosnian' solution proposals regarding the Libyan question was the proclamation of the annexation of Tripolitania and Cyrenaica on 5 November 1911.[72] The Ottoman government protested to this Italian initiative, proclaiming it null and contrary to the treaties of Paris in 1856 and Berlin in 1878.

The attitude of the European powers towards the invasion of Tripolitania and Cyrenaica was a clear confirmation of the growing international weight of Italy.[73] The desire of the various powers to maintain good relations with Italy gave the government in Rome great leeway during the war against the Ottoman Empire, which was exploited to occupy the Libyan coast and the islands of the Dodecanese. The attempts to mediate and to find a negotiated solution to the conflict, often concocted with the aim of curbing Italian designs, proved ineffective in the face of the Giolitti government's decision to go ahead with its own plans. Because of the difficulties in defeating Arab resistance in Tripolitania and Cyrenaica, since April 1912 rumors started spreading that the Italian government was planning military attacks against Constantinople in the Aegean Sea to force the Ottomans to surrender and compel a peace. After Italian actions of naval blockade in the Red Sea and bombing the port of Beirut on 24 February 1912,[74] there was a widespread belief in Europe that the next Italian step would be to attack the Dardanelles and Constantinople. On 18 April a squadron of Italian naval vessels bombarded two fortresses on the Straits of Dardanelles.[75] Between 28 April and 21 May, Italian naval forces occupied Rhodes and several islands of the Aegean Sea, the so-called Dodecanese Islands. As a reaction the Ottomans decided to close the Straits of Dardanelles to the ships of neutral states.[76] Italian occupation of the Dodecanese Islands aroused concern in France and Great Britain. The French and British feared that Italy would try to annex the islands.[77] This was unacceptable for Paris and London because it would change the political and military balance in the eastern Mediterranean to their disadvantage.

Italian dynamism in the Eastern Mediterranean worried French and British diplomacy and made it clear that Italy was gaining a new importance in that geopolitical area. On 25 February 1912 Paul Cambon emphasized that, after the Italian conquest of Tripolitania, France and Great Britain would have to live in Africa with a disturbing and inconvenient neighbour, able to build a large naval base in Tobruk and to allow access to ports and coal deposits for the German fleet. Hence it was necessary to force Italy into an alliance with France and Great Britain.[78] Since autumn 1911 the two ambassadors in Rome, the British Rodd and the French Barrère, were convinced that an agreement with Italy was necessary.[79] According to Barrère, the conquest of Tripolitania would oblige Italy to devote more attention to the Mediterranean problems, forcing it to strengthen its relations with France and Great Britain; it was necessary, however, that this possible Italian approach be encouraged by a 'bienveillante et amicable' attitude in London and Paris.[80] But in the following years there were no positive diplomatic results about the project of a tripartite agreement regarding the status of the Mediterranean among Italy, France and Great Britain. On 15 October the Italian-Ottoman peace preliminaries were signed in Ouchy,[81] and three days later, on 18 October, the peace treaty was signed in Lausanne.[82] In autumn of 1912, in the aftermath of the Ottoman-Italian war, the British and French formally proposed to Italy the conclusion of an agreement on the political status of the Mediterranean, but Giolitti and San Giuliano left the initiatives from London and Paris unanswered.[83] The projects of a Mediterranean Entente between Italy, France and Britain were never implemented.

Liberal Italy, First World War and the 'mutilated victory' (1914–22)

As Luigi Salvatorelli rightly noticed, in the aftermath of the war in Libya the Triple Alliance seemed revitalized, and the relations between Italy and France weakened.[84] Not by chance, a renewed treaty of the Triple Alliance was signed in Vienna on 5 December

1912,⁸⁵ and was to come into force on the expiry of the existing treaty, that is, on 8 July 1914, and last theoretically until 1920.⁸⁶ The government in Vienna, anxious to preserve the Triple Alliance at the height of the Balkan War, agreed to attach a protocol to the treaty of alliance, drawn up by the German foreign secretary Kiderlen and Italian Foreign Minister San Giuliano, that in addition to recognizing Italian sovereignty over the Libyan territories, declared that the Italian-Austrian accords of 1900–1 and 1909 on the Balkans were not modified by the renewal of the treaty of alliance between Italy, Austria-Hungary and Germany.⁸⁷ Notwithstanding the efforts of the European powers to circumscribe the Italo-Turkish War, the Italian conquest of Libya inflicted a heavy blow on the Ottoman Empire, weakening it further and providing the Balkan Christian states with the opportunity for a definitive showdown with the Turkish enemy. Under the pressure of tsarist diplomacy, Greece, Bulgaria, Montenegro and Serbia concluded a series of defensive and offensive alliances in the first few months of 1912 aimed at preparing a war of liberation against Turkey, and embarked on a military conflict in the fall of the same year.⁸⁸ The Turkish military proved incapable of resisting the offensive of the Balkan League, which in a short space of time conquered most of the European territories of the Ottoman Empire.

The hypothesis of the partition of the Ottoman Near East became again a diplomatic reality. Giolitti's and San Giuliano's support for the Triple Alliance can be explained in part by the conviction that the carve-up of Asiatic Turkey among the European great powers was imminent, and that Italy therefore needed the backing of the Triple Alliance to defend its own interests in the Eastern Mediterranean.⁸⁹ The conclusion of a new Italo-Austro-German naval convention in June 1913⁹⁰ was an indication of San Giuliano and Giolitti's determination to remain allied to Germany and Austria-Hungary and to use that alliance as a tool of Italy's foreign policy, partly with a view to reinforcing Italy's position with respect to France, which was perceived as a dangerous rival.⁹¹ Meanwhile, after the conquest of the Dodecanese Islands, Italy started developing an economic penetration in south-western Anatolia, in the region of Adalia/Antalya. So, Italy showed its desire to take part in the possible partition of the Ottoman Empire and started to prepare for it.

The assassination of Francis Ferdinand and his wife by pan-Serbian nationalists was the pretext used by the government in Vienna to enact a plan that a section of the Habsburg leadership had been cherishing for many years: the violent suppression of independent Serbia and the annexation of many Serbian territories destined to become part of a future Yugoslav entity dominated by the Croatians and integrated into the Habsburg Empire. On the Habsburg side the war against Serbia was conceived as a unilateral action to be carried out without consultations with Italy. The government in Vienna wanted to face the Italians with a *fait accompli*. At the root of this choice lay Austria's distrust of its Italian ally.

The broadening of the conflict into a European war and the inability of Austria and Germany to gain a rapid victory wrecked the Habsburg calculation. But these Habsburg plans and German support for them explain the failure of Austro-German diplomacy to involve Italy in the fighting. As Bernhard von Bülow himself noted,⁹² the Italian government was ready to support the military initiatives of Austria-Hungary politically and even to consider intervening in the war on the side of its allies.⁹³ This was what the Italian ambassadors to Berlin and Vienna, Riccardo Bollati and Giuseppe Avarna, advised, and it was a hypothesis that the government in Rome seriously considered.[94]

The refusal by the government in Vienna to give Italy some Habsburg territories and the shortsightedness of German diplomacy made Italian collaboration with the Austrian war plans impossible and threw the Triple Alliance into political crisis. The impossibility of reaching a territorial agreement with Austria-Hungary induced the Italian government to remain neutral in a conflict that, between the end of July and the beginning of August, saw Germany enter the field on the side of Austria-Hungary, and Russia, France and Great Britain do the same in defense of Serbia and of a Belgian state whose neutrality had been violated by the German invasion.

From the beginning of August until the death of San Giuliano in October 1914 there was a *de facto* phase of stagnation and lull in Italian foreign policy: this was partly the result of deterioration in the health of San Giuliano, gravely ill and unable to handle a heavy burden of work, but it derived chiefly from the Italian desire to await the outcome of the military operations and to carry out a major buildup of arms before taking a final decision.[95]

Italian foreign policy regained momentum with the appointment of Sidney Sonnino as Minister for Foreign Affairs.[96] Apart from Giolitti, Sonnino was the only Italian politician having the necessary range of skills (experience, thorough grasp of international questions, energy, tough negotiating skills and the capacity to make decisions) to lead Italian diplomacy in that political situation.

Sonnino's appointment was favourably received in Berlin, as his sympathies for German culture and the Triple Alliance were well known.[97] Indeed between November 1914 and February 1915 Salandra and Sonnino, with the approval of the king and Giolitti, who controlled the parliamentary majority that supported the government, reopened negotiations with Vienna and Berlin with the aim of finding an accord on the basis of Article VII: the objective was to obtain the surrender of Austrian territories inhabited by Italians or considered necessary to the strategic security of the state as a compensation for the new Habsburg conquests and for Italy's neutrality. At the same time the Italian government continued to work on defining its own plans of territorial expansion, in the eventuality of either a compensated neutrality or a military intervention on the side of the Triple Entente.

Once the Austro-Hungarian unwillingness to give serious and concrete consideration to the Italian demands for compensation had become clear, in February 1915 Salandra, Sonnino and the king decided in favour of a military intervention against Vienna, and in March began talks with the powers of the Entente to determine the nature of Italy's future participation in the world war.

The fundamental stages in the evolution of Italian foreign policy between 1914 and 1915 are now widely known. The studies of Luigi Albertini,[98] Alberto Monticone,[99] Mario Toscano,[100] Brunello Vigezzi,[101] Leo Valiani,[102] Hugo Hantsch,[103] Friedrich Engel-Janosi,[104] Pietro Pastorelli[105] and Luciano Monzali have exhaustively reconstructed the long negotiations between Italy and the Austrians and Germans in search of an agreement on Italian neutrality and the simultaneous diplomatic talks that led to the conclusion of the Treaty of London on 26 April 1915,[106] and the subsequent declaration of war on Austria in May.

The London Treaty showed clearly that Italy wanted to enter the war to complete the 'Risorgimento', that is, to pursue a program of territorial expansion aimed at achieving those Alpine and Adriatic territories that would guarantee to the Italian state military security and hegemony at its borders and the union of most of the Italian population living in the Habsburg empire. One can see that in the London treaty of April 1915 the African colonial problems, the future of the Ottoman Empire, the Middle East, had secondary importance compared to European territorial requests. Article VIII of the London Treaty guaranteed full Italian sovereignty on Rhodes and the Dodecanese Islands. Article IX foresaw that in case of total or partial partition of Turkish Asia, Italy would obtain 'une part équitable dans la région mediterranéenne avoisinant la province d'Adalia ou l'Italie a dejà acquis des droits et des intérêts qui ont fait l'objet d'une convention italo-britannique'.[107] Italy gained as well all the rights and privileges that the Ottoman Sultan had received by the Lausanne treaty of 1912 (Article X) and the possibility to have compensations in Northern and Eastern Africa if Great Britain and France would annex German colonies (Article XIII). Clause XII engaged Italy and the Entente to preserve the independence of the Islamic Holy places and of Arabia. The articles regarding Africa and Asia showed that in 1915 the Rome government had an interest to participate to the eventual partition of the Ottoman Empire and to enlarge its colonial possessions in Africa, but this was no longer the core of Italian foreign policy, now all focused on the war against Austria-Hungary.

After the intervention in war, the evolution of the international context and of the war gradually pushed Italian diplomacy to change its political aims and to give more importance to the Middle East and to Africa. The French, British and Japanese conquests in Asia and Africa drew the attention of Italian public opinion and made understandable the global dimensions of the war underway. The weakening of the Ottoman Empire and the spreading of news of secret treaties among London, Paris and St. Petersburg and on the future of Turkey and the Middle East scared the Rome government, but at the same time aroused fantasies and appetites of conquest amongs Italian leading groups. So from 1916 the Italian governments led by Salandra and then by Paolo Boselli, always with Sidney Sonnino as foreign minister, decided to resume a policy of colonial expansion in the Near East and in Africa. This was something that the other great powers had already begun to plan. Great Britain, France and Russia had prepared the partition of the Ottoman Empire with the secret agreements of 1915–16. So, from the Italian perspective Rome's demands would be necessary to preserve the balance of power in the Mediterranean and in the Middle East in anticipation of British, French and Russian expansion.

The chance to open the negotiations on the Middle East with the Allies came after the formal Italian declaration of war on Germany on 25 August 1916. Soon after, Sonnino demanded from the Entente powers the communication of the secret treaties on Straits and on the arrangements of the Ottoman dominions, negotiated excluding Italy.[108] The communication request was accompanied by a demand for a new discussion of future of the Ottoman Empire and of Italian interests in Middle East. In November 1916 Italian diplomacy presented its demands, based on the request of the future control of large parts of south-western Anatolia: the regions of Adalia/Antalya and Smirne/Izmir and the *vilayets* di Aidin/Aydin, Konia e Adana. Italian claims were fundamentally a specification and a putting into effect of what had been foreseen by article IX of the London treaty of 1915.

After long and harsh negotiations, Italy obtained recognition of most of its claims with the exchange of notes between 18 and 21–22 August 1917, held in Paris and London, known as the St. Jean de Maurienne agreements. In case of victory in the war with these agreements Italy obtained the Turkish regions of Adalia/Antalya, Aydin, Konia, Adana and Izmir. So, a great slice of Anatolia would become Italian. It appeared for a while a great diplomatic success for the Italians. But the evolution of relations between Italy and the Allies during 1918 would soon show that the application of the St. Jean de Maurienne agreements would be difficult. The German and Ottoman military defeat and the disintegration of the Habsburg empire quickly destroyed the political unity within the Entente powers. Liberal Italy's ambition to play a major role in the Balkans and in the Near East clashed with political designs of Great Britain and France and their ideas of a new post-war international order. To counter Italian influence in the Balkans, Great Britain, France and the United States began favouring the birth of a great united Yugoslav state while, to forestall Italy's expansion in Anatolia, they supported Greeks' dream to re-create a Greater Greece which would include southern Albania, Izmir and most of Western Anatolia. Not fully aware of the Allies' mistrust and hostility, after the end of the war Italian public opinion and political leadership were caught by an expansionist passion and frenzy. The war had cost a great effort and the loss of many lives as well as the strength for further warfare. Italy's engagement in the war had to be compensated. The territorial gains foreseen in the London Treaty of April 1915 were not enough. Strong became domestic pressures increased on the the Rome government to obtain more Adriatic territories (Fiume/Rijeka, Spalato/Split) and more colonies, not only in Anatolia but also in Africa. In autumn 1918 the Orlando government asked the Allies that the future peace conference would guarantee the creation of an exclusive Italian area of influence in the Horn of Africa, with the creation of an Italian protectorate of Ethiopia, and the enlargement of the borders of the Italian colony of Libya.[109]

A great weakness of Italian diplomatic positions became the worsening of relations with the United States, which entered the war only in 1917 but had a decisive role in the military victory on the Western front against German armies. The United States had no territorial ambitions in Europe and in the Middle East but showed a kind of ideological hostility to Italian territorial aims. According to American president Woodrow Wilson, while France and Great Britain were civilizing powers, Liberal Italy was not a fully democratic and advanced country and pursued a reactionary expansionist foreign policy, obsessed with search, conquest of strategic borders and mistrustful towards the project of the League of Nations.

So, when in January 1919 the Paris Peace conference began, Liberal Italy was in a difficult political position of strong diplomatic isolation. At the same time, the Italian Liberal establishment was becoming politically weaker even domestically. The Socialist party, ruled by the extremist and pro-Bolshevik wing, and the new Catholic political movement, the *Partito Popolare Italiano*, were getting stronger and gaining more and more consent from an Italian population tired of the war and of economic sacrifices. To survive politically the Liberal governments (between 1918 and 1922 led by Orlando, Nitti, Giolitti, Bonomi and Facta) sought after important foreign policy successes. Another consequence of the crisis of the Liberal state was declining to play an international global role and the decision to focus all its energy only on Italian territorial questions.

In fact the Italian participation at the Paris peace conference was characterized by a defensive attitude against British, French and American attempts to discuss and reduce the territorial gains the London Treaty of 1915 and the St. Jean de Maurienne agreements had guaranteed to Liberal Italy.

After some early skirmishes in the Supreme Council at the beginning of April 1919, the diplomatic clash of Italy, the United States and the British and French exploded between 19 and 24 April. Because of Allied opposition to Italian demands in the Eastern Adriatic and Wilson's lack of respect towards the Rome government, Prime Minister Orlando and the Italian delegation left the conference and went back to Rome to receive a new vote of confidence from the parliament.[110] The departure of the Italian delegates, and the prolonged absence of the delegation from Paris were two major mistakes. The absence of Italian delegates slowed down negotiations to find territorial compromises and aggravated ill feelings and resentment of the Allied governments against Italy. From early May the diplomatic disagreements between Italy and the Allies became wider and deeper, regarding more and more not only the Adriatic question but also the Near East and Africa. French, British and American delegates exploited skilfully the Italian absence from the peace conference to weaken Italian positions in Anatolia and diminish Italian rights in Africa. With the news of Italian landings on Turkish coasts of Anatolia, on 6 and 7 May the Allies gave a free hand to the Greeks to occupy Izmir, already promised to Italy in 1917. At the same time, the three big powers decided the distribution of the international mandates on the former German colonies, a distribution that benefitted France, Great Britain and the British Dominions and completely excluded Italy.

Irritated by these unilateral initiatives of the Allies, the Rome government went back to the Paris Peace conference on 7 May. Harshly criticized at the domestic level, weakened internationally, Orlando and Sonnino engaged doggedly to negotiate a territorial agreement on Italian claims in Europe, Asia and Africa.[111] But despite many attempts, and a French effort to mediate between Wilson and the Italians, the Rome government failed to obtain a favourable border with Yugoslavia, an international mandate on Anatolia or some territorial compensations in Africa.[112] The inability to solve the Italian territorial questions at the peace conference weakened and delegitimized the Orlando government, which eventually resigned on 19 June 1919.

The new Italian government, led by the economist Francesco Saverio Nitti with Tommaso Tittoni as foreign minister, marked the return to power of the wing of the Liberal movement ruled by Giovanni Giolitti. Within the new government, Nitti, lacking diplomatic skills and experience, delegated to Tittoni the management of foreign policy.[113] A convinced imperialist, Tittoni decided to give more importance to expansion in the Near East and Africa. To scale down British and French hostility Italy accepted improving relations with Greece by signing the Tittoni-Venizelos agreement on 29 July 1919, which recognized Greek territorial aims in Southern Albania and in Izmir, ceded all Dodecanese Islands, except Rhodes, to Athens and left open the future possibility of a return of Rhodes to the Greek government if the British surrendered Cyprus to Greece.

But Tittoni's attempts to convince the British and the French to concede to Italy substantial territorial gains in Anatolia and in Africa failed. By some exchanges of notes in September 1919 he obtained only some minor territorial adjustments in Libya, the cession of Giubaland/Jubaland in Eastern Africa and some guarantees concerning the economic and legal rights of the big Italian community in Tunisia.[114]

Facing a stalemate in the negotiations on the Adriatic question because of Wilson's intransigent refusal to recognize Italian control of Rijeka, Tittoni resigned November 1919, to be replaced by the lawyer Vittorio Scialoja. From this moment Nitti played a major role in Italian diplomatic activity. He tried to improve relations with the British to convince them to favour a quick solution to the Italian-Yugoslav controversy on borders, also at cost of important territorial sacrifices. Despite British sympathy, Nitti did not achieve a final solution to the Adriatic controversy with the Yugoslavs. Nor did he obtain substantial successes in the Near East and Africa. Italy signed the peace treaty with the Ottoman Empire, the Sèvres Treaty, on 10 August 1920. By the Sèvres Treaty and the Tripartite British-French-Italian Accord which accompanied it, Italy gained the recognition of an exclusive Italian zone of influence in Southern and Western Anatolia within the Ottoman state, excluding the region of Izmir given to Greece. The Dodecanese was formally to become Italian, also if a Greek-Italian treaty signed on 10 August 1920 confirmed Italy's promise to surrender these Aegean islands to Athens. But facing the growing strength of the Turkish nationalist movement led by Kemal Ataturk, the so much desired Italian sphere of influence in Anatolia was a concession without much usefulness and with no possibility to become reality. Great Britain showed its hostility to Italian plans of absorption of Ethiopia, and Nitti managed to get only a simple exchange of notes (10-13 April 1920) that formalized the British transfer to Italy of Jubaland, of the Giarabub/Jarabub oasis and of some desert territories at the boundaries between Libya and Egypt.

Unable to solve the Adriatic conundrum, attacked by the growing nationalist far right groups and by the far left, Nitti was obliged to resign. On 15 June 1920 Giovanni Giolitti returned to power after six years of political isolation.[115] He chose as foreign minister a young career diplomat, Carlo Sforza, former under-secretary in the Nitti governments and together with Salvatore Contarini, secretary general of the Italian Ministry for Foreign Affairs, a key figure in Italian diplomacy.[116]

Sforza had been a convinced supporter of Italian intervention in the world war and had strong and close links with the French ambassador in Rome, Camille Barrère. He believed that Liberal Italy had to restore relations with the Western powers and to modernize its foreign policy by espousing with determination the principle of national self-determination in Europe and in the Middle East, looking for not only territorial expansion but more and more economic influence.

Former Italian High Commissioner in Constantinople, Sforza knew the strength of Turkish nationalism. He decided not to ratify the Turkish peace treaty and denounced the Tittoni-Venizelos agreement, opening the way to the development of secret contacts with the Turkish nationalists led by Kemal Ataturk. Italy started to supply the Kemalists with weapons and ammunition and signed on 13 March 1921 an Italian-Turkish treaty foreseeing the Rome engagement to support Turkish sovereignty on Thrace and Izmir and to withdraw Italian troops from Anatolia after the ratification of a future new peace treaty.[117]

Thanks to an obliging Italian policy on the German question, the Giolitti government improved relations with France. By exploiting the growing isolation of Yugoslav diplomacy after the political decline of Woodrow Wilson, Italy convinced the Belgrade government to close the Adriatic controversy by signing the so-called Rapallo treaty on 12 November 1920. It was a very favourable agreement for Italy which got control of Trieste, Istria, Zadar/Zara and several Adriatic islands. In exchange, Yugoslavia won Italian recognition of its sovereignty on most of Dalmatia and support for its territorial integrity and independence.[118] Between the end of 1920 and the first months of 1921 Sforza exploited the fear of Habsburg restoration in Central Europe to gather support among Yugoslavs, Romanians and Czechoslovakians. He signed an anti-Habsburg convention with Yugoslavia on 12 November 1920, to which Czechoslovakia adhered, and supported the birth of the Little Entente among Belgrade, Bucharest and Prague. But Sforza's foreign policy, with his realism about Italy's concrete possibilities of expansion and the new emphasis on economic influence rather than territorial conquests, was harshly criticized by the Italian right-wing parties, especially the rising Fascist movement led by the former Socialist Benito Mussolini. Italy's relations with Great Britain deteriorated because of Italian support of nationalist movements in Middle East, like the Turkish Kemalists, the Egyptian nationalists and the anti-British government of King Amanullah in Afghanistan.[119] After harsh and difficult parliamentary debates on foreign policy, which showed the weakness of the government's consent, on 27 June 1921, Giolitti resigned.[120]

In July 1921 a new government was formed, led by the Liberal-Socialist reformer Ivanoe Bonomi,[121] with the career diplomat Pietro Tomasi Della Torretta.[122] This Bonomi government and those led by his successor Luigi Facta, a politician close to Giolitti, with Carlo Schanzer as foreign minister, were very weak politically and obliged to pursue a foreign policy based on a nationalist agenda so as to gather support from the strong right-wing parties. Both Della Torretta and Schanzer, in desperate need to use foreign policy to relaunch the prestige of their governments, tried to strengthen Italy's international role by building close relations with Great Britain.[123] Italian diplomacy hosted the Genoa Conference in spring 1922 to favour European economic recovery and improve relations with Bolshevik Russia.[124] During the conference Schanzer strongly supported British interests and points of view. Afterwards he tried to negotiate a general political treaty with London, which would guarantee new Italian colonial successes in Near East and in the Horn of Africa, but Lloyd George did not show interest in giving concessions and in helping the weak and powerless Italian Liberal governments.[125] Neglected and ill-supported by the Western powers, Liberal Italy was to succumb to the rise of the Fascist movement led by Benito Mussolini at the end of October 1922.

The friend of the British: Mussolini's foreign policy (1922–32)

Mussolini's accession to power in October 1922 marked the end of Liberal hegemony in Italy and the beginning of a political process which would eventually transform the country from a Liberal and pluralist democracy to an authoritarian dictatorship from 1925 onwards.[126] Despite the strongly nationalist ideology which characterized the Fascist movement, the international reaction to the designation of the Fascist leader as prime minister ('presidente del Consiglio') and foreign minister was neither hostile nor negative. Especially France and Great Britain, mistrustful of Italian Liberals too prone to improve relations with Germany and untrustworthy, saw positively a new political leader like Mussolini, who extolled Italian participation in the Great War and promoted a strongly anti-German nationalism. For British politicians and diplomats, the authoritarian tendencies of the Fascists were not necessarily negative: after all, Italy was viewed as an Oriental and backward country, not mature for parliamentary and democratic government.

Lacking diplomatic experience and wishful to lure support from conservative and establishment Liberals, Mussolini confirmed Salvatore Contarini as secretary-general of the Italian Foreign Ministry. Until his resignation in March 1926 Contarini, a Sicilian Conservative Liberal, had a strong impact on Italian foreign policy. He pushed Mussolini to improve relations with neighbouring countries like Yugoslavia and Austria and advised him to build close cooperation with the Western powers, France, Great Britain and United States.[127] Mussolini followed his advice, and one can notice that until the early 1930s Italian foreign policy was substantially moderate and conservative, aspiring to consolidate Italy's rank and prestige as one of the victors of the First World War. Aware of the weakness of his position, the Fascist leader was keen on using foreign policy as an instrument of domestic politics, so as to strengthen his popularity among Italians.

Mussolini's attempts to create close diplomatic cooperation with Great Britain had considerable success, and between 1924 and 1933 Fascist Italy followed a coherent pro-British foreign policy. The aim of this pro-British course was to enhance Italy's status and influence in the Mediterranean area, in the Middle East and Central and Eastern Europe, and to have diplomatic support against France, with which relations had sharply deteriorated since 1924. The London governments showed much more benevolence and attention towards Mussolini than to his Liberal predecessors. Keeping Fascist Italy friendly was seen as a way of maintaining stability and order in the Near East and Europe in an international context whereby the victory of the Kemalist nationalists in Turkey and the consolidation of the Soviet Union created sources of instability and danger for British imperial interests.

So during the negotiations held in Lausanne for a new Turkish peace treaty, signed on 24 July 1923, the British government refused Mussolini's demand to renegotiate the attribution of mandates in Middle East but accepted to recognize Italian control of the Dodecanese Islands and Rhodes. In 1924–5 the London government ceded definitively Jubaland and the Jarabub region on the Libyan-Egyptian border to Italy. The British conservative government agreed as well to sign an agreement on Ethiopia in December 1925, which revived the old British-French-Italian Treaty of 1906 and confirmed British recognition of the Italian right to have an economic sphere of influence in the Abyssinian state in exchange for Rome's recognition of British interests in the Tsana Lake region. Italian participation to the Locarno treaties of 1925 was reciprocated by British support to Italy's hegemony in Albania.

So, the 1920s Mussolini was able to build good relations with the UK, a real British-Italian Entente in the Mediterranean and in the Middle East, but did not forge a solid diplomatic cooperation with the new Turkish Republic. Kemal Ataturk, who had fought against the Italians in Tripolitania and Cyrenaica in 1911–12, was mistrustful of Italian intentions, knowing that within the Fascist party there were some, like for instance Francesco Coppola, who thought that Italy should not give up the project of creating an Italian colony in Anatolia. A Turkish-Italian treaty of friendship, signed in 1928, failed nevertheless to create an effective partnership between the two countries. In the early 1930s the Italian decision to build new menacing military infrastructure on the Dodecanese Islands and the signing of the Four Powers Pact without Ankara's participation in 1933[128] aroused Turkish suspicions against Italian intentions in the Near East.[129] Fearing an aggressive new Italian expansionism, Turkey decided to improve relations with Great Britain and France.

While accepting the existing international political and territorial order in the 1920s and early 1930s Fascist Italy pursued an active policy of peaceful economic and cultural expansion in the Mediterranean and Middle East. Italy had consistent economic interests in the former territories of the Ottoman Empire now under the control of Great Britain and France, for instance the influential presence of financial institutions like the Banco di Roma and of maritime navigation companies as such as the Lloyd Triestino. Ancient Italian communities were still living in the main Middle Eastern towns and were particularly strong in Egypt. Continuing the strategy of Liberal Italy, the Fascist regime tried to open new Italian consulates and schools to promote trade and commerce in that geopolitical area, attempting to conquer economic influence, particularly in those Middle Eastern states which had become independent, such as as Iran, Turkey and Afghanistan. The sale of armaments was deemed a very useful tool to create good political cooperation with those states. But a serious limitation to Italian possibilities was the lack of financial resources and capital to invest in the Middle East. The Fascist state deemed it important as well to potentiate and create cultural institutions to favour and develop cultural relations with the Asian peoples. The *Istituto per l'Oriente*, founded by Amedeo Giannini in 1921,[130] was strengthened by the Fascist regime and became a useful tool of Italian cultural diplomacy with the Arab world. The *Istituto per il Medio ed Estremo Oriente*,[131] created by Giovanni Gentile and Giuseppe Tucci, had the goal to promote economic and cultural relations with India, China and Japan, for instance by supporting exchanges between Italian and Asiatic universities, by giving scholarships to study in Italy and by organizing research and archaeological missions.

After 1929 and the signing of the Lateran treaties between the Italian state and the Vatican, Italian Catholic institutions and clergy in Middle East very often became a useful tool of Fascist Italy's influence and propaganda in Asia and Africa.

A peculiarity of the Italian Fascist propaganda was the creation of Fascist party cells among Italian communities abroad, the so-called 'Fasci all'estero'. These became instruments to promote Fascist ideology and propaganda among Arab intellectuals, and it is not possible to underrate the influence of Italian Fascism in the development of Arab nationalism, especially in Lebanon, Syria and Egypt.

Mussolini's great design: The search for Italian predominance in the Mediterranean Sea (1932–40)

In the 1930s internal and international developments pushed Mussolini to pursue a more active and ambitious foreign policy. In domestic politics, the Fascist authoritarian regime was more permanent and stronger after the 1929 agreements with the Holy See. The rise of national socialism in Germany, with Hitler's appointment as chancellor in 1933, opened new possibilities for Italy's diplomatic strategy[132] as it progressively disrupted European stability, broke French–German cooperation and enhanced Italian importance in European politics. A clear sign of Mussolini's will to pursue a more dynamic international action was his choice to return to be Italian foreign minister in 1932. Within Italian diplomacy, since 1932 some expressed the idea that Italian support against the rising menace of German revisionism could bring territorial prizes in Africa. According to Raffaele Guariglia, director of Political Affairs in Italian Foreign Ministry, Italy should support French positions and interests in Europe asking in exchange for French help to guarantee once and for all Italian absorption of Ethiopia.[133]

After some failed attempts to find common ground with Hitler, Mussolini decided to espouse Guariglia's strategy and began a clear political rapprochement with France[134] which would result in the Laval-Mussolini agreements signed on 7 January 1935. With these agreements the Italo-French alliance of war times was reborn. Fascist Italy accepted participation in the anti-German coalition Paris was trying to build to defend the European political order and in exchange it obtained French recognition of Italian predominance in Ethiopia and support in the future absorption of the African state under Italian colonial rule.

A few months afterwards, in October 1935, Italy launched a military campaign against Ethiopia and a serious global crisis broke out. Italian hopes of a quick and painless absorption of Ethiopia with French and British help soon vanished. The Ethiopian adventure proved to be more dangerous and difficult than foreseen.[135] The diplomatic clash that exploded between Italy and the League of Nations' coalition led by London put the Italian state in a dangerous state of isolation. In those months Mussolini developed a strong hostility towards the French and British political leaders, accusing them of being instinctively anti-Italian, anti-Fascist and politically unreliable. To come out of his international isolation, from January 1936 the duce decided to resume contacts with Nazi Germany,[136] and in the following months a new German-Italian cooperation came to life, based on Italian recognition of Germany's predominant interests in Austria, Nazi support of Italian conquest of Ethiopia and a reciprocal diplomatic partnership.[137]

Military victory in the Horn of Africa in May 1936 foiled the serious risk of the Fascist regime's breakdown and fall. On the contrary, Mussolini and Italian Fascism were strengthened by the conquest of Ethiopia. The African success convinced the duce that the time was ripe to start a process of radical 'fascistizzazione' of Italian society, that is, the transformation of the Fascist regime into a totalitarian state.

At the same time, the military victory was deemed a success of Fascism, of its ideology and its organization, which had to continue its international expansion. As Renzo De

Felice remarked, Mussolini began to overrate his political talents and capabilities, thinking himself a great world leader whose destiny was to build a Fascist civilization for the whole mankind. Fascist Italy, a young and vigorous nation, had to become not just a Euro-Mediterranean power, as it was already, but a great world power, creating together with Nazi Germany and Imperial Japan a new international order and destroying the hegemony of Britain and France, corrupt and decadent Liberal democracies. Together with his son in law, Galeazzo Ciano, appointed foreign minister in June 1936, Mussolini developed a new Italian foreign policy with ambitions and outlook that were enlarged excessively.[138] Abandoning the old Italian search for balance of power in the Mediterranean, from 1936 onwards the Fascist state began to strive for a conquering political and military hegemony in the Middle East, choosing an overtly anti-British and anti-French expansionist policy. The partnership with Germany became pivotal, the so-called Axis policy, as Mussolini said in a public speech in November 1936. Not a true alliance, but a preferential partnership, based on the fact the German expansionism towards Eastern and Central Europe was compatible with the new Italian designs in the Middle East and in the Mediterranean area. Clear display of this new Fascist dynamism was the Italian military intervention in the Spanish Civil War in 1936, with the obvious goal of weakening the strategic positions of the Western Liberal democracies in the Mediterranean.[139] Not by chance, Fascist Italy came to be perceived as a revisionist and destabilizing power, and its relations with states like Turkey, fearful of being a possible goal of Fascist imperialism, deteriorated irreversibly.[140]

Italian presence in the Middle East grew stronger after 1936. Until 1935 Italian Middle East strategy had shown a certain sympathy for the Zionist movement, especially for the revisionist wing led by the pro-Fascist and pro-Italian Vladimir Jabotinsky. This political sympathy brought the Fascist regime to opening a Jewish section of the naval school of Civitavecchia in 1934.[141] But after the Ethiopian war, Italian foreign policy became more and more anti-Jewish and pro-Arab. It is possible to notice that, on a political and propaganda plan, the support of Arab nationalism became a permanent feature of Italian foreign policy.[142] For instance, in 1936 Fascist Italy started giving money and weapons to pan-Arab nationalist movements, like that led by the mufti of Jerusalem, Hai Amin Husayni, and sympathized more and more with Egyptian nationalism. Starting from 1938, the year of the establishment of the anti-Jewish racial laws in Italy, the Fascist state sided openly against any project of a Jewish state in the Middle East and supported strongly Arab positions in the Palestine question. Anyway, it must be underlined that the pro-Arab Fascist policy was strongly opportunistic. It wished to stir up turmoil in British and French dominions and colonies so as to convince London and Paris to surrender to Italian demands. When, in April 1938, with the so-called Easter agreements, Italy and the UK seemed to have found a temporary entente on the Mediterranean and Eastern problems, Mussolini stopped the aid to the anti-British Arab nationalists and toned down the anti-British character of Fascist propaganda in Middle East.[143]

Despite Mussolini's hopes, 1938 saw a marked weakening of Fascist Italy's position in world international relations. The union of Austria and Germany in March and the Munich agreements on 29 September 1938 enhanced Nazi Germany's military and political power and made it the predominant power in Central Europe. At the same time, the attempted improvement of relations with Western countries failed. The anti-French propaganda campaign unleashed by the Rome government to compel Paris to open negotiations so as to give Italy some territorial compensations, a campaign which culminated in provocative anti-French demonstrations in the Italian Chamber in November 1938,[144] worsened relations between France and Italy to deteriorate and convinced London and Paris to intensify military cooperation against the growing Fascist menace.

Fearful of a possible war as a consequence of the breakdown with France, on 1 January 1939 Mussolini decided finally to accept the German proposal to negotiate a formal treaty of alliance between the powers that had signed the Anti-Komintern pact, Germany, Italy and Japan.[145] The road was open, after Japanese withdrawal from the negotiations, to the future finalization of the Italian–German alliance treaty, The Pact of Steel, in May 1939. In March 1939 the German violation of the Munich agreements and the break-up of Czechoslovakia showed the impossibility for Fascist diplomacy to control and influence Hitler's international actions.[146] Despite his personal disappointment with the Germans, after some days of reflection Mussolini decided to keep on with the firm intention of signing a political and military alliance with Hitler, but gave also the new directive to accelerate Italian taking of control of those European territories deemed strategically vital and part of the Italian sphere of influence.[147] Italy spurred the resurgence of anti-Yugoslav Croatian nationalism[148] and invaded independent Albania, despite the fact the Albanian king had been a good friend and ally of Italy for many years.[149] After obtaining a formal German declaration stating that Germany had no aims and claims in the Mediterranean Sea, deemed by Berlin an 'Italian lake', and that Croatia was part of the Italian sphere of influence,[150] Mussolini decided to sign the Pact of Steel. This public treaty, an offensive political and military alliance, gave the international community the clear message that Italy and Germany were getting ready for war and definitively tied Mussolini to Hitler.

In fact, the Pact of Steel was, together with the Molotov-Ribbentrop agreements, an element that accelerated the rapid escalation to the world war. Again, Mussolini and Ciano were caught by surprise by Hitler's dynamism. Despite promises to the Italians to wait for three years before launching an open war, he attacked Poland on 1 September 1939. Italian military unpreparedness and the uncertitude about the final result of the war involving Paris, London and Berlin advised Mussolini to postpone Rome's military intervention. If the duce had become an ideologue, he had not yet lost all his pragmatism and opportunism. So Mussolini spent the period of time between September 1939 and May 1940 getting ready for the moment to fulfil his projects of expansion in the Mediterranean and waiting for a clear military result in the French-British-German war.[151]

The Allies' battlefield defeat in May 1940 seemed to the eurocentric Mussolini a clear sign of the ending of the war with a German triumph. So, thinking that a new 1870 was happening, the duce pushed Italy into the war against France and Great Britain in June 1940. The goals of Italian entry into the war were to participate in the division of the booty, to build and create an Italian *Lebensraum*, but also to strengthen Italy in front of the disquieting and dangerous German imperialism, by reforming a full Italian–German alliance put in jeopardy by the neutrality decision of Mussolini in September 1939.[152]

The march to the catastrophe: Fascist Italy's foreign policy towards the Middle East (1940–3)

The goal of the intervention of Fascist Italy in the Second World War was the establishment of Italian preponderance in the Mediterranean and the Middle East. This Italian hegemony had to be built by the creation of an exclusive sphere of influence dominated by Rome, which would embrace old and new colonies, protectorates, allies and clients. According to Mussolini, Ciano and the Italian Foreign Affairs Ministry, Fascist Italy's war aims consisted of the conquest of many African and Asiatic territories (Tunisia, parts of Algeria and Morocco, Sudan, Tchad, Aden), the establishment of an Italian protectorate in Egypt, the concession of many military and naval bases on the Arabian Peninsula and in the Middle East and the creation of exclusive and privileged relations with some partially independent Arab states (Lebanon, Syria, Iraq).[153] Italian politicians and diplomats developed plans about the political future of Iran, Afghanistan and India only after Japan's attack on the United States in December 1941. According to Adolfo Alessandrini, the chief of the India bureau in the Italian Foreign Affairs Ministry, in the case of Tripartite powers' military victory, Iran should become part of the Italian sphere of influence. Italy also wished the return of Amanullah, former Afghan king in exile in Rome, to power in Afghanistan. Afghanistan should enlarge greatly its territories including in Soviet, British and Iranian regions, becoming a sort of buffer state tied to Italy, at the border between the Italian sphere of influence in the Middle East, the German one in Russia and the Japanese one in India and in the Indian Ocean.[154]

During the Second World War, the Italians sought to intensify contacts and cooperation with Arab political leaders (Amin el Husseini, Rashid Ali al-Gailani, King Farouq of Egypt). By using a well-oiled propaganda machine, for instance the Arab-speaking Radio Bari, Fascist Italy developed and stimulated strong anti-British and anti-Jewish feelings in the Middle East. But Italian support for Arab nationalism was fundamentally ambiguous and ambivalent. Italian Fascism wanted to mobilize Arab nationalists against the British, but it did not want full independence of the Arab states because its aim was the establishment of Italian predominance in the region. Not by chance, despite Arab pressures, Italy was reluctant to grant binding public or secret declarations supporting full Arab independence. The most important and explicit act of Italian support for Arab nationalism, the secret exchange of notes between Ciano, Rashid Ali al-Gailani and Amin el Husseini on 28 April 1942, was just a very generic and not binding declaration of sympathy towards the Arab cause.[155]

Another element of weakness of Italian policy towards the Middle East was the existence of a not too hidden competition between Rome and Berlin for the partition and delimitation of the respective areas of exclusive influence in that geopolitical region. Despite many repeated declarations by Hitler to Mussolini and Ciano according to which the Mediterranean and the Middle East were areas reserved to Italian *Lebensraum* and preponderance, many German diplomats, politicians and high military officers were against Italian hegemony in Middle East. The German minister in Iran, Ettel, and in Turkey, von Papen, thought Third Reich's interest was to ensure the control of the Iraqi and Iranian oil resources and of the most important communication and transport routes, avoiding total Italian control of them. To achieve this aim it was advisable to limit and obstruct Italian expansionist ambitions and goals by protecting Turkey and Iran and by supporting full independence for the Arabs.[156] In the German Ministry of Foreign Affairs' view, the promise to the Italians of political *désintéressement* and no interference did not mean giving up the pursuit of German economic, cultural and strategic interests. Fascist Italy should accept German participation in the exploitation of oil resources, to the common protection of the communication and transport routes and to archaeological and cultural missions in Middle East. Anyway, it was pivotal not to let Middle Eastern politicians to think that Germany did not show interest towards that geopolitical area.

In fact, despite being united by an alliance treaty (the Tripartite Pact), Germany, Italy and Japan did not turn out to be able to develop a common policy and action towards the Asiatic peoples. The Japanese, for instance, distrustful of Berlin, were reluctant to cooperate with the Germans and blocked for a long time any project of a united Tripartite propaganda supporting full Indian independence.[157] Hitler and many German leaders were afraid of a too extended and successful Japanese expansion in Asia and considered Tokyo a possible future rival power.[158] During 1942, with the new Italian–German advance in Northern Africa, the Rome government seemed to abandon its reluctance towards the Arab cause and began to push strongly in favour of a more determined Tripartite propaganda action supporting Arab and Indian national movements, bumping into German disinterest and obstructionism.[159] In spring 1942 Japan its changed its attitude and declared it was favourable to a common public Tripartite declaration supporting the independence of India and the Arabs.[160] Mussolini tried to convince Hitler to accept this Japanese proposal during their conversations in Klessheim on 29 April 1942,[161] but the *Führer* was utterly contrary and hostile, and the project of common declaration died.[162]

As is well known, the military events in Mediterranean Africa between end 1942 and the early months of 1943 dealt the lethal and fatal blow to the Italian Fascist regime. The British victory at El Alamein and the American landing in North Africa showed the Italian ruling class that the defeat of Italy was by now inevitable.[163] The military crisis of Mussolini's dictatorship had a strong impact at the domestic level, disintegrating its internal support. Aware of the weakening of his power positions, Mussolini worked towards a new diplomatic strategy: he tried, in vain and without success, to convince Hitler to negotiate and close a separate peace treaty with the Soviet Union and to concentrate all Italian–German military resources to defend Italy in the Mediterranean.[164] Many Italian diplomats, high military officers faithful to the Savoy dynasty and Fascist politicians, for instance Ciano and the former ambassador in London Dino Grandi, on the other hand, started to push for a quick and immediate Italian exit and abandonment of the war through a separate peace with the British and the Americans. Ciano tried to convince Mussolini to open peace negotiations with London and Washington, but the duce refused because he believed the Tripartite could still win the war.¹⁶⁵ Mussolini decided, instead, to dismiss his son-in-law and other untrustworthy Fascist ministers from government at the beginning of February 1943.¹⁶⁶

Mussolini resumed the office of foreign minister and put the former governor of Dalmatia, Giuseppe Bastianini, at the head of the administrative structure of the Ministry of Foreign Affairs as under-secretary.¹⁶⁷ Bastianini was a faithful Fascist, ready to obey to the duce's orders.¹⁶⁸ But in those months, the collapse of the Fascist state became clear, completely subjugated to Germany and under the risk of invasion from the Allies. During 1943, Italian diplomacy, by now aware of their country's weakness, gave more and more attention to propaganda activity, trying to justify and legitimize the Italian–German alliance as an attempt to unify European civilization and nations against the external threat of Soviet Russia and the United States. Keen on rebalancing the alliance with Germany, Bastianini attempted to convince the Nazi government to fight, with more intensity and intelligence, the propaganda war against the United Nations' coalition by giving more consideration to the rights of the small European nations and by relaunching the theme of the battle against communism as a war to defend Europe. But his idea of an anti-communism European Charter met lack of interest and opposition on Hitler's and Ribbentrop's part. Italian diplomats tried as well to relaunch the propaganda to support the Arab and Islamic independence movements. Bastianini and the general director of European and Mediterranean Affairs of the Ministry of Foreign Affairs, Leonardo Vitetti, asked insistently to the Germans to publish the secret declaration in favour of Arab independence prepared in 1942, but to no avail.¹⁶⁹ According to Italian diplomats, propaganda was the only weapon left to support the resistance of the Arab peoples against British-American imperialism. The Americans and the British had promised future independence to the Arabs: a prolonged silence from the part of Italy and Germany was very counter-productive.¹⁷⁰

The strongest Italian expression of support towards Arab nationalists was the project of declaration for the Arab peoples that Bastianini proposed to the German government in July 1943. In this document Fascist Italy declared independence and freedom of the Arab countries in the Middle East (Iraq, Syria, Palestine, Lebanon, Transjordan) as one of the most important goals of Italian and German war efforts and foreign policies. Rome and Berlin were ready to accept the formation of a united Pan-Arab state and opposed the creation of a Jewish national home or state in Palestine.¹⁷¹ No word was made on Egypt and the Maghreb countries: Fascist Italy still dreamt of a Mediterranean empire.¹⁷²

The project of the German–Italian declaration was not fulfilled because of the fall of Mussolini at the end of July 1943.

Looking for a new role in the Middle East: Post-Fascist Italy and the search for the Arab world's friendship

The fall of the Fascist regime was a political initiative of a coalition of forces: the Savoy Monarchy, the Italian military and some Fascist dissidents. The new prime minister, General Pietro Badoglio, led the negotiations with the British and the Americans-Americans which brought about the Italian armistice in September 1943. In the following years Italy definitely lost its international autonomy and became an object of great powers' designs.[173]

But Italian diplomats and the new democratic and anti-Fascist politicians showed great determination in returning to play a role in international politics, especially in the Mediterranean area. In the rebuilding of a new post-Fascist Italian foreign policy, particularly important was the role of Renato Prunas, appointed secretary general of the Italian Foreign Ministry in November 1943, an office that he maintained until 1946. As Roberto Gaja noted,[174] Prunas, de facto foreign minister until 1945, established some of the strategic directives that would bring Italy to the successful reinsertion in European and Mediterranean politics and to the re-assumption of an international role.[175] Prunas perceived between 1944 and 1945 that the United States could become the most important political, economic and military ally and support for Italian foreign policy. Moreover, he strove to improve relations and to reconcile Italy with France, the Soviet Union[176] and Austria, paving the way for making the French the most vocal supporters for Italian participation in the European integration process and to the Atlantic Alliance. Prunas favoured a conservative Italian foreign policy that would abandon the Fascist ideological dreams and go back to the traditions of Italian diplomacy rooted in political realism and *raison d'état*. Prunas agreed with Alcide De Gasperi, foreign minister between the end of 1944 and 1946 and prime minister between 1945 and 1953, and Carlo Sforza, foreign minister between 1947 and 1951, that Italy should develop a policy of reconciliation and peace with former enemies and victims of Fascist imperialism (especially Greece and Turkey) and intensify relations with all the Mediterranean states, especially the Arab countries.[177] But at the same time post-Fascist Italy was determined to remain a colonial power and between 1945 and 1949 fought hard to preserve some of its former colonies, in particular Tripolitania, Eritrea and Somalia. The colonialist feelings of an important part of Italian public opinion and the need of the Christian-Democrat-led governments to show a will to defend strongly Italy's interests against the propaganda of right-wing and left-wing opposition parties (the neo-Fascists, monarchists, the communists), explain the determined and long diplomatic battle that post-Fascist Italy fought to preserve and maintain part of its African empire.[178]

It must be said that not everyone in Italian diplomacy agreed with this colonialist strategy. Pietro Quaroni,[179] former Italian minister in Afghanistan and Soviet Union, and from 1947 ambassador to France, thought that there had been a political reawakening of the Asian and African peoples, who would not accept any more European rule. It was a mistake trying to reclaim the former colonies.[180] Instead, Italy should adapt and accept these changes and try to become a point of attraction and support to the needs of economic development of these peoples.

The diplomatic battle to obtain the restitution of the former colonies was destined to defeat. After the Second World War, the British wished to punish the Italians and to reduce strongly Italian influence and presence in the Mediterranean and in the Middle East to better guarantee London imperial interests in those areas,[181] while the Americans thought rightly that Italy did not possess the necessary economic and financial resources to take control and manage its former colonies.[182] Some Italian diplomats and politicians knew that Italian colonialism was a lost cause[183] and, after the failure of the Italian-British agreement of 1949 (the so-called Bevin-Sforza agreement), they decided to change strategy radically. To react to unilateral British initiatives supporting the establishment of Cyrenaica as an independent state, the De Gasperi government decided at the end of May 1949 to proclaim publicly Italian sympathy and support for the principle of national self-determination for the peoples of Eritrea and Tripolitania.[184] The abandon of the territorial demands on Libya and Eritrea reconciled Italy with the Arab and Latin American states and allowed the Italian state to improve its international image.

Opting to leave the colonies was part of the ideological renewal that Italian foreign policy underwent after the Second World War. The discovery of American political culture, the Cold War, the decolonization process obliged Italian diplomats and politicians to a rethinking of the role of Italy in the world and of the ways of better defending national interests.[185] The great challenge of Prunas, De Gasperi, Sforza and their success was to find a way of regaining influence and power in the international arena despite the defeat in the Second World War, the crisis of the European national states and the loss of military power as a non-nuclear middle-range state.[186] The Cold War was an unexpected opportunity for Italy. To contain and counter Soviet Union and international communism, the Western world led by the United States needed allies and was ready to look for them among the former Fascist enemies. The entry in the Western bloc, the participation in the Atlantic alliance and the new supranational European organizations allowed the progressive relaunch of the Italian role in world with new instruments and values.

Also, after 1949, abandoning the dream of a return to Africa as a colonial power, Italy was able to develop effective international activity in the Middle East, regaining some economic, cultural and political influence. Particularly relevant in this context was the establishment of good relations with Israel and Egypt, the signing of a friendship treaty with Lebanon in 1949, the first agreement of this kind with an Arab country, and economic penetration in Iran, which culminated in the oil agreements of 1957, establishing the Italian oil agency, ENI, as a major player in international energy markets.

The concept of Italian anti-colonialism has been used to interpret this new Italian policy in the Middle East.[187] This concept does not fully explain the ambiguity and complexity of Italian policies in Africa and Asia in the 1950s and in the 1960s. Perhaps it is more useful to speak of a 'double-track' strategy, which, on the one hand, proclaimed publicly Italian support towards the national emancipation movements in Asia and Africa, and on the other, it was careful to preserve and maintain Rome's alignment with Western interests in the Middle East and in Africa.[188] Indeed, during the 1950s the Italian attitude towards the decolonization process was very moderate and ambiguous, always avoiding open and formal refusal of colonialism.[189] As the Italian ambassador in Washington, Manlio Brosio, noticed in 1956, 'you cannot be utterly anti-colonialist as long as the most important NATO States have colonies'.[190] In the early 1960s the Rome government more clearly espoused a position of refusal and condemnation of colonialism.[191]

During the 1960s Italian activism in the Middle East grew.[192] The centre-left governments led by Amintore Fanfani and Aldo Moro tried to build a strong economic and cultural Italian role in the Middle East by intensifying relations with the Arab states.[193] With Turkey and Iran, trade and economic cooperation was good but political relations were not particularly close and intimate. Ankara privileged economic relations with Western Germany and military and political partnership with Washington.[194] Iran as well viewed the United States as the most important economic and political ally and also when Teheran showed the will to consider Europe and Japan important partners in the process of internal modernization, Italy did not gain a pivotal role. Because of growing Italian cooperation and sympathy with the Arab world, relations between Israel and Italy worsened during the 1960s. Most of the Italian leaders defended the Israeli right of existence and independence but criticized Israeli obsession for military power and strategic hegemony in the region, as well as its lack of will to foster and favour the development of a peace process in the Middle East.[195] From 1967 Italian politicians and diplomats gave growing attention to the problem of the Arab Palestinian refugees, viewed as not only a humanitarian emergency but also as a political problem, to be solved through the two-state solution in Palestine.

Notes

1 Rechberg to Apponyi, 29 June 1860, *Il problema veneto: Il problema veneto e l'Europa 1859-1866* (Venice: Istituto Veneto di Scienze, Lettere e Arti, 1966), Austria, doc. 99; see too ibid., docs 94, 101, 153, 169.
2 For Cavour's foreign policy, see: Rosario Romeo, *Cavour e il suo tempo* (Rome-Bari: Laterza, 1969-84), vol. 3; Franco Valsecchi, *L'Europa e il Risorgimento. L'alleanza di Crimea* (Florence: Vallecchi, 1968); Angelo Tamborra, *Cavour e i Balcani* (Turin: ILTE, 1958); Luca Riccardi, Prefazione, in *Storia & Diplomazia. Rassegna dell'Archivio Storico del Ministero degli Affari Esteri e della Cooperazione Internazionale*, n. 1-2, January-December 2015, p. 8.
3 See for example: *I Documenti diplomatici italiani* (Rome: Libreria dello Stato-Istituto Poligrafico dello Stato, 1952-) (henceforth DDI), series I, vol. 11, Menabrea to Maffei, 29 January 1869, doc. 57; ibid., Menabrea to Pepoli, 29 January 1869, doc. 58; ibid., Menabrea to Maffei, 26 April 1869, doc. 278.
4 DDI, I, 10, Menabrea to Bertinatti, 26 February 1868, doc. 128.
5 On the policy of the last government of the Right on the Eastern question the analysis carried out by Gaetano Salvemini remains fundamental, drawing on documents belonging to the Robilant family that are only partly reproduced in the DDI: Gaetano Salvemini, *La politica estera italiana dal 1871 al 1915* (Milan: Feltrinelli, 1970), 165-97. Also useful: Enrico Decleva, *L'Italia e la politica internazionale dal 1870 al 1914. L'ultima fra le grandi potenze* (Milan: Mursia, 1974), 35-40; Rinaldo Petrignani, *Neutralità e alleanza. Le scelte di politica estera dell'Italia dopo l'Unità* (Bologna: Il Mulino, 1987), 107-20; Luciano Monzali, *Italians of Dalmatia. From Italian Unification to World War I* (Toronto: University of Toronto Press, 2009), 92-110.
6 Visconti Venosta to Robilant, 2 March 1875, DDI, II, 6, doc. 77.
7 Out of the very extensive international literature on the Balkan and Eastern crisis between 1875 and 1878 we recommend: William L. Langer, *European Alliances and Alignments, 1871-1890* (New York: Knopf, 1931); William Norton Medlicott, *Bismarck, Gladstone and the Concert of Europe* (London: University of London, 1956);

István Diószegi, *Die Aussenpolitik der Oesterreichisch-Ungarischen Monarchie 1871–1877* (Wien: Böhlau, 1985); Franz-Josef Kos, *Die Politik Oesterreich-Ungarns während der Orientkrise 1874/75–1879. Zum Verhältnis von politischer und militärischer Führung* (Wien: Böhlau, 1984); George Hoover Rupp, *A Wavering Friendship: Russia and Austria 1876–78* (Cambridge, MA: Harvard University Press, 1941); Francis Roy Bridge, *From Sadowa to Sarajevo: The Foreign Policy of Austria-Hungary, 1866–1914* (London: Routledge and Kegan Paul, 1972); Ettore Anchieri, *Costantinopoli e gli Stretti nella politica russa ed europea dal trattato di Qüciük Rainargi alla convenzione di Montreux* (Milan: Giuffrè, 1948), 53–62.

8 DDI, II, 7, Melegari to Robilant, 14 October 1876, doc. 483.
9 On Italo-British relations in 1878: Dwight E. Lee, *The Proposed Mediterranean League of 1878*, in 'Journal of Modern History', 1931, 33–45.
10 See for instance the results of Francesco Crispi's journey to Germany and other European capitals in 1877: DDI, II, 8, docs 45, 64, 90, 102, 109, 111, 123, 129, 137, 139, 141, 145, 167, 178; *Documents diplomatiques français 1871–1914* (Paris: Imprimèrie Nationale, 1929–59) (henceforth DDF), I, 2, docs 202, 205, 206, 211; Francesco Crispi, *Politica estera. Memorie e documenti* (Milan: Treves, 1912), 1–69; Petrignani, *Neutralità e alleanza. Le scelte di politica estera dell'Italia dopo l'Unità*, cit. 130–40; Christopher Duggan, *Francesco Crispi 1818–1901: From Nation to Nationalism* (London/New York: Oxford University Press, 2002).
11 On the diplomatic action of the Cairoli-Corti government: DDI, II, 10; Luigi Albertini, *The Origins of the War of 1914* (London: Oxford University Press, 1952–7), 3 vols, in particular I; Petrignani, *Neutralità e alleanza. Le scelte di politica estera dell'Italia dopo l'Unità*, cit., pp. 147–55.
12 DDI, II, 7, doc. 11.
13 On Italy and the Triple Alliance: Luigi Chiala, *Pagine di storia contemporanea. III. La Triplice e la Duplice Alleanza (1881–1897)* (Turin: Roux, 1898); Petrignani, *Neutralità e alleanza. Le scelte di politica estera dell'Italia dopo l'Unità*; Alfred Francis Pribram, *The Secret Treaties of Austria-Hungary, 1879–1914* (Cambridge, MA: Harvard University Press, 1921); Francesco Salata, *Per la storia diplomatica della Questione Romana. Da Cavour alla Triplice Alleanza* (Milan: Treves, 1929); Langer, *European Alliances*; Luigi Salvatorelli, *La Triplice Alleanza. Storia diplomatica 1877–1912*, ISPI, Milan 1939; Albertini, *The Origins of the War of 1914*, I; Fritz Fellner, 'Der Dreibund. Europäische Diplomatie vor dem Ersten Weltkrieg', in *Vom Dreibund zum Völkerbund. Studien zur Geschichte der internationalen Beziehungen 1882–1919* (Salzburg: Oldenbourg, 1994), 19–81; Holger Afflerbach, *Der Dreibund. Europäische Grossmacht-und Allianzpolitik vor dem Ersten Weltkrieg* (Wien: Böhlau, 2002); Monzali, *Italians of Dalmatia*, 137–51; Monzali, 'Österreich in der Aussenpolitik des Liberalen Italien 1866–1915. Einige Überlegungen/L'Austria nella politica estera dell'Italia liberale 1866–1915. Alcune riflessioni', in Andreas Gottsmann and Romano Ugolini (eds), *Österreich-Ungarn und Italien im Ersten Weltkrieg/Austria-Ungheria e Italia nella prima guerra mondiale* (Wien: Österreichische Akademie der Wissenschaften, 2019), 75–98.
14 On the figure of Mancini and his career as a jurist and politician: Zecchino Ortensio (ed.), *Pasquale Stanislao Mancini: L'uomo, lo studioso, il politico* (Naples: Guida, 1991); Antonio Droetto, *Pasquale Stanislao Mancini e la scuola italiana di diritto internazionale del secolo XIX* (Milan: Giuffrè, 1954); Carlo Zaghi, *P. S. Mancini, l'Africa e il problema del Mediterraneo 1884–1885* (Rome: Casini, 1955); Monzali, *Italians of*

Dalmatia; Afflerbach, *Der Dreibund. Europäische Grossmacht-und Allianzpolitik vor dem Ersten Weltkrieg*, 99–110.
15 Pasquale Stanislao Mancini, *Discorsi parlamentari di Pasquale Stanislao Mancini* (Rome: Camera dei Deputati, 1896–7), VIII, 553, speech at the session of 7 December 1881.
16 DDI, II, 14, doc. 686, Mancini to Robilant, 20 April 1882.
17 Francis Harry Hinsley, 'International Rivalry 1885–1895', in Ernest Alfred Benians, James Butler and Charles Edmund Carrington (eds) *The Cambridge History of the British Empire, Vol. III, The Empire-Commonwealth 1870–1919* (Cambridge: Cambridge University Press, 1959); Carlo Giglio, *La politica africana dell'Inghilterra nel XIX secolo* (Padova: CEDAM, 1950), 438–50.
18 DDF, I, 4, Saint-Hilaire to de Noailles, 4 June 1881, d. 29. See as well *ivi*, de Noailles to Saint-Hilaire, 29 May 1881, d. 27.
19 DDI, II, 19, doc. 396, Robilant to Nigra, 30 March 1886.
20 *Testo del trattato separato tra l'Italia e l'Austria-Ungheria*, 20 February 1887, in DDI, II, 20, doc. 540; also published in *Die Grosse Politik der Europäischen Kabinette 1871–1914* (Berlin: Deutsche Verlagsgesellschaft für Politik und Geschichte, 1922–7) (hereafter GP), 3, doc. 571; and Pribram, *The Secret Treaties of Austria-Hungary, 1879–1914*.
21 The best political biography of Francesco Crispi is the one by Duggan, *Francesco Crispi 1818–1901*; also useful are the pages devoted to Crispi by Gioacchino Volpe and Sergio Romano: Gioacchino Volpe, *Italia moderna* (Florence: Sansoni, 1973); Sergio Romano, *Crispi. Progetto di una dittatura* (Milan: Bompiani, 1973); see, too, Fausto Fonzi, *Crispi e lo 'Stato di Milano'* (Milan: Giuffrè, 1972); Luciano Monzali, *Guerra e diplomazia in Africa orientale. Francesco Crispi, l'Italia liberale e la questione etiopica* (Rome: Società editrice Dante Alighieri, 2020).
22 On Francesco Crispi's foreign policy: Gaetano Salvemini, 'La politica estera di Crispi', in *La politica estera italiana dal 1871 al 1915* (Milan: Feltrinelli, 1970); Renato Mori, *La politica estera di Francesco Crispi (1887–1891)* (Rome: Edizioni di Storia e Letteratura, 1973); Enrico Serra, *La questione tunisina da Crispi a Rudinì ed il 'colpo di timone' alla politica estera italiana* (Milan: Giuffrè, 1967); Monzali, *Guerra e diplomazia in Africa orientale. Francesco Crispi, l'Italia liberale e la questione etiopica*; William L. Langer, *The Diplomacy of Imperialism, 1890–1902* (New York: Alfred A. Knopf, 1935); Carlo Giglio, *L'articolo XVII del trattato di Uccialli* (Como: Cairoli, 1967); Carlo Conti Rossini, *Italia ed Etiopia dal trattato di Uccialli alla battaglia di Adua* (Rome: Istituto per l'Oriente, 1935); Cedric James Lowe, *The Reluctant Imperialists: British Foreign Policy, 1878–1902* (London: Macmillan, 1967); Pierre Milza, *Français et italiens à la fin du XIXe siècle. Aux origines du rapprochement franco-italien de 1900–1902* (Rome: Ecole française de Rome, 1981), two vols.
23 On Italo-German relations between 1887 and 1890: Langer, *European Alliances*; Massimo Mazzetti, *L'esercito italiano nella Triplice Alleanza. Aspetti della politica estera 1870–1914* (Naples: ESI, 1974); Norman Rich, *Friedrich von Holstein. Politics and Diplomacy in the Era of Bismarck and Wilhelm II* (Cambridge: Cambridge University Press, 1965), I: 193–203, 247–8.
24 On this: Francesco Guida, *La Bulgaria dalla guerra di liberazione sino al trattato di Neuilly 1877–1919. Testimonianze italiane* (Rome: Bulzoni, 1984); Francesco Guida, Armando Pitassio and Rita Tolomeo, *Nascita di uno Stato balcanico: la Bulgaria di Alessandro di Battenberg nella corrispondenza diplomatica italiana 1879–1886* (Naples: ESI, 1988).

25 Salvatorelli, *La Triplice Alleanza. Storia diplomatica 1877–1912*, 141–3.
26 GP, vol. 10, Von Hatzfeldt to Von Holstein, 31 July 1895, docs 2371, 2372; *ivi*, Von Hatzfeldt to German Foreign Ministry, 3 August 1895, d. 2375.
27 DDI, II, 27, docs 405, 421, 428, 434, 475.
28 DDI, II, 27, *Colloquio del presidente del Consiglio e ministro dell'Interno, Crispi, con il viceammiraglio Accinni e il capitano di vascello Bettolo*, 16 November 1895, d. 458.
29 DDI, II, 27, docs 506, 524, 533, 558.
30 A detailed reconstruction of the Italo-Austrian military negotiations at the end of the 1980s in Mazzetti, *L'esercito italiano nella Triplice Alleanza. Aspetti della politica estera 1870–1914*, 95–105. On Italo-Habsburg relations under Crispi, see Afflerbach, *Der Dreibund. Europäische Grossmacht-und Allianzpolitik vor dem Ersten Weltkrieg*, 231–50; Monzali, *Italians of Dalmatia*, 164–74.
31 DDI, II, 27, Blanc to Nigra, 12 January 1896, doc. 739; ibid., docs 782, 787; GP, 10, docs 2369, 2370.
32 DDI, II, 27, docs 779, 815.
33 DDI, II, 27, doc. 793.
34 DDI, II, 27, docs 852, 913.
35 On the conflict between Italy and Ethiopia in 1895–6: Monzali, *Guerra e diplomazia in Africa orientale*.
36 On the foreign policy of the Rudinì governments: Salvatorelli, *La Triplice Alleanza. Storia diplomatica 1877–1912*, 215–20; Enrico Serra, *Camille Barrère e l'intesa italo-francese* (Milan: Giuffrè, 1950); Serra, *La questione tunisina da Crispi a Rudinì*; Enrico Decleva,*Da Adua a Sarajevo. La politica estera italiana e la Francia 1896–1914* (Bari: Laterza, 1971); Luciano Monzali, *L'Etiopia nella politica estera italiana 1896–1915* (Parma: Università di Parma, 1996); Afflerbach, *Der Dreibund. Europäische Grossmacht-und Allianzpolitik vor dem Ersten Weltkrieg*, 413–15.
37 DDI, III, 1, doc. 40, Caetani to Nigra and Lanza, 26 March 1896.
38 Pribram, *The Secret Treaties of Austria-Hungary, 1879–1914*, 314–19; DDI, III, 1, doc. 92, Lanza to Caetani, 1 May 1896; Albertini, *The Origins of the War of 1914*, I.
39 DDI, III, 1, doc. 87, Caetani to Nigra and Lanza, 26 April 1896.
40 In this connection: DDF, I, 12, doc. 321, Billot to Berthelot, 13 March 1896; ibid., Billot to Hanotaux, 26 May 1896, doc. 390.
41 On the difficult Italo–British relations in those years: DDF, I, 12, docs 240, 245, 313, 405; Lowe, *The Reluctant Imperialists*; James L. Glanville, *Italy's Relations with England, 1896–1905* (Baltimore: Johns Hopkins University Press, 1934); Enrico Serra, *L'intesa mediterranea del 1902. Una fase risolutiva nei rapporti italo-inglesi* (Milan: Giuffrè, 1957); Arthur Marsden, 'Salisbury and the Italians in 1896', *Journal of Modern History* 40 (1968), 91–117; Cedric J. Lowe and Frank Marzari, *Italian Foreign Policy, 1870–1940* (London: Routledge and Kegan Paul, 1975).
42 On the rapprochement between Italy and France from 1896 onward: Milza, *Français et Italiens à la fin du XIXe siècle. Aux origines du rapprochement franco-italien de 1900–1902*, II; Decleva, *Da Adua*; Pierre Guillen, *L'expansion 1881–1898* (Paris: Imprimèrie Nationale, 1984).
43 Monzali, *L'Etiopia*, 55–75.
44 On this see the observations of Decleva, *Da Adua*, 81–5.
45 On Pelloux: Luigi Pelloux, *Quelques souvenirs de ma vie* (Rome: Istituto per la storia del Risorgimento, 1967).
46 Milza, *Français et Italiens à la fin du XIXe siècle. Aux origines du rapprochement franco-italien de 1900–1902*, II; DDF, I, 14, docs 512, 527, 529, 535, 552.

47 On this: Luigi Peteani, *La questione libica nella diplomazia europea* (Florence: Cya, 1939); Pietro Silva, *Il Mediterraneo dall'Unità di Roma all'impero italiano* (Milan: ISPI, 1942), 356–66; Serra, *Barrère*, 67–70.
48 An in-depth examination of the national conflicts within the Ottoman Empire and the attitude of the European powers in Langer, *The Diplomacy of Imperialism*. A fine study of the Armenian question is the one by Francesco Sidari, *La questione armena nella politica delle grandi potenze dalla chiusura del Congresso di Berlino del 1878 al trattato di Losanna del 1923* (Padua: CEDAM, 1962). See too: *Documenti diplomatici italiani sull'Armenia* (Florence-Venice: Oemme, 1999–2000) series II, vols 1, 2, 3. On Macedonia: *Austro-Hungarian Documents Relating to the Macedonian Struggle 1896–1912* (Thessaloniki: Institute for Balkan Studies, 1976); Fikret Adanir, *Die makedonische Frage, ihre Entstehung und Entwicklung bis 1908* (Wiesbaden: Steiner, 1979).
49 Salvatorelli, *La Triplice Alleanza. Storia diplomatica 1877–1912*, 198; Langer, *The Diplomacy of Imperialism*.
50 On this: Decleva, *Da Adua*, 173–80.
51 *British Documents on the Origins of the War, 1898–1914* (London: HMSO, 1927–38) (henceforth BD), 1, docs 352, 355, 356, 359, 360, 361; Serra, *L'intesa mediterranea*.
52 On the Italian penetration of Albania and Montenegro: DDF, II, 1, docs 4, 365; *ivi*, II, 2, doc. 201; *ivi*, II, 3, doc. 62.
53 DDI, III, 5, doc. 751, Prinetti to Nigra, 31 August 1901.
54 GP, 18, part 2, doc. 5731, Von Bülow to Von Wedel, 9 March 1902; DDI, III, 6, doc. 329, Prinetti to Nigra, 7 April 1902.
55 Still useful on the figure of Giolitti and his ideas, even if full of inaccuracies, are his memoirs: Giovanni Giolitti, *Memoirs of My Life* (London: Chapman and Dodd, 1923); see too *Dalle carte di Giovanni Giolitti. Quarant'anni di politica italiana* (Milan: Feltrinelli, 1962), 3 vols. His political activity has been studied and discussed at great length by historians, but there is no truly complete and satisfactory biography, nor any close examination of Giolitti's thought and action in the international field. However, we refer the reader to: Sergio Romano, *Giolitti lo stile del potere* (Milan: Bompiani, 1989); Nino Valeri, *Giovanni Giolitti* (Turin: Utet, 1972); Giovanni Spadolini, *Giolitti: un'epoca* (Milan: Longanesi, 1985); Luigi Albertini, *Venti anni di vita politica*, ed. Luciano Magrini (Bologna: Zanichelli, 1950–3), 5 vols, in particular series I, vols 1 and 2; Rosario Romeo, *L'Italia liberale: sviluppo e contraddizioni* (Milan: Il Saggiatore, 1987); Alberto Aquarone, *L'Italia giolittiana* (Bologna: Il Mulino, 1988); Volpe, *Italia moderna*, II and III; Giorgio Candeloro, *Storia dell'Italia moderna* (Milan: Feltrinelli, 1974), vol. VII; Aldo A. Mola, *Giolitti. Lo statista della nuova Italia* (Milan: Mondadori, 2003).
56 On the Italian attempts to counter Austro-Russian collaboration on the introduction of reforms in Ottoman Macedonia: BD, 5, docs 23, 33, 150; DDF, II, 4, docs 230, 277, 283, 295, 303, 307, 308; ibid., 6, doc. 62; GP, 19, part 1, docs 5996, 5999; ibid., 22, docs 7394, 7397, 7417, 7507, 7720; Francesco Tommasini, *L'Italia alla vigilia della guerra. La politica estera di Tommaso Tittoni* (Bologna: Zanichelli, 1934–41), 5 vols, I: 409–20, II: 15–20, III: 489–94.
57 On this: Marta Petricioli, *Archeologia e Mare Nostrum. Le missioni archeologiche nella politica mediterranea dell'Italia 1898–1943* (Rome: Levi, 1990); Daniel J. Grange, *L'Italie et la Méditerranée (1896–1911)* (Rome: Ecole française de Rome, 1994); Monzali, *L'Etiopia*, pp. 301–9; Tommasini, *L'Italia alla vigilia della guerra*, II 57–60, III 199–206.

58 Tommasini, *L'Italia alla vigilia della guerra*, IV and V; Albertini, *The Origins of the War of 1914*, I; Momtchilo Nintchitch (Ninčić), *La crise bosniaque (1908-1909) et les Puissances européennes* (Paris: Costes, 1937), 2 vols; Bernadotte E. Schmitt, *The Annexation of Bosnia, 1908-1909* (New York: Fertig, 1970); Aleš Skřivan, *Deutschland und Österreich-Ungarn in der europäischen Politik der Jahre 1906-1914* (Hamburg: Dölling und Galitz, 1999).

59 On Italo-Russian relations and the conclusion of the Racconigi Agreement: Tommasini, *L'Italia alla vigilia della guerra*, IV and V; Guido Donnini, *L'accordo italo-russo di Racconigi* (Milan: Giuffrè, 1983); Anchieri, *Costantinopoli e gli Stretti*, 114-20.

60 On the negotiations that led to the exchange of notes between Italy and Austria: Tommasini, *L'Italia alla vigilia della guerra*, V; Donnini, *L'accordo italo-russo di Racconigi*; Luciano Monzali, 'Sidney Sonnino e la politica estera italiana dal 1878 al 1914', in *Il colonialismo nella politica estera italiana 1878-1949. Momenti e protagonisti* (Rome: Società editrice Dante Alighieri, 2017), 42-6.

61 For an analysis of the Libyan question in the foreign relations of the Liberal Italy: Francesco Malgeri, *La guerra libica 1911-1912* (Rome: Edizioni di Storia e Letteratura, 1970); Paolo Soave, *Fezzan: il deserto conteso (1842-1921)* (Milan: Giuffrè, 2001); Gianpaolo Ferraioli, *Politica e Diplomazia in Italia tra XIX e XX secolo. Vita di Antonino di San Giuliano (1852-1914)* (Soveria Mannelli: Rubbettino, 2007); Peteani, *La questione libica nella diplomazia europea*; Silva, *Il Mediterraneo dall'Unità di Roma all'Unità d'Italia*; Salvatorelli, *La Triplice Alleanza. Storia diplomatica 1877-1912*. On the influence of the Libyan conflict on the outbreak of the First World War: Sidney B. Fay, *The Origins of the World War* (New York: Free Press, 1966); Albertini, *The Origins of the War of 1914*, I; Pierre Renouvin, *La crise européenne et la première guerre mondiale* (Paris: PUF, 1948); Bernadotte E. Schmitt, *The Coming of the War, 1914* (New York: Fertig, 1966); Klaus Hildebrand, *Das vergangene Reich. Deutsche Aussenpolitik von Bismarck bis Hitler 1871-1945* (Stuttgart: Deutsche Verlags-Anstalt, 1995).

62 On Italian attitude during the Second Moroccan crisis: DDI, IV, 7-8, docs 26, 41, 42, 54, 65, 68, 76, 91, 92, 97, 107, 138; BD, 7, docs 273, 445; DDF, II, 14, docs 11, 52.

63 BD, 7, doc. 445; DDI, IV, 7-8, doc. 104; Salvatorelli, *La Triplice Alleanza. Storia diplomatica 1877-1912*, 397. On German perception of Italian intention to solve by force the Tripolitania question: GP, 30, part 1, docs 10819, 10821, 10822.

64 In this connection: Memorandum by the Foreign Minister San Giuliano, 28 July 1911, in *Dalle carte di Giovanni Giolitti*, III, doc. 49; ACS, CGG, portfolio 23, San Giuliano to Giolitti, 4 September 1911; ibid., portfolio 22, Antonio di San Giuliano, Memorandum, 13 September 1911, enclosure with San Giuliano to Giolitti, 13 September 1911.

65 ACS, CGG, portfolio 22, Avarna to San Giuliano, 28 July 1911. Very useful on the genesis of the Italian decision to conquer Tripolitania and Cyrenaica is Malgeri, *La guerra libica (1911-12)*, 97-110. See too: Enrico Serra, *I diplomatici italiani, la guerra di Libia e l'imperialismo*, in Enrico Serra and Christopher Seton-Watson (eds), *Italia e Inghilterra nell'età dell'imperialismo* (Milan: Angeli, 1990), 146-64; DDI, IV, 7-8, docs 108, 120-1; GP, 30, part 1, docs 10841, 10842, 10847, 10848, 10849; *Österreich-Ungarns Aussenpolitik von der Bosnischen Krise 1908 bis zum Kriegsausbruch 1914* (Wien: Österreichischer Bundesverlag, 1930) (from now OEU), 3, docs 2585, 2595, 2607, 2654; Ferraioli, *Politica e diplomazia in Italia tra XIX e XX secolo. Vita di Antonino di San Giuliano (1852-1914)*, 377-90; Richard J. Bosworth,

Italy, the Least of the Great Powers: Italian Foreign Policy before the First World War (Cambridge: Cambridge University Press, 1979).
66 For instance Louis, the French ambassador in Saint Petersburg: DDF, II, 14, doc. 308. See also ibid., d. 353, Jules Cambon to de Selves, 24 September 1911.
67 DDI, IV, 7–8, doc. 240.
68 DDI, IV, 7–8, docs 244, 245, 250, 256, 257, 259.
69 DDF, II, 14, doc. 361.
70 GP, 30, part 1, docs 10883, 10887, 10888; DDF, II, 14, docs 402, 406, 411, 419; DDI, IV, 7–8, docs 332, 340, 246, 248, 368, 372. On Austrian-Hungarian attitude towards Italian invasion of Tripolitania: OEU, 3, docs 2655, 2713, 2714, 2738, 2809, 2878, 2932, 2996, 3056, 3108; Franz Conrad Von Hötzendorf, *Aus meiner Dienstzeit, 1906–1918* (Wien-Berlin: Rikola, 1921), vols 2, II 218.-230.
71 DDF, II, 14, docs 467, 478, 492; Timothy W. Childs, *Italo-Turkish Diplomacy and the War over Libya 1911–1912* (Leiden: Brill, 1990), 71–5.
72 DDI, IV, 7–8, docs 410, 411; GP, 30, part 1, docs 10917, 10918; OEU, 3, doc. 2874; Ferraioli, *Politica e diplomazia in Italia tra XIX e XX secolo. Vita di Antonino di San Giuliano (1852–1914)*, 421–30.
73 On the diplomatic history of the war in Libya in 1911–12: Ferraioli, *Politica e diplomazia in Italia tra XIX e XX secolo. Vita di Antonino di San Giuliano (1852–1914)*; William C. Askew, *Europe and Italy's Acquisition of Libya 1911–1912* (Durham, NC: Duke University Press, 1942); Albertini, *Venti anni*, I, 2; Salvatorelli, *La Triplice Alleanza. Storia diplomatica 1877–1916*; Volpe, *Italia moderna*, III; Malgeri, *La guerra libica 1911–1912*; Childs, *Italo-Turkish Diplomacy and the War over Libya 1911–1912*; Christopher Seton-Watson, 'British Perceptions of the Italo-Turkish War 1911–12', in Serra and Seton-Watson, *Italia e Inghilterra*, 111–45; C. J. Lowe, 'Grey and the Tripoli War, 1911–1912', in F. H. Hinsley (ed.), *British Foreign Policy under Sir Edward Grey* (Cambridge: Cambridge University Press, 1977), 31–325; Afflerbach, *Der Dreibund. Europäische Grossmacht-und Allianzpolitik vor dem Ersten Weltkrieg*, 686–96; Luciano Monzali, *A Half-Hearted Friendship: France and Italian Conquest of Tripolitania and Cyrenaica*, in L. Micheletta and A. Ungari (eds), *The Libyan War 1911–1912* (Newcastle upon Tyne: Cambridge Scholars, 2013).
74 Askew, *Europe and Italy's Acquisition of Libya 1911–1912*, 191–2.
75 DDI, IV, 7–8, docs 780, 782, 784; DDF, III, 2, doc. 361; OEU, 4, docs 3525, 3534; Askew, *Europe and Italy's Acquisition of Libya 1911–1912*, 201–5.
76 Askew, *Europe and Italy's Acquisition of Libya 1911–1912*, 212–15. On Ottoman reaction to Italian attacks and occupations: Childs, *Italo-Turkish Diplomacy and the War over Libya 1911–1912*, 133–40.
77 DDF, III, 3, docs 9, 21, 28, 36, 40.
78 DDF, III, 1, doc. 516.
79 DDF, II, 14, doc. 475; BD, 9, tome 1, docs 368, 419; Askew, *Europe and Italy's Acquisition of Libya 1911–1912*, 246–50; Gianluca André, *L'Italia e il Mediterraneo alla vigilia della prima guerra mondiale. I tentativi di intesa mediterranea (1911–1914)* (Milan: Giuffrè, 1967).
80 DDF, III, 3, doc. 160.
81 The text of the preliminary Italian-Ottoman agreement is published in DDI, IV, 7–8, docs 1066, 1067.
82 The text of the peace treaty is published in DDI, IV, 7–8, doc. 1077.
83 DDF, III, 4, docs 285, 342, 393, 497, 518; BD, 9, tome 1, docs 423, 427, 428, 429; Askew, *Europe and Italy's Acquisition of Libya 1911–1911*; André, *L'Italia e il*

Mediterraneo alla vigilia della prima guerra mondiale. I tentativi di intesa mediterranea (1911–1914); Ferraioli, *Politica e diplomazia in Italia tra XIX e XX secolo. Vita di Antonino di San Giuliano (1852–1914)*, 535–40.

84 Salvatorelli, *La Triplice Alleanza. Storia diplomatica 1877–1912*.
85 ACS, CGG, portfolio 12, Avarna to San Giuliano, 5 December 1912.
86 Pribram, *The Secret Treaties of Austria-Hungary, 1879–1914*.
87 GP, 3, part 2, docs 11272, 11273, 11275, 11277; OEU, 4, docs 4424, 4505, 4522, 4524; ACS, CGG, portfolio 12, San Giuliano to Bollati, 5 November 1912; ACS, CGG, portfolio 22, Pansa to San Giuliano, 15 November 1912; ibid., San Giuliano to Giolitti, 15 November 1912; Pribram, *The Secret Treaties of Austria-Hungary, 1879–1914*; Salvatorelli, *La Triplice Alleanza. Storia diplomatica 1877–1912*, 457; Albertini, *The Origins of the War of 1914*, I; Volpe, *Italia moderna*, III, 457–67.
88 On the origins and course of the Balkan Wars: Ernst Christian Helmreich, *The Diplomacy of the Balkan Wars, 1911–1912* (Cambridge, MA: Harvard University Press, 1938); Albertini, *The Origins of the War of 1914*, I; Afflerbach, *Der Dreibund. Europäische Grossmacht-und Allianzpolitik vor dem Ersten Weltkrieg*, 721–30; Raymond Poincaré, *Au service de la France. Neuf années de souvenirs* (Paris: Plon, 1926), vols 1 and 2; John D. Treadway, *The Falcon and the Eagle: Montenegro and Austria-Hungary, 1908–1914* (West Lafayette: Purdue University Press, 1983); Katrin Boeckh, *Von den Balkankriegen zum Ersten Weltkrieg. Kleinstaatenpolitik und ethnische Selbstbestimmung auf dem Balkan* (Munich: Oldenbourg, 1996).
89 Andrè, *L'Italia e il Mediterraneo alla vigilia della prima guerra mondiale. I tentativi di intesa mediterranea (1911–1914)*, 147–50; Marta Petricioli, *L'Italia in Asia minore. Equilibrio mediterraneo e ambizioni imperialiste alla vigilia della prima guerra mondiale* (Florence: Sansoni, 1983).
90 On the genesis of the naval convention: Mariano Gabriele, *Le convenzioni navali della Triplice* (Rome: Ufficio storico della Marina militare, 1969), 324–40.
91 On the Italian vision of the Triple Alliance: Decleva, *Da Adua*, 416–18; Brunello Vigezzi, *Da Giolitti a Salandra* (Florence: Vallecchi, 1969), 3–52; Volpe, *Italia moderna*, III.
92 Bernhard vonBülow, *Memoirs of Prince von Bülow* (Boston: Little, Brown, 1931–2), 4 vols, in particular vol. 3.
93 On the Italian attitude toward the international crisis of July 1914: Albertini, *The Origins of the War of 1914*, II and III; Mario Toscano, 'L'Italia e la crisi europea del luglio 1914', in *Pagine di storia diplomatica contemporanea. I. Origini e vicende della prima guerra mondiale* (Milan: Giuffrè, 1963), 125–40; Pietro Pastorelli, *Dalla prima alla seconda guerra mondiale. Momenti e problemi della politica estera italiana (1914–1943)* (Milan: LED, 1997), 15–30; Brunello Vigezzi, *L'Italia di fronte alla prima guerra mondiale. I. L'Italia neutrale* (Milan: Ricciardi, 1966); Vigezzi, *L'Italia unita e le sfide della politica estera dal Risorgimento alla Repubblica* (Milan: Unicopli, 1997), 129–40; William A. Renzi, *In the Shadow of the Sword: Italy's Neutrality and Entrance into the Great War 1914–1915* (New York: Peter Lang, 1987); Alberto Monticone, *La Germania e la neutralità italiana: 1914–1915* (Bologna: Il Mulino, 1971); Leo Valiani, *The End of Austria-Hungary* (New York: Knopf, 1973); Monzali, 'Sidney Sonnino e la politica estera italiana'; Monzali, *Italians of Dalmatia*.
94 DDI, IV, 12, doc. 524, Bollati to San Giuliano, 25 July 1914.
95 In this connection: DDI, V, 1, docs 54 and 55, San Giuliano to Salandra, 4 August 1914; Antonio Salandra, *La neutralità italiana 1914–1915* (Milan: Mondadori, 1928).

96 On the figure of Sidney Sonnino and his foreign policy vision: Paola Carlucci, *Il giovane Sonnino fra cultura e politica (1847-1886)* (Rome: Istituto di Storia del Risorgimento Italiano-Archivio Izzi, 2002); Luciano Monzali, 'Sidney Sonnino e la politica estera italiana nell'età degli imperialismi europei', in Pier Luigi Ballini (ed.), *La politica estera dei Toscani. Ministri degli Esteri nel Novecento* (Florence: Polistampa, 2012), 13–53; Monzali, 'La politica estera di Sidney Sonnino e i fini di guerra dell'Italia (1915-1917). Alcune riflessioni', in Pietro Neglie and Andrea Ungari (eds), *La guerra di Cadorna 1915-1917* (Rome: Ufficio storico SME, 2018); Monzali, 'Sidney Sonnino and Serbia', in Vojislav Pavlović (ed.), *Serbia and Italy in the Great War* (Belgrade: Institute for Balkan Studies, 2019), 81–120; Pier Luigi Ballini (ed.), *Sidney Sonnino e il suo tempo* (Florence: Olschki, 2000); Pier Luigi Ballini (ed.), *Sidney Sonnino e il suo tempo 1914-1922* (Soveria Mannelli: Rubbettino, 2000); Geoffrey A Haywood, *Failure of a Dream: Sidney Sonnino and the Rise and Fall of Liberal Italy, 1847-1922* (Florence: Olschki, 1999).
97 Monticone, *La Germania e la neutralità italiana: 1914-1915*, 58–65.
98 Albertini, *Venti anni di vita politica*, II, 1.
99 Monticone, *La Germania e la neutralità italiana: 1914-1915*.
100 Mario Toscano, *Il patto di Londra. Storia diplomatica dell'intervento italiano (1914-1915)* (Bologna: Zanichelli, 1934); Toscano, *La Serbia e l'intervento in guerra dell'Italia* (Milan: Giuffrè, 1939); Toscano, 'Le origini diplomatiche dell'art. 9 del patto di Londra relativo agli eventuali compensi all'Italia in Asia Minore', *Storia e Politica*, no. 3 (1965), 342–84; Toscano, 'Rivelazioni e nuovi documenti sul negoziato di Londra per l'ingresso dell'Italia nella prima guerra mondiale', *Nuova Antologia*, August 1965, 433–57, September 1965, 15–37, October 1965, 150–7, November 1965, 295–312; Toscano, 'L'Intervento dell'Italia nella prima guerra mondiale. Le carte Imperiali e la preparazione del negoziato', *Nuova Antologia*, 1968, 303–23, 461–73; Toscano, 'Imperiali e il negoziato per il patto di Londra', *Storia e Politica*, no. 2 (1968), 177–205.
101 Vigezzi, *L'Italia di fronte alla prima guerra mondiale. I. L'Italia neutrale*; Vigezzi, *I problemi della neutralità e della guerra nel carteggio Salandra-Sonnino (1914-1917)* (Milan: Ricciardi, 1962); Vigezzi, *Da Giolitti a Salandra* (Florence: Vallecchi, 1969).
102 Valiani, *The End of Austria-Hungary*.
103 Hugo Hantsch, *Leopold Graf Berchtold. Grandseigneur und Staatsmann* (Graz: Verl. Styria, 1963), 2 vols.
104 Friedrich Engel-Janosi, *Österreich und der Vatikan 1846-1918* (Graz: Verl. Styria, 1958), 2 vols.
105 Pastorelli, *Dalla prima alla seconda guerra mondiale*.
106 On the negotiations between Italy and the Entente in the spring of 1915 see too: Luciano Monzali, 'Alcune considerazioni sul Patto di Londra e la politica estera italiana fra il 1914 e il 1915', in Andrea Ciampani and Domenico Maria Bruni (eds), *Istituzioni politiche e mobilitazioni di piazza* (Soveria Mannelli: Rubbettino, 2018), 267–83; Monzali, *Italians of Dalmatia*; Giovanni Orsina and Andrea Ungari (eds), *L'Italia neutrale 1914-1915* (Rome: Rodorigo, 2016); H. James Burgwyn, *The Legend of the Mutilated Victory: Italy, the Great War and the Paris Conference, 1915-1919* (Westport: Greenwood Press, 1993); Michael Boro Petrovich, 'The Italo-Yugoslav Boundary Question 1914-1915', in Henry I. Roberts (ed.), *Russian Diplomacy and Eastern Europe 1914-1917* (New York: King's Crown Press, 1963), 178–90; Wolfram W. Gottlieb, *Studies in Secret Diplomacy during the First World War* (London: Allen and Unwin, 1957), 135–401.

107 The text of the London agreement in Antonio Salandra, *L'Intervento [1915]. Ricordi e pensieri* (Milan: Mondadori, 1930), 156–60. See also: Toscano, 'Le origini diplomatiche dell'art. 9 del patto di Londra relativo agli eventuali compensi dell'Italia in Asia Minore'.

108 On the agreements about the partition of the Ottoman Empire during the First World War and the role of Italy: Harry N. Howard, *The Partition of Turkey: A Diplomatic History, 1913–1923* (Norman: University of Oklahoma Press, 1931); Anchieri, *Costantinopoli e gli Stretti*; M. Toscano, *Gli accordi di San Giovanni di Moriana. Storia diplomatica dell'intervento italiano (1916–1917)* (Milano: Giuffrè, 1936); L. Riccardi, *Alleati non Amici. Le relazioni politiche tra l'Italia e l'Intesa durante la prima guerra mondiale* (Brescia: Morcelliana, 1992); Guglielmo Imperiali, *Diario 1915–1919* (Soveria Mannelli: Rubbettino, 2006). Useful documentation in DDI, V, vols 6, 7, 8.

109 René Albrecht Carrié, *Italy at the Paris Peace Conference* (Hamden: Archon Books, 1966); Luciano Monzali, 'La politica estera italiana nel primo dopoguerra 1918–1922. Sfide e problemi', *Italia contemporanea*, nos 256–7 (2009), 379–406; Paolo Soave, *Una vittoria mutilata? L'Italia e la conferenza della Pace di Parigi* (Soveria Mannelli: Rubbettino, 2020).

110 Luigi Aldrovandi Marescotti, *Guerra diplomatica. Ricordi e frammenti di diario (1914–1919)* (Milan: Mondadori, 1936), 221–39; Paul Mantoux, *Les Délibérations du Conseil des Quatre (24 mars – 28 juin 1919)* (Paris: CNRS éditions, 1955), 2 vols, I, 115–20, 277–80.

111 Luciano Monzali, 'Il governo Orlando-Sonnino e le questioni coloniali africane alla Conferenza della Pace di Parigi del 1919', *Nuova Rivista Storica*, no. 1 (2013), 67–132; Francesco Salata, *Il nodo di Gibuti. Storia diplomatica su documenti inedita* (Milano: ISPI, 1939), 291–6; Giovanni Buccianti, *L'egemonia sull'Etiopia (1918–1923). Lo scontro diplomatico fra Italia, Francia e Inghilterra* (Milan: Giuffrè, 1977), 83–90; Mario Toscano, 'Il problema coloniale italiano alla conferenza della pace', in *Pagine di storia diplomatica contemporanea* (Milan: Giuffrè, 1963), 2 vols, I.

112 On the negotiations between Italy, the Entente and Wilson in those months: Luciano Monzali, *Italiani di Dalmazia 1914–1924* (Firenze: Le Lettere, 2007); Luca Riccardi, *Francesco Salata tra storia, politica e diplomazia* (Udine: Del Bianco, 2001); Ivo John Lederer, *Yugoslavia at the Paris Peace Conference* (New Haven, CT: Yale University Press, 1963); Marta Petricioli, *L'occupazione italiana del Caucaso: 'un ingrato servizio' da rendere a Londra* (Milan: Giuffrè, 1972); Pietro Pastorelli, *L'Albania nella politica estera italiana* (Napoli: Jovene, 1970); Luca Micheletta, *Italia e Gran Bretagna nel primo dopoguerra* (Rome: Jouvence, 1999), 2 vols, I; Francesco Caccamo, *L'Italia e la «Nuova Europa». Il confronto sull'Europa orientale alla conferenza di pace di Parigi (1919–1920)* (Milan: Luni, 2000).

113 On Nitti governments' foreign policy: Francesco S. Nitti, *Edizione nazionale delle opere di Francesco Saverio Nitti. Scritti politici. Diario di prigionia, Meditazioni dell'Esilio* (Bari: Laterza, 1967), V; Enrico Serra, *Nitti e la Russia* (Bari: Dedalo, 1975); Paolo Alatri, *Nitti, D'Annunzio e la questione adriatica (1919–20)* (Milan: Feltrinelli, 1959); Micheletta, *Italia e Gran Bretagna nel primo dopoguerra*; Monzali, *Italiani di Dalmazia 1914–1924*; Monzali, *Il colonialismo nella politica estera italiana*; Monzali, *Francesco Tommasini, l'Italia e la rinascita della Polonia indipendente* (Rome: Accademia Polacca, 2018).

114 ASMAE, portfolio 472, *Milner to Tittoni*, London, 13 September 1919; ibid., *Tittoni to Milner*, 16 September 1919. On Tittoni's colonial designs: Monzali, Il *colonialismo nella politica estera italiana*, 165–222.

115 On the new Giolitti government: Valeri, *Giovanni Giolitti*, 287–95.
116 On Carlo Sforza: Carlo Sforza, *L'Italia dal 1914 al 1944 quale io la vidi* (Rome: Mondadori, 1944); Sforza, *Fifty Years of War and Diplomacy in the Balkans: Pashich and the Union of the Yugoslavs* (New York: Columbia University Press, 1940); Sforza, *Pensiero e azione di una politica estera italiana. Discorsi e scritti* (Bari: Laterza, 1924); Sforza, *Makers of Europe. Portraits and Personel Impressions and Recollections* (New York: Elkin Mathews & Marrot, 1930); Maria Grazia Melchionni, 'La politica estera di Carlo Sforza nel 1920–21', *Rivista di Studi politici internazionali* (1969), in particular 541–5; Melchionni, 'La convenzione antiasburgica del 12 novembre 1920', *Storia e Politica*, nn. 2 e 3 (1972), 224–64, 374–417; Giancarlo Giordano, *Carlo Sforza. La diplomazia 1896–1921* (Milan: Angeli, 1987); Giordano, *Carlo Sforza. La politica 1922–1952* (Milan: Angeli, 1992); Micheletta, *Italia e Gran Bretagna nel primo dopoguerra*, I; Livio Zeno, *Carlo Sforza. Ritratto di un grande diplomatico* (Firenze: Le Monnier, 1999); Monzali, *Italiani di Dalmazia 1914–1924*; Monzali, 'Riflessioni sulla cultura della diplomazia italiana in epoca liberale e fascista', in Giorgio Petracchi (ed.), *Uomini e Nazioni. Cultura e politica estera dell'Italia del Novecento* (Udine: Gaspari, 2005).
117 Micheletta, *Italia e Gran Bretagna nel primo dopoguerra*, I.
118 The Rapallo agreements of November 1920 (the Anti-Habsburg agreement and the border treaty) are published in Amedeo Giannini, *Documenti per la storia dei rapporti fra l'Italia e la Jugoslavia* (Rome: Istituto per l'Europa Orientale, 1934), 36–40. See as well: Riccardi, *Francesco Salata*, 264–80; Monzali, *Italiani di Dalmazia 1914–1924*, 191–220.
119 Luciano Monzali, *Un Re afghano in esilio a Roma. Amanullah e l'Afghanistan nella politica estera italiana 1919–1943* (Florence: Le Lettere, 2012).
120 On the fall of the Giolitti government: Renzo De Felice, *Mussolini il fascista. La conquista del potere 1921–1925* (Turin: Einaudi, 1966), 101–5; Monzali, *Italiani di Dalmazia 1914–1924*; *British Documents on Foreign Affairs: Reports and Papers from the Foreign Office Confidential Print* (Washington, DC: University Publications of America, 1983–), II, F, 4, Buchanan to Curzon, 27 June 1921, doc. 327.
121 De Felice, *Mussolini il fascista. La conquista del potere 1921–1925*, 101–10; Danilo Veneruso, *La vigilia del fascismo. Il primo ministero Facta nella crisi dello Stato liberale in Italia* (Bologna: Il Mulino, 1968), 18–30.
122 On Della Torretta: Luciano Monzali, 'Cancellare secolari fraintendimenti. Appunti sulle relazioni fra l'Italia liberale e la Prima Repubblica Austriaca', *Römische Historische Mitteilungen* 60 (2018), 329–66; Micheletta, *Italia e Gran Bretagna nel primo dopoguerra*, II, 405–7; Giorgio Petracchi, *Da San Pietroburgo a Mosca. La diplomazia italiana in Russia 1861–1941* (Rome: Bonacci, 1993), 170–5.
123 Micheletta, *Italia e Gran Bretagna nel primo dopoguerra* II, 595–605.
124 On the Genoa Conference: Carole Fink, *The Genoa Conference: European Diplomacy, 1921–1922* (Chapel Hill: University of North Carolina Press, 1984); Stephen White, *The Origins of Détente: The Genoa Conference and Soviet-Western Relations, 1921–1922* (Cambridge: Cambridge University Press, 1985); Giorgio Petracchi, *La Russia rivoluzionaria nella politica italiana. Le relazioni italo-sovietiche 1917–25* (Bari: Laterza, 1982), 214–20; Matteo Pizzigallo, *Alle origini della politica petrolifera italiana (1920–1925)* (Milan: Giuffrè, 1981), 94–110.
125 Monzali, 'La politica estera italiana nel primo dopoguerra 1918–1922. Sfide e problemi', 379–406; Micheletta, *Italia e Gran Bretagna nel primo dopoguerra*, II, 672–90.

126 To understand Mussolini's personality and ideas a necessary reading are the works of Renzo De Felice, the most important historian of Fascist Italy: De Felice, *Mussolini il fascista. La conquista del potere 1921-1925*; De Felice, *Mussolini il duce. Gli anni del consenso 1929-1936* (Turin: Einaudi, 1974); De Felice, *Mussolini il duce. Lo Stato totalitario 1936-1940* (Turin: Einaudi, 1981); De Felice, *Mussolini l'alleato. I L'Italia in guerra 1940-1943* (Turin: Einaudi, 1990), 2 vols. Useful also: Emilio Gentile, *The Italian Road to Totalitarianism* (London: Routledge, 2009); Gentile, *The Origins of Fascist Ideology, 1918-1925* (New York: Enigma Books, 2005); Gentile, *The Sacralization of Politics in Fascist Italy* (Cambridge, MA: Harvard University Press, 1996).

127 On Fascist Italy's foreign policy in the 1920s: Ruggero Moscati, 'La politica estera del fascismo. L'esordio del primo ministero Mussolini', *Studi politici* (September 1953–February 1954); Moscati, 'Gli esordi della politica estera fascista. Il periodo Contarini-Corfù', in *La politica estera italiana dal 1914 al 1943* (Turin: ERI, 1963), 39–60; Ettore Anchieri, 'L'esordio della politica estera fascista nei documenti diplomatici italiani', in *Il sistema diplomatico europeo: 1814–1939* (Milan: Angeli, 1977), 197–215; Anchieri, 'L'affare di Corfù alla luce dei documenti diplomatici italiani', in ibid., 217–30; Raffaele Guariglia, *Ricordi 1922–1945* (Naples: ESI, 1949); Pietro Pastorelli, 'La storiografia italiana del dopoguerra sulla politica estera fascista', *Storia e politica* (1971), 575–600; Pastorelli, *Italia e Albania 1924–1927. Origini diplomatiche del trattato di Tirana del 22 novembre 1927* (Florence: Rivista di studi politici internazionali, 1967); Alan Cassels, *Mussolini's Early Diplomacy* (Princeton, NJ: Princeton University Press, 1970); Giampiero Carocci, *La politica estera dell'Italia fascista (1925–1928)* (Bari: Laterza, 1969); Ennio Di Nolfo, *Mussolini e la politica estera italiana 1919–1933* (Padova: Cedam, 1960); H. James Burgwyn, *Italian Foreign Policy in the Interwar Period 1918–1940* (London: Praeger, 1997); Luciano Monzali, *Antonio Tacconi e la Comunità italiana di Spalato* (Venice: Società dalmata di storia patria, 2008); Monzali, *Il sogno dell'egemonia. L'Italia, la questione jugoslava e l'Europa centrale* (Florence: Le Lettere, 2010); Monzali, *Gli italiani di Dalmazia e le relazioni italo-jugoslave nel Novecento* (Venice: Marsilio, 2015); Francesco Lefebvre D'Ovidio, *L'Intesa italo-francese del 1935 nella politica estera di Mussolini* (Rome: Selbstverl, 1984); D'Ovidio, *L'Italia e il sistema internazionale. Dalla formazione del governo Mussolini alla grande Depressione (1922–1929)* (Rome: Edizioni di Storia e Letteratura, 2016).

128 De Felice, *Mussolini il duce. Gli anni del consenso*, 442–67; Jean-Baptiste Duroselle, *France and the Nazi Threat: The Collapse of French Diplomacy 1932–1939* (New York: Enigma Books, 2004); Francesco Salata, *Il Patto Mussolini. Storia di un piano politico e di un negoziato diplomatico* (Milan: Mondadori, 1933).

129 Luciano Monzali, 'Giuliano Cora e le relazioni italo-bulgare nella prima metà degli anni Trenta', in Stefano Baldi and Alexandre Kostov (eds), *140 Anni di Relazioni fra Italia e Bulgaria. Diplomazia, Economia, Cultura (1879–2019)* (Tendril: Sofia, 2019), 111–38.

130 Luciano Monzali, 'Amedeo Giannini e la nascita della storia delle relazioni internazionali in Italia', *Storia contemporanea*, no. 4 (1994), 493–525.

131 On Ismeo: Valdo Ferretti, 'Politica e Cultura: origini e attività dell'Ismeo durante il regime fascista', *Storia contemporanea*, no. 5 (1988), 779–819; Antonino Di Giovanni, 'Giuseppe Tucci, l'IsMEO e gli orientalismi nella politica estera del fascismo', *Annali della Facoltà di Scienze della formazione, Università degli studi di Catania*, no. 11 (2012), 74–94; Enrica Garzilli, *L'esploratore del Duce. Le avventure di Giuseppe Tucci e la politica italiana in Oriente da Mussolini a Andreotti. Con il carteggio di Giulio*

Andreotti (Rome: Memori Asiatica, 2012); Oscar Nalesini, 'Orrori e nefandezze di un esploratore. Note in margine di una recente biografia di Giuseppe Tucci', *Annali dell'Università degli Studi di Napoli L'Orientale di Napoli*, no. 73 (2013), 201–79; Mario Prayer, *Internazionalismo e nazionalismo culturale. Gli intellettuali bengalesi e l'Italia negli anni Venti e Trenta* (Rome: Bardi, 1996), 30–40; Prayer, 'Italian Indologists and Modern India, 1913–1941', in Arun Bandopadhyay and Sanjukta Das Gupta (eds), *In Quest of the Historian's Craft: Essays in Honour of Professor B. B. Chauduri* (New Delhi: Manohar, 2018), 147–79.

132 De Felice, *Mussolini il duce. Gli anni del consenso*; Jens Petersen, *Hitler e Mussolini. La difficile alleanza* (Rome: Laterza, 1975).

133 DDI, VII, 11, Guariglia to Grandi, 18 February 1932, d. 226, also printed in Guariglia, *Ricordi*, 144–71. On Guariglia's ideas: Raffaele Guariglia, 'Un ambasciatore monarchico nell'Italia repubblicana. Raffaele Guariglia e la politica estera italiana (1943–1958)', in Luciano Monzali and Andrea Ungari (eds), *I monarchici e la politica estera italiana del secondo dopoguerra*: (Soveria Mannelli: Rubbettino, 2012), 159–242; Lowe and Marzari, *Italian Foreign Policy*, 147–8.

134 On the brief Italian–French reconciliation: De Felice, *Mussolini il duce. Gli anni del consenso*; Duroselle, *France and the Nazi Threat*; Giovanni Buccianti, *Verso gli accordi Mussolini-Laval. Il riavvicinamento italo-francese fra il 1931 e il 1934* (Milan: Giuffrè, 1984); Salvatore Minardi, 'L'accordo militare segreto Badoglio-Gamelin del 1935', *Clio*, no. 2 (1987), 271–300.

135 On the Italian-Ethiopian war: De Felice, *Mussolini il duce. Gli anni del consenso*; Renato Mori, *Mussolini e la conquista dell'Etiopia* (Florence: Le Monnier, 1978); Giorgio Rochat, *Militari e politici nella preparazione della campagna d'Etiopia. Studio e documenti 1932–1936* (Milan: Angeli, 1971); Franklin. D. Laurens, *France and the Italo-Ethiopian Crisis, 1935–1936* (L'Aja: Mouton De Gruyter, 1967); William Norton Medlicott, 'The Hoare-Laval Pact Reconsidered', in David Dilks (ed.), *Retreat from Power: Studies in Britain's Foreign Policy of the Twentieth Century* (London: Macmillan, 1981), vol. I, 118–38; Alessandro Lessona, *Memorie* (Rome: Lessona, 1963), 149–80.

136 Regarding relations between Berlin and Rome in those years: Manfred Funke, *Sanzioni e cannoni 1934–1936. Hitler, Mussolini e il conflitto etiopico* (Milan: Garzanti, 1972); Gerhard L. Weinberg, *The Foreign Policy of Hitler's Germany. Diplomatic Revolution in Europe 1933–1936*, vol. I, *Diplomatic Revolution in Europe (1933–1936)* (London: Humanities Press, 1970), 232–40; *Akten zur Deutschen Auswärtigen Politik 1918–1945*, Göttingen, 1950–95 (henceforth ADAP), C, IV, 2, d. 485; Jürgen Gehl, *Austria, Germany and the Anschluss* (London: Oxford University Press, 1963).

137 DDI, VIII, 3, dd. 275, 282, 384, 614; De Felice, *Mussolini il duce. Gli anni del consenso*; Mori, *Mussolini e la conquista dell'Etiopia*. On the French perception of the German-Italian reconciliation: DDF, II, 1, dd. 121, 135, 209, 211, 360.

138 De Felice, *Mussolini il duce. Gli anni del consenso*; De Felice, *Mussolini il duce. Lo Stato totalitario 1936–1940*; Ennio Di Nolfo, 'Le oscillazioni di Mussolini: la politica estera fascista dinanzi ai temi del revisionismo', *Nuova Antologia*, no. 2176 (1990), 172–95; Fulvio D'Amoja, *La politica estera dell'Impero. Storia della politica estera fascista dalla conquista dell'Etiopia all'Anschluss* (Padova: Cedam, 1967); Rosaria Quartararo, *Roma fra Londra e Berlino. La politica estera fascista dal 1930 al 1940* (Rome: Bonacci, 1980); Fortunato Minniti, *Fino alla guerra: strategie e conflitto nella politica di potenza di Mussolini 1923–1940* (Neaples: ESI, 2000).

139 On Italian intervention in Spain: John F. Coverdale, *Italian Intervention in the Spanish Civil War* (Princeton, NJ: Princeton University Press, 1975); De Felice, *Mussolini il duce. Lo Stato totalitario*.
140 Regarding Italian–Turkish relations: Maria Antonia Di Casola, *Turchia neutrale, 1943–1945: la difesa degli interessi nazionali dalle pressioni alleate* (Milano: Giuffrè, 1981–4), 2 vols.
141 On Italy and the Zionist movement in Palestine: Sergio Minerbi, *L'Italie et la Palestine 1914–1920* (Paris: Presses universitaires de France, 1970); Minerbi, 'Il progetto di un insediamento ebraico in Etiopia (1936–1943)', *Storia contemporanea*, no. 6 (1986), 1083–137; Minerbi, 'Italia e Palestina nel carteggio Jabotinsky – Sciaky', *Nuova Storia Contemporanea* 2 (2006), 149–56; Renzo De Felice, *Il fascismo e l'Oriente. Arabi, ebrei e indiani nella politica di Mussolini* (Bologna: Il Mulino, 1988).
142 De Felice, *Il fascismo e l'Oriente. Arabi, ebrei e indiani nella politica di Mussolini*; Arturo Marzano, *Onde fasciste. La propaganda di Radio Bari (1934–1943)* (Rome: Carocci, 2015); Nir Arielli, *Fascist Italy and the Middle East (1933–40)* (Basingstoke: Palgrave Macmillan, 2013).
143 For an analysis of Italian-British growing antagonism in the second half of the 1930s: De Felice, *Mussolini il duce. Lo Stato totalitario*; Donatella Bolech Cecchi, *L'accordo di due Imperi. L'accordo italo-inglese del 16 aprile 1938* (Milan: Giuffrè, 1977); Cecchi, *Non spezzare i ponti con Roma. Le relazioni fra l'Italia e la Gran Bretagna dall'accordo di Monaco alla seconda guerra mondiale* (Milan: Giuffrè, 1986); Quartararo, *Roma tra Londra e Berlino. La politica estera fascista dal 1930 al 1940*.
144 On French-Italian relations: Duroselle, *France and the Nazi Threat*; De Felice, *Mussolini il duce. Lo Stato totalitario*; Alessandra Giglioli, *Italia e Francia 1936–1939* (Rome: Jouvence, 2001); Monzali, *Un ambasciatore monarchico nell'Italia repubblicana. Raffaele Guariglia e la politica estera italiana*.
145 Mario Toscano, *The Origins of the Pact of Steel* (Baltimore: Johns Hopkins University Press, 1967), 101–5.
146 Galeazzo Ciano, *Diario 1936–1943* (Milan: Rizzoli, 1990), 226–64; R. De Felice, *Mussolini il duce. Lo Stato totalitario*.
147 De Felice, *Mussolini il duce. Lo stato totalitario*, 585–95; Pastorelli, *Dalla prima alla seconda guerra mondiale*, 132–5; Ciano, *Diario*, 267.
148 Ciano, *Diario*, 262–74; Alfredo Breccia, *Jugoslavia 1939–1941. Diplomazia della neutralità* (Milan: Giuffrè, 1978).
149 Alberto Basciani, 'Tra politica culturale e politica di potenza. Alcuni aspetti dei rapporti tra Italia e Albania tra le due guerre mondiali', *Mondo Contemporaneo* 2 (2012), 91–114; Basciani, *L'illusione della modernità: il Sud-Est dell'Europa tra le due guerre mondiali* (Soveria Mannelli: Rubbettino, 2016); Bernd J. Fischer, *King Zog and the Struggle for Stability in Albania* (New York: Columbia University Press, 1984); Fischer, *Albania at War, 1939–1945* (London: Hurst, 1999); Massimo Borgogni, *Tra continuità e incertezza. Italia e Albania (1914–1939). La strategia politico-militare dell'Italia in Albania fino all'operazione «Oltre Mare Tirana»* (Milano: Angeli, 2007); Ciano, *Diario*, 286–7; Luca Micheletta, *La resa dei conti. Il Kosovo, l'Italia e la dissoluzione della Jugoslavia (1939–1941)* (Rome: Edizioni Nuova Cultura, 2008).
150 Toscano, *The Origins of the Pact of Steel*; Ribbentrop to Ciano, 20 March 1939, *Documents on German Foreign Policy, 1918–1945* (London: HMSO, 1949–) (hereafter DGFP), series D, 6, doc. 55.
151 On Italian plans in the Mediterranean Sea: Davide Rodogno, *Fascism's European Empire: Italian Occupation during the Second World War* (Cambridge: Cambridge

University Press, 2006); H. James Burgwyn, *Mussolini Warlord: Failed Dreams of Empire, 1940-1943* (New York: Enigma Books, 2012).

152 For a thorough and complete analysis of the diplomatic and political process that brought to Italian intervention into the Second World War see: Gianluca Andrè, *La guerra in Europa (1°settembre 1939-22 giugno 1941)* (Milan: ISPI, 1964); De Felice, *Mussolini il duce. Lo Stato totalitario*; Macgregor Knox, *Mussolini Unleashed, 1939-1941: Politics and Strategy in Fascist Italy's Last War* (Cambridge: Cambridge University Press, 1986).

153 DDI, IX, 5, docs 65, 114, 549. On the Arab policy of Fascist Italy: De Felice, *Il fascismo e l'Oriente*; Renzo De Felice, *Mussolini l'alleato 1940-1945. I L'Italia in guerra 1940-1943: 1 Dalla guerra "breve" alla guerra lunga* (Turin: Einaudi 1990); Lukasz Hirszowicz, *The Third Reich and the Arab East* (London: Routledge and Kegan Paul, 1966); Lorenzo Medici, *Colonialismo al tramonto. La neutralità dell'Iraq durante la seconda guerra mondiale* (Perugia: Guerra, 1998).

154 De Felice, *Il fascismo e l'Oriente*, 340-8; Milan Hauner, *India in Axis Strategy: Germany, Japan, and Indian Nationalists in the Second World War* (Stuttgart: Klett-Cotta, 1981), 414-30. See also Monzali, *Un re afghano in esilio a Roma*, 79; Hirszowicz, *The Third Reich and the Arab East*.

155 The text in DDI, IX, 8, d. 488. On this declaration: Monzali, *Un re afghano in esilio a Roma*, 75-80; De Felice, *Il fascismo e l'Oriente*. See also ADAP, D, XI, 1, docs 57, 58, 146.

156 ADAP, D, IX, d. 277; ADAP, D, XI, d. 146; Hirszowicz, *The Third Reich and the Arab East*, 85-94.

157 Hauner, *India in Axis Strategy*, 411-20; DDI, IX, 8, docs 125, 256.

158 DDI, IX, 8, Lanza d'Ajeta to Ciano, 11 March 1942, d. 358.

159 Hauner, *India in Axis Strategy*, 423-30.

160 DDI, IX, 8, d. 450; De Felice, *Il fascismo e l'Oriente*, 348-9; Hauner, *India in Axis Strategy*, 670-1.

161 DDI, IX, 8, d. 492, *Colloquio del capo del Governo Mussolini con il cancelliere del Reich Hitler*, 29 April 1942.

162 On the Tripartite powers' attitude toward Indian independence: Hauner, *India in Axis Strategy*, 455-70; De Felice, *Il fascismo e l'Oriente*.

163 Frederick William Deakin, *The Brutal Friendship: Mussolini, Hitler and the Fall of Italian Fascism* (New York: Harper and Row, 1962); De Felice, *Mussolini l'alleato. I L'Italia in guerra (1940-1943). 2 Crisi e agonia del regime*.

164 De Felice, *Mussolini l'alleato. I L'Italia in guerra (1940-1943). 2 Crisi e agonia del regime*; Ennio Di Nolfo, *La Repubblica delle speranze e degli inganni. L'Italia dalla caduta del fascismo al crollo della Democrazia Cristiana* (Florence: Ponte delle Grazie, 1996), 31-56; Di Nolfo, *Vaticano e Stati Uniti 1939-1952 (Dalle carte di Myron C. Taylor)* (Milan: Angeli, 1978), 50-70; Toscano, *Dal 25 luglio all'8 settembre. Nuove rivelazioni sugli armistizi fra l'Italia e le Nazioni Unite* (Florence: Le Monnier, 1966), 141-80; Pastorelli, *Dalla prima alla seconda guerra mondiale. Momenti e problemi della politica estera italiana 1914-1943*, 155-73.

165 Ciano, *Diario*, 693.

166 Simona Colarizi, *La seconda guerra mondiale e la Repubblica* (Turin: UTET, 1984), 174.

167 Giuseppe Bastianini, *Uomini, cose, fatti. Memorie di un Ambasciatore* (Milan: Vitagliano, 1967); Egidio Ortona, *Diplomazia di guerra. Diari 1937-1943* (Bologna: Il Mulino, 1993).

168 De Felice, *Mussolini l'alleato. I L'Italia in guerra (1940-1943). 2 Crisi e agonia del regime*.
169 ADAP, E, VI, docs 29, 74, 115; DDI, IX, 10, docs 320, 358, 381, 393; Hirszowicz, *The Third Reich and the Arab East*.
170 DDI, IX, 10, d. 381.
171 This was the text of the proposed declaration: 'Le Potenze dell'Asse che hanno manifestato costantemente la loro amicizia verso i paesi Arabi del Vicino Oriente, e la loro comprensione e simpatia per le loro aspirazioni, intendono riconfermare formalmente le direttive della loro politica. Le Potenze dell'Asse dichiarano pertanto: che esse considerano la libertà e l'indipendenza dei paesi Arabi del Vicino Oriente (Iraq, Siria, Palestina, Libano e Transgiordania) come uno degli obiettivi della loro politica; che esse sono pronte a riconoscere la piena sovranità e indipendenza di tali paesi ed a consentire alla loro unione, qualora questa sia desiderata dalle popolazioni interessate; che esse sono contrarie a qualunque soluzione della questione palestinese – compreso il progetto di un focolare nazionale ebraico in Palestina – che contrasti con le aspirazioni e con gli interessi del popolo arabo.' *Progetto di dichiarazione per i paesi Arabi,* Annex to *Babuscio Rizzo to Alfieri,* 5 July 1943, DDI, IX, 10, d. 472.
172 DDI, IX, 10, docs 15, 47, 85, 124, 147, 235, 264.
173 Toscano, *Dal 25 luglio all'8 settembre*; Di Nolfo, *La Repubblica*; Pastorelli, *Dalla prima alla seconda guerra mondiale*; Elena Aga Rossi, *Una nazione allo sbando. L'armistizio italiano del settembre 1943* (Bologna: Il Mulino, 1993).
174 Roberto Gaja, *L'Italia nel mondo bipolare. Per una storia della politica estera italiana (1943-1991)* (Bologna: Il Mulino, 1995).
175 On Prunas' diplomatic action: Mario Toscano, 'La ripresa delle relazioni diplomatiche fra l'Italia e l'Unione Sovietica nel corso della seconda guerra mondiale', *La Comunità Internazionale* (1962), 34–72; Toscano, 'La ripresa delle relazioni diplomatiche fra l'Italia e la Francia nel corso della seconda guerra mondiale', *Storia e Politica* (1962), 523–604; Toscano, *Designs in Diplomacy: Pages from European Diplomatic History in the Twentieth Century* (Baltimore: Johns Hopkins University Press, 1970); Gaja, *L'Italia nel mondo bipolare. Per una storia della politica estera italiana (1943-1991*; Gaja, 'Renato Prunas ed i rapporti italo-francesi dal 1943 al 1945', *Affari Esteri*, no. 67 (1985), 376–86; Gaja, 'La svolta di Salerno: una notte a Minori', in Enrico Serra (ed.), *Professione diplomatico* (Milan: Angeli, 1988), 88–95. See as well: Gianluca Borzoni, *Renato Prunas diplomatico (1892-1951)* (Soveria Mannelli: Rubbettino, 2004); Pietro Quaroni, *Il mondo di un ambasciatore* (Milan: Ferro, 1965), 315–21; Ennio Di Nolfo and Maurizio Serra, *La gabbia infranta. Gli Alleati e l'Italia dal 1943 al 1945* (Rome: Laterza, 2010); Mauro Conciatori, '1943: la diplomazia italiana dopo l'8 settembre. I diplomatici italiani di fronte alle conseguenze dell'annuncio dell'armistizio', *Storia delle relazioni internazionali* (1990), 99–234.
176 Paolo Spriano, *Storia del Partito comunista italiano. Volume quinto. La Resistenza. Togliatti e il partito nuovo* (Turin: Einaudi, 1975); Elena Aga Rossi and Victor Zaslavsky, *Togliatti e Stalin. Il PCI e la politica estera staliniana negli archivi di Mosca* (Bologna: Il Mulino, 1997); Toscano, 'La ripresa delle relazioni diplomatiche fra l'Italia e l'Unione Sovietica nel corso della seconda guerra mondiale'; Roberto Morozzo Della Rocca, *La politica estera italiana e l'Unione Sovietica (1944-1948)* (Rome: Goliardica, 1985).
177 DDI, X, 5, docs 135, 211; DDI, X, 6, d. 9, Sforza to Prunas, Quaroni e Carandini, 3 June 1947; Matteo Pizzigallo, *La diplomazia italiana e i Paesi arabi dell'Oriente*

Mediterraneo (1946-1952) (Milan: Angeli, 2008); Pizzigallo (ed.), *Amicizie mediterranee e interesse nazionale 1946-1954* (Milan: Angeli, 2006); Pizzigallo (ed.), *L'Italia e il Mediterraneo orientale 1946-1950* (Milan: Angeli, 2004); Federica Onelli, *All'alba del neoatlantismo. La politica egiziana dell'Italia (1951-1956)* (Milan: Angeli, 2013).

178 John H. Spencer, *Ethiopia at Bay: A Personal Account of the Haile Sellassie Years* (Algonac: Reference, 1984); Yohannes Okbazghi, *Eritrea: A Pawn in World Politics* (Gainesville: University Press of Florida, 1991); Gianluigi Rossi, *L'Africa italiana verso l'indipendenza 1941-1949* (Milan: Giuffrè, 1980); Harold G. Marcus, *Ethiopia, Great Britain and the United States, 1941-1974: The Politics of Empire* (Berkeley: University of California Press, 1983); Giovanni Buccianti, *Libia: petrolio e indipendenza* (Milan: Giuffrè, 1999); Angelo Del Boca, *Gli italiani in Africa orientale. IV. Nostalgia delle colonie* (Milan: Mondadori, 1992); Del Boca, *Gli italiani in Libia* (Rome-Bari: Laterza, 1988); Carlo Sforza, *Cinque anni a Palazzo Chigi. La politica estera italiana dal 1947 al 1951* (Rome: Atlante, 1952).

179 On Pietro Quaroni: Pietro Quaroni, *Ricordi di un ambasciatore* (Milan: Garzanti, 1954); Quaroni, *Valigia diplomatica* (Milan: Garzanti, 1956); Quaroni, *Il mondo di un ambasciatore*; Monzali, *Un Re afghano in esilio a Roma. Amanullah e l'Afghanistan nella politica estera italiana 1919-1943*; Monzali, 'Pietro Quaroni e l'Afghanistan', *Nuova Storia Contemporanea* 1 (2014), 109-22; Monzali, 'Pietro Quaroni e la questione delle colonie africane dell'Italia: 1945-1949', *Nuova Rivista Storica* 2 (2015), 459-97; Bruna Bagnato, *L'Italia e la guerra di Algeria (1954-1962)* (Soveria Mannelli: Rubbettino, 2012); Stefano Baldi (ed.), *Un ricordo di Pietro Quaroni* (Rome: UNAP Press, 2014); Gaja, *L'Italia nel mondo bipolare*, 38.

180 DDI, X, 2, Quaroni to De Gasperi, 30 September 1945, d. 589.

181 See William R. Louis, *The British Empire in the Middle East, 1945-1951: Arab Nationlism, the United States and Postwar Imperialism* (Oxford: Oxford University Press, 1985).

182 On American attitude towards Italian colonial demands: Harold G. Marcus, *Ethiopia, Great Britain and the United States, 1941-1974*; Jeffrey A. Lefebvre, *Arms for the Horn: US. Security Policy in Ethiopia and Somalia, 1953-1991* (Pittsburgh, PA: University of Pittsburgh Press, 1991).

183 DDI, X, 7, d. 217, Quaroni to Sforza, 3 February 1948; Gastone Guidotti, *Un ricordo di Carlo Sforza*, 'Affari Esteri', 1972, n. 15, 78-84; Piero Craveri, *De Gasperi* (Bologna: Il Mulino, 2006), 500.

184 DDI, XI, 2, docs 972, 1002, 1003, 1022, 1023; Sforza, *Cinque anni a Palazzo Chigi*, 119-30.

185 Luciano Monzali, *Mario Toscano e la politica estera italiana nell'era atomica* (Florence: Le Lettere, 2011); Monzali, 'Pietro Quaroni e la questione delle colonie africane dell'Italia: 1945-1949', 459-97.

186 On De Gasperi's foreign policy: Francesco Malgeri, *De Gasperi. Volume II. Dal fascismo alla democrazia (1943-1947)* (Soveria Mannelli: Rubbettino, 2009); Pier Luigi Ballini, *De Gasperi. Volume III. Dalla costruzione della democrazia alla 'nostra patria europea' (1948-1954)* (Soveria Mannelli: Rubbettino, 2009); Mario Toscano, *Storia diplomatica della questione dell'Alto Adige* (Bari: Laterza, 1968); Toscano, *Pagine di storia diplomatica contemporanea*, II; Pietro Pastorelli, *La politica estera italiana del dopoguerra* (Bologna: Il Mulino, 1987); Pastorelli, *Il ritorno dell'Italia nell'Occidente. Racconto della politica estera italiana dal 15 settembre 1947 al 21 novembre 1949* (Milan: LED, 2009); Antonio Varsori, *L'Italia*

nelle relazioni internazionali dal 1943 al 1992 (Rome-Bari: Laterza, 1998); Varsori, *La Cenerentola d'Europa? L'Italia e l'integrazione europea dal 1947 ad oggi* (Soveria Mannelli: Rubbettino, 2010); Luca Riccardi, *Il 'problema Israele'. Diplomazia italiana e PCI di fronte allo Stato ebraico (1948-1973)* (Milan: Guerini, 2006); Ennio Di Nolfo, *La Guerra Fredda e l'Italia 1941-1989* (Florence: Polistampa, 2010); Guido Formigoni, *La Democrazia Cristiana e l'alleanza occidentale (1943-1953)* (Bologna: Il Mulino, 1996); Ennio Di Nolfo, Romain H Rainero and Brunello Vigezzi (eds), *L'Italia e la politica di potenza in Europa (1945-50)* (Milan: Marzorati, 1990); Bruna Bagnato, *Storia di un'illusione europea. Il progetto di unione doganale italo-francese* (London: Lothian Press, 1995); Luciano Monzali, *Gli italiani di Dalmazia e le relazioni italo-jugoslave nel Novecento* (Venice: Marsilio, 2015); Lorenzo Medici, *Dalla propaganda alla cooperazione. La diplomazia culturale italiana nel secondo dopoguerra (1944-1950)* (Padua: CEDAM, 2009).

187 For instance: Bruna Bagnato, *Vincoli europei echi mediterranei. L'Italia e la crisi francese in Marocco e in Tunisia* (Florence: Ponte delle Grazie, 1991); Bagnato, 'Alcune considerazioni sull'anticolonialismo italiano', in Ennio Di Nolfo, Romain H. Rainero and Brunello Vigezzi (eds), *L'Italia e la politica di potenza in Europa (1950-1960)* (Milano: Marzorati, 1992), 298-317.

188 On Italian foreign policy in the 1950s and 1960s: Luciano Monzali, 'Aldo Moro, Italian Ostpolitik and Relations with Yugoslavia', in Massimo Bucarelli, Luca Micheletta, Luciano Monzali and Luca Riccardi (eds), *Italy, Tito's Yugoslavia and International Politics in the Age of Détente* (Bruxelles: Peter Lang, 2016), 199-216; Monzali, *Mario Toscano e la politica estera italiana nell'era atomica*; Italo Garzia, Luciano Monzali and Massimo Bucarelli (eds), *Aldo Moro, l'Italia repubblicana e i Balcani* (Nardò: Besa, 2011); Guido Formigoni, *Storia d'Italia nella Guerra Fredda (1943-1978)* (Bologna: Il Mulino, 2016); Varsori, *L'Italia nelle relazioni internazionali dal 1943 al 1992*; Formigoni, *La politica estera italiana negli anni della Guerra Fredda. Momenti e attori* (Padova: Antenore, 2005); Riccardi, *Il 'problema Israele'. Diplomazia italiana e PCI di fronte allo Stato ebraico (1948-1973)*; Federico Imperato, *Aldo Moro e la pace nella sicurezza. La politica estera del centro-sinistra 1963-1968* (Bari: Progedit, 2011); Luigi Vittorio Ferraris (ed.), *Manuale della politica estera italiana 1947-1993* (Rome: Laterza, 1996); Bruna Bagnato, *Prove di Ostpolitik. Politica ed economia nella strategia italiana verso l'Unione Sovietica 1958-1963* (Florence: Olschki, 2003); Alessandro Brogi, *L'Italia e l'egemonia americana nel Mediterraneo* (Florence: La Nuova Italia, 1996); Leopoldo Nuti, *Gli Stati Uniti e l'apertura a sinistra. Importanza e limiti della presenza americana in Italia* (Rome: Laterza, 1999); Nuti, *La sfida nucleare. La politica estera italiana e le armi atomiche 1945-1991* (Bologna: Il Mulino, 2007); Egidio Ortona, *Anni d'America. La diplomazia 1953-1961* (Bologna: Il Mulino, 1986); Ortona, *Anni d'America. La cooperazione 1967-1975* (Bologna: Il Mulino, 1989); Giuseppe Spagnulo, *Il Risorgimento dell'Asia. India e Pakistan nella politica estera dell'Italia repubblicana (1946-1980)* (Firenze: Le Monnier, 2020).

189 For instance: Zoppi to Ministero degli Affari Esteri, 2 April and 30 October 1956, published in Gian Paolo Calchi Novati, *Il canale della discordia. Suez e la politica estera italiana* (Urbino: Quattro Venti, 1998), 77-80, 178-80; Rossi Longhi to Brosio, 10 and 28 October 1956, ibid., 162-4, 166-7. See also: Manlio Brosio, *Diari di Washington 1955-1961* (Bologna: Il Mulino, 2008).

190 Brosio, *Diari di Washington 1955-1961*, 173.

191　Angela Villani, *L'Italia e l'Onu negli anni della coesistenza competitiva (1955–1986)* (Padova: Cedam, 2007).
192　On Amintore Fanfani: Agostino Giovagnoli and Luciano Tosi (eds), *Amintore Fanfani e la politica estera italiana* (Venice: Marsilio, 2010); Luca Riccardi, 'Tra Stati Uniti ed Egitto: Fanfani e la crisi di Suez', *Nuova Storia Contemporanea*, no. 6 (2009), 81–98; Riccardi, 'Fanfani, la politica estera e la crisi mediorientale', *Nuova Storia Contemporanea*, no. 5 (2010), 69–100; Evelina Martelli, *L'altro atlantismo. Fanfani e la politica estera italiana (1958–1963)* (Milan: Guerini, 2008).
193　On Italy's policy toward the Middle East in the postwar years the books of Luca Riccardi are particularly important: Riccardi, *Il 'problema Israele'. Diplomazia italiana e PCI di fronte allo Stato ebraico (1948–1973)*; Riccardi, *La «grandezza» di una Media Potenza. Personaggi e problemi della politica estera italiana del Novecento* (Rome: Società Dante Alighieri, 2017); Riccardi, *L'internazionalismo difficile. La «diplomazia» del PCI e il Medio Oriente dalla crisi petrolifera alla caduta del muro di Berlino (1973–1989)* (Soveria Mannelli: Rubbettino, 2013). See also: Ferraris (ed.), *Manuale della politica estera italiana 1947–1993*; Luciano Monzali, 'Aldo Moro e la politica estera dell'Italia repubblicana nel Mediterraneo (1969–1978). Momenti e problemi', in Italo Garzia, Luciano Monzali and Federico Imperato (eds), *Aldo Moro, l'Italia repubblicana e i Popoli del Mediterraneo* (Nardò: Besa, 2013), 68–124; Rosario Milano, *L'ENI e l'Iran (1962–1970)* (Napoli: Giannini, 2013); Roberta La Fortezza, *Cedri e ulivi nel giardino del Mediterraneo. Storia delle relazioni diplomatiche italo-libanesi tra il 1943 e il 1958* (Soveria Mannelli: Rubbettino, 2020); Massimo De Leonardis (ed.), *Il Mediterraneo nella politica estera italiana del secondo dopoguerra* (Bologna: Il Mulino, 2003); Ilaria Tremolada, *All'ombra degli arabi. Le relazioni italo-israeliane 1948–1956: dalla fondazione dello Stato ebraico alla crisi di Suez* (Milano: M & B, 2003); Tremolada, *Nel mare che ci unisce: il petrolio nelle relazioni tra Italia e Libia* (Udine: Mimesis, 2015); Mario Toscano, *La 'Porta di Sion'. L'Italia e l'immigrazione clandestina ebraica in Palestina 1945–1948* (Bologna: Il Mulino, 1990); Spagnulo, *Il Risorgimento dell'Asia. India e Pakistan nella politica estera dell'Italia repubblicana (1946–1980)*.
194　On Italian–Turkish relations: ACS, AA, series V, underseries 1, portfolio 127, Ministero degli Affari Esteri, *Documentazione per l'incontro tra l'on. le Ministro e il Ministro degli Affari Esteri di Turchia Ihsan Sabri Caglayangil (14 settembre 1969)* (September 1969).
195　Riccardi, *Il 'problema Israele'. Diplomazia italiana e PCI di fronte allo Stato ebraico (1948–1973)*, 203–20.

4

Italy's foreign policy and the Palestinian question

Luca Riccardi

The origins of Italy's policy in the Middle East

Italy's return to democracy, after its defeat in the Second World War, forced the country to completely revise its foreign policy. All the principles that had informed its policy in the first half of the twentieth century – expansionism, colonialism, the ambition to join the ranks of the Great Powers – had to be abandoned. The 'intense and tormented post-war period'[1] was therefore a time of economic and social reconstruction, but also of a search for a new international position[2] in line with the principles of the new democratic republic. While Italy's traditional interests remained the same, they had to be pursued in the context of its new status as a 'medium power' on the international scene. This meant focusing on the Mediterranean and particularly the troubled eastern region, from the perspective of a country that needed to rebuild itself after the war, and taking into account the Cold War and Italy's place as an ally of the United States. The Italian government continued to be firmly focused on maintaining the balance in the Mediterranean Basin, where a large part of its economic interests still lay, and where many Italian communities still lived, in the main cities of the Mediterranean area and throughout the Arab world.[3] From this perspective, the contrast between Israel and Arab countries represented from the start a 'serious threat to peace',[4] a peace that became Italy's main objective in the region.

Italy had to deal, on the one hand, with the rise on the international scene of Arab countries, following decolonization, and, on the other hand, with the birth and development of the State of Israel, whose defense soon became one of the guiding principles of US policy in the Middle East. In the 1950s, the series of Italian governments led by the Christian Democrats developed a new policy, called neo-Atlantism, which intended to combine Italian interests, especially in the Mediterranean, with the increasing international problems caused by the evolution of the Cold War.[5] The protagonists of this period were certainly Amintore Fanfani and Aldo Moro, who both served more than once as prime ministers and foreign ministers. In the Middle East, their policy was always sympathetic to Arab countries while continuing to support the right to exist of the State of Israel.[6] This approach, which remained the guiding principle of Italian Middle Eastern policy for at least forty years, was termed *equidistanza* or 'equidistance'.

At the time of the Six-Day War crisis, in June 1967, Moro was head of the government and Fanfani the foreign minister. Although public opinion was largely in favour of Israel, they elaborated a new policy centered on the principle that the question of Palestinian refugees had to treated as a 'political' problem, as opposed to a purely humanitarian one.[7] More specifically, from that moment on, Italian diplomacy adopted as its starting point Resolution 242 of the UN Security Council, that is, the request that Israel withdraw from Occupied Territories, but also that Arab countries recognize the State of Israel. In general, the Palestinian question became a permanent part of the Italian foreign-relations agenda.[8]

This line of action met with the approval of the Vatican state which was worried by the developments in Palestine, especially with regard to the situation of Christian sites in the Holy Land. Its approval, for Roman Catholic politicians like Moro and Fanfani, was politically very important. After the Six-Day War, the position of the Vatican slowly evolved until, towards the mid-1970s, it too became a supporter of a 'political' solution to the Palestinian question.[9] This made relations between the Vatican and the State of Israel increasingly difficult.

The Middle East and Europe: The Yom Kippur War

The fourth Arab–Israeli conflict broke out while Italy was experiencing a severe economic crisis aggravated by the 'first serious symptoms of an involution of the political-institutional system'.[10] The international oil crisis[11] following the measures taken by oil-producing Arab countries against Israel and in support of Egypt and Syria, further aggravated the Italian internal situation. The fragile government led by the Christian Democrat Mariano Rumor relied on a quarrelsome alliance between the center and the Socialist Party, which tottered under the impact of the economic crisis. Aldo Moro, who was the foreign minister, immediately understood that the response to the oil crisis could not be only national.[12] All European countries, to some extent, had been hit hard by the 'sanctions' launched by oil-producing countries. This led the nine members of the European Economic Community to intensify their cooperation and try to overcome their differences over the Middle East. In the eyes of Italian diplomacy, the situation in the European community seemed rather fragmentary:

> France had a very philo-Arab position, like the UK; Italy, the German Federal Republic, Belgium, Luxembourg, Ireland had a more balanced one; Holland and Denmark were very pro-Israel.[13]

The effectiveness of the Arab strategy, however, led to a revision of European policy which up to then had been paralysed by cross-vetoes. On 6 November 1973, after a few fruitless meetings, the Political Committee, in which all member states were represented, issued a statement in which it reaffirmed the need for implementing Resolution 242. This in itself would have been enough to irritate Israel, but the Committee also officially took a position in favour of the 'legitimate rights of the Palestinians', which had to be taken in account 'to establish a just and lasting peace'.[14]

After a French initiative, this was followed in the coming months by the establishing of a Euro-Arab forum, serving as a permanent form of cooperation between the EC and the Arab world. This initiative was meant to contribute to the modernization of Arab economies and societies. The practical results were few, but the initiative represented an interesting effort to transform the oil crisis into an opportunity for the cooperation of two 'worlds' that seemed distant but were in many ways complementary.[15] Europe's initiative was obviously also meant to obtain a softening of the restrictions by Arab countries that had expressed the intention of modulating oil sales based on the attitude of their European partners towards the State of Israel.

Israel seemed to have been progressively marginalized by European diplomacy.[16] Moro was particularly pleased with European decisions because they coincided with the line followed up to then by the Italian government. On the other hand, he feared their consequences for Italy's already deteriorating relations with the United States, which strenuously supported Israel. For this reason, inside the EC, notwithstanding his personal beliefs, Moro had ensured that Italy adopt an 'intermediate position'.[17] For Moro, in line with the traditional policy of the Italian Republic, good relations with the United States had to remain a central tenet of Italy's foreign policy as well as that of the entire EC.

In the following months, as the rise of oil prices was severely damaging the Italian economy, Moro continued to support the rights of Palestinians. He declared that the Palestinians were 'not looking for assistance, but for a motherland'.[18] This position was not dictated by 'sentimentalism, nor by any particular hostility towards Israel'.[19] Rather it was the result of his political realism, which made him see the solution of the Palestinian question as an element of stability and a premise for an end to the Middle Eastern conflict. A similar line was adopted in the course of 1974 by the international community and in particular by the UN. In November 1974, Yasser Arafat, leader of the Palestinian Liberation Organization (PLO) was invited to speak at the General Assembly in New York. His success irritated both Israel and the United States.[20]

In general, Moro's policy was always that of reinforcing relations with Arab countries without damaging the fundamental relations with Washington. To carry out this difficult objective, Moro took a few important initiatives. Starting from the Yom Kippur War, he negotiated, with the crucial help of the secret services, an agreement with the PLO, named 'Iodo Moro' or 'Moro agreement', in which the Italian government allowed the PLO to use Italy as a basis for its logistics and the passage, transit of Palestinian military groups. The PLO pledged in turn not to launch attacks from Italy besides, of course, avoiding any attacks on Italian soil.[21] The most important political consequence of the agreement was the establishing 'in disguise' of an informal diplomatic delegation of the PLO in Rome. With many limits, this delegation became the interlocutor of the Foreign Ministry and in general of Italian political leaders.[22]

The Italian government participated in the conference of oil-consumer countries organized by the US government in February 1974 in Washington. The idea was to create a Western counter-cartel to oppose the initiatives of OPEC. The Italian government decided to participate also to reassure the United States, which was preoccupied by Italy's pro-Arab policy, and to satisfy components in the government majority that were hostile to its policy. Significantly, the leadership of the delegation was assigned to the vice-president of the government and leader of the Republican Party, Ugo La Malfa, a 'firm advocate of a policy of loyalty towards the US'.[23]

While Moro's strategy in regards to the Arab–Israeli conflict was not meant to lead Italy to take an anti-US course it did seek to preserve Italy from the dangers of a highly complex international situation. During the Washington conference, as Italian minister of foreign affairs, he carried out a tour of various Arab capitals aimed at reinforcing the economic and political ties with the Middle East.[24] He stated,

> The relations between Italy and the Arab world, like those between Europe and the Arab world, are in line with a tradition, they follow a profound reasons, they are essential for the future of our continent.[25]

In Moro's view, there was no contradiction between this policy and Italy's traditional post-war support of the United States or the pro-Western stance of the EC.

The Declaration of Venice and the Middle East in the early 1980s

After Moro's tragic assassination in 1978 by the Red Brigades, his legacy was taken up by another Christian Democrat politician, Emilio Colombo, who had already served as prime minister in 1970–2, and was foreign minister from 1980 to 1983. When Colombo acquired the latter position, there had just been some important developments in the Middle East. In 1979, the Israel-Egypt peace process had culminated with the signing of the Treaty of Washington on 26 March. In those same weeks, an Islamic revolution guided by the ayatollah Khomeini had taken place in Iran, sparking Islamic radicalism in the region. As a result, oil prices which had remained stable for some time, had suddenly risen.[26] On both occasions, the position taken by the Italian government did not completely coincide with that of Washington. For US diplomacy, the peace between Egypt and Israel was the 'cornerstone' of a 'global solution'; for Giulio Andreotti, who during the first half of 1979 was still prime minister, it was 'the first step towards the achievement of a fair and lasting peace'.[27] The difference ultimately revolved around the Palestinian question and the status of Jerusalem. As for Iran, the Rome government, while deploring the excesses of the revolution, adopted a prudent stance, waiting to see the way the situation in the new country evolved.[28]

Notwithstanding the efforts made in the second half of the 1970s, Italy's Middle Eastern policy had failed to achieve any concrete results other than that of maintaining cordial relations, in different ways, with the various components of the Arab world. The boundary to Italy's collaboration had always remained, however, the right to exist of the State of Israel. Notwithstanding Italy's reservations towards Israeli policy, Italy had always condemned its delegitimizing by its adversaries. This had been true even within the UN, where, on 10 November 1975, the majority of the General Assembly voted in favour of a resolution that equated Zionism with a form of racism and racial discrimination.[29]

The developments in the Middle Eastern scenario provided new opportunities for Italy and Europe. The leading figure in this case was doubtless the French President Giscard d'Estaing who in early 1980 toured the Arab countries, reaffirming his support for Palestinian self-determination, but reinforcing it with another important request: the participation of the PLO in all peace negotiations. D'Estaing's initiative stimulated the EEC Italian presidency to a new 'activism'.[30] Led by Colombo, who was supported by the new prime minister, the Christian Democrat Francesco Cossiga, an important result was achieved. At a European summit held in Venice, on 13 June 1980, a declaration was approved that not only acknowledged the right of the Palestinian people 'to fully exercise their right to self-determination', but also their right to participate in future negotiations through the PLO.[31] The declaration also admonished the State of Israel not to undertake any 'unilateral initiative' in relation to Jewish settlements in the Occupied Territories or the status of Jerusalem.

The United States viewed this evolution in European policy with a certain diffidence. Its goal was still the achievement of the Camp David objectives, which had been subscribed to by Egypt and Israel. The United States insisted that Europeans avoid 'any action that could make these negotiations more difficult'.[32] But the effort of Secretary of State Muskie to convince the Europeans to desist failed. President Carter was left with no choice but to accept the declaration, at least on the surface. A few days later, he told King Hussein of Jordan that the European declaration was not 'incompatible with the Camp David process'.[33] In reality, the United States had many reservations about the European policy and particularly about the actions undertaken by Colombo.[34]

The Italian government had a different view. Colombo had grasped the importance for Europe and for Italy of a solution to the Palestinian question in the larger context of the Arab–Israeli conflict. The declaration of Venice was a 'qualitative change'[35] in the European and Italian capacity to intervene in the negotiations on the Middle East. In fact, for Italian Prime Minister Cossiga, it was one of the 'two true initiatives'[36] with an international scope that were undertaken in the period he was head of the government.[37]

The declaration gave a new authority on the Middle Eastern question to the EC and to Italy, to the point that Egypt – in the wake of the increasingly difficult negotiations with Israel on the application of the part of the Camp David agreements that concerned the Palestinians – began to look to Europe as the political entity that could unfreeze the negotiations. However, this never happened, also due to the Israeli government's lack of trust in Europe and its reluctance to allow it to get involved in the peace process. Thus the possibility of a mediation by the EC or by specific European countries never became a reality. Nevertheless Italy, including all its various political components, continued to consider the Middle East as one of the main concerns of its international policy.

Soldiers and diplomacy

The evolution of the political situation in the Middle East in 1981 offered Italy the opportunity to play a role in important political events. This combined with changes in Italy's internal political situation. The discovery of the involvement of numerous prominent members of the Italian upper classes in the secret masonic lodge Propaganda Due (P2) and the ensuing political crisis, led to the nomination for the first time of a non-Christian Democrat as head of government: the leader of the small Republican Party, Giovanni Spadolini. His action was marked by a 'moralizing intervention'[38] at various levels, helped by an improved economic situation. On the international scene, Spadolini sought to adopt a more assertive role, proposing Italy as a mediator in a number of complicated situations that had developed in the Middle East.[39] This mediation was achieved through Italy's armed forces, which were used as a peace-keeping corps in multilateral scenarios.

The general situation favoured this new Italian protagonist attitude. The role of the UN, in those years, was hindered by the resurgence of the Cold War, caused by the USSR's invasion of Afghanistan and, later, by the failure of the negotiations on Euromissiles.[40] The friction between the United States and the USSR paralysed the Security Council, preventing it from diplomatically and militarily intervening when necessary. Its role was therefore taken up by a group of Western countries, which intervened to fill a void in the Mediterranean that threatened to undo the little progress made in the peace process. The first objective was the application of the peace treaty between Israel and Egypt with restitution by Israel, of the Sinai peninsula. The operation was to be supervised by soldiers of the United States and European countries that had volunteered: France, the UK, the Netherlands and Italy.

The importance of this event lay mostly in its European dimension. The four countries adhered to the US project through a declaration that presented the mission in continuity with the traditional policy of the EC in the Middle East, centered on the Declaration of Venice. Furthermore, the initiative had the 'political backing' of the Ten who had published a declaration in support of the initiative. The Italian government, in line with the ideas of Spadolini and Colombo, pursued the initiative in close collaboration with two fronts (the 'dual anchorage'): Europe and the United States. The collaboration with Washington was thus integrated into the initiative with the unanimous support of all the members of the EEC.[41]

After this first mission, which ended on 25 April 1982, Italy decided to commit in first person to the solution of the Lebanon crisis. On 6 June 1982, Israeli troops had entered Lebanon launching the operation 'Peace in Galilee', with the goal of definitely wiping out the Palestinian presence in the south of Lebanon.[42] Italy's condemnation of the invasion, immediately voiced in the name of the government by Foreign Minister Colombo, was followed by Italy's offer to send a military force, in a multilateral context, to help calm down the political situation.[43] The specific task of the Italian force, which numbered about five hundred units, in coordination with the French and the United States, was to escort outside of Beirut a few thousand Palestinian fighters and transfer them to Syria, and also to supervise the evacuation of a large number of Syrian soldiers, allowing them to cross the 'green line' that separated the sectors in Beirut, preventing any contact with Israeli forces. As soon as the mission was over and the international force had withdrawn, Palestinian camps in Beirut were assaulted by Phalangist militia with the tacit approval of the Israelis, and a large number of civilians were massacred.[44] The Italian force was obliged to return to protect the remaining Palestinian civilians,

Although this second leg of the mission lasted longer, ending only in February 1984, it failed to achieve the restoration of the sovereignty of the Lebanese state, which Italy, along with the United States and France, had as its main goals.

Italy's military presence was associated with a certain diplomatic activity. The Lebanese president, Gemayel, had visited Rome in 1982, and in November of the same year, Colombo traveled to Beirut, still in a state of civil war, to offer US$100 million for the reconstruction of the country.[45] But most of Italy's efforts continued to focus on the search for a solution to the Palestinian question. The undisputed protagonist of this effort was the Christian Democrat leader Giulio Andreotti. At the beginning of this period, Andreotti was somewhat at the margins of the political scene. After having been prime minister five times and minister several more times, he was now simply president of the Foreign Affairs Commission of the Chamber of Deputies. On the other hand, for many years he had never made a mystery of his interest in the Middle East question.[46] He now put to use his extensive network of national and international political contacts, also thanks to the mediation of the Italian Communist Party. In fact, it was thanks to some members of the PCI that, in September 1982, Andreotti managed to secure the participation of Arafat in the World Interparliamentary Union. Arafat's visit was a remarkable media success. On the other hand, it evidenced the divisions among Italy's political currents on the role of the PLO. Prime Minister Spadolini, who openly supported Israel, refused to meet him.[47] The president of the Republic, the socialist Pertini, after some hesitation, due to his volatile character and the pressures received by his entourage, who insisted on prudence, decided instead to receive Arafat in the form reserved for heads of state.[48] Colombo also met with Arafat, in line with his policy of making Italy a mediator among the various components of the Western countries. In line with the Declaration of Venice, Colombo believed that no peace project would ever succeed without the direct involvement of Palestinian organizations. His meeting with Arafat was the culmination of an intense series of contacts Colombo had had with the PLO in his three years as foreign minister.[49]

The Craxi-Andreotti period

The political elections of 1983, with the rise of the Socialist Party, seemed to undermine the traditional political balance centered on the hegemony of the Christian Democrats.[50] Bettino Craxi, leader of the Italian Socialist Party, became prime minister. Craxi's objective was to make the Socialist Party a fundamental actor in the Italian political scene, undermining the PCI–DC opposition that had dominated Italian politics since 1948, forcing the PSI to remain in a subservient position, first towards the PCI and then towards the DC.[51] Craxi wanted his party to represent the new emergent productive social sectors in Italy, which were contributing to its modernization and helping overcome the economic crisis of the 1970s.

Craxi's antagonist appeared to be Andreotti who had been nominated foreign minister. Andreotti was the oldest leader of the DC, on the surface the representative of the old guard, which was now declining in favour of a new, more dynamic, generation of politicians. Moreover, in the previous years the two leaders had repeatedly and openly clashed over various questions.[52] Notwithstanding this unlikely basis, in the almost four years in which they held their posts in the government, Craxi and Andreotti managed to develop a shared vision and policy on a number of international questions, such as Italy's relations with the United States and the USSR, European integration and the peace process in the Middle East.[53]

Both believed that the European Community could play a crucial role in the Middle East. After the multinational expedition in Lebanon had ended in 1984, Craxi and Andreotti decided to exploit the Italian presidency of the EC in the first semester of 1984 to carry out 'a strong initiative' on the Israeli–Palestinian conflict.[54] For this purpose, they launched a series of preliminary contacts with Arab leaders to pave the way for a resumption of peace talks.[55] The main element of the Italian strategy, in this phase, was convincing the PLO to adopt a different political strategy. Specifically, without undermining Palestinian internal unity, Craxi and Andreotti, in the name of Europe, wanted to convince Yasser Arafat to free himself from the conditioning of the most extreme wings of his movement and to definitely give up the use of armed force, in order to become an acceptable interlocutor in the eyes of Israel. The United States, given its preferential relations with Israel, should have appreciated a more moderate stance by the PLO, and the USSR, too, had shown a certain interest in Italy's strategy, and could have supported from the outside, contributing its ties with some of the governments more hostile to Israel, starting with Syria.[56]

The tour of Arab capitals undertaken by Craxi and Andreotti in the last months of 1984 ended in Tunis, on 6 December 1984, where they met with Arafat himself. The Italians asked Arafat to elaborate a 'set of proposals'[57] to be presented as a Jordanian-Palestinian joint action, for the purpose of establishing direct negotiations with Israel. The final goal had to be the creation of 'a confederate union of two states', Jordan and the Palestinian state, which would be finally recognized by Israel.[58]

This strategy, however, met many obstacles. Some of these were internal. Minister of Defense Spadolini did not approve it, seeing it as a threat to Italy's friendly relations with Israel. During a trip to Israel, at the end of 1984, he tried to assuage Prime Minister Peres, who had manifested his hostility to Italy's initiative, to the point of canceling a visit to Rome planned for January 1985. Spadolini's trip was also meant to assuage the concerns of the more pro-Israel current in the Italian parliamentary majority.[59] In general, Italy continued with its traditional policy of 'equi-distance'.

But the most serious blow against Italy's strategy came from the one who should have been its greatest supporter: the European Community. At the European Council held in Dublin on 3–4 December 1984, Craxi and Andreotti asked for a 'specific initiative' in the form of a 'new Declaration' that would develop 'on that of Venice' and of a 'contact mission' of the presidency with the various Arab countries.[60] This proposal, however, failed due to the inability of member states to overcome their differences. In the end, only generic conclusions were reached which, while declaring the EC's support for any initiative by member states in favour of peace talks, did not call for any direct involvement by the EC itself.[61]

Other problems came from the dynamics of the Middle East. The agreement stipulated between Arafat and King Hussein on 11 February 1985,[62] which had to provide the basis for the negotiations with Israel, was a rather generic one. This offered a pretext to Israel to reject the proposal, which would have paved the way, even if not in clear-cut terms, to a future independent Palestinian state.

The Italian government too had reservations about the agreement. Craxi stated that it was 'unsatisfactory' although being 'no doubt a step forward'.[63] Following the policy of 'equi-distance' in the same period, the Italian government had sought to get closer to Israel, which had always had problematic relations with Italy. A major turning point was the arrival in Rome, on 18 February 1985, of Shimon Peres, the first Israeli prime minister to ever visit Italy. This visit was considered the culmination of this phase of Italy's strategy for the Middle East[64] and provided an occasion for a partial rapprochement between the two governments, albeit between 'lights and shadows'.[65]

Craxi, however, used the results of this meeting to convince Arafat to engage in direct negotiations with Israel. He gave him what was certainly a touched-up version of the talks, saying Peres had appeared willing to cooperate and had displayed a 'responsible and sincere' attitude.[66] Arafat was therefore invited to accept the conditions demanded, especially in terms of the composition of the delegation that had to begin negotiations.[67] The crux of the matter, for Craxi, was armed struggle. If the PLO renounced 'terrorist tactics', Israel's opposition to negotiation, even if it did persist, would seem much less defensible, from a political perspective.

In any case, however, Peres continued to be against direct negotiations with the PLO. In this uncertain situation, negotiations dragged on until the resurgence of the military clash between Palestinians and Israeli and the divisions among Arab leaders put an end to them. It was only with the outbreak of the *Intifada*, in December 1987, that negotiations were to resume again. Italy and Europe had failed.

The hijacking of the *Achille Lauro*

During this interlude, the Italian governments had to deal with several problems tied to the unresolved Palestinian question. On 7 October 1985, a Palestinian commando took control of the *Achille Lauro*, an Italian cruise ship carrying several hundreds of passengers, some of them US citizens. This led to a confused situation, with interventions by Egyptian, Italian and Palestinian authorities, in an effort to find a solution that would not harm the hostages. In reality, this did not happen because the terrorists killed a US citizen of Jewish origin. The killing, however, was kept secret while Arafat, through the mediation of Abu Abbas, the head of the organization to which the terrorists belonged, negotiated with Egyptian president Mubarak the surrender of the terrorists in return for their immunity. After they had disembarked, news of the murder emerged, and the plane that was transferring the terrorists to Tunis was intercepted by US aviation and forced to land at the Nato base of Sigonella, in Sicily. This led to a military confrontation between Italy, claiming the right of sovereignty, and whose military had taken control of the plane, and the United States demanding that the terrorists be handed over, including the mediator Abbas, whom they believed to be in reality the man behind the whole operation. In the end, the terrorists were arrested, to be tried by an Italian tribunal, while Abbas was allowed to leave on a plane.[68]

The events produced a crisis in Italian politics on three fronts. There was a major rift between the United States and the Italian government. However, the alliance was crucial to both countries, and a reconciliation was soon achieved.[69] Italy's relations with Israel also became strained. Israeli public opinion, backed by its government, began to accuse the Italian government of being 'tolerant towards terrorism', and Craxi responded in kind.[70] Finally, there were problems also within the Italian majority that supported the government. The leader of the small Republican party, Spadolini, threatened to withdraw his support, and a crisis was avoided only thanks to the determination of Craxi, who took the occasion to reaffirm in Parliament his support for a Palestinian state:

> I oppose the use of armed struggle by the PLO, not because I do not think it has a right to it, but because I am convinced that an armed struggle will not lead to any solution ... however, I do not question the legitimacy of the use of armed struggle; this is a different matter.

There was only one solution: 'land in return for peace'.[71] It is interesting to note that, on this point, Craxi's position had the full support not only of Andreotti and most Christian Democrats, but also of the communist party in the opposition, who were generally very hostile to Craxi's government.[72]

The Intifada and its consequences

On 7 December 1987, a Palestinian revolt broke out in Gaza that soon spread to all the Occupied Territories. The revolt undermined the precarious balance in the Middle East, leading the various actors to adopt new strategies. The EC voiced its concern over the growing violence and openly sided with the Palestinian protesters.[73] Throughout the following year, Italian diplomacy, still led by Andreotti, put pressure on Arafat asking that he accept resolution 242 and reject terrorism in order to pave the way to future negotiations.[74] Craxi, now only the head of the Socialist Party, but still an authoritative international leader, worked to bring Hussein and Arafat closer, in view of a future confederation between Jordan and the Palestinian Territories which had to serve as an interlocutor for Israel.[75] During this phase, the EC, and especially the socialist group in the European Parliament, served as a 'stage' for Arafat to ask the international community and the United States in particular to adopt a different stance.[76]

On 15 November 1988, in Algiers, the National Palestinian Council accepted the UN resolutions as the basis for an international peace conference and the formal proclamation of the State of Palestine,[77] a decision that was met with great favour in Italy and Europe. The Israeli government tried to convince the Italian government to moderate its enthusiasm, but met with little success. This was to be expected, considering how the decisions taken by the Palestinians seemed completely in line with the European policy centered on the Venice resolution.[78] In this case too, the line of the Italian government coincided almost completely with that of the communist opposition. The new secretary of the PCI, Achille Occhetto, was the first Western leader to meet with Arafat after the Palestinian meeting in Algiers. Offering Arafat the support of the PCI, Occhetto pointed out that this support was shared by all major Italian political elements: 'With Andreotti and Craxi, we are all saying pretty much the same things.'[79] This was proven by the talks that Arafat later had in Rome, on 23 December 1988, with the new prime minister Ciriaco De Mita, in the presence of Andreotti, who was again foreign minister. The cordial tenor of the meeting seemed to anticipate a qualitatively different type of relation, one between 'State and State'.[80]

Italian diplomacy however did not neglect the Israeli front. In April 1989, De Mita and Andreotti paid an official visit to Israel. Prime Minister Shamir had come up with an alternative strategy: elections were to be held in the Occupied Territories in order to produce a local Palestinian leadership alternative to the PLO, with which the Israelis were to negotiate 'a transitory agreement on self-government'.[81] The Italian government, starting with De Mita himself, tried to get the Palestinians to consider the agreement but met with firm opposition by the PLO.[82]

The immediate consequence of the new Palestinian policy was a formal change in the official relations between Italy and the PLO. In May 1989, the government, following parliamentary motions almost unanimously approved, decided to change the status of the Palestinian diplomatic representation in Rome, which up to then had been based in other Arab embassies. On 29 May 1989, the PLO office in Rome became a diplomatic body officially recognized by the Italian government as the representative of the Palestinians.

Italy in short was playing its role in that 'magic moment' in which a solution to the Palestinian question seemed possible. In the years to come, however, the Palestinian question was conditioned by the end of the Cold War, the resumption of the military confrontation between Israel and the armed Palestinian fringes, the rise of the Islamic-Nationalist faction of Hamas and then the Gulf War, followed by the Madrid and Oslo agreements. Events in which Italy, along with Europe in general, while continuing to follow them with interest, was no longer able to play any role.

Notes

1 Guido Crainz, *Storia della Repubblica: L'Italia dalla Liberazione ad oggi* (Rome: Donzelli, 2016), 3–65.
2 Antonio Varsori, *L'Italia nelle relazioni internazionali dal 1943 al 1992* (Rome: Laterza, 1998), 43–81; Pietro Pastorelli, *Il ritorno dell'Italia nell'Occidente* (Milan: LED, 2009); Luigi Vittorio Ferraris, *Manuale della politica estera italiana 1947–1993* (Rome: Laterza, 1996), 3–89.
3 An example in Marta Petricioli, *Oltre il mito: L'Egitto degli italiani (1917–1947)* (Milan: Bruno Mondadori, 2007).
4 Sforza to Prunas e Prina Ricotti, 26 aprile 1948, DDI, s. X, vol., VII, doc. 617.
5 The bibliography on neo-Atlantism is vast. See Evelina Martelli, *L'altro atlantismo: Fanfani e la politica estera italiana (1958–1963)* (Milan: Guerini, 2008); Guido Formigoni, *Storia d'Italia nella Guerra fredda (1943–1978)* (Bologna: Il Mulino, 2016), 250–8; Massimo De Leonardis, 'L'Italia: «alleato privilegiato» degli Stati Uniti

nel Mediterraneo?', in Massimo De Leonardis (ed.), *Il Mediterraneo nella politica estera italiana del secondo dopoguerra* (Bologna: Il Mulino, 2003), 61-93.

6 See Agostino Giovagnoli and Luciano Tosi (eds), *Amintore Fanfani e la politica estera italiana* (Venice: Marsilio, 2010); Francesco Perfetti, Andrea Ungari, Daniele Caviglia and Daniele De Luca (eds), *Aldo Moro nell'Italia contemporanea* (Firenze: Le Lettere, 2011), 300-809; on Italian Middle Eastern politics see, among other things, Giampaolo Calchi Novati, *Mediterraneo e questione araba nella politica estera italiana* in *Storia dell'Italia repubblicana,* vol. II, *La trasformazione dell'Italia: sviluppo e squilibri,* tomo 1, *Politica, economia, società* (Turin: Einaudi, 1995), 195-263; Luca Riccardi, *La «grandezza» di una Media Potenza. Personaggi e problemi della politica estera italiana del Novecento* (Rome: Società Editrice Dante Alighieri, 2017), 199-305.

7 See the intervention by Aldo Moro at the UN Assembly General in Luciano Tosi (ed.), *Sulla scena del mondo: L'Italia all'Assemblea generale delle Nazioni Unite 1955-2009* (Naples: Editoriale Scientifica, 2010), d. 23.

8 See Daniele Caviglia and Massimiliano Cricco, *La diplomazia italiana e gli equilibri mediterranei. La politica mediorientale dalla guerra dei Sei giorni al conflitto dello Yom Kippur (1967-1973)* (Soveria Mannelli: Rubbettino, 2006); Luca Riccardi, *Il «problema Israele». Diplomazia italiana e PCI di fronte allo Stato ebraico (1948-1973)* (Milan: Guerini, 2006), 203-467.

9 Silvio Ferrari, *Vaticano e Israele dal secondo conflitto mondiale alla guerra del Golfo* (Florence: Sansoni, 1991), 183-4.

10 Piero Craveri, *La repubblica dal 1958 al 1992* (Milan: Tea, 1995), 489-601.

11 On the Yom Kippur War one of the most recent studies is by Asaf Siniver (ed.), *The Yom Kippur War: Politics, Legacy, Diplomacy* (Oxford: Oxford University Press, 2013). For the US position see also Henry Kissinger, *Crisis: The Anatomy of Two Major Foreign Policy Crises* (Toronto: Simon & Schuster, 2003), 7-417.

12 Riccardi, *Il «problema Israele»,* 449.

13 Ducci to Gaja and to many embassies, 8 November 1973, p. 1 in AM, ACS, b. 57.

14 'Dichiarazione sul Medio Oriente dei nove governi della CEE (Bruxelles, 6 novembre 1973)', in Ministero degli Affari Esteri, *Italia e Medio Oriente (1967-1973)* (Rome: Servizio Storico e Documentazione s.d.), 177-8.

15 On this initiative see Silvio Labbate, *Illusioni mediterranee: il dialogo euro-arabo* (Florence: Le Monnier, 2016).

16 Luca Riccardi, 'Sempre più con gli arabi. La politica italiana verso il Medio Oriente dopo la guerra del Kippur', *Nuova Storia Contemporanea* 6 (2006), 57-82.

17 Antonio Varsori, *La Cenerentola d'Europa? L'Italia e l'integrazione europea dal 1947 a oggi* (Soveria Mannelli: Rubbettino, 2010), 289.

18 Comunicato ANSA, *Discorso del ministro degli esteri alla Commissione esteri del Senato,* 21 January 1974, AM, b.76, f. 1.

19 Roberto Ducci, *I Capintesta* (Milan: Rusconi, 1982), 53.

20 Andrew Gowers and Tony Walker, *Yasser Arafat e la rivoluzione palestinese* (Rome: Gamberetti, 1994), 153-62; Xavier Baron, *I Palestinesi. Genesi di una nazione* (Milan: Baldini & Castoldi, 2002), 263-6.

21 Salvatore Sechi, 'Su Moro, Arafat, Gheddafi e la strage di Bologna', *Nuova Storia Contemporanea* 6 (2000), 132-5; Miguel Gotor, *Il memoriale della Repubblica. Gli scritti di Aldo Moro dalla prigionia e l'anatomia del potere italiano* (Turin: Einaudi, 2011), 337-43.

22 Luca Riccardi, *L'Internazionalismo difficile. La «diplomazia» del PCI e il Medio Oriente dalla crisi petrolifera alla caduta del muro di Berlino (1973-1989)* (Soveria

Mannelli: Rubbettino, 2013), 94; Alberto La Volpe, *Diario segreto di Nemer Hammad ambasciatore di Arafat in Italia* (Rome: Editori Riuniti, 2002).
23 Ferraris, *Manuale della politica estera italiana*, 273; on La Malfa: Lorenzo Mechi, *L'Europa di Ugo La Malfa. La via italiana alla modernizzazione (1942-1979)* (Milan: Franco Angeli, 2003).
24 Luca Riccardi, 'Da Colombo ad Andreotti e Craxi: spunti di ricerca sulla politica mediorientale dell'Italia negli anni Ottanta', in Gianvito Galasso, Federico Imperato, Rosario Milano and Luciano Monzali (eds), *Europa e Medio Oriente (1973-1993)* (Bari: Cacucci, 2017), 18.
25 *Discorso del ministro degli Esteri alla Commissione Esteri del Senato*, 21 January 1974, 3.
26 Marcella Emiliani, *Medio Oriente. Una storia dal 1918 al 1991* (Rome: Laterza, 2012), 217-22, 329-40; Farian Sabahi, *Storia dell'Iran* (Milan: Bruno Mondadori, 2006), 158.
27 Andreotti-Christopher meeting, Rome, 19 March 1979, ACS, PCM, CD, b. 32, f. *Medio Oriente*, 2 and 5.
28 *Consiglio di Sicurezza delle Nazioni Unite. Richiesta di sanzioni contro l'Iran*, appunto, 29 December 1979, ACS, PCM, Cons.Dipl, b. 15 f. *Iran*.
29 Alessandro Polsi, *Storia dell'ONU* (Rome: Laterza, 2006), 119-20.
30 Ferraris, *Manuale della politica estera italiana*, 379.
31 AP, S.-CD, VIII legislatura Disegni di legge e relazioni, Documenti, *Dichiarazione del Consiglio europeo sul Medio Oriente*, 13 June 1980, 223.
32 Department of State to Multiple Posts, 19 May 1980, FRUS, 1977-80, vol. IX, *Arab-Israeli Dispute*, August 1978-December 1980, doc. 368.
33 Memorandum of Conversation, 18 June 1980, ibid., n. 379.
34 Emilio Colombo, *Per l'Italia per l'Europa. Conversazione con Arrigo Levi* (Bologna: Il Mulino, 2013), 167.
35 'Intervista al presidente Emilio Colombo', in Cricco Caviglia, *La diplomazia italiana e gli equilibri mediterranei*, 144.
36 Francesco Cossiga and Piero Testoni, *La passione e la politica* (Milan: Rizzoli, 2000), 260.
37 Francesco Cossiga was prime minister until 18 October 1980.
38 Craveri, *La repubblica*, 861.
39 Enrica Costa Bona and Luciano Tosi, *L'Italia e la sicurezza collettiva. Dalla Società delle Nazioni alle Nazioni Unite* (Perugia: Morlacchi, 2007), 262-3.
40 Olav Njølstad, 'The Collapse of Superpower Détente, 1975-1980', in Melvin P. Leffler and Westad Odde Arne (eds), *The Cambridge History of the Cold War*, III, *Endings* (Cambridge: Cambridge University Press, 2010), 135-55, in particular 149-55; on the Italian position see Leopoldo Nuti, *La sfida nucleare. La politica estera italiana e le armi atomiche 1945-1991* (Bologna: Il Mulino, 2007), 347-93.
41 Riccardi, *Da Colombo ad Andreotti e Craxi*, 25-7.
42 On this see, among others, Avi Shlaim, *Il muro di ferro. Israele e il mondo arabo* (Bologna: Il Ponte, 2003), 445-63.
43 Intervention by Foreign Minister Emilio Colombo, AP, CD, VIII legislatura, Discussioni, 11 June 1982, 48096-48097.
44 Giuseppe Lissi and Massimo Ramaioli, 'Questione libanese, forze di pace in Medio Oriente e impegno dell'Italia', in Silvio Beretta and Mugnaini Marco (eds), *Politica estera dell'Italia e dimensione mediterranea: storia, diplomazia, diritti* (Soveria Mannelli: Rubbettino, 2009), 123-58, in particular 128-42.
45 Ferraris, *Manuale della politica estera italiana*, 385.

46 Giulio Andreotti, *Diari 1976–1979. Gli anni della solidarietà* (Milan: Rizzoli, 1981), 274–9, notes of 15–19 November 1978.
47 Valentino Baldacci, *Giovanni Spadolini: la questione ebraica e lo stato d'Israele* (Florence: Polistampa, 2013), 130.
48 Riccardi, 'Da Colombo ad Andreotti e Craxi', 30; Antonio Maccanico, *Con Pertini al Quirinale. Diari 1978–1985* (Bologna: Il Mulino, 2014), 231–2.
49 Ferraris, *Manuale della politica estera italiana*, 381.
50 Craveri, *La repubblica*, 920.
51 On Craxi's politicy see, among others, Colarizi Simona and Marco Gervasoni, *La cruna dell'ago. Craxi, il partito socialista e la crisi della Repubblica* (Rome: Laterza, 2006), 151–89. Piero Craveri, 'L'irresistibile ascesa e la drammatica caduta di Bettino Craxi', in Gennaro Acquaviva and Luigi Covatta (eds), *Il crollo. Il PSI nella crisi della prima Repubblica* (Venice: Marsilio, 2012), 661–84.
52 Massimo Franco, *Andreotti. La vita di un uomo politico, la storia di un'epoca* (Milan: Mondadori, 2008), 136–50; Massimo Pini, *Craxi. Una vita, un'era politica* (Milan: Mondadori, 2006), 202.
53 A few references are in Francesco Lefebvre D'Ovidio and Luca Micheletta (eds), *Giulio Andreotti e l'Europa* (Rome: Storia e Letteratura, 2017); Luciano Monzali, *Giulio Andreotti e le relazioni italo-austriache 1972–1992* (Merano: Alphabeta Verlag, 2016); Ennio Di Nolfo, 'Il PSI, Craxi e la politica estera italiana', in Covatta Acquaviva, *Il crollo*, 685–712.
54 Gennaro Acquaviva and Antonio Badini, *La pagina saltata della storia* (Venice: Marsilio, 2010), 81.
55 Antonio Badini, 'Intervento', in Ennio Di Nolfo (ed.), *La politica estera italiana negli anni Ottanta* (Manduria: Lacaita, 2003), 37.
56 Riccardi, 'Da Colombo ad Andreotti e Craxi', 34; for the Soviet policy see Galia Golan, *Soviet Policies in the Middle East: From World War II to Gorbachev* (Cambridge: Cambridge University Press, 1990), 140–96.
57 Badini, 'Intervento', 37.
58 *Appunto* del MAE, s.d. (February 1985), GA, b. 485.
59 Baldacci, *Giovanni Spadolini*, 145.
60 Bottai to many embassies, 12 January 1985, GA, b. 498.
61 Ferraris, *Manuale della politica estera italiana*, 390; Session of the European Council, Dublin, 3 and 4 December 1984, *Conclusions*, aei.pitt.edu/1400/1Dublin_dec_1984.pdf, pp. 233–4.
62 Shlaim, *Il muro di ferro*, 478.
63 Riccardi, 'Da Colombo ad Andreotti e Craxi', 37; Bottai all'ambasciata di Tunisi, 25 February 1985, GA, b. 485.
64 Matteo Gerlini, 'Il caso Achille Lauro e le sue conseguenze', in Di Nolfo, *La politica estera italiana negli anni Ottanta*, 99.
65 Bottai to the embassy in Tunis, 25 February 1985, GA, b. 485.
66 Ibid.
67 Ibid.
68 A complete reconstruction of the entire event is in Matteo Gerlini, *Il dirottamento dell'Achille Lauro e i suoi inattesi e sorprendenti risvolti* (Milan: Mondadori, 2016).
69 On this, see the testimony of the Italian ambassador in Washington at the time, Rinaldo Petrignani, in Di Nolfo, *La politica estera italiana negli anni Ottanta*, 131–45.
70 Riccardi, 'Da Colombo ad Andreotti e Craxi', 44.
71 AP, Debates, 6 November 1985, 32789–32790.

72 Riccardi, *L'internazionalismo difficile*, 686.
73 Riccardi, 'Da Colombo ad Andreotti a Craxi', 51–2.
74 Antonio Varsori, *L'Italia e la fine della guerra fredda* (Bologna: Il Mulino, 2013), 99
75 Moreno to MAE, 22 August 1988, GA, b. 484.
76 Calamia to MAE, 15 September 1988, GA, b. 484.
77 AP, Debates, 6 November 1985, 32789–32790.
78 *Appunto per l'On. Ministro*, 18 November 1988, GA, b. 484.
79 Riccardi, *L'internazionalismo difficile*, 725.
80 Ferraris, *Manuale della politica estera italiana*, 399.
81 Shlaim, *Il muro di ferro*, 516.
82 Varsori, *L'Italia e la fine della guerra fredda*, 103–4.

5

Cultural diplomacy in the Middle East: The Italian contribution

Lorenzo Medici

Investigating Italian cultural diplomacy in the Middle East over the three considered decades is a demanding task, considering the scarcity of archival sources. However, some reading keys are available to scholars. In particular, the first half of the 1970s can be linked directly to the cultural policy promoted in the Middle East by Aldo Moro, whose characteristics remained unchanged in the following years. The cultural policy promoted by Moro in North Africa and the Middle East between the late 1960s and the early 1970s, when the Christian Democrat statesman held the offices of prime minister and foreign minister on several occasions,[1] was part of a process which had started immediately after the Second World War, when cultural soft power became an important tool for Italy's foreign policy. The country's cultural tradition had already represented an important diplomatic resource in the Liberal period and the Fascist regime. During Mussolini's dictatorship, cultural diplomacy contributed to spreading not only Italian language and culture but also Fascist social and political values. In the wake of the Ethiopian war, Fascist ideological radicalization and Italy's rapprochement with Nazi Germany, new measures of targeted political propaganda complemented the regime's cultural diplomacy.[2] Following the fall of the regime and the end of the Second World War, the new ruling elite considered it fundamental to enhance the country's cultural resources since it had lost, after the defeat, effective diplomatic instruments of political and economic influence. Consequently, cultural diplomacy had the goal of promoting the image of a new, democratic and anti-Fascist Italy, engaged on the international scene and willing to foster political and commercial relations.[3] On these premises, Italian cultural diplomacy was assigned a long-term task, based on cultural exchanges aimed at influencing the ruling classes and opinion makers, who in turn would act on the public opinion of the respective countries. Therefore, during the Cold War, Italy did not promote propaganda campaigns, unlike the leading countries of the Western alliance engaged in the front line in countering the Soviet propaganda offensive. On the contrary, the Italian government pursued a cultural policy based on dialogue and cooperation, according to the principles of UNESCO. In the context of a broader political vision, attentive to multilateral diplomacy, the governments of the Italian Republic chose a path already traveled by Fascism, but with instrumental motivations. The new address, far from being inspired by the politics of power and the unilateral affirmation of Italian culture, although careful to protect the country's interests, was realized with UNESCO membership, where Italy was admitted in 1947. Multilateral cultural cooperation also characterized bilateral cultural diplomacy, based on dialogue and mutual exchange to the point that it was preferred to use the term *cultural cooperation*.[4] Similarly to the Liberal and Fascist periods, the Mediterranean was one of the main areas of the Italian Republic's cultural promotion. Unlike Great Britain and France, Italy did not have a colonial empire to defend. The loss of colonies, with the peace treaty of 1947, allowed the Italian government to present itself as a disinterested partner, and facilitated cultural relations, besides political and economic ones.[5] Moreover, Italy maintained a low profile within the Western military alliance, while the United States was assuming the role of Western leader in the Mediterranean as well.[6] Both conditions proved helpful in relations with the Arab countries.[7] Indeed, from the mid-1950s, Italy pursued a 'neo-Atlantic' policy that aimed, even within the Atlantic Pact, to establish a bridge between North and South and to increase its own political and economic role in the Mediterranean.[8] Within this context, cultural relations were intended to facilitate political and commercial relations with the countries of the region.[9]

As in other regions, also in North Africa and the Middle East, Italian cultural diplomacy pursued long-term goals and promoted cultural exchanges, dialogue and cooperation, as envisioned by UNESCO. After the closure, of numerous institutions due to the world conflict, especially public and private schools and sections of the 'Dante Alighieri', cultural and educational activities were progressively resumed and strengthened, despite the shortage of financial resources.[10] In the 1950s, Italian cultural centers and institutes opened in Beirut, Istanbul, Ankara, Cairo and Tripoli; in the 1960s in Algiers, Tunis, Tel Aviv (with the Haifa section), Baghdad and Tehran.[11] This was made possible also by the establishment of cultural agreements and scientific and technical cooperation which, in many cases, provided for the reciprocal opening of cultural institutions. Agreements were signed with Algeria, Egypt, Jordan, Iran, Iraq, Israel, Lebanon, Libya, Morocco, Oman, Saudi Arabia, Syria, Tunisia, Turkey and Yemen.[12] The main activities of the cultural institutes and centers consisted of courses in Italian language and literature, but also in Arabic literature. The lectures and classes were held mainly in Italian, and in some cases in Arabic. Besides hosting libraries, the institutes organized conferences, monographic courses, 'Lectura Dantis', art history lessons, musical concerts, theatrical performances and film screenings, and provided scholarships for local students to study in Italy. The cultural programs focused mainly on topics that had the approval of the Middle Eastern and North African countries' elites, and often related to distant times, such as the Roman and medieval ages, the Renaissance, and the results of archaeological missions. These themes, along with other and more recent ones, also applicable to the colonial period, were not presented as an expression of an Italian primacy, as had happened during Fascism, but were meant to highlight the existence of a common civilization in the Mediterranean Basin.[13] Alongside the initiatives of the institutes, there were those of the schools abroad, both public (mainly in Morocco), and legally recognized (they spread in Lebanon and in Egypt), and private (in Algeria, Saudi Arabia, Egypt, Israel, Lebanon, Morocco, Syria,

Tunisia and Yemen). The government largely subsidized the last two school types, administered by religious orders or private companies.[14] Also the archaeological missions maintained an important role. Since the late 1940s the Ministry of Foreign Affairs supported the resumption of excavations in Palestine and in Jordan, while the Italian Archaeological School of Athens resumed its activities in Greece, Turkey and Libya. In the 1960s, the *Farnesina* financed a vast program of excavations conducted by Italian universities in Syria, Egypt, Sudan, Malta, Tunisia and Algeria. The common theme was the running of investigations that revealed the historical and cultural convergences among the civilizations of the region.[15] In the years when Aldo Moro led Italian foreign policy, cultural promotion followed the guidelines of dialogue and cooperation with the ultimate goal of safeguarding peace. Cultural cooperation was a fundamental component of Italian foreign policy as it fostered mutual understanding between peoples and allowed to mitigate the economic and social imbalances still existing in the world.[16] The spirit of the Italian action would reportedly not have been 'aggressive and ideological', but 'of understanding and of concord among peoples; … for this reason, rather than speaking about relations with other countries, it was preferred to speak about cooperation with them in all the various sectors'.[17] The cornerstone of Italian cultural diplomacy remained mutual exchange: 'we cannot speak of cultural "export", without integrating the concept with that of cultural "import" …; and the whole can be defined … cultural "cooperation".'[18] Under-secretary for Foreign Affairs Dionigi Coppo argued that cultural diplomacy should have

> operated in the long term and represented universals values. … Our cultural policy does not have the purpose of propaganda or a nationalistic intent. It takes place both bilaterally and on a multilateral level and is based on the principle of cooperation. It means mutual understanding, agreement, exchange, education for international comprehension, contribution to human improvement, to human civilization. It is the donation of one's own culture, it is the acquisition of another culture, it is the common creation of a new culture.[19]

With the newly independent, 'culturally younger' countries, relations had to become an opportunity for an exchange of experiences designed to pursue mutual enrichment and reach long-term goals: 'Making an efficient cultural policy does not mean imposing the own culture.'[20] Just as in previous years, Prime Minister Moro paid particular attention to the Mediterranean. His effort was meant to favour the political-diplomatic action carried out by the Italian government for the solution of the Arab–Israeli conflict, and to avoid the worsening of the confrontation between the two superpowers, increasingly involved in the Middle Eastern crisis. What the Italian government feared above all was the growing political and military penetration of Moscow and the consequences deriving from the closure of the Suez Canal, which would weaken Italy's traditional political, economic and cultural ties with the countries of the area.[21] The 1973 Yom Kippur War and the decision by Arab countries to use the oil weapon to isolate Israel from its allies further reinforced the pro-Arab policy that, since the 1967 crisis, the Italian foreign minister had tried to impose on pro-Israeli government forces.[22] As part of a broader traditional approach with which Italy supported multilateral diplomacy and international organizations,[23] Moro and his government promoted an active role for the United Nations and Europe for a policy of peace and cooperation. Believing that the solution of the Middle East problem constituted an element of the East–West dialogue, in 1972 Italy proposed to set up a conference on security and cooperation in the Mediterranean, following the example of the European one.[24] Moreover, Italy made a fundamental contribution to the elaboration of a Mediterranean policy of the European Economic Community: the declaration made by the European Community in November 1973 for the application of UN Resolution 242 and the legitimate rights of the Palestinians, was followed in July 1974 by the launch of the Euro-Arab Dialogue.[25] The action carried out on the political and economic levels would be assisted by cultural diplomacy, entrusted with the task of fostering friendly relations with countries throughout the region, in order to set in motion currents of sympathy and friendship towards Italy. Cultural institutes in North Africa and the Middle East, to which in the 1970s were added those of Alexandria, Haifa (independent from the Tel Aviv one) and Rabat,[26] endured to be considered the 'main instruments of Italian cultural presence abroad' and the first interpreters of classical cultural cooperation, the humanistic one.[27] Despite the constant lack of resources, also due to the limited financial participation of local authorities, the institutes continued to provide courses in Italian language and literature, conferences, art exhibitions, book shows, theatre, film and music events (such as the Italian lyrical season in Cairo), and to coordinate the distribution of scholarships.[28]

Alongside the activities of the institutes, there were those of Italian lectureships in universities and local high schools (Algiers, Jerusalem, Haifa, Teheran, Beirut, Cairo, Alexandria, Damascus, Tunis, Ankara, Istanbul and Aden),[29] courses of Italian schools abroad, both state and subsidized (particularly in Morocco, Lebanon and Egypt),[30] and the excavations of archaeological missions (in the 1970s conducted mainly in Algeria, Libya, Malta, Egypt, Syria, Israel, Tunisia, Turkey, Iraq and Iran).[31] Moreover, starting from the twentieth century's second post-war period, the activities and language courses held by the 'Dante Alighieri' resumed also in Alexandria, Cairo, Tunis, Jerusalem, Haifa, Casablanca, Rabat and Tangier.[32] However, soon traditional cultural diplomacy was no longer considered effective to achieve the intended objectives. In addition to the humanistic field, the scientific one should be developed and, above all, that of technical cooperation. To this end, Italy's Foreign Ministry officials completed the reorganization of Italian cultural promotion abroad with the relaunching of technical assistance, which already had important applications in previous years.[33] For the Christian Democratic statesman, it was necessary to eliminate the economic and cultural imbalances which generated poverty and conflict and prevented developing countries from expressing their full potential. The inclusion of technical assistance into cultural cooperation would allow more easily combining the pursuit of national goals with the ideals of social progress and justice among the nations.[34] Technical cooperation would prove to be useful also for the pursuit of national interests, strengthening political and commercial relations with the Mediterranean countries, especially in relation to the Italian need for energy sources. The basis of this action was the belief that Italy had a model to export and was 'free from any suspicion of hegemonic will, significant stains of colonialism and sense of superiority'.[35] Attention to these aspects of cultural cooperation was also linked to the debate within the United Nations Organization which, following the entry of the newly independent countries, had outlined the objective of an effective reduction of the gap between the world's North and the South, and called on the industrialized countries to cooperate.[36] An important role in obtaining this result was entrusted to education, so much so that already at the beginning of the 1960s UNESCO, under the leadership of the director-general, Italian Vittorino Veronese, had launched an action plan for the literacy and education of adults in the Third World.[37] Therefore, a technical direction of Italian schools abroad would contribute to the professional training of citizens of the assisted countries, along with specialization courses, the granting of scholarships and the creation of technical education centres on site, so that the manufacturing plants of the developing countries were controlled and managed by local cadres.[38] Above all, technical assistance should be strengthened through better coordination and greater financial resources. Previously, decree no. 18 of 15 January 1967 had conferred the competences related to scientific and technical cooperation to the Directorate General of Cultural Relations (Direzione Generale per le Relazioni Culturali – DGRC) of the Ministry of Foreign Affairs.[39] Italy's new policy was implemented with law no. 1222 of 15 December 1971 on technical cooperation with the developing countries.[40] It gave structured and original regulation to this sector and put together various related subjects (civil volunteering, delivery of experts and equipment, aid to Somalia, etc.) until then regulated by separate and often conflicting legislative provisions, and provided funds for a five-year period. The law transformed the DGRC into the Directorate General for Cultural, Scientific and Technical Cooperation, in which a special Service for Technical Cooperation was established with developing countries. The new name indicated the desire to implement a cultural policy abroad that, alongside the dissemination of traditional subjects, promoted the transmission of scientific and technological knowledge in order to stimulate the economic growth of developing countries by training companies' workforce and encouraging the modernization of institutions.[41]

The agreements for cultural, scientific and above all technical cooperation were important tools at the disposal of this new direction of Italian cultural diplomacy. With these agreements, concluded since the 1950s but relaunched by law no. 1222, Italy undertook to provide developing countries the technical assistance they needed on the basis of the requests and priorities they presented. In the early 1970s, the signing of these agreements was also reached with the Mediterranean countries: Tunisia (August 1969, an additional protocol was signed in August 1971); Morocco (January 1970); Iran (September 1970); Algeria (June 1971); Lebanon (July 1971); Israel (November 1971); Syria (the technical cooperation of December 1972 followed to the cultural one of December 1971); Saudi Arabia (February 1973); Libya (February 1974); Iraq (July 1974); Egypt (April 1975).[42] These agreements put into practice the provisions of law no. 1222 of 1971 and provided for: the Italian commitment for the preparation of studies and projects likely to contribute to the economic and social development of the beneficiary country; initiatives for the professional training of craftsmen and technicians; the sending from Italy, at the request of the local government, of experts (from skilled workers to university teachers) in the various branches of applied sciences, as well as cooperators and civil service volunteers; the granting of scholarships. The parties undertook to organize traineeships for technical and professional training, to host information and study missions, to participate in the construction and equipment of vocational training centers and technical institutes, and to exchange scientific and technical documentation and patents. The creation of mixed commissions for the formulation and examination of concrete technical assistance proposals and, on the Italian side, the granting of non-repayable grants – often destined to Italian companies or to companies with a prevalent Italian participation – for the preparation of studies and projects entrusted to them by the beneficiary countries. Finally, Italy would provide free technical-scientific equipment to improve health and social structures.[43]

The agreements should have allowed Italy to become a privileged partner of the countries of the region on political, economic and social levels, strengthening above all commercial relations. Participation in the development plans of the Arab countries would have opened up new perspectives for economic agreements, relating in particular to energy sources, so as to redress the Italian trade balance, in sharp deficit after the oil shock following the Yom Kippur War.[44] In addition to the agreements, among the instruments of the renewed cultural diplomacy initiated by law no. 1222 there were, as we mentioned, schools operating in developing countries.[45] In the Middle East, schools were frequented largely by native students, and progressively performed technical assistance functions, adopting a professional training scheme.[46] The model to follow was the protocol signed with Egypt in March 1970 which, meeting the requests presented by the Egyptians to train specialists in the technical-professional field, foresaw the creation in Cairo of a technical-industrial institute, managed by the order of the Salesians (a Roman Catholic educational religious order founded in 1859) and financially supported by the Italian government.[47] Even the archaeological missions were increasingly characterized as initiatives related to technical assistance, through the participation of local scholars and staff. Always within the framework of technical cooperation were the actions carried out on the multilateral level, such as the Italian participation in the rescue, conducted in the early 1970s by UNESCO, of the Philae island temples in Egypt, after the one carried out in the previous decade of the Abu Simbel temples, both threatened by the construction of the Aswan Dam on the Nile River.[48] The focus on technical cooperation in the Middle East was confirmed by the strong presence of experts and volunteers sent mainly to this area,[49] but above all by the amount of allocated funds. Law no. 1222 of 1971 established an allocation of 50 billion liras for the following five years.[50] The estimated Foreign Affairs budget for 1972, allocated 17.5 billion to cultural and scientific cooperation, with an increase of 20 per cent over the previous year, while technical cooperation received 9.5 billion, equal to a 50 per cent increase.[51] On an approved budget of 7.5 billion, if 2.7 billion lira went to Somalia, the icon of Italian cooperation, the countries of the 'Mediterranean Basin and the Arab World' were assigned 1.4 billion and those of the 'Middle and Far East' (which included both Yemens, Iraq and Iran) 260 million.[52] However, in 1973 the allocations for cultural, scientific and technical cooperation increased by only 5 per cent.[53] Following the oil crisis of the same year a difficult period began, characterized by lower funding, which made Italian action less incisive.[54] Indeed, the political and economic crisis, experienced by Italy in the second half of the 1970s, had profound repercussions also on cultural, scientific and technical cooperation, both due to the greater attention given by governments to internal issues compared to international ones and, above all, because of the strong reduction in the expected funding. The action initiated by Moro in favour of the development of technical assistance with law no. 1222 of 1971, in order to better meet the demands of the Mediterranean countries and, consequently, to strengthen the Italian political and economic position, was slowed down. However, the initiative of the Christian Democrat statesman provided the necessary legislative and programmatic coordinates to operate with greater incisiveness in the following years, through the important instrument of cultural cooperation in a region of vital interest to Italy. Actually, these premises defined the Italian cultural diplomacy in the Mediterranean and the Middle East in the following decades which, from the point of view of political-diplomatic relations, constituted a complex period, characterized by recurrent crises and tensions: the Lebanese civil war, the Iranian revolution, the Soviet intervention in Afghanistan, the US bombing of Tripoli, the Iran–Iraq War, the Israeli Lebanon invasion, the Sigonella Crisis, the Gulf War, the Algerian Civil War.[55] Because of these events, Italy's cultural action in the area suffered setbacks. For example, the cultural institute in Tripoli suspended activities in 1969–76 (1976 was the year in which the institute also suffered a fire), following Colonel Gaddafi's *coup d'état* and the subsequent deterioration of relations with Italy that provoked the expulsion in 1970 of Italian citizens living in the country.[56] After the normalization of Italy–Libya affairs, the publication of a new series of the 'Quaderni dell'Istituto Italiano di Cultura di Tripoli' created the conditions for the resumption of cultural activities in Tripoli. However, the institute closed again in 1992–99, following the economic embargo decided by the United Nations against Libya, which was held responsible for the Lockerbie bombing.[57] Also the cultural institute in Baghdad closed following the Iraqi invasion of Kuwait in 1990 and the subsequent Gulf War, which caused the breakdown of diplomatic relations. The Baghdad institute remained closed throughout the 1990s.[58] The cultural Institute in Tehran closed in November 1986 after a diplomatic crisis which also caused the expulsion of three Italian diplomats and the recall by Iran of the Iranian ambassador in Rome, following a comedy scene hosted by the television show *Fantastico* broadcast by the first channel of the Italian public network. The scene targeted Ayatollah Khomeini, Iran's political and religious leader, at the time engaged in the war against Iraq. Until then, the Italian Institute in Teheran was the only Western cultural center still open, after the closure of the American, British and French ones following the Iranian Revolution.[59] It is worth mentioning the absence of retaliation on the Italian side towards the Cultural Center of the Islamic Republic of Iran in Rome, which remained open.[60] In other cases, the Italian governments' attitude towards dialogue and cooperation overcame these standstills. For example, the Italian institute in Beirut remained open through all the years of the civil war (1975–90). In 1985, when the Green Line divided the city into East Beirut and West Beirut, in addition to the Hamra headquarters, a branch of the institute was opened in Zouk Mikhael, a predominantly Christian area, in the same building that housed the Italian embassy, and an informal section worked at the St. Elie School of the Carmelite Fathers in Tripoli.[61] Likewise, the Italian institute of Algiers did not stop its activity despite the long civil war of 1991–2002, even though from October 1994 to January 1999 the institute reduced its outside activities and focused on Italian-language courses that never stopped, as well as offering the possibility of using the library.[62]

Actually, beyond the difficulties encountered by some of them, the majority of cultural centers in the Middle East accomplished the goal of promoting the Italian language and culture abroad, and the establishment of a place of meeting and dialogue for cultural and foreign operators, such as a reference point for Italian communities abroad.[63] Alongside the deeds of the cultural institutes, the functions of the Italian-language readerships (established in Rabat, Algiers, Tunis, Tripoli, Benghazi, Cairo, Alexandria, Beirut, Amman, Damascus, Aleppo, Istanbul, Ankara, Izmir, Jerusalem, Tel Aviv, Haifa, Tehran, Jeddah, Riyadh and Sanaa) remained important; as did the educational programs of public and private schools, often religious (existing in Morocco, Algeria, Tunisia, Libya, Egypt, Lebanon, Israel, Palestine, Jordan, Syria, Iran, Iraq, Turkey, Saudi Arabia and Yemen).[64] In turn, the cultural agreements were strengthened with the approval of executive programs drawn up by the bilateral commissions provided for in the agreements themselves. In particular, executive programs were concluded with: Iran (February 1978); Iraq (November 1986); Morocco (June 1990); Algeria (October 1992); Jordan (December 1992, after the cultural agreement signed in October 1975); Egypt (December 1993); Oman (June 1993, after the cultural agreement signed in April 1988); Israel (November 1994); Turkey (June 1995); Tunisia (September 1995, after a new cultural agreement signed in September 1981); Syria (April 1996).[65] Finally, the function of the sections of the Dante Alighieri[66] and that of the archaeological missions[67] remained of great importance. A report published some years ago by the Italian Ministry of Foreign Affairs highlighted how in the long run Italian cultural policy in the Mediterranean and the Middle East achieved significant objectives. The study of the Italian language has seen, in fact, a steady rise in the universities and schools of the countries of the region – historically speaking English or French as a second language. In 2001, for example, almost eighteen thousand students participated in over a thousand courses organized by Italian institutes of culture in the region, while no statistical data were given about the more-attended Italian-language classes in schools and universities.[68] However, a recent official publication indicated that the number of students of the Italian-language courses directly supported by the ministry fell to around eleven thousand.[69]

Beyond these figures, partial and difficult to collect and to verify, the cultural diplomacy promoted by Italy in the Middle East contributed to the definition of an image of Italy as a country supporting dialogue and cooperation, in order to foster its political and economic roles in the region.

Notes

1 Moro was foreign minister from August 1969 to June 1972 and then from July 1973 to November 1974, before becoming president of the council until July 1976.
2 Lorenzo Medici, *Dalla propaganda alla cooperazione. La diplomazia culturale italiana nel secondo dopoguerra (1944–1950)* (Padova: Cedam, 2009), 1–71; Laura Fotia, 'La diplomazia culturale del regime fascista: una rassegna storiografica', *Mondo Contemporaneo* 1 (2018), 73–90.
3 Medici, *Dalla propaganda alla cooperazione* ... cit., 73–220.

4   Lorenzo Medici, 'Aspetti e momenti della partecipazione italiana all'UNESCO', in Federico Romero and Antonio Varsori (eds), *Nazione, interdipendenza, integrazione: Le relazioni internazionali dell'Italia (1917-1989)* (Rome: Carocci, 2006) II, 85-103; Medici, *Dalla propaganda alla cooperazione* ... cit.; Medici, 'L'Italia nell'Unesco fra guerra fredda e decolonizzazione', in Luciano Tosi (ed.), *In dialogo: La diplomazia multilaterale italiana negli anni della guerra fredda* (Padova: Cedam, 2013), 143-74.
5   Gianluigi Rossi, *L'Africa italiana verso l'indipendenza (1941-1949)* (Milan: Giuffrè, 1980).
6   See: Alessandro Brogi, *L'Italia e l'egemonia americana nel Mediterraneo* (Florence: La Nuova Italia, 1996); Elena Calandri, *Il Mediterraneo e la difesa dell'Occidente, 1947-1956. Eredità imperiali e logiche di guerra fredda* (Florence: Manent, 1997); Luca Riccardi, *La grandezza di una media potenza. Personaggi e problemi della politica estera italiana del Novecento* (Rome: Società editrice Dante Alighieri, 2017).
7   Luca Riccardi, *Il 'problema Israele': Diplomazia italiana e PCI di fronte allo Stato ebraico (1948-1973)* (Milan: Guerini e Associati, 2006), 101.
8   See: Massimo de Leonardis, 'La politica estera italiana, la Nato e l'Onu negli anni del neoatlantismo (1955-1960)', in Luciano Tosi (ed.), *L'Italia e le organizzazioni internazionali. Diplomazia multilaterale nel Novecento* (Padova: Cedam, 1999), 201-33; Agostino Giovagnoli and Luciano Tosi (eds), *Un ponte sull'Atlantico. L'alleanza occidentale 1949-1999* (Milan: Guerini e Associati, 2003); Evelina Martelli, *L'altro atlantismo. Fanfani e la politica estera italiana (1958-1963)* (Milan: Guerini e Associati, 2008).
9   See: Bruna Bagnato, *Vincoli europei echi mediterranei. L'Italia e la crisi francese in Marocco e in Tunisia 1949-1956* (Florence: Ponte alle Grazie, 1991); Giampaolo Calchi Novati, *Il Canale della discordia. Suez e la politica estera italiana* (Urbino: Quattro Venti, 1998); Massimo de Leonardis (ed.), *Il Mediterraneo nella politica estera italiana del secondo dopoguerra* (Bologna: Il Mulino, 2003); Alberto Tonini, *Il sogno proibito. Mattei, il petrolio arabo e le 'sette sorelle'* (Florence: Polistampa, 2003); Matteo Pizzigallo (ed.), *L'Italia e il Mediterraneo orientale 1946-1950* (Milan: Franco Angeli, 2004); Bruna Bagnato, *Petrolio e politica. Mattei in Marocco* (Florence: Polistampa, 2004); Riccardi Luca, *Il «problema Israele»*... cit.; Matteo Pizzigallo (ed.), *Amicizie mediterranee e interesse nazionale, 1946-1954* (Milan: Franco Angeli, 2006); Matteo Pizzigallo, *La diplomazia italiana e i Paesi arabi dell'Oriente mediterraneo (1946-1952)* (Milan: Franco Angeli, 2008); Bruna Bagnato, *L'Italia e la guerra d'Algeria (1954-1962)* (Soveria Mannelli: Rubbettino, 2012); Matteo Pizzigallo (ed.), *La politica araba dell'Italia democristiana: studi e ricerche sugli anni Cinquanta* (Milan: Angeli, 2012).
10 ASMAE, Gabinetto (1943-58), b. 83 (1944-7), 6, 2/13, Istituti e scuole all'estero - Finanziamenti, promemoria, il ministro degli Esteri, De Gasperi, al presidente del Consiglio, Parri, Roma, 14 luglio 1945; ivi, progetto di lettera, De Gasperi al ministro del Tesoro, Federico Ricci, Roma, s.d. [November 1945]. For a general overview of the Italian cultural policy in the Mediterranean, see: Gennaro de Novellis, *L'Italia nella cultura mediterranea*, 'Quadrivio', II, 1962, 6, 9-29; *Atti del I Convegno su: La presenza culturale italiana nei paesi arabi: storia e prospettive. Napoli, 28-30 maggio 1980* (Rome: Istituto per l'Oriente, 1982), 225-86; *Atti del II Convegno su: La presenza culturale italiana nei paesi arabi: storia e prospettive. Sorrento, 18-20 novembre 1982* (Rome: Istituto per l'Oriente, 1984); Lorenzo Medici, 'La diplomazia culturale della repubblica italiana nel Mediterraneo', in Daniela Melfa, Alessia Melcangi and Federico

Cresti (eds), *Spazio privato, spazio pubblico e società civile in Medio Oriente e Africa del Nord, Atti del convegno SeSaMO, Catania 2006* (Milan: Giuffrè, 2008), 553–69.

11 Ministero degli Affari Esteri, Direzione Generale delle Relazioni Culturali, *Istituzioni culturali e scolastiche italiane all'estero. 30 Marzo 1961* (Rome: Ministero degli Affari Esteri, 1961), *passim*; *Istituzioni culturali e scolastiche italiane all'estero. 1° Gennaio 1968* (Rome: Ministero degli Affari Esteri, 1968), *passim*; *La promozione della cultura italiana all'estero* (Rome: Istituto Poligrafico e Zecca dello Stato, 1996), *passim*.
See also: Franco Foschi, *Sugli istituti italiani di cultura all'estero. Note e riflessioni* (Florence: Vallecchi, 1980), *passim*. In 1952 the Center for Italian-Arab relations was created in Rome as an autonomous section of the *Istituto per l'Oriente*; 'Il Centro per le Relazioni Italo-Arabe', *Informazioni Culturali* VIII (1955), 6, 14–15.

12 Ministero degli Affari Esteri, Servizio del contenzioso diplomatico dei trattati e degli affari legislativi, *Accordi culturali e di cooperazione scientifica e tecnica fra l'Italia ed altri stati* (Rome: Ministero degli Esteri, 1972), *passim*.

13 On the activities of cultural institutes in the Mediterranean, see the specific sections dedicated to them by the journals: 'Informazioni Culturali', 'Il Veltro', 'Quadrivio', 'Esteri' e 'Affari Esteri'. See also: 'Rapporti culturali internazionali', *Rivista di Studi Politici Internazionali* XXV (1958), 1, 71–80; Foschi, *Sugli istituti italiani di cultura…* cit., 82–3, 93–7, 210–21, 241–56; Ministero degli Affari Esteri, *La promozione della cultura italiana…* cit. for some examples: 'L'Istituto Italiano di Cultura di Beirut', *Informazioni Culturali* VIII (1955), 6, 8–10; 'La cultura italiana a Beirut', *Informazioni Culturali* X (1957), 7–8, 16–18; Giuseppe Valentini, 'Cultura italiana nel Libano', *Quadrivio* I (1961), 3, 67–76; 'Inaugurazione del Centro Italiano di Cultura ad Algeri', *Informazioni Culturali* XIII (1960), 5, 14; Fernando Caruso, 'L'Istituto Italiano di Cultura di Teheran', *Il Veltro* XIV (1970), 1–2, 183–7; Luigi Polacco, 'La presenza della cultura italiana nella Turchia di oggi', *Il Veltro* XXIII (1979), 2–4, 483–91.

14 Ministero degli Affari Esteri, *La cooperazione culturale scientifica e tecnica* (Rome: Ministero degli Affari Esteri, 1971), 167 et sqq; Medici, *La diplomazia culturale della repubblica italiana nel Mediterraneo…* cit., 562.

15 Ibid., 565.

16 Ministero degli Affari Esteri, *La cooperazione culturale scientifica e tecnica…* cit., 1971, V.

17 Ibid., 14.

18 Ibid., 16.

19 Ibid., 15.

20 Ministero degli Affari Esteri, *La cooperazione culturale scientifica e tecnica* (Rome: Ministero degli Affari Esteri, 1973), 20.

21 Ministero degli Affari Esteri, *Italia e Medio Oriente, 1967–1974* (Rome: Servizio storico e documentazione, 1974); Luigi Vittorio Ferraris (ed.), *Manuale della politica estera italiana, 1947–1993* (Rome: Laterza, 1996), 255–76; Daniele Caviglia and Massimiliano Cricco, *La diplomazia italiana e gli equilibri mediterranei. La politica mediorientale dell'Italia dalla guerra dei Sei Giorni al conflitto dello Yom Kippur (1967–1973)* (Soveria Mannelli: Rubbettino, 2006); Riccardi, *Il «problema Israele»…* cit., 309–88, 441–67.

22 Luca Riccardi, 'Sempre più con gli arabi. La politica italiana verso il Medio Oriente dopo la guerra del Kippur (1973–1976)', *Nuova Storia Contemporanea* X (2006), 6, 57–82.

23 Enrica Costa Bona and Luciano Tosi, *L'Italia e la sicurezza collettiva. Dalla Società delle Nazioni alle Nazioni Unite* (Perugia: Morlacchi, 2007).

24 Aldo Moro, 'Il contributo italiano alla causa della pace nel mondo', *Relazioni Internazionali* XXXV (1971), 12, 289–92; Moro, *L'Italia nell'evoluzione dei rapporti internazionali, Discorsi, interventi, dichiarazioni e articoli recuperati e interpretati da Giovanni Di Capua* (Rome: Ebe; Brescia: Moretto, 1971), 279–81; 'Moro espone a Montecitorio l'azione internazionale dell'Italia', *Relazioni Internazionali* XXXVIII (1974), 32–3, 825–8; 'La costante azione dell'Italia per la pace e la distensione fra i popoli', in Aldo Moro (ed.), *Scritti e discorsi*, VI, *1974–1978* (Rome: Cinque Lune, 1990), 3165–77; Aldo Moro, *Discorsi parlamentari*, II, *1963–1977* (Rome: Camera dei Deputati, 1996), 1400–1. See: Luca Riccardi, 'Aldo Moro e il Medio Oriente (1963–1978)', in Francesco Perfetti, Andrea Ungari, Daniele Caviglia and Daniele De Luca (eds), *Aldo Moro nell'Italia contemporanea* (Florence: Le Lettere, 2011), 551–83; Italo Garzia, Luciano Monzali and Federico Imperato (eds), *Aldo Moro, l'Italia repubblicana e i popoli del Mediterraneo* (Besa: Besa, 2013); Federico Imperato, Rosario Milano and Luciano Monzali (eds), *Fra diplomazia e petrolio. Aldo Moro e la politica italiana in Medio Oriente (1963–1978)* (Bari: Cacucci, 2018).

25 Riccardi, *Sempre più con gli arabi...* cit.; see also: Silvio Labbate, *Illusioni mediterranee: il dialogo euro-arabo* (Florence: Le Monnier Università, 2016); Labbate, 'The Beginning of the Euro-Arab Dialogue and the Trans-Atlantic Relations (1973–1975)', *Nuova Rivista Storica* CI (2017), 2, 347–70.

26 Ministero degli Affari Esteri, *La promozione della cultura italiana ...* cit., 75, 103, 131.

27 Ministero degli Affari Esteri, *La cooperazione culturale...* cit., 1971, 47.

28 For some examples of the activities of the institutes see: ACS, AM, b. 130, f. 32, Ministero degli Affari Esteri, Segreteria Generale, *Visita in Tunisia del Ministro degli Affari esteri On. Aldo Moro (4-6 settembre 1970); Relazioni culturali fra l'Italia e la Tunisia*, Roma, s.d.; ibid., b. 130, f. 43, Ministero degli Affari Esteri, Segreteria Generale, *Riunione dei capi missione in paesi arabi e del Mediterraneo (Tunisi, 6 settembre 1970); Relazioni culturali e di assistenza tecnica con Marocco, Algeria, Tunisia, Libia, R.A.U. e Sudan*; Roma, s.d.; ibid., b. 130, f. 48, Ministero degli Affari Esteri, Segreteria Generale, *Incontro del Ministro degli Affari Esteri Aldo Moro con il Ministro degli Affari Esteri della R.A.U., M. Riad (21-22 settembre 1970); Rapporti culturali con la R.A.U*, Roma, s.d.; ibid., b. 135, f. 97, Ministero degli Affari Esteri, Segreteria Generale, *Visita in Italia del Ministro degli Affari Esteri dell'Impero dell'Iran, Sig. Ardeshir Zahedi (24-26 maggio 1971); Rapporti culturali italo-iraniani*, Roma, s.d.; ibid., b. 135, f. 101, Ministero degli Affari Esteri, Segreteria Generale, *Visita del Ministro degli Affari Esteri On. Aldo Moro nella Repubblica Algerina Democratica e Popolare (15-18 giugno 1971); Rapporti culturali italo-algerini*, Roma, s.d.; ibid., b. 137, f. 122, Ministero degli Affari Esteri, Segreteria Generale, *Visita a Roma del Ministro degli Affari Esteri della Repubblica Turca, Bayülken (17 febbraio 1972), Rapporti culturali e di cooperazione scientifico-tecnica tra Italia e Turchia*, Roma, 8 febbraio 1972; ibid., b. 157, f. 24, Ministero degli Affari Esteri, Segreteria Generale, *Visita dell'Onorevole Ministro in Arabia Saudita (1°-3 febbraio 1974); Cooperazione culturale, scientifica e tecnica fra l'Italia e l'Arabia Saudita*, Roma, s.d. See also: Medici, *La diplomazia culturale della repubblica italiana nel Mediterraneo...* cit. 563–4.

29 Ministero degli Affari Esteri, *La cooperazione culturale...* cit., 1973, 54–7.

30 Ibid., 64–9.

31 Ibid., 1971, 79–80; ibid., 1973, 99–100; see: 'Missioni archeologiche italiane nel Mediterraneo', *Il Veltro* XV (1971), 3–4, 462–6; 'Missioni archeologiche italiane nel Mediterraneo', *Il Veltro* XV (1971), 5–6, 624–6; 'Missioni archeologiche italiane nel

Mediterraneo', *Il Veltro* XVI (1972), 1–2, 116–20; 'Missioni archeologiche italiane all'estero', *Il Veltro* XXII (1978), 3–4, 389–420.

32 'Cronache della 'Dante Alighieri'. Le scuole della 'Dante Alighieri' all'estero', *Il Veltro* XV (1971), 1, 155–6; 'Cronache della 'Dante Alighieri'. L'opera culturale e sociale della 'Dante Alighieri' per le comunità italiane all'estero', *Il Veltro* XV (1971), 1, 496; see: https://dantealighieri-ilcairo.weebly.com/index.html.

33 Ministero degli Affari Esteri, *La cooperazione culturale...* cit., 1971, 122. Moro's declaration was made in July 1970.

34 Ministero degli Affari Esteri, Servizio per la Cooperazione Tecnica con i Paesi in via di sviluppo, *Quaderni della cooperazione con i paesi in via di sviluppo, 1. Repertorio dei programmi 1972–1975* (Rome: Ministero Affari Esteri, 1976), 22.

35 Elena Calandri, 'L'Italia e l'assistenza allo sviluppo dal neoatlantismo alla Conferenza di Cancún del 1981', in Varsori Romero (ed.), *Nazione, interdipendenza, integrazione...* cit., I, 2005, 265; see also: Calandri, *Prima della globalizzazione. L'Italia, la cooperazione allo sviluppo e la guerra fredda 1955–1995* (Padova: Cedam, 2013).

36 Alessandro Polsi, *Storia dell'Onu* (Rome: Laterza, 2006), 93–100; Angela Villani, *L'Italia e l'Onu negli anni della coesistenza competitiva (1955–1968)* (Padova: Cedam, 2007), 343–434.

37 Fernando Valderrama, *A History of Unesco* (Paris: Unesco, 1995), 139–41; Sara Banchi, 'Il 'valore dell'educazione': la svolta degli anni sessanta nelle politiche dell'Unesco', in Antonio Varsori (ed.), *Sfide del mercato e identità europea. Le politiche di educazione e formazione professionale nell'Europa comunitaria* (Milan: Franco Angeli, 2006), 53–85; Medici, *Aspetti e momenti...* cit., 92; Medici, 'Organizzazioni internazionali e soft power: il caso dell'Unesco', in Marco Mugnaini (ed.), *Nazioni Unite e sistema internazionale* (Milan: Franco Angeli, 2018), 181–200.

38 ACS, AM, b. 130, f. 43, Ministero degli Affari Esteri, Segreteria Generale, *Riunione dei capi missione in paesi arabi e del Mediterraneo (Tunisi, 6 settembre 1970); Relazioni culturali e di assistenza tecnica con Marocco, Algeria, Tunisia, Libia, R.A.U. e Sudan*, Roma, s.d.

39 Ministero degli Affari Esteri, *La cooperazione culturale...* cit., 1971, 7.

40 Ibid., 1971, VII.

41 Ministero degli Affari Esteri, *Linee direttrici per una politica italiana di assistenza ai paesi in via di sviluppo* (Rome: Ministero Affari Esteri, 1970); Luigi Vittorio Ferraris, 'La politica italiana di cooperazione allo sviluppo', in Tosi (ed.), *L'Italia e le organizzazioni internazionali...* cit., 327–40; Calandri, *L'Italia e l'assistenza allo sviluppo...* cit., 253–70; Tosone Lorella, 'Trade and aid. L'Italia alla Conferenza delle Nazioni Unite sul Commercio e lo Sviluppo (1964–1972)', in Luciano Tosi (ed.), *In dialogo...* cit., 227–60; Borruso Paolo (ed.), *L'Italia in Africa. Le nuove strategie di una politica postcoloniale* (Padova: Cedam, 2015).

42 Ministero degli Affari Esteri, *Accordi culturali...* cit., passim; *La legislazione italiana*, vols XXVI-XXXVII (Milan: Giuffrè, 1969–76) passim. Many of these agreements were signed during the meetings, both held in Rome and in the capitals of North Africa and the Middle East, among the leaders of the Mediterranean countries and Moro (or Giuseppe Medici, when he was head of the *Farnesina* since June 1972 to July 1973). Technical cooperation agreements with the Mediterranean countries were also concluded in the following years, both on the bilateral level and, as hoped by the Italian government, on the multilateral one. Some examples on this regard were the economic, technical, financial and commercial cooperation agreements signed by the member states of the EEC and by the Council of the European Communities

with Algeria, Tunisia and Morocco (April 1976), and with Egypt, Jordan, Syria and Lebanon (January 1977).

43 About the characteristics and purposes of the agreements see: Ministero degli Affari Esteri, *La cooperazione culturale*... cit., 1971, 58–9; ibid., 1973, 139; 149–51. For some examples: ACS, FAM, b. 135, f. 97, Ministero degli Affari Esteri, Segreteria Generale, *Visita in Italia del Ministro degli Affari Esteri dell'Impero dell'Iran, Sig. Ardeshir Zahedi (24–26 maggio 1971)*; *Rapporti culturali italo-iraniani*, Roma, s.d.; ibid., b. 135, f. 101, Ministero degli Affari Esteri, Segreteria Generale, *Visita del Ministro degli Affari Esteri On. Aldo Moro nella Repubblica Algerina Democratica e Popolare (15–18 giugno 1971)*; *Rapporti culturali italo-algerini*, Roma, s.d.; ibid., b. 136, f. 105, Ministero degli Affari Esteri, Segreteria Generale, *Visita in Italia del Ministro degli Affari Esteri della Repubblica libanese Khalyl Abouhamad (14–15 luglio 1971)*; *Rapporti culturali e di Assistenza tecnica*, Roma, s.d.; ibid., b. 157, f. 24, Ministero degli Affari Esteri, Segreteria Generale, *Visita dell'Onorevole Ministro in Arabia Saudita (1°-3 febbraio 1974)*; *Cooperazione culturale, scientifica e tecnica fra l'Italia e l'Arabia Saudita*, Roma, s.d.; ibid., b. 157, f. 27, Ministero degli Affari Esteri, Segreteria Generale, *Visita in Italia del Presidente del Consiglio dei Ministri libico, maggiore Jalloud (21–25 febbraio 1974)*; *Colloqui dell'On. Presidente con il Primo Ministro libico: questioni rientranti nei grandi temi della collaborazione economica e tecnologica che intendiamo sviluppare con la Libia*, Roma, 21 February 1974; ibid., b. 159, f. 44, Ministero degli Affari Esteri, Archivio, *Documentazione Iraq (16–19 luglio 1974)*; *Accordo di cooperazione economica e tecnica tra l'Italia e l'Iraq*, Roma, 17 July 1974.

44 Silvio Labbate, *Energia made in Italy. Le cooperazioni italiane oltre frontiera. Dagli albori alle crisi petrolifere degli anni Settanta* (Rome: Aracne, 2012).

45 Ministero degli Affari Esteri, *Linee direttrici*... cit., 6.

46 ACS, FAM, b. 130, f. 43, Ministero degli Affari Esteri, Segreteria Generale, *Riunione dei capi missione in paesi arabi e del Mediterraneo (Tunisi, 6 settembre 1970)*; *Relazioni culturali e di assistenza tecnica con Marocco, Algeria, Tunisia, Libia, R.A.U. e Sudan*, Roma, s.d.; See also: Ministero degli Affari Esteri, *La cooperazione culturale*... cit., 1971, 53.

47 Ibid., b. 130, f. 48, Ministero degli Affari Esteri, Segreteria Generale, *Incontro del Ministro degli Affari Esteri Aldo Moro con il Ministro degli Affari Esteri della R.A.U., M. Riad (21–22 settembre 1970)*; *Rapporti culturali con la R.A.U.*, Roma, s.d.

48 Brunozzi Raffaella, *Il contributo italiano alla campagna internazionale dell'Unesco per il salvataggio dei monumenti di Abu Simbel*, Tesi di Laurea, Università degli Studi di Perugia, Facoltà di Scienze Politiche, Corso di Laurea in Scienze Politiche, a.a. 2005–6.

49 Ministero degli Affari Esteri, *La cooperazione culturale*... cit., 1973, 157 et sqq.

50 Ibid., 140.

51 Ibid., 11.

52 Ibid., 146.

53 Ibid., 12.

54 Calandri, *L'Italia e l'assistenza allo sviluppo*... cit., 266.

55 Luca Riccardi, *L' ultima politica estera. L'Italia e il Medio Oriente alla fine della prima Repubblica* (Soveria Mannelli: Rubbettino, 2014); Paolo Soave, *Fra Reagan e Gheddafi. La politica estera italiana e l'escalation libico-americana degli anni '80* (Soveria Mannelli: Rubbettino, 2017); Matteo Gerlini, *Il dirottamento dell'Achille Lauro e i suoi inattesi e sorprendenti risvolti* (Milan: Mondadori education, 2016); Massimo Bucarelli and Luca Micheletta (eds), *Andreotti, Gheddafi e le relazioni italo-libiche* (Rome:

Studium, 2018); Galasso, Imperato, Milano and Monzali (eds), *Europa e Medio Oriente*... cit.; Imperato, Milano and Monzali (eds), *Fra diplomazia e petrolio*... cit.

56 Lorenzo Medici, *Moro, l'Italia repubblicana e la Libia. Momenti e problemi delle relazioni bilaterali*, Garzia, Monzali and Imperato (eds), *Aldo Moro*... cit., 302–40.

57 https://iictripoli.esteri.it/iic_tripoli/it/istituto/chi%20siamo/storia. See also: Kenny MacKaskill, *The Lockerbie Bombing: The Search for Justice* (London: Biteback, 2016).

58 AP, CD, *XIII Legislatura, Allegato B ai Resoconti, Seduta del 14 novembre 2000*, 34573. Even today, the institute is not an active center, having no longer resumed activities, as a consequence of the Second Gulf War; AP, CD, S, *XVII Legislatura, Disegni di Legge e Relazioni, Documenti*, doc. LXXX n. 5, 24.

59 Piero Benetazzo, 'I fulmini di Khomeini', *La Repubblica*, 28 November 1986; see: Dario Marchetti, 'Quella volta che Anna Marchesini fece infuriare l'Iran', *La Stampa*, 30 July 2016. The building of the former Italian institute of culture has been put up for sale in the summer 2017. https://ambteheran.esteri.it/ambasciata_teheran/it/ambasciata/news/news/2017/06/vendita-immobile-ex-istituto-italiano.html.

60 http://rome.icro.ir/index.aspx?siteid=209.

61 Ministero degli Affari Esteri, *La promozione della cultura italiana*... cit., 82; see also: https://iicbeirut.esteri.it/iic_beirut/it/istituto/chi_siamo/storia.

62 Ministero degli Affari Esteri, *La promozione della cultura italiana*... cit., 76; see also: https://iicalgeri.esteri.it/iic_algeri/it/istituto/chi_siamo/storia.

63 Ministero degli Affari Esteri, *La promozione della cultura italiana*... cit., 9–43.

64 Ministero degli Affari Esteri, *Istituzioni culturali*... cit., *passim*; Carlo Cirvilleri, *Le istituzioni scolastiche, educative e culturali all'estero* (Firenze: Le Monnier, [1988] 1993), 65–73, 76–9.

65 Ministero degli Affari Esteri, Direzione Generale delle Relazioni Culturali, *La promozione della cultura italiana*... cit., 46–8.

66 'La 'Dante Alighieri' in Medio Oriente: la cultura strumento di pace', *Inform*, 236, 12 December 2003, http://comunicazioneinform.it/archivio/art/art_03/03n236a4.htm.

67 Ministero degli Affari Esteri, Direzione Generale delle Relazioni Culturali, *Missioni archeologiche italiane. La ricerca archeologica, antropologica, etnologica* (Rome: L'Erma» di Bretschneider, 1997).

68 Emanuela Ulivi, 'Italiano, sempre più studiato nel Mediterraneo', *Corriere della Sera*, 1 October 2006.

69 *L'italiano nel mondo che cambia. Stati generali della lingua italiana nel mondo, Firenze, 21-22 ottobre 2014*, Ministero degli Affari Esteri e della Cooperazione Internazionale, pp. 43–4; https://www.esteri.it/MAE/approfondimenti/2014/2014italiano_nel_mondo_che_cambia.pdf.

6

The EU, Italy and the Middle East: The Euro-Arab dialogue

Silvio Labbate

During the 1973 oil crisis the Arab sanctions put Europe in a very difficult stance. Among the attempts made to solve such a difficult situation was the French initiative launched in December 1973: the Euro-Arab Dialogue (EAD). Thought to be an alternative strategy to the Washington deals, this choice incurred strong opposition from the White House; antagonism which stemmed from the European Community's (EC) pro-Arab declaration of 6 November, which also troubled relations with Israel.

Despite the fact that attempts to make this type of collaboration permanent failed, the EAD was a significant moment both in the field of international relations and in the history of Western European governments.[1] Within this EC effort, the role played by Italy was in some aspects very significant. The importance of Arab oil supplies had already in earlier years pushed the Italian government closer to the countries on the southern shore of the Mediterranean; a state of affairs that escalated before and during the Yom Kippur War, especially with Aldo Moro as foreign minister. Notwithstanding this, Italy also later played an active role within the EAD scenario.

The purpose of this chapter is to examine the role played by Italy during the long and troubled evolution of the Euro-Arab project which led the EC to develop a real foreign policy by participating directly in the solving of the Middle East (ME) issue. There is no literature on the Italian position within the EAD. The archival documents currently available, however, allow a reconstruction of how it developed within European foreign policy and, more generally, against the scenario of transnational diplomatic relations.

The EU, Italy and the Middle East before the 1973 oil crisis

Prior to 1973 relations between the Arab world and the EC had been poor. This was true even though the European Global Mediterranean Policy was formulated in April 1972 through the negotiation of a series of bilateral trade and cooperation agreements with some Mediterranean countries.[2] As a matter of fact, after the Suez Canal crisis the EC's political influence in the area was considerably reduced and all attempts to reach any common agreement at the beginning of the 1970s was primarily blocked because of the susceptibility of some partners to bilateral pressure from Israel. Nevertheless in 1972 the EC Commission took the initiative to overcome this impasse, sending a memorandum to the EC Council of Ministers (13 October 1972) about the idea of starting a direct relationship between countries which were exporters and importers of energy.[3] Another attempt was made in April 1973: the Commission urged the EC Council of Ministers to start a *climat de confiance* with the oil producing countries.[4] With probable increasing difficulties for energy supply on the horizon, any action of a single country was likely to be unsuccessful, while in the scenario of realizing a European energy policy, a direct and friendly relationship with the Arab petroleum-exporting states would have been useful.[5] Among the attempts by individual countries to obtain direct energy supplies were those of Italy, a state completely dependent on oil importation from the Mediterranean area. Since Mattei's era, in fact, Italy had attempted to improve relations with ME governments in an effort to overcome internal energy shortages.[6] After the murder of the president of ENI, Italy's national oil company, in 1962, however, the Italian energy policy could no longer find a way to solve its problems. At the beginning of the 1970s, then, the situation in the Peninsula was still very complicated. Difficulties really began to emerge when the Arab countries planned new measures to destabilize the international oil market through constant increases in crude oil's price, anticipating by a few months the heavy sanctions of autumn 1973. At this point the Italian government was forced to look for a different foreign policy: on one hand, it wanted to avoid any Mediterranean initiative that Washington could consider unfriendly; on the other hand, it tried to distance itself from the US pro-Israeli policy. In this way, the Farnesina – the Italian Ministry of Foreign Affairs – attempted to became 'a privileged interlocutor' in the ME area.[7] The appointment of Aldo Moro as head of the Ministero degli Affari Esteri (MAE) – the Italian foreign office – reinforced this trend, and Italy decided on a closer approach to the Arab world in a context where national energy necessities increasingly demanded a non-conflictual relationship with oil-producing countries.[8]

As a matter of fact, the Italian approach to Mediterranean governments was undermined by energy dependence. This was also the case before the 1973 oil crisis, and one of the protagonists of this closer approach policy was Foreign Minister Moro. Already in 1971, for instance, in the report on the activity of the EC of that year, he underlined 'the need to speed up the development of a Community energy policy that [would] allow Europe to rely on its own energy structure appropriate to its status as a large consumer and importer of petroleum products, and guarantee reliable supplies at low prices'.[9] In other words, Moro urged European partners to start cooperating with the Mediterranean oil-producing countries; the Italian minister's interest in the area of Arab countries, then, was already evident in this action. Nevertheless, the times were not yet ripe and Italy, as well as the EC, would be found unprepared for the new punitive measures adopted by the Arab countries after the outbreak of the Yom Kippur War – this, despite Washington, based on detailed internal analysis, predicting the imminent outbreak of an energy crisis and repeatedly asking Brussels too to collaborate in this area.[10] In any case, the pro-Arab policy adopted by Moro after the 1973 oil crisis had been developed much earlier – a policy that would also be the basis for future

Euro-Arab cooperation. The attitude of Italy to the ME region, therefore, was a starting point for developments in the following years.

The birth of Euro-Arab cooperation

On 5 November 1973 the nine-member Organization of the Arab Petroleum Exporting Countries (OAPEC) announced their decision to cut crude production by 25 per cent, in comparison to September levels, and threatened to make a further 5 per cent reduction.[11] The new measures pushed the EC partners to adopt a new, markedly pro-Arab joint declaration during the Brussels meeting on the following day.[12] This choice put Europe in a difficult position with Israel and, above all, the United States. In fact, although Washington recognized that difficulty in obtaining sufficient oil supplies was behind the Nine's decision,[13] America could not accept such a sharp division in policy between the two shores of the Atlantic.[14] Nevertheless, Western European governments were in panic over the oil shortage; and Paris and London were prominent in their attempts to make bilateral accords with oil producers with the purpose of achieving privileged positions.

Italy reacted to the Arab sanctions by following the same path, trying to regain the traditional character of "bridge" country in the approach toward the southern shore of the Mediterranean states. This scenario, the general worsening of relations with the oil producers, gave Italy the chance to develop a new type of collaboration, connecting oil imports to financial initiatives. With this in mind, Moro went on an official mission to the Mediterranean area: from 25 January to 3 February 1974 he visited its main cities, smoothing the way for the start of important economic negotiations for his country.[15] It was in this way that Italy officially started what was known as Moro's pro-Arab policy, very similar to French initiatives. Then, in the framework of Paris's actions in favour of the Arab countries, President Pompidou called for a summit of the Nine to examine the ME crisis and lay down the basis for cooperation between the League of Arab States (LAS) and the EC. It was held on 15 December 1973 in Copenhagen and a delegation of four Arab ministers attended. The diplomatic delegates of Algeria, Sudan, Tunisia and the United Arab Emirates asked the European partners to improve their relations with the Arab world, starting with collaboration in the economic, technical and cultural sectors. This situation was very probably contrived by the Quai d'Orsay, but it was very difficult for Brussels to ignore such an application which could bring undeniable and important advantages. Notwithstanding this, the December 1973 Kissinger proposal to 'establish an *energy action group* ... for collaboration in all areas of the energy problem' had to be considered.[16] In January 1974 Nixon invited the foreign ministers of all the Western countries to a conference of the principal oil-consuming nations to be held in Washington the following February. Now, EC relations with the Arab world had to take into account the wishes of the White House. In fact, the idea of European collaboration with the LAS gave the White House a new cause for disagreement.[17] Despite this, as requested by the four Arab ministers in Copenhagen, during the EC Political Committee summit in January the Quai d'Orsay introduced an alternative strategy to that of Washington: for Paris the time was ripe to develop a dialogue with the Arab world – the EAD – essentially based on economic cooperation.[18] Behind the French proposal was the wish to operate in full autonomy from the United States; this would have caused not inconsiderable problems for the European partners in their relationship with the United States – as well as with Israel. Faced with this situation Washington announced its opposition to the project and accelerated the process of convening the energy conference. Kissinger, in particular, was very suspicious about the Arabs' real motivation for proposing a dialogue with the EC – it could be a trick to ask for weapons and to fight Israel; in addition, as he directly told Foreign Minister Moro, he thought that the European initiative would have a damaging effect on the American attempts to achieve both a peaceful resolution of the ME conflict and in general a peace process in the area.[19]

For Italy participation in the French idea offered several opportunities in foreign policy. As stressed by the Director General of Political Affairs of Farnesina, Roberto Ducci, to Moro, there were considerable effects to the *détente*, in an international equilibrium which had already been severely tested by the war and the sanctions of the Arab countries; and the EAD could be directly linked to Italy's Mediterranean policy by developing a strategy beneficial to the peninsula's interests.[20] Ducci's advice was welcomed by the Italian foreign minister who decided to support the French initiative as part of the efforts to improve relations with the Arab world to obtain oil benefits. In doing this however, Italy received the inevitable protests from Israel. For instance, in February 1974 the Israeli ambassador Sasson strongly criticized both Italy's position on ME problems and its favouring of French ideas that would 'tip the European balance in favor of the Arabs'.[21]

There were also a lot of misgivings within the Nine regarding the EAD. London, for instance, only reservedly supported the French project trying to mitigate its most controversial and less advantageous aspects for Great Britain and cancelling its strong anti-American characteristics. On 18 January the EC working group of ME experts discussed the Paris proposal: there was, despite some reservations (Dutch and Danish), general agreement that the initiative – which had an economic cooperation target – had to have a political nature and target.[22] In spite of this, some European partners did not believe that this would be acceptable to Washington; consequently, they decided to constantly inform Washington on the Nine's intentions, provoking the predictable negative reaction in Paris. Nonetheless, at the EC Political Committee meeting of 6–7 February, the political directors substantially adopted the French proposal, accepting in principle the EAD; the European partners also decided to plan a conference of the ministers of foreign affairs concerned, inevitably provoking a new negative reaction from the White House.[23] It was against this background that the summit promoted by Nixon to discuss international energy problems took place and, as is well known, the divergences between French and American policies were officially manifested there. Even so, there were no doubts about the necessity of the EAD among the Nine, and even the British succeeded in withstanding pressure from Washington, refusing to disavow the EC line.[24] Therefore, the EC Council of Ministers on 4 March finally announced their decision to begin the EAD which could eventually lead to the establishment of a long-term economic, technical, and cultural cooperation with the Arabs. The Nine reached a compromise that foresaw only the start of the first phase of the established cooperation on 6–7 February, postponing discussions about how to proceed to the following meeting. In particular, London – supported by Bonn – registered their reservation on the necessity to connect the initiative to consultation with the United States – as strongly requested by Kissinger.[25] Notwithstanding this, the Washington reaction to this last EC decision was very vigorous: in the Department of State there was 'strong irritation' at the failure of the EC to consult the White House over this approach to the Arabs.[26] The Secretary of State accused the Western European governments of deliberately subverting trans-Atlantic solidarity; the main issue was the lack of consultation, but also the reference to a meeting of the ministers of foreign affairs with the Arabs caused considerable annoyance: it appeared to be a deliberate gesture on the part of the Nine to develop their own identity in opposition with the United States.[27] The White House pressure achieved results during the EC Political Committee summit of 12–13 March, when the UK did not remove its reservations regarding the project, and the Nine officially took note of the temporary impossibility of effecting the decisions of 4 March; there was no real unity of intentions about how the EAD would continue.[28] Nevertheless, the situation appeared very delicate: if the EC had decided, because of American pressure, to revoke the previous decisions, France would certainly have stopped the whole process of European cooperation – as it had threatened to do – thereby opening the doors to the risk of general disintegration. Equally, a negative reaction was to be expected from the Arab world to the point of jeopardizing – very probably – future relations. An important compromise was reached during the informal meeting of the Nine's foreign ministers held at Schloss-Gymnich, near Cologne, on 21–22 April 1974: the Presidency of the European Council (PEC) was allowed to consult allies or other friendly states about issues covered within the European Political Cooperation (EPC).[29] In other words, there was an agreement – the so-called 'Gymnich formula' – whereby the Western European governments would inform and consult the United States on their foreign policy deliberations.[30]

The next step for the EAD was the Bonn EC ministerial summit of 10 June 1974 when the Nine adopted a text that specified the areas and the means of developing their cooperation with the Arab countries.[31] Regarding trans-Atlantic relations, the Western European governments opted for direct contact with Washington, giving concrete application to the principle of the consultations – according to the 'Gymnich formula' – which, however, as it was well specified, were not to have been either automatic or institutionalized. Furthermore, the Nine decided to eliminate from the EAD those issues that could not be discussed because they were potentially controversial and divisive: for instance, both oil questions and political matters were removed – satisfying American wishes. Anyway, the dialogue with the Arabs after the Bonn decisions appeared very different from France's initial intentions. The Quai d'Orsay wished to create an alternative cooperation to the Washington pact, but times had changed: the 1973 oil shock was almost over, and Kissinger was succeeding in obtaining discreet successes thanks to so-called 'shuttle diplomacy'. A series of factors was therefore determining the start of a new climate, more extended and cooperative, in the complex patchwork of trans-Atlantic relations. As a consequence, the foreign ministers of the Nine laid down the basis of the collaboration with the Arab countries, according to an institutionalized structure linked to the highest authorities of each partner; in this way it was possible to synchronize and unify EC policy and make relations with the LAS easier. The White House remained worried about the whole initiative, which could potentially strengthen the more radical Arab positions.[32] However, any further American criticism was postponed to the future evolution of the project. Washington seemed to have received valid assurances about the possible anti-American developments of the collaboration with the Arabs; as shown by the later documentation, the European partners – London *in primis* – had in fact promised the White House not to turn the dialogue into a political exchange, not interfering in any way in the American policy in the ME.[33] It was a circumstance that went beyond the principle of the consultations established in Bonn on 10 June, or with the 'Gymnich formula'; de facto, this set a strict limit both on the project of cooperation itself, and on the autonomous development of EC foreign policy. In other words, the White House seemed to control the project, managing its evolution. Washington then applied a sort of silent consent, limiting itself to checking the situation and receiving daily all the updates from Europe. Throughout this process, Italy merely backed the Quai d'Orsay initiatives, trying not to take up a strong position against the United States and Israel; for Italian diplomacy, in fact, the EAD always seemed an opportunity to pursue in order to improve relations with the Arab world and to obtain those essential energy benefits. On the other hand, Palazzo Chigi continued to work on its relationships with the ME governments; for instance, thanks to Moro's journey in early 1974 to the main cities of the area, the Peninsula started promising negotiations in Riyadh to increase oil imports from Saudi Arabia and signed an agreement with Libya for a sizeable increase in supplies of crude. As well as this, the basis was created in many countries for introducing cooperation based on the use of so-called petrodollars in exchange for an increase and improvement in Italian technical, scientific, financial and, above all, industrial presence.[34] This, of course, also encouraged the evolution of EAD. During the visit of the United Arab Emirates foreign minister, Ahmed Khalifa El Suwaidi, in Italy (23–24 July 1974), in fact, both parties openly declared their support for the initiative, hoping to start as soon as possible. The UAE minister was invited by Moro and also met with the President of the Italian Republic Giovanni Leone.[35] This episode clearly showed Italy's positive intentions towards the EAD project and, although not decisive, surely created the premise for its early launch.

The dialogue and Italy's role

On 31 July 1974 the first official meeting took place, in Paris, between the Kuwaiti Foreign Minister, Sheikh Sabah Al-Jaber; the LAS Secretary-General, Mahmoud Riad; the President of the European Commission, François-Xavier Ortoli; and the new EC delegate of the PEC, Jean Sauvagnargues, in order to discuss the organization of the EAD.[36] In this negotiation phase, Italian participation was marginal. Rome's representatives merely supported the EC delegates in the consultation to get the Euro-Arab cooperation off the ground. Even so, it is important to point out how Italy offered all its support for the success of the project. It was in Paris then that the EAD was at last consecrated; it was the official constitutive act which would provide a departure point for concrete and effective collaboration between the parties. However, it was clear that its structure and its possible results could have also provoked policy consequences in relation to the development and the stability of the Arab world. In general all EC members were aware of the difficulties of conducting a dialogue between countries so divergent in background and experience. As a matter of fact, Britain and France had a long history of dealing with the Arabs, while Ireland and Denmark, for instance, were very new to this issue. On the Arab side, national rivalries, enormous differences in wealth and general inexperience in carrying out multilateral technical negotiations could create problems. For these reasons extreme prudence was indicated: it was necessary to first weigh up the possibility of a critical situation occurring. EAD political issues were included in this; they could still potentially be a bone of contention with Washington. Indeed, the Arabs wanted the EC to play a greater role in the ME because of the close geographical historical and cultural ties between the two parties involved. They wanted the Europeans to have a better understanding of the Arab point of view to correct what they regarded as a pro-Israel bias.[37] In this scenario the role of Italy could be important thanks to the traditional friendly policy demonstrated in favour of the countries on the southern shore of the Mediterranean. On 1 August 1974, Moro defined the EAD as 'the natural complementarity and continuity of the European and Arab world', stressing how important it was for Italy.[38] In discussions between European partners, it was the Italian minister who had to relaunch into the dialogue the action program devoted to aiding developing countries, anticipating what would become a constant in North-South relations.[39] Notwithstanding this, during an EAD joint preliminary meeting in October, political issues really began to be the centre of the debates. The Lebanese delegates – Lebanon held at that time the presidency of the LAS Council – in fact, underlined that, because of the ample attendance of states of the Mediterranean area, the dialogue would necessarily have to also deal with ME questions; otherwise, some Arab countries would be deeply disappointed and the whole project would be put in danger.[40] This specification worried the Europeans; the possibility referred to was the principal threat to the success of the EAD, especially as regarded trans-Atlantic limits and constraints. Nevertheless, it would have been difficult for the EC to refuse to listen if some Arab state had made a declaration on the general political situation in the ME at the first General Committee (GC) meeting;[41] this encounter, decided in Paris in July, was to take place for the first time in the French capital on 26 November. The situation worsened after the 7th Summit of the Arab Conference (Rabat, 28 October 1974): the political aspect as an indispensable condition of the EAD was confirmed. The position of the Palestine Liberation Organization (PLO) as the sole legitimate representative of the Palestinian people had been recognized. Then, at the beginning of November Riad officially asked the PEC that a Palestinian delegation be allowed to attend the EAD discussions, albeit initially with observer status only within the GC.[42] The EC Political Committee had a long and controversial debate, but did not succeed in reaching a unitary position; only the French – supported in a very unclear way by the Italians[43] – were prepared to admit the PLO as observer. After all, the joint international implications of such an important choice were manifold and directly involved the relationship with Washington. The consequent EC refusal to comply with this request caused the LAS to decide to suspend the GC meeting.⁴⁴ As a result, the EAD was frozen for several months. Despite all of this, at the beginning of 1975 it seemed clear that the PLO should participate in the EAD if it were to be saved from failure. The issue was taken up again by FitzGerald, the Irish foreign minister and new PEC delegate. Following this, at the next EC foreign ministers meeting in Dublin (13 February 1975) the Nine accepted a compromise proposed by the French and decided to suggest to the Arab states that, as a temporary alternative to the GC summit, the PLO delegates participate in the EAD as member of a unified LAS delegation.⁴⁵ According to the so-called 'Dublin formula', joint expert working groups would meet to start a preliminary part of the dialogue before reaching an agreement about the GC – and on the kind of PLO participation within it. In this way the Europeans focused their attention only on technical matters of the Euro-Arab cooperation, also suggesting that the GC problems might be solved in the future. Thus, the Nine would provisionally go beyond the issue to officially recognize the PLO delegates, but it would permit them to participate. This solution was accepted by the Americans; after all, the White House knew well enough that the Nine were unlikely to have affected a foreign policy which did not accord with that of the United States. Nonetheless, during the next summit of the LAS Council (26 April 1975) the Arabs agreed to accept the 'Dublin formula', starting the EAD with the expert working groups meetings.⁴⁶ The currently available archival documentation does not allow us to understand the Italian position well, but Rome fully supported the Irish initiative; and Italy undoubtedly played an important role in bilateral relations. Immediately after the LAS meeting, in fact, Italian Foreign Minister Mariano Rumor went to Cairo (27–29 April 1975), headquarters of the LAS: Sadat declared that he was pleased with the solution achieved to re-establish the EAD, emphasizing the importance of Europe and especially of Italy in a more direct and concrete approach to the problems of the Arab world.⁴⁷ The first EAD working group rendezvous was held in Cairo (10–15 June 1975) and in the final Joint Memorandum the Nine succeeded in eliminating any direct reference to the more pressing political issues. The Cairo agreement represented an important appreciation of the task carried out by the EC within the Mediterranean area. Notwithstanding this, and despite appearances, it had not been easy to reach this agreement: according to Klaus Meyer, negotiations nearly broke down more than once, but in the end common sense prevailed.⁴⁸ Anyway, the meeting was a success; a confirmation of this was the fact that the parties agreed to meet again in Rome the following month. On this occasion Italy played a central role, although there were many fears about it: Rome did not seem to promise the same guarantees as Dublin. The Italian representative, Cesare Regard, in the organization of the July event gave the impression that he was not up to the situation – UK Foreign Secretary Callaghan had even talked about 'signs of panic' – requiring direct support from the EC group of experts.⁴⁹ The US ambassador in Rome, Volpe, also had some doubts about Italian abilities; he underlined how nervous Rumor was following his taking over of the PEC.⁵⁰ Despite these preambles, the second EAD working group summit (22–24 July 1975) was again a success: the experts drew up a final memorandum containing the guidelines that the Euro-Arab cooperation was to follow in the future.⁵¹ Once more, the underlying political issue of the dialogue was suppressed; the Arab side pushed for the inclusion in the final memorandum of a recommendation that a GC meeting should take place – with no date specified – but the Europeans were successful in avoiding this. The first-rate diplomatic role played by Regard and his collaborators in dodging the new Arab requests to include political issues in the EAD and the accurate communications given to Washington pushed Kissinger to express his personal appreciation to the Italians for their work in the PEC.[52] On the other hand, the GC issue – which could reopen the question of PLO participation – still remained an open question after the Italian summit. In Rome the Arabs had fixed that the next summit of the LAS Council – foreseen for autumn – was supposed to decide if the EAD would continue or not, and eventually if the GC summit would occur before or after the new experts' rendezvous in November. Nonetheless, the Nine still had different opinions about official Palestinian participation in the EAD, as emerged at the EC foreign ministers' Political Consultations in Venice (11–12 September 1975).[53] However, the time then seemed ripe for developing a different collaboration with the Arabs, and EC acceptance of a GC meeting could now be considered a concrete possibility. After all the international scenario was changing rapidly at that time and many situations were entirely new; for example, the Vietnam War had ended, the dictatorial regimes of Greece, Portugal and Spain had succumbed, and the great ascent of the socialist parties in Europe risked completely changing the pre-existing framework of international relations. In other words, the prudent and worried atmosphere in the EC towards the EAD was gradually changing; perhaps indeed the positive results of Cairo and Rome had succeeded in dispelling the last taboos in this sense, making dialogue appear even more like a potential opportunity not to be missed. Furthermore, the Sinai Interim Agreement signed on 4 September 1975 considerably modified the terms of the ME question. Even if the Nine did not think about taking unilateral political action contrary to American wishes, they seemed to feel themselves freer to face this issue without the risk of strong US pressure. Even so, the Mediterranean issue remained very complex, and the Europeans sought to avoid any action that could interfere with the ME negotiation process.[54] Nevertheless, as Regard reported during the meeting of the EAD Coordinating Group of the Nine (Rome, 2 October), following the conclusion of the Sinai Agreement, Egyptians felt bound to do something for the PLO. According to the Italian delegate, the Arabs might regard a continued refusal on the part of the Nine to convene the GC summit as a demonstration of a lack of interest on the part of the Europeans in dialogue.[55] Then, the LAS Council (18–22 October 1975) agreed to accept the third expert working group meeting of November in Abu Dhabi, but Riad formally asked the Nine to fix a date for the summons of the GC.[56] This request was not connected with the new experts' rendezvous, but the LAS's secretary-general clearly indicated that 'the dialogue would soon run into the sands if the Europeans went on blocking the General Commission'.[57] He also remarked that in the GC the Palestinians would only be observers, without voting rights – as in the UN. According to Regard, 'in the circumstances … the Nine risked disaster if they did not meet Riad's request'. The French – as usual – agreed to accept PLO participation, and the Italians were inclined to support them; the British, however, could not accept this as long as the Palestinians rejected Israel's right to exist. As a matter of fact, London had an identical position to that 'suggested' by Washington; the line adopted by the EC majority foresaw that the Arabs might be persuaded to apply the 'Dublin formula' in the GC summit.

Riad preferred not to propose this demand to his Arab colleagues before the November meeting, because it would have meant its certain failure; so it was decided to postpone the issue until after the expert working groups' summit.[58] The Europeans, then, succeeded in putting off the more pressing political issues in the EAD, thus again satisfying American wishes. Consequently, the Abu Dhabi rendezvous (22–25 November 1975) could begin; but, at the inaugural meeting the speech of the LAS's secretary-general, introducing the political issues in the EAD, surprised the Europeans. Riad said it was convinced of the urgent need to schedule the GC summit, considered as a vital body of the machinery of the dialogue. The Abu Dhabi meeting, therefore, had to be a starting point for a new EAD phase.[59] The Nine had no alternative but to accept this course. Abu Dhabi, then, had brought to an end the type of collaboration that had so far taken place. At this point the Europeans seemed to understand that political matters could not be excluded. This primarily meant greater European involvement in the ME's pressing problems, with the obvious remonstrations that this would incur from the United States and Israel. Moreover, some EC partners – the Dutch *in primis* – appeared to believe recognition of the PLO to be inevitable. However, the Italian ambassador, Roberto Gaja, Secretary-General of the *Farnesina*, immediately reassured the White House that Italy would continue to resist such pressures.[60] The Abu Dhabi meeting, then, marked the end of the first phase of the EAD characterized by the expert working groups' rendezvous to open the political stage of the Euro-Arab cooperation. It was in this new setting that the GC meetings took place: the first meeting was held in Luxembourg (18–20 May 1976), with the Europeans succeeding in reapplying the advantageous 'Dublin formula', and in avoiding any unwanted diplomatic involvement.[61] Notwithstanding this, ME issues were the main reason for disagreement both within the LAS and in the relationship between the latter and the EC, undermining any chance of a successful outcome to the project. The subsequent GC rendezvous – Tunis (10–12 February 1977), Brussels (26–28 October 1977) and Damascus (9–11 December 1978) – never succeeded in overcoming this stumbling block. This, despite the announcement of the so-called 'London Declaration' of June 1977[62] and the subsequent 'Venice Declaration' of June 1980.[63]

The maneuvering spaces available to Italian diplomacy in this second part of the project were therefore very limited; Rome attempted to maintain good relations with Arab governments, supporting the EC's line. For instance, in March 1977 the MAE's head, Arnaldo Forlani, went to Egypt and met President Sadat, Foreign Minister Fahmi and Riad; furthermore, on the 26th of the same month, Syrian President Assad received a message from Forlani expressing Italy's commitment to the encouragement of the EAD.[64] In the light of this pledge, on the occasion of Israeli Foreign Minister Dayan's visit to Rome (9–12 January 1978), the Farnesina was concerned with the criticisms Italy could be receiving.[65] Moreover, following the signing of the peace treaty between Cairo and Tel Aviv (26 March 1979) – which led to the expulsion of Egypt from the LAS – Italy was among the first of those Western European countries that called for action to ensure the continuation of the EAD.[66] When Riad's substitute as LAS's general secretary, Chedli Klibi, went to Rome both in January and in May 1980 – following Italy's taking over of the PEC – and, meeting with the Italian foreign minister, tried to resume the dialogue, the premises for the 'Venice Declaration' were laid down.⁶⁷ At the EC meeting in Venice of the heads of state and government (12–13 June), therefore, Rome played an important role in the choices that were made and that brought Europe to a direct commitment to Middle Eastern issues. However, despite the Thorn mission in the Middle East and the first EAD political meeting in Luxembourg (12–13 November 1980), the Euro-Arab project came to a standstill in the following years.⁶⁸

Conclusions

Despite the fact that attempts to make this type of collaboration permanent had failed, the EAD represented an important development opportunity for both sides: expectations and hopes that, on both sides, gradually disappeared over the years in an increasingly evolving and ever-complex international scenario. However, some of the choices seemed really difficult to make, especially in view of the pressing problem of Palestine, resulting in long and difficult negotiations from the outset. This turbulent process was also surely partly due to the originality of the project and the intricate arguments it dealt with, to which, in the early stages, was added the White House's hostility: Washington's fears of seeing a real instrument capable of lending itself to Arab pressure on the EC brought to light the weaknesses and divisions in the European camp, putting the creation of any hypothetical cooperation at risk of failure. Washington's stance in fact excluded from negotiations two important issues, the energy issue, the real motive for EC interest in the EAD, and – at least during the early years – a direct involvement in the Middle East peace question. This demonstrated once again the persistent American capacity to direct the decisions of the Nine. All this contributed to establishing a project decidedly different from that which the Quai d'Orsay had imagined during the difficult months of the 1973 oil crisis.

Nevertheless, the enormous dichotomies on the goals to be given to the EAD also had a considerable impact: the Europeans continued to push for technical, economic and cultural cooperation, but the Arabs did not budge from their insistence on including political issues in the negotiations. The wish of several Arab countries to join the project as a means of applying pressure in order to obtain diplomatic concessions, first among them being the official recognition of the PLO as the only legitimate representative of the Palestinian people, and of having greater contractual strength to the detriment of Israel – in the framework of the regional dispute – were among the main reasons for the eventual lack of cooperation.

Despite everything, Italy played an important role in the evolution of the EAD. This was also thanks to their traditional friendly policy demonstrated in favour of the countries on the southern shore of the Mediterranean, in a context where national energy supplies indicated a non-conflictual relationship with the oil producer countries. In several stages of the Euro-Arab project Rome was in fact particularly active and, despite some doubts, proved to be equal to the other European partners. It was no coincidence that a decisive step was taken in Venice, and the phase of European direct involvement in the Middle East began, a result which, even up to the last moment, no one would have thought possible. Furthermore, although there are not many archive documents available, the Italian diplomatic contribution was an undeniable attempt to make a success of the EAD. In the following period, Italy continued to seek to keep the project alive, within the Middle East policy stance taken by President of the Council Bettino Craxi and Foreign Minister Giulio Andreotti. In the 1980s, in fact, there was an intense cycle of visits to Arab countries: even if the goal of these meetings was to improve bilateral agreements, it was also an opportunity to speak about EAD. In January 1985, for instance, Andreotti met in Rome the LAS's Secretary-General Klibi, and Euro-Arab cooperation was at the centre of the debate.[69] A last attempt to resume the dialogue was also made by Andreotti in October 1988 in Tunis, meeting Klibi again,[70] but the project failed to survive the Iraqi invasion of 2 August 1990 and the consequent Gulf conflict.

Notes

1 For Western European governments, the author refers to the European Economic Community governments.
2 For a study on the EC Mediterranean and foreign policy see, for instance, David Allen and Alfred Pijpers (eds), *European Foreign Policy-Making and the Arab-Israeli Conflict* (The Hague: Martinus Nijhoff, 1984); David Allen, Reinhardt Rummel and Wolfang Wessels, *European Political Cooperation: Towards a Foreign Policy for Western Europe* (Oxford: Butterworth-Heinemann, 1982); Federica Bicchi, *European Foreign Policy Making toward the Mediterranean* (New York: Palgrave Macmillan, 2007); Ricardo Gomez, *Negotiating the Euro-Mediterranean Partnership: Strategic Action in EU Foreign Policy?* (Aldershot: Ashgate, 2003); Daniel Möckli, *European Foreign Policy during the Cold War: Heath, Brandt, Pompidou and the Dream of Political Unity* (London: Tauris, 2009).
3 'Necessary Progress in Community Energy policy, Communication from the Commission to the Council forwarded on 13 October 1972', Brussels, 4 October 1972, *Bulletin of the European Communities*, Supplement, 11/72.
4 *Orientations et actions prioritaires pour la politique énergétique communautaire, Communication de la Commission au Conseil, Commission des Communautés Européennes*, Brussels, 19 April 1973, HAEU, EN, n. 81.
5 For European energy policy the author refers to the attempts to create collaboration in this sector between Belgium, France, Federal Republic of Germany, Italy, Luxemburg and the Netherlands (also including UK, Ireland and Denmark from 1973 with the accession of these countries into the EC).
6 Cf. Silvio Labbate, *Il governo dell'energia. L'Italia dal petrolio al nucleare, 1945–1975* (Firenze: Le Monnier, 2010); Labbate, 'Italy and the Development of the European Energy Policy: From the Dawn of the Integration Process to the 1973 Oil Crisis', *European Review of History* 20 (2013), 67–93.
7 Cf. Massimiliano Cricco, 'Dalla genesi del secondo piano Rogers alle premesse della guerra dello Yom Kippur (1970–1973)', in Daniele Caviglia and Massimiliano Cricco (eds), *La diplomazia italiana e gli equilibri mediterranei: La politica mediorientale dell'Italia dalla guerra dei Sei Giorni al conflitto dello Yom Kippur, 1967–1973* (Soveria Mannelli: Rubbettino, 2006), 95.

8   For further investigation on Moro and the Italian energy policy, see Silvio Labbate, 'Aldo Moro e la politica energetica dell'Italia', in Francesco Perfetti, Andrea Ungari, Daniele Caviglia and Daniele De Luca (eds), *Aldo Moro nell'Italia contemporanea* (Firenze: Le Lettere, 2011), 705–34.
9   *Report on the activities of the ECC for the year 1971 by the Minister of Foreign Affairs (Moro)*, Camera dei Deputati, V Legislatura, 27 December 1971, HAEU, EM, nn. 27–8.
10 Cf. Silvio Labbate, 'Energy and Transatlantic Relations: From the Attempts to Establish a European Policy to the Eve of the 1973 Oil Crisis', *Journal of European Integration History* 20 (2014), n. 1, 105.
11 Cf. Daniel Yergin, *The Prize: The Epic Quest for Oil, Money and Power* (New York: Simon & Schuster, 1991), 606–32.
12 *Tel. n. 508 from Brussels to the FCO*, Brussels, 6 November 1973, TNA, FCO, *The Year of Europe: America, Europe and the Energy Crisis, 1972–1974*, Documents on British Policy Overseas, s. III, vol. IV, Keith Hamilton and Patrick Salmon (eds) (London: Routledge, 2006), doc. 375.
13 For Nine the author refers to the nine European partners.
14 Cf. *Tel n. 1122 From Sir Philip Adams, British Ambassador in Cairo, to the FCO*, Cairo, 8 November 1973, TNA, FCO, *The Year of Europe*, doc. 382.
15 Cf. *Discorso del ministro Moro alla Commissione Esteri della Camera*, Rome, 28 February 1974, ACS, AM, 1, Scritti e discorsi 1953–78, annuali, b. 29.
16 *Tel n. 1534 From Sir Alec Douglas-Home, SecState for the FCA, to UK Representative in Brussels*, London, 13 December 1973, TNA, FCO, *The Year of Europe*, doc. 457.
17 For further examination see Silvio Labbate, 'The beginning of the Euro-Arab Dialogue and the Trans-Atlantic relations (1973–1975)', *Nuova Rivista Storica* CI (2017), II, 347–70.
18 For a survey of the EAD see, for instance, David Allen, 'The Euro-Arab Dialogue', *Journal of Common Market Studies* 4 (1977), 323–42; Allen and Andrin Hauri, 'The Euro-Arab Dialogue, the Venice Declaration and Beyond', in Daniel Möckli and Victor Mauer (eds), *European-American Relations and the Middle East* (London: Routledge, 2010), 93–107; Nijmeddin Al-Dajani, 'The Euro-Arab Dialogue: The Arab Viewpoint', in Edmond Völker (ed.), *The Euro-Arab Cooperation* (Leyden: Sijthoff, 1976), 213–21; Haifaa A. Jawad, *Euro-Arab Relations: A Study in Collective Diplomacy* (Reading: Ithaca Press, 1992); Silvio Labbate, *Illusioni mediterranee: Il dialogo euro-arabo* (Firenze: Le Monnier, 2016).
19 Cf. *Memorandum of Conversation between SecState (Kissinger) and Italian Foreign Minister (Aldo Moro)*, Brussels, 10 December 1973, NARA, NPMP, Presidential Henry Alfred Kissinger MemCons.
20 Cf. *Memorandum by the MAE Director General of Political Affairs, Roberto Ducci, to the Minister of Foreign Affairs, Aldo Moro*, Rome, 13 January 1974, ACS, AM, s. 6, MAE, Visite e questioni diverse, b. 31.
21 *MAE internal memorandum, Conversations with Israel's ambassador (R. Tancredi)*, Rome, 13 February 1974, GA, Israele e Palestina, 2, Israele-Italia, 1949–2007, f. 1, b. 478.
22 Cf. *MAE internal memorandum*, DGAP, Ufficio IX, Rome, 19 January 1974, ACS, AM, s. 6, MAE, Visite e questioni diverse, b. 31.
23 Cf. *MAE internal memorandum for the Foreign Minister Moro (Ducci)*, Rome, 1 March 1974, ACS, AM, s. 6, MAE, Visite e questioni diverse, b. 40.
24 Cf. *Tel n. 436 from Sir Alec Douglas-Home, SecState for FCA, to UK Representative in Washington*, London, 20 February 1974, TNA, FCO, *The Year of Europe*, doc. 558.

25 Cf. *Meeting Minutes between Michael S. Weir, Counsellor and Head of Chancery of UK Mission in New York, and Alan Campbell, Assistant Under-SecState for FCA*, London, 6 March 1974, TNA, FCO, *The Year of Europe*, doc. 564.
26 *Internal memorandum (Craig), NENAD*, 6 March 1974, TNA, FCO 30/2513.
27 Cf. *Tel n. 817 from Sir Peter Ramsbotham, British Ambassador in Washington, to the FCO*, Washington, 7 March 1974, TNA, FCO, *The Year of Europe*, doc. 565. See also Henry Alfred Kissinger, *Years of Upheaval* (Boston: Little, Brown, 1982), 899–900.
28 Cf. *EAD: Waiting for the British, Tel n. 3722 from the US Embassy in Bonn to the SecState (Hillenbrand)*, Bonn, 8 March 1974, Access to Archival Databases AAD, NARA, RG 59, GRDS, CFPF, ET, 1/1/1974 - 12/31/1974.
29 Cf. *European Role in Mideast, Tel n. 6406 from the US Embassy in Bonn to the SecState (Cash)*, Bonn, 23 April 1974, AAD, NARA, RG 59, GRDS, CFPF, ET, 1/1/1974 - 12/31/1974.
30 Cf. Christopher Hill and Karen E. Smith (eds), *European Foreign Policy. Key Documents* (London: Routledge, 2000), 97–8; Simon J. Nuttall, *European Political Cooperation* (Oxford: Clarendon Press, 1992), 18.
31 Cf. *Note du Secrétaire Général adjoint (SGa) de la CCE, Klaus Meyer, à l'attention de Monsieur le Président Ortoli et al.*, Brussels, 24 June 1974, HAEU, KM, n. 39.
32 Cf. *EC/Arab, Tel n. 15597 from the US Embassy in Paris to the SecState (Stone)*, Paris, 26 June 1974, AAD, NARA, RG 59, GRDS, CFPF, ET, 1/1/1974 - 12/31/1974.
33 Cf. *EAD Hits Snag, Tel n. 15322 from US Embassy in London to the SecState (Spiers)*, London, 22 November 1974, AAD, NARA, RG 59, GRDS, CFPF, ET, 1/1/1974 - 12/31/1974.
34 Cf. *Discorso del ministro Moro alla Commissione Esteri della Camera*, Rome, 28 February 1974, ACS, AM, 1, Scritti e discorsi 1953–78, Annuali, b. 29.
35 Cf. *Visita del ministro degli esteri dell'Unione emirati arabi a Roma (23–24 luglio)* in MAE-Servizio Storico e Documentazione, *1974. Testi e Documenti sulla politica estera dell'Italia* (Rome: Tipo-litografia L. Chiovini 1975), 331–32.
36 Cf. *EPC: Record of the ME Experts' meeting on Paris on 2 August 1974*, Paris, 2 August 1974, TNA, FCO, 96/157.
37 Cf. *EAD: Objectives*, Paper produced by the FCO, London, 24 September 1974, TNA, FCO, 96/158.
38 A. Moro, *Scritti e discorsi*, G. Rossini (ed.), vol. VI, 1974–8 (Rome: Cinque Lune, 1990), 3168.
39 Cr. *Premier programme d'action du dialogue euro-arabe, Note du SGa de la CCE, Klaus Meyer, à Monsieur De Kergorlay, Directeur général adjoint, et Monsieur Durieux, Directeur à la DG VIII*, Brussels, 3 October 1974, HAEU, KM, n. 39.
40 Cf. *Note du SGa de la CCE, Klaus Meyer, à l'attention de M. le Président François-Xavier Ortoli et al.*, Brussels, 16 October 1974, HAEU, KM, n. 39.
41 The GC had to be composed of the representatives of all of the twenty-nine countries concerned and had the task of formulating the theoretical framework of the project.
42 Cf. *EAD, Note du SGa de la CCE, Klaus Meyer, à l'attention de Monsieur le Président Ortoli et al.*, Brussels, 8 November 1974, HAEU, KM, n. 39.
43 In fact, the Italians seemed to be inclined to support the French, but in a telegram to Washington, the Deputy General Director of Political Affairs of the Farnesina explicitly stated, 'The [EC] ministers agreed, with reluctant French consent, that PLO should not rpt not be allowed to sit in on Euro-Arab dialogue, even with observer status' (Cf. *EC Ministerial, November 18, Tel. n. 16177 from US Embassy in Rome to the

Secretary of State, Rome, 19 November 1974, AAD, NARA, RG 59, GRDS, CFPF, ET, 1/1/1974–12/31/1974).

44 Cf. *EAD - PLO Participation, Tel n. 27602 from US Embassy in Paris to the SecState (Rush)*, Paris, 19 November 1974, AAD, NARA, RG 59, GRDS, CFPF, ET, 1 January 1974–12 December 1974.

45 Cf. *February 13 Foreign Ministers' Meeting: EAD, Tel n. 317 from US Embassy in Dublin to the SecState (Rendahl)*, Dublin, 14 February 1975, AAD, NARA, RG 59, GRDS, CFPF, ET, 1 January 1975–12 December 1975.

46 Cf. *Note du SGa de la CCE, Klaus Meyer, à l'attention de M. Roland de Margerie, M. Hannay, M. de Sedouy*, Brussels, 29 April 1975, HAEU, KM, n. 40.

47 Cf. *Visita al Cairo del ministro on. Mariano Rumor (27-29 aprile)* in MAE-Servizio Storico e Documentazione, *1975. Testi e Documenti sulla politica estera dell'Italia* (Rome: Tipo-litografia L. Chiovini 1976), 166–73.

48 Cf. *Note du SGa de la CCE, Klaus Meyer, à l'attention de MM. Les membres de la Commission*, Brussels, 16 June 1975, HAEU, KM, n. 40.

49 Cf. *EAD, Meeting of Coordinating Group, Dublin, 20 June, Tel from the FCO to the PEC*, London, 23 June 1975, TNA, FCO, 30/3031.

50 Cf. *EC: Partial Schedule, Upcoming Meetings in Italy, Tel n. 9359 from US Embassy in Rome to the SecState (Volpe)*, Rome, 30 June 1975, AAD, NARA, RG 59, GRDS, CFPF, ET, 1 Janury 1975–12 December 1975.

51 Cf. *Joint Working Paper, Internal Note (R.Q. Braithwaite, Head of European Integration Department–FCO)*, Rome, 24 July 1975, TNA, FCO, 30/3037.

52 Cf. *Italian PEC, Tel n. 175300 from the SecState to the US Embassy in Rome (Kissinger)*, Washington, 25 July 1975, AAD, NARA, RG 59, GRDS, CFPF, ET, 1 January 1975–12 December 1975.

53 Cf. *EC Foreign Ministers Political Consultations, Venice: EAD, Tel n. 08199 from the US Mission to the EC to the SecState (Greenwald)*, Brussels, 15 September 1975, AAD, NARA, RG 59, GRDS, CFPF, ET, 1 January 1975–12 December 1975.

54 Cf. *EAD, Tel n. 15088 from the US Embassy in London to the SecState (Richardson)*, London, 30 September 1975, AAD, NARA, RG 59, GRDS, CFPF, ET, 1 January 1975–12 December 1975.

55 Cf. *EAD, Meeting of the Co-ordinating Group–Rome 2 October 1975*, Rome, October 2, 1975, TNA, FCO, 30/3039.

56 Cf. EAD, *Tel from PEC to all COREU*, Rome, 23 October 1975, TNA, FCO, 30/3039.

57 *EAD: Meeting of the General Commission, Tel from PEC to all COREU*, Rome, 25 October 1975, TNA, FCO, 30/3039.

58 Cf. *EAD - Mission de la Présidence de la délégation Européenne auprès du Secrétariat de la Ligue Arabe au Caire (5-6 novembre)*, Tel from PEC to all COREU, Rome, 7 November 1975, TNA, FCO, 30/3040.

59 Cf. *Speech Delivered By H. E. Mahmoud Riad, Secretary General of the LAS at the Inaugural Meeting of Euro-Arab Experts in Abu Dhabi*, Abu Dhabi, 22 November 1975, TNA, FCO, 30/3042.

60 Cf. *Preparations for European Council Meeting: Rome, December 1-2-Conversation with Ambassador Gaja, Tel. n. 279393 from the SecState to US Embassy in Rome*, Washington, 26 November 1975, AAD, NARA, RG 59, GRDS, CFPF, ET, 1 Janury 1975–12 December 1975.

61 Cf. *Euro-Arab Dialogue, General Committee Luxembourg, 18–20 May 1976, Internal note*, London, 21 May 1976, TNA, FCO, 98/194.

62 Cr. 'Political Cooperation–Statement on the Middle East', *Bulletin of the European Communities*, 6/77, 62.
63 Cr. *Déclaration du Conseil Européen sur le Moyen-Orient, Venice, 12–13 juin 1980*, Venice, 13 June 1980, HAEU, KM, n. 44.
64 Cf. *Egitto. Visita del ministro degli Esteri, on. Forlani (12–14 marzo)* in MAE-Servizio Storico e Documentazione, *1977. Testi e Documenti sulla politica estera dell'Italia* (Rome: Istituto Poligrafico e Zecca dello Stato, 1979), 175–7 and 16.
65 Cf. *MAE Internal Memorandum, Visit of Israeli Foreign Minister Dayan to Rome (January 9–12, 1978) – Ideas for Conversations on political Issues*, Rome (not dated), GA, Israele e Palestina, 8, Personalità israeliane, f. 10, b. 480. Actually, the EAD did not appear among the topics discussed (cf. *The Diplomatic Councilor of the President of the Council of Ministers, Conversation between the President of the Council, Mr Andreotti and the Foreign Minister of Israel Dayan*, Rome, 10 January 1978, ibid.).
66 Cf. 'Riunione del Consiglio dei ministri degli Esteri (Bruxelles, 20 novembre)', in MAE-Servizio Storico e Documentazione, *1979: Testi e Documenti sulla politica estera dell'Italia* (Rome: Istituto Poligrafico e Zecca dello Stato 1981), 279.
67 Cf. 'Medio Oriente. Visita del Segretario Generale della Lega Araba, Chedli Klibi (Roma, 22 maggio)', in MAE-Servizio Storico e Documentazione, *1980: Testi e Documenti sulla politica estera dell'Italia* (Rome: Istituto Poligrafico e Zecca dello Stato 1983), 290.
68 Cf. Dialogo euro-arabo (Lussemburgo, 12–13 novembre), in ibid., 382–5.
69 Cf. 'Medio Oriente. Colloquio tra il ministro degli Esteri on. Andreotti ed il segretario generale della Lega Araba Klibi (Roma, 8 gennaio)', in MAE-Servizio Storico e Documentazione, *1985: Testi e Documenti sulla politica estera dell'Italia* (Rome: Istituto Poligrafico e Zecca dello Stato, 1990), 235.
70 Cf. 'Visita del Ministro degli Esteri on. Andreotti (Tunisi, 22 ottobre)', in MAE-Servizio Storico e Documentazione, *1988: Testi e Documenti sulla politica estera dell'Italia* (Rome: Istituto Poligrafico e Zecca dello Stato, 1993), 290.

7

Italy and the Lebanese 'civil' war

Roberta La Fortezza

Speaking of 'civil' war with reference to the fifteen years of clashes which ravaged Lebanon[1] starting from 1975 is at least reductive. The Lebanese war theatre was in fact characterized by the intertwining of a set of dynamics, interests, tensions, historical events, equilibrium and disequilibrium, not only internal but also external, so complicated and confused that the Lebanese context becomes an enigma almost impossible to solve, an 'intricate tangle of complex problems and conflicting interests'.[2] If undoubtedly the war acquires the connotation of a 'civil' conflict in connection with the historical tensions between Muslims and Christians, on the other hand, it cannot be defined merely as a religious conflict, given that its development also involves many other directives and perspectives. The intra-religion conflict; the Palestinian question and the internal 'civil' war within the Palestinian Movement, divided those who supported Arafat[3]'s approach 'a gun and an olive branch'[4] and those who took a stand against such an approach; the interests of the two Lebanese neighbours, Israel and Syria, their internal and relational dynamics within the regional context; the conflicts, the regional revolutions and even the peace agreements: all of these were the protagonists, sometimes invisible, sometimes more manifest, of the Lebanese 'civil' war. It is in this precise, highly precarious context that the Italian government's action, first political-diplomatic and then military, will take place.

Italy and the first phases of the Lebanese war

The structuring and the subsequent hardening of the political struggle conducted by the PLO provoked enormous upheavals in the region in the years between 1960 and 1970. By the beginning of the following decade, the Palestinian issue had definitely assumed political relevance[5] and had become the key point in the redefinition of the regional governance and, at the same time, the first and deepest limitation in the research for possible solutions. When in 1975 Lebanese tensions burst, disclosing the essential link between the Palestinian issue and the dilemma of the same stability of the Land of the Cedars, the Italian government immediately had a clear idea of the situation: the implosion of Lebanon had to be framed in the more general context of the region along with its inconsistencies, with a particular reference to the political escalation of the Palestinian refugees issue and their national liberation movement. The evolution of the Lebanese situation could not be understood without reference 'to the stagnation of the negotiation dynamics'[6] in the Israeli-Palestinian issue, to the problem of the acceptance of the principle according to which the Palestinian people should have an independent homeland and state[7] and to that of the recognition of the PLO as the legitimate representative in the negotiation process. After all, the problem of the recognition of the PLO as legitimate representative of the Palestinian people was one of the central dilemmas of Italian politics: such recognition was seen by a large number of Italian politicians as the only possible way to show their concrete support for the Palestinian right to self-determination and for the recognition of their national rights and, in particular, as the bravest deterrence measure against Israel.[8] From 1976, when Syria's presence in the Lebanese context was becoming more and more evident, Italian politics focused on the requests of unconditional withdrawal of the Syrian army, whose operations were directed by Hafiz al-Assad. The Italian parliamentary opposition, in particular, kept requesting the government for a strong and urgent intervention so that Lebanon would not become the sacrificial victim of the Syrian regime;[9] they demanded the withdrawal of the Syrian troops from Lebanon, called for Italian pressure on Syrian authority in that direction,[10] for the solution of the Palestinian issue and the guarantee of the integrity and unity of Lebanon. Italian commitment to the issue of 'Lebanon's political unity and territorial integrity'[11] would have actually become a permanent feature of Italian international policy throughout the long Lebanese conflict. It was seen as the only possible means to restore stability in the region and to avoid the exacerbation of the crisis. In this respect, as a matter of fact, Rome's perspective proved to be farsighted: a crucial role in the Lebanese 'civil' war was actually played by the two neighbouring countries, Israel and Syria, which had their own interests, each in its own way, in the little former Ottoman province of Lebanon. Syrian appetites first and then Israeli ones could have had a determining role in marking the definitive disappearance of the country of Lebanon as an autonomous and independent entity. If France had already established its role as guardian of the independence of this little state, since its creation, surrounded by possible threats, Rome, too, in that moment of greatest need, stood in defence of the sovereignty of the country with which it had shared a long history of friendly relations. In August 1976, Enrico Berlinguer drew the attention of the Italian government to the necessity to undertake 'an immediate and effective initiative' in order to contribute to 'bringing a definitive end to the Palestinian massacre and to the bloodbath which causes every day hundreds of deaths and injuries among the populations of Lebanon'.[12] The solution proposed by the secretary of the Italian Communist Party (PCI) was to promote a dialogue among all Lebanese forces with 'the full participation of the representatives of the Palestinian people'.[13] Therefore, in this respect, it was further stressed how the Lebanese question was inextricably linked to the long-standing issue of the recognition of the PLO as a decisive interlocutor at the negotiating table. Syrian intervention represents, in the PCI leader's speech, the main obstacle to the start of this dialogue and to the achievement of a truce. According to Berlinguer, the Syrian army served the interests of international imperialism forces and of the most reactionary forces both of the State of Israel and of the Arab countries, which are now giving the impression, in an increasingly clear way, that their actions are aimed at the achieving of a sort of 'final solution'[14] of the Palestinian issue: a solution, in other words, which aims at the extermination of these people. We cannot passively witness the cold and ruthless execution of this tragedy. Nor can we simply make pleas, requests, invocations.[15]

Giulio Andreotti, head of the Italian government from July 1976 to August 1979, was the one to announce to the Chamber of Deputies that the Foreign Minister Arnaldo Forlani had organised a meeting with the Italian ambassadors to Middle Eastern countries in order to 'have them report about the situation and to study the possible coordinated actions to support all the initiative aimed at achieving terms of truce and providing assistance to the population involved'.[16] In Italian political circles, it was clear that Lebanon not only constituted an 'act of atrocious genocide of an entire population, defenceless and innocent',[17] but represented also a dangerous hotbed of conflict in the Mediterranean.[18] In this context, Italy, for its own vocation of peace and for the interests it had in the area, had to assume a

specific fostering task in the adoption of interventions and measures aimed at bringing an end to a situation, tragic from a human outlook and in evident violation of the international laws on human rights.[19]

For the first two years of the crisis, Italy considered Lebanon as a 'victim', on one hand, of the international impasse in the Israeli-Palestinian negotiation, and, on the other hand, of Syrian appetites. When, on 16 October 1976, a settlement was reached in Riyadh, Italy and the whole international community were deceived into thinking that the war was over, and that Lebanon could begin again to build peace. In fifteen years of war, there was an infinite series of truces: the 'end of the Lebanese war' was announced in November 1976, again in 1982, twice, and yet again in 1987. But the war restarted every time, destroying everything they managed to rebuild in the meantime, and above all destroying every faint illusion of achieving peace. While the international community was misled into thinking that the Lebanese issue was already settled, and while the main focus was the difficult situation of Lebanon which was dealing with 'the serious problem of the reconstruction',[20] on 14 March 1978, Israel launched the operation '*Litani*' by occupying the southern Litani River area. Italian politics focus shifted, in a natural yet sudden way, from the northern border of Lebanon to the southern one, that is from Syria to Israel. In particular, the target of the accusations was the unscrupulous policy that Israel was pursuing in Lebanon. Gorla and Pinto, members of the Italian parliament, questioned the government about what position Italy intended to take concerning the serious attack perpetrated by Israel against the Palestinian people in Lebanese territory. The same members of the Italian parliament, in fact, stressed how the Israeli attack went far beyond the logic of retaliation, proving to be ultimately a genuine invasion against the territorial integrity of Lebanon 'aimed at the genocide of the Palestinian people'.[21] Following Israeli action, the Lebanese crisis reached such an extent that the security of the entire Middle East region was endangered[22] and carried also the risk of complicating the relations between the two superpowers: the Israeli direct invasion, endorsed and supported by US policy, challenged Syria, Russia's ally. The danger was so inherent in the Israeli action that Ezer Weizman, Ministry of Defence, during the press conference hastened to announce: 'I hope ... that Syria will understand that it is an operation limited to southern Lebanon'.[23] At that point Italy addressed the United Nations and the European Economic Community (EEC), stressing the need to find a global solution to the Lebanese crisis. In fact, the United Nations decided to intervene to restore the *status quo,* with Security Council Resolution no. 425 of 19 March 1978,[24] in response to a Lebanese request, and the UNIFIL (United Nations Interim Force in Lebanon) mission was established, with the purpose of supervising the withdrawal of Israeli forces from southern Lebanon, the cessation of the hostilities and assisting the Lebanese government in reasserting its authority in the area involved in the conflict. The repercussions from the Lebanese crisis in the entire area started to be particularly evident, and the peace process emerged as a 'priority interest for Europe'.[25] In this respect, the farsighted approach that Italy tried to pursue was that of a collective responsibility for the future of Lebanon and of the Mediterranean. The Italian government, along with the other eight members of the EEC, wanted to make sure that the integrity of Lebanon would be preserved, and that the intervention of forces which could further undermine the already precarious political situation would be avoided.[26] As a matter of fact, Lebanon in 1978 was already saturated with 'foreign bodies': Palestinians, Syrians, Israelis and now the international community. In 1979, the III Foreign Affairs Committee briefly reviewed the military interventions in Lebanon: firstly the 'green helmets' of the Arab Deterrent Force (ADF) and consequently Syrian interference in Lebanese affairs; then 'the southern territory has been occupied for some months by the Israelis', for some time in spring 1978, according to the committee, Iraqi units had operated in Lebanon; finally UN 'blue helmets' arrived.[27] In 1979 the situation did not yet allow the realization that Lebanon's response to this plethora of foreign elements would be the natural one of the immune system of an assaulted, wounded and torn body. With the beginning of the new decade, the Lebanese question started, for the Italian state, to take on new and scary forms, which did not concern the international scenario but Italy's own internal dynamics. There were several interpellations by various members of the Italian parliament referring to the issue of the training camps for Palestinian guerrilla fighters in Libya, Yemen and Lebanon. In fact, there were rumours about the presence of some Italians in those training camps. The horrendous nightmare of a coordination, or even an interaction, between Italian domestic terrorism and the international one was emerging. On 3 February 1981, Prime Minister Forlani, answering the interpellations made on the question up to that moment, confirmed that, according to Italian intelligence agencies, some records of those camps documented the passage of some Italians. The same Italian intelligence agencies, Forlani reported, stressed that 'such structures often responded to national defence systems, or in any case for different purposes; systems that used in various ways mercenaries and elements from diverse backgrounds'.[28] In addition to data, episodes and information, more or less ascertained, about this affiliation between international and Italian domestic terrorism, a comprehensive political evaluation could not be conducted – Forlani further pointed out – without taking into account the observation that there was a convergence of motivations and goals between the two kinds of terrorisms:

> When we speak of terrorist international connections, we have to consider the analysis in relation to the events characterizing the international scene and to evaluate in a careful and objective way the actions which contributed to the destabilization in various regions of the world. These actions have given rise to the suspicion that there might exist or insert international strategies aimed at fomenting crisis situations.[29]

While, from the point of view of internal security, the looming scenarios were hardly reassuring, the beginning of the new decade led, instead, to a certain optimism with regard to the international dynamics in relation to the Lebanese situation. A hopeful attitude arose from the speech of the Italian Foreign Affairs Minister, Emilio Colombo, at the beginning of October 1981:

> Some encouraging signs are provided by the evolution in Lebanon, where, despite the general picture of widespread anarchy prevailing in some parts of the country, some room for manoeuvre has been preserved for possible diplomatic actions. These find their premise in the preservation of the 'ceasefire' declared last year on July 24th in Southern Lebanon, committing both Israel and the PLO, and also in the still open perspectives of a possible national reconciliation among Lebanese factions, participating in the existing operation through the Arab quadripartite committee.[30]

Colombo's optimism would be swept away some months later, when on June 3rd, 1982 Israel launched a new version, on a notably larger scale, of the 1978 operation. This time the operation was called 'Peace of the Galilee' and would not have been limited to penetrating southern Lebanon, but would have reached the gates of Beirut. A new phase of the war in Lebanon was now starting, the one we could define as the 'Israeli phase'. The Lebanese crisis, from the Italian point of view, was now a situation increasingly charged with uncertainties and dangers, such as jeopardizing the political unity and the same territorial integrity of the country and consequently the security of the entire Middle Eastern region. The Israeli action of 1982 stirred up 1978 fears of a more extensive regional conflict and even of the participation of global actors. The question addressed to the Italian government was always the same: what initiatives they wanted to undertake to preserve political unity and territorial integrity of Lebanon. The government's most concrete answer would arrive precisely following the situation that arose after the 'Peace in Galilee' operation, when Italy would combine its diplomatic approach with the military intervention.

'The continuation of politics by other means': The Italian military involvement in Lebanon

Between the end of the 1970s and the beginning of the 1980s, Italy started to show a stronger inclination towards a more active role and towards the assumption of greater responsibilities in the Middle Eastern region. The first act of this more active phase, also from the military point of view of Italian politics, was Rome's willingness to participate in the Multinational Force and Observers (MFO) deployed in the Sinai. Starting from 1979, Italy participated in the mission ITALAIR, which provided air support for UN ground forces involved in the UNIFIL mission operating in southern Lebanon.[31] This first participation in the peace operation in Lebanon demonstrated, as Arnaldo Forlani pointed out in October 1980, Italian willingness to 'actively contribute to the preservation of peace and to the gradual solution of the problems of an area to which our country is tied by culture and history'.[32] In this respect, the Italian commitment in Lebanon of 1982 was the culmination of this new political-diplomatic approach. Lebanon was, in fact, a long-standing friend of the Italian peninsula, a country with which it had shared thousands of years made of political, economical and cultural relations. Notwithstanding the complexity, the difficulty and the destruction, both political and military, persisting in Lebanon, the ancient friendly country would show also in the 1980s, in the middle of war, how different and more intimate its relation with Italy was, even compared with the one the old Maronites' refuge had with France. It was mostly the policy of impartiality, which reached its highest level precisely in the Lebanese situation, to further protect and preserve the Italian mission in Beirut. The idea of the establishment of the first Multinational Force in Lebanon (MNF) began to emerge in June 1982, immediately after the Israeli invasion of the Land of the Cedars, within the framework of negotiations and then of the definition of the Habib[33] *Plan* designed to bring an end to the hostilities between Israel, Lebanon and the PLO.[34] Precisely in the context of such an agreement, Lebanon officially asked the United States, France and Italy to participate in the multinational force to be deployed in Lebanon for a maximum of thirty days, renewable. Based on the results of the negotiations conducted by Habib, the MNF had the specific tasks of allowing the evacuation of the Palestinian guerrillas from West Beirut which was still besieged by the Israelis, facilitating the clearing of the armed Palestinian resistance and guaranteeing their safety until the boarding of the ships that would take the guerrillas to Tunisia, Jordan, the Sudan, Yemen and Iraq or on the entire overland transfer along the corridor towards Damascus. The Italian choice to take part in the MNF, participation which had been expressly requested by Lebanon, above all by virtue of that particular trust and friendship towards the Italians, fitted perfectly with the humanitarian approach to the Lebanese crisis Italy had maintained throughout the 1970s; but it also had political bases, both in its motivations and, even more, in its consequences. If, from the humanitarian point of view, the evacuation of the Palestinian guerrillas would have resulted in the cessation of the Israeli indiscriminate bombing, from the political perspective, safeguarding the evacuation of the Palestinians would mean also ensuring 'the survival, at least potential, of their political movement'.[35] The political consequence, conscious or not, reasoned or not, of that military action was that of ensuring a future for the PLO, although 'in countries and horizons far from Lebanon and thus even further away from the land claimed by the Palestinians'.[36] For Italy it was also a 'tangible sign of the constant commitment in favour of dialogue and negotiation, which alone can lead to the creation of a climate of greater trust between Arabs and Israelis'.[37] So, from the Italian perspective, such a military mission could not be absolutely separated from the political intent and, above all, should be contextualized within both the management of the Lebanese crisis and more generally of the Arab–Israeli conflict and of the entire international issue which reverberated around the Middle East. This idea fully reflected the political-diplomatic approach Italy had adopted since the start of the crisis. On 26 August 1982, the ITALCON contingent, composed of five hundred soldiers from the Bersaglieri regiments, landed in Beirut in order to support the eight hundred French paratroopers and the eight hundred US marines landed in the previous days. MNF forces would later be supported *in loco* also by approximately three thousand soldiers of the Lebanese army and two thousand officers of the internal security force. In less than two weeks the evacuation of more than ten thousand Palestinians was accomplished. Militarily speaking, the mission was a success; within a few days the evacuation was carried through without incident and even succeeded in completing the mission earlier than the ultimate time limit. Between 10 and 15 September, the three MNF contingents left Lebanon before the time limit, upon Lebanese request. The return to the homeland of the Italian forces was done in view of the request of the Lebanese government; nevertheless much criticism was made against the decision to withdraw the multinational forces from Beirut. The main concern was the fate of the Palestinian refugees left without protection after the withdrawal of the MNF, and some important persons, such as Berlinguer and Craxi, drew attention to the necessity to send the MNF back to Lebanon. During those hot days of August, when the MNF was still on Lebanese territory, caught up in the euphoria of a new end of the war, some particular episodes were ignored and seen simply as complaints about a new 'foreign body'. Yet, some days later, those same episodes would have become premonitory signs of the new massacres which were about to be carried out. The reorganisation of the balances resulting from the removal of the Palestinian guerrillas would have terrible consequences once again on the civilian population. The fear for what could happen started to grow more and more tangible: as soon as the multinational force was due to leave the field open to the phalangist militias, these would enter West Beirut. This was exactly what happened in mid-September, when the Christian militias not only found the field open, but also sought vengeance for the death of the newly elected president, Bachir Gemayel, hero of the Christian resistance. The result of that reorganisation of the balances and of the desire of revenge were the Sabra and Shatila massacres.[38] Following the terrible carnage in the Palestinian camps, the Italian Communist Party accused the government of having failed to take all the possible measures to avoid the withdrawal of the peacekeeping force, leaving 'the Palestinians unarmed and defenceless'.[39] The government rejected such criticism; according to Colombo, not only it would have been unreasonable not to respect the demand of the Lebanese government, but it was also necessary to consider that 'there were some attempts, also by the Italian ambassador in Beirut, both addressed to the outgoing President Sarkis, and to the elected President, Benchir Gemayel, and also to other Lebanese authorities, to discuss with them the duration of the permanence of the MNF beyond the period necessary to complete the evacuation of the Palestinians'.[40] Nevertheless, despite the justifications and the unquestionable absence of evil intent in the choices made in September, there remained that natural sense of guilt for not having understood what consequences the evacuation was going to have and for having left Beirut before having first ascertained the fate of the Palestinian people. This exact sense of guilt, the political embarrassment of having made promises then brutally broken, the shame of being so close to the place of the massacre and not being able to understand, the will to conclude something which seemed hanging suspended, all contributed to bring the MNF back to Beirut less than two weeks from its premature departure. Towards the end of September, Italian, French and US soldiers went back, as in a déjà vu, to Lebanon.[41] This time, the peacekeeping multinational force would remain in the Levantine country until the Lebanese army would be ready to take the place of the MNF armies to ensure the safety of the civilian population. West Beirut was divided among the three contingents of the Multinational Force: US marines took the airport zone, covering the area up to Khalde; French paratroopers occupied good part of the commercial area of West Beirut; lastly, the operational area of the Italians included Sabra and Shatila, as well as Burj al-Barajne and its adjacent Shiite neighbourhoods. The territorial deployment of the contingents was also based on a political logic:[42] the Americans were deployed as buffer between the Israelis and other forces, assuming that they would be more capable of handling their Israeli ally; the French were deployed to guard the phalangists, because they thought that the Christians would be more open towards the country that had protected them for over a century; Italians, at last, being a Mediterranean people and in view of that friendship towards the Arab-Muslim people, would more easily win the favour of the Lebanese and the Palestinians in the refugee camps. In this second mission, the Italian contingent, guided by General Franco Angioni,[43] numbered of a little more than two thousand men. It was the most complex and risky military engagement led by Italian armed forces since the end of the Second World War: two thousand soldiers, almost all of them conscripts, thousands of kilometres away from their home, deployed in a very difficult mission, both militarily and politically, in a country torn apart by internal struggles and by dangerous and often incomprehensible dynamics. The goals of the mission were presented by Minister Colombo on 23 September 1982: 'to avoid further shedding of innocent blood' ensuring above all the safety of the civilian populations, 'to stop that escalation of violence that others did not know how to or did not want to dominate', to facilitate the restoration of the sovereignty and political authority of the central government over the capital and to facilitate the resumption, as soon as possible, of the negotiations for the total withdrawal from Lebanon of all the foreign forces 'based in Lebanon against the wishes of the legitimate authorities of that country'.[44] It was a peacekeeping mission, and the rules of engagement, set by institutional bodies and not by the then minister of defence, Lelio Lagorio, were exclusively defensive. In this sense, the army was a sort of 'peace weapon' which should not be introduced in the local military dynamics, but rather should pursue, exactly as Rome was doing in politics, equidistance and neutrality between the parties. For Italy, the decision to 'militarize' its political approach, adhering to a mission much more complex than the prior one, originated from the strategic belief that the military presence *in loco* would help the political scheme by creating a climate of greater trust and cooperation among all the actors of the Lebanese theatre and the international community. It was not a *politique muscle* or a policy based on sheer balances of power: the idea was that of a broader-based strategy which could support the diplomacy and the negotiations through the military mission. Starting from this strategic framework, the Italian military action differed considerably from that of the other contingents: on one hand, the army worried about pursuing purposes which could be defined as almost 'humanitarian';[45] on the other hand, the Italian tactical approach, contrary to that of the United States, for example, was constantly that of patrolling and of creating direct contact with the locals. This direct contact with the population remained, as Fisk himself stresses, constantly humble: 'They were humble men with none of the swagger and arrogance that Americans and French troops often unwittingly demonstrated towards the Lebanese.'[46]

For the first months following the arrival in Beirut of the second MNF, the situation remained relatively calm: after the evacuation of the guerrillas, the focus was back on peace and on the end of the war. But, soon, as it was at that point sadly conceivable, war started again. In this new context, the main problem of the MNF was to keep an iron neutrality between the parties. This was what the United States and France were lacking, and that, on the contrary, was the main feature of the Italian intervention. When war restarted, the Americans and French began to take sides more and more openly with President Gemayel, not seen as the man able to resolve the internal Lebanese conflicts, but rather as the most reliable ally for the West in a clear bipolar perspective. Americans and French kept training the phalangist army and providing it with equipment, using increasingly the despised Deuxième Bureau for intelligence gathering. At the same time, the United States continued to consolidate its alliance with Israel and with the phalangists. In short, the MNF became progressively an instrument of support of the Maronite-Phalangist government, losing its status of peacekeeping mission playing in a more active way the leading role in local military events. In spring 1983, approximately six months after the arrival of the second MNF, the first attacks against the international contingent took place: Lebanon began to rebel also against the new, too-intrusive guests, and the idyll of the MNF started to turn into a nightmare. On 16 March 1983, it was the turn of Italy: five soldiers of Battaglione San Marco on patrol were injured during an attack; one of them, Filippo Montesi, died from complications four days later at the Hospital Celio in Rome. On 12 August unidentified persons opened fire with automatic firearms on a group of Italian soldiers; on 5 September, when the war in Lebanon was definitely beginning again with the rebellion of the Muslim neighbourhoods and the clashes in Shuf, the Italian camp was bombed. The situation escalated when the VI US fleet opened fire on Druse posts in order to help Gemayel's army, while the French started their air raids against the guerrillas on Metn Hills. The MNF was no longer a peacekeeping force, but had become involved in the Lebanese war, giving support to the Phalangists in an open war against Lebanese Muslims. The differences and tensions existing also within the political schemes of the MNF became evident when Andreotti, during a meeting with Mitterrand in Venice during those days of October, openly criticised 'the unfortunate military operation' of France.[47] On 23 October 1983 at 6.20 am a car bomb exploded in front of the American base; exactly twenty seconds later, a second suicide bomber caused an explosion in French headquarters. The two attacked were the ones that had become involved in the war. Also, the Italians prepared to receive the same treatment from that country torn apart and exhausted by years of war; but they were spared. Was it for the military and political neutrality they were able to demonstrate; for their human involvement towards local populations; for the help they gave to the Shiites; or by pure chance? There are still many questions about those days of 1983. Probably the truest answer to that question, however seemingly banal, can be found in the speech of Sandro Pertini, President of the Republic, visiting the Italian contingent in Beirut on 4 November 1983: 'Italian soldiers know how to win the love of the people, because they are good, generous, ready to help the civilian population'.[48]

Already in the weeks following the attack, the requests for withdrawal of the Italian contingent began to arrive; nevertheless, it was only in the first months of 1984 that the decision to leave Lebanon started to take shape. Even though the Italian political-diplomatic strategy was profoundly different from that of the other MNF members, it cannot be disregarded that the Multinational Force was, at this point, a new divisive factor and that the entire image of the MNF was now tarnished because of the political-diplomatic decisions of the French and Americans, despite the fact that Italy had followed a different policy. When on 17 February President Reagan signed the withdrawal order of US military forces, the Italian contingent also was summoned back to its homeland. Although the Italian contingent had been the first to announce a reduction of its soldiers, from two thousand to fourteen hundred at the beginning of the new year, it was the only one to continue its mission of protection of civilians, as done for seventeen long months until the last day in Beirut, when General Angioni embarked on the naval vessel which took him back to his homeland, in compliance with the orders of Rome.

In the years following the military mission, Italian policy focused more on the result and the evaluations about the effectiveness of the Italian mission on Lebanon and its war. After all, it was the first expedition of Italian soldiers across Italian borders after the Second World War, and this raised a new issue. In the midst of the Cold War, the Italian defence system was designed and developed to protect the national borders from the possible risk deriving from the bipolar clash; consequently the doubts about the abilities to move within a scenario like the Lebanese one were legitimate and totally understandable. In spite of these initial doubts, Italy came out of the Lebanese experience strengthened and more aware of its own military and political force. The Italian mission in Beirut ended up being a political success and a highly valuable operational experience for the armed forces, which contributed to the outlining of the new Italian model, which would be further improved once again in Lebanon in the twenty-first century. From a political perspective, the Italian mission in Beirut was a way to redeem Italy's name within the international context, allowing attainment of the objectives for which Italian policy had been constantly striving ever since the end of the Second World War: showing Italy to be a medium power and having the right to sit with equal dignity at the table with the major world powers to discuss the fate of its vital area, the Mediterranean. Therefore, Lebanon was an essential feature of the more general scheme of the Italian 'projection' in the Mediterranean, giving to Italy the opportunity to reinforce its position therein and to accelerate the growing process of assuming responsibilities in this theatre vital for the country. Italian commitment qualified also as a response to those who accused Rome of being disinterested in Middle Eastern issues, delegating the safety of its area of vital interest to the United States. Nevertheless, the Italian approach in the region was extremely different from the American one; in fact, the latter saw Middle Eastern crises merely as the transposition of the bipolar clash. In this context, the Lebanese crisis, the support to Gemayel and the political alliance with Israel were clearly meant as actions against Syria, and therefore against the Soviet Union. The Italian political and diplomatic class, on the contrary, had become aware that the game being played in the Mediterranean had more local causes than global ones, even though often fomented by the global ones. The war in Lebanon went on for some years, until the implementation of the agreements of Ta'if and was subject to a series of new transformations: on one hand the overwhelming role played by the Shiite groups, with Hezbollah taking the field; on the other hand there were the distressing data about the intra-confessional conflicts regarding all the Lebanese religious communities, Christians,[49] Shiite and Sunnis, and even the internecine clash within the same Palestinian movement; eventually the kidnapping season,[50] started surreptitiously in 1982 with the kidnapping of David Dodge, president of the American University of Beirut, reached its peak. In this delicate and complex context, the requests for help addressed to Italy continued, above all made by Arafat to defend the Palestinian people; such requests would eventually become a suggestion for a new edition of the MNF.[51] According to Arafat, to the Palestinians, to the Lebanese and to the Arab world in general, Italy was for sure the most reliable interlocutor, understanding and friendly, to discuss issues with. For its part, Italy showed also in the last part of the Lebanese war the same fears displayed during the initial stages: in 1988 the main concern was still that there might be a repartition of the country.[52] Italy would then focus on diplomacy in order to avoid a similar situation and above all to help the Lebanese to move towards the election of a president who could be supported by all factions and could promote national reconciliation and constitutional reforms.[53] Besides, towards the end of the 1980s the attention of the Italian political and military classes was drawn to the necessity to deal with the new threats arising in another war theatre: the one between Iran and Iraq.

Notes

1 About the Lebanese civil war, see Béchara Ménassa Benassar, *Anatomie d'une guerre et d'une occupation (1975–1978)* (Paris: Ed. Galilée, 1978); Benassar, *Paix d'Israel au Liban* (Paris: Ed. L'Orient-Le Jour, 1983); Denise Chamoun, *Histoire du Liban Contemporain*, Vol. II (1943–1990) (Paris: Fayard, 2004); Georges Corm, *Le Proche-Orient éclaté (1956–2000)* (Paris: Gallimard, 2001); Charles Helou, *Mémoires*, Vols

I, II, III, IV and V (Beirut: Imprimerie Saint Paul, 1995); Antoin Jabre, *La guerre du Liban* (Paris: Belfond, 1980); Samir Kassir, *La guerre du Liban (1975-1982)* (Paris: Ed. Karthala-Cermoc, 1994); Jonathan Randall, *Going All the Way: Christian Warlords, Israeli Adventurers, and the War in Lebanon* (New York: Vintage Books, 1984); Itamar Rabinovich, *The War for Lebanon, 1976-1983* (Ithaca, NY: Cornell University Press, 1984); Benny Morris, *Vittime. Storia del conflitto arabo-sionista 1881-2001* (Milan: BUR Rizzoli, 2001); Robert Fisk, *Il martirio di una nazione. Il Libano in guerra* (Milan: Il Saggiatore Tascabili, 2010); George Corm, *Le Liban contemporain: Histoire et société* (Paris: Autrement, 2003); Jean Sarkis, *Histoire de la guerre du Liban* (Paris: PUF, 1993); Abdallah Naaman, *Le Liban, Histoire d'une nation inachevée*, Vols I, II and III (Paris: Glyphe, 2015); Edgar O'Ballance, *Civil War in Lebanon, 1975-1992* (London: Palgrave Macmillan, 1998); John Bulloch, *Death of a Country: The Civil War in Lebanon* (London: Weindenfeld and Nicolson, 1977); Elizabeth Picard, *Lebanon: A Shattered Country, Myths and Realities of the Wars in Lebanon* (New York: Revisede Edition Picard, 2002); Dilip Hiro, *Lebanon: Fire and Embers, A History of the Lebanese Civil War* (London: Weidenfeld & Nicolson, 1993); MariusDeeb, *Syria's Terrorist War on Lebanon and the Peace Process* (New York: Palgrave Macmillan, 2003); Robert Fisk, *Pity the Nation: The Abduction of Lebanon* (New York: Nation Books, 2002); Farid Al-Khazen, *The Breakdown of the State in Lebanon, 1967-1976* (London: I.B. Tauris, 2000); Ahmad Beydoun, *Le Liban: Itinéraire dans une guerre incivile* (Beirut: Karthala-Cermoc, 1993); Joseph G. Chami, *Le Mémorial de la guerre 1975-1990* (Beirut: Chemaly & Chemaly, 2002); Helena Cobban, *The Making of Modern Lebanon* (London: Hutchinson, 1985); Marius Deeb, *The Lebanese Civil War* (London: Praeger, 1980); Thomas Friedman, *From Beirut to Jerusalem* (London: Collins, 1990); Theodor Hanf, *Coexistence in Wartime Lebanon: Decline of a State and Rise of a Nation* (London: I.B. Tauris, 1993); William Harris, *Faces of Lebanon: Sects, Wars, and Global Extensions* (Princeton, NJ: Princeton University Press, 1993); Sune Haugbolle, *War and Memory in Lebanon* (Cambridge: Cambridge University Press, 2010); Michael Johnson, *All Honourable Men: The Social Origins of War in Lebanon* (London: I.B. Tauris, 2002); Aïda Kanafani-Zahar, *Liban – La guerre et la mémoire* (Rennes: Presse Universitaire de Rennes, 2011); Samir Kassir, *La guerre du Liban: De la dissension nationale au conflit régional* (Paris: Karthala, 1994); Samir Khalaf, *Civil and Uncivil Violence in Lebanon: A History of the Internationalization of Communal Conflict* (New York: Columbia University Press, 2002); Jean Said Makdisi, *Beirut Fragments: A War Memoir* (New York: Persea Books, 1990); Alain Ménargues, *Les secrets de la guerre du Liban: Du coup d'état de Béchir Gémayel aux massacres des camps palestiniens* (Paris: Albin Michel, 2004); Franck Mermier (ed.), *Mémoires de guerres au Liban (1975-1990)* (Paris: Actes Sud, 2010); Selim Nassib, *Beirut: Frontline Story* (London: Pluto Press, 1983); Tabitha Petran, *Struggle over Lebanon* (New York: Monthly Review Press, 1987); Jonathan Randall, *The Tragedy of Lebanon: Christian Warlords, Israeli Adventurers and American Bunglers* (London: Chatto & Windus, 1983); Yezid Sayigh, *Armed Struggle and the Search for a Palestinian State: The Palestinian National Movement, 1949-1993* (Oxford: Oxford University Press, 1997); Fawwaz Traboulsi, *A History of Modern Lebanon* (London: Pluto Press, 2007); Ghassan Tueni, *Une guerre pour les autres* (Paris: J. C. Lattes, 1985); Lucia Volk, *Memorials and Martyrs in Modern Lebanon* (Bloomington: Indiana University Press, 2010); Samir Khalaf, *Civil and Uncivil Violence in Lebanon* (New York: Columbia University Press, 2002).

2 AP, CD, 11 August 1976.

3   About the Arafat figure see Amnon Kapeliouk, *Arafat l'irriducibile* (Florence: Ponte alle Grazie, 2004)
4   The reference is to Arafat's speech during the Twenty-Ninth Session of the United Nations General Assembly, 13 November 1974.
5   Daniele Caviglia, *La diplomazia italiana e gli equilibri mediterranei: la politica mediorientale dell'Italia dalla guerra dei sei giorni al conflitto dello Yom Kippur (1967–1973)* (Soveria Mannelli: Rubbettino, 2006), 36.
6   AP, CD, 19 February 1976.
7   AP, CD, 31 October 1979.
8   See Fabio Tana, 'L'evoluzione del dibattito tra i partiti', in Fabio Tan (ed.), *La lezione del Libano* (Milan: Ipalmo – Franco Angeli, 1985).
9   AP, CD, 29 July 1976.
10 AP, CD, Foreign Affairs Committee, 6 October 1976.
11 AP, CD, 19 February 1976.
12 AP, CD, 10 August 1976
13 Ibid.
14 The III Foreign Affairs Committee also spoke of the 'final solution', AP, CD, Foreign Affairs Committee, 6 October 1976.
15 AP, CD, 10 August 1976.
16 AP, CD, 11 August 1976.
17 AP, CD, 10 August 1976.
18 Ibid.
19 Ibid.
20 AP, CD, 8 February 1978.
21 AP, CD, 4 April 1978.
22 AP, CD, 12 October 1979.
23 Robert Fisk, *Pity the Nation: Lebanon at War* (Oxford: Oxford University Press, 2001), 124.
24 The text of the Resolution is available online at http://www.un.org/fr/documents/view_doc.asp?symbol=S/RES/425 (1978) (accessed 19 February 2018).
25 AP, CD, 12 October 1979.
26 Ibid.
27 Ibid.
28 AP, CD, 3 February 1981.
29 Ibid.
30 AP, CD, 1 October 1981.
31 Ibid.
32 AP, CD, 22 October 1980.
33 Philip Habib was Ronald Reagan's special envoy to the Middle East.
34 Alain Brouille, 'La force multinationale d'interposition à Beyrouth (21 août–13 septembre 1982)', *Annuaire Français de Droit International* 28 (1982), 293–336.
35 Fabio Tana (ed.), *La lezione del Libano*, 14.
36 Ibid.
37 AP, CD, 30 August 1982.
38 Refer in particular to the Report of the Israeli Kahan Commission.
39 AP, CD, Foreign Affairs and Defense Committee, 23 September 1982.
40 Ibid.
41 On 1 February, a few dozen British soldiers join the multinational contingent.

42 Because of the small size of their contingent, the British were not assigned a specific sector as the other international forces. They were located in the southeastern part of the city, near the presidential palace.
43 See Franco Angioni, *Un soldato italiano in Libano* (Milan: Rizzoli, 1984).
44 AP, CD, Foreign Affairs and Defense Committee, 23 September 1982.
45 Shortly after the arrival of the Italian contingent in Beirut, General Angioni requested the dispatch of a field hospital for the Italian military forces. Therefore, a hospital with a maximum capacity of six thousand units arrived in Beirut, but the Italian contingent consisted of only two thousand men. For this, the hospital was immediately made available to the local population for which it became a reference point.
46 Fisk, *Pity the Nation*, 451.
47 'Mitterrand', *Rivista 30 giorni*, http://www.30giorni.it/articoli_id_4661_l1.htm (accessed 19 February 2018).
48 Refer to the Sandro Pertini Speech.
49 ILS, GA, Israel and Palestine, b. 487, f. 2, Report for official visit in Italy of PLO President Arafat, April 1990.
50 ILS, GA, Israel and Palestine, b. 488, f. 4, Notes about kidnappings of American, French and Italian citizens in Lebanon.
51 ILS, GA, Israel and Palestine, b. 487, f. 1, General Secretary Foreign Office, 23 February 1987.
52 ILS, GA, Israel and Palestine, b. 489, f. 9, Letter from US Secretary of State, George Shultz, to Andreotti, 28 November 1988.
53 ILS, GA, Israel and Palestine, b. 487, f. 1, Message about Lebanon from US Secretary of State to Giulio Andreotti, 23 November 1988.

8

The Sigonella crisis: The Middle East and the Atlantic alliance

Matteo Gerlini

The hidden issue of missiles

According an old interpretation, the crisis of the *Achille Lauro* and Sigonella was a confrontation between two dimensions of Italian foreign policy. The first dimension was the transatlantic relations, marked by the nuclear armaments issues and by the so-called Second Cold War: in such a dimension the Italians agreed and shared the Americans' political options. The second dimension was Italian diplomacy towards the Arab countries, towards the Arab–Israeli conflict, towards the Palestine Liberation Organization (PLO) and so towards the problem of terrorism by a 'Middle Eastern matrix', as the press at the time used to headline it: this dimension was not in agreement with the United States. Conversely, in this field, the two diplomacies were expected to keep different positions, if not conflicting ones, due to the fact that the US government considered first the reasons of the Israeli government, whereas the Italian president of the minister's council and his minister of foreign affairs had a pro-Arab policy. They were so close to the Arabs as to show an understanding towards terrorism.[1] Such a version, popular because of easy understanding, was wrong at that times and it is more wrong today, thanks to recently available sources.

The main error of this version is ignorance of the basic agreement between the transatlantic relations of Bettino Craxi's government and its policy towards the Middle East. Giulio Andreotti was considered by most newspapers as the prominent pro-Arab[2] member of the Italian government, but actually he was not involved in Middle East affairs until 1978. In that year he received from US President Jimmy Carter a request of diplomatic support for the Arab–Israeli peace process, so that happened when he was already a senior Italian politician.[3] The following Italian initiatives towards the Arab–Israeli conflict were willingly subsidiaries to the US ones, and when some criticism was raised by some members of the American government, it was eventually more formal than substantial. It is meaningless to stress how the form is relevant, especially in diplomacy, but getting out by the representation of the daily papers, it is evident how the whole of Italian foreign policy perceived itself as ancillary sometimes, supporting other times, regarding the peace plan(s) promoted by the United States.[4] How to implement the various plans was a divisive problem both for Italians and Americans, and this problem caused some confrontation among policymakers. It was not the position towards the Arab–Israeli conflict, clear and shared, because everybody agreed on the necessity of peace. Rather, it was the various options for the peace agreement which divided the government of the United States[5] so strongly that sometimes the statements were contradictory, as in the *Achille Lauro* hijacking.

To understand what was at stake in the outcome of the *Achille Lauro* hijacking, it is necessary to reconstruct the Euromissiles debate, started in 1978–9. The quarrelsome issue of nuclear armaments entered a new phase after the Soviet decision to deploy new intermediate-range ballistic missiles, the SS-20. For the Russians, it was modernizing in compliance with the commitments for the limitations of armaments, but it was doubtlessly an improvement of the arms systems targeting Western Europe. The SS-20 substituted the aged SS-4 and SS-5, deployed since the 1960s, but the new missiles carried three nuclear warheads instead of one and were propelled with solid instead of less effective liquid fuel.[6] Nevertheless, the North Atlantic Treaty Organization (NATO) too was already debating its deployment of new ballistic missiles as proposed by US Secretary of Defence James Schlesinger in 1975.[7] But when in 1976 the Russians began the deployment of the SS-20, the long-standing debate around the US commitment to the defence of Western Europe against the perceived Soviet threat was renewed.[8] The liability of American assurances for Western Europe's security, the cornerstone of the Atlantic alliance, was tested. A difficult process started, in which the military options were the outcome of the intergovernmental and political bargaining inside the alliance structures. Recent historical scholarship has identified the role of German chancellor Helmut Schmidt in the harsh debate around the deployment of NATO ballistic missiles – the so-called Euromissiles – appropriate to match the Warsaw Pact SS-20. In the complex functioning of NATO, the High Level Group was the committee which, after thorough evaluations, proposed in July 1979 to deploy a combination of Pershing II and BGM-109 G Gryphon missiles for approval of the member states.[9]

For the leadership of the Italian socialist party, the Euromissiles debate was a quarrelsome turning point, because it meant a final change of position towards NATO, and therefore a change in the international position of the party itself. The so-called 'autonomist' internal current, led by party chair Bettino Craxi, seized the opportunity to gain trust from the Americans and from some Italian institutions bodies, such as the armed forces, for which Atlantism was a basic feature.[10] Craxi entered staunchly into the party's debate, putting the Socialists on strongly Atlantic positions, winning against internal opponents, who seemed the majority before the party direction meeting of October 1979. Nevertheless, the votes of the socialists were crucial to the approval of the parliamentary motion of 6 December 1979, which gave to the government, chaired by the Christian Democrat Francesco Cossiga, the mandate to agree with the deployment of the Euromissiles in Italian territory. Andreotti, at that moment free from government roles, in the parliamentary debate was looking for a motion with broader consensus, possibly including the Communist Party.[11] Anyway, Cossiga participated in the North Atlantic Council, the highest organ of NATO, reporting the availability of the Italian Republic to deploy the new weapons on its territory.

With that meeting, the Italian facilities were included in the list of available sites for the Euromissiles, but at the same time the North Atlantic Council approved the so-called dual-track decision, with a clause which made the actual deployment contingent upon an expected Soviet turning back on the SS-20.[12] To be applied, such a clause needed a less aggressive attitude from the Soviet side, or rather, a less besieged perception, but it was quite unrealistic coming at the time of the Soviet invasion of Afghanistan. The coalition of the parties in the Italian parliament during the second government chaired by Cossiga gained the participation of the socialist party. The socialists gained relevant ministries, such as Defence, obtained by Lelio Lagorio, an autonomist leader, in a phase of big changes for NATO and for the constellation of bases on which the alliance was built.

The Mediterranean and the Italian governments

The NATO bases were the fortresses of the Atlantic organization, committed to defending Western European governments in the Cold War, and they were the physical place where the Allied armed forces became integrated with the superpower military system. American supremacy in the Mediterranean was grounded on the system of bases,[13] needed so that the US Sixth Fleet could counter the Fifth Eskadra of the Soviet navy, called by NATO Sovmedron (Soviet Mediterranean Squadron). In foreign policy doctrine, the attitude of the President of the United States, Ronald Reagan, was similar to the one of Craxi in identifying a Soviet expansionistic drive. For the socialists it was more imperative that NATO stand out, turning off the détente and tackling the armaments race, holding back the Soviets and compelling them to open a negotiation.[14] Some American intellectuals, experts of the Italian world, who had known Craxi personally since the 1970s, bridged these elective affinities.[15] Michael Ledeen was probably the most famous, at the time a young historian often in Italy, where he wrote an interview on Fascism with the prominent historian of the time, Renzo De Felice.[16] In the same period, Ledeen was an expert for US intelligence and then, with the election of Reagan, he became a White House consultant with an excellent network in Israel.[17]

The Italian government shifted to a new five-party coalition,[18] in which the president of the council of ministers was the Republican Giovanni Spadolini, while Lagorio continued to keep the Defence ministry, following directly the process of deployment of the Euromissiles. The technical and political timing of deployment was influenced by the opening in October 1980 of East–West negotiations, in the spirit of the dual-track decision, but promptly suspended until 30 November 1981.[19] In 1981 the Italian government built a missile-launch site in Comiso, Sicily, close to a relevant airborne base, very important since the early years of NATO, in the Sigonella site.[20] Sigonella was called the 'Hub of the Med' by the US Navy, which was sharing it with the Italian air force. Indeed, the international military role of the Italian Republic was promptly changing with the participation of the Italian armed forces in the multinational missions in Sinai and Lebanon. This military engagement intertwined with Italian diplomatic efforts towards the peace process. Both were marked by the effect of the most serious attack against a Jewish community in the history of the Republic, on 9 October 1982. Terrorists of the Abu Nidal group, a Palestinian anti-PLO organization, struck with grenades and machine guns at the exit of the synagogue in Rome, killing a child, Stefano Gay Taché, and wounding thirty-nine.[21] Abu Nidal called the attack a retaliation for the Sabra and Chatila massacres, but, in fact, the main political target was the Italian engagement in Lebanon.[22]

Just less than two months after the attack, the second Spadolini government fell, and after the political elections of 1983 the renewed five-party coalition agreed on Craxi as president of the council.[23] In the new government, the minister of defence was Spadolini, while Andreotti was appointed minister of foreign affairs. The first Euromissiles, the Cruise, arrived in Sigonella in November 1983,[24] to be moved and deployed in Comiso after Parliament had voted in favour of their hosting in the national territory.[25]

In the first steps of the new government Craxi demonstrated his availability to question the Euromissiles choice towards resuming negotiations between the blocks.[26] The same year 1984 was marked by the opening of a new wave of international terrorism, retaliation and covert operations, in whose frame was the *Achille Lauro* hijacking. A catalyst of the tensions was the peace process option of the making of a Jordan-Palestinian commission, which was expected to negotiate with Israel. The Italians supported this option, with an agreement with the king of Jordan, Hussein bin Talal, and PLO president Yasser Arafat, but they had to face a heterogeneous front of opposition. On 11 February 1985, Arafat and Hussein publicly struck a vague deal, 'a first step towards a wider agreement', as the Italian MFA noted, thus avoiding defining the acceptance or not of the 242 UN resolution of 1967.[27]

Between terror and peace

It is necessary to continue to follow the intertwining of both plans, the Euromissiles and peace process, to understand how in 1985 it was an understanding of the Italian government with the Americans and with Soviets too, which provided viability to the Italian initiative. In early January 1985, a letter by Reagan anticipated to Craxi the topics which US diplomacy was addressing for the negotiations on the limitation of armaments and on the Strategic Defense Initiative.[28] In the following March, Craxi and Andreotti met with Reagan in Washington, in the frame of their state visit in the United States. Craxi delivered a speech in a session of the Congress, and had a bilateral, very friendly meeting with Reagan on several issues, among them the peace process. When Craxi demanded Reagan trust Arafat to support him on the path of negotiation in return to Arafat renouncing terrorism, Reagan asked the interpreter if he had understood correctly. After the surprise, Reagan passed the ball to Craxi, who had to demonstrate the reliability of his proposal.[29] A major sponsor of the visit was the US ambassador to Italy Maxwell Rabb, appointed in 1981, a staunch supporter of Craxi and convinced of his reliability in relations with the United States. During the trip, Rabb established a friendly relationship with Craxi and his diplomatic counsellor, Antonio Badini, whom he trusted in the agonizing days of the *Achille Lauro* hijacking.[30]

On the Middle Eastern chessboard, two facts were relevant to recall on the eve of the *Achille Lauro* hijacking. The first one was when on 21 May 1985 Shimon Peres, head of the Israeli government, negotiated an exchange of prisoners with Ahmed Jibril, leader of the Popular Front for the Liberation of Palestine – General Command, a Syrian-obeying organization. In return for three Israeli prisoners of war in Lebanon, the Israeli government freed 1,150 jailed Palestinians. Jibril and the Syrian-oriented groups gained major credit in the occupied territories,[31] but also Peres got more internal consensus in the attempt to go ahead with the peace process.

The second fact was the following: 14 June, a Lebanese terrorist group hijacked a TWA Athens–London airliner with layover in Rome. More than one hundred passengers were kept hostages for three days, flying several times between Algiers and Beirut. Robert D. Stethem, of the US Navy, was shot onboard and his corpse thrown off onto the airstrip. Eventually, in Beirut, the Shiite militias took the hostages, freeing them in several groups, up to the end of the month. The hijacking was declared as the answer to the attack against the Hezbollah party's leader, the Sheik Mohammed Hussein Fadlallah: a car bomb prepared by the CIA and paid by the Saudis, but incredibly the Sheik was unhurt during the explosion that caused eighty casualties.[32] The hijackers and the US government negotiated with the mediation of the Syrian government, supported by the Iranian one. The hostages were released in return for the liberation of prisoners detained in Greek and Israel jails. The United States limited the human losses, but paid the price of asking the liberation of prisoners and let the hijackers free.[33] Reagan declared the nation under attack, tried to obtain from the Syrian President Hafiz al Assad the liberation of US citizens kidnapped in Lebanon and the arrest of the TWA hijackers, but the dialogue was interrupted.[34]

The Jewish holiday of Yom Kippur was on 25 September 1985. In the Cypriote port of Larnakes, a yacht was assaulted by three men who declared themselves members of Force 17, the armed group of Arafat's party, al Fath. Onboard were three Israeli citizens, who were killed regardless of a negotiation attempted by the Cypriotes. Some Italian newspapers believed the three Israelis to be Mossad agents.[35]

In retaliation, the Israel government authorized an air raid against the PLO headquarter in Tunis, the 'Wooden leg' operation. On 30 September Israeli airfighters bombed the PLO premises, which, after the evacuation from Beirut were located just out of Tunis city. They killed fifty-six Palestinians and fifteen Tunisians, but not Arafat, who had been advised of the action.[36] While the Soviet Union censored the aggression, Reagan called the bombing a legitimate defensive act,[37] before calling back his assertion thanks to a statement of the Secretary of State George Shultz[38] In Italy, for the first time, almost nobody endorsed the Israeli action. Craxi asked for a clear position of rejection by Arafat against the Larnakes attack, and by the US government against the legitimation of the Israeli bombing. Then he argued with Peres, with heavy accusations between them: Peres stated Craxi colluded with terrorism, Craxi called Peres a terrorist.[39]

The planned visit in Italy of the Israeli Minister of Tourism, Avraham Sharir, was cancelled by Lagorio, who held the homologous ministry in the Craxi government.[40] A relevant aspect in the hot international debate, neglected by the Italian press, was the alleged assistance of NATO with the Israel air raid. The Arab newspapers, including the more moderate ones, went so far as to credit the news of refuelling during the flight of the Israeli fighters by a plane of the Atlantic Alliance. This allowed them to fly from Israel to Tunis, out of the range of F-15 Eagles. The NATO spokespersons denied the rumours, but not enough to quell the claim of the Arab press, which debated an evident technical question as the refuelling of the fighters.[41] Overall, the political meaning of the Arab version marked a new phase in debating Middle Eastern terrorism: it was the first time a NATO military asset was mentioned in the frame of Israel's counterterrorism. In the Arab world, the perception of a shift in the role of the alliance shed a different light on what was going on in the Sigonella airbase after the *Achille Lauro* hijacking.

The hijacking[42]

On 7 October 1985, the Italian transatlantic *Achille Lauro* was cruising the Mediterranean for the second time that year. After having disembarked some of the passengers in Alexandria for a visit to the historical sites, the ship headed to Port Said to wait for those passengers. During the short trip, a Palestinian group kidnapped the passengers while they were in the dining room. The terrorists ordered the ship's captain to head for Tartharbourbor, Syria. Using the radio onboard the Palestinians contacted the Egyptian authorities, asking to give notice of the kidnapping. For reasons still unknown, the Egyptians refused to do so, and the news reached the organs of information from the coastal radio station in Gothenburg, Sweden, which acted as a radio bridge between the ship and the Egyptians. The terrorists asked for the liberation of Palestinians prisoners from the jails of Israel, otherwise, they would begin to kill the hostages. All of the governments whose citizens were among the passengers of the ship came into action, and also the Americans, certainly the most organized to deal with a terrorist attack. Both governments prepared plans for a military action to free the ship, but without agreeing on a common operation. Instead, both governments arranged to ask the PLO to try to contact the kidnappers. Therefore, the PLO representatives went to Port Said, but at that point the ship was already in the waters in front of Tartus, and the Syrians offered a channel to negotiate with the terrorists. It was now 8 October, and although Andreotti agreed, Craxi did not, following the American request to refuse any negotiations with terrorists, and the contact was interrupted. As the channel was closed, the terrorists secretly killed the US passenger Leon Klinghoffer, and his body was thrown into the sea. The terrorists threatened to kill another US passenger, while they ordered the captain to head for Libya. While the ship was sailing there, the Italian special forces were about to go into action, despite the Americans pressing to leave the field to their special forces only. The reason was the extreme difficulty of action, which had no precedent, and the lack of trust of the US military in the capability of the Italian special forces. During this short stalemate, the PLO negotiator persuaded, by radio, the hijackers to surrender in return of setting them free. The terrorists decided to surrender to Egyptian authorities, stopping the ship at Port Said, in an agonizing situation, with a hovering helicopter and naval movements around the *Achille Lauro*. It seemed to be the beginning of an American military action or perhaps Egyptian. On the afternoon of 9 October, four Palestinians left the ship in the hands of Egyptian port authorities. The consular investigation immediately verified the disappearance of Klinghoffer and his plausible murderer, while the hijackers were held by the Egyptians, who did not intend to proceed against them. The PLO offered itself as a judging court, but this hypothesis was immediately discarded. The Italian government, despite having guaranteed immunity to the hijackers, after the discovery of the murder asked to obtain the four kidnappers. On the 10th, the terrorists were put aboard an Egyptian airliner together with the Palestinian negotiators: Hani el Hassan, the PLO's intelligence officer, and Abu Abbas, head of the liberation front in Palestine, a splinter-group of the Popular Front for the Liberation of Palestine that the hijackers belonged to. As the plane took off, the Tunisian government closed all the airports precautionarily. While the aircraft was expected in the Roman airport of Ciampino, it was intercepted by US fighters from the carrier *Saratoga*, at that moment hosted in the port of Dubrovnik. The fighters ordered the Egyptian pilot to land at the Sicilian NATO base of Sigonella, and he obeyed.

The Americans obtained from Craxi the permission to land at the Sigonella base although the planes had probably already touched the ground in the first minutes of 11 October. In fact, in addition to the intercepted Egyptian plane, also transport aircrafts carrying American special forces, who were about to assault the Egyptian plane to take all the Palestinians on board and presumably bring them to the United States, landed in Sigonella. The Italian soldiers stationed at the base, stood between the plane and the US special forces, while breaking news via Agenzia Stampa Nazionale Associata (ANSA) from Palazzo Chigi reported that the Egyptian plane had landed in Sigonella. Thus, the veil of secrecy placed by the Americans on the operation was lifted; the Italians would have benefited from the secrecy, because they would not have given any account for this sort of extraordinary rendition. Therefore, the US government went on, asking Italian authorities to hand the Palestinians over to them. George Shultz, secretary of state, telephoned Andreotti, who denied permission. Reagan, interpreted by the Italian-speaking Ledeen, called Craxi, claiming both the four hijackers and the two PLO leaders, but perhaps Craxi took time. The Italian magistrate of Syracuse went to the base, and in collaboration with the Americans, proceeded to identify the four hijackers. He organized the transfer of some US passengers from the *Achille Lauro* to Sigonella, for an identification of the hijackers. The four Palestinians waited in the Italian barracks of Sigonella, the two negotiators remained on board the aircraft, but the Egyptian plane was denied permission to take off for Egypt. Therefore, the Egyptian port authorities blocked the *Achille Lauro*, which was leaving, holding it until the plane had taken off from the base. In the afternoon the magistrates of Genoa, the responsible prosecutors, arrived, and authorized the departure of the plane for Ciampino with the two leaders of the PLO. US newspapers were on sale with news of the confrontation between the two armed forces in Sigonella, which the Italian government had managed to keep hidden. The Italian government was cautious for other possible US force actions, and when at ten that evening the plane left for Ciampino, there were two more serious violations of Italian airspace by the Americans, afraid that the Egyptian plane would flee, and they were intending to intercept it again. Meanwhile, the US embassy began to present documents proving Abu Abbas's primacy in the hijacking. Ambassador Maxwell Rabb had agreed with Craxi and his undersecretary, Giuliano Amato, for the detainment in Italy of the two Palestinian negotiators for investigations, but the

American violations led Craxi to radically change his position. Before midnight on the 11th, the plane landed at Ciampino and the two Palestinian negotiators remained on board with two Egyptian soldiers, while the remaining passengers and members of the crew and of the armed escort got off.

The climate in the United States was difficult: in California, Jewish extremists killed Alex Odeh, the American Palestinian representative and supporter of the option of negotiating with the PLO. In Italy, before the dawn of the 12th, the American embassy presented the dossier needed for the indictment of the two Palestinian negotiators to the head of the cabinet of Ministry of Justice. But the ministry considered the US trials insufficient, and its response arrived at one o'clock in the afternoon at Palazzo Chigi, where Andreotti and Amato remained to represent the government. After receiving the decision, the Americans asked for a new assessment, aware that the Egyptian plane was about to take off again, curbed only by the fear of a new interception and possible shooting down of the aircraft. Therefore, Andreotti authorized the transfer of the two Palestinians to a Yugoslavian airliner to Belgrade. The Americans provided evidence to the Rome attorney's office, but when the magistrates arrived at the Fiumicino airport, where the two Palestinians and the Egyptian jet had been transferred, it was too late: the Yugoslavian flight had already left. This opened up a harsh and unprecedented diplomatic crisis between Italy and the United States, narrated through the meetings in Washington and Rome of the representatives of the two countries, while the respective public opinions flared up. In Italy, Spadolini disagreed with the decision taken by Craxi and Andreotti to let the Palestinian negotiators go free. On the 13th, the *Achille Lauro* was released by the Egyptian authorities.

The crisis

The tension in the public opinion of the United States and Italy was rising, increasing the concern of the government, according to what the Italian ambassador to the United States Rinaldo Petrignani reported to Luigi Cavalchini, head of cabinet of the minister of foreign affairs, on 14 October. The ambassador suggested challenging Shultz with the behaviour of the United States and preparing to respond to the US reply regarding Craxi's promise during the telephone call with Ledeen to retain the 'four plus two' by contrasting 'improper use of our bases'.[43] That same day, the leaders of the Italian republican party disagreed with its own government's decision to set free the two Palestinian negotiators.

On 15 October in Brussels, in the midst of a meeting of the North Atlantic Council, Shultz and Andreotti finally had a chance to discuss what had happened. Here, Andreotti mentioned the difficulties that the Euromissiles deployment would meet if the clamor on the Sigonella base persisted on the American side. The press release issued by the Farnesina, as soon as Andreotti returned from Brussels, disclosed to the media the news of the clarification he had with Shutz, and announced the forthcoming joint communiqué. Ruggiero phoned Petrignani to tell him that the meeting had gone 'quite well', but just as Andreotti met Shultz, in Washington Petrignani was a guest of Clare Boothe Luce, upon her request.[44]

Former US ambassador to Italy and Reagan's strong supporter, Boothe wanted to listen to Petrignani on the reasoning of the Italians, knowing the country well and appreciating its Catholic faith. She assured Petrignani that she would talk to Reagan, pleading the Italian government's case to dissuade easy riders of popular moods that would lead to a scenario full of risky wild cards.[45]

Instead, on the way back to the United States, Shultz sent a brief message from the plane to Petrignani, addressed to the Italian government. In the first point of the note, Shultz declared that he 'did not consider appropriate' the joint statement of the Italian and the US governments, the Italian and the US ones, on the whole affair. For Shultz, after the exchange of views with Andreotti, the disagreement remained. The secretary of state closed by reiterating that relations between the United States and Italy were broad, deep and strong, and that they would continue from this point.[46]

Back in Rome, Andreotti had told the press what the Americans already knew, namely that the destination of the Egyptian Boeing, rejecting Tunis, was the Roman airport of Ciampino.[47]

At the time of receiving the secretary of state's message, Petrignani double-checked if Shultz had been aware of developments in the Italian domestic situation, and he was told that the head of US diplomacy was aware of all the necessary elements, 'even those coming from Rome'. Andreotti immediately commented on Shultz's statements as 'a turnaround', as he had agreed with the secretary of state the joint communiqué after the meeting in Brussels.[48] Subsequently, Andreotti believed that it was not Shultz who did not approve the document, but someone not better identified in the government. Therefore, according to what is read in his later memories, he phoned Vernon Walters; senior CIA leader, Italian-speaking, and Catholic, Walters was then ambassador to the UN and a member of the presidential cabinet. He was told by Andreotti that, without a correction to Shultz's statement, the Italian delegation would fail to attend the New York summit on 24 October.[49] It is not possible to date this call exactly, even if it must have happened more or less in those hours, since Amato confirmed to Petrignani that Craxi was of the same opinion, so that he could communicate it through the official routes.[50] Reagan was very keen on this meeting, as he intended to discuss with the G-7 heads of East–West relations, with a view to the upcoming meeting with Gorbachev on 19–20 November in Geneva. The first US-USSR meeting after six years of frost. French president François Mitterrand had already indicated that he did not want to participate, so the Italian presence was even more relevant to the success of the American meeting.[51]

At the same time, Christian Democratic senator Francesco D'Onofrio, who knew the American reality, phoned Petrignani to check if there had really been any pressure on the Italian republicans by the US government. He then told the ambassador to convey to the Americans the certainty that Spadolini's position would not be a majority in the country.[52] In fact, in the afternoon of 16 October, the Republican leadership withdrew its support to the government, withdrawing its ministers. In the Italian institutional system of that time, it meant the fall of the government.

From Washington, Petrignani confirmed the changed general attitude, both of the media outlets and of Reagan's spokesman. During a previous day's lunch offered in New York for the 'FIAT Day', Petrignani spoke with Steve Forbes, publisher of

Forbes magazine, and former Secretary of State Henry Kissinger: both agreed on the usefulness of closing the incident, recognizing that both governments could not behave differently: 'We had to get mad and you had to set him free.'[53]

The turning point

On the same morning of the 17th, Rabb recorded a change of tone even in Andreotti's speeches, which had abandoned the usual subtle style to shift to direct and heavy comments on US conduct in the post-hijacking.[54] On that day, Craxi intervened in the Chamber of Deputies before presenting his resignation, according to a strategy suggested by the president of the Chamber herself, the communist Nilde Iotti. The leadership of the communist party had in fact decided to support both Craxi and Andreotti in the parliamentary debate. Craxi's speech received wide approval, especially from the Communists, while only the so-called secular parties and the neo-Fascist Italian social movement, were critical.

On 18 October, Secretary-General of the Ministry of Foreign Affairs Renato Ruggiero, was invited to lunch at Villa Taverna, where he reported to Rabb some considerations expressed by Craxi. He said that one element the United States seemed to fail to grasp or understand was that Craxi had been under enormous pressure from Mubarak to release the Egyptian plane and the two Palestinians. Mubarak was acting from a position of weakness: the crowds in Cairo would have inflamed the streets, debasing the role of Mubarak in front of the entire Arab world, if his request had not been accepted. Craxi believed that Italy's sovereignty had been offended by what had happened in Sigonella, especially about the American fighter which took off from there towards Ciampino, following the Egyptian plane. Subsequently Ruggiero added that the delayed request to land in Sigonella by the interceptors and the Egyptian plane expressed a lack of trust in Italy. So for the Italians a gesture was needed in front of the American public, to calm the press campaign against Italy underway in the United States.[55]

The day before, the head of the Spanish government, Felipe Gonzalez, had told Craxi that what had happened between the United States and Italy on this matter would – unless there were changes of course – put at risk the result of the Spanish referendum on NATO. When Rabb countered that the Americans also needed a gesture from the Italians, and that they had to keep in mind that from the US point of view Craxi was wrong essentially because he had not kept his word. Ruggiero replied that Craxi was a proud, hotheaded man: it was impossible for him to apologize. In any case, Ruggiero said, time was running out; Craxi would not take part in the 24 October meeting in New York unless something – something for him to understand as a public gesture – was made to dampen the 'press war' between the United States and Italy. Craxi, added Ruggiero, would remain on the Italian political scene for a long time, having already marked the political landscape with its Atlanticist and pro-American positions. Certainly, there would not be a reversal of 180 degrees; however, if the dispute continued, it would have caused early elections. Craxi would then 'have embraced a sort of Gaullist platform' that would have won votes extolling national sovereignty, and this would have caused serious problems in the medium term for relations between Italy and the United States. Rabb would do what he could, even if the officials in Washington were still, 'justly and understandably', furious. Commenting to Shultz the dialogue with Ruggier, Rabb acutely noted that Craxi was torn between opposing feelings: on one hand the nationalist flattery was the harbinger of consensus, while, on the other hand the desire to be one of the world leaders who participated in the meeting on 24 October. Summarizing 'conflicting instincts', Rabb believed that Craxi wanted to return to the Atlantic by going to New York, but he would never do so without the certainty of not being criticized by the Italian press and the US government. The ambassador agreed with Ruggiero: Craxi had a long future ahead of him; moreover, it would have been impossible to create a stable democratic government in Italy without the participation of the socialists.[56]

The later events confirmed a serious change in tone and substance in the attitude of the Americans. Despite the bitterness of the exchanges between Andreotti and Shultz, Italian diplomacy continued to insist to the White House 'the extreme importance of an American initiative to end the persistent unfortunate phase of polemics', until Rozanne L. Ridgway, 'assistant secretary' for European affairs, told Petrignani that President Reagan's special emissary would be available to meet Craxi the same day.[57] Ridgway revealed to Petrignani the contents of Reagan's message, of which the presidential emissary would have been the bearer, but also disclosed the formal invitation that the president of the United States would make to Craxi for the meeting in New York on 24 October. She confirmed that the presidential emissary appointed to go to Craxi would be Deputy Secretary of State John C. Whitehead.[58] Reagan's letter to Craxi, already known and widely cited in the reconstructions of the crisis published in the Italian press, has become particularly famous for the effect the opening formula, 'Dear Bettino', as he used before the crisis, had on the Italian readers. In the short message, Reagan confined to trivial differences of views between friends and durable allies everything that had happened between the two governments in the previous days, specifying that he had never had any doubt about the intention of the Italians to put the hijackers on trial.[59] After receiving immediately the unofficial translation of the letter, Solomonic Andreotti noted, on the same sheet: 'the reason never stands on one side'.[60]

When the meeting ended, it was ten in the morning in Washington. In the evening, at the reception of the National Italian American Foundation (NIAF), Reagan participated. During his greeting speech, addressing Petrignani in front of the Italian-Americans gathered in the hall, the president said that 'the friendship between our two countries was indisputable'. The hall exploded in a long liberating applause.[61] The Italian-Americans had worked hard for this meeting, remembers Badini: divided souls, troubled and hit by the attacks of the US press on Italy, yet deeply proud of the patriotic pride that Craxi had reactivated.[62]

The end of the crisis

Even the Italian Republicans had changed their attitude, finding themselves to be the only ones guilty of a crisis of many faces and that perhaps had been exploited by many for easy advantages. When the leadership of the party started a substantial reversal, with a declaration issued the day after the letter from Reagan, the crisis of the five-party coalition began to see a possible internal solution, without changes in the majority.[63]

On the 20th there were two meetings, of which there had never been any news before, for very understandable reasons. Hugh Montgomery first met Andreotti and then Cossiga, who in July of that year was elected president of the Republic. Montgomery had been a CIA executive since its foundation, then Reagan placed him in charge of the State Department's information service, a post he had left early in 1985 to become Walters's deputy at the United Nations. Montgomery also knew Italy well, having served at the CIA station in Rome.

Cossiga said he was struck by a phenomenon that, in its early stage could not be considered alarming, but that now had to induce a serious pause for reflection. The story had aroused a wave of nationalism that, given recent Italian history, could not be overlooked. Maybe it was an exaggerated concern, but he was troubled by the comments that hovered among ordinary citizens. Equally worrying was the discomfort of the armed forces, which accused the civil authorities of having abandoned them, wounding their honour.[64]

In the comments for the department closing the report, sent ten days after the meeting, Rabb wrote to agree with Montgomery regarding the points raised by Cossiga, and in an even more direct way than Andreotti had done, in particular regarding the question of nationalism that also alarmed the embassy. But even more important was the reading of the violations of Italian airspace collateral effects, which were no longer just problems between the two governments but also between the Italian government and the armed forces.[65] This made the question of Comiso's base, the site where the Euromissiles were deployed, even more concrete: Sigonella was the airbase of Comiso. This made it even more urgent to repair the fractures.

Therefore, a side meeting was arranged the same day, 24 October in New York, during the meeting of the Western allies. It formally sanctioned the end of hostilities. In about twenty-five minutes, concluded in the presence of the press, Reagan, Shultz and the National Security Advisor Robert McFarlane met Craxi, Andreotti, Badini and Petrignani. The absence of Rabb, who should have participated according to protocol, was clearly noted. Andreotti, we learned from a subsequent document, introduced the possibility of restricting the use of Italian bases granted to the United States solely to NATO purposes. Craxi essentially repeated the speech he made to Whitehead, with perhaps a significant difference, because he said that Abu Abbas had never left the Egyptian plane, protected by escort and under diplomatic immunity. Of course, it was untrue, as he got off when the Boeing had landed in Fiumicino, to board the Yugoslav airplane. But Reagan, a consummate politician, did not reply to Craxi, who at the end of the meeting for the sake of the photographers held out his hand, saying 'friends like before'.[66]

Notes

1 A good example was a previous chapter by the author: Matteo Gerlini, 'Il caso "Achille Lauro" e le sue conseguenze', in Ennio Di Nolfo (ed.), *La politica estera italiana negli anni Ottanta* (Venice: Marsilio, 2007), 99. An interpretation believed by the press,

as reviewed by Emanuela Primiceri, *Il sequestro dell'Achille Lauro e il governo Craxi. Relazioni internazionali e dibattito politico in Italia* (Manduria: Lacaita, 2005), *passim*.
2. Guido Quaranta, 'Giulio d'Arabia', *L'Espresso* (20 October 1985).
3. As implicitly demonstrated by Luigi Cavalchini, 'I rapporti col mondo arabo', in Ennio Di Nolfo and Mario Barone (eds), *Giulio Andreotti. L'uomo, il cattolico, lo statista* (Soveria Mannelli: Rubbettino, 2010), 115–17.
4. Matteo Gerlini, 'Il pentapartito e il processo di pace arabo-israeliano', in Silvio Pons and Adriano Roccucci and Federico Romero (eds), *L'Italia contemporanea dagli anni Ottanta a oggi*, vol. I, *Fine della Guerra fredda e globalizzazione* (Rome: Carocci, 2014), 345–55.
5. A classic reference is Leonard S. Spiegel, *The Other Arab Israeli Conflict: Making America's Middle East Policy from Truman to Clinton* (Chicago: University of Chicago Press, 1986), with the more recent Douglas Little, *American Orientalism: The United States and the Middle East since 1945* (London: I.B. Tauris, 2003), *passim*.
6. It's still useful to refer to Raymond L. Garthoff, *Détente and Confrontation: American-Soviet Relations from Nixon to Reagan* (Washington, DC: Brookings Institution, 1994), 935–75.
7. Leopoldo Nuti, *La sfida nucleare: La politica estera italiana e le armi nucleari (1945–1991)* (Bologna: il Mulino, 2007), 348–53.
8. The following reconstruction is based on David Holloway, 'The Dynamic of Euromissile Crisis, 1977–1983', in Leopoldo Nuti, Frédéric Bozo, Marie-Pierre Rey and Bernd Rother (eds), *The Euromissiles Crisis and the End of the Cold War* (Washington, DC: Woodrow Wilson International Center for Scholars; Stanford, CA: Stanford University Press, 2015), 11–28.
9. Holloway, 'The Dynamics of the Euromissiles Crisis, 1977–1983', 16–17.
10. Leopoldo Nuti, *L'esercito italiano nel secondo dopo guerra, 1945–1950: La sua ricostruzione e l'assistenza militare alleata* (Rome: Ufficio storico dello Stato maggiore dell'esercito, 1989).
11. Luca Giurato, 'Dal PSI e dalla DC due voci contro il governo Cossiga', *La Stampa* (1 December 1979).
12. Holloway, 'The Dynamic of Euromissile Crisis, 1977–1983', 17.
13. Liliana Saiu, *Basi e strutture militari degli Stati Uniti in Italia: Il negoziato 1949–1954* (Rome: Aracne, 2014); Elena Calandri, *Il Mediterraneo e la difesa dell'Occidente (1947–1956)* (Florence: Manent, 1997).
14. It's clarifying the path followed by the articles appeared on the Socialists review Mondoperaio from 1977 onwards is really clarifying: Luciano Vasconi, 'Carter e la coesistenza', *Mondoperaio* 2 (February 1977); the roundtable coordinated by Federico Cohen, 'La difesa dell'Europa', *Mondoperaio* 2 (February 1980), rapidly followed by Victor Zavlasky, 'Neo Stalinismo e politica di potenza', *Mondoperaio*, 10 (October 1980).
15. Giuseppe Sacco, *Critica del nuovo secolo* (Rome: Luiss University Press, 2006), 668–83.
16. Michael Ledeen (ed.), *Intervista sul fascismo* (Rome-Bari: Laterza, [1975] 1997).
17. Pino Buongiorno, 'Tre squilli nella notte', *Panorama*, 27 October 1985; John J. Mearsheimer and Stephen M. Walt, *The Israel Lobby and US Foreign Policy* (London: Penguin, 2008), 160–4.
18. Simona Colarizi, *Storia politica della Repubblica: Partiti, movimenti e istituzioni 1943–2006* (Rome: Laterza, 2011), 141–7.
19. Holloway, 'The Dynamic of Euromissile Crisis, 1977–1983', 19.
20. Nuti, *La sfida nucleare*, 384.

21 Arturo Marzano and Guri Schwartz, *Attentato alla sinagoga, Roma, 9 ottobre 1982: Il conflitto israelo-palestinese e l'Italia* (Rome: Viella, 2013).
22 Giuseppe Zaccaria, 'Terroristi di "giugno nero" gli assassini della Sinagoga', *La Stampa* (11 October 1982).
23 Simona Colarizi and Marco Gervasoni, *La cruna dell'ago: Craxi, il Partito socialista e la crisi della Repubblica* (Rome: Laterza, 2005).
24 'Sigonella si prepara a ricevere i Cruise', *La Stampa*, 14 November 1983.
25 Nuti, *La sfida nucleare*, 388.
26 Antonio Badini and Gennaro Acquaviva, *La pagina saltata della storia* (Venice: Marsilio, 2010), 30–6.
27 ILS, GA, s. Israele-Palestina, b. 481, MAE, DGAP, Appunto, Accordo Hussein- Arafat (Amman, 11 febbraio 1985), Rome, no date.
28 ILS, GA, s. Personalità, 'Bettino Craxi', Messaggio del presidente Reagan, traduzione non ufficiale, seg., 5 January 1985.
29 Badini and Acquaviva, *La pagina saltata della storia*, 74–5.
30 Ibid., 66–7.
31 ILS, GA, s. Israele-Palestina, b. 488, MAE, Tel. da Italdipl Tel Aviv a Esteri Roma, Espulsione di esponenti palestinesi, 28 November 1985.
32 Bob Woodward, *Veil: The Secret Wars of the CIA, 1981–1987* (New York: Simon & Schuster, 2007), 397–8.
33 Richard C. Thornton, 'The Hijacking of TWA-847: A Strategic Analysis', in Jussi M. Hanhimaki and Bernhard Blumenau (eds), *An International History of Terrorism: Western and Non-Western Experiences* (London: Taylor and Francis, 2013), 124–6.
34 David C. Wills, *The First War on Terrorism: Counter-terrorism Policy during the Reagan Administration* (New York: Rowan & Littlefield, 2003), 112–28.
35 'Chiedevano la liberazione di venti compagni i terroristi che hanno sequestrato lo yacht', *Corriere della sera*, 26 September 1985.
36 Sandro Ottolenghi, Giovanni Porzio and Carlo Rossella, 'Ore 10, Arafat deve morire', *Panorama*, 13 October 1985.
37 'Solo Reagan approva il raid', *La Repubblica*, 2 October 1985, 3.
38 Enrico Franceschini, 'Reagan rettificato da Shultz "condanniamo ogni violenza"', *La Repubblica*, 3 October 1985, 2.
39 Alvaro Ranzoni, 'Perché Craxi ha rotto con Peres', *Panorama*, 13 October 1985.
40 Lelio Lagorio, conversation with the author, web: http://www.leliolagorio.it/documenti/medio_oriente.pdf (accessed 9 April 2016).
41 Fiamma Nirenstein, 'Ma Israele non è terrorista. Colloquio con Giorgio La Malfa'; and Guido Quaranta, 'La violenza crea solo violenza: Colloquio con Giulio Andreotti', *L'Espresso*, 13 ottobre 1985.
42 The following reconstruction is a synthesis of Matteo Gerlini, *Il dirottamento dell'Achille Lauro e i suoi inattesi e sorprendenti risvolti* (Milan: Arnoldo Mondadori Education, 2016), 58–166.
43 ILS, GA, Achille Lauro, b. 193, MAE, Appunto, Gabinetto del ministro, per il Presidente Andreotti, 14 ottobre 1985.
44 Rinaldo Petrignani, in Di Nolfo (ed.), *La politica estera italiana negli anni ottanta*, 139.
45 Ibid.
46 CPLGC, Appunto per l'on. Presidente del Consiglio, Rome, 16 October 1985.
47 RRPL, CMC, NSC, Achille Lauro, b. 91131, WHSR, cable, from AmEmbassy Rome to SecState WashDC, Achille Lauro hijacking – Italy and Abu el Abbas, 12 October 1985.

48 ILS GA, Achille Lauro, 193, Appunto per l'On. Presidente del Consiglio, Rome, 16 October 1985; RRPL CMC, NSC, Achille Lauro, b. 91131, WHSR, cable, from AmEmbassy Rome to SecState WashDC, Italian version of Shultz-Andreotti meeting, 15 October 1985.
49 Alessandro Silj (ed.), *L'alleato scomodo. I rapporti fra Roma e Washington nel Mediterraneo: Sigonella e Gheddafi* (Milan: Corbaccio, 1998), 171–2.
50 Petrignani, in Di Nolfo (ed.), *La politica estera italiana negli anni ottanta*, 141.
51 Badini and Acquaviva, *La pagina saltata della storia*, 115–20.
52 Petrignani, in Di Nolfo (ed.), *La politica estera italiana negli anni ottanta*, 140.
53 ILS GA, MAE, Tel. da Italdipl Washington a Esteri Roma, Nota telegrafica per l'on. Ministro (Petrignani), 17 ottobre 1985.
54 RRPL CMC, NSC Records, s. Achille Lauro, b. 91131, WHSR, cable, from AmEmbassy Rome to SecState WashDC, Achille Lauro hijacking: Foreign ministry reacting, 17 October 1985.
55 USDSVRR, Case n. F-2006–06074, doc. n. C18606002, From AmEmbassy Rome to SecState, Wash. DC, The US-Italian discord and Craxi's October 24 trip to New York, 18 October 1985.
56 Ibid.
57 ILS GA, Achille Lauro, b. 193, Tel. da Italdipl Washington a esteri Roma, messaggio personale del presidente Reagan per l'onorevole presidente del consiglio, viaggio a Roma di emissario presidenziale, n. 2372 18 October 1985.
58 ILS GA, Achille Lauro, b. 193, da Italdipl Washington a esteri Roma, messaggio personale del presidente Reagan per l'onorevole presidente del consiglio, viaggio a Roma di emissario presidenziale, n. 2374 18 ottobre 1985.
59 ILS GA, Achille Lauro, b. 193, lettera, President Reagan to His Excellency Bettino Craxi, Washington, 18 October 1985.
60 ILS, GA, Achille Lauro, b. 192, MAE, appunto manoscritto, no date, no place.
61 Petrignani, in Di Nolfo (ed.), *La politica estera italiana negli anni ottanta*, 145.
62 Antonio Badini, conversation with the author, 5 May 2005.
63 'Quattro partiti dicono Craxi', *La Stampa*, 19 October 1985.
64 USDSVRR, Case n. F-2006–06074, doc. n. C18606000, Tel. from AmEmbassy Rome to SecStae WashDC, Discussion of the Achille Lauro affair with President Cossiga, 30 ottobre 1985. Partially published in Fondazione Craxi, *La notte di Sigonella* (Milan: Mondadori, 2015).
65 Ibid.
66 Petrignani, in Di Nolfo (ed.), *La politica estera italiana negli anni ottanta*, 146–7; Paolo Garimberti, 'Craxi-Reagan, amici come prima', *La Stampa*, 25 October 1985, 7.

9

Gaddafi and the troubled relations with Italy

Paolo Soave

Italy and Libya after the Second World War: A new start

Historically, most Italian attempts to achieve the profile of Mediterranean power implied establishing special relations with Libya. In the colonial era the region including Tripolitania, Cyrenaica and Fezzan was mainly considered as the North African shore (the so-called 'quarta sponda'),[1] but once the kingdom of Libya achieved its independence Rome started seeing it as a new relevant strategic partner. After the Second World War the demographic presence in North Africa of some Italian communities was a pivotal tool for the new foreign policy practised by Rome, so different from the past and aimed at promoting Mediterranean relations inspired by peaceful coexistence, democracy and multilateral cooperation.[2] The 'surrender of rights'[3] over the colonies imposed by the peace treaty first forced Italy to search for an old style diplomatic compromise in order to maintain some influence on Libya, the so-called Bevin-Sforza agreement, and then, after its failure, to turn to a post-colonial policy. This change was part of a wider process aimed at reshaping the international role of Italy, no longer able, according to Ambassador Pietro Quaroni, to act as a relevant power.[4] Driving the country towards the Western block, as a national leader Alcide De Gasperi was perfectly aware of the need of a democratic and representative foreign policy, aimed at creating a space of international autonomy, even beyond NATO, urged not only by socialists and communists, but also by the DC and the Catholic world. To some extent, since then, the more Italian foreign policy was sensitive to national political instability, the more it would try to intensify its pro-Third World approach.[5]

Despite the action of the United Nations, the independence of Libya emerged as a consequence of the previous alliance between the UK and Idris es Sanusi, rather than as a starter of a wider process of decolonization, which eventually was delayed for some years. The Cold War, on the contrary, was already forcing the powers to oppose each other geopolitically, and the main Western partners of Italy, the United States and the UK, simply considered Rome no longer able to keep control over an area of increasing strategic relevance for the Mediterranean balance of power. The new kingdom of Libya was a typical case of neocolonialism, soon subject to a strong economic and military Anglo-American influence.[6] As the Cold War contributed to outline the strategic relevance of the Mediterranean Basin, Italy tried to carry on regional dialogue and cooperation even beyond ideological or strategic barriers.[7] During the 1960s, Italy was once again an appreciated regional partner, an emerging industrial power, with a friendly and sensitive approach to the social and economic needs of backward countries. The Italian formula seemed to be fit for everyone, so after an early sympathy for Israel, as a post-colonial and pro-socialist state, a strong movement supporting the Palestinian issue and the Arab world arose in Italy.[8] However as Arab–Israeli tensions escalated in wars, and Libya was transformed into an Anglo-American military base, the positive Italian regionalism was jeopardized by the globalization of the Cold War.[9] Starting with the Suez Crisis the USSR was involved in Middle East tensions. If regionalism was devoted to preserving unity, the Cold War exploited political tensions favouring local discord. Moreover, Italy was strictly dependent on NATO security and worried by the increasing militarization of the Middle East. American support to Israeli defense was considered in Italy the main reason for the strict relations between countries like Egypt and Syria with the USSR in order to acquire arms supplies. For many reasons Libya was the acid test of the Italian regional approach in opposing Cold War divisive effects, its most advanced attempt and eventually the best result of its foreign policy. As Italy was the bulwark of Western strategic influence in the Mediterranean, Idris was required to oppose Nasser pan-Arabism and acted prudently, avoiding any meaningful engagement in the Arab–Israeli crisis.

Despite many difficulties, the Italian community still remained the élite of the poor in Libyan society and in 1956 a bilateral agreement gave evidence of the common interest in removing the past and starting a new profitable era, in compliance with the United Nations resolution 388 on post-colonial relations. Italy committed to transfer to the Libyan authorities the former colonial properties as well as to refund Tripoli for colonial and war damages, as Libya acknowledged the social and economic role of the Italians.[10] Hopefully it was the turning point of the bilateral relations, as confirmed a year after with the agreement between ENI, the Italian oil company, and the Libyan government.[11] Eni's chairman, Enrico Mattei, was the most ambitious supporter of the so-called 'neoatlantismo', the new foreign policy pursued by Italy since the mid-1950s and aimed at achieving a wider international autonomy.[12] It was especially turned to the Arab countries and inspired by the need of energy supplies as well as by the search for a wider political consensus after the end of the so-called De Gasperi centrism. Mattei was to some extent an economic nationalist convinced that the development of Italy was not negotiable, even with its allies. To Mattei the 'veto' posed by NATO on relations with anti-Israeli or pro-Soviet countries seemed simply unfit for Italy. In 1957 Mattei was succesful in completing with the Shah Reza Pahlavi a revolutionary oil agreement particularly favourable to the producer, a kind of war declaration to the so-called 'seven sisters', the strongest Western oil majors. In the same year Mattei tried to do the same with Libya, which was not as advanced as Iran in the oil industry, but Idris was forced by the Americans to reject the treaty reached by Mattei and Libyan Prime Minister Ben Halim.[13] However, despite the strong influence of Standard Oil of New Jersey, which had discovered a huge oil field in Libya, Mattei was able to take part in the local competion, obtaining a first contract in 1959.[14] Once removed the past without a serious national debate, Italy was once again on the verge of a new social-economic influence in Libya, providing for new strategic investments, at least until September 1969, when some young officers seized power in Tripoli.[15]

The advent of Gaddafi: A junior Nasser

The political change in Libya was commonly considered the consequence of Idris's loss of consensus as well as of emerging of Israeli–Arab tensions after the Six-Day War.[16] According to Henry Kissinger, US national security advisor, the coup had been inspired by the rising Arab nationalism led by Nasser. Kissinger's main concern was focused on US regional influence, no longer able to support the moderate regimes after the reduction of the peripheral engagements imposed by the Nixon doctrine. Gaddafi was imagined to be just more inclined to social reforms than Idris, hostile to moderate Tunisia and less handy for the Western powers.[17] With experience in a British military academy, he was the young, unknown leader of the least relevant country in the Middle East, a son of the desert with permanent injuries from the colonial times and finally a devoted admirer of Nasser.[18] Soon after the coup he announced a reformist program aimed at providing Libya with a common identity and some solid social bases.[19] A new interpretation of the Sharia deprived the old religious elites of any social and political relevance, concentrating in Gaddafi's hands any power over tribes and military forces. The ambition for a non-aligned Libya, freed from any influence, was announced with the Third Way theory.[20] As a tough answer to the failure of decolonization, the first terrific decision taken by Gaddafi was the expulsion of the Americans and the British from their military bases in Wheelus Field and El Adem. He clearly explained that this move was not the end of the relations with the Western powers, but a turning point for a better consideration of the Libyan national interests and for a new international and more autonomous posture.[21] The American ambassador in Libya, Joseph Palmer, suggested a soft reaction: on a long-term perspective, once having achieved some political stabilization, the new leader was expected to become a new ally in order to prevent Soviet influence over the Mediterranean. This point of view was widely shared at the Department of State as well as in Europe.[22] Far from considering the expulsion from Wheelus Field a first step to a new Nasserism, the Nixon administration did not suffer any strategic loss because of the advent of the new ballistic missiles. A soft approach in order to appease Gaddafi as well as Arab nationalism, thus preserving the American economic interests in Libya, was consistent with the preference for a light engagement in the Middle East.[23] However, when in 1970 Gaddafi announced the revolutionary nationalization of the oil industry, the Americans started bewaring of the new Libyan leader.[24] He proved to be the first Arab leader exploiting this resource in foreign policy, then widely followed by the other producers after the Yom Kippur War. Within a few years the increasing oil revenues permitted Gaddafi to purchase a huge amount of arms in order to improve the regional influence of Libya as an emerging country devoted to pan-Arabism. Even more concerning was the fact that the USSR was to become the leading arms supplier of Libya by 1974.[25] Analysts started wondering if Gaddafi would be able to do better than Nasser in establishing an effective alliance with Moscow, not only a simple partnership, in order to change the balance of power in the Middle East. The answer still remained quite reassuring: Gaddafi was too unpredictable for the Soviets as well as Libya being unable to offer sea facilities to the Soviet Navy.[26] However, after the loss of that strategic presence, the United States had even suffered serious damage of its economic interests in Libya. Having misunderstood Gaddafi, someone at the Department of State as well as at the White House was forced to admit that a new factor of regional instability had arisen.[27] Despite Libya being short of staff to operate its new military systems, Tunisia, Iran and Egypt became aware of the emerging threat to regional stability.[28] The most interesting case was Egypt: Sadat's deep change in foreign policy, with openings to Israel and the United States, made the country no longer a model but a border enemy for Libya. Egyptian military officers declared to be ready to punish Gaddafi with a military initiative in the event of American consent. They were confident that in case of preemptive attack against Tripoli no serious reaction would come from Moscow, and in 1977 the border tensions eventually erupted in a short war between Egypt and Libya.[29] Camp David was a turning point: the complete change of the Egyptian approach to the regional dispute forced Libya, fiercely opposing the treaty with Israel, to isolation. Gaddafi reacted by intensifying his support to many forms of radicalism, but what he really achieved was only widespread criticism even by his Italian partners.[30]

Reshaping relations again: Moro's answer to Gaddafi

The political stability of Libya was a strategic asset for Italian interests, admitted Roberto Gaja, general secretary of the Ministry for Foreign Affairs. For him even the military presence of British and American soldiers in Libya was a positive factor of stability.[31] This appraisal was dramatically confirmed when Italy experienced the same hostility.[32] On 21 July 1970, Gaddafi announced the expulsion of about twenty thousand Italians living in Libya. According the trade advisor of the Italian embassy in Tripoli, Morrone, the general amount of goods seized from the Italians was more than US$100 million. Moreover, ambassador Folchi noticed that, unlike France, Italy had no Mirage war planes to offer in order to keep Colonel Gaddafi friendly.[33] In expelling Italians, he wanted not to remove the long-term economic relations with Italy but to relaunch them on different bases. As the Italian community still represented the social elite of Libya, it had to pay the consequences of the the new political course, based on the myth of anti-colonialism.[34]

As for the Americans, the Italian reaction was very prudential. Despite the decision happening quite unexpectedly and causing a deep concern, Minister for Foreign Affairs Aldo Moro opted for the moderate way.[35] Italian astonishment was confirmed by the misunderstanding of the Egyptian role: while Moro was hopeful in Nasser's mediation in order to appease Gaddafi, it was clear that Egypt, far from playing as a honest broker, was interested in replacing the Italian influence over Libyan society with its own workers.[36] However Libyan Minister for Foreign Relations Buyasseer clearly explained the new political course to Moro, and that it aimed at removing the treaty of 1956 and opening a new era in bilateral relations.[37] Even the serious issue of the rights of the expelled Italians was a critical point for Italy, and eventually Rome preferred not to raise new tensions with Tripoli and try to match as much as possible the claims. Unprepared, Moro and most Italian politicians supposed Gaddafi was only pressing Italy in order to obtain new economic advantages and not really pursuing a revolutionary course. As Libya represented the acid test of the new democratic and peaceful Italian foreign policy, no tough reaction was acceptable for a country which had been a former colonial power. Moreover, economic relations with Libya were particularly strategic in order to secure cheap energy supplies for the industrial development. Moro argued that in case of intense economic relations between the two countries it would have been easier to coexist with Gaddafi. On 5 May 1971, Moro was in Tripoli to offer Gaddafi some cooperation for the launch of the Libyan national petrochemical industry, a real turning point in bilateral relations.[38] On 25 February 1974, Jalloud, Gaddafi's closest advisor, signed in Rome a bilateral agreement on scientific and economic cooperation. As Italian oil imports reached thirty million tons a year, a plan for new Libyan refineries was approved by the two governments.[39] ENI became a strategic investor in Libya, as were other private and public Italian companies offering new projects and joint ventures in a country which was short of hospitals, schools, streets and other basic social facilities. However the Moro way in dealing with Gaddafi was not easily accepted in Italy, raising some nationalistic reactions for its supposed weakness. While the advent of Gaddafi, despite the first move, really enhanced bilateral economic advantages, the main problem in experiencing a troubled lasting relationship with him was the lack of political comprehension. For many years, as Italy did not face its past, the Colonel tried to fire the emerging Libyan identity with strong anti-colonial rhetoric, even establishing the so-called 'day of hate' against Italy.

Eventually the Moro way was largely successful in strenghtening economic relations and in stabilizing the Libyan political scenario. The Italian–Libyan affair gained increasing relevance according the formula of balanced and integrated cooperation between an industrial power, not invasive and respectful of the local characters, and a backward oil producer. To some extent, it was a case of 'indispensable cooperation' because, on the one hand, Italy could not obtain elsewhere the same cheap conditions in purchasing energy supplies; on the other hand, Libya could not achieve technological assistance and investments avoiding the risk of neocolonialism.[40] In few years Italy and Libya widened the field of their cooperation to culture and technology, and many companies got a role in the Libyan economy and society. In the 1970s, even Fiat, the most important Italian private company, tied up relations with Libya.

The success of Moro's formula was confirmed by two factors. First, for about forty years, all along the Gaddafi era, the Italian governments followed the same political path, deciding to tolerate the Colonel's harsh attacks basically in exchange for good business and stable relations. This point proved to be stronger than the Libyan concern for the fact that Italy was a NATO member which hosted some American military bases that could hit Libya any moment. Secondly, the success of Moro's formula was confirmed by the critics coming from the Western allies. For the Americans the Italian–Libyan special relationship was hardly acceptable, even if considering the need of safe and cheap energy supplies, the moral issue in order to prevent new conflicts with

Tripoli after the colonial era and the general interest in Mediterranean stability.[41] In the 1970s, two points created some concern in the Americans: oil and arms supplies. After the Yom Kippur conflict, the oil consumptions were a matter of solidarity among the Western powers as Kissinger tried to argue promoting a common front of consumers facing the producers. Despite the international crisis, ENI was the only Western company preserved by the Libyan constrains and, according to the Americans, this was a matter of unfair competition or a lack of solidarity among Western companies. Moreover, as Gaddafi was moving towards closer cooperation with the USSR, the Italian bilateral relations with countries unfriendly to the Western block and Israel caused concern.[42] US diplomats outlined in their reports the increasing economic relevance of the bilateral relations between Italy and Libya, offering less attention to the political reasons. They concluded that Gaddafi seemed to appreciate only a point of Italian foreign policy, the friendly approach towards the Arab world, but eventually they underrated the possible contribution to Middle East stability coming from good bilateral relations between Rome and Tripoli.[43] In some talks the Italian executives of the Ministry of Industry and Foreign Affairs were suggested by the American diplomatic staff in Rome to turn the industrial production from oil to atomic energy, in order to avoid a dangerous addiction to Libya.[44] Even more astonishing was the investment of the Libyan Arab Foreign Bank which purchased 9.1 per cent of Fiat shares in December 1976. Cesare Romiti, general manager of the Italian company, explained to the American consul in Turin that Fiat had decided to satisfy the Libyan ambition to take some part in the Western financial world in a moment when the Italian company was short of cash.[45]

Another point of the Italian soft approach to Libya was the availabilty to sell advanced arms, which was opposed by the Americans in case some US components or patents were involved, in order to prevent any unfriendly use against Israel.[46] Eventually, the Libyan complaints reached Italy.[47] Maybe the most interesting defense of the Italian soft approach to Gaddafi was made by President Giovanni Leone in a summit when he said that by tolerating the Colonel's insolence, Italy was giving evidence of its international responsibility in order to prevent an alliance between the USSR and Libya.[48] Consequently in 1978 Libyan Minister for Foreign Affairs Ali Triki signed in Rome a new agreement of economic and scientific cooperation which opened his country to a new increasing Italian elite represented by Eni's personnel. Sometimes the Italian government was asked by its allies to convince Gaddafi to be more moderate, especially as concerned the Camp David agreement. In this case the failure of diplomatic efforts proved the lack of any Italian political influence over Gaddafi and the distance between Rome and Tripoli in relation to the peace process in the Middle East.[49] Despite the expulsion of the Italian community, the 1970s were a golden age in the bilateral relations between Italy and Libya, economically rather than politically.

By the way Gaddafi himself contributed to the increasing isolation of Libya supporting international terrorism, especially after the attack in Fiumicino airport, on December 1973.[50] The Libyan leader broadly compromised the Italian effort to promote Libya as a reliable partner for the Western countries and eventually only Rome continued to appreciate the political stability imposed by Gaddafi.[51]

Troubled years: Terrorism and the global Cold War on the Italian–Libyan special relationship

The emergence of international terrorism inspired by the Arab–Israeli tensions was a serious issue for Italian foreign policy in the Mediterranean, especially in order to stay consistently on the same course regarding the regional interests with the Western strategic alliance. While in the 1970s Nixon and Carter pursued a soft way in dealing with Gaddafi and matched quite well with Italian tolerance of the Libyan regime, after 1981 President Reagan imposed a turning point, arguing that terrorism was the other face of the Cold War. As the bipolar confrontation was on the verge of a possible turn because of the crisis of the USSR, fighting the states supporting terrorism and indirectly tied to Moscow, especially for the purchase of arms, gave Reagan the chance to relaunch the international profile of the United States and impose some pressure on the Soviets.[52] As Reagan was oriented to end the detente and win the Cold War, his doctrine really oriented the foreign and security policy turning to a global approach to regional issues, from the Middle East to Latin America.[53] According to Westad's interpretation, Reagan widely contributed to globalizing the Cold War.[54] In the Middle East the Americans experienced the lowest point of their influence in October 1983, when the slaughter of marines in Lebanon caused by an 'act of war using the medium of terrorism', according to George Shultz, brought Reagan to call back the troops from that country.[55] The Middle East had slowly slipped into the Cold War starting from the Suez Crisis. As the only stable alliance in the region was the US–Israeli one, the Arabs tried to exploit the bipolar confrontation in order to gain some advantages. However no Arab leader was able to establish a real political and strategic alliance with the USSR, and even arms supplies, which came particularly copiously from Moscow, never forced the balance of power and, eventually, the peace process in favour of the Arabs.[56] The same happened for Gaddafi, who was never considered by Soviet leaders a reliable partner, as American intelligence assumed.[57] Combining a hostile approach towards the United States with a huge amount of Soviet arms, he was automatically enrolled in the list of enemies.[58] Even if only a minor troublemaker, Libya became a test case for the United States, and Reagan was particularly capable in exploiting the wave of national indignation for the long series of terroristic attacks against civil targets, as the polls led by *ABC* and the *Washington Post* clearly showed.[59] Against Libya the United States practised every aspect of coercive diplomacy, from diplomatic isolation to sanctions and eventually the use of force.[60] Since 1981 the US administration had adopted some economic measures in order to cut the Libyan oil revenues which financed the purchase of arms.[61] The sanctions were harshly debated by American and European oil companies, fiercely opposed by Gaddafi and, eventually, Reagan proved unwilling to wait a long time in order to take some advantage from the economic constraints on Libya. The next step of the escalation, the use of force, was debated inside the administration between the 'hawks' gathered around George Shultz and the 'doves' led by Caspar Weinberger, but eventually approved as 'preemptive and retaliatory strikes against terrorists'.[62] Before the use of force other moves involving the CIA were taken by the administration in order to create some pressure on Gaddafi and eventually provoke his political downfall.[63]

The perspective of a military confrontation in the Mediterranean between the two most relevant strategic partners of Italy caused deep concern in the Craxi government. The socialist leader and his Minister for Foreign Affairs, Andreotti, were trying to relaunch some international activism and one of the most relevant points was the Italian contribution to the peace process in the Middle East.[64] At the same time, in the years of the so-called second Cold War, Craxi had proved to be a reliable strategic ally accepting the deployment in Italy of new missiles in Comiso, quite close to Libya, causing new disappointment in Gaddafi. Despite his hostile rhetoric against Italian strategic subordination to the United States, the Colonel was always involved in the regional dialogue and cooperation pursued by Rome. An escalation between Americans and Libyans in the Mediterranean would have been particularly dangerous for Italy. As Giulio Andreotti was able to get Gaddafi's trust introducing the theme of some Italian economic reparatory act for the past, in 1984 he was asked by the Libyan leader to mediate with Reagan in order to remove the tensions between Tripoli and Washington.[65] To some extent, as Andreotti recognized, Gaddafi relied on Italian mediation to avoid the international isolation imposed by the Americans. Concerning this, Reagan and Shultz replied to Andreotti to be no longer interested in Gaddafi's words but only in some evidence of goodwill coming from Tripoli, starting from condemnation of terrorism against American targets.[66] Andreotti, who acted as mediator without conviction, was always very careful in balancing the alliance with the United States with the Italian interest for Libya as regional partner. At the same time he was available to use his influence over Gaddafi in order to facilitate the secret mission in Libya of the American ambassador to the Holy See, William Wilson. The mission eventually did not succed in preserving American oil interests in Libya and caused some embarrassment in Reagan's administration when it was unveiled by Gaddafi. It clearly showed that the White House's approach in dealing with the Libyan leader was not so monolithic as officially stated by Reagan and Shultz.[67]

However the Italian effort to maintain the same course of foreign policy with the United States and Libya was harshly tested from 1985 to 1986. In October 1985 the Sigonella crisis pushed Italian and US forces to the verge of a conflict over the capture of the terrorists responsible for the hijacking of the *Achille Lauro* and the murder of the American citizen Leon Klinghoffer.[68] The two allies clearly had divergent attitudes towards the terrorists and Mediterranean security. The difference between the American global approach defined by the Cold War was tackled by the Italian regional way, aimed at preserving relations with all actors, especially Arafat's PLO and Egypt. Despite the tensions Craxi and Reagan soon restored good personal relations, and the American administration admitted the existence of different ways in dealing with violence, and that the diplomatic one was the way pursued by Italy. Moreover, the Americans recognized that Craxi had been successful with Italian public opinion in posing the Sigonella crisis in terms of national sovereignty. Unusually for an Italian leader, he was acting in such a proud and effective way that ambassador Raab suggested considering him as a long-term partner.[69] Once again the Middle East and the Mediterranean represented the geopolitical preferred area for some Italian autonomy.

Less than a year later, a somewhat similar crisis occurred again involving Libya and the United States. After new terroristic attacks, from the end of 1985 to 1986, Reagan definitely decided to strike against Gaddafi.⁷⁰ The final step of the escalation was announced by the American decision to conduct some naval drills on March, close to the disputed Sidra waters.⁷¹ After the attacks at Vienna and Fiumicino airports in December 1985, with some evidence of Libyan responsibility, the Italian government had more difficulties in carrying on its moderate and regional policy and eventually was forced by the events to follow Washington by way of the embargo on Tripoli, even if only partially practised.⁷² Craxi and Andreotti tried in any possible way to avoid a military clash in the Mediterranean. Both opposing actors were hard for Italian diplomacy to handle. Gaddafi was really worried by the prospects of an American military attack, but as he was not about to repudiate his foreign policy, he was just trying to avoid international isolation. When he asked the Maltese premier, Bonnici, to involve Italy in a wide Mediterranean peace conference, even Craxi meant to subordinate this possible way out for Libya upon a formal condemnation of terrorism, and this initiative fell down.⁷³ While the socialist leader was not particularly tolerant of the Colonel and refused to restore high-level relations with Libya, the talks between the diplomat Alessandro Quaroni and Jalloud contributed to securing economic bilateralism for better moments.⁷⁴ In order to enhance the Italian position in the Mediterranean, Craxi visited a prominent leader and a respected partner of the Americans, Mubarak.⁷⁵ The talks with the Americans definitely failed when in March 1986 George Shultz was in Rome. The serious difference between the global approach of the United States and the regional vision of Italy emerged once again as in the Sigonella crisis and finally the Secretary of State ironically wished Italy good luck in trying to soften Gaddafi through diplomacy.⁷⁶

The escalation forced even Italy to consider Libya as a potential threat for its security, especially in order to secure a few thousands Italians who were working in Tripolitania and Cyrenaica.⁷⁷ However, the most relevant political and diplomatic effort sustained by the Italian government in order to prevent the final step of force was with Europe. The European Community was very late in becoming aware of the crisis and in general about terrorism. Apart from the cultural and political differences in approaching the issue of political violence, the Twelve were moving towards regional dialogue with the Arabs in order to define a common Mediterranean space.⁷⁸ In a few months some meetings were devoted by the ministers of foreign affairs to the issue of terrorism. On 14 April 1986, the Twelve produced their best effort recognizing the Libyan threat and adopting progressive measures to isolate Tripoli and force Gaddafi to repudiate terrorism. The European solution was focused on an international conference, including the Mediterranean actors as well as the most relevant extra-European powers.⁷⁹

The common effort was too late and not particularly effective, according to the United States. After having visited the most important European capitals, Vernon Walters, Reagan's envoy, was in Italy just in time to talk with Craxi and Andreotti after the meeting in the Hague and some hours before the American attack.⁸⁰ Walters's task was not to debate with the European allies as to how to deal with Gaddafi, but just to inform them that the United States would attack Libya soon. The European tour of Walters was not easy: Margaret Thatcher hardly accepted to allow the American planes to leave from British bases in order to reach Libya. Andreotti and Craxi used rational arguments trying to convince the Americans to postpone military action: the use of force could escalate new tensions in the Mediterranean, creating new troubles for

Italy. Moreover, despite his unpredictable or hostile behaviour, Gaddafi was providing the Libyan stability, and the Americans had not prepared a political alternative. The prospect of anarchy, as well as a stronger alliance between Tripoli and Moscow in case of political survival of Gaddafi, were even worse. American indifference to the fate of Gaddafi and the Libyan leadership sounded really stunning to the Italians. Craxi and Andreotti tried also to play the European card emphasizing the results of the Hague summit, but the Americans proved not to be particularly interested in preserving at least a formal role for the European Community in the Mediterranean crisis. Walters said only that the Americans had the evidence of Libyan responsibility for the *La Belle* disco terroristic attack in Berlin, a 'smoking gun', and that the announced military action was only aimed at punishing Gaddafi.

The goal was particularly limited, even in military or strategic terms, and the lack of European solidarity was considered quite disappointing by Walters. The last appeal posed by Andreotti was a plea for more time in order to secure the positions of the Italians who were in Libya. Many years after, the real purpose of the Italian government was unveiled: its intelligence warned Gaddafi of the imminent attack, maybe to save his life.[81] This further move aimed at preserving bilateral relations was not so meaningful: Gaddafi was personally aware of the American military threat, which had been announced by the Soviets. In the same hours, the American air raid came like a new case of the old 'gunboat diplomacy' pursued in the Mediterranean in the early 1980s.[82] Far from removing the causes of terrorism as well as to provoke the collapse of Gaddafi's regime, the air raid was a slap in the face to the European allies who had pursued a diplomatic solution of the crisis, which Shultz admitted.[83] It was also a move to test the Soviet reaction in the global Cold War: from Moscow came only a formal condemnation of the American conduct, as expected by Reagan.

Apparently Italy suffered the most: deeply humbled by the lack of any Libyan defense under the American bombing, Gaddafi reacted by trying to launch some missiles towards the Loran station on the Italian island of Lampedusa. More paradoxical than stunning, the Libyan leader searched for an easy political relaunch against a partner who was too moderate for a tough reaction and at the same time too much interested in preserving at any cost the bilateral relations with Tripoli. In doing so the failure of the Libyan missile attack contributed to its political aim, as Craxi decided not to retaliate.[84] As the American escalation and its culminating point in April 1986 dropped Italian–Libyan relations to their lowest level after the expulsion of the Italian community in 1970, the interest for arguing economic cooperation survived both in Rome and in Tripoli.

Despite some scholars have argued that Reagan led the first war on terror many years before 11 September 2001, soon after the raid on Libya the American interest in pursuing this goal collapsed.[85] According to its Political Affairs' General Direction of the Ministry for Foreign Relations, Italy had to move beyond American protection and pursue the lifting of the economic embargo in order to relaunch bilateral relations with Libya. The only change before the crisis was the emphasis posed for the first time by the Craxi government on the Libyan responsibilities in causing Mediterranean instability, as confirmed during the Tokyo summit in May 1986. However Craxi and Andreotti argued with their Western allies about the opportunity to ease the economic embargo in order to bring Tripoli to repudiate terrorism.[86] Far from removing the sanctions, the Americans started admitting that Gaddafi was a long-term problem and proved to be more available to cooperate with the Europeans in order to face the Libyan threat with diplomatic or economic means.[87] Once again Italy acted, promoting a Libyan redemption, at least until the airliner explosion over Lockerbie, in December 1988, which definitely confined Gaddafi to international condemnation and isolation.

After the Cold War: From isolation to rehabilitation

In the 1990s the Libyan position was no longer sustainable, as Gaddafi had lost any international support. In bad conditions the ties with Italy assumed high relevance in order to secure the Libyan political stability, as Craxi clearly showed when he declared that Italy was ready to take responsibilities for its colonial crimes.[88] In 1991, Andreotti's goodwill proposal turned to commitment to removing the mines from Libya and giving information about the deportees, in exchange for Gaddafi's pledge to repudiate the production of chemical weapons. Even if reluctantly, Italy respected United Nations resolution 748 which since 31 March, 1992, extended the embargo to force Libya to deliver the individuals responsible for Lockerbie.[89]

Even in the so-called 'Seconda Repubblica', with a new party system emerging from the action led by the judiciary against the old political forces, Italy started working towards a slow removal of the severe conditions that could push Gaddafi's regime into economic crisis and eventually political instability. In 1996 the Prodi government authorized ENI to sign a new agreement for a gas pipeline as the first step of a new era of economic investments. Inaugurated in 2004 by Berlusconi and Gaddafi, Greenstream, the longest sea pipeline in the Mediterranean, is a physical link aimed at definitely stabilizing economic integration between Libya and Italy, whatever the changing political conditions.[90]

Giving evidence of realism, the Colonel contributed to overcoming the worst moment delivering the perpetrators of Lockerbie in 1999, repudiating mass destruction weapons and opposing the spread of Al Qaeda in his country. A stunning, full rehabilitation occurred when he was upgraded to strategic partner of the European Union to contain migratory flows across the Mediterranean. Representing the African Union, Gaddafi was received in Brussels by Romano Prodi, chair of the European Commission, in April 2004.[91] In 2008 these positive conditions led Italy to the special relationship with Libya through a new general deal of friendship and economic cooperation signed by Berlusconi and Gaddafi, which was eventually suspended by Rome in 2011 under the Western military campaign promoted to remove the Colonel[92]. Since then Italy is still searching for a new stability in Libya as a condition for restoring the special relationship with Tripoli and for a safer Mediterranean.

Conclusion

From the 1970s to the 1990s, relations between Italy and Libya were widely influenced by the Gaddafi's unpredictable behaviour. Trying to promote himself as a new

Nasser and Libya as new regional power, on one hand he got the economic advantages from the bilateral relations with Italy and, on the other hand, he exploited the political weakness of Rome and its weak participation into NATO. As economic relations improved through those years, shaping 'indispensable cooperation' and a sort of complementarity between an industrial power and an energy supplier, the political dialogue was almost nonsense, and Gaddafi appreciated only the Italian sympathy for the Arab world. The soft approach introduced by Moro since 1970 remained the best answer to Gaddafi's tough rethoric in order to preserve economic relations and prevent new threats in the years of emerging international terrorism and Cold War confrontation. The political misunderstanding between Tripoli and Rome was a matter of post-colonialism rather than real decolonization. While Italy never elaborated its past in national terms and simply tried to go beyond, Gaddafi never cast off the historical heritage and instead exploited it in order to define a common Libyan identity. These contradictions turned into a crisis when the superpowers interfered in the Mediterranean, making Gaddafi isolated and forcing Italy to take some distance from Tripoli. Despite some personal changes, there was a stunning continuity in Italy's moderate approach to the Colonel, practised by every government even beyond the Cold War with the 'Seconda Repubblica' and its new parties. The history of the economic interpenetration between these two countries was clearly successful, one of the most relevant for the Italian foreign policy in the second post-war period. Moreover, it contributed to the stability of the Mediterranean at least until 2011, when long-term Italian fears about a post-Gaddafi scenario were confirmed.

Notes

1 For Italian colonialism in Libya, see Luciano Monzali, *Il colonialismo nella politica estera italiana, 1878–1949: Momenti e protagonisti* (Rome: Dante Alighieri 2017); Massimo Borgogni and Paolo Soave, *Italia e Libia: Un secolo di relazioni controverse* (Rome: Aracne, 2015); Federico Cresti, *Non desiderare la terra d'altri: la colonizzazione italiana in Libia* (Rome: Carocci, 2011), Paolo Soave, *Fezzan: il deserto conteso (1842–1921)* (Milan: Giuffré, 2001), Angelo Del Boca, *Gli italiani in Libia*, 2 vols (Rome: Laterza, 1986); Sergio Romano, *La quarta sponda: la guerra di Libia, 1911–1912* (Milan: Bompiani, 1977); Jean Louis Miège, *L'imperialismo coloniale italiano dal 1870 ai giorni nostri* (Milan: BUR, 1976).

2 For a general approach to the history of Italian foreign policy, see Luca Riccardi, *La grandezza di una media potenza: personaggi e problemi della politica estera italiana del Novecento* (Rome: Dante Alighieri, 2017); Giuseppe Mammarella and Paolo Cacace, *La politica estera dell'Italia: dallo Stato unitario ai giorni nostri* (Rome: Laterza, 2010); Sergio Romano, *Guida alla politica estera italiana: da Badoglio a Berlusconi* (Milan: BUR, 2004); Liliana Saiu, *La politica estera italiana dall'Unità a oggi* (Rome: Laterza, 1999); Antonio Varsori, *L'Italia nelle relazioni internazionali dal 1943 al 1992* (Rome: Laterza, 1998); Luigi V. Ferraris (ed.), *Manuale della politica estera italiana 1947–1993* (Rome: Laterza, 1996); Roberto Gaja, *L'Italia nel mondo bipolare. Per una storia della politica estera italiana (1943–1991)* (Bologna: Il Mulino, 1995); Antonio Varsori, *La politica estera italiana nel secondo dopoguerra* (Milan: LED, 1993);

Paolo Cacace, *Venti anni di politica estera italiana (1943–1963)* (Rome: Bonacci, 1986); Pietro Pastorelli, *Dalla prima alla seconda guerra mondiale: momenti e problemi della politica estera italiana, 1941–1943* (Milan: LED, 1986).

3 Gianluigi Rossi, *L'Africa italiana verso l'indipendenza (1941–1949)* (Milan: Giuffré, 1980).

4 Luciano Monzali, 'Pietro Quaroni e la politica estera italiana (1944–1947)', in Stefano Baldi (ed.), *Un ricordo di Pietro Quaroni* (Rome: Ministero Affari Esteri e della Cooperazione Internazionale, 2014), 39–50. For the relevance of the colonial issue in the Italian foreign policy after the Second World War, see Gaja, *L'Italia nel mondo bipolare*, 129–31.

5 For some considerations on the connection between national and foreign policy in Italy, see James E. Miller, *La politica estera di una media potenza: il caso italiano da De Gasperi a Craxi* (Manduria: Lacaita, 1992).

6 For the Libyan strategic relevance in a Cold War perspective, see Giovanni Buccianti, *Libia: petrolio e indipendenza* (Milan: Giuffré, 1999).

7 Massimo de Leonardis (ed.), *Il Mediterraneo nella politica estera italiana del secondo dopoguerra* (Bologna: Il Mulino, 2003).

8 On the emerging of an Italian pro-Arab attitude see Luca Riccardi, *Il problema Israele: diplomazia italiana e PCI di fronte allo Stato ebraico, 1948–1973* (Milan: Guerini, 2006); Ferraris (ed.), *Manuale della politica estera italiana 1947–1993*, 63.

9 Odd A. Westad, *The Global Cold War: Third World Interventions and the Making of Our Times* (Cambridge: Cambridge University Press, 2007).

10 Massimiliano Cricco, 'Gheddafi e l'Italia negli anni Settanta. Dall'espulsione della comunità italiana dalla Libia alla firma degli accordi di cooperazione economica tra Roma e Tripoli', in Daniela Melfa, Alessia Melcangi and Federico Cresti (eds), *Spazio privato, spazio pubblico e società civile in Medio Oriente e in Africa del Nord* (Milan: Giuffré, 2008), 530.

11 Ilaria Tremolada, *Nel mare che ci unisce. Il petrolio nelle relazioni tra Italia e Libia* (Milan: Mimesis, 2015).

12 See Nico Perrone, *Enrico Mattei* (Bologna: Il Mulino, 2012).

13 Ben Halim and Mustafa Ahmed, *Libya: The Years of Hope – The Memoirs of Mustafa Ben-Haim, Former Prime Minister of Libya* (London: AAS Media, 1994). On Mattei's challenge to the international oil market, see Leonardo Maugeri, *L'arma del petrolio: questione petrolifera globale, guerra fredda e politica italiana nella vicenda di Enrico Mattei* (Florence: Loggia de' Lanzi, 1994).

14 Massimiliano Cricco, *Il petrolio dei Senussi: Stati Uniti e Gran Bretagna in Libia dall'indipendenza a Gheddafi (1949–1973)* (Florence: Polistampa, 2002), 88.

15 Idris received no help from the UK as the treaty signed on 29 July 1953 had set aid only for threats coming from outside Libya and not regarding coups, see Ettore Anchieri, *La diplomazia contemporanea* (Padova: Cedam, 1959), 330–2.

16 Walter Laqueur, *Il nuovo terrorismo: Fanatismo e armi di distruzione di massa* (Milan: Corbaccio, 2002), 208. After the Suez crisis Nasser alleged Idris to favour the presence of British troops along the border with Egypt, Renzo De Felice, *Ebrei in un paese arabo: gli ebrei nella Libia contemporanea tra colonialismo, nazionalismo arabo e sionismo (1835–1970)* (Bologna: Il Mulino), 112–17.

17 FRUS, 1969–72, Foundations of Foreign Policy, vol. I, The Modern World, a Single 'Strategic Theatre', Attachment to the Memorandum From the President's Assistant for National Security Affairs (Kissinger) to President Nixon, 29 September 1969, 115–16.

18 On Gaddafi: Alison Pargeter, *Libya: The Rise and Fall of Qaddafi* (New Haven, CT: Yale University Press, 2012); Angelo Del Boca, *Gheddafi: una sfida dal deserto* (Rome: Laterza, 2001); Mansour El-Kikhia, *Qaddafi's Libya: The Politics of Contradiction* (Gainsville: University Press of Florida, 1997); Janice Monti Belkaoui and Ahmed Riahi Belkaoui, *Qaddafi: The Man and His Policies* (Avebury: Aldershot, 1996); David Blundy and Andrew Lycett, *Qaddafi and the Libyan Revolution* (London: Weidenfeld and Nicholson, 1987); Lisa Anderson, *The State and Social Transformation in Tunisia and Libya, 1930–1980* (Princeton, NJ: Princeton University Press, 1986).

19 Anna Baldinetti, *The Origins of the Libyan Nation: Colonial Legacy, Exile and the Emergency of a New Nation-State* (London: Routledge, 2010), 20–6. According Campanini, the Libyan revolution driven by Gaddafi was an indirect product of Nasserism: Massimo Campanini, *Storia del Medio Oriente* (Bologna: Il Mulino, 2010), 143.

20 For the shaping of the Jamahiriyya: Massimiliano Cricco and Federico Cresti, *Gheddafi. I volti del potere* (Rome: Carocci, 2011), 65–78; Mahmoud Mustafa Ayoub, *Islam and the Third Universal Theory: The Religious Thought of Mu'ammar al Qadhadhafi* (London: Paul Kegan International, 1991).

21 Christopher Blanchard and James Zanotti, 'Libya: Background and U.S. Relations', *Congressional Research Service* (8 February 2011), 4.

22 Edward Haley, *Qaddafi and the United States since 1969* (New York: Praeger, 1984), 4–5.

23 See Antonio Donno and Giuliana Iurlano (eds), *Nixon, Kissinger e il Medio Oriente (1969–1973)* (Florence: Le Lettere 2010).

24 For the birth of the National Oil Company see Del Boca, *Gheddafi*, 39–44.

25 NARA, CFPF, ET, RG 59, From US Mission NATO to Secretary of State, 'The Situation in the Mediterranean', 1 June 1974; GA, URSS, 691, CIA ER 77-10296, 'August 1977 Communist Aid to the Less Developed Countries of the Free World', 1976.

26 NARA, NIE 11/4–82 'The Soviet Challenge to US Security Interests', 10 August 1982.

27 FRUS, 1969–72, Foundations of Foreign Policy, vol. I, Off the Records Remarks by President Nixon, Chicago, Illinois, 16 September 1970, pp. 250–2; From Secretary of State to American Embassy, London, Situation in the Southern Region, 6 March 1975.

28 NARA, CFPF, Tels., RG 59, Ford Administration, ACDA Director Fred Ikle, 6 January 1975; Ford, Kissinger, Shah, 15 May 1975; From American Embassy to Secretary of State, 'FRG Nuclear Interests in Libya', 16 January 16 1976.

29 NARA, CFPF, Tels., RG 59, From Secretary of State to American Embassy, Tunis, 'General Gamasy on Threat from Libya', May 13, 1976; From American Embassy, Tripoli, to Secretary of State, 'Qhadhafi's Concern Egypt, USSR and U.S.', 7 September 1976.

30 Geoff Simons, *Libya: Te Struggle for Survival* (London: MacMillan, 1993); Ronald Bruce St. John, *Qaddafi's World Design: Libyan Foreign Policy, 1969–1987* (London: Saqi Books, 1987). Concerning Gaddafi's support to international terror, see Brian Lee Davis, *Qaddafi, Terrorism, and the Origins of US Attack to Libya* (New York: Praeger, 1990). Gaddafi was defined 'a minor troublemaker' by Walter Laqueur, 'Reflections on Terrorism', *Foreign Affairs* 65, no. 1 (1986), 95. Many times Kissinger mentioned Gaddafi as a paradigm of destabilization, NARA, GRF-0314, Ford Administration, Ford, Kissinger, Scowcroft, Cabinet War Room, White House, 20 and 24 August 1974.

31 Gaja, *L'Italia nel mondo bipolare*, 186.
32 Arturo Varvelli, *L'Italia e l'ascesa di Gheddafi: la cacciata degli italiani, le armi e il petrolio (1969–1974)* (Milan: Baldini and Castoldi Dalai, 2009).
33 Cricco, 'Gheddafi e l'Italia negli anni Settanta', 502.
34 Del Boca, *Gheddafi*, 45–7.
35 ACS, AM, Scritti e discorsi, 1969, 22, 488, Intervento di Aldo Moro in Commissione Esteri, Rome, 12 September 1969.
36 Varvelli, *L'Italia e l'ascesa di Gheddafi*, 16–17.
37 ACS, AM, Ministro degli Esteri, f. 139, 2,3, Intervento di Moro alla Commissione Esteri, Rome, 4 August 1970.
38 ACS, AM, f. 24, 513, Dichiarazione di Aldo Moro al termine dell'incontro con Gheddafi, 5 May 1971.
39 NARA, CFPF, ET, RG 59, From US Mission NATO to Secretary of State, Report of Recent Allied Contacts with Arabs, 13 March 1974.
40 Paolo Soave, 'Italia e Libia: la cooperazione indispensabile (1956–2011)', in *Afriche e Orienti*, nos 1–2 (2013), 158–72.
41 Varvelli, *L'Italia e l'ascesa di Gheddafi*, 50.
42 NARA, CFPF, ET, RG 59, From American Embassy, Rome, to Secretary of State, Italian Government Views on Libyan Developments and Energy Cooperation, 7 September 1973.
43 NARA, CFPF, ET, RG 59, From US Mission NATO to Secretary of State, Report of Recent Allied Contacts with Arabs, 13 March 1974.
44 NARA, CFPF, ET, RG 59, From American Embassy, Rome, to Secretary of State, Alternative Energy Sources, 17 January 1974.
45 NARA, CFPF, ET, RG 59, From American Council, Turin, to Secretary of State, Libyan Assistance to Fiat, 3 December 1976.
46 NARA, CFPF, ET, RG 59, From American Embassy, Rome, to Secretary of State, Italian APC Sales to Libya, 9 January 1974; Military Sales to Libya, 28 November 1974.
47 Ferraris, *Manuale della politica estera italiana*, 281.
48 NARA, CFPF, ET, RG 59, Memorandum of Conversation, Ford-Leone, Rome, 3 June 1975; Ford, Leone, Moro, Memorandum of Conversation, 6 January 1975.
49 Del Boca, *Gheddafi*, 132–7.
50 Giuseppe Paradisi and Rosario Priore, *La strage dimenticata. Fiumicino, 17 dicembre 1973* (Reggio Emilia: Imprimatur, 2015).
51 ACS, AM, f. 25, 535, Intervento di Aldo Moro alla Commissione Esteri, 27 October 1975, Rome.
52 NARA, RG 263, CIA, Security National Intelligence Estimate 11/2-81 'Soviet Support for International Terrorism Violence', 27 May 1981.
53 Cheryl Hudson and Gareth Davies, *Ronald Reagan and the 1980s: Perceptions, Policies, Legacies* (New York: Palgrave Macmillan, 2008); David Mervin, *Ronald Reagan and the American Presidency* (New York: Longman, 1990). On the impact of Reagan's presidency over the Cold War, see John Louis Gaddis, *The Cold War* (London: Allen Lane, 2006); Raimond Leonard Garthoff, *Détente and Confrontation: American-Soviet Relations from Nixon to Reagan* (New York: Brookings Institution, 1985).
54 Westad, *The Global Cold War*, 373–410.
55 George Shultz, *Turmoil and Triumph: My Years as Secretary of State* (New York: Charles Scribner's Sons, 1993), 232.
56 Massimiliano Trentin and Matteo Gerlini (eds), *The Middle East and the Cold War: Between Secrity and Development* (Newcastle upon Tyne: Cambridge Scholars,

2012); William Quandt, *Soviet Policy in the October 1973 War: A Report Prepared for the Office of the Assistant Secretary of Defense/International Security Affairs* (Santa Monica: Rand Corporation, R-1864-ISA, May 1976).

57 NARA, NIE 11-6-70 'Soviet Policies in the Middle East and Mediterranean Area', March 5, 1970; RG 263, NIE 'Intelligency Memorandum Prospects for Soviet Naval Access to Mediterranean Shore Facilities', 2 August 1976.

58 Mattia Toaldo, *The Origins of the US War on Terror: Lebanon, Libya and American Intervention in the Middle East* (London: Routledge, 2013), 125–54.

59 ILS, GA, s. Stati Uniti, Reagan, b. 591, Ambasciatore Petrignani al Ministro degli Esteri, Washington, 1 November 1985.

60 Tim Zimmermann, 'Coercive Diplomacy and Libya', in Alexander George and William Simons (eds), *The Limits of Coercive Diplomacy* (Boulder: Westview Press, 1994), 204–28.

61 RRL, NSDD 16 'Economic and Security Decisions for Libya', 10 December 1981.

62 NARA, RR-NSC, NSPP, NSDD 138, 'Combating Terrorism', 3 April 1984.

63 Bob Woodward, *Veil: The Secret Wars of the CIA, 1981–1987* (London: Headline, 1987), 365–444.

64 For the Italian foreign policy in the Craxi's years see Ennio Di Nolfo (ed.), *La politica estera italiana negli anni Ottanta. Gli anni di Craxi* (Venice: Marsilio, 2007).

65 For the relevance of the Andreotti-Gaddafi relations see Luca Micheletta and Massimo Bucarelli (eds), *Andreotti, Gheddafi e le relazioni italo-libiche* (Rome: Studium, 2018).

66 ILS, GA, s. Stati Uniti, Reagan, b. 591, Ambasciatore Petrignani al Ministro degli Esteri, Washington, 25 August 1984.

67 ILS, GA, s. Stati Uniti, b. 609, William Wilson, Colloquio Wilson-Andreotti, Rome, 11 January 1986.

68 Matteo Gerlini, *Il dirottamento dell'Achille Lauro e i suoi inattesi e sorprendenti risvolti* (Milan: Mondadori Università, 2016).

69 FOIA, Department of State, US Embassy Rome to Department of State, Rome, 18 October 1985.

70 NARA, RR-NSC, NSPP, NSDD 205 'Acting Against Libyan Support of International Terrorism', 8 January 1986.

71 ILS, GA, s. Stati Uniti, Shultz, b. 606, Ambasciatore Petrignani al Ministro degli Esteri, Washington, 22 March 1986. Petrignani announced the American will to cause the clash with the Libyans, as admitted by Reagan in his diaries, Ronald Reagan, *Reagan Diaries* (New York: HarperCollins, 2007), 398–401.

72 ILS, GA, s. Stati Uniti, Whitehead, Ambasciatore Petrignani al Ministro degli Esteri, Washington, 13 January 1986. The Italian government suspended the arms supplies but Petrignani was invited to declare to the Americans that for Italy it would be impossible to implement a full embargo to Libya.

73 ILS, GA, s. Craxi, b. 271, 'Presidente Craxi a Stoccolma', 14–15 March 1986.

74 ILS, GA, s. Stati Uniti, b. 606, Ministro degli Esteri, 'Tensioni nel Mediterraneo', s.d.

75 FOIA, Department of State, From secretary of State to U.S. Embassy Athens, 'Italian Perspective on Prime Minister on Craxi's Visit to Cairo', Washington, 18 January 1986.

76 IlS, GA, s. Stati Uniti, 'Colloquio Andreotti-Shultz', Rome, 30 March 1986.

77 ILS, GA, s. Europa, b. 371, Direzione generale Emigrazione e Affari Sociali, Ministero Affari Esteri, 'Unità di Crisi, Comunità italiana in Libia', Rome, 12 April 1986.

78 Silvio Labbate, *Illusioni medititerranei. Il dialogo euro-arabo* (Florence: Le Monnier, 2016).

79 ILS, GA, s. Europa, b. 371, 'Dichiarazione dei Dodici sul terrorismo internazionale e la crisi mediterranea', Incontro ministeriale straordinario sulla cooperazione politica europea, Ministero degli Esteri, The Hague, 14 April 1986.
80 ILS, GA, s. Stati Uniti, b. 609, f. 423, Vernon Walters, 'Incontro Craxi-Walters', 'Incontro Andreotti-Walters', Rome, 14 April 1986.
81 'I libici rivelano 20 anni dopo: così Craxi salvò Gheddafi', *Corriere della Sera*, 31 October 2008.
82 Joseph Stanik, *El Dorado Canyon: Reagan's Undeclared War with Qaddafi* (Annapolis: Naval Institute Press, 2003); Robert Venkus, *Raid on Qaddafi: The Untold Story of History's Longest Fighter Mission by the Pilot Who Directed It* (New York: St Martin's Press, 1992).
83 Shultz, *Turmoil and Triumph*, 687.
84 Bettino Craxi, *Io parlo e continuerò a parlare. Note e appunti sull'Italia vista da Hammamet* (Milan: Mondadori, 2014), 34–5.
85 David Wills, *The First War on Terrorism: Counter-terrorism Policy during the Reagan Administration* (New York: Rowman & Littlefield, 2003), 10.
86 ILS, GA, Stati Uniti, b. 609, 'Visita di Walters', September 1986.
87 RF, NSC, Memorandum for Frank C. Carlucci from Robert B. Oakley 'Anniversary Assessment of the USG Policy Towards Libya', Washington, 12 January 1987.
88 Del Boca, *Gheddafi*, 356.
89 Ibid., 242–3.
90 'Eni Greenstream', http://www.greenstreambv.com/it/pages/gasdotto/gasdotto-greenstream.shtml (accessed 21 March 2018).
91 Giampaolo Malgeri, 'Le relazioni fra Italia e Libia', in Matteo Pizzigallo (ed.), *Il ponte sul Mediterraneo. Le relazioni fra l'Italia e i paesi arabi rivieraschi (1989–2009)* (Rome: Editrice Apes, 2011), 177.
92 Fabio Casini, 'Gheddafi. La fine di un dittatore', in Massimo Borgogni and Paolo Soave (eds), *Italia e Libia. Un secolo di relazioni controverse* (Rome: Aracne, 2015), 201–26.

10

Italy and Algeria: A resilient connection

Azzedine Layachi

Introduction

Being the largest country in Africa and strategically located in the north of the continent, and only hundreds of miles from the Spanish and Italian shores, Algeria was naturally destined to have intense interactions with its neighbours to the north, that is, the south-western European countries, especially France, Italy and Spain. Throughout the centuries, the area occupied today by Algeria and the rest of the North Africa region known as the Maghreb served as a transit area for people moving to and from Africa, Europe and the Middle East.

French colonial policy opened the country to European settlers and extracted substantial economic and geostrategic benefits. The local population was subdued by large-scale and systematic raids – known as *razzias* – which destroyed villages, burned crops, indiscriminately killed thousands of people of all ages, and tortured, humiliated and expelled more from their lands and villages. After Algeria was annexed administratively to France in 1848, the colonization of the land was increased by bringing in more European settlers, mainly French, Italians, Maltese and Spaniards of low socioeconomic status. This settlement colonization destroyed the local social and economic structures and increased the impoverishment of the indigenous population through property confiscation, punishing taxation, and forced mass migration from fertile lands. In 1962, after a bitter seven-and-a-half-year war, Algeria finally became an independent state.

Algeria 1973–99

The colonial policies and the long war of independence dislocated and unsettled Algerian society and its diverse communities. Upon independence, the majority of Algerians were suffering from illiteracy – estimated at 90 per cent – poverty, unemployment – around 70 per cent – poor health conditions and extremely limited services. The basic infrastructure was also dismal due to the war for independence and the colonial policy of building it mostly where European settlers lived. As a result, the newly independent country and its leadership started almost from scratch in building a functioning state, an integrated society and a viable economy. However, disagreement among the post-independence leaders made the start slow and difficult.

Serious divisions put in jeopardy the revolution that was underway and the frail FLN (The National Liberation Front). The party's success at unifying the ranks of the resistance to colonialism unraveled quickly due to doctrinal disagreements and a power struggle between civilian, military, internal and exiled leaders. Factional rivalries remained a constant feature of Algeria until today.

The first president of independent Algeria, Ahmed Ben Bella, was overthrown on 19 June 1965 by Defense Minister Colonel Houari Boumediene, who ruled the country at the head of the Council of the Revolution. Boumediene promised to reestablish the principles of the revolution, end corruption and personal abuses, eliminate internal divisions, and build a socialist economy based on industrialization and comprehensive agrarian reform.

Under Boumediene, Algeria pursued a socialist mode of development. The state became responsible for production, employment, welfare and social protection. It controlled most foreign trade, manufacturing, retail, agriculture, utilities and banking. All major foreign business interests and most large domestic businesses were nationalized. By the early 1970s, almost 90 per cent of the industrial sector and more than 70 per cent of the industrial workforce were under state control. By the end of the 1970s, the country had made noticeable progress in human development, especially in health, education and poverty reduction. However, the development strategy pursued proved later to be incapable of dealing with various challenges.

The industrialization program did not stimulate national development as planned and became a source of financial drain. The agricultural sector suffered from neglect and remained underdeveloped and poorly organized. The 1971 Agrarian Revolution policy failed and agriculture production declined dramatically, causing frequent food shortages, increased dependence on food imports and urban migration.

When Boumediene died suddenly in December 1978 of a rare kidney ailment, the military chose Colonel Chadli Bendjedid as new president. Under him, the country faced serious challenges throughout the 1980s, including a declining economy, rapid population growth, increasing unemployment, and by the end of the decade, a sharp drop in energy prices. State revenues – highly dependent on hydrocarbon exports – fluctuated wildly and eventually declined drastically when oil prices dipped by 40 per cent in 1986. In response to the crisis, Bendjedid initiated a semblance of economic liberalization, which included a shift away from heavy industry and toward agriculture, light industry, and consumer goods. Public enterprises were broken up into smaller units, and several small state firms were privatized. Subsidies were reduced, and price controls were lifted. The economy was also slowly opened to limited foreign investment, and efforts were made to expand and revitalize the domestic private sector.

The economic reforms ended up causing more hardship on the masses. Unemployment and prices increased, and the industrial output of the non-hydrocarbon sector declined drastically. By the end of the 1980s, Algeria was on the brink of a social explosion. It faced rapidly declining export revenues which undermined the state's capacity to meet its social-welfare expenditures and its ability to maintain security and stability. A high foreign debt stressed the country's finances. Furthermore, the generation gap between an aging leadership and a youthful society increased the social tensions. There was a clear disconnect between a ruling elite which based its legitimacy on independence-war credentials and a population whose 70 per cent were under the age of thirty and with no memory of the war.

After several weeks of strikes and work stoppages, the expected social explosion did finally happen in the first week of October 1988. Thousands of Algerian youth participated in violent riots for six days in several cities. It was the most violent public demonstrations since independence.

Startled by events, state leaders reacted with a swift military repression that killed five hundred people and imposed a state of siege. As if to make up quickly for the harsh repression, President Bendjedid carried out sweeping institutional reforms which included a constitutional amendment that separated the FLN party from the state, restructured executive and legislative authority, strengthened presidential powers, eliminated the commitment to socialism, ended the one-party system and introduced freedom of association and free multiparty, and multicandidate, elections.

In 1989, sudden and full-fledged political liberalization dismantled the single-party system and allowed the birth of an independent press, a myriad of civic associations and sixty-two new parties representing a wide variety of political tendencies. The most prominent party was the Front Islamique du Salut (Islamic Front of Salvation, known by its French acronym as FIS). The FIS's radical rejection of the existing order and its plan to establish an Islamic republic governed by strict Islamic morality and the Shari'a (Islamic Law) were the bedrock of this movement's popular appeal.

In the country's first multiparty local elections in June 1990 the FLN was badly defeated by the new Islamist party FIS. The Islamist party secured 853 of the 1,520 local councils (55 per cent) and 32 of the 48 provincial assemblies (67 per cent). The FLN won only 487 local and 14 provincial constituencies (Wilaya). Capitalizing on this victory in local elections, the Islamists demanded early presidential elections and a new electoral redistricting, claiming that the existing district scheme undermined their strength. They confronted the government by organizing civil disobedience and sit-ins in main city squares in Algiers, calling for a general strike and inciting army officers to rebel against the regime. The urban sit-ins ended in June 1991 when, throughout Algeria, the army moved to disband the Islamists and imposed a state of siege and martial law. Thousands of Islamists, including top FIS leaders Abassi Madani and Ali Belhadj were arrested and sentenced to twelve years in prison, which they served fully.

The legislative elections, which were originally scheduled for June, took place on 26 December 1991. To the surprise of many people, the FIS won 188 seats out of 430 in the first round and the FLN obtained merely 16 seats. Surprised by the unexpected results, many people, including the military establishment, feared for Algeria's fate, especially because some FIS leaders had declared democracy a heresy. Runoff elections planned for the following month were cancelled in January 1992 by a military intervention which pushed President Bendjedid to resign on 11 January, and later banned the FIS. Thousands of FIS supporters were jailed in makeshift detention centres in the south of the country.

The repression pushed thousands of Islamist militants to go underground and escalate violent attacks – which had started a year earlier – against the state and anyone who disagreed with them, especially intellectuals, journalists and academics. Among the violent groups that contributed to turning the 1990s into a 'Dark Decade' was the a FIS's military wing, the Islamic Salvation Army (AIS), the Armed Islamic Groups (GIA), which quickly became notorious for its indiscriminate violence against civilians, and the Salafist Group for Preaching and Combat (GSPC), which joined the al-Qaeda network in 2006 and changed its name to al-Qaeda in the Islamic Land of the Maghreb (AQIM). Since then, AQIM has extended its actions to the rest of the Maghreb and the Sahel region.

The Islamists carried out killings of not only military and police personnel, but also civilians, including known journalists, professors, poets, doctors, nurses and civil servants. The victims have also included simple citizens accused of either cooperating with the state or refusing to help the Islamist cause. Many foreigners were killed as well. There was not a single day that did not bring with it a sad toll of violence against civilians. The violence against civilians was in both urban centres and remote villages. Many people – sometimes hundreds – were killed every week, and frequently in the most vicious way. Infants, teenagers, women and men were often decapitated, with their heads left in a public place as a warning to the living. Thousands of women were kidnapped and raped, and many of them killed. Entire villages were decimated, such as Bentalha, south of Algiers, in September 1997.[1]

Close to two million people were displaced from their villages, especially in what became known as the 'Triangle of Death' which included the regions of Blida, Médéa and Aïn Defla, all south of Algiers.

The state security forces responded to the escalating violence with a massive crackdown against the Islamists and anyone suspected of aiding them. Thousands of alleged militants were imprisoned and scores were killed. There were rumors that the army, in its counter-insurgency response, was itself engaged in the killing of civilians, camouflaged as acts of Islamist groups; they were also acts suspected of being revenge collective punishment that killed large numbers of civilians whenever security officers were assassinated. The security forces were also accused of intentionally not aiding people being massacred by hordes of Islamists. Evidence of this has been presented in many publications of first-hand witness accounts.[2] From 1992 to 1999 the armed conflict had claimed around two hundred thousand lives, caused substantial destruction of infrastructure, displaced scores of people and isolated Algeria in the international arena.

Rather than live in this climate of sheer terror and intimidation, thousands of Algerian fled the country and sought refuge in other countries, Europe being the favored destination. Others went to Italy and Spain. It has been estimated that around five hundred thousand had left the country since the start of the internal war in 1992, and sought asylum almost anywhere in the world if they could not make it to France.

In that environment of widespread violence in the north of the country, the military rulers were unable to assemble a civilian government which commanded the confidence and respect of all Algerians. As a consequence, the country was temporarily ruled by a High State Council headed, at first, by Defense Minister General Khaled

Nezzar, and then by independence war hero Mohamed Boudiaf, who returned from exile in Morocco. However, within six months, he was assassinated by one of his security details on 29 June 1992 while he was addressing an attentive audience in the eastern city of Annaba. The whole event was seen live on television. Boudiaf, who had stimulated high hopes among the masses, was followed by Ali Kafi, leader of the independence war veterans' organization, and then in 1995 by Lamine Zeroual, a retired general who became the first leader to be elected since the 1980s. He won a six-year term with 61 per cent of the vote in the first multiparty presidential election in the history of independent Algeria. In spite of the high hopes placed in Zeroual's ability to end the crisis, political violence increased. At that moment, many Algerians and international observers expected the state to collapse and feared that the worst would happen after an Islamist military victory.

The economic and social infrastructure was also being destroyed by the violent campaign. Telephone centres, food stocks, public utility vehicles, and schools were targeted. By preventing the normal operations of the country and halting the flow of foreign aid and investment, the Islamists have succeeded in stopping Algeria's economic and social development.

In the midst of the terrible cycle of violence, Algeria became isolated internationally due to the disruption of normal relations with other countries, the assassination of foreign workers by Islamist groups, and the uneasy situation the country's rulers found themselves in due to the cancellation of an electoral process that was generally viewed as fair and to the harsh repression that ensued.

Most Western countries did not openly support the Algerian government as it battled the first wide-scale armed rebellion the region. Some countries, such as France, even refused to sell to the Algerian government anti-guerilla weapons systems, such as attack helicopters equipped with night-vision capabilities. The difficulties the Algerian security services were having in taming the Islamist guerilla spread doubts about the survival of the regime and made the United States and some European countries hesitate in lending open support to the Algerian military as the violence went on unabated.

A break finally happened towards the end of the 1990s as the army started to get the upper hand in the war and succeeded in undermining the cohesion of the rebel groups by infiltrating them and instigating conflicts among their leaders. President Zeroual was also instrumental in this break when he started secret negotiations with one group, the Islamic Army of Salvation, for an amnesty for its troops if they gave up the fight and surrendered their weapons. However, a faction of hardliners in the military, known as the 'Eradicators' rejected such a plan, opting instead for a continuation of the war, which they were certain to win. Because of this resistance to his peace initiative, and invoking health reasons, Liamine Zeroual resigned in fall 1998 from the presidency, well before the end of his term.

As the military in charge of the country sought a new, suitable, president, they welcomed a candidate they had previously rejected when he sought to replace Boumediene in 1978: Abdelaziz Bouteflika who was foreign minister at that time thought of himself as the natural heir to Boumediene. After being brushed aside by the military as a potential president in 1978, Bouteflika went into self-exile in Arab

Gulf states for around twenty years. When he returned in the late 1990s, he appeared at that time as the best person who could pull the country out of its crisis. He had some popular appeal and was not involved at all in the turmoil of the Dark Decade.

Bouteflika won the presidency in a election held in March 1999 and, within months of taking office, he put a 'National Concorde' law to a referendum; it was widely approved mostly because it raised hopes that Algeria's nightmare would soon end. The National Concorde amnestied from legal prosecution all Islamist militants who were not guilty of a blood crime or rape if they surrendered by 13 January 2000. Thousands of armed elements accepted the deal and stopped fighting. However, many others did not and maintained their violent activities. In 2000, violence in the centre and eastern part of the country diminished, but increased in the west, including in the regions of Oran, Mostaganem, Mascara, and Sidi Bel Abbes. Even though these regions were less targeted in previous years, they were not entirely spared by the Islamist violence that has engulfed the country since 1992. The surrender seemed to involve mostly AIS with whom President Zeroual had initiated negotiations.

The GIA and GSPC had rejected the amnesty offer. However, the GIA was almost nearing the end of its existence for many reasons, including a combination of improved state counter-insurgency efforts, internal dissent over leadership, a number of brutal internal purges, infiltration by the security services, the withdrawal of support from international Islamist groups, and a series of brutal civilian massacres in the mid- and late 1990s, and the killing of seven Trappist monks. In September 1997, the GIA issued its final 'communiqué' and was not heard from since then.

Italy and the war for Algerian independence

Italy's geographical proximity to North Africa allowed for recurring interactions between the northern and southern sides of the Mediterranean Sea throughout the centuries. The interaction between Italy and Algeria took on many forms and focused on different areas.[3]

Algeria's relations with Italy are said to have began in 1958 when Enrico Mattei met members of the Provisional Government of the Republic of Algeria in exile in Omsk, Siberia. Mattei was then president of the national energy company Ente Nazionale Idrocarburi (National Hydrocarbons Authority), better known as ENI. Mattei, who was the architect of Italy's state-owned energy sector, helped publicize the Algerian independence struggle and helped funnel support to the nationalists. He even worked with the Algerian delegation at the Evian talks about independence and helped prepare a draft treaty with France on the exploitation of Sahara resources. Unfortunately, Mattei died in a suspicious plane crash in October 1962, shortly after Algeria's independence.[4] The French were suspected of being behind his death because they were fairly upset about his relations with the Algerian nationalists.[5]

The book published in 2012 by Bruna Bagnato *L'Italia e la guerra d'Algeria* (Italy and the Algerian War 1954–62) argues that the start of Algeria's war of independence was met with almost total indifference in Italy. However, that changed when the Algerian independence struggle finally caught Italy's attention in 1958 thanks to

Enrico Mattei.[6] After that, official Italy became torn between its obligation to be on the side of France (a military ally and fellow European state) and its strong interest in the Algerian struggle for independence. This conflict, and the way Mattei forced Italy to pay attention to it and to support the Algerian nationalists, may have ushered in the elements of the nascent Italian foreign policy toward North Africa and the Middle East. This development might be best understood in the context of Italy's search for a third foreign policy path beyond the post-Second World War competing tracks of Atlanticism and Europeanism.[7] Instead of choosing between the two when dealing with its neighbors on the southern shores of the Mediterranean Sea, Italy tried to pursue its national interest through a Mediterranean policy which, at times, appeared to clash with the overall guidelines of both Europeanism and Atlanticism, as was the case with embracing Algeria's nationalists in the 1950s and early 1960s.

After Algeria became independent, Italian film director Gillo Pontecorvo made probably the best movie on the Algerian war of independence as it was fought in the streets of the capital: *La battaglia di Algeri* (*The Battle of Algiers*) which was released in 1968. Using a documentary style, and in black and white, the movie relays the drama and agony of Algeria's war of independence, especially its guerrilla aspect in an urban setting. It shows what motivates the nationalists, how they organize and conduct their disruptive operations (called 'terrorism' by the French). It also shows the other ugly side of the war: the wide-scale use of horrible torture and extra-judicial killing by the French paratroopers sent to pacify the city in the late 1950s. The movie, which was banned in France, became famous for its quality and its inspiration for people struggling for freedom and against colonialism and oppression. After the United States invaded Iraq in 2003 and encountered guerrilla-style resistance, the US military made its top officers involved in that war watch the movie because of its detailed portrayal of how a guerrilla force resists invader and organizes their struggle with limited material and human resources.

Between the Mattei meeting with the Algerian nationalists in 1958 and the production of *The Battle of Algiers*, Italian interest had increased substantially, mostly in solidarity with the nationalists. While the war was raging, Italians organized demonstrations, information events, and 'Algeria Week' across the peninsula. A group of Italian intellectuals and politicians wrote to Secretary General of the United Nations Dag Hammarskjold, asking him to help bring peace to Algeria. An Italian Peace Committee of Algeria was created to call attention to what was happening there and to support the independence of Algeria. Representatives of the GPRA were invited to speak at a solidarity event at the Teatro dei Satiri in Rome on 11 December 1961. According to several accounts, Italy often gave free passage to agents of the FLN and also served as transit route for weapons going to the Algerian guerrillas, much to the dislike of France.[8]

Prosperity of economic relations: The natural gas connection

Following Algeria's independence, relations with Italy started to grow slowly on a bilateral basis as well as in the context of European initiatives and, later, European

Union ones. The main economic interest pursued by Italy in Algeria was – and still is – natural gas.

As early as the 1970s, as Italy started looking into expanding its natural gas consumption, discussion began about importing gas from Algeria by liquefied natural gas (LNG) ships or via pipeline. Discussions at the government level began on the project and involved the state-owned energy companies ENI, its subsidiaries Saipem and Snamprogetti, and the Algerian state company Sonatrach. After the LNG shipping option was dismissed due to cost and security considerations, ENI started developing a plan in the early 1970s for an underwater pipeline between Algeria and Italy through Tunisia. The two countries decided to build a 'Transmed' pipeline which became operational in 1983 with the first delivery of Algerian natural gas to Italy. Another pipeline linking Algeria to Spain through Morocco was built and started delivering Algerian gas under the Mediterranean to Spain in 1996. The pipeline to Italy was realized fairly quickly, mostly because ENI, a politically well-connected company, successfully pushed the project forward as a necessity for Italy's security of supply and obtained all the needed backing from the Italian and other European governments.

The Transmed investment proved worthwhile for both Italy and Algeria. Today, the North African country is Italy's second supplier of natural gas after Russia. It provides 32.7 per cent of Italy's consumption needs, an average of 22.6 Bcm a year). Italy's remaining gas needs have been met by Russia (29 per cent, 20 Bcm) and Libya (13 per cent, 9 Bcm). Even though most of Italy's needs in natural gas are met by these three suppliers (75 per cent of total consumption and 88 per cent of total imports),[9] the Italians are aware of the risks of overdependence on such a small number of suppliers. If one of them fails to deliver contracted quantities for any reason, Italy would find itself in a bind.

An additional natural gas pipeline bringing more Algerian gas to Italy and Europe has been discussed for many years since Transmed became operational, but it had difficulty getting off the ground for many reasons, including cost. At some point the idea seemed to have been abandoned. However, in recent years, the project was back on track as Italy and Algeria finally agreed to go ahead with the new Algeria-Sardinia Italy Gas Pipeline known as Galsi. The pipeline is to be built by a consortium of companies called Galsi which include Sonatrach, Edison, Enel and Hera Group. The pipeline, connecting Algeria to Italy through Sardinia, will be 837 km long (565 km under water). Sonatrach owns a 41.6 per cent interest in Galsi, Edison 20.8 per cent, Enel 15.6 per cent, Hera 10.4 per cent and the region of Sardinia 10.4 per cent.[10] However, the exact start of the project has not been decided yet. The delay is due to gas pricing issues. It is said that the Algerian side wants firm sales contracts and an acceptable price on future deliveries. Once it comes online, the pipeline is expected to supply up to 8 billion cubic meters of natural gas.

To lessen the vulnerability linked to dependency on only three suppliers (Libya, Russia and Algeria), Italy, along with other European states, has also been participating in a project to build a US$40 billion international gas pipeline that would bring gas to Europe by way of the Trans Adriatic Pipeline (TAP). However, the final stage of the 3,500 km (2,200-mile) corridor which goes through Italy has been halted by the government that came to power in summer 2018. Italy's new environmental minister objected to the project and called it 'pointless'. TAP, which will bring gas to Western Europe from central Asia, is said to be 'a cornerstone of the European Union's energy security policy which aims to wean the bloc off Russian gas supplies'.[11] This TAP project, which has become the centre of diatribe and controversy between members of the governing coalition in Italy, may make the Galsi project look more reasonable than before, and its construction may start in the near future.

The EU gas market has three main sources of imports: Russia, Norway and Algeria. The Mediterranean pipelines which bring gas to and through Italy today are the Green Stream from Libya and the Trans-mediterranean Pipeline (Transmed) from Algeria. If the current Italian political deadlock on TAP is resolved, new gas imports will be flowing by 2020 through the Trans-Adriatic Pipeline connecting Puglia to Azerbaijan, via Georgia, Greece, Turkey, and Albania. Also, if Galsi, the second pipeline from Algeria is ever realized, Italy will be set for the foreseeable future in terms of energy supply. Not only its own energy needs will be secure and regular, but European dependence on Russian gas will also be somewhat attenuated.

The Sant'Egidio peace mediation: A failed 'parallel diplomacy'

Sympathy for the Algerian independence movement was not the only time the Italians felt concerned about turmoil in Algeria and tried to do something to help find a solution to it. When Algeria was in the midst of horrible violence during the 'Dark Decade', when the war reached its paroxysm in the mid-1990s, the Sant'Egidio Community of Rome[12] tried to bring together all concerned parties in the conflict with the aim of brokering a resolution of the conflict. In 1990, the Community had become involved in mediation efforts between warring factions in the Mozambique civil war. It successfully mediated a solution to the conflict though the Rome General Peace Accords of 1992.[13] A few years later, it attempted a peace initiative in the Algerian conflict.

In Algeria at that time, after dialogue attempts between the government and the two jailed FIS leaders failed, the state turned to a firmer repression of radical Islamists while opening up to moderate, non-violent, opposition parties, both religious and secular. The FIS was not included in those efforts.

It was in that tense and violent context that the Sant'Egidio Community organized in 8–13 January 1995 a meeting in Rome of the Algerian League of Human Rights and seven opposition parties, including the banned FIS which was represented by its exiled leadership. The gathering engaged in intense debates and negotiations over an agreement that became known as the Rome Platform[14] for resolving the Algerian crisis. This initiative failed mainly because the Algerian government rejected the idea of the meeting and its final product.

The Sant'Egidio initiative stimulated mixed reactions. Some praised it as a unique opportunity where representatives of the key players in the Algerian conflict finally met and agreed on a set of democratic principles and a commitment to non-violence, but others – including the Algerian government – denounced it as foreign interference in the internal affairs of the country, and also as a ploy to give legitimacy to the violent and intolerant Islamist factions that were leading a war against the Algerian state and the civilian population. In the end, the Sant'Egidio initiative failed to move the belligerents toward an actual settlement of the conflict. That would happen three years later when President Zeroual started direct negotiations with the Islamic Army of Salvation (AIS, the armed wing of FIS).

The Sant'Egidio mediation and conciliation efforts in the Algeria case were also criticized by the Catholic bishops of Algeria, such as Pierre Claverie, the bishop of Oran, and Henri Teissier, the archbishop of Algiers. Both agreed that the Rome Platform had been signed without first getting the radical Islamists to end their ruthless campaign of violent attacks and assassinations. Both believed that the Rome meeting, in fact, gave the violent factions a legitimacy they did not deserve. Soon after, Bishop Claverie was killed, along with his driver in 1996.

Criticism of the Sant'Egidio initiative came also from the Italian ambassador to Algeria from 1996 to 1998, Franco de Courten. In his published memoirs, Ambassador de Courten gave a very critical account of the religious community's work. In his lengthy account about this, the ambassador mentioned, among other things, the difficulty the Italian government found itself in when the Algerian government expressed concern about what was termed the 'parallel diplomacy' conducted by the Sant'Egidio Community.[15]

It appeared, at first, that the centre-left government, headed by Prime Minister Prodi, did not see any problem with the initiative. However, when relations between the two countries became uneasy as a result of this,[16] and as Islamist violence continued unabated in Algeria in spite of the commitment to the non-violence made by the FIS in Rome, Foreign Minister Lamberto Dini was dispatched to Algiers to clear things up and, in a way, apologize for the tensions between the two countries caused by this event and to indicate that the Sant'Egidio initiative was dead.

In that same period, the conflict intensified in violence and destruction as neither the government nor the armed groups were willing to compromise with their opponents. The hardliners within the regime, known as the 'eridecateurs', did not seem willing to stop the fight until the opponent was destroyed or surrendered. The same logic seemed to move the armed groups. The conflict was not yet ripe. Those within the regime who sought a compromise – known as the 'conciliateurs' – failed to get dialogue going with the Islamist opposition. Sant'Egidio also failed because of the lack of ripeness of the conflict, a condition finally reached by the end of the 1990s when, finally, a truce was welcomed by most sides.

This conflict cost the lives of two hundred thousand people, including 120 foreigners, between 1993 and 2010. Among them were around twenty Italian citizens working in Algeria or on business visit, such as the seven sailors killed in the middle of the night on their boat *Lucina* on 8 July 1994. Their throats were slit as they slept on the boat, which was transporting semolina and was docked at the port of Jijel, 350 km east of Algiers.

It took a few years after the failed Sant'Egidio initiative before Italy's relations with the Algerian government were back on the agreeable track of the past. Cooperation in the economic and security fields developed thereafter.

The Algeria-Italy natural gas connection has been mutually beneficial to both countries, but it also brought with it some embarrassing corruption cases involving Italian companies. In 2013 Paolo Scaroni, the CEO of ENI, was suspected of having paid US$265 million in bribes to Algerian officials in exchange for multibillion-dollar contracts with Sonatrach. Saipem, an ENI subsidiary, was also at the centre of a corruption probe for having paid intermediaries – mostly Algerians – about 198 million Euros between 2007 and 2010 to secure contracts worth 8 billion Euros with Sonatrach. On 19 September 2018, a court in Milan, found Saipem and a its former CEO Pietro Tali guilty of corruption. The court handed down prison sentences, seized 197.9 million Euros from Saipem and fined it 400,000 Euros.

Besides hydrocarbons, other areas of transaction between Italy and Algeria have included important investments in each other's economies in recent years. Italy, the fourth largest source of foreign direct investment in Algeria after Turkey, France and Spain, has been exploring more business opportunities in Algeria's industry, services, tourism, telecommunications and construction sectors.

Italian and Algerian officials often speak of a strategic alliance between the two countries which started in the late 2000s and involves cooperation between security forces, such as the Algerian Gendarmerie and the Italian Carabinieri; intelligence sharing on networks of radical groups; cooperation in helping Libya solve its crisis; and discussions on ways and means to lessen human trafficking and unwanted migration to Italy by sea. Italy aims to create a protective net around its maritime borders against risks posed by such migration and is equally concerned about potential instability in Algeria which can threaten the supply of natural gas and unleash a large number of unwanted migrants. Relations between the two countries have come to encompass the important areas of security, migration, energy supply and development. As a result, the connection between them has acquired crucial importance in the pursuit of Italy's national interest in the Mediterranean Basin and is likely to remain resilient in the face of potential challenges that might come in the future.

Notes

1. John R. Schindler, 'Two Decades Later, Algeria Protects Mystery of Bentalha Massacre', *Observer*, 12 September 2017, https://observer.com/2017/09/two-decades-later-algeria-protects-mystery-of-bentalha-massacre/. As this article indicates, there is still a strong suspicion that the security forces housed not far from Bentalha were aware of the massacre and did not intervene as a punishment for a population which may have voted for FIS in 1991, and also as a way to discredit the Islamists.
2. Habib Souaidia, *La Sale Guerre* (Paris: La Découverte, 2001); Hisham Aboud, *La mafia des Généraux* (Paris: J.C. Lattès, 2002); Nesroulah Yous, *Qui a tué à Bentahla?* (Paris: La Découverte, 2000); Youcef Bedjaoui, Abbas Aroua and Meziane Ait-Larbi (eds), *An Inquiry into the Algerian Massacres* (Geneva: Hoggar Press, 1999).
3. For the Italo–Algerian relations, see Luigi V. Ferraris, *Manuale della politica estera italiana 1947–1993* (Rome: Laterza, 1996), 166 et sqq.
4. Gumbel Andrew, 'Autopsy May Solve Deadly Mystery of the Mattei Affair', *The Independent*, 29 August 1997, https://www.independent.co.uk/news/world/

autopsy-may-solve-deadly-mystery-of-the-mattei-affair-1247785.html. See also his informative obituary 'Italian Oil Chief Dies in Air Crash: Mattei, Long Stormy Figure, Killed with 2 Near Milan', *New York Times*, 27 October 1962, https://timesmachine.nytimes.com/timesmachine/1962/10/28/89883718.pdf.

5 See *Enrico Mattei et l' Algerie pendant la Guerre de Libération Nationale*, 'Summary of Proceedings of a Colloquium organized by the Italian embassy, the Direction Générale des Archives Nationales d' Algérie, ENI and the Algerian Office National de la Culture et de l'Information, in Algiers on Decembre 7, 2010', https://baldi.diplomacy.edu/diplo/texts/cantini_Mattei_FR.pdf. On ENI and Algeria, useful also is Rosario Milano, 'L'ENI e l'Algeria (1963–1973)', in Italo Garzia, Luciano Monzali and Federico Imperato (eds), *Aldo Moro, l'Italia repubblicana e i popoli del Mediterraneo* (Besa: Nardò, 2013), 498–533.

6 Bruna Bagnato, *L'Italia e la Guerra d'Algeria 1954–1962* (Soveria Mannelli: Rubbetino, 2012). A French version of the book was published in 2017. See also Romain Rainero, 'L'Italie entre amitié française et solidarité algérienne', in Rioux Jean-Pierre (ed.), *La Guerre d'Algerie et les Français* (Paris: Fayard, 1990), 429–50.

7 Also known as trans-Atlanticism, Atlanticism is a foreign policy which supports close relations between Europe, the United States and Canada, with NATO as a central focus. Europeanism refers to a foreign policy that is independent of transatlantic relations and built on a European Union-centered perspective.

8 Stéphane Mourlane, 'The Algerian War in Franco-Italian Relations (1958–1962)', *World Wars and Contemporary Conflicts* 217 (2005), 77–90.

9 Nicolò Sartori, 'The Southern Gas Corridor: Needs, Opportunities and Constraints', *Documenti IAI, Istituto Affari Internazionali*, June 2011.

10 'Hydrocarbons Technology', *Algeria Sardinia Italy Gas Pipeline (Galsi)*, 2018, https://www.hydrocarbons-technology.com/.../algeria-sardinia-italy-gas-pipeline-galsi/.

11 Massimiliano Di Giorgio, 'Exclusive: Italy's New Government to Review TAP Gas Pipeline', *Reuters*, 6 June 2018, https://www.reuters.com/article/us-tap-italy-exclusive/exclusive-italys-new-government-to-review-tap-gas-pipeline-idUSKCN1J21SI.

12 On the international diplomacy of Sant'Egidio Community, Roberto Morozzo della Rocca (ed.), *Making Peace: The Role Played by the Community of Sant'Egidio in the International Arena* (London: New City, 2013); Morozzo della Rocca, *Fare pace: La diplomazia di Sant'Egidio* (Cinisello Balsamo: San Paolo, 2018).

13 Roberto Morozzo della Rocca, *Mozambico: una pace per l'Africa* (Milan: Leonardo, 2002).

14 The Rome document was signed by the following personalities: Ali Yahiya, representing the Algerian Human Rights League (LADDH); Abdelhamid Mehri, representing the National Liberation Front (FLN); Hocine Aït Ahmed and Ahmed Djeddai, representing the Socialist Forces Front (FFS); Rabah Kebir and Anwar Haddam, representing the Islamic Salvation Front (FIS); Louisa Hanoune, representing the Workers Party (PT); former president of Algeria Ahmed Ben Bella and Khaled Bensmain, representing the Movement for Democracy in Algeria (MDA); Abdallah Djaballah, representing the Islamic Renaissance Movement (Ennhda) party; Ahmed Ben Mouhammed, representing the Contemporary Muslim Algeria movement (JMC).

15 Franco De Courten, *Diario d´Algeria* (Soveria Mannelli: Rubbettino, 2003). See Sandro Magister, 'St. Egidio and Algeria. An Ambassador´s Disturbing Revelations', *L'Espresso*, 29 December 2003, http://chiesa.espresso.repubblica.it/articolo/7005%26eng%3Dy.html.
16 According to the Italian ambassador, Algeria may have even threatened to stop the delivery of natural gas on which Italy depends heavily.

Part Three

Italy and the greater Middle East

11

Italy and Turkey: Between Europe and the Middle East (1969–93)

Federico Imperato

Italy and Turkey – between convergence and crisis in the Mediterranean (1969–80)

The 1970s in both Italy and Turkey were characterized by an array of parallel internal difficulties, reaching extremes with the emergence of the phenomenon of a very ideological form of terrorism, on the one hand, and an economic crisis, which was the reflection of a paradigm shift in facing the problems of energy and raw material supply on the other. Indeed, rather than abundance, scarcity of energy resources was the theme of the day; a problem that – albeit strictly economic – was combined with the political and military conflicts that had inflamed Middle Eastern geopolitics since the period immediately after the Second World War.

The June 1968 Italian elections brought about a sudden halt to the experience of the centre-left and saw a return to a period of governmental instability. Aldo Moro, one of the leaders of the Christian Democracy (DC), found himself in a minority within his own party, which in turn witnessed his detachment from the majority current and the assumption of a more leftist position. Thereafter, the Apulian statesman was engaged in deep political reflection, questioning the prevalent direction within the DC, the starting point of which being the identification of 1968 as a turning point. The youth and worker protests alongside the social phenomena of the following years, such as the so-called 'strategia della tensione' ('strategy of tension') and terrorism, originated internally from a failure to complete the set of reforms embarked upon by the centre-left, and which were abandoned immediately afterwards following the summer crisis of 1964. However, from an international point of view, the anti-Vietnam War demonstrations and protests which united public opinion in the vast majority of Western countries, and the new rift within the communist bloc caused by the Prague Spring, which followed the Hungarian uprising of the previous decade, demonstrated how the USA–USSR-centred bipolarity, based on a nuclear stalemate, was no longer able to keep up with the complexity and polycentrism of the international system. From this, Moro obtained two ways out, both domestically and internationally, destined to undermine the relationship of loyalty – almost faith – which tied Rome to its American ally. The failure to stabilize the Italian political system, even after joining the government with the Italian Socialist Party (PSI), led Moro to develop a 'strategy of attention' towards the PCI (Italian Communist Party), led by Enrico Berlinguer. He appeared to increasingly dislike the Brezhnev Doctrine, and was more inclined to support the Italian democratic system in the face of the growing anti-system protests, such as extreme right-wing and far-left political terrorism. This 'strategy of attention' towards the PCI was accompanied at an international level by a re-launch of the diplomatic initiatives towards Eastern Europe and the Mediterranean. It was a confirmation of the fact that there were no separate 'universes' such as the blocs formed during the early Cold War and, therefore, international cooperation had to serve as a modern alternative to the power politics still practised by the two superpowers.[1]

In Turkey, on the other hand, the governmental experience of Süleyman Demirel, leader of the AP (Adalet Partisi – Justice Party), and prime minister of Turkey since 1965, was marked by initially positive trends, subsequently followed by reversal. Until 1969, Turkish economic growth had been high, and real incomes had risen almost continuously; however, 1969 was to mark the exact turning point. The annual increase in national income, which, according to the estimates of the five-year plan inaugurated in 1967, ought to have been 7 per cent, failed to reach 6.4 per cent, falling to 4.8 per cent in 1970;[2] to this was added the political violence of extreme right-wing and far-left political groups, who also protested, among other things, during the visit of the US Sixth Fleet, between July 1968 and February 1969 – thus attesting to the climate of intense anti-Americanism due to Washington's lack of support for the Turkish position on Cyprus.[3] These factors all conspired to provoke a crisis within the Ankara government. In February 1970, the right wing of the AP voted with the opposition, forcing Demirel to resign. The situation worsened towards the end of the year, when forty-one deputies and senators left Demirel's party in order to found a new political movement, the Democratic Party (Demokratik Parti – DP), whose name recalled Adnan Menderes's former party, outlawed by the military coup of 1960.[4] This paralysis of Demirel's government, weakened by numerous defections within the very same AP, led to intervention by the military. On 12 March 1971, an ultimatum by the Chief of the Armed Forces led to the resignation of the Demirel government, to be replaced thereafter by an exponent of the right wing of the CHP (Cumhuriyet Halk Partisi – Republican People's Party), Nihat Erim, who was immediately supported by the old Kemalist leader İsmet İnönü.[5]

Erim's rise to power did not lead to any stabilization of Turkish political life, which, on the contrary, showed increasingly deep signs of crisis. In April 1972, Erim too was forced to resign,[6] being replaced in leadership of the government by Ferit Melen – one of the leaders of the CGP (Cumhuriyet Güven Partisi – Republican Reliance Party), itself an offshoot of the CHP. The CHP was trapped between the divergent political directions of the two leaders, the elder İsmet İnönü, one of the party's founders and a close collaborator of Mustafa Kemal Atatürk, and the younger Bülent Ecevit, who, between May and November 1972, was to prevail – thus forcing İnönü to abandon the presidency first and then any office within the party that he himself had helped found fifty years before.[7]

The prolonged Turkish crisis was without doubt a reflection of an internal situation that was unable to guarantee any stable and prolonged progress in terms of economic and social structures; however, it could also not avoid being affected by the geopolitical turbulence in the eastern Mediterranean during the 1960s and 1970s. The question posed by Cyprus seemed to have no positive answers. As far as the Cyprus question was concerned, there were now three different theses and three different political camps respectively – each one somewhat ambiguous. Whereas Greece claimed to recognize and respect Nicosia's independence, it also hoped one day to reach the long-awaited *enosis* (ένωσις – union); the Cypriot government, on the other hand, formally maintained its commitment to the goal of *enosis* with Greece, while fiercely defending its sovereignty; finally, Turkey recognized the independence of Cyprus, yet wanted to transform it into a federal state, a state within which the Turkish minority would have its claims to autonomy recognized.[8]

The Turkish military intervention in Cyprus in the summer of 1974, following the coup d'état of 15 July of that same year by Greek officers of the Cypriot National Guard, had no real effect on the bilateral relations between Italy and Turkey, which were above all strong in terms of commerce – in spite of the fact that Italy had not adopted a favourable position towards the regime in Ankara with regard to the Cyprus question.[9] Italy approved the UN resolution of 1 November 1974, calling for the withdrawal of all foreign armed forces present in Cyprus as well as the establishment of a constitutional authority decided by mutual agreement between the two respective communities. The proclamation of the Turkish Federated State of Cyprus in February 1975 provoked condemnation from Rome, alongside the EEC, which were in favour of the independence, sovereignty and territorial integrity of the island. At the United Nations, this led to the approval of Security Council Resolution 367 (12 March 1975) inviting both the Greek and the Turkish communities of Cyprus and the governments of Ankara and Athens to resume negotiations in order to reach a planned solution.[10]

Italian foreign policy towards the Mediterranean area, which became even stronger in the late 1960s and early 1970s, guaranteed renewed focus on Turkey, regarded as being an important point of contact between Europe and Asia. This objective corresponded to Italy's existing foreign policy requirements during the republican era, and it was the development of a policy of dialogue rather than a policy of power – the pursuit of specific national interests within the framework of European integration and loyalty to the alliances on which Rome's international policy had been decided since the end of the Second World War. It was within this context, that the visit of Italian Prime Minister Mariano Rumor, accompanied by Minister for Foreign Trade Vittorino Colombo, and Under-Secretary for Foreign Affairs Mario Zagari, to Ankara (5–8 June 1969), was to be an excellent opportunity to affirm an agreement of common goals between Italy and Turkey in terms of the development of a coherent Mediterranean policy.[11]

In August 1969, Aldo Moro's appointment as minister of foreign affairs in the second Rumor government led to a far greater political emphasis on both Eastern Europe and the so-called Third World.[12] Within this context, Turkey – a bridge between Europe and Asia – which, moreover, shared an Atlantic bond with Italy, constituted a central element. Moro went to Turkey on 29 April 1970, after a stopover in Bulgaria. A central element of the talks that the Italian minister of foreign affairs held with his Turkish counterpart, Çağlayangil, was the situation in the Middle East, whose regional equilibrium was in a perpetually unstable state owing to the incessant tensions that had resulted in full-blown conflict between Arabs and Israelis. On that occasion, the Turkish foreign minister expressed a certain concern, accompanied by a degree of pessimism, on a possible solution to the question, an attitude that, according to Moro, confirmed that 'caution [was]… always demonstrated [by Ankara] in the face of any initiative that could give grounds to greater Turkish commitment in the Middle Eastern conflict'.[13] Experts in the Ministry of Foreign Affairs had also defined the Arab–Israeli conflict as a thorn in the side for Turkey, for further attracting Soviet presence in the region.[14] Moro urged Çağlayangil to 'follow the development of events with utmost attention and contribute with every means available to the United Nations so as to achieve a just and lasting peace, according to Security Council Resolution of November 1967'.[15] At the end of the talks with Çağlayangil, Moro expressed his satisfaction with the progress of Italo-Turkish relations. He affirmed that 'in matters of Mediterranean politics Turkey is a constant point of reference for Italy'.[16] The one element of dissatisfaction in the bilateral relations between Rome and Ankara was the impossibility, on the Italian side, of prolonging the military assistance to Turkey that had been initiated by a resolution approved by the Atlantic Council on 15 December 1965, thereby establishing that the Italian government, from 1965 onwards, would grant Turkey an annual contribution of 750 million lire to be allocated to military supplies purchased in Italy for Turkish defence needs. Albeit with a delay, the Italian government had contributed to the payment of the contributions until 1968; however, subsequent financial difficulties and a lack of specific legislation that would have also guaranteed continued assistance legislatively, led Moro to make only a brief reference to Rome's favourable position in terms of increasing the already substantial aid received by Turkey within the framework of the OECD and EEC.[17]

The overall positive trend in the bilateral relations between Italy and Turkey saw further confirmation in the fact that Moro, on his official visit to Turkey, decided to hold a meeting of the HOMs in the Middle East in Istanbul, in which Italian diplomatic representatives in the area participated. According to the Italian minister of foreign affairs himself, during the meetings held between 30 April and 1 May, the diplomatic representatives in the Middle East expressed their appreciation for the Italian government's line in the region, which aimed at avoiding the escalation of conflict as well as controlling the inflow of armaments. On the other hand, concern was indeed raised about the continued retreat of Western positions in the area, to the advantage of Soviet interests,[18] and the serious Arab–Israeli situation – also deemed as being detrimental to Western interests. It is interesting to note a widespread expectation within the Arab world for greater direct Italian involvement in the issue, which, nonetheless, did not lead to any policy change.[19]

Moro's return at the head of the Ministry of Foreign Affairs in the third Rumor government had been ushered in with relatively low-profile diplomatic activity, with visits to two countries somewhat on the fringes of international relations – Bulgaria and Turkey. However, on more in-depth analysis, it would be difficult to ignore the traits common to both countries, traits which went beyond their different and contrastive international positions. In terms of Bulgaria and Turkey, the commonality of being geographically part of south-eastern Europe and the Mediterranean confirmed Italian foreign policy guidelines, which aimed at making the *Mare Nostrum* the cradle of international détente, thereby a model of coexistence between differing political systems that could be an exportable alternative to the bipolarism of the two global superpowers.

Meanwhile, on the Turkish side, the main concern in pursuing dialogue with Italy was supposedly to find support for Turkish requests for full association with the European Common Market. The approaching expiry of the twelve-year period leading up to the transitional phase led Turkish Foreign Minister Ümit Hayuk Bayülken to visit the main capital cities of Western Europe, including Rome, where he arrived on 17 February 1972. Turkey sought inclusion within the beneficiary states in the Generalised Scheme of Preferences (GSP) that the EEC applied (from 1 July 1971) to developing countries, as well as a rebalancing of its own association agreement in light of the accession of the UK, the Republic of Ireland and Denmark to the Common Market. On that occasion, Italian Minister of Foreign Affairs Aldo Moro confirmed that Rome would do its best to arrive at a Community decision favourable to the inclusion of Ankara within the GSP in addition to a rebalancing of Turkey's association agreement, on which, moreover, the Council of Ministers of the EEC had already authorized the Commission to negotiate an additional protocol for the definition of the necessary changes.[20] The Additional Protocol signed between the EEC and Turkey in Brussels came into force on 1 January 1973 and thus marked the beginning of the twelve-year transitional phase that, in 1985, was to have established the customs union. Tax and customs barriers were abolished on many Turkish products (with the notable exception of textiles), while the EEC continued its financial commitment to Ankara.[21] Turkish insistence on association with the European Economic Community was justified by the difficult economic circumstances that Turkey was experiencing – exacerbated by a conflictual social situation and by a large demographic increase which, although typical of a developing country, rendered the quest for any solution all the more complex. These were all factors that the technical government led by Ferit Melen – who had succeeded Erim in April 1972 – would have to face while seeking to garner support in Europe.[22]

Nevertheless, in the mid-1970s, the agreement between Rome and Ankara on Mediterranean issues was to go through a period of great difficulty as a result of the Cyprus crisis – a precursor of important repercussions in terms of the geopolitical structures in the region. On 2 December 1974, introducing his fourth government to the Italian Senate, a DC-PRI (Italian Republican Party) coalition, Moro also focused on the situation in the Mediterranean and the Middle East and, when dealing with the Cyprus question, stated that a possible solution would only be realistic if the governments of Greece and Turkey became aware of the fact that 'what [should have] encouraged both sides to come to some kind of agreement was indeed greater than that which divided them'.[23]

The Cyprus question played an important role in leading the Ankara government to pursue a foreign policy of greater independence with respect to the other Atlantic allies – the United States in particular. The United States did not fully support Turkey with regard to the ensuing controversy that surrounded the Eastern Mediterranean island. Furthermore, the whole Cypriot issue was to see a sudden resurgence in the summer of 1974 with the coup against Archbishop Makarios led by the pro-Greek forces of Sampson which in turn led the Ankara government to occupy the north-eastern part of the island – an occupation that caused Washington to implement an arms embargo on Turkey. Indeed, the controversy that divided Ankara and Athens – a knotty diplomatic game in which Washington also became involved – was far more complex, and included both the Cyprus question itself as well as the issues surrounding the territorial boundaries of the Greek Aegean islands off the Turkish coast and the exploitation of the continental shelf, whose subsoil was thought to be rich in hydrocarbons; the invasion of Cyprus by the Turkish military was to occur thanks to armaments that had been supplied by the United States. The problem lay in the fact that the Turkish-American agreement for the sale of armaments to Ankara contained a specific clause: arms were to be used only for defence purposes and not for aggression. Thus began a complex trilateral dispute involving the United States, Greece and Turkey, which ended with a vote in the US Congress, despite the contrary opinion of President Gerald Ford, in favour of both the appeal and the embargo.[24] The Turkish government's disapproval of Washington's actions was evident in Ankara's announcement of a possible interruption in negotiations on bilateral defence agreements as well as the potential closure of a number of military bases that had been granted for use to the United States. Turkey's reaction to NATO was equally harsh, with threats of a possible revision of the Turkish contribution to the integrated military command in the event of any continuation of the embargo.[25] This greater independence of Turkish foreign policy was borne witness to by the threat of dismantling US bases on Turkish territory, which – along with a decision already taken by Greek Prime Minister Konstantinos Karamanlis for Greece to leave integrated NATO controls – jeopardized the south-eastern flank of the Mediterranean in terms of the Atlantic alliance and was to the full advantage of the USSR.

Moro, at the head of the Italian Ministry of Foreign Affairs, demonstrated a typical sense of proportion and circumspection in proceeding towards a diplomatic solution to the long and arduous crisis in Cyprus. With regard to the question of military bases, he decided not to respond publicly, rather entrusting the task of encouraging a concerted solution of the issue by a mission of the Director of the Political Affairs of the Italian Ministry of Foreign Affairs – Roberto Ducci – in Athens and Ankara.[26] The Ducci mission did not lead to any tangible results, having to clash with the weakness of Greece, which was struggling with its difficult transition from dictatorship to democracy, on the one hand, and with Turkey in terms of its boldness, its strong advantages gained in the field and its complete unwillingness to renounce its territorial claims, on the other.[27]

The US Congress's decision in February 1975 to suspend arms shipments to Turkey led the military's general staff in Ankara to make immediate countermoves. There was the immediate opening of negotiations with other potential arms suppliers, among which France, West Germany and Italy should be mentioned – nations whose governments were more than willing to replace the United States in equipping the Turkish armed forces.[28]

In any case, the Cyprus question failed to compromise bilateral relations between Italy and Turkey. Italian financial support of the Turkish government within the context of NATO[29] and the support given to the association of Turkey in the EEC constitute two solid examples of Italy's focus on the Mediterranean Basin and the Middle East, and how it was evident that Turkey played a role as a bridge between Europe and Asia. Trade was mainly driven by incentives after Turkish Deputy Prime Minister Necmettin Erbakan's visit to Rome (16-20 December 1976), which led to the signing of a cooperation agreement seeking to bring political meaning to the Mediterranean framework.[30]

On the other hand, despite the bilateral plan becoming a community plan, greater difficulties arose. These were linked to Ankara's complicated financial predicament resulting from the oil crisis of 1973-4 as well as three years of US embargo from 1974 to 1977 – a consequence of Turkey's invasion of Northern Cyprus. In October 1978, the Turkish government led by Bülent Ecevit suspended the gradual association process that had been envisaged by the Ankara Agreement (1963) so as to prioritize internal issues. Ecevit's aim was to revise the terms of this agreement – calling for a five-year extension to proceed with tariff reduction, thereby protecting the Turkish economy from the potentially destabilizing effects of the Customs Union.[31] Acute difficulties existed between the EEC and Turkey, from political, diplomatic and economic points of view, and the Ankara government called for association on different terms, especially with regard to agricultural products and the free movement of work forces. In addition, Turkish agricultural products were directly in competition with those of other Mediterranean countries in the Community, such as Italy and, in anticipation of its accession, Greece. It was thus difficult for Brussels to be able to engage with Ankara beyond a certain limited scope. A similar argument applied to the issue of free movement of Turkish workers in the continental area, especially given the worrying period of unemployment that afflicted Europe in the second half of the 1970s.[32] Meanwhile, Turkish unemployment numbered approximately 3.5 million, thus painting a rather bleak picture of the Turkish economy – an economy whose exports to industrialized nations had suffered devastating effects from the international economic crisis and whose balance of payments deficit in 1977 had reached a figure of US$3 billion while foreign debt amounted to US$11 billion. Oil prices, which rose considerably after 1973, forced Turkey to pay increasingly more for its crude oil imports on which the national economy for the most part depended. Nevertheless and despite this, the EEC did indeed remain Turkey's main trading partner and, as late as 1979, imports from EEC countries accounted for around 38 per cent of the total, while Ankara sent 50 per cent of total exports to Western European countries.[33]

The relations between Italy and Turkey during the 1980s

The beginning of the 1980s in Italy and Turkey were marked by important internal changes that would have a notable effect on both countries' international relations.

In Italy, the phenomenon of political and social instability was exacerbated by the emergence of terrorism from both the extreme right and left, which, under the shadow of irregular activities, carried out by certain elements within the Italian armed forces and intelligence service, even cast doubt on the effective survival of an entire political and institutional system. The attack at the heart of this system came with the kidnapping and assassination of a major figure in Italian politics – Aldo Moro. Those fifty-five days – 16 March to 9 May 1978 – had an effect on political circles as well as public opinion in a similar way to what had happened in Italy after 8 September 1943 – dealing the initial, fateful blow to a system whose definitive end would be put off for more or less another decade. The so-called *linea della fermezza (no negotiations with the terrorists line/policy)* supported unanimously by both the DC and the PCI was rather a symptom of weakness. At least in terms of the DC, the very unity of the party was what was aimed at, perceived as being the only remaining hope of salvation – a basic condition for survival and, therefore, conservation of power. This firmness served exclusively to unify the forces within Italian politics, albeit a unity that contained an effective power vacuum as far as the state was concerned. Under those feverish and dramatic circumstances within Italy there was in fact a complex web of intervention and collateral strategies, originating within the corrupt fibres of Italian politics and bureaucracy as well as from the vested interests of foreign powers, which had none other than the enrichment and consolidation of personal power as goals. Nevertheless, in the short term, the system managed to keep going, even witnessing a decade of new economic impetus in Italy – one of the reasons for greater activism on Rome's part as far as foreign policy alongside the increasing authority of the Italian government within the international arena was concerned.[34]

The kidnapping of Moro and its tragic conclusion also marked the peak of the terrorist offensive. But terrorism was incapable of garnering strength or popular support and thus moved from overthrowing the social order to mass revolution. In a purely incidental way, the end of this phenomenon coincided more or less with the adhesion of the Italian government to the NATO Dual-Track Decision (Euromissiles), which, on the one hand, saw an end to DC-PCI governments of 'national unity' on a domestic level and a return to centre-left coalitions with Bettino Craxi's socialists – ever more distant from the communists – whereas, on the other hand, it meant a strengthening of Italy's position within NATO in terms of foreign policy. The marginalization of Berlinguer's PCI within the institutions was also brought about by a resurgence of the bipolar dispute between the United States and the USSR, of which the following factors (in addition to the international debate regarding the deployment of the aforementioned Euromissiles) were important: the Soviet invasion of Afghanistan and the military coup in Poland. The US reaction to this revival of 'power politics' by Moscow, after about a decade of détente, was witnessed by the new orientation of the Strategic Defence Initiative (SDI), which in turn had further important effects on the road towards the crisis of political unanimism in foreign policy as well as the widening of the gulf between the Italian left and government policy.[35]

The situation in Turkey was, if possible, far more serious than in Italy and therefore necessitated even more drastic solutions. The problems that had been gripping Turkey for about a decade were also typical of those in other Southern European countries. First, there was considerable political instability: the coalition governments ruling Turkey between 1973 and 1980 were all weak. The bitter dialectic between the two major Turkish political parties, Süleyman Demirel's AP and Ecevit's CHP, prevented any agreement from being reached in the only coalition that would have been able to lead to a large and stable majority – thus intensifying the influence of small extremist groups and polarizing the entire Turkish political framework.[36] In this state of paralysis, it was impossible to resolve the two other problems that Turkey was facing: political violence and the economic crisis. The phenomenon of terrorism, from both the extreme right and left in Turkey shook the entire country to the core. The number of victims of political violence increased rapidly from about 230 in 1977 – of which 39 were during a demonstration on 1 May in Taksim Square, Istanbul – to a body count ranging from 1,200 to 1,500 two years later. In the year before the military coup, there were over two thousand victims, including thirty-five the day before the eve of the pronouncement, which occurred on 12 September 1980. The economy was also in a ruinous situation; inflation had hit hard and in some regions stood at 104 per cent; unemployment was endemic – counting for about a fifth of the workforce; goods, even basic supplies, were unavailable, and foreign debt was soaring.[37] It was in this dire state of affairs, on 12 September 1980, that the armed forces seized power, dissolved parliament, deposed the government and suspended all political parties along with the two radical trade union confederations – the socialist DİSK (Confederation of Progressive Trade Unions of Turkey – Türkiye Devrimci İşçi Sendikaları Konfederasyonu) and the ultra-nationalist MİSK (Confederation of Turkish Nationalist Workers Unions – Türkiye Milliyetçi İşçi Sendikaları Konfederasyonu). Military power and authority did indeed bring order to the country, with terrorism defeated and dissent mollified. In 1982 a new constitution was drawn up that regulated Turkish public life in highly restrictive terms, limiting press freedom as well as trade union freedom and individual rights and liberties.[38]

The new course set by the military, in terms of the economy, was marked by a growth in exports and a gradual freeing up of the internal market. On the one hand, this signalled a certain decline in relations between Ankara and the European Community whereas, on the other, it instilled new confidence among international investors, who granted new funds and subsidies to Turkey through the IMF and the OECD. In fact, an initial aid package had already been granted to the Ankara government in 1979 – before the coup – placing faith in Turgut Özal, who, as part of Demirel's cabinet, had been the architect of a package of economic reforms inspired by the IMF. These funds, totalling US$300 million, came from the IMF itself along with other subsidies coming from the OECD, which granted Ankara 'emergency aid' amounting to US$906 million. Other credits were granted by a consortium of international bankers for US$400 million and by the World Bank for another US$160 million.[39] Italy (ranking third in terms of contribution of funds) made an important contribution to OECD fund provision to Ankara totalling US$115 million – after the United States and West Germany with US$295 million, respectively – then followed by France, Japan and the European Economic Community with US$100 million, Switzerland with US$37 million, the UK with US$33 million and subsequent funds from other minor countries.[40]

The situation in Turkey led to its suspension from the Council of Europe. The European countries were particularly sensitive to Turkish domestic developments. Indeed, the coup d'état brought about a climate of discontent and mistrust, not to mention explicit condemnation among European governments and public opinion that was to poison relations to a certain extent. A consequence of this was the imposition of visa requirements on Turkish travellers by the major European countries – with the exception of Italy and the UK. Furthermore, European public opinion was apprehensive about the want of any progress in the establishment of a civilian government and excesses in the Turkish fight against terrorism – there were rumours and reports of torture in Turkish prisons.[41] Turkey's suspension from the Council of Europe came in May 1981, when the Turkish deputies' mandate expired and which, in the absence of an elected parliament, could not be renewed.[42] In actual fact, this provision was not formalized, and the Council of Europe itself partially reversed it on 28 January 1982. The text approved at that day's session by a very tight majority conceded that fundamental human rights had indeed been violated in Turkey with the advent of the dictatorship – recognizing in particular that some political prisoners had also been subjected to torture, in addition to which the suspension of parliamentary activities and the dissolution of political parties was also decried. Moreover, a further cause for condemnation was the fact that the political parties themselves had been excluded from the work of the Constituent Assembly of Turkey which was working on the new fundamental law. In contrast, it was also nonetheless recognized that the situation in which General Kenan Evren's military had intervened had been unsustainable owing to the terrorism that had been ravaging the country; all of this rendered such an action tantamount to obligatory.[43] At the same time, the European Parliament also sent the Turkish government, at the behest of socialist and communist groups, a request to 're-establish democratic institutions and practices' within two months, threatening otherwise to suspend the associate relationship with the EEC.[44] This request arrived on 21 January 1982, when both the suspension of the deputies' mandate in Ankara (members of the dissolved Turkish National Assembly) and EEC-Turkey association were reaffirmed. The same intransigence was to be witnessed with regard to the issue of economic aid, to which Strasbourg remained deeply hostile.[45] Even the Italian government, speaking through its Minister of Foreign Affairs, Emilio Colombo, in the Chamber of Deputies on 3 March 1982, held a steadfast position with regard to the potentially authoritarian route on which Turkey was headed. In fact, Rome had no intention of making any concessions on fundamental principles of human rights and political liberties, as well as its hope to see a 'fully democratic and pluralist structure restored as soon as possible'; Colombo wanted to emphasise appreciation for the strong bond between the European Community still felt in Ankara and which might prove decisive in avoiding a 'painful involution as much towards exasperated nationalism as desperate, yet risky, Islamic solidarity'.[46]

Another point of conflict between Turkey and the EEC continued to be the question of Cyprus. After the 1974 Turkish invasion and the consequent military clashes, the de facto situation was that of a stalemate between the two communities – the Greek-Cypriots concentrated in the southern part of the island and the Turkish-Cypriots in the northern part. On 15 November 1983, the Northern Turkish administration proclaimed its independence, declaring itself to be the Turkish Republic of Northern Cyprus. Condemnation from the ten countries of the European Community was unanimous – referring to UN Security Council Resolution n. 541/1983, which had defined any attempt to create a Turkish Republic of Northern Cyprus as being 'invalid and worsening in terms of the Cypriot situation'; the resolution was supposed to have provided a basis for the restoration of the territorial integrity and unity of the Republic of Cyprus. The ten EEC nations appealed to the Turkish government for intervention on the issue and also for it to exercise its influence on the Turkish-Cypriot community in order to revoke its decision.[47]

The US position was in many ways even more delicate for a number of reasons: first, Turkey shared two thousand kilometres of common border with the USSR and, moreover, strategic control of the Dardanelles that provided it with the opportunity to counter Russian access to the Eastern Mediterranean. These factors alone would suffice in order to outline the strategically important role that Turkey played in terms of the entire Atlantic alliance,[48] and therefore the United States could not condemn a coup that might guarantee the pacification of the country in question, along with a certain level of efficiency, that Washington itself deemed necessary given the volatility of the southern Mediterranean and the Middle East during the late 1970s and the early 1980s.[49] At the beginning of the 1980s, the international geopolitical situation seemed to be in rapid evolution, and the policy of international détente seemed to have reached a definitive crisis. With the onset of the 1980s, the crisis of the détente, which in those early months played out its final moves in Poland, the Iran–Iraq War and the arrival of Reagan at the White House all became new factors that directly involved Turkey. The heightening of international tensions thus emphasized Turkey's strategic importance even more. In this sense, the generals who had seized power with the coup of 12 September 1980 played their hand well in emphasising this aspect in an effort to secure political and economic aid from the West. In the words of the generals, Turkey wanted to continue to be a bulwark against Soviet expansionism in the Eastern Mediterranean and in the Persian Gulf, thereby strengthening its position as a fundamental link in the Atlantic alliance. This image was perfectly compatible with Reagan's outlook, and he soon expressed his support for the Turkish generals. At that time, friendship with Turkey in the new US administration was guaranteed by the presence of the US Secretary of State Alexander Haig, who, on his appointment as NATO Supreme Commander (1974–9), had striven successfully to see an end to the military embargo against Turkey.[50] In fact, during the 1980s, the main US concerns in the Middle East were primarily the Iranian Revolution, and secondly the Iran–Iraq War. From this point of view, Turkey was able to represent a strong geopolitical ally for Washington in the region. For its part, the military regime in Ankara also looked at the coming to power of Khomeini in Tehran and the Iranian Islamic Republic with utmost suspicion – fearing its influence on Islamic groups within Turkey itself.[51]

All of this inevitably led to an intensification of the arms trade between the Western powers and Turkey and in which Italy was also a main player. In April 1984, at the end of the Atlantic Council in Istanbul, Italian Minister of Defence Giovanni Spadolini exchanged views on the prospects of bilateral cooperation in the defence sector with his Turkish counterpart, Zeki Yavuztürk, who, a few days later on 9 May, saw to negotiations for the supply of fifty-two Alenia G222 military transport aircraft to Turkey with conditions that also provided for a number of financial benefits.[52]

The arrival of Giulio Andreotti[53] as minister of foreign affairs (starting in 1983) strengthened the traditional understandings between Italy and Turkey on themes of bilateral relations, Mediterranean policies and the European Economic Community. During the mid-1980s in particular, the Mediterranean was yet again an area of great international instability, above all due to Libyan activities under Colonel Gaddafi, which saw Libya become a hub of terrorism along with the PLO and, to a lesser extent, Syria.[54] The Reagan administration dealt with international terrorism through pressure and reprisals against Libya, in which Italy also participated despite its traditionally pro-Arab stance. Washington's staunch determination in the fight against terrorism led to direct Italian involvement, which provided NATO and the US Sixth Fleet with air and naval bases for incursions on Libyan territory. However, the government in

Rome undertook a rather different approach, that is to say enduring on one hand and mediating on the other – as far as possible – in order to avoid the worst outcome, and in this sense the Craxi government enjoyed the full support of Turkey. During the talks held by Andreotti in Ankara on a visit at the end of January 1986, an agreement was reaffirmed not to support sanctions against Libya as they were considered to be of questionable effectiveness. As far as Turkey's accession to the EEC was concerned, Andreotti renewed Italian support of the Turkish government, while, on a bilateral level, an agreement was signed on 2 October 1986 for cooperation in the fight against organized drug-trafficking and terrorism, which included six-monthly meetings and the creation of expert sub-commissions.[55]

In April 1987, Turkey officially requested accession to the EEC. The European response was a refusal, but a refusal that did seek to leave the door slightly ajar – the EEC offered membership of the single customs union instead of full membership. Negotiations proceeded slowly and with difficulty, as the European Community demanded full observance of European rules on intellectual property, labelling and free trade, while Turkey, for its part, sought financial benefits. On the occasion of Turkish Prime Minister Turgut Özal's visit to Rome (5–6 October 1988), the Italian government reiterated its full support for Turkey's accession to the EEC, in relation to which there were no political and economic obstacles, as well as the Italian government's readiness for the implementation of policies that would facilitate Turkish cohesion within the Community. In this sense, the turbulence of the international system during the late 1980s and early 1990s did also enkindle hope in terms of a special collaborative relationship between Italy and Turkey within the Community – be it the creation of a Mediterranean axis to counter the northern axis post-German reunification or with regard to security from the perceived threat posed by the demographic pressures coming from the southern shores of the Mediterranean. Nonetheless, the difficult human rights situation in Turkey, especially in terms of the Kurdish minority and a new economic recession, were to delay Turkey's participation in the Customs Union until 1995.[56]

Notes

1 For the evolution of Moro's external and internal political strategy during the period, see Gianni Baget Bozzo and Giovanni Tassani, *Aldo Moro: Il politico nella crisi 1962/1973* (Florence: Sansoni, 1983), 311 et sqq.; Giorgio Campanini, *Aldo Moro: Cultura e impegno politico* (Rome: Studium, 1992); Andrea Ambrogetti (ed.), *Aldo Moro e la crisi della forma partito* (Naples: Edizioni Scientifiche Italiane, 1993); Guido Formigoni, *Aldo Moro. L'intelligenza applicata alla mediazione politica* (Milan: Centro Ambrosiano, 1997); Fabio Vander, *Aldo Moro: La cultura politica e la crisi della democrazia italiana* (Genoa: Marietti, 1999); Felice La Rocca, *L'eredità perduta. Aldo Moro e la crisi italiana* (Soveria Mannelli: Rubbettino, 2001); Augusto D'Angelo, Moro, i vescovi e l'apertura a sinistra (Rome: Studium, 2005); Antonello Di Mario, *L'attualità di Aldo Moro negli scritti giornalistici (1943–1978)* (Naples: Tullio Pironti, 2007); Francesco Saita, *Aldo Moro politico. Dalla Costituente a via Caetani sviluppo e crisi del pensiero di uno statista* (Rome: Reality Book, 2008); Pietro

Panzarino, *Aldo Moro e le convergenze democratiche. Il dialogo nel carteggio DC-PCI durante il governo delle astensioni (1976–1978)* (Treviso: Piazza Editore, 2008); Corrado Guerzoni, *Aldo Moro* (Palermo: Sellerio, 2008); Giovanni Galloni, *Trent'anni con Moro* (Rome: Editori Riuniti, 2008); Luciano Conte, *Aldo Moro. L'eredità di un laico cattolico* (Cosenza: Falco Editore, 2008); Angiola Filipponio and Aldo Regina (eds), *In ricordo di Aldo Moro: Atti del Convegno (Bari, 20 giugno 2008)* (Milan: Giuffré, 2010); Mondo Contemporaneo (ed.), *Aldo Moro nella storia dell'Italia repubblicana* (Milan: Franco Angeli, 2011); Francesco Perfetti, Andrea Ungari, Daniele Caviglia and Daniele De Luca (eds), *Aldo Moro nell'Italia contemporanea* (Florence: Le Lettere, 2011); Pietro Panzarino, *L'eredità politica di Aldo Moro: Pensiero e azione di un uomo libero (1976–1978)* (Venice: Marsilio, 2011); Federico Imperato, *Aldo Moro e la pace nella sicurezza: La politica estera del centro-sinistra 1963–1968* (Bari: Progedit, 2011); Italo Garzia, Luciano Monzali and Massimo Bucarelli (eds), *Aldo Moro, l'Italia repubblicana e i Balcani* (Nardò: Besa, 2011); Italo Garzia, Luciano Monzali and Federico Imperato (eds), *Aldo Moro, l'Italia repubblicana e i popoli del Mediterraneo* (Nardò: Besa, 2013); Alfonso Alfonsi (ed.), *Aldo Moro nella dimensione internazionale: Dalla memoria alla storia* (Milan: Franco Angeli, 2013); Federico Imperato, *Aldo Moro, l'Italia e la diplomazia multilaterale: Momenti e problemi* (Nardò: Besa, 2013); Giovanni Mario Ceci, *Moro e il PCI: La strategia dell'attenzione e il dibattito politico italiano (1967–1969)* (Rome: Carocci, 2013); Pietro Panzarino, *Il centro-sinistra di Aldo Moro (1958–1968)* (Venice: Marsilio, 2014); Renato Moro and Daniele Mezzana (eds), *Una vita, un paese: Aldo Moro e l'Italia del Novecento* (Soveria Mannelli: Rubbettino, 2014); Piero Doria, *Il contributo di Aldo Moro alla costruzione della democrazia italiana* (Rome: Aracne, 2015).

2   On Turkish history, see Luca Pietromarchi, *Turchia vecchia e nuova* (Milan: Bompiani, 1965), particularly 187–434; Antonello Biagini, *Storia della Turchia contemporanea* (Milan: Bompiani, 2002); Erik J. Zürcher, *Storia della Turchia. Dalla fine dell'impero ottomano ai giorni nostri* (Rome: Donzelli, 2007), 251–407; Lea Nocera, *La Turchia contemporanea. Dalla repubblica kemalista al governo dell'AKP* (Rome: Carocci, 2011). A far more extensive corpus is available in English: Stanford J. Shaw and Ezel Kural Shaw, *History of the Ottoman Empire and Modern Turkey, Vol. 2: Reform, Revolution and Republic. The Rise of Modern Turkey, 1808–1975* (Cambridge: Cambridge University Press, 1977); Resat Kasaba (ed.), *The Cambridge History of Modern Turkey, Vol. 4: Turkey in the Modern World* (Cambridge: Cambridge University Press, 2008). For specifics, see Donatella Viti, 'Difficile momento per la Turchia', *Relazioni Internazionali*, 23 January 1971, 83.

3   'Manifestazioni antiamericane in Turchia', *Relazioni Internazionali*, 3 August 1968, 766; 'Manifestazioni antiamericane in Turchia', *Relazioni Internazionali*, 15 February 1969, 120. Another famous demonstration of hostility towards the United States is known as the 'Komer Incident', named after the US ambassador to Turkey Robert W. Komer, who, while visiting the *Middle East Technical University* (METU) in Ankara on 6 January 1969, was faced with the protests of a group of students from ultra-left-wing organizations who set fire to his car; see Nasuh Uslu, *The Turkish-American Relationship between 1947 and 2003: The History of a Distinctive Alliance* (New York: Nova Science, 2003), 33–4.

4   'Nuova formazione politica in Turchia', *Relazioni Internazionali*, 10 October 1970, 943.

5   Donatella Viti, 'I militari turchi scendono in campo', *Relazioni Internazionali*, 20 March 1971, 276–7.

6 Donatella Viti, 'Le dimissioni di Erim', *Relazioni Internazionali*, no. 17, 22 April 1972, 415.
7 'Si dimette l'erede di Ataturk', *Relazioni Internazionali*, no. 20, 13 May 1972, 496.
8 ACS, AM, s. 5 et sqq. 1, b. 137, f. 122, Appunto. Oggetto: Turchia, Rome, 8 February 1972, 2; 'Cipro e petrolio tra Ankara e Atene', *Relazioni Internazionali*, no. 16, 20 April 1974, 417.
9 Luigi Vittorio Ferraris (ed.), *Manuale della politica estera italiana 1947-1993* (Bari: Laterza, 1998), 289-90. For Italian initiatives in the aftermath of the 1974 Cyprus crisis, see the statements of Minister of Foreign Affairs Aldo Moro to the Italian Foreign Affairs Committee on 1 August 1974: 'Distensione fra i popoli', Aldo Moro, *L'Italia nell'evoluzione dei rapporti internazionali* (Rome: EBE-Moretto, 1986), 498-9. The Cyprus problem is not handled exhaustively in terms of Italian historiography with the following being exceptions: G. P. C. N. [Gian Paolo Calchi Novati], 'La grave tensione di Cipro. Il futuro costituzionale e il contrasto greco-turco', *Relazioni Internazionali*, no. 1, 4 January 1964, 5-7; Bruno Grandi, *Profili internazionali della questione di Cipro* (Milan: Giuffré, 1983). A larger corpus is available in other languages: Christopher Hitchens, *Hostage to History: Cyprus from the Ottomans to Kissinger* (London: Verso, 1997); Melek Firat, 'La politique étrangère de la République de Chipre d'après les archives turques d'Ankara', *Études Balkaniques. Cahiers Pierre Belon*, no. 5 (1998), 185-204; Firat, 'Les politiques Chipriotes de la Turquie de 1945 à 2001', *GREMMO Monde Arab Contemporain. Cahiers de Recherche*, no. 9 (2001), 53-62; Aytug Plümer, *Cyprus 1963-64: The Fateful Years* (Lefkoşa: Cyrep, 2003); David Hannay, *Cyprus: The Search for a Solution* (London: I.B. Tauris, 2005); William Mallinson, *Cyprus: A Modern History* (London: I.B. Tauris, 2005); James Ker-Lindsay, *The Cyprus Problem: What Everyone Needs to Know* (Oxford: Oxford University Press, 2011).
10 Enrica Costa Bona and Luciano Tosi, *l'Italia e la sicurezza collettiva: Dalla Società delle Nazioni alle Nazioni Unite* (Perugia: Morlacchi, 2007), 241-2.
11 'Il viaggio del presidente Rumor in Turchia: Volontà di cooperazione ispira I rapporti italo-turchi', *Relazioni Internazionali*, no. 24, 14 June 1969, 508.
12 Baget Bozzo, Tassani, *Aldo Moro*, 424.
13 ACS, AM, s. 5, et sqq. 1, b. 128, f. 19, 'Tel. in arrivo n. 17443 dall'Ambasciata d'Italia ad Istanbul (Mondello) al Ministero degli Affari Esteri. Oggetto: Messaggio On.le Ministro su colloqui avuti con Autorità turche', Istanbul 1 May 1970, 3.
14 ACS, AM, s. 5, et sqq. 1, b. 128, f. 19, Appunto. Oggetto: Politica estera turca', n.d. (April 1970), 11-12. On several occasions the Soviet Union had tried to obtain a favourable - from a Soviet position - revision to the clauses of the 1936 Montreux Convention, which included, among other things, different tonnage limits in terms of military shipping passing through the Dardanelles - depending on whether the States concerned were riparian or non-riparian: ibid., 11.
15 ACS, AM, s. 5, et sqq. 1, b. 128, f. 19, 'Brindisi del Ministro degli Affari Esteri Onorevole Moro al pranzo offertogli ad Ankara dal Ministro degli Affari Esteri Caglayangil', 2.
16 Francesco Ricciu, 'L'On. Moro in Turchia', *Relazioni Internazionali*, no. 19, 9 May 1970.
17 ACS, AM, s. 5, et sqq. 1, b. 128, f. 19, 'Appunto: Turchia - Situazione economica e rapporti economici con l'Italia', pp. 16-17; ACS, AM, s. 5, et sqq. 1, b. 128, f. 19, 'Tel. in arrivo n. 17211 dall'Ambasciata d'Italia ad Ankara al Ministero degli Affari Esteri. Oggetto: Tel. a firma On.le Ministro per il Presidente della Repubblica e per l'On.le Presidente del Consiglio', Ankara, 30 April 1970, 1-2.

18 ACS, AM, s. 5, et sqq. 1, b. 128, f. 21, 'Tel. in arrivo n. 17474 dall'Ambasciata d'Italia ad Istanbul (Mondello) al Ministero degli Affari Esteri. Oggetto: Disciplina afflusso armamenti in Medio Oriente', Istanbul, 1 May 1970, 1.
19 ACS, AM, s. 5, et sqq. 1, b. 128, f. 21, 'Tel. in arrivo n. 17475 dall'Ambasciata d'Italia ad Istanbul (Mondello) al Ministero degli Affari Esteri. Oggetto: Riunione nostri Ambasciatori accreditati in Paesi Medio Oriente, RAU e Turchia, presiedute da On.le Ministro', Istanbul, 1 May 1970, 1.
20 ACS, AM, s. 5, et sqq. 1, b. 137, f. 122, 'Colazione offerta dall'On. Ministro in onore del Ministro degli Esteri turco (17 febbraio 1972)' 2; Enrico Serra, L'Europa nei colloqui italo-turchi', *Relazioni Internazionali*, no. 9, 26 February 1972, 211.
21 Franco Taiana, 'Turchia ed Europa', Valeria Fiorani Piacentini (ed.), *Turchia e Mediterraneo allargato. Democrazia e democrazie* (Milan: Franco Angeli, 2005), 275–80; Carola Cerami, 'La svolta degli anni '70 nei rapporti fra Turchia e Comunità europea: come superare il modello interpretativo dell'avvicinamento-allontanamento', Antonio Varsori (ed.), *Alle origini del presente. L'Europa occidentale nella crisi degli anni Settanta* (Milan: Franco Angeli, 2007), 99–101.
22 On Turkey's difficulties during the early 1970s, see Donatella Viti, 'Difficile momento per la Turchia', *Relazioni Internazionali*, 23 January 1971, 83–4; Viti, 'La Turchia nella morsa delle contraddizioni', *Relazioni Internazionali*, no. 47, 20 November 1971, 1134; Viti, 'Le dimissioni di Erim', *Relazioni Internazionali*, no. 17, 22 April 1972, 415.
23 Italian Senate, session held on 2 December 1974, in Aldo Moro, *Discorsi parlamentari*, vol. II 1963–1977 (Rome: Camera dei Deputati, 1996), 1514.
24 Valerio Pellizzari, 'Il nodo di Cipro fra Turchia e Grecia', *Relazioni Internazionali*, no. 18, 10 July 1976, 676–7.
25 Donatella Viti, 'Iniziativa autonomistica dei turco-ciprioti', *Relazioni Internazionali*, no. 8, 22 February 1975, 172–3.
26 Paolo Soave, 'L'Italia e la crisi cipriota', Garzia, Monzali and Imperato (eds), *Aldo Moro, l'Italia repubblicana e i popoli del Mediterraneo*, 182–4.
27 Ibid., 188–9.
28 Donatella Viti, 'Grande destra in Turchia', *Relazioni Internazionali*, no. 14, 5 April 1975, 322.
29 On this argument see Aldo Moro's personal correspondence archive held at the Central State Archives, in particular: ACS, AM, s. 3, et sqq. 2, et sqq. 2, b. 71, f. 202: 'Lettera del Ministro degli Affari Esteri Amintore Fanfani al Ministro del Commercio Estero Giusto Tolloy', Rome, 7 December 1967, 1.
30 Ferraris, 289.
31 Taiana, 'Turchia ed Europa', 278–9.
32 Ibid.
33 Ibid., 279–80.
34 Piero Craveri, *La Repubblica dal 1958 al 1992* (Turin: UTET, 1995), 733–46. Regarding the case of Aldo Moro an extensive bibliography exists including among others: Leonardo Sciascia, *L'affaire Moro* (Palermo: Sellerio, 1978); Sergio Flamigni, *La tela del ragno: Il delitto Moro* (Milan: Kaos, 1993); Agostino Giovagnoli, *Il caso Moro: Una tragedia repubblicana* (Bologna: Il Mulino, 2005); Vladimiro Satta, *Il caso Moro e i suoi falsi misteri* (Soveria Mannelli: Rubbettino, 2006); Miguel Gotor, *Il memoriale della Repubblica: Gli scritti di Aldo Moro dalla prigionia e l'anatomia del potere italiano* (Turin: Einaudi, 2011).
35 On Italian foreign policy during the 1980s, see Ennio Di Nolfo (ed.), *La politica estera italiana negli anni ottanta* (Venice: Marsilio, 2007); Leopoldo Nuti, *La sfida nucleare*.

La politica estera italiana e le armi atomiche 1945-1991 (Bologna: Il Mulino, 2007), 347-93; Antonio Varsori, *La Cenerentola d'Europa? L'Italia e l'integrazione europea dal 1947 a oggi* (Soveria Mannelli: Rubbettino, 2010), 331-74.

36 Zürcher, *Storia della Turchia*, 318-19.
37 Donatella Viti, 'La Turchia sotto i militari', *Relazioni Internazionali*, no. 38, 20 September 1980, 815.
38 Zürcher, *Storia della Turchia*, 340-1.
39 'Il salvataggio della Turchia', *Relazioni Internazionali*, no. 28, 14 July 1979, 621.
40 'Gli aiuti alla Turchia', *Relazioni Internazionali*, no. 20, 16 May 1981, 439.
41 Pietro Sormani, 'La Turchia dei generali e l'Europa', *Relazioni Internazionali*, no. 14, 4 April 1981, 289.
42 Pietro Sormani, 'Sospesa la Turchia dal Consiglio d'Europa', *Relazioni Internazionali*, no. 21, 23 May 1981, 465.
43 'Europa e Turchia', *Relazioni Internazionali*, nos 3-4, 6 February 1982, 55-56.
44 'Ultimatum di Strasburgo alla Turchia', *Relazioni Internazionali*, no. 16, 18 April 1981, 348.
45 'Europa e Turchia', loc. 56.
46 'El Salvador e Turchia nel discorso di Colombo alla Camera dei deputati', *Relazioni Internazionali*, no. 10, 13 March 1982, 189.
47 ILS, GA, s. Europa, b. 363, f.: 'Lussemburgo 9 aprile 1984, Declarations des Dix – 27 mars 1984', 8.
48 Donatella Viti, 'La Turchia e gli interessi dell'Occidente', *Relazioni Internazionali*, no. 9, 3 March 1979, 182.
49 Viti, 'La Turchia sotto i militari', 182.
50 Sormani, 'La Turchia dei generali e l'Europa', 289.
51 Zürcher, *Storia della Turchia*, 394.
52 Ferraris, 452-3.
53 On Giulio Andreotti, see Giuseppe Romeo, *La politica estera italiana nell'era Andreotti (1972-1992)* (Soveria Mannelli: Rubbettino, 2000); Nicola Tranfaglia, *La sentenza Andreotti. Politica, mafia e giustizia nell'Italia contemporanea* (Milan: Garzanti, 2001); Giorgio Galli, *Il prezzo della democrazia. La carriera politica di Giulio Andreotti* (Milan: Kaos, 2003); Massimo Franco, *Andreotti. La vita di un uomo politico, la storia di un'epoca* (Milan: Mondadori, 2008); Mario Barone and Ennio Di Nolfo (eds), *Giulio Andreotti. L'uomo, il cattolico, lo statista* (Soveria Mannelli: Rubbettino, 2010); Antonio Varsori, *L'Italia e la fine della guerra fredda. La politica estera dei governi Andreotti (1989-1992)* (Bologna: Il Mulino, 2013); Luca Riccardi, *L'ultima politica estera. L'Italia e il Medio Oriente alla fine della Prima Repubblica* (Soveria Mannelli: Rubbettino, 2014); Paolo Gheda and Federico Robbe, *Andreotti e l'Italia di confine. Lotta politica e nazionalizzazione delle masse (1947-1954)* (Milan: Guerini e Associati, 2015); Luciano Monzali, *Giulio Andreotti e le relazioni italo-austriache 1972-1992* (Merano: Alpha & Beta, 2016).
54 On Gaddafi's Libya, see Massimiliano Cricco, *Il petrolio dei Senussi: Stati Uniti e Gran Bretagna in Libia dall'indipendenza a Gheddafi (1949-1973)* (Florence: Polistampa, 2002); Angelo Del Boca, *Gheddafi: Una sfida dal deserto* (Bari: Laterza, 2010); Massimiliano Cricco and Federico Cresti, *Gheddafi: I volti del potere* (Rome: Carocci, 2011); Federico Cresti and Massimiliano Cricco, *Storia della Libia contemporanea: Dal dominio ottomano alla morte di Gheddafi* (Rome: Carocci, 2012).
55 Ferraris, 453.
56 Ibid.

12

Partners in rivalry: Britain, ENI and the Tehran oil agreements of 1971

Bruno Pierri

Introduction

ENI has always been the maverick amongst western oil companies. ... Signor Cefis ... suggested ... that a radical change is needed in the relationship between producer and consumer governments. This would undermine the international oil companies' traditional role as buffers between producer and consumer, and lead to direct negotiations for long-term contracts. ... This position may indeed be reached one day, but it is not in the interests of our companies or of HM Government that it should be expedited.[1]

From these few words, we can easily realize how tense the relations between oil majors and the Italian state hydrocarbon corporation were. In 1971, in fact, ENI (Ente Nazionale Idrocarburi, the National Hydrocarbons Authority) had been almost the only large oil company to reject invitations to participate in the industry's cooperative arrangements leading to the Tehran agreements of 14 February. According to British government officials, the Italians had a long-standing suspicion of the same international oil industry on which they still felt dependent.[2] Instead, Downing Street had backed the oil companies in negotiating together in response to the demands of the producers, and hoped ENI would at last side with the other Western administrations in resisting more outrageous requests.[3]

As far as the Middle East was concerned, the 1969 ENI report argued that its associate partners in that area had a profitability rate of 60 to 70 per cent a year, while in Europe the majors deliberately kept their partners in a state of low income. In light of this, the big companies were accused, sometimes with the collusion of their parent governments, of harming a common European energy policy and the diversification of supplies, thus shifting high costs to consuming countries. Hence, according to ENI, it was necessary for the Italian government to back the national corporation in finding new energy sources abroad and achieving closer economic and industrial relations with producing governments.[4] In the meantime, a watershed for global energy balance had occurred on 1 September 1969 with the Free Officers' coup in Libya, led by

Muammar Gaddafi against King Idris. British interests in Libya were considerable, almost equalizing Iranian annual production. Moreover, almost all drillings were operated by American companies, although some of the most substantial discoveries in the previous years had been made by small American and European firms, making the oil trade share of the majors drop from 90 to 75 per cent in 1968. Therefore, the ownership of the industry and the control over international marketing was becoming less centralized.[5] Consequently, overall oil talks were taking place between the two Atlantic countries in 1970, during which the British and Americans agreed that the most important issue was security of supply, while in early May the majors had managed to reach an agreement with the Shah, establishing the principle according to which the producing country had the right to directly market its own oil.[6] In the meantime, on 2 September 1970 in Tripoli a pivotal agreement was signed. Until then, in fact, industrial democracies and oil companies had been made blind by illusions regarding an American energy surplus which could decrease prices, and the estimation that any producer would always be ready to push prices down and augment output in order to make the highest profits possible.[7] The new agreement had established an increase from US$2.23 to US$2.53 a barrel for the posted price of Libyan crude,[8] as well as a further two-cent growth for the following five years. Finally, the income tax was increased from 50 to 58 per cent.[9]

The Conference of Caracas and ENI's attitude

What happened in Tripoli had had immediate repercussions, for in November in Tehran the posted price had been increased by nine cents a barrel and the tax ratio shifted to 55 per cent. Whitehall regarded Iran as a safe source of oil and the government did not usually interfere with the companies' commercial policies; however, in this case Downing Street was ready to put discreet pressure on them.[10] On the other hand, Britain had important interests at stake in Iraq. In this case, the available documentation shows how the Anglo-Italian rivalry in the Mesopotamian country had been developing for years by then. As evidence of this, we can quote the dialogue in 1967 between British Secretary of State George Brown and his Italian equivalent, Amintore Fanfani, on the negotiations taking place between ENI and the Iraqi Petroleum Company, an affiliate of BP, and whose assets had been almost entirely expropriated six years earlier. The fact that the Italian corporation was dealing with the Iraqi government, which was supposed to reach an agreement on compensation with British Petroleum first, was not really welcomed by the British, who accused the Italians of making things more difficult by taking IPC stolen property. Therefore, Brown asked his Italian colleague to keep out of the field while the British-American company was trying to settle its differences with the Iraqis.[11]

Whether they liked it or not, the Western powers had to take note that times had changed and that sometimes oil producers opted for power instead of economic benefits. Within this context, the Persian Gulf area, and Iran in particular, played a pivotal role in American interests. On the basis of the Nixon Doctrine, the balance of power in the region was to be guaranteed by relying on local conservative powers, and this theory was appreciated by Tehran.[12] Such a situation made exporters for the first time aware that the energy market was favouring them, also on the basis of the fact that non-OPEC producers allocated a good portion of their output to the domestic market, thus leaving to the Organization a very wide share of the international market.[13] As a confirmation of this in December the OPEC Conference of Caracas issued Resolution 120, establishing the principle that those companies not accepting taxes and royalties imposed by OPEC would be denied supplies. The producers stated that the minimum tax on oil incomes would be generally increased to 55 per cent, while Resolution 124 approved any measure decided by Libya to acquire an additional price for better freight conditions. The crux of the new system was the concept of regionalization, through which OPEC aims were separately negotiated on the basis of geographical location. Hence, two main areas of negotiations were framed, the Persian Gulf and the Mediterranean, and the beginning of the talks was to take place a month after the end of the Conference.[14] Meanwhile, the Shah made a major television speech, stressing the need to further increase prices in view of the decline of the purchasing power of the US dollar and the British pound in the previous years, which had resulted in producers earning substantially less.[15] In addition to that, it is important to specify that the Shah did not particularly favour any specific independent company; rather, he aimed at achieving the highest benefit from foreign enterprises, not only in terms of higher prices but also as concerned facilities and know-how acquisition.[16]

To this clear message from the producers to take over their own oil, the companies felt the need of a joint approach to counter the danger. As evidence of that, suffice it to remind what the companies' counsel, John J. McCloy, stated:

> The leapfrogging or whipsaw effect came into full play.[17] Yet, I think there was still a reasonable hope that outstanding issues between the companies and the producing governments could be solved until, in December 1970, a whole series of demands emanated from an OPEC conference in Caracas.[18]

In opposition to the two resolutions, the companies agreed that it was not possible to negotiate on any other basis than reaching agreement simultaneously with all producers. Moreover, the independents insisted upon the so-called 'Safety Net Agreement' designed to supply oil to any company cut off in a reprisal action, by proportionally sharing the burden with other corporations according to their production.[19] In the talks taking place in New York in January 1971, during which the main issue to debate was the problem of how to avoid antitrust laws, all of the Seven Sisters had been represented as well as the leading independents. ENI was practically the only absentee. What the oilmen sought was collaboration between governments and companies, with the justification that the enterprises were now facing a cartel more formidable than themselves. Such an initiative marked a complete reversal from the attitude the majors had had for the previous ten years. While in the past, in fact, they did not even want to recognize the existence of OPEC, now they claimed to negotiate with the organization as a whole, thus helping the cartel to acquire more strength.[20]

On the other hand, American diplomacy was aligned to the Iranian posture, as there was the risk for radicals to prevail in overall deals.[21] It was crystal clear how the White

House aimed at favouring such reliable allies like Iran and Saudi Arabia, who had no intention to involve all OPEC members in negotiations.[22] The Nixon administration had everything to lose by taking sides or trying to moderate a settlement, especially since the companies had by then concluded that the Gulf States would get what they wanted.[23] Stability of supplies had priority on prices, and in order to have it granted any unilateral action was to be avoided. Hence, it was much better for the companies to accept the producers' conditions.[24] To add evidence, suffice it to quote a CIA estimate dating back to 14 November 1970, in which it was warned that in the following ten years the oil producing countries would try more and more to gain control of their own output. As far as oil companies were concerned, the report continued, they would see their traditional role diminished, while direct dealings between consuming and producing governments would increasingly take place. Until then, Arab countries had always been motivated by a desire for more income, being highly dependent on oil revenues to run their economies, and that was why it was unlikely for them to use oil as a political weapon against the West in case of resumption of hostilities between them and Israel, although some interruption of oil shipments would be inevitable. However, it could not be excluded that one or more major producers might decide to risk oil revenues for political aims.[25] Although American policymakers could not exclude that producers might adopt radical measures, they seemed convinced that in the end an agreement would be reached. After all, it was true that prices were much lower, in terms of purchasing power, than those of the previous decade. Moreover, Washington's experts were persuaded that even a substantial increase in prices would be accepted in exchange for stability of supplies and costs. Such an optimistic stance was based on the estimation that an extreme measure like oil-flow interruption implied an economic strength that at the moment only Libya and Kuwait enjoyed, while Saudi Arabia had too high financial interests abroad to choose such a drastic policy. Hence, oil questions had to be discussed from a strictly economic point of view, although from a long-term perspective everybody knew that producers would seek political advantage.[26]

Actually, the majors shared the same concern on stability of supplies. As evidence of this, the companies had proposed a five-year agreement with an annual posted price adjustment clause in line with world inflation. What is particularly interesting, as reminded by Francesco Petrini, is the fact that this clause had not been requested by OPEC, thus implying that the corporations were not worried about stability of markets and continuity of business, while higher taxes would have been shifted to individual consumers through higher prices or tax deductions.[27] Within OECD as well, the general feeling was to leave companies free to run negotiations, giving them only very discreet diplomatic support. In this way, they believed the dispute would be managed on a strictly commercial level.[28]

The British-Italian talks on ENI and the Middle East

With reference to the Italian approach, almost any kind of reflection highlighted the need to pursue an alternative policy with regard to multinational oil companies, as in case of serious energy crisis Italy could have gained better market conditions. Being almost entirely dependent on imported Middle Eastern crude, in the short term the only way to follow was by reaching a compromise with producers. In November 1970, ENI had issued an in-depth study, according to which a policy somewhat different from that of the majors seemed more coherent with a strategy of crude oil exploration, as it was always vital to keep an attitude welcomed by producing countries.[29] Therefore, the state corporation chose not to join the majors in the decision to pursue a global negotiation with producers.[30] However, in order to implement direct contacts without the intervention of the companies, it was necessary for both contracting parties to earn visible profits, not only in terms of oil incomes, as the majors could afford to pay higher prices than consuming governments. In light of this, ENI was thinking of establishing relations between groups of consumers, such as EEC countries and groups of producers, such as Gulf regimes, with the aim of importing crude oil at relatively low prices, on the one hand, and supplying investment goods and technical assistance to industrial development, on the other. Such agreements could have been negotiated on a government-to-government level and reached only within a frame of stability.[31] The Italian hydrocarbon corporation was setting up an outlook of economic and political collaboration between European consumers and Middle Eastern producers which paved the way to a period of confrontation between two different kinds of attitude towards energy problems. Such an approach broke the path the Italian government, and in particular Giuseppe Saragat, a few months before being elected as president of the Republic, had requested ENI to walk, in order not to provoke tensions and misunderstandings with the majors.[32] As a confirmation of this, the president of the Republic did not absolutely agree with ENI's intention for bilateral deals. By quoting a meeting he had with BP Chairman Sir Eric Drake, on 25 February 1971, we know that he wished the companies to pursue a unified approach. Instead, ENI had been a problem for the Italian government for the last twenty years.[33] We may say that London was talking to Saragat in order for the latter to put discreet pressure on Palazzo Chigi to tame the Italian state corporation and make it follow the majors' path.

Instead, this was exactly the opposite of what the chairman of ENI, Cefis, stated a few weeks afterwards. In a report delivered to the Italian Chamber of Deputies, in fact, he suggested that the negotiations should not be left to the companies, since they only represented their own interests. According to the chairman, the EEC had to take the initiative in order to either: (a) reach long-term agreements between producers and European consumer countries, under which Europe would be supplied with oil, at the same time participating in the development of producing countries; or (b) set up joint ventures between state-owned companies of developing countries and those of the consumers, covering the whole industry process, from prospecting to distribution.[34] Naturally, ENI was backed by the Italian association of industrialists, which in the same days released a report on the energy supply problem, highlighting how the market had changed in the very last period, making supplies less flexible due to political factors in the producing countries. In such a context, the best thing to do seemed to be acting on a communitarian level with the aim of diversifying fuels and supplies. What Confindustria was suggesting was a process of economic integration with producing countries.[35] Such an outlook became even more urgent if we quote what the vice chairman of ENI, Raffaele Girotti, said in those days. According to him, in fact, in 1985 oil was supposed to cover around 80 per cent of Italy's energy needs, coming above all from the Middle East. Therefore, because of the way that it was structured, the energy industry could no longer satisfy national supplies. As a matter of fact, the physical safety of oil supplies was no longer guaranteed by the big companies, as the problem could by then only be solved through political action towards the producers. What happened in Tehran, therefore, showed that producers no longer regarded the oil industry in terms of export revenues but, instead, as a tool of economic development that until then had not been accomplished. The most important part of such a report is certainly the one criticizing the companies' achievements in Tehran and Tripoli. Girotti stressed that the majors had negotiated higher costs which could be easily shifted to individual consumers. In particular, the agreement had generated negative inflationary effects which was difficult for the consumers' economies to stand. Moreover, this was only a period of truce and new crises already surfaced on the horizon, while the majors were gradually losing power on what affected the security of European supplies most. To face such a problem, Italy could not afford to be absent from the energy industry network, moulded according to new and closer relations between consuming and producing governments.[36]

On the contrary, the Petroleum Division of the British Department of Technology did not really think that any government-to-government deal could ever alter the strong bargaining stance of producers.[37] The atmosphere of distrust was so evident that the British suspected the Italian attitude was aimed at doing business with the producers when all other companies were subject to retaliation. With reference to EEC policies, instead, the Italians were supposed to play quite an active role in shaping the European stance towards energy issues. While it was not realistic to postpone direct country-to-country deals indefinitely, it was not in the interest of British companies to speed up the process.[38] To this we also have to add the situation of attrition between Rome and Washington on the Arab–Israeli dispute, as the former was more willing to trust Arab claims, while the latter had the security of the Jewish State as a starting point for any kind of talks. Moreover, the Italians thought that the conflict had to be solved within the aegis of the United Nations.[39]

Therefore, Aldo Moro was very active in the diplomatic arena at the beginning of the 1970s, initiating a series of visits to several Middle Eastern capitals to favour economic partnership between Italy and the Arab countries as well as Israel. The statesman's activism in the area was underlined by the British embassy, stating how Italy had moved into a new diplomatic phase. The Apulian politician's journeying may have not achieved any visible outcome, but it had the effect of showing that the right place for Italy in Middle Eastern questions was on the Arab side of a neutral line.[40] In 1971, in fact, ENI planned to activate production in its main concession in Libya, and the talks between the Italian foreign minister and Qaddafi in May paved the way to further accords involving several Italian enterprises, of course with ENI enjoying the lion's share.[41] Concerning this, Ilaria Tremolada's thesis is that the Libyans knew very well how badly they needed Italian technology, but above all they wanted to be sure that their exports to Italy would increase year by year. Both governments realized how much they needed each other, especially in a period during which the relations between the Libyan military junta and British and American companies were deteriorating. Had they relinquished their interests in oil exploration in the North African country, ENI might have represented quite a valid alternative, thus becoming the crux of the relationship between Rome and Tripoli and a good resource for Italy's Middle Eastern policy.[42] The consuming governments could not totally supersede the role of the companies, but at the same time it was no longer possible to passively wait for events and negotiations to take place. Instead, the governments were supposed to directly deal with producers to ameliorate supply conditions and set up a parallel oil network.[43]

The aftermath of the Tehran Agreements

On 14 February 1971, a five-year agreement was reached in Tehran between Persian Gulf producers and oil companies. The producers, who gained an immediate increase in oil revenues, had their taxation brought up to 55 per cent, up to US$3.5 billion by 1975. In exchange they committed themselves not to claim any other increase for the following five years, regardless of what competitors requested.[44] The agreements were a real breakthrough, leading pricing relations to a phase where producers played a more assertive role. For the first time, OPEC had been recognized as a world power by the majors, as well as by the industrial establishment of consuming countries. Moreover, producers had by then acquired the ability to plan prices for a certain span of time, irrespective of movements of supply and demand, thus showing how pricing had become independent from market variations.[45] The greatest change from the majors' point of view, however, involved the success in regaining effective control of foreign and domestic competition while shifting profits from extraction to operations downstream, thus making a lot of profits from distribution, refining and related petrochemicals operations.[46] The immediate consequence of the agreements was the 51 per cent nationalization of French assets in Algeria, just a few days afterwards.[47] The North African government, however, had always claimed that their aim was control of the remaining Algerian energy sources. In virtue of this, the only brake to a sensitive increase of prices was the consideration that the Western world could soon turn to alternative sources.[48] On 20 March, another agreement was reached in Tripoli, signed on 2 April. In this case, the companies accepted a barrel price increase from US$2.55 to US$3.32, as well as a tax increase from 50 to 55 per cent.[49] To quote what Executive Secretary Theodore Eliot said to Kissinger on the upcoming Libyan negotiations, there is no doubt that it had become impossible to reject what the military junta claimed. While the companies' business in Libya was certainly a major US interest, Eliot said that what was at stake was also the North African country's political position in the Mediterranean, its financial ability to influence events in the Middle East and the Maghreb, and the young officers' stance towards the Soviet Union. There was no immediate alternative to that regime, enjoying an unprecedented amount of leverage over Western Europe, which acquired around a fifth of its oil needs from Libya.[50] With regard to the British government, Foreign Secretary Alec Douglas-Home welcomed the new accord, stating that the companies had played the role of buffer between producers' claims and consumers' interests, thus proving the correct choice of Downing Street not to intervene in the negotiations.[51]

Producers had by then acquired the power to maintain a common front and increase prices and the level of taxation, while consumers had practically no countervailing influence. Nevertheless, British experts still relied on the assumption that major producers had no real alternative market to Western Europe and Japan.[52] On the other hand, the Italian government, and Aldo Moro in particular, had since the late 1960s been using all possible diplomatic skills to facilitate ENI's presence in several producing countries.[53] In such a context of growing tension between producers and consumers, the state corporation pursued a policy of autonomy from the majors by maintaining a neutral stance after the signature of the aforementioned agreements, on grounds that the multinationals were becoming a sort of tax collector on behalf of producers at the expense of consumers.[54] In the meantime, Walter Levy, oil advisor to both the British and the American governments, stated that the big companies were no longer the best way to conciliate national and private interests, at the same time favouring development in producing countries. This situation of weakness was also due to consumer countries' policies, which were no longer appropriate for a sellers' energy market. As a matter of fact, the companies were by then willing to accept producers' claims, as they knew the costs would be offloaded onto retail consumers. Therefore, the new accords had changed the role of the companies, turning them from representatives of American foreign policy into agents of producing countries. Thus, the consequent price increase was practically giving birth to a sort of 'taxation without representation', and that was why the United States was supposed to arrange a 'consumer cartel' to negotiate with producers,[55] who had by then perfectly realized that the demand for oil had become so high and frenzied that consumers were ready to pay well above official prices.[56] Despite this warning, the American administration was not ready to completely change the approach to international energy questions, as Washington experts were reasonably sure that, due to the massive profits gained through the two agreements, the two main Gulf producers would not claim further burdensome requests from both an economic and a political point of view.[57]

With regard to the other parent country, Whitehall had always relied on Shell and BP for various reasons, such as their importance for the balance of payments, and the need to keep oil issues separate from Britain's political role on the Middle Eastern chessboard.[58] However, the most worrying thing regarding European oil relations was that the old continent had no real alternative energy source to those of the Middle East, therefore increasing dependence on them and being unable to face Arab hostility.[59] As a producer as well as a consumer country, London had an interest in preserving the oil industry structure of those times, but British policymakers tacitly accepted that producers would soon be more involved in oil operations, while British commissioners in an enlarged EEC were recommended to hold key posts in order to ensure maximum influence on energy matters.[60] In the meantime, within the Foreign and Commonwealth Office there were doubts about the profitability of an accord that some officers regarded as too expensive for individual customers and consuming governments as well.[61] Moreover, it was by then well known that future exploitation of oil would either take the form of partnership between national and foreign companies, or service contracts, under which companies would work on behalf of producer governments, or production solely by national oil companies, with crude oil marketed through supply contracts with foreign companies.[62] In addition, a Shell report of April 1971 clearly stated that the oil industry would need no less than US$540 billion for the following decade, in order to carry out further investments to satisfy the growing demand. The study also reminded how most of this amount of money could not come from the financial market, for the companies had limited resources available. Therefore, further price increases were inevitable in order to allow the multinationals to be almost completely independent in the global scenario.[63] Meanwhile, recent agreements had imposed a burden of 140 million pounds sterling on the 1971 British balance of payments, and the government, although agreeing that in the near future it might be necessary to take a more active role and cohesive line, tried to put pressure on the Italian executive, hoping that ENI would finally join with the other companies in resisting the most outrageous demands of producers.[64] Whitehall reminded how important oil companies had been in granting increasing volumes of oil supplies at costs which had contributed to post-war economic prosperity. What mattered most, international corporations provided quite a flexible system of supply which bilateral agreements, though not necessarily negative, put in jeopardy, thus making consumers run a security risk. According to the British government, it was not certain that oil supply terms were best negotiated through country-to-country deals.[65]

In fact, as Giuliano Garavini and Francesco Petrini argue, the origins of the price escalation may be dated back to the foundation of OPEC a decade earlier and the development strategy adopted first of all by its most densely populated members, traditionally in favour of higher prices and oil reserves preservation to respond to other commodities they imported, and whose costs were booming in the same span of time.[66] Hence, the management of oil output had become the best tool in the hands of the producers to plan and power their own development and industrialization process.[67] The whole oil industry – quoting Algerian Oil Minister Belaid Abdessalam – had become a question of 'planting oil and combustion gas to harvest factories ..., diversify production and set up an organized and progress-oriented national economy'.[68] Within this context, what ENI denounced was the absence of a supranational energy strategy, both on a communitarian and a global level. By virtue of this, an independent policy was regarded as the best way to pursue national interests. Moreover, since Italy lacked those resources other countries were exploring and about to exploit in different areas of the world, keeping the political credit ENI had gained in the previous years in the Middle East appeared as a sort of guarantee in case of crisis.[69] Such a change of perspective was regarded as even more urgent on grounds that in one year Italy's oil imports had increased by more than 3 per cent, and the Middle East's share amounted to around 60 per cent, while only a year before it was estimated at less than 55 per cent.[70] The Italian state enterprise managed to run only about 20 per cent of Italy's whole national energy consumption, thus playing only a marginal role in the world oil industry.[71] This meant that the Italian economy was too openly affected by the repercussions of international economic and political tensions; hence, it was no longer advisable to grant access to oil supplies through the majors. In light of this, ENI claimed a privileged role, by specifically requesting the government to back the company's contacts with producers and favour the crude produced and purchased by ENI on the national market.[72] Crude oil exploration within the international scenario, was consequently to be carried out also through direct deals with producing governments, allowing benefits for both Italian energy needs and the producers' development.[73]

Conclusions

In the early 1970s, the companies had by then lost the freedom to mould OPEC crude output. In particular, they could no longer react to market developments without any reference to the wishes of producers. On the contrary, the latter were by then able to increase the posted price against the will of the former.[74] Such a situation was also favoured because demand was growing faster than the supply of energy. Actually, the expansion of alternative sources, especially nuclear facilities, was rather slow, thus making spare capacity extremely limited.[75] By then, producers were able to respond to the inflation impact, for the Tehran and Tripoli agreements had presupposed quite a stable dollar at less than 3 per cent yearly inflation. Moreover, the Caracas Resolution 122 of 1970 had established that, in case of variation in the exchange rate of the currencies of major industrialized countries affecting the purchasing power of OPEC members, posted or tax-reference prices should be adjusted so as to reflect such changes.[76] As a matter of fact, inflation started growing at a considerable rate, reaching about 78 per cent between 1970 and 1972. Since oil transactions were estimated in dollars, in real terms the price per dollar agreed only a few months previously was falling, while the price of imported goods from industrialized countries was rising. Therefore, the basis of the deal had been undermined, and further price increases were required both to compensate inflation and to maintain the real value of a commodity traded in dollars.[77] Concerning this, in the year after the Tehran agreements the producers' tax incomes had increased by 30 per cent due to real market prices – despite the companies' profits in the same temporal segment having doubled. This was evidence of how the international market developed much faster than, and in a different way from, accords between companies and producers.[78] To further worsen the situation, we must not forget the Nixon administration's decision of 15 August 1971 to suspend dollar convertibility into gold and the consequent devaluation of US currency. With around 80 per cent of world oil transactions occurring in US dollars, it was inevitable for prices to hike again, so much so that in January 1972 in Geneva new agreements between the companies and OPEC Gulf countries were necessary to adjust the posted price by another 8.9 per cent. What Gulf States complained about was that they purchased 60 per cent of their imports from the industrialized nations of Western Europe and Japan, which had re-valued their prices by an average of 11 per cent on the US dollar. According to an American intelligence memorandum, however, most international companies had not been imposed with an additional burden, while producers had been sustaining losses in terms of reduced purchasing power.[79] In the year following the Tehran and Tripoli agreements, producers' revenues were augmented by around 30 per cent, but the companies' profits had increased even more, thus also being useful to finance alternative energy sources.

Events since the Libyan September 1970 accords had managed to stimulate regional solidarity, showing a greater degree of collaboration among producers, which in the past had been practically unknown. They had gained the conviction that they held the whip hand, at last.[80] However, most OPEC oil was to be sold in Europe and Japan, although mainly through American companies and their affiliates. Regarding this, Joe Stork reminds us how there had been some suspicion that the Nixon Administration saw higher prices also as a way to slow down the Japanese economy, whose exports were annoying American corporations a lot. At the same time, all the talks of a shortage crisis were shelved by the end of the year, when major oil companies registered an astonishing 36 per cent jump in overseas earnings.[81] In the summer of 1971, Walter Levy published an article in 'Foreign Affairs', estimating that the oil producers' revenues would rise to US$18.5 billion in 1975, while Europe's bill for oil imports would increase by US$5.5 billion.[82] The market had radically changed, so much so that the development and the growth of the world economy had become dependent on imported oil, rather than domestically produced coal, especially in Western Europe, whose governments were initially relieved by lacking supply disruptions. However, Professor Morris A. Adelman, one of the preeminent authorities on the economies of mineral resources and Professor of Economics at Massachusetts Institute of Technology, thought otherwise, stating that the genie was by then out of the bottle and that OPEC governments would soon be back for another slice of the cake. In a word, they had tasted blood, as Francisco Parra writes, and perceived that some countries, namely the United States, were not adamantly opposed to higher prices and taxes. What the companies really disliked, instead, was the loss of control on the oil industry and the prospect of OPEC's ever-escalating demands.[83] Concerning this, it is interesting to quote what George Piercy and Henry Schuler, on behalf respectively of the Standard Oil Company of New Jersey and the Nelson Hunt Company, testified before the Subcommittee on Multinational Corporations of the Senate Foreign Relations Committee several years after the Tehran and Tripoli agreements. According to the two functionaries, those negotiations had been a real tragedy for the companies. The momentum in oil deals had passed over OPEC and the producing states, while at the same time the companies recognized the flat price in force during the previous decade, thus realizing that producers had had a serious purchasing power problem.[84]

In conclusion, what stands out from the available documentation is the distrust the British authorities had towards the Italian approach on oil questions. ENI had always been seen as a maverick, as a sort of oil company without oil trying to leak in a market which had been taken for granted for a very long time by the British and American majors. London claimed to rely on a laissez-faire tradition, therefore complaining about the Italian policy to interfere with market deals. However, by reading archival records there are doubts about the reliability of such an attitude. Actually, it is more likely that the Italians were regarded as commercial rivals, especially in times of emergency. In order to add evidence to this, suffice it to say that during the 1973 crisis the British government directly dealt with the Iranians and the Saudis on the best way to invite the producers to invest in the UK, as long as Britain showed readiness to help with the industrial development of those countries.[85] Even clearer was the view of the British Chancellor of the Exchequer Denis Healey, when he asked whether there was any way in which the British government could be of more direct help.⁸⁶ The British ministers' visits to the oil producing countries were not so different from what Italian statesmen had done a few years previously. The difference was that Italy found itself in a ceaseless situation of shortage, depending on foreign areas for practically all of its energy needs, while Britain was concerned about its balance of payments due to the massive price increase, and wanted to limit the damage while waiting for North Sea production to be activated. Now there was a shortage of oil, and the companies had to accept that producers were by then in the position to make the best decisions for themselves.⁸⁷ A new era of international economic relations had begun, and what the British seemed not to have accepted was that Western Europe needed a level of solidarity and collaboration that London was not ready to accept. Oil producers were about to dismantle the old concession system, with the consequent majors' monopoly. While the companies aimed at higher and higher profits, thus in a way giving up the role of buffer between consumers and producers, it had become inevitable for governments to get involved in the negotiation process. It took a while for the British to realize that they could no longer take the lead in the Middle East.

Notes

1 *Oil: Points to Raise – Italian Attitude*, 5 May 1971, in TNA, FCO 17/1489, Confidential.
2 *Visit of the Italian Prime Minister to London 27–30 June 1971: Oil – Brief by the Foreign and Commonwealth Office, in Consultation with the Department of Trade and Industry and the Treasury*, 21 June 1971, in TNA, FCO 33/1504, Part C, IMV (71) 14, Confidential.
3 *Record of a Meeting between the Prime Minister and the Foreign and Commonwealth Secretary and Signor Emilio Colombo, Prime Minister of Italy and Signor Aldo Moro, Italian Foreign Minister at 10 A.M. on Monday, 28 June 1971 at Chequers*, 30 June 1971, in TNA, FCO 33/1506, Part E, WR J/548/5, Confidential.
4 *L'Italia e l'ENI: situazione e problemi dell'intervento pubblico nell'industria petrolifera*, in TNA, FCO 67/171, MOP 311/1, 1968/1969.
5 *Memorandum Prepared in the Central Intelligence Agency: Prospects for US Access to World Oil over the Next 15 Years or So*, 28 August 1969, in Edward C. Keefer (gen. ed.) and Linda Qaimmaqani (ed.), FRUS, vol. XXXVI, *Energy Crisis, 1969–1974*, doc. 8, Secret, 25–35.
6 *Memorandum from Harold Saunders of the National Security Council Staff to the President's Assistant for International Economic Affairs (Flanigan): Iranian Consortium Settlement*, 7 May 1970, in NARA, NPMP, NSC,, Files, Box 601, Country Files, Middle East, Iran, vol. II, 6/1/70-12/70, Secret, Exdis.
7 Henry Alfred Kissinger, *Years of Upheaval* (Boston: Little, Brown, 1982), 858.
8 The posted price is an artificial price representing the basis from which payments to producing governments are estimated. Royalties are a posted price percentage. Therefore, taxation is estimated on the posted prices minus production costs and royalties.
9 Ian Seymour, *OPEC: Instrument of Change* (New York: St. Martin's Press, 1981), 70.

10 *Outline Brief for Anglo-American Oil Talks – 3 December 1970: Item 2(a) Iran*, in TNA, FCO 67/445, C399891, Confidential.
11 T. W. Garvey to Oil Department: *ENI and IPC*, 27 June 1967, in TNA, FCO 54/30, OD 193/5, Confidential.
12 Michael A. Palmer, *Guardians of the Gulf: A History of America's Expanding Role in the Persian Gulf, 1833–1992* (New York: Free Press, 1992), 87–8.
13 Silvio Labbate, *Il governo dell'energia: l'Italia dal petrolio al nucleare (1945–1975)* (Milan: Mondadori Education S.p.A., 2010), 121–2.
14 Seymour, *OPEC*, 75–6.
15 *Priority Tel. No. 5566 0930Z from Amembassy Tehran to StateDept Washington DC: Confrontation between Oil Consortium and Iran-OPEC Appears Imminent*, in NARA, RG 59, Central Files 1970–3, PET 6, IRAN, Confidential.
16 Rosario Milano, *L'ENI e l'Iran (1962–1970)* (Napoli: Giannini Editore, 2013), 240.
17 Venezuela had introduced legislation to raise its profits share to 60 per cent and fix prices unilaterally, without any reference to negotiation with the companies. Daniel Yergin, *The Prize: The Epic Quest for Oil, Money and Power* (London: Simon & Schuster, 1993), 580.
18 John M. Blair, *The Control of Oil* (New York: Vintage Books Editions, 1978), 223.
19 Ibid., 224.
20 Anthony Sampson, *The Seven Sisters: The Great Oil Companies and the World They Made* (London: Hodder and Stoughton, 1983), 229–30.
21 *Tel. 301 from AmEmbassy Tehran to SecState Washington DC: Oil Situation – Briefing of Consortium Negotiators*, 19 January 1971, Immediate, Action SS-45, OP191510Z, in NARA, RG 59, Central Files 1970–3, PET 3 OPEC, Secret, Exdis.
22 *Tel. 310 Section Two from AmEmbassy Tehran to SecState Washington DC: Oil Situation – Piercy Views*, 20 January 1971, Immediate, Action SS-45, OP201530Z, in NARA, NPMP, NSF, Middle East 1969–74, Country File Iran, vol. III, Jan 1, 1970–Aug 31, 1971, b. 602, f. 1, Secret, Exdis.
23 *Memorandum from C. Fred Bergsten of the National Security Council Staff to the President's Assistant for National Security Affairs (Kissinger): International Oil Situation*, 1 February 1971, Secret, in FRUS 1969–76, vol. XXXVI, doc. 84, 207–9.
24 *Tel. 018185 from SecState Washington DC to AmEmbassy Tehran: Oil Situation*, 3 February, 1971, Immediate, Origin SS-45, OP030106Z, in NARA, NPMP, NSF, Middle East 1969–74, Country File Iran, vol. III, 1 January 1970–31 August 1971, b. 602, f. 1, Secret, Exdis.
25 *NIE 20/30–70: Security of Oil Supply to NATO and Japan*, 14 November 1970, Secret, Controlled Dissem, in www.foia.cia.gov.
26 *Memorandum for Mr. Henry A. Kissinger: World Oil Situation*, 25 January 1971, 7101152, Secret, Exdis, in NARA, NPMP, NSC Institutional Files, b. H-180, f. NSSM 114.
27 Francesco Petrini, *Imperi del profitto: Multinazionali petrolifere e governi nel XX secolo* (Milan: Franco Angeli, 2015), 237.
28 *Research Department Memorandum: The Tehran Oil Agreement (February 1971)*, 13 November 1972, in TNA, FCO 51/242, Departmental Series, Research Department, D.S. No. 45/72, RR 6/6, Confidential – UK Eyes A.
29 *I problemi dell'Eni nel mercato internazionale*, Appunto ENI, novembre 1970, in ASENI, BB, I. 5, 422.
30 *Situazione degli approvvigionamenti di petrolio*, Telespresso n. 077/1690/C, DGAE, Ufficio VIII MAE a PCM, al Ministero del Bilancio, al Ministero del Tesoro, al

Ministero Industria e Commercio, al Ministero Partecipazioni Statali, all'ENI, 25 gennaio 1971, in ASENI, BB, II. 4, 441.
31 *Alcune considerazioni sulla possibilità di instaurare rapporti diretti tra Paesi produttori e Paesi consumatori per l'approvvigionamento di petrolio*, Servizio Pianificazione Energia ed Idrocarburi, 19 aprile 1971, in ASENI, BB. II. 4, 441.
32 Labbate, *L'Italia e l'Eni di fronte alle crisi petrolifere degli anni Settanta*, Nuova Rivista Storica, 98/2, 2014, 490.
33 *Meeting with President Saragat*, 25 February 1971, in TNA, FCO 67/582, ML 311/1.
34 *Saving Tel. No. 6 from British Embassy, Rome, to FCO: Oil*, 18 March 1971, in TNA, FCO 67/582, ML 311/1, Unclassified.
35 Confederazione Generale dell'Industria Italiana: Direzione Generale per i Rapporti Economici, Problemi e prospettive dell'approvvigionamento energetico italiano, April 1971, in TNA, FCO 67/582, ML 311/1, Unclassified.
36 *Problemi dell'approvvigionamento degli idrocarburi e dei combustibili nucleari: relazione presentata dall'Ing. Raffaele Girotti, Vice Presidente dell'ENI, alla riunione del 23 aprile 1971 della Commissione Consultiva dell'Energia*, in TNA, FCO 67/582, ML 311/1, Unclassified.
37 *Derek Eagers to R. H. Ellingworth: Italian Attitudes to Oil Questions*, 10 May 1971, in TNA, FCO 67/582, ML 311/1, Confidential.
38 *Oil: Points to Raise*, undated, in TNA, FCO 67/582, ML 311/1, Confidential.
39 Massimiliano Cricco, 'Dalla genesi del secondo piano Rogers alle premesse della guerra dello Yom Kippur (1970–1973)', in Daniele Caviglia and Massimiliano Cricco (eds), *La diplomazia italiana e gli equilibri mediterranei: La politica mediorientale dell'Italia dalla guerra dei Sei Giorni al conflitto dello Yom Kippur (1967–1973)* (Soveria Mannelli: Rubbettino, 2006), 106–10.
40 *British Embassy, Rome, to Sir Alec Douglas-Home*, 16 October 1970, in TNA, FCO 33/1094, WRJ 2/1 (2/45), Confidential and Guard.
41 Massimiliano Cricco, 'Aldo Moro e la cooperazione economica con i Paesi arabi', in Francesco Perfetti, Andrea Ungari, Daniele Caviglia and Daniele De Luca (eds), *Aldo Moro nell'Italia contemporanea* (Florence: Le Lettere, 2011), 625–6.
42 Ilaria Tremolada, *Nel mare che ci unisce: Il petrolio nelle relazioni tra Italia e Libia* (Milan: Mimesis, 2015), 233.
43 *V. Giovagnoni: OCDE Riunione a Parigi del 20.01.1971, Rapporto confidenziale*, 23 gennaio 1971, in ASENI, EE, s. Rapporti con le organizzazioni nazionali e internazionali, b. 442, f. 1fc8.
44 *Intelligence Note – OPEC Oil: Persian Gulf Anchored, Mediterranean Next*, 18 February 1971, RECN-3, in NARA, RG 59, Central Files 1970–3, PET 3 OPEC, Confidential.
45 Fadhil J. Al-Chalabi, *OPEC and the International Oil Industry: A Changing Structure* (Oxford: Oxford University Press, 1980), 82.
46 Richard C. Thornton, *The Nixon Kissinger Years: The Reshaping of American Foreign Policy* (New York: Paragon House, 1989), 83.
47 In July 1970, the Algerian government had already unilaterally increased the posted price from 78.6 cents to US$1.21 a barrel. Hence, for the first time, a producing country had managed to impose a higher price with no element of agreement. Frank Brenchley, *Britain and the Middle East: An Economic History 1945–87* (London: Lester Crook, 1989), 201.
48 *J. R. Johnson to J. R. A. Bottomley: Oil Review*, 13 May 1971, in TNA, POWE 63/709, C399891, Confidential.

49 *Tel. 56087 from the Department of State to Certain Diplomatic Posts*, 2 April 1971, 2311Z, Confidential, Priority, in FRUS, 1969–76, vol. XXXVI, doc. n. 88, 214.
50 NIE 36.5–71: *Libya*, 30 April 1971, Secret, in Edward C. Keefer ed., FRUS, 1969–76, vol. E-5, Part 2, *Documents on North Africa, 1969–1972*, doc. 74.
51 *Douglas-Home to Certain Posts: Libyan Oil Negotiations*, 7 April 1971, in TNA, FCO 67/608, ML 423/1, Part C, Confidential.
52 *A Reply to the Questions in the Note Attached to Mr. R. H. W. Bullock's Letter of 6th April, 1971*, 26 April 1971, in TNA, POWE 63/709, C399891, Confidential.
53 Elisabetta Bini, 'A Transatlantic Shock: Italy's Energy Policies between the Mediterranean and the EEC, 1967–1974', *Historical Social Research* 39, no. 4 (2014), 153.
54 *Untitled Notice*, 7 March 1971, in ASENI, BB. III.1, 442, DE, f.. Organismi nazionali e internazionali.
55 Petrini, *Imperi del profitto*, 237.
56 Leonardo Maugeri, *The Age of Oil: The Mythology, History, and Future of the World's most Controversial Resource* (Westport, CT: Praeger, 2006), 107.
57 *Intelligence Memorandum Prepared in the Central Intelligence Agency: Saudi Arabia's Changed Financial Outlook*, April 1971, ER IM 71-70, Secret, No Foreign Dissem, in Edward C. Keefer, gen ed, Linda W. Qaimmaqami, and Adam M. Howard, eds, FRUS, 1969–76, vol. XXIV, *Middle East Region and Arabian Peninsula, 1969–1972; Jordan, September 1970*, doc. 148, 469–78.
58 Petrini, Imperi del profitto, 253.
59 W. J. Levy, *First Thoughts on Energy Policy in an Enlarged European Community*, June 1971, in TNA, POWE 63/709, C399891, Confidential.
60 *Report of the Interdepartmental Working Group on International Oil Questions: Cover Note by the Chairman*, undated, in TNA, PREM15/1144, C395830, Confidential.
61 *M. P. Hannam from British Embassy Tripoli to FCO: Libyan Oil Agreement*, 22 April 1971, in TNA, FCO 67/608, Confidential.
62 *Anglo-US Talks: 28 and 29 October 1971. Item 1 (a) – Participation and the Future of the Concessionary System*, October 1971, in TNA, FCO 67/570, C395833, Confidential.
63 Petrini, *Imperi del profitto*, 259.
64 *Record of a Meeting between the Prime Minister and the Foreign and Commonwealth Secretary and Signor Emilio Colombo, Prime Minister of Italy, and Signor Aldo Moro, Italian Foreign Minister, at 10 a.m. on Monday, 28 June 1971, at Chequers*, 30 June 1971, in TNA, PREM 15/500, Confidential.
65 *The Role of the International Oil Companies*, 26 July 1971, in TNA, FCO 67/582, ML 311/1, Unclassified.
66 Giuliano Garavini and Francesco Petrini, 'Continuity or Change? The 1973 Oil Crisis Reconsidered', in Antonio Varsori and Guia Migani (eds), *Europe in the International Arena during the 1970s: Entering a Different World* (Bruxelles: P.I.E. Peter Lang, 2011), 214.
67 Giuliano Garavini, *Dopo gli imperi: l'integrazione europea nello scontro Nord-Sud* (Milan: Mondadori Education S.p.A., 2009), 204.
68 Joe Stork, *Il petrolio arabo* (Turin: Rosenberg & Sellier, 1978), 179.
69 Ilaria Tremolada, 'L'ENI in Arabia Saudita: dalla concessione mineraria alle conseguenze dello shock petrolifero del 1973', *Nuova Rivista Storica* 98, no. 2 (2014), 583.

70 Tabella N. 18: Stato di previsione della spesa del Ministero delle partecipazioni statali per l'anno finanziario 1973 – Annesso N. 4, *Conto consuntivo Ente Nazionale Idrocarburi (E.N.I.), Esercizio finanziario 1971*, 16, in www.senato.it.
71 *Appunto per Girotti*, 23 February 1971, in ASENI, Presidenza Raffaele Girotti, b. 127, f. 3717.
72 *Sfligiotti a Girotti*, 16 February 1971, in ASENI, Presidenza Raffaele Girotti, b. 127, f. 3717.
73 Massimo Bucarelli, 'L'ENI e il petrolio dell'Iraq negli anni Settanta: tra crisi energetiche e nazionalismo arabo', *Nuova Rivista Storica* 98, no. 2 (2014), 687.
74 Louis Turner, *Oil Companies in the International System* (London: Royal Institute of International Affairs/George Allen & Unwin, 1978), 129–30.
75 Francisco R. Parra, *Oil Politics: A Modern History of Petroleum* (London/New York: Tauris, 2004), 114.
76 Seymour, *OPEC*, 96.
77 Fiona Venn, *The Oil Crisis* (London: Pearson Education, 2002), 152.
78 Parra, *Oil Politics*, 176–9.
79 *Intelligence Memorandum Prepared in the Office of Economic Research, Central Intelligence Agency: Oil Companies Compensate for Dollar Evaluation: The Geneva Agreement*, February 1972, in FRUS, 1969–76, vol. XXXVI, doc 110, ER-IM 72-15, Confidential, pp. 264–8.
80 Christopher R. W. Dietrich, '"First Class Brouhaha": Henry Kissinger and Oil Power in the 1970s', in Elisabetta Bini, Giuliano Garavini and Federico Romero (eds), *Oil Shock: The 1973 Crisis and its Economic Legacy* (London: I.B. Tauris, 2016), 50.
81 Joe Stork, *Middle East Oil and the Energy Crisis* (London: Monthly Review Press, 1975), 175.
82 James Bamberg, *British Petroleum and Global Oil, 1950–1975: The Challenge of Nationalism* (Cambridge: Cambridge University Press, 2000), 466.
83 Parra, *Oil Politics*, 143–4.
84 Bennet H. Wall, *Growth in a Changing Environment: A History of Standard Oil Company (New Jersey) 1950–1972 and Exxon Corporation 1972–1975* (New York: McGraw-Hill, 1988), 808.
85 *Department of Trade and Industry to the Prime Minister: Middle East Oil and Investment*, 13 December 1973, in TNA, FCO 96/117, ME 12/324/1, Part A, Confidential.
86 *Chancellor's Visit to Saudi Arabia: Notes of a Meeting at the Ministry of Finance on Monday 9 December at 4.30 pm*, 13 December 1974, in TNA, T 277/2880, Confidential.
87 Charles More, *Black Gold: Britain and Oil in the Twentieth Century* (London: Continuum, 2009), 142.

13

Italy and the Iranian Revolution

Rosario Milano

The fleeing of the Shah and the subsequent resignation of Shapour Bakhtiar's last imperial government were not the only events that characterized the Iranian revolution. On the contrary, these two events, along with the return of Imam Khomeini, wiped out the weak balance of power on which the anti-Pahlavi coalition had been founded and started a new articulated revolutionary process.[1] The provisional government, established by the Iranian Revolutionary Council (*Shury-e-Enqelab-e-Eslami*), officially took office on 13 February 1979, led by the Liberal leader Mehdi Bazargan. The executive was composed of the representatives of the Movement for the Freedom of Iran and the National Front, but excluded both the representatives of the left movements and the Shiite clergy. The revolution offered the world the reassuring face of the heirs of Mohammad Mossadegh, determined to promote the rapid normalization of the country to limit the effects of institutional turmoil and to prevent the rise of the radical Islamic factions. The declared non-alignment of revolutionary Iran and the objective of creating a new order in the Middle East constituted the necessary conditions on which a new and non-conflictual relationship with the two world superpowers was to be found. For the provisional government of Iran, such a priority was inextricably linked to the challenge of building an autonomous internal consensus. The Iranian economy was weakened by twelve months of political disturbances that caused the collapse of hydrocarbon production, so that the economic recovery of Iran represented the main task of Bazargan's executive. The interest of the provisional executive for rapid economic recovery matched the expectations of Western governments and international companies operating in that country. Also for Italy, in the first months of 1979 the priority was to guarantee the safeguarding of economic interests and the security of the Italian communities that still lived in Iran. During the following weeks, Giulio Tamagnini, the ambassador of Italy in Tehran, had several meetings with the authorities of the new Iran. On 4 March, he met with Mehdi Bazargan and his deputy Abbas Amir-Entezam, who expressed their intention to resume the export of crude oil in the short term, and who showed their appreciation towards Italian companies that decided to remain during the revolution and that were already committed to the resumption of productive activities. He also saw Ali Ardalan, minister of economy and finance, who went into detail on the guidelines of Iran's new economic policy, stressing particularly the new regime's aim to mobilize all national resources to support full employment in the country. The collapse of productive activities caused the unemployment of approximately three million people, between 25 and 30 per cent of the total Iranian workforce, a social bomb ready to explode again. Despite widespread public statements against the major infrastructural works that the Shah had planned, which the opposition had heavily contested, the provisional government revealed the intention to evaluate the political opportunity of every single industrial project on a case-by-case basis, excluding, however, the continuity of investments in the nuclear sectors, which favoured the Shah and his family members. The orientation of the executive seemed favourable to the activities of many of the Italian companies engaged in Iran, but appeared to be threatening the realization of Bandar Abbas's major work, since the revolutionaries considered that one of most prominent by-products of the corrupted Pahlavi regime.[2] On 5 March 1979, Bazargan announced that Iranian oil production and maritime traffic from Abadan had resumed. Evidently, production had then fallen to 2 million barrels a day, of which only 1.35 million was for export, compared to the 6.5 million produced a day in the recent past, and the new government had to stop the erosion of Iranian market shares. The day before, the Italian ambassador had had a talk with the president and general manager of the NIOC (National Iranian Oil Company) Hassan Nazih, who outlined the implications of the new Iranian oil policy, whose primary objective was the sale of crude oil through the cash market and long-term contracts signed with the governments of consumer countries, such as Italy.[3] Ambassador Giulio Tamagnini reported all of these positive indications towards Italy, one of the first countries that proved ready to come back to Persia, and he also collected precise information regarding the political purpose of the provisional executive to promote the resumption of the Italian companies' activities.[4] However, the appreciation shown by the members of government was not sufficient to guarantee the safety of Italian companies and their workers still present in Iran. Indeed, the interruption of the industrial activities caused strong pressure by Iranian workers as even the Italian oil facilities in Marun and Ahwaz were literally assaulted by the masses of Iranian unemployed. Tamagnini then not only committed himself to ensuring the continuity of the economic and diplomatic engagement of Italy in Iran, but invited the Italian operators to adopt the utmost caution towards the Iranian situation. It was in fact 'a new country, a new society', constantly evolving, characterized by a struggle for hegemony that involved uncertainty and imposed the constant change of ministries and of course of interlocutors.[5] Giulio Tamagnini then suggested to those economic subjects whose 'recent work in this country can allow wage demands or other claims from local workers' to postpone the resumption of their activities, an attitude also adopted by the embassies of Germany and Great Britain, while, the ambassador said, the French seemed to have 'not yet focused on the Iranian problem'. The first mission to Iran of Giorgio Mazzanti, the chairman of Ente Nazionale Idrocarburi (ENI), the Italian state-owned company in the field of oil and gas, took place between 9 and 13 March 1979, followed by a second visit in mid-April. Together with Mazzanti, two key figures went to Iran, Carlo Sarchi and Marcello Colitti, who well knew the Iranian pre-revolutionary reality. The delegation and the Italian ambassador in Tehran had meetings with the leaders of the provisional government and of the NIOC, and there emphasized the 'political viewpoint' of the mission. The Iranians appreciated the work of ENI during the meetings, an element that was proudly reiterated in the statements of the company's top management and the Italian press. All the problems related to the activities of the companies of the ENI holding were discussed with the Iranians, problems that were common to all the companies who were still working in that country. The main issues that hindered the full resumption of activities consisted in the collection of debts and the application of clauses for the revaluation of contracts, as well as the crucial problem of public order. Despite these critical issues, the new president of ENI tried to actualize a stable form of cooperation between ENI and NIOC in the branch of energy supplies, using the short-term needs of the revolutionary regime in Tehran as leverage, but also trying to enhance the heritage represented by the traditional bilateral relations between the two countries. Mazzanti hoped to be able to complete the service agreement that the Italian company was pursuing since the early 1970s, when the then president Raffaele Girotti had tried in vain to seduce the Shah with the 'Iran connection' project. Now, ENI received received a 'cordial rejection' by the Iranians, who considered that type of agreement premature in that phase of reconstruction, since this would have bound the economy of the country. Italian expectations received only partial confirmation in Iran, as evidenced by the contract signed on 16 May 1979 by Agip and NIOC for the supply of 12,000 barrels a day until the end of the year and by the achievement of the agreement for the delivery to the Iranian state company of 35,000 barrels per day of crude oil obtained from the reserves of the companies Sirip and Iminoco.[6]

The beginning of the second Iranian revolution: The attack on the 'great Satan'

The middle-class members of the Iranian revolutionary coalition tried to manage the excessively anti-Western tones, aiming, as we have seen, at the normalization and development of lots of opportunities offered by post-revolutionary Iran. Some members of the Bazargan government seemed to be under the illusion of being able to face those challenges despite the state of anarchy in Iran, characterized by the selective and progressive demolition of the armed forces, which hid the dual nature of revolutionary power in Iran. The provisional government therefore tried to lay the groundwork of economic and foreign policies in order to achieve national independence, but failed to offer effective short-term solutions to the problems of the economy, such as the increasing unemployment of Iranians.[7] The dispute among the different sides of the revolution emerged violently in March 1980, during the campaign for the referendum on the adoption of State as a form of Government and again in August after the election of the assembly of experts, which were two critical moments within the process that would have led to the birth of the *velayat-e faqih (guardianship of the jurist)* and to the success of the Mullahs' radical movement, represented by the Islamic Republican Party. Urban terrorism and firefights among political movements were fomented by the ongoing revolt in the ethnically non-Iranian provinces, especially those inhabited by the Kurds, where the *Pasdaran* were forced to intervene militarily.

Through Khomeini, the clergy accused the army and the government of being the most responsible for the difficulties of the country, because they had 'little faith in God'. It appeared clearly that the government was weak compared to the power that the clergy held in the whole Iranian society, and was so completely unable to influence the evolution of Iranian political life. On the following 1 September, the leader of the provisional government resigned, but then was forced to withdraw his resignation. During the celebration of the twenty-fifth anniversary of the Algerian revolution, on 1 November, Bazargan met Zbigniew Brzezinski, President Carter's National Security Advisor, in Algiers. This was one of Bazargan's last acts, certainly his last international appearance as a leader of the provisional government, as he was now accused of colluding with the United States and was forced to resign after the assault on the US Embassy in Tehran. The occupation of the US Embassy in Tehran and the subsequent seizure of fifty-seven US citizens working there was carried out by a group of Iranian students, self-defined as ones 'following the way of the Imam' (*Khat-e Imam*), and this marked the beginning of the second phase of the Iranian revolution.[8] There followed the gradual declining of the Liberal phase of the Iranian revolution, which led to the appointment of more and more radicals at the top jobs in key ministries, imposing a decisive change of political direction on the government, which affected the oil minister, justice and foreign affairs. Under the leadership of Hassan Nazih, the production of hydrocarbons in Iran reached the figure of almost four million barrels a day, which was a progressive increase even if still lower than the 35 per cent of levels recorded before the revolution. Thanks to a courageous and dynamic policy, characterized by a fighting spirit and a survival instinct, proposing advantageous commercial formulas for the buyers, Iran quickly increased the national production and signed new sales agreements.[9] After the governmental reshuffle that took place in September, Ali Akbar Moinfar headed the newly established Ministry of Oil, replacing Nazih as the key high-ranking political personality in the management of the Iranian hydrocarbon resources. He changed the initial approach of his predecessors supporting a different oil policy characterized by higher prices and lower production levels. His objective was to limit the levels of production, balancing the consequent reduction of hydrocarbon income by imposing higher prices, an artificially fixed price of US$35 per barrel. The ambition of the minister was jeopardized by the diplomatic tensions related to the hostage issue and, above all, the oil price policy of Moinfar – aimed at bringing the oil price closer to that of other world energy sources – was unsustainable because of the price of US$28 per barrel required by the Saudis. In the end, the minister was forced to record the dramatic decline in exports until they were completely suspended during the following April 1980.[10] The absolute uncertainty of Iran's internal and international relations represented a major hurdle on the way of normalization of that country. The referendum of 10 October established in Iran the institutional system called *velayat-e faqih*, and that, among many doubts, represented the only certainty for the opponents of the IRP (Islami Republican Party) and for foreigners. The Soviet invasion of Afghanistan also offered another fundamental support to the radicalisation and victory of Khomeini. The first post-Pahlavi Iranian elections on 25 January 1980 were held in a tense political atmosphere marked by the widespread intervention of the corps of *Pasdaran* in the provinces of the country. The effects of the astonishing victory of Adolhassan Bani Sadr, immediately supported by all the Western world, would have been annulled by the hostage crisis, and in the meanwhile the European countries simply would have observed quite passively the decline of the first and last democratic president of the Republic of Iran. The Iranian turmoil and the main issue represented by the occupation of the embassy fully involved political and public debate in Italy. Italy also was facing a dramatic phase of redefinition of the political domestic equilibrium when the government of Rome assumed the presidency of the European Economic Community (EEC), and that forced Italy to intervene in the Iranian question.[11] Therefore, Giulio Tamagnini also represented the EEC during the early dramatic phases of the American hostage crisis. The reaction of the Carter administration to the crisis was focused on the preparation of economic and financial measures, like stopping crude oil imports from Iran and freezing Iranian funds and assets in the United States, as well as sending more warships to the Gulf. The United States tried to impose a discussion in UN headquarters about the multilateral adoption of similar sanctions against the violation of international law by Iranians, but the Soviet veto deprived the US initiative of the necessary legitimacy. For several months the adoption of voluntary measures was embarrassing for not only the EEC members but even the Washington administration, which insistently asked Europe to take joint initiatives, even clamorous, such as withdrawing ambassadors and the closure of diplomatic offices in Iran. European prudence emerged on the diplomatic level and was therefore confirmed by the attitude of the community countries concerning the sanctions against Iran. The ambassadors of the EEC, reunited by Tamagnini, reiterated their perplexities, since Europe could not adopt measures without the legitimacy of the UN. For Tamagnini these sanctions were inappropriate. He thought instead that for the whole Western world a dialogue with the Iranians was necessary, without dividing the world into good and bad. If on the one hand condemnation of the serious violation of international law was inevitable, on the other hand Italian diplomacy, along with the German Federal Republic, constantly tried to moderate the attitude of the EEC, which should have continued the path indicated by the Resolution 457 of the Security Council. After all, despite the economic situation becoming progressively worse, the Iranians gave no sign of giving up and, even in the case of economic war against the entire Western countries establishment, they proved to be self-confident. Not only Tamagnini but Bani Sadr also criticized the students, taking a moderate position about the issue of seizure and asking attention to the need for Iran to find a negotiating solution to the situation in the short term. Giulio Tamagnini was one of the first to point out the success of Bani Sadr, an Iranian leader whose views were formed abroad during his fifteen-year exile. His election was the most effective response to the invasion of Shiite clergy in Iran, since he was considered capable of solving the hostage crisis and winning the underground confrontation between secularists and the clergy.[12]

Italy and the election of Bani Sadr

Beyond the general importance conferred to the presidency of Bani Sadr, the election of the former minister of the economy seemed to represent an important opportunity to develop favourable conditions for Italian firms operating in Iran. The Iranian economic expansion had been limited by the decisions of the Revolutionary Council, which suspended the contract with the Consortium and all the contractual formulas were deemed incompatible with the law regarding relations between state-owned companies and private companies that were active in Iran. Beyond the limits imposed by Iranian law and the difficult international condition of the country, what limited the exchange between Iran and the other economies was the difficulty for foreign companies to adapt themselves to the changed conditions of the Iranian market, which required more work and less earnings, and that also required consolidating the private channels of trading, perhaps even more important than in the past in Iran.[13] Tamagnini considered in a very positive way some reassuring acts by the Tehran authorities, such as the payment of some arrears for the benefit of Italian companies, which came precisely in the spring of 1980 and seemed to encourage Italian permanence in Iran. The searches for continuity and the economic goals were strictly connected and for several reasons could not be abandoned because of the presence of workers and their families, as well as of the diplomatic staff still present in Iran. Companies such as Impregilo, ENI, Montedison, Italstrade and Condotte came back to Iran pushed by their needs and by the invitations of the Iranians and diplomats of Italy. In this period in which Italy and Iran tried to rebuild their bilateral relations, Italy had to manage in the first months of 1980 the serious embarrassment created by the Agusta helicopter issue, a problem that overlapped the bigger theme of relations between European countries and the United States, therefore, linked to the attitude of the Community with regard to relations between the Iranians and the Americans.[14] The relationship between the Pahlavi dynasty and Agusta had particularly flourished thanks to the high-quality weapons produced by the Italian company, which profited from the positive trend of bilateral relations with Iran and, above all, could be counted on because of the special relationship between the House of Savoy and the ruling house in Iran. Agusta consolidated its successful relationship with Iran, focusing on the re-export of goods produced under the large US companies' license, such as the famous forty-four-seater CH-47Cs Chinook helicopter. The last contract that the Shah had signed with Agusta in 1979, was negotiated by the heir of the House of Savoy. The contract provided the delivery of sixteen Chinook helicopters, supplies of spare parts and maintenance services for a total value of US$425 million. After the revolution, the provisional government reduced the initial order, limiting its validity to the goods and services that had already been paid for by Iran. The occupation of the Embassy and the related sanctions, however, required Italy to suspend the supply although a team of Iranian pilots were already in Italy to bring helicopters back home, since those helicopters were produced under license of US company Boeing Vertol. The issue was reported by Tehran, protested for the delivery block of what already paid. The Iranian government insisted on calling the issue 'humanitarian' because, meanwhile, there was the flood of Khuzestan and those helicopters were necessary to help people affected by that natural disaster. After visiting Paris, on 12 February 1980, the minister of foreign affairs of the Islamic Republic of Iran, Sadegh Ghotbzadeh, arrived in Rome. His Italian counterpart, Attilio Ruffini, and Minister Siro Lombardini promised the Iranian politician that they would release the supply of spare parts for helicopters, considering it to be a legitimate decision, given that Iranians had already paid for them. The ongoing delays in releasing the supply generated a tough reaction by Iranians, then seriously determined not only to obtain the helicopters but to one more time test European loyalty to Washington. On 28 February, Hassan Ghadiri, the first secretary and press officer of Iran's embassy in Rome, formulated precise allegations against Italy in relation to the Agusta supplies and therefore to the drama represented by the flood in Khuzestan. However, the trade was suspended for a second time, contrary to what was promised to Ghotbzadeh, as the US government renewed its veto on the supply of helicopters by Agusta, right before the diplomatic crisis of March 1980.[15] In fact, the supply of helicopters should be considered an important element in the relations between the United States and Iran, and became extremely critical following the failed UN mission in Tehran (10 March). Then the US administration effectively created common cause against the Tehran regime by proposing the application of collective solidarity measures on a voluntary basis. European countries seemed to be against the hypothesis of breaking diplomatic relations, since these were considered essential for many governments in Iran, a country that in that historical phase was full of pitfalls but also of opportunities. After the humiliating conclusion of the UN commission's journey, Khomeini took a new position in favour of the students, determined to elicit a more decisive reaction by Washington. Carter announced the breach of diplomatic relations and the adoption of new and more stringent sanctions on 7 April. The United States forced the Western world to choose whether or not to follow the United States as the situation escalated.[16] On 9 April, the US Ambassador to Italy, Richard Gardner, was received by Director of the Italian Foreign Ministry Franco Maria Malfatti, a meeting that preceded taking office of the Cossiga government on 15 April. Then, Iran was facing the danger of an alignment of Europe with US positions. On 11 April 1980, Foreign Minister Ghotbzadeh summoned the EEC ambassadors and the ambassadors of New Zealand, Australia and Japan to discuss the issue, launching an implicit but firm warning against Euro-Atlantic solidarity on the issue of sanctions. Oil minister Moinfar pointed out to Western diplomats that in those days the Revolutionary Council should have evaluated more than fifty contracts that had been previously suspended. The main holders of these contracts were European companies. During the Council of Ministers of the EEC of Luxembourg, the European countries wrote a Solomonic 'Declaration on Iran'. The EEC countries expressed their solidarity with the United States, announcing the adoption of some minor measures and postponing the adoption of economic and financial sanctions after the convocation of the Iranian parliament. The US attempt to organize an expedition to free the hostages failed in the desert near Tabas on 24 April 1980. This shocked the world, creating the fear of a military escalation, and it had very serious consequences, creating a further element of embarrassment among US partners. Italian Foreign Minister Emilio Colombo condemned this American military action, a strong stance that was applauded by the members of the Communist Party but contested by social democrats, Liberals and republicans. The minister criticized the use of force by the United States and distanced himself from President Carter, who had kept his European allies in the dark about his intentions. After the failed blitz, Italian cultural institutions and the embassy kept a distance from the violence used in Tehran against the diplomatic offices of Western countries, such as the British, accused of connivance with the United States. The subsequent statements of Colombo during the debate in the Chamber of Deputies and in the Senate on international politics were, however, used to rectify the government's tone on this issue, legitimating the United States and its frustration and impatience due to their relationship with Iran after what had happened. The following summit of heads of state and government on 28 April substantially confirmed the decisions of the foreign ministers of the EEC. The European Community once again appeared to be torn between the strategic alliance with the United States and the necessity to protect their own interests, as Europeanism still appeared to be blurred in the background of these prevailing elements. During the Naples Council of Ministers (17–18 May), it was questioned what kind of measures should have been taken, without using any military measures or punitive economic sanctions. The EEC countries decided to apply some of the harshest economic sanctions against Tehran, but Europe wanted to wait for the general elections before taking any measures against Iran. The decisions taken in April aroused criticism within the EEC for seeming to be too much like the US initiatives, even after the disastrous adventure in the desert and the consequent resignation of the US Secretary of State.[17] Europe seemed to be turning its back on the Iranians, who then experienced the most critical moment in terms of international relations. Iran feared the effects of complete isolation and insisted more on trade relations with the Eastern countries of Europe and non-EU countries.[18] The EEC Council of Naples decided to ban the exports and re-export of goods to Iran, excluding food and medicines, and member states were obligated to restrict the supply of transport services in the European ports in favour of Iranian ships. It was conditional and cosmetic solidarity, and everybody in Europe hoped that Iran could produce more legislative and administrative instruments to persuade withdrawal of the decisions that were taken in the Naples summit. The necessity to offer solidarity to the United States did not erase Europeans' scepticism regarding the effectiveness of the sanctions, and the substantial failure of those measures proved the artificiality of the European consensus.[19] Despite the imposition of the sanctions, Iranian imports increased by 12 per cent during the year 1980, that is US$64 billion, thanks to the diversification of the Iranian sales channels that crossed Turkey and the Soviet Union. In the last quarter of 1980, and increasingly after the conflict against Iraq, 29 per cent of total Iranian imports went through the Soviet channel, compared to the 6 per cent of 1979, thus leading to an increase of 31 per cent of Iranian-Soviet exchange.[20]

The Italian government led by Francesco Cossiga also implemented sanctions, concentrating on administrative interventions in the export licensing sector. For Italy, as for all members of the EEC, unemployment and the consequent sanctions were an obstacle to the development of economic and commercial relations. The measures adopted by the Council of Luxembourg, which involved the partial reduction of diplomatic staff in Iran, proved to be problematic because they were in clear contrast with the practical needs of the European countries and with the request for accreditation of the ambassador to European countries. During one of the last meetings with the Iranian oil minister, the Italian ambassador tried to outline the framework of bilateral relations between the two countries. During the meeting, Tamagnini focused his attention on the information about the progress of works by Italian companies in Iran during the first eighteen months of the revolution, as well as on the general aspects concerning the Iranian regime's policy. The Italian companies had several problems on an operational level and on the financial side, since the companies were suffering in terms of credit because of the late payments of the Iranians, who in turn could use the pretext of sanctions to justify their non-fulfillment. Saipem, a private company founded in 1956 to operate in the oil services, was tied down with the connection work Igat I–Igat II, and was forced to suspend the works for financial reasons. They did not find a solution concerning the adjustment of the contract and for the payments, money that they needed to repair the plants damaged during the revolutionary period. In the overall framework, even if we consider all these difficulties, what was emerging were the economic opportunities in Iran for Italy, a country that has always been appreciated in Iran, especially following the Venice Declaration.[21] The new Italian ambassador in Tehran, Francesco Mezzalama, therefore received precise instructions from Colombo and Malfatti, with whom Mezzalama had long cooperated, and this confirmed the vivid and strong interest in monitoring and improving the partnership with Tehran. The Italian ambassador was aware of the the necessity of keeping an open dialogue with the Iranians waiting for the issue of US hostages to be resolved.[22] On 28 May 1980, the assignment of the Iranian parliament (*majlis*) marked another step towards institutional normalization and to a solution of the hostage crisis, an issue that was clearly closely connected with the struggle for power between Bani Sadr and a part of the Shiite clergy.[23]

Europe between the end of sanctions and the conflict over the Shatt al-Arab

The progressive affirmation of Khomeini in Iran received a new external input thanks to Saddam Hussein's attack on Khuzestan. As the issue of hostages had already helped to set apart the representatives of the revolutionary establishment opposing the radical religious, Bani Sadr was finally defeated because of the consequence of the conflict between Iran and Iraq. The solution of the hostage crisis had seemed to be making Europe able to respond to Tehran's request to improve their economic relations. Despite the stigmatization of the attitude taken by the EEC in the dispute against the United States, the Iranians showed with facts that they were ready to choose Europe as the first partner of Iran.[24] The conflict stopped, once again, the speedy growing of the economic expectations of the European countries in Iran and forced the EEC to cope with the conciliation of a common diplomatic stance over the war and the growth of commercial and political relations with the Tehran regime.[25] Notwithstanding the decision of the EEC to take a neutral position on the conflict, the next invitation issued by the European institutions to not export lethal items to the two countries at war created new misunderstandings between Europeans and Iranians. In fact, the Western countries and the Middle Eastern regimes gave implicit support to Iraq while maintaining an appearance of neutrality; their support was justified on geopolitical grounds, but it also had economic motivations.[26] In the short run, the conflict caused several problems to the European states, such as the threat to energy security of the West and navigation through the Strait of Hormuz.[27] In fact, the Iraqi attacks damaged the main Iranian oil terminals and therefore the country's export capability, menacing the lives of civilians and of foreign staff, as well as foreigner economic interests and investments. The war in Iran forced the progressive evacuation of some of the Italian companies' hydrocarbon facilities that were still active.[28] The ambiguous European attitude hurt therefore the sensitivity of the Islamic Republic's representatives and risked jeopardizing the ongoing relationship between Iran and European members. On 5 December an Iranian delegation in Rome launched an appeal to the EEC for an explicit condemnation of the aggression. According to the Iranians, after the Iraqi attack the EEC had been indifferent: the silence of Europe was unacceptable and discriminatory, since the EEC had until then shown itself to be sensitive to human rights violations in every part of the world, with attention to the violations committed against the US prisoners and against ethnic-religious minorities in revolutionary Iran. Despite the role that Iraq carved out in the context of US policy in the Gulf as a supplier of crude oil to Italy, Iran remained a more important economic partner for Italy than Iraq. The support of the West in favour of Saddam was therefore reinforced considering national interests, but as Malfatti and the new ambassador Francesco Mezzalama affirmed, Iran played a strategic role for Italy, being a 'bigger, stronger, richer' country. A lot of Italy's direct investments were concentrated in Persia and these needed to be safeguarded. Even public companies were involved, and several contracts were extremely difficult to resolve. That is why the economic activities in Iran required the commitment of the government.[29]

The ongoing conflict fuelled the fears related to Iran's ability to preserve the unity and independence of the country. The decline of Iranian oil's production also seemed unstoppable and destined to drag down the entire economy of the country and the Islamic revolution itself. Mohammad Gharazi, Moinfar's successor as oil minister, had to deal with several issues: the legacy of the revolution in this delicate sector, the problems related to the effects of Minister Moinfar's initiatives and the consequences of the war on the Shatt al-Arab.[30] Many of the critical elements of Iran's economic policy had been underestimated for a very long time by the leaders of the IRP. Iran was helped by the increased prices applied by the producing countries starting from the 58th OPEC Conference of Algiers. The decisions taken by the exporters' cartel helped to make Iranian oil competitive again, especially for the benefit of the southern hemisphere's countries and the Soviet bloc that increased their oil imports thanks to the 'barter agreement' formula. Beginning in September 1981 under the auspices of the new minister, Gharazi, there were also important changes to Iranian oil policy. Iran began to produce crude oil to finance the war, and to cope with it the Ininan government completed definitive cancellation of the contracts of the former Consortium companies (8 September 1981) and desiged a technical committee to allocate the seized areas of research to the new firms.[31] The disastrous economic and material situation of the country paradoxically attracted the attention of economic operators from all over the world, who began to go to Tehran frequently, just as they did at the time of Reza Pahlavi's regime.[32] ENI itself expressed interest in Iranian crude oil again, also because even Iraqi crude oil export was suffering the effects of the war. In the previous months, the members of the Italian delegations had tried to go through the Iranian chaos, obtaining a supply contract by NIOC, whose execution was however suspended almost immediately due to logistical difficulties and to well-known financial problems. On November 1981, a delegation from ENI went to Iran to explore the possibility of signing contracts to purchase oil and to look for new opportunities in the field of services for the extraction of hydrocarbons. The unresolved difficulties between Iran and ENI remained the debts owed by the previous regime and those due to the companies that worked for ENI. Iranian policymakers reaffirmed that Iran hoped to establish relations with the companies that were independent from multinationals like the Italian ones and, thanks to the renewed dynamism of its Iranian hydrocarbons policy, one of Eni's firms signed a new agreement concerning the works provided by Igat II.[33]

The summer of 1981 marked the beginning of a new institutional earthquake in Iran for which the former president of the Islamic Republic Bani Sadr was forced to leave the country. The second phase of the Iranian revolution ended with the definitive affirmation of the IRP as sanctioned through the election of the hojatoleslam Ali Khamenei as president of the Islamic Republic of Iran on 2 October 1981. Since then the IRP have taken full control over all the institutions of the country, a 'new country' that, however, would have continued to be a key economic partner with Italy.[34]

Notes

1 Said Amir Aryomand, *The Shadow of God and the Hidden Imam: Religion, Political Order and Social Change in the Sh'ite Iran from the Beginning to 1890* (Chicago: University of Chicago Press, 1984); Aryomand, *The Turban of the Crown: The Islamic Revolution in Iran* (Oxford: Oxford University Press, 1988), 135–6; Marcella Emiliani, Marco Ranuzzi de' Bianchi and Erika Atzori, *Rivoluzione, clero e potere in Iran* (Bologna: Odoya, 2008), 108–14; Renzo Guolo, *La via dell'Imam: L'Iran da Khomeini ad Ahamadinejad* (Rome: Laterza, 2007), 28 et sqq.; Dilip Hiro, *Iran under the Ayatollah* (London: Routledge & Kegan Paul, 1987), 108; Michael Ledeen and William Lewis, *Dèbacle: The American Failure in Iran* (New York: Vintage, 1981), 216–33; Luca Riccardi, *L'internazionalismo difficile: La diplomazia del PCI e il Medio Oriente dalla crisi petrolifera alla caduta del muro di Berlino 1973-1989* (Soveria Mannelli: Rubbettino, 2013), 275–87; Farian Sabahi, *Storia dell'Iran* (Milan: Bruno Mondadori, 2006), 184; Sepehr Zabih, *Iran since the Revolution* (London: Croom Helm, 1982), 16.

2 ILS, GA, b.1282, *Tel. da Tramagnini per il MAE*, 3 March 1979; ASENI, DE, b. 165, f. 1742, 'Riunione al Ministero degli Affari esteri sulla situazione in Iran', nota firmata A. Donadelli per il Dr Sarchi, 7 March 1979. See Rosario Milano, 'L'ENI e l'Iran (1973-1978)', *Nuova Rivista Storica*, May–August (2014), no. II, 603–65.

3 Shaul Bakhash, *The Politics of Oil and Revolution in Iran: A Staff Paper* (Washington, DC: Brookings Institute, 1982), 3 et sqq. See Rosario Milano, *L'ENI e l'Iran 1963-1970* (Napoli: Giannini, 2013).

4 ASENI, EE, b. 201, f. 5, *Appunto 'Riunione Cipe'*, 12 March 1979.

5 ILS, GA, b. 1282, *Tel. da Iatldipl Teheran, Tamagnini, al MAE*, 5 March 1979; ILS, GA, b. 1282, *Tel. da Italdipl Teheran, Bondioli, al MAE*, 9 April 1979.

6 ASENI, b. 166, f. 174C, *Tel. dell'Ambasciata di Italia in Iran per il Ministero degli Affari esteri*, 27 April 1979; ASENI, b. 166, f. 174C, *Tel. dell'Ambasciata di Italia in Iran per il*

Ministero degli Affari esteri, 5 May 1979. See Milano, *L'ENI e l'Iran (1963–1970)*, cit.; Milano, 'L'ENI e l'Iran (1973–1978)'.
7   TNA, FCO 8/3603, *Note on the IPU Spring Meeting*, 14 April 1980.
8   TNA, BT 241/2929, *Arm Exports to Iran*, 4 May 1979; Hiro, *Iran under the Ayatollah*, 317; Ray Takeyh, *Guardians of the Revolution* (Oxford: Oxford University Press, 2009), 28–9; Ledeen and Lewis, *Dèbacle*, 256–75; Emiliani, de' Bianchi and Atzori, *Rivoluzione, clero e potere in Iran*, 143.
9   TNA, FCO 8/3638, *Internal FCO-MED, M.J. Williams*, 3 January 1980.
10 TNA, FCO 8/3602, *Tel. from British Embassy in Teheran, D.N. Reddaway, to FCO-MED, D. Coates*, 14 May 1980.
11 See Giampaolo Calchi Novati, 'Mediterraneo e questione araba nella politica estera dell'Italia', in various authors, *Storia dell'Italia repubblicana*, vol. II, *La trasformazione dell'Italia: Sviluppo e squilibri* (Turin: Einaudi, 1995); Ennio Di Nolfo (ed.), *La politica estera italiana negli anni Ottanta* (Manduria: Lacaita, 2003); Luigi Vittorio Ferraris (ed.), *Manuale della politica estera italiana 1947–1993* (Rome: Laterza, 1996); Giuseppe Mammarella and Paolo Cacace, *La politica estera dell'Italia: Dallo Stato unitario ai giorni nostri* (Rome: Laterza, 2006); Riccardi, L'internazionalismo difficile, 286–7; Antonio Varsori, *L'Italia nelle relazioni internazionali dal 1943 al 1992* (Rome: Laterza, 1998).
12 TNA, FCO 8/3602, *NATO Expert Working Group 6–8 February 1980*, 13 February 1980.
13 ASENI, EE, b. 134, f. 3, *Lettera da Agip, E. Barbaglia, per E. Egidi*, 9 April 1980. ASENI, EE, b. 115, f. 1, *Memorandum per Carlo Sarchi da parte di N. Ghaffary*, 12 April 1980. Siegmund Ginzberg, 'Più morbido l'Iran sul Petrolio', *L'Unità*, 13 December 1979; Giulio Tamagnini, *La caduta dello scià:. Diario dell'ambasciatore italiano a Teheran 1978–1989* (Rome: Edizioni Associate, 1990), 194–5.
14 TNA, FCO 8/3665, *Tel. from British Embassy in Teheran, J. Graham, to FCO-MED*, 6 January 1980; G. Tamagnini, 258–9.
15 *TNA, FCO 8/3633, FCO-MED, A.C. Miers 5 March 1980; TNA, FCO 8/3633, Tel. from British Embassy in Rome, P.E. Pellew, to FCO-MED, A.C. Miers, 24 March 1980*; TNA, FCO 8/3633, *Tel. from British Embassy in Rome, W.G. Adams, to FCO-MED, A.C. Miers*, 5 March 1980.
16 TNA, FCO 8/3589, *Internal FCO-MED, C.LG. Mallaby*, 17 October 1980; FCO 8/3589, *Iran-US bilateral relations 1980*. See Riccardi, *L'internazionalismo difficile*, 359.
17 TNA, FCO 8/3597, *Tel. from British Embassy in Teheran, J. Graham, to FCO-MED*, 13 May 1980.
18 Siegmund Ginzberg, 'Tutti – tranne gli stupidi – comprano e vendono in Iran', *L'Unità*, 23 May 1980; ASENI, EE, b. 115, f. 1, *Tel. dal MAE, Bucci, a ENI*, 8 June 1980.
19 TNA FCO 8/3603, *Tel. from British Embassy in Washington, Handerson, to FCO-MED, A.C. Miers*, 28 January 1980; TNA, FCO 8/3611, *Tel. from British Embassy in Washington, Handerson, to FCO-MED, A.C. Miers*, 19 May 1980. See Hiro, *Iran under the Ayatollah*, 323 et sqq.
20 TNA, FCO 8/4036, *Tel. from Copenaghen CoreEu to La Haye Coreu*, 9 January 1981.
21 ASENI, EE, b. 115, f. 1, *Tel. da Ambasciata d'Italia al MAE*, 29 June 1980. See Milano, *L'Eni e l'Iran (1963–1970)*; Milano, *L'Eni e l'Iran (1973–1979)*.
22 Francesco Mezzalama, *L'avventura diplomatica. Ricordi di carriera* (Soveria Mannelli: Rubbettino, 2006), 204–7.

23 ILS, GA, 1282, *Tel. da Italdipl Teheran, Tamagnini, al MAE*, 28 May 1980; TNA, FCO 8/3597, *Tel. from British Embassy in Teheran, J. Graham, to FCO-MED, A.C. Miers*, 20 May 1980.
24 TNA FCO 8/4037, *Report of the Meeting of Community Head of Mission*, S. Barrett, 21 April 1981; E. Rouleau, 'I. L'Union Sacrée', *Le Monde*, 6 June 1981; TNA, FCO 8/4036, *Tel. from British Interest Section, S. Barrett, to FCO-MED*, 3 February 1981.
25 TNA, FCO 8/4036, *Tel. from FCO-MED, F.M. Wogan, to M. Bullard*, 31 March 1981; TNA, FCO 8/4036, *FCO-MED, F.M. Wogan, to British Interest Section, S. Barrett*, 29 April 1981. TNA, FCO 8/4037, *From British Interest Section, S. Barrett, to Cor EU The Hague*, 21 April 1981; TNA, FCO 8/4037, *Tel. from the UK Delegation to NATO, P.F. Ricketts, to FCO-MED, M.J. Lamport*, 22 May 1981.
26 ASENI, EE, b. 201, f. 5, *Il ministro delle Partecipazioni statali, Gianni De Michelis, al ministro del Petrolio della Repubblica d'Iraq, Tahe Abdul Karim*, 3 May 1980. ASENI, EE, b. 201, f. 5, *Visita in Iraq dal 26 al 30 luglio 1982*, 23 August 1982. See Massimo Bucarelli, 'L'ENI e il petrolio dell'Iraq negli anni Settanta: tra crisi energetiche e nazionalismo arabo', *Nuova rivista Storica*, no. II, May–August (2014), 667 et sqq.; Haim Shemesh, *Soviet-Iraq Relations, 1968–1988: In the Shadow of the Iran-Iraq Conflict* (Boulder, CO: Lynne Rienner, 1992); Maziar Behrooz, *Rebels with a Cause: The Failure of the Left in Iran* (London: Tauris, 1999).
27 Igor Man, 'Se la nostra nazione sarà in pericolo faremo saltare tutti i pozzi del Golfo', *La Stampa*, 24 September 1980. ASENI, EE, b. 201, f. 5, *N.73/8*, 26 September 1980; ASENI, EE, b. 201, f. 5, *Tel. da MAE, DGAP-Uff.VII, Bucci, a ENI*, 3 October 1980; TNA FCO 8/4037, *Tel. from Rome CorEu to London Cor Eu*, 26 July 1981; ASENI, EE, b. 201, f. 5, *Tel. da DiEst ENI, R. Santoro, a SNAM – Divisione Trasporti Marittimi, Ing. Leonardi*, 26 September 1981.
28 ASENI, EE, b. 201, f. 5, *Lettera di A. Grandi per l'Ambasciatore F. Malfatti*, 22 September 1980; TNA, FCO 8/4408, *Conversation with Malcom Simpson about obsolete American weapons, FCO-MED, W.G. Clare*, 1 February 1982.
29 Mezzalama, 204–7. See ASENI, EE, b. 128, f. 1, *Promemoria C. Sarchi per il Dr. Di Donna*, 5 May 1980; ASENI, EE, b. 201, f. 5, *Promemoria Eni DiEst, R. Pollack*, 27 March 1981.
30 TNA, FCO 8/4064, *Tel. from British Interest Section in Teheran, Commercial Dept., to FCO, G. Asley*, 31 August 1981; TNA, FCO 8/4064, *Tel. from British Interest Section in Teheran, J. McCredie, to FCO*, 31 August 1981; TNA, FCO 8/3625, *'Economic Situation after Four Weeks of War', from British Interest Section in Teheran, M. Bundy, to FCO-MED, A.C. Miers*, 19 February 1981; TNA, FCO 8/4061, *British Interest Section in Teheran, J. McCredie, to FCO-MED, M.J. Lamport*, 23 September 1981. TNA, FCO 8/4061, *Letter from British Interest Section in Teheran, N.A. Ling, to FCO-MED, M.J. Lamport*, 9 November 1981.
31 TNA, FCO 8/4061, *Internal FCO-MED, D. Coates*, 21 October 1981; TNA, FCO 8/4061, *Tel. from British Interest Section in Teheran, J. McCredie, to FCO-MED, A.C. Miers*, 27 August 1981; ASENI, b. 191, f. 31, *Promemoria Missione in Iran 2–6.XI.1981, A. Moriniello per R. Santoro*, 12 November 1981.
32 TNA, FCO 8/4061, *Tel. from British Interest Section in Teheran, J. McCredie, to FCO-MED, A.C. Miers*, 30 April 1981; TNA, FCO 8/4061, *Tel. from Trade Department to British Interest Section in Teheran, J. McCredie*, 20 May 1981; TNA, FCO 8/4094, *Iran: some thoughts on leaving, S.J. Barret*, 15 July 1981.

33 ASENI, DE, b. 193, f. 12, *Appunto per il Presidente,* 15 January 1982; ASENI, DE, b. 191, f. 31, *Promemoria Missione in Iran 2–6.XI.1981, A. Moriniello per R. Santoro,* 12 November 1981.
34 TNA, FCO 8/4094, *Iran: some thoughts on leaving, S.J. Barret,* 15 July 1981; TNA, FCO 8/4033, *Tel. from British Embassy in Teheran, C.S. Rundle, to FCO-MED, D. Coates,* 16 September 1981.

14

Italy, King Zahir and the Soviet occupation of Afghanistan, 1979–89

Luciano Monzali

The strange friendship: Afghanistan and Italy from Amanullah to the Soviet invasion of 1979

During the twentieth century, Italy played quite a significant role in the political events of Afghanistan.[1] It was the first Western European country to recognize in 1921 the independence of the Afghan state when it ceased to be a British protectorate and in the following years it helped the economic modernization of this state, which was ruled by Amanullah as an emir and then as a king. Deposed by a tribal revolt inspired by the British in 1929, Amanullah went into exile in Italy, where he lived until his death in 1960. In the 1930s and 1940s, Rome became the centre of the political machinations of Amanullah to regain power from his successors and relatives, Nadir and Zahir. After the Second World War, when the dream of regaining power with the support of Fascist Italy and Nazi Germany had vanished, Amanullah decided to reconcile with Zahir by giving up every claim to the Afghan throne and by declaring his submission to the ruling king in 1948.[2] Zahir himself started visiting Italy and liked it, spending long holidays there from the 1950s onwards. He was staying in Italy when in July 1973 his cousin Daoud/Daud, the former prime minister, organized a coup d'état with the support of the communists and established a republic with himself as president. The new regime was strongly nationalist and authoritarian. Zahir decided to assume a cautious attitude toward Daoud. One month after the coup, the king abdicated formally and Dauod allowed various members of the royal family to leave Afghanistan and promised to respect and guarantee Zahir's private properties.[3]

Seeing as he was already used to travelling to Italy, Zahir decided to establish his residence in exile in Rome and went to live in a villa in the suburbs of the Italian capital. He led a very private life but did not give up the idea of regaining power in Kabul. Several Afghan politicians, public servants and intellectuals gravitated around him and ended up forming the so-called 'Group of Rome', which would play a significant role in Afghan political events of the following decades.[4]

Once in power, Daoud, an extreme Pashtun nationalist, reopened the boundaries controversy with Pakistan and adopted a friendly attitude towards the Soviet Union.

He tried to pursue an authoritarian modernization of Afghan society, garnering the support of the communists who were part of his government. After some time, however, fearful of an excessive strengthening of the communists in bureaucracy and in the armed forces, Daoud decided to expel them from the government and to distance Afghanistan from Moscow, moving quite close to Imperial Iran, which was ready to give huge loans to the Afghan government. In an increasingly tense political climate, in April 1978, after the killing of a communist representative, Mir Akbar Khyber, Daoud ordered the arrest of many leaders of the Afghan Communist Party (the People's Democratic Party of Afghanistan, also known as PDPA). In retaliation, some communist military officers organized a coup d'état which, quite unexpectedly, succeeded. With the government buildings surrounded and then bombed by the rebels' military planes, Daoud, his relatives and many ministers surrendered and were killed by the conspirators.[5]

The communists formed a revolutionary government led by Prime Minister Nur Mohammad Taraki, and by Deputy Prime Minister and Foreign Affairs Minister Hafizullah Amin. Despite strong Soviet economic and political support, the weakness of this new government and lack of popular consent for it were soon evident. Attempts to use coercion to implement a vast programme of social reforms (e.g. land reform, the emancipation of women, compulsory development of literacy among the masses) stirred unrest and revolt in the conservative and traditionalist countryside. Harsh and heated conflicts broke out within the Communist Party between the dominant Khalq faction and rival Parcham Group. In autumn 1979, the anti-communist rebellion led by Islamic fundamentalists and followers of Zahir, and supported by Iran and Pakistan, grew stronger in the whole country. In October 1979, a bloody feud erupted within the PDPA, with Amin removing Taraki from office and, despite Soviet pressure to let him live, having him killed together with many other communist exponents seen as a possible political menace. Once Amin gained power, he secretly tried to improve relations with the United States, but Moscow found out about this.

In an international context marked by rising tension with the United States and worried by Khomeyni's rise to power in Iran, the Soviet government decided to organize a direct military intervention in Afghanistan to overthrow Amin and enable the Parcham faction of the PDPA to rule. On Christmas Eve 1979, Soviet military forces invaded Afghanistan. The KGB special forces forced their way into the prime minister's palace in Kabul and killed Amin, several of his relatives and his aides. Babrak Karmal, the leader of the Parcham group, became the new Afghan prime minister.

Italy and the Soviet invasion of Afghanistan

Italian public opinion and the country's political parties harshly condemned the Soviet invasion of Afghanistan. Moscow's initiative violated the national self-determination principle that was so important to Italians. Prime Minister Francesco Cossiga summoned the Council of Ministers on 29 December to discuss the Afghan matter, and they prepared and voted for a communiqué inviting all the parties involved in the conflict to conform to the principles and norms of the United Nations Charter. The aim of this move was a return to normality without foreign interventions, allowing the Afghan people to decide their own destiny.[6] On 9 January 1980, during a parliamentary debate on Afghanistan,[7] the Italian government harshly condemned the Soviet military intervention.[8] Moscow had interfered heavy-handedly in the internal situation of an independent state like Afghanistan, changing the political situation in Central Asia. Italy was very worried by the possible consequences of this move by the Russians on the détente policy which the government in Rome wanted to preserve. According to Italy, a prerequisite for the continuation and progress of détente was that the Soviet military occupation of Afghanistan come to an end.[9] The Italian Communist Party (PCI), due to the good confidential contacts it had with the Soviet Union and the international communist movements, was not caught by surprise when the Russians invaded Afghanistan. The Italian communist leaders had known for several months about the difficult Afghan internal situation and the possibility of a Soviet intervention.[10] The PCI had seen the communist takeover of Afghanistan in 1978 in a positive light as the Afghan communists wanted to reform their society by overcoming feudalism, giving land to farmers and freeing women from conditions akin to slavery.[11] But very soon, the Afghan Communist Party was torn apart by internal conflicts, and news of expulsions, arrests and murders reached Rome.[12] The first reaction of the PCI to the Soviet invasion was an article published in *Unità*, the Communist Party newspaper, on 29 December 1979, which expressed the view that the change of government in Kabul and the Soviet military intervention were worrying and dangerous.[13] Russia's actions were considered a violation of the independence and autonomy of Afghanistan, and the PCI looked unfavourably on military interventions that undermined the principles of independence, sovereignty and non-interference in internal affairs, which they believed should always be respected.[14] On 4 January 1980, the Central Committee of the Party gathered and agreed to support the proposal of the PCI's General Secretary, Enrico Berlinguer, to condemn these Soviet actions, as they were seen as an initiative which aggravated international tensions and showed excessive hegemonic Soviet ambitions.[15]

The PCI not only condemned the Soviet invasion but was also harshly critical of the American strategy of sanctions and counter-measures against Moscow. According to the Italian communists, the American policy of reprisal damaged Europe's interests and threatened world peace. Instead, what was necessary was a continuation of the diplomatic dialogue with Moscow and of the negotiations regarding arms control. The Italian communists decided to strongly oppose the Atlantic alliance's decision to deploy American missiles in Europe. During the period spanning the end of December and the beginning of January 1980, the government in Rome initiated consultations with Washington and the European allies,[16] then decided to recall the Italian diplomatic representative from Kabul and to suspend all kinds of aid to Afghanistan. In the following weeks, the Cossiga government cancelled all forms of economic cooperation with the Afghan state and decided to participate in a European programme of food aid for Afghan refugees in Pakistan. Regarding the Soviet Union, after some immediate and minor reprisals (the cancellation of some state visits and of a symposium of Italian and Soviet historians, and the refusal to let a Soviet scientific research ship dock in Italy), the government in Rome focused on acting in concert with its European Economic Community partners. As president of the

European Economic Community (EEC), Italy ordered the Community states not to step in and replace the agricultural exports to Russia which had been blocked as a result of American sanctions, and it decided to apply the Coordinating Committee on Multilateral Export Controls (COCOM) rules to high-technology exports to the Soviet Union.[17] However, within the Italian political establishment there were more than just a few critics of the harsh American strategy of countermeasures employed against the Soviet Union. The anti-American position of the PCI was shared not only by the pacifist wing of Italian Catholicism but also by the Conservative politician and Christian Democrat Giulio Andreotti. In the months in question, Andreotti, who was a bit politically isolated after the end of the season of cooperation with the PCI, planned to get back into the full swing of political life in some way or to become president of the Republic by supporting a close partnership between the Christian Democrats and the communists. In his view, excessive compliance with the American decision to totally and radically oppose the Russians was wrong because it was against Italian national interests and weakened the political leadership of Enrico Berlinguer, the general secretary of the PCI, who was willing to free his party from Soviet influence but was strongly conditioned by the anti-American and pro-Soviet sympathies of a large part of the communist militants. Andreotti harshly criticized Carter's policies, especially the decision to quickly deploy the Pershing and cruise missiles to Europe and his choice for economic sanctions against Soviet Russia. According to the Christian Democrat, Carter's positions were mainly a way of trying to secure more votes in the elections.[18] Due to strong popular opposition to the boycotting of the Olympics in Russia, in May 1980 the Italian government advised the Italian Olympic Committee not to go to Moscow because of the Soviet occupation of Afghanistan but left the final decision to the Committee itself. On 19 May, the Cossiga government declared that it would not send its representatives to the Olympic ceremonies in Moscow and that it would not allow its national anthem to be played or the Italian flag to be displayed. The following day, though, the Italian Olympic Committee voted to go to the Olympics in the Soviet Union.[19] According to Gardner, the former American ambassador in Rome, it was a typical 'Italian compromise' and a diplomatic defeat for the United States.[20] During the first half of the 1980s, the Afghan matter continued to engage Italy, its political parties and its public opinion. The presence in Rome of the former Afghan king, Zahir, made the Italian capital the international centre of the monarchist opposition to the Afghan communist regime, the so-called 'Group of Rome'. The Afghan monarchists in Rome represented the tribes who were loyal to the Durrani royal family and had their strongholds in the Pakistani towns of Quetta and Peshawar. Their political aim was the expulsion of the Soviets from Afghanistan and the restoration of the monarchy. The Italian government supported Zahir's followers cautiously and quietly as it was afraid of riling Moscow. Another reason for Italian prudence was the fact that many Western governments – along with Pakistan and Saudi Arabia, strong political and economic supporters of the Afghan anti-Soviet resistance – did not look favourably on Zahir and his political designs. The Saudis, Pakistanis and Americans accused the Monarchists of not being very active in the fight against the Soviets, and preferred to support Islamic fundamentalists like the Pashtuns Burhanuddin Rabbani and Gubuddin Hekmatyar and the Tajik Ahmed Shah Massud, who accused Zahir of being pro-Russian. In fact, the Islamabad government wanted to politically dominate the future post-Soviet Afghan government and thought the Islamists would be more reliable and loyal allies to Pakistan than Zahir. The Americans and many Western governments accepted this Pakistani strategy despite knowing from some polls carried out in the Afghan refugee camps that the majority of the Afghan people preferred Zahir to any other political and military leader.[21]

But in Italy the Soviet occupation of Afghanistan also became a heated theme of internal political debate. The attitude towards Soviet occupation was one of the subjects of a violent and harsh ideological and political diatribe between the Italian left-wing parties, the Socialists and the Communists. The Socialist Party and its leader, Bettino Craxi, as well as some progressive Liberal representatives deemed it to be a moral and political duty to support the fight of the Afghan rebels and patriots against Soviet occupation, which, in their view, was very similar to the Eastern European anti-Soviet dissidents' battle for freedom.[22] Craxi and the Socialists also saw in the Afghan matter the chance to use a political theme that could make the PCI feel uneasy and put them on the defensive as they were reluctant to engage in initiatives regarding Afghanistan for fear of further irritating the Soviet Union. The Socialist magazine *Mondoperaio*, inspired by Federico Coen and Carlo Ripa di Meana,[23] organized an international Symposium in Rome on 'The Left for Afghanistan' in September 1980. On that occasion, the International Committee for Solidarity with the Afghan Resistance was formed and was presided over by the philosopher and jurist Norberto Bobbio, along with the Socialist politician Margherita Boniver as deputy president and Carlo Cristofori as secretary.[24] In the following years, the Committee collected funds and campaigned in Italy and Europe in favour of the Afghan rebels, sending missions to Pakistan and coming into contact with the Afghan anti-communist parties. The attention and sympathy of Italian public opinion regarding the Afghan resistance was intense and permanent, as testified to by the frequent articles in the Italian press and news on Afghanistan during the 1980s. Sandro Pertini, the Italian president of the Republic, was very sympathetic towards the cause of the Afghan partisans and condemned the Soviet occupation of this country several times.[25] In August 1983, Craxi was appointed prime minister and Giulio Andreotti became foreign minister, a role the latter would hold until 1989. Craxi and Andreotti wished to strengthen Italy's role and influence in international affairs, especially in terms of the European integration process and Middle Eastern politics.[26] Regarding Afghanistan, the Craxi government tried both to be supportive of the right of the Afghan people to determine their own political destiny and to favour a political solution to the conflict based on a compromise which would allow Moscow to quickly withdraw its armed forces without losing too much prestige on an international level.

As he was sympathetic to the plight of the Afghan refugees, Craxi established a commission on human rights in Afghanistan which answered to the prime minister's office and was chaired by Paolo Ungari, a jurist with strong ties to the Italian Republican Party (Partito Repubblicano Italiano, PRI). The commission's task was to study the situation of the Afghan refugees in Pakistan, report back to the Italian government on this and propose initiatives to improve their living conditions.

Italy, Zahir and the Afghan question after Gorbachev's rise to power

During the 1980s, Italian diplomacy favoured the efforts of the United Nations (UN) to promote peace in Afghanistan by, for instance, keeping the lines of communication open between the warring parties and the regional powers through the vice secretary-general of the UN, Diego Cordovez.[27] Italy was also in favour of relaunching the negotiations using third parties, such as Romania, as intermediaries.[28] In April 1984, Andreotti flew to Moscow and met Soviet Foreign Minister Gromyko. During the talks with his Soviet colleague, the Italian politician underlined the importance of, and the urgency for, the end of the Afghan conflict and the withdrawal of Soviet troops.[29] Gorbachev's rise to power in 1985 did not initially bring about changes in the Soviet policy towards Afghanistan so, in May 1985, Craxi and Andreotti went to Russia to meet him. A few days earlier, Maurizio Teucci, an expert on Afghan matters and the head of Bureau XI of the Farnesina's Political Affairs Directorate, had met the Afghan general Abdul Wali (an aide to the former king Zahir) to discuss the political situation in Afghanistan.[30] Wali confirmed the establishment of the Islamic Unity of Afghanistan Mujahideen, which had grouped together the most important resistance leaders based in Peshawar (the radical fundamentalists Hekmatyar, Khalis, Rabbani and Abdul Rassul Saiyaf, and the moderate Islamists Mohammadi, Gailani and Mujaddedi). Because of heavy pressure from the Americans and the growing military danger posed by the Russians, Pakistan had at long last accepted to support the unity of the Afghan resistance. Zahir himself also supported the initiative because he saw it as the first step towards the creation of a united front comprising all the anti-Soviet forces. The former king gave his backing to the resistance without raising the matter of monarchical restoration.[31] According to Wali, the Gorbachev leadership created hope in a future political solution to the Afghan conflict; it was time for a political initiative from the Western countries, in particular Italy, a country which had good relations with the Soviet Union and at the same time always showed great sensitivity towards the Afghan problem.[32] During their visit to Moscow, Craxi and Andreotti engaged in long talks with Gorbachev and Foreign Minister Gromyko.[33] The Afghan matter was included in these discussions, and the Italians asked for a speedy solution to the conflict, but to no avail: the Soviet leaders continued to defend their policies regarding Afghanistan. In March 1986, during the funeral of the Swedish Socialist leader Olaf Palme, Craxi had an interesting conversation on Afghanistan with Indian Prime Minister Rajiv Gandhi,[34] who wanted a political and honourable end to the Afghan conflict. The Soviets wanted to withdraw but felt they needed guarantees against American interference through Pakistan. Pakistan was not in a hurry to stop the conflict because thanks to this it received huge amounts of economic and military aid from the United States. The weapons that Pakistan had been given had created a military build-up in the region and were a great worry to India in particular.[35] An accurate and precise analysis of the military situation in Afghanistan in 1987, after the failure of the Soviet attempts to bring an end to the Afghan resistance and the open American intervention in the conflict by their furnishing Stinger missiles to the Afghan partisans, was made by the Italian chargé d'affairs in Kabul, Pietro Ballero, when he left

Afghanistan at the end of his diplomatic mission.[36] In the Italian diplomat's view, there was a military stalemate in Afghanistan. The Soviet troops occupied the most important towns and the North-South communication route (Heratan/Mazar-e-Sharif/the Salang pass/Kabul/Jalalabad), but the resistance hindered Soviet control of the countryside and of many roads. Nearly half of the Afghan population lived in towns under Russian control. Military operations had shown a lack of efficiency of the Soviet armed forces. Apart from some special units, the Red Army seemed badly trained, with old, low-quality weapons and very backward and badly organized physical and psychological assistance for the troops.[37] After the military occupation of Afghanistan, Moscow had, at first, supported the PDPA's revolutionary programme but this resulted in political failure so the Soviets insisted that the PDPA adopt a moderate approach, transforming the Afghan government programme into a kind of moderate nationalist progressivism. Features of this new strategy were the calling of a Loya Jirga, the demotion of Karmal, the end of the land reform, discussions with local notables, respect for the Islamic religion, the promise of considerable provincial autonomy and a striving for national reconciliation.[38] According to Ballero, Moscow just wanted a loyal government in Kabul; it did not matter if it was ineffective and powerless. The Afghan population was fiercely anti-Russian and was skeptical and indifferent towards the Kabul regime. The mujahideen had no common or coherent political programme beyond being against the Soviets and the PDPA government. The party leaders living in Peshawar had refused any reconciliation with the communists and any idea of a coalition government, but their influence in Afghanistan was limited and survived only thanks to the fact that they were the channel for the financial and military support given by the West and the Islamic countries to the partisans. According to the Italian diplomat, the Afghan people wanted Zahir to return to power, and the former king appeared to be the only figure capable of uniting and pacifying the country.[39] As mentioned previously, India was very interested in the Afghan matter. Between 1987 and 1988, the Indian ambassador in Rome, Akbar Mirza Khaleeli, entered into direct talks with Zahir. Khaleeli told the Italian diplomat Norberto Cappello that the Indian government also wanted a political solution to the Afghan conflict because it was the only way of reducing the tension in the region and weakening the strategic role of Pakistan in American foreign policy.[40] In February 1988, the Indian Deputy Minister of Foreign Affairs, Natwar Singh, came to Rome and met Zahir. Singh later told the Italian undersecretary of Foreign Affairs, Gilberto Bonalumi, that Zahir seemed to be a very reserved and prudent man, perhaps due to the fact he had lived abroad for too long to still have the contacts with the Afghan society that were pivotal if he wanted to play an important political role.[41] India was ready to cooperate in order to help bring about peace in Afghanistan; it was not opposed to the idea of a UN multinational peace force in Afghanistan, but perhaps it was a bit too early to discuss this. In 1987, the Soviet leadership's will to accelerate the withdrawal of its own troops from Afghanistan grew stronger, and in September of that year Soviet Foreign Minister Shevardnadze formally communicated to American Secretary of State Shultz Moscow's decision to withdraw. The new Soviet strategy gave impetus and political meaning to the negotiations between Afghanistan and Pakistan that the UN, under the guidance of Assistant Secretary-General Diego Cordovez, had been trying to foster and keep alive since 1982.[42] The UN pushed for a solution to the Afghan conflict based on the connection between the start of the Soviet withdrawal and international engagements related to Afghanistan's status taken by the interested powers, a diplomatic approach which was looked upon favourably by Moscow.⁴³ The amelioration of the relations between the Soviet Union and the United States, as testified by the Gorbachev–Reagan summit in Washington and the signing of the medium-range missiles agreement in December 1987, made the development of international negotiations on Afghanistan easier. Gorbachev's announcement in February 1988 that by the end of the year all Soviet troops would leave Afghanistan and go back home, weakened the negotiating position of Moscow. The role of the Americans was decisive, with Washington using its influence to convince Pakistan to sign agreements on Afghanistan, which were, however, based on a fragile and changing regional and international political situation and therefore only minimally binding. The negotiations on Afghanistan were finally successful and the so-called Geneva peace agreements were signed in the Swiss town on 14 April 1988 and came into force on 15 May of the same year.⁴⁴ The Geneva peace agreements were seen in a positive light by the Italian diplomacy. The Soviet withdrawal from Afghanistan eliminated a big obstacle to the East–West détente, gave Soviet–American cooperation a crucial role in solving international crises, and was an important contribution to the stabilization and development of European–Soviet relations.⁴⁵ According to the head of Bureau VI of the Farnesina's Political Affairs Directorate, Benedetto Amari, it was mainly foreign policy reasons that pushed Gorbachev to accept the Geneva treaties and to accelerate the end of the Soviet military presence in Afghanistan. Moscow felt the need to improve its image in Third World countries and in the United Nations. There was also the will to overcome one of the obstacles, as well as the Cambodian crisis, which hampered the improvement of relations with Communist China. But what was perhaps most important was Gorbachev's desire to use the withdrawal from Afghanistan as a tool to ameliorate relations with Western Europe and the United States. The Geneva agreements encouraged the chances of success of the upcoming fourth Gorbachev–Reagan summit and allowed a progressive détente in American–Soviet relations and pacification of the international system, pivotal to letting the Soviet leader concentrate on internal problems.⁴⁶ The Geneva agreements were guaranteed by Moscow and Washington, but they were not very effective and did not last long. The mujahidin did not accept the peace treaties and went on fighting against the Kabul government with the support of Pakistan⁴⁷ and tacit American consent. But despite the violations of the Geneva agreements, the Soviets carried on withdrawing from Afghanistan, and the last Soviet soldier left the country on 15 February 1989.

Striving for reconciliation: Italian diplomacy and negotiations between Zahir and the Soviets

The government in Rome wanted to participate in the pacification and reconstruction process in Afghanistan started by the Geneva peace process. An example of this was the Italians' financial contribution of US$14 million to the aid plan organized and coordinated by Sadrudding Aga Khan, the UN representative for aid to Afghanistan.⁴⁸

They also wanted to help the Soviet government to avoid an embarrassing complete political and diplomatic defeat in the Afghan conflict. With the Gorbachev administration, the already cordial Soviet–Italian relations had intensified. The Italian political class, both the centre-left parties which led the government and the PCI, looked favourably on the internal and international initiatives of Gorbachev and supported the process of reform and democratization in the Soviet Union.[49] Italian public and private economic firms, which had always had a passion for the Eastern countries,[50] also supported closer relations with the Soviet Union. In addition, there were serious foreign policy and Italian national interest reasons that pushed the Italians to adopt closer contacts with Moscow. During the Cold War, Italy had opposed the expansionist and hegemonic aims of Soviet Russia but it was not in favour of the disintegration of the Soviet Union, deeming that possibility to be a danger to peace and stability in Europe. Therefore, the government in Rome strongly supported the activity and political survival of the reformist Gorbachev administration. Regarding Afghanistan, Italian Foreign Minister Andreotti met Gorbachev in February 1987 and confirmed Italian and European wishes for a fast political and peaceful end to the conflict, expressing satisfaction with the growing signs of a new Soviet policy in the country.[51] The close ties between Zahir's Rome Group and the Italian diplomacy convinced the Farnesina, led by Secretary-General Bruno Bottai, of the chance of becoming a mediator between Moscow and the former king to try and form an Afghan national reconciliation government which also included communists and was not hostile to the Soviet Union. At the end of October 1988, Bottai let Zahir know that the Soviet diplomacy was interested in engaging in direct talks with him. The former king answered that he was ready to meet Soviet emissaries, but only in absolute secrecy.[52] On 4 November, a Soviet delegation led by Yulii Michailovič Vorontsov, deputy minister of foreign affairs and ambassador in Afghanistan,[53] met Zahir in Rome. The following day, Soviet diplomats Alexseev and Artemov met Bottai to thank Italian diplomacy for having facilitated contacts with the Afghan Rome Group. The meeting had been useful to inform Zahir on the situation in Afghanistan and the determined will of Moscow to promote national reconciliation there. Their impression was that Zahir could influence Afghan political events.[54] Bottai said that Italy wanted to be informed of the developments of the contacts between the Soviet Union and Zahir, and was convinced that the choice of national reconciliation was the only way of solving the Afghan conflict.[55] On 9 November, General Wali, a close aide of Zahir, met the head of Bureau XI of the Farnesina's Directorate of Political Affairs, Leopoldo Ferri di Lazara, to thank Italian diplomacy for having made the talks with the Soviets possible. Wali said that talks with Pakistani officials were also under way and declared Zahir's readiness to intensify cooperation with the government in Rome.[56] The Italian Ministry of Foreign Affairs decided to inform Washington about the discussions taking place between Zahir, Pakistan and Moscow. Meanwhile, the leader of the alliance of the Afghan Resistance parties, Burhanuddin Rabbani, went to Washington and met President Reagan and Secretary of State Shultz, who were about to be succeeded by the new George W. Bush administration.[57] According to the Italian ambassador in the United States, Rinaldo Petrignani, Rabbani was confident of an approaching military victory for the mujahidin and refused any compromise with the PDPA. The Afghan politician asked the Americans for their view on a possible return of Zahir to Afghanistan, underlining that only two parties out of seven of the Peshawar alliance supported the former king. The American administration declared that it was not against the return of Zahir if the Afghan political parties could come to an agreement on it. Reagan and Shultz confirmed the total American support of the Resistance forces and of the political regime they would establish in Afghanistan.[58] On 7 January 1989, Soviet Foreign Affairs Minister Eduard Shevardnadze met Andreotti in Paris.[59] The Soviet minister expressed his satisfaction with the outstanding state of Italian–Soviet relations, which had reached a new level and intensity after the visit of Italian Prime Minister Ciriaco De Mita to Moscow in October 1988, and showed interest in the possible political role of Zahir in Afghanistan. Zahir could play an important part in the pacification of Afghanistan, and Shevardnadze asked Italy to incite the former king to make an urgent decision on this. Zahir could use the Soviet presence to strengthen his influence in Afghanistan. According to Andreotti, it was vital for the timetable of Soviet withdrawal to be respected and for a peaceful transition to be implemented. Zahir, as the former king, had to be impartial towards the political factions and parties, but Andreotti accepted to personally transmit Shevardnadze's message to the Afghan exile in Rome. In mid-January, Andreotti met Zahir in Rome. The Roman minister communicated Shevardnadze's statements to Zahir and confirmed Italian readiness to facilitate communication between the former king and the Soviet government.[60] Meanwhile, the last phase of Soviet withdrawal came to an end. The Soviets kept their promise and, on 15 February, the last Russian soldier left Afghanistan.[61] After the Soviet withdrawal, Vorontsov decided to meet Zahir again and asked Italy for help.[62] Before the meeting between Vorontsov and Zahir, which took place on 21 February, the Foreign Ministry Secretary-General, Bottai, went to Zahir's residence to inform the former king in advance of some Soviet views on the future of Afghanistan.[63] The Soviets wanted the creation of an Afghan national unity government that could create the conditions for pacification of the country. Moscow was interested in Zahir's participation in the national reconciliation process and wanted him to make a public declaration supporting it. Bottai underlined Italy's desire to help bring about peace in Afghanistan in order to avoid further bloodshed in this stricken country. Zahir explained to Bottai that every section of the anti-communist resistance was completely hostile to the chief of the PDPA Kabul government, Mohammed Najibullah,[64] and it was not possible to go against public opinion. Political progress was possible only if a new government, representative of the majority of the Afghan people and not imposed by one warring party, came to power. A ceasefire was not realistic now because it would favour the pro-Soviet forces, which were better organized than the Resistance. Bottai gave Zahir confirmation of Italy's support and sympathy for his future actions and activities.[65] On 20 February, the Italian secretary general had a long talk with Vorontsov to discuss the Afghan situation after Soviet withdrawal.[66] Bottai stressed Italy's concern over the difficult political situation in Afghanistan and its possible negative repercussions on East–West relations. Italy had always played a constructive role in Afghanistan and wanted to help in the reconstruction process by, for example, supporting the humanitarian project of the Aga Khan. According to Vorontsov, the Afghan factions and parties had not fully understood that the Soviet withdrawal had completely changed the situation and that there was a serious risk of total anarchy. The Soviets had made several mistakes, including thinking they could run the country in a centralized way from Kabul despite the fact that the Afghans had mainly a tribal and religious identity and the capital was of limited importance to them. Moscow's idea was to weaken and hinder those groups of the Resistance which wanted a purely military solution to the conflict. To this end, it was important to stop supplying weapons to the warring parties, but the Americans' attitude towards Afghanistan was rigid and uncooperative, unlike the one they adopted in other regional crises. Pakistan's attitude was also worrying. After Zia ul-Haq's death, the civilians were back in power with the election of Benazir Bhutto as president. In Vorontsov's view, the Pakistani military and secret services had opted for a dangerous and intransigent policy in Afghanistan which was not shared by Bhutto and which could provoke a war with the Soviet Union as the Soviets could not tolerate Pakistani penetration into Afghanistan. Bhutto, according to the Soviet diplomat, was a kind of prisoner of the Pakistani military, which was single-handedly in charge of the country's defence and was participating in a huge drug-trafficking operation in Afghanistan.[67] Vorontsov stressed that Zahir could play a positive political role in Afghanistan. He was very popular with the Pashtuns in the South and also with some Islamic traditionalist fighters but time was running out, and Zahir needed to act if he wanted to have the chance of a political role.[68] During this time, the Italian government pushed hard to give Zahir a role in the Afghan political process and dialogue since it saw him as the right man to lead the pacification process. But Pakistan, the United States and the UK were not in favour of this strategy and preferred the option of a clear political and military victory of the anti-communist resistance and the fall of the Najibullah regime. According to many American officials, Zahir was 'a great pasta eater in his villa outside Rome',[69] who had done nothing to stop the Soviet occupation of Afghanistan.

Epilogue

As we know, in the years following the Soviet withdrawal, Zahir did not go back to Afghanistan. Pakistan, the Afghan Islamic parties and the Americans were against a political role of the former king in post-communist Afghanistan. Zahir, whom an Islamic terrorist tried to kill in Rome in 1991, carried on living in Rome until 2002, when he flew back to his native country.

During the 1980s, Italian foreign policy showed a constant interest in the Afghan conflict. The government in Rome, the Italian political parties and public opinion were against the Soviet invasion of Afghanistan and showed sincere sympathy towards the fight of the Afghan people against foreign occupying forces. But, as opposed to the United States and other European allies, Italy still wanted a political, not just a military, solution to the Afghan conflict – one based on a diplomatic agreement between the Afghan parties and the global and regional powers. This explains the strong Italian support for the monarchist groups gathered around the former king, Zahir. After Gorbachev became leader of the Soviet Union, Italian diplomacy tried to help the cooperation between Zahir and the Soviets, aiming at fostering a project of national reconciliation and union among all the Afghan political parties and factions.

These Italian efforts and projects were not successful. Italian diplomacy and government underestimated the tragic and heavy legacy of many years of war and violence and the mark that all this had left on Afghan society. Any idea of pacification and national reconciliation was impossible. But an important contribution to the failure of the Italian efforts of pacification came from the United States, which preferred complete and absolute victory by the anti-communist mujahidin rather than the creation of an Afghan government in which the former Afghan communists and Zahir had a significant role to play.

Notes

1   On Italian–Afghan relations in the twentieth century, see Luciano Monzali, *Un Re afghano in esilio a Roma: Amanullah e l'Afghanistan nella politica estera italiana 1919-1943* (Firenze: Le Lettere, 2012); Monzali, 'La politica estera italiana e l'occupazione sovietica dell'Afghanistan (1979-1989). Note e documenti', in Gianvito Galasso, Federico Imperato, Rosario Milano and Luciano Monzali (eds), *Europa e Medio Oriente 1973-1993* (Bari: Cacucci, 2017), 285–336. Regarding Afghanistan's history, see Amin Saikal, *Modern Afghanistan: A History of Struggle and Survival* (London: Tauris, 2006); Egidio Caspani and Ernesto Cagnacci, *Afghanistan crocevia dell'Asia* (Milan: Vallardi, 1951); William Kerr Fraser Tytler, *Afghanistan: A Study of Political Developments in Central and Southern Asia* (Oxford: Oxford University Press, 1953); Elisa Giunchi, *Afghanistan: Storia e società nel cuore dell'Asia* (Rome: Carocci, 2007); Martin Ewans, *Afghanistan: A New History* (London: Routledge, 2002); Thomas Barfield, *Afghanistan: A Cultural and Political History* (Princeton, NJ: Princeton University Press, 2010); Ludwig W. Adamec, *Afghanistan's Foreign Affairs to the Mid-Twentieth Century. Relations with the USSR, Germany and Britain* (Tucson: University of Arizona Press, 1974); Eugenio Di Rienzo, *Afghanistan: Il 'Grande Gioco', 1914–1947* (Rome: Salerno Editrice, 2014).
2   ASMAE, DGAP, Afghanistan, b. 3, Calisse to Italian Foreign Ministry, 25 November 1948; TNA, FO, 983/25, British representative in Kabul to Foreign Office, 1° December 1948.
3   Saikal, *Modern Afghanistan*, 174, 300.
4   See James F. Dobbins, *After the Taliban: Nation-Building in Afghanistan* (Washington, DC: Potomac, 2008); Barnett R. Rubin, *Afghanistan from the Cold War through the War on Terror* (Oxford: Oxford University Press, 2013), 9–18, 99–100; Florian Krampe, 'The Liberal Trap: Peacemaking and Peacebuilding in Afghanistan after 9/11', in Mikael Eriksson and Roland Kostić (eds), *Mediation and Liberal Peacebuilding: Peace from the Ashes of War?* (London: Routledge, 2013), 57–75.
5   On Afghanistan in the 1970s and 1980s and the great powers' policies, see Saikal, *Modern Afghanistan*; Odd Arne Westad, *The Global Cold War: Third World Interventions and the Making of Our Times* (Cambridge: Cambridge University Press, 2007), 299 et sqq.; Raymond L. Garthoff, *Détente and Confrontation: American-Soviet Relations from Nixon to Reagan* (Washington, DC: Brookings Institution, 1994), 977 et sqq.; Joseph J. Collins, *The Soviet Invasion of Afghanistan: A Study in the Use of Force*

in Soviet Foreign Policy (Lexington, MA: Lexington Books, 1986); Milan Hauner, *The Soviet War in Afghanistan: Patterns of Russian Imperialism* (Philadelphia: University Press of America, 1991); John Fullerton, *The Soviet Occupation of Afghanistan* (Hong Kong: Far Eastern Economic Review, 1983); Anthony Hyamn, *Afghanistan under Soviet Domination, 1964-91* (Houndsmills: Macmillan, 1992); Raja Anwar, *The Tragedy of Afghanistan: A First-Hand Account* (London: Verso, 1988), 92 et sqq.; Rodric Braithwaite, *Afgantsy: The Russians in Afghanistan 1979-89* (Oxford: Oxford University Press, 2011).

6 On Italy's political events in the 1980s, see Piero Craveri, *La Repubblica dal 1958 al 1992* (Turin: UTET, 1995), 638 et sqq.; Francesco Barbagallo, *Enrico Berlinguer* (Rome: Carocci, 2007), 269 et sqq.; Aurelio Lepre, *Storia della prima Repubblica. L'Italia dal 1942 al 1992* (Bologna: Il Mulino, 1993), 284 et sqq.; Massimo Pini, *Craxi: Una vita, un'era politica* (Milan: Mondadori, 2006); Simona Colarizi and Marco Gervasoni, *La cruna dell'ago: Craxi, il partito socialista e la crisi della Repubblica* (Rome: Laterza, 2005); Antonio Varsori, *La Cenerentola d'Europa? L'Italia e l'integrazione europea dal 1947 a oggi* (Soveria Mannelli: Rubbettino, 2010); Luca Riccardi, *L'internazionalismo difficile. La 'diplomazia' del PCI e il Medio Oriente dalla crisi petrolifera alla caduta del muro di Berlino (1973-1989)* (Soveria Mannelli: Rubbettino, 2013).

7 AP, CD, Meeting of 9 January 1980, 7190 et sqq. See Luigi Vittorio Ferraris (ed.), *Manuale della politica estera italiana 1947-1993* (Rome: Laterza, 1996), 488.

8 AP, CD, Meeting of 9 January 1980, Sarti's speech, 7244-9.

9 Ibid., 7245.

10 On the Italian communists and the Afghan matter, see Antonio Rubbi, *Il mondo di Berlinguer* (Rome: Napoleone, 1994), 157-68. Also see Silvio Pons, *Berlinguer e la fine del comunismo* (Turin: Einaudi, 2006), 169-71.

11 Rubbi, *Il mondo di Berlinguer*, 158.

12 Ibid., 160-1.

13 *Forte preoccupazione*, *L'Unità*, 29 dicembre 1979.

14 Ibid.

15 Rubbi, *Il mondo di Berlinguer*; 158 et sqq.; Pons, *Berlinguer e la fine del comunismo*, 169-71.

16 See *Documents on British Policy Overseas* (London: Routledge, 2012), s. III, vol. 8, docs 11, 13; *Akten zur Auswärtigen Politik der Bundesrepublik Deutschland 1979* (München: Oldenbourg, 2010), vol. 2; *Akten zur Auswärtigen Politik der Bundesrepublik Deutschland 1980* (München: Oldenbourg, 2011), vol. 1.

17 ILS, GA, s. Afghanistan, b. 32, Italian Ministry of Foreign Affairs, Memorandum, 21 January 1980, with annexes; ibid., Italian Ministry of Foreign Affairs, Memorandum, 22 January 1980.

18 Richard N. Gardner, *Mission Italy: Gli anni di piombo raccontati dall'ambasciatore americano a Roma 1977-1981* (Milan: Mondadori, 2004), 321-2, 338. Also see: ILS, GA, b. 1009, Andreotti a La Rocca, 15 June 1980; Giulio Andreotti, *I Diari segreti* (Milan: Solferino, 2020), 63 et sqq.

19 Ferraris, *Manuale della politica estera italiana 1947-1993*, 367.

20 Gardner, *Mission Italy*, 353.

21 See Steve Coll, *La guerra segreta della Cia* (Milan: Rizzoli, 2004), 142.

22 Simona Colarizi and Marco Gervasoni, *La cruna dell'ago: Craxi, il partito socialista e la crisi della Repubblica* (Rome: Laterza, 2005), 42 et sqq.

23 See Federico Coen and Paolo Borioni, *Le cassandre di Mondoperaio: Una stagione creativa della cultura socialista* (Venice: Marsilio, 1999), 55; Carlo Ripa Di Meana, 'Bettino Craxi e il dissenso. Una lunga e grande storia', in Andrea Spiri (ed.), *Bettino Craxi, il socialismo europeo e il sistema internazionale* (Venice: Marsilio, 2006), 191–218.
24 The proceedings are published in Federico Coen (ed.), *La sinistra per l'Afghanistan* (Venice: Marsilio, 1981).
25 Text of the speech: http://presidenti.quirinale.it/Pertini/documenti/per_disc_31dic_82.htm. On Pertini, president of the Republic, see Antonio Maccanico, *Con Pertini al Quirinale: Diari 1978-1985* (Bologna: Il Mulino, 2014); Marco Gervasoni, *Le armate del president: La politica del Quirinale nell'Italia repubblicana* (Venice: Marsilio, 2015), 91 et sqq.
26 On the foreign policy of the Craxi-Andreotti governments, see Giulio Andreotti, *L'URSS vista da vicino* (Milan: Rizzoli, 1988); Andreotti, *Gli USA visti da vicino* (Milan: Rizzoli, 1989); Gennaro Acquaviva and Antonio Badini, *La pagina saltata della Storia* (Venice: Marsilio, 2010); Roberto Gaja, *L'Italia nel mondo bipolare. Per una storia della politica estera italiana (1943–1991)* (Bologna: Il Mulino, 1995), 201 et sqq.; Ennio Di Nolfo (ed.), *La politica estera dell'Italia negli anni Ottanta* (Manduria: Lacaita, 2003); Gennaro Acquaviva and Luigi Covatta (eds), *Il PSI nella crisi della prima Repubblica* (Venice: Marsilio, 2012); Luigi Guidobono Cavalchini, 'I rapporti con il mondo arabo', in Mario Barone and Ennio Di Nolfo (eds), *Giulio Andreotti. L'uomo, il cattolico, lo statista* (Soveria Mannelli: Rubbettino, 2010), 105–44; Luciano Monzali, *Gli Italiani di Dalmazia e le relazioni italo-jugoslave nel Novecento* (Venice: Marsilio, 2015); Monzali, *Giulio Andreotti e le relazioni italo-austriache 1972–1992* (Merano: Alfabeta, 2016); Francesco Lefebvre D'Ovidio and Luca Micheletta (eds), *Giulio Andreotti e l'Europa* (Rome: Edizioni di Storia e Letteratura, 2017).
27 For an accurate analysis, see Diego Cordovez and Selig S. Harrison, *Out of Afghanistan: The Inside Story of the Soviet Withdrawal* (Oxford: Oxford University Press, 1995).
28 ILS, GA, Afghanistan, b. 32, Ercolano to Andreotti, 12 May 1984.
29 Andreotti, *L'Urss vista da vicino*, 194.
30 ILS, GA, Afghanistan, b. 32, Direction of Political Affairs Ministry of Foreign Affairs, Bureau XI, Teucci, Memorandum, 24 May 1985.
31 Ibid.
32 Ibid.
33 Andreotti, *L'URSS vista da vicino*, 241.
34 ILS, GA, Bettino Craxi, b. 271, Badini, Memorandum, 17 March 1986, annex from Badini to Quaroni, 17 March 1986.
35 Ibid.
36 ILS, GA, Afghanistan, b. 32, Ballero, Memorandum on the Afghan situation from March 1983 to September 1987, annex from Ballero to Andreotti, September 1987.
37 Ibid.
38 On the Soviet policy of national reconciliation in Afghanistan, see Braithwaite, 274 et sqq.; Antonio Giustozzi, *War, Politics and Society in Afghanistan, 1978–1992* (London: Hurst, 2000), 120 et sqq.
39 Ballero, Memorandum on the Afghan situation from March 1983 to September 1987.
40 ILS, GA, Afghanistan, b. 32, Cappello, Memorandum, 26 January 1988.
41 ILS, GA, Afghanistan, b. 32, Bonalumi to Andreotti, 5 February 1988.

42 Raymond L. Garthoff, *The Great Transition: American-Soviet Relations and the End of the Cold War* (Washington, DC: Brookings Institution, 1994), 721; Cordovez and Harrison, *Out of Afghanistan*; Riaz M. Khan, *Untying the Afghan Knot: Negotiating Soviet Withdrawal* (Lahore: Sang-e-Meel, 2005).
43 Westad, *The Global Cold War*, 376.
44 The Geneva peace agreements consisted in: a bilateral treaty of mutual non-interference between Pakistan and Afghanistan, a Pakistani–Afghan agreement on the voluntary return of the refugees to Afghanistan, a declaration on the international guarantees signed by Moscow and Washington, and a treaty signed by Pakistan, Afghanistan, the United States and the Soviet Union on the 'Interrelationships for the Settlement of the Situation Relating to Afghanistan'. The Geneva agreements called for the existing borders to be respected, the right to return for the refugees, the survival of the Najibullah government, which was ready to start a national reconciliation process, and the withdrawal of the Soviet forces from Afghanistan by 15 February 1989. The text of the Geneva peace agreements is published in Cordovez and Harrison, *Out of Afghanistan*, 389–97. Regarding the negotiations that led to these agreements, see: Cordovez and Harrison, *Out of Afghanistan*; William Maley, 'The Geneva Accords of April 1988', in Amin Saikal and William Maley (eds), *The Soviet Withdrawal from Afghanistan* (Cambridge: Cambridge University Press, 1989), 12–28. Also see the Soviet documentation published by the digital archive of the Wilson Center: digitalarchive.wilsoncenter.org, e.g. *Ronald Reagan on Afghanistan*, 10 December 1987; http://digitalarchive.wilsoncenter.org/document/117246, *Conversation between M.S. Gorbachev and US Vice President George H.W. Bush*, 10 December 1987. A Soviet interpretation of these agreements can be found in Eduard Shevardnadze, *The Future Belongs to Freedom* (London: Sinclair-Stevenson, 1991), 67–70. Also see Garthoff, *The Great Transition*, 736.
45 ILS, GA, Afghanistan, b. 32, General Direction of Political Affairs, Bureau VI, Amari, Memorandum for the General Director of Political Affairs, 16 April 1988.
46 Ibid.
47 On Pakistan's attitude towards the Geneva treaties, see ILS, GA, Afghanistan, b. 32, Fornara to the Ministry of Foreign Affairs, 17 April 1988; Monzali, 'La politica estera italiana e l'occupazione sovietica dell'Afghanistan', 324 et sqq.
48 See the ANSA press communiqués of 19 July 1988 in ILS, GA, Afghanistan, b. 32.
49 On Italian–Soviet relations, see Roberto Gaja, *L'Italia nel mondo bipolare: Per una storia della politica estera italiana (1943-1991)* (Bologna: Il Mulino 1995); Sergio Romano, *Memorie di un conservatore* (Milan: Longanesi, 2002), 176 et sqq.; Bruna Bagnato, *Prove di Ostpolitik: Politica ed economia nella strategia italiana verso l'Unione Sovietica (1958-1963)* (Florence: Olschki, 2003); Giorgio Petracchi, 'L'Italia e l'Ostpolitik', in Ennio Di Nolfo (ed.), *La politica estera dell'Italia negli anni Ottanta*, 293–318; Fabio Bettanin, 'Le relazioni fra Italia e Urss nella prima fase della distensione', *Mondo contemporaneo* 2 (2009); Alessandro Salacone, *La diplomazia del dialogo. Italia e Urss tra coesistenza pacifica e distensione (1958-1968)* (Rome: Viella, 2017); Fabio Bettanin, Michail Prozumenikov, Adriano Roccucci and Alessandro Salacone, *L'Italia vista dal Cremlino. Gli anni della distensione negli archivi del Pcus 1953-1970* (Rome: Viella, 2015); Luca Riccardi, 'Appunti sull'Ostpolitik di Moro', in Italo Garzia, Luciano Monzali and Massimo Bucarelli (eds), *Aldo Moro, l'Italia repubblicana e i Balcani* (Nardò: Besa – Salento Books, 2012), 58–88.
50 Gaja, *L'Italia nel mondo bipolare*, 243–4.

51 *Record of Conversation between M.S. Gorbachev with Italian Minister of Foreign Affairs Giulio Andreotti*, 27 February 1987, http://digitalarchive.wilsoncenter.org/document/117234.
52 ILS, GA, Afghanistan, b. 32, Bottai to the Italian Embassy in Moscow, 31 October 1988.
53 On the Soviet will to use Zahir politically, see *Report of the Soviet Ambassador Y. M. Vorontsov, concerning the current political situation inside Afghanistan and the possibilities of solving the Afghan question*, 3 February 1989, http://digitalarchive.wilsoncenter.org/document/113128. Also see the Memoirs of Gorbachev's adviser, Andrei Grachev, in Andrei Grachev, *Gorbaciov's Gamble: Soviet Foreign Policy and the End of the Cold War* (Cambridge: Polity Press, 2008), 100 et sqq.
54 ILS, GA, Afghanistan, b. 32, Bottai to the Italian Embassy in Moscow, 5 November 1988.
55 Ibid.
56 ILS, GA, Afghanistan, b. 32, Ferri, Memorandum, 9 November 1988.
57 ILS, GA, Afghanistan, b. 32, Petrignani to the Italian Ministry of Foreign Affairs, 9 November 1988.
58 Ibid.
59 See an account in: ILS, GA, Afghanistan, b. 32, Perlot to the Italian Embassy in Moscow, 9 January 1989; ibid., Perlot, Memorandum, 9 January 1989.
60 Andreotti, *Gli Usa visti da vicino*, 264.
61 For an Italian analysis of this process and its consequences in Kabul, see ILS, GA, Afghanistan, b. 32, Italian Ministry of Foreign Affairs, Memorandum, 30 January 1989; Monzali, 'La politica estera italiana e l'occupazione sovietica dell'Afghanistan (1979–89). Note e documenti', 330–1.
62 ILS, GA, Afghanistan, b. 32, Bottai to the Italian Embassy in Moscow, 9 February 1989.
63 ILS, GA, Afghanistan, b. 32, Bottai to the Italian Embassy in Bonn, Islamabad, Moscow, and others, 20 February 1989.
64 For some information on Mohammed Najibullah, see C. Andrew, V. Mitrokhin, *L'Archivio Mitrokhin*, 389 et sqq.
65 Bottai to the Italian Embassy in Bonn, Islamabad, Moscow, and others, 20 February 1989.
66 ILS, GA, Afghanistan, b. 32, Bottai to the Italian Embassy in Bonn, Islamabad, Moscow, and others, 21 February 1989.
67 Ibid.
68 Ibid.
69 Coll, *La guerra segreta della CIA*, 215. On the Italian attempts to convince the Washington government to support Zahir, see Monzali, 'La politica estera italiana e l'occupazione sovietica dell'Afghanistan', 333–4.

15

Italy and Pakistan, 1971–91

Giuseppe Spagnulo

Italy and the consolidation and development of the Pakistani state (1948–70)

Italy established diplomatic relations with Pakistan in August 1948, exactly one year after the creation of the aforementioned state, following the end of the Anglo-Indian Empire and its partition with the Indian Union.[1] Since the creation of Pakistan, Italy had looked at this new Muslim country as being of interest in two main ways. First, from an economic/commercial perspective, aimed at exploiting the decolonization and the 1947 partition in order to increase its exports and the economic access of the main national companies in a geopolitical area which, until then, had been completely reserved for British colonial power. Second, from a political perspective aimed at considering the new Pakistani state as potentially destined to increase its influence in the Muslim world and especially in the Middle East thanks to its size, its demography (in 1947, Pakistan was the most populated Islamic country in the world), the strength of its army, and not least because of the prestige obtained by having succeeded in freeing itself both from London rule and from the inclusion in a state with a Hindu majority, as would have happened if the territory of British India had remained united and which is what the Indian Congress Party had long claimed.[2]

Therefore, Italy would have looked at Pakistan as the Far Eastern part of an area (spreading eastward from the southern Mediterranean to include the entire Middle East and Afghanistan) in which to extend its attempt to define its own 'Islamic policy'. This attempt would have had to face the diminished spaces of autonomy granted to Italy by its resized post-war possibilities, by the redefinition of international order according to the bipolar criteria of the Cold War and by its decision to join the 'Atlantic bloc' in 1949. Just by virtue of this choice, Italy tried to carve out an intermediary role for itself, a sort of 'bridge' between the Western world and the Islamic world, taking advantage of a geographical position which lent itself almost naturally to such a function and which had thus already served as a connection between these two worlds during very different historical moments.[3] Pakistan also regarded Italy with respect, seeing it as a linking country between America, Asia and Africa with which it could develop a friendly understanding and collaborative relationship, as was actually the case.[4]

In the 1950s, an Italian political presence in Asia began, leading to a buzz of activity, with a series of exchange visits between Asian and Italian government figures. The aim was to strengthen ties with these countries, many of which had just become independent, to foster economic relations and to exchange ideas on international politics with their leaders. Moreover, countries like India and Pakistan itself began to be considered fundamental by the government of Rome, 'not only for the stability and welfare of Asia but also for the consolidation of peace in the world'.[5] Without a doubt, the most important event in the Italy–Pakistan political relations of the 1950s was the visit of Foreign Minister Gaetano Martino during one of the stages of his 'long journey in Asia'.[6] It was the first official trip of an Italian foreign minister 'beyond the Suez Canal',[7] deemed necessary in view of the major developments in international politics and the importance assumed by Asia, whose lack of interest would be accompanied by a decisive removal of Italy from a framework of relationships of primary importance shortly after the end of the Korean War and the Bandung Conference which kicked off the beginning of the Non-Aligned Movement.[8]

This Italian activism brought about good results in Pakistan: a series of commercial agreements and technical cooperation laid the basis for the constant presence of Italy among the main architects of the economic development of the 'Land of the Pure'. The Italy–Pakistan bond of friendship was certainly also favoured by their shared position on international political alignment. In fact, in order to get out of an insecure relationship with its neighbour-rivals, India and Afghanistan, which was exacerbated by an internal instability inherited from the Partition, the Pakistani government soon chose a clear and unambiguous side in the context of the Cold War: an alliance with the United States and the Western bloc.[9] Moreover, Pakistan's weak situation (a polymorphic state divided into two sections located over a thousand kilometers from one another) pushed its rulers to move away from Liberal-democratic government hypotheses and to adopt authoritarian solutions that culminated in a military coup d'état which took place in October 1958 at the hands of army commander-in-chief Mohammad Ayub Khan, assisted by Pakistani President Iskander Mirza, who was also forced to resign and go into exile after a few days.[10]

In general, it can be said that starting from the second half of the 1950s there was a twofold Italian political orientation towards the Indian subcontinent. This orientation was directly linked to the international positions of the subcontinent's two major countries (India and Pakistan) and also to the evolution of the Middle Eastern political context, with the division between some more pro-Western countries (Turkey, Iran, Saudi Arabia and Iraq until 1958, and Pakistan itself) and others (Nasser's Egypt, Syria, Algeria, etc.) that were distinguishing themselves by carrying on with a neutralist and anti-imperialist policy very similar to that of Indian leader Jawaharlal Nehru.[11] Thus, on the one hand, good Italian–Pakistani relations were facilitated by common international alliances while on the other the government of Rome tried not to cut itself off from the congeniality of a country like India. In the first years since independence, India had acquired great prestige in much of the Arab world as well as in Asia and Africa with its non-alignment policy, not to mention the special relationship that Nehru had established with Tito's Yugoslavia, namely with countries that were decisive for Italian foreign policy.

In the intricate context of the Indian subcontinent, Italy then tried to carve out the role of a 'bridge' for itself, attempting to at least avoid taking positions on thorny issues which would be regarded as unpleasant by one country or the other (e.g. the neverending issue of Kashmir) and trying, where possible, to collaborate with both. It was a foreign policy that reflected Italy's limited decision-making power in this geopolitical area, traditionally considered remote by the Italian political class or, at any rate, mainly reserved for more powerful countries.[12]

In fact, during the turbulent crisis that hit the Indian subcontinent in the 1960s, Italy tended to adopt the general guidelines of its Western allies but often distinguished itself by not excessively exposing itself to a partisan bias, avoiding favouring either India or Pakistan. Thus, in 1962, Italy supported the government of Nehru in a very bland manner in the brief conflict with China despite pressure from the United States to encourage greater interventionism of the Western world in an anti-Chinese capacity.[13] Italy's lukewarm attitude, which did not stray far from simple statements of solidarity with India and the sending of some blankets for the Indian army, was probably a response to the need not to complicate relations with Pakistan, which in addition to feeling betrayed by its Western allies (who were arming its worst enemy) and internationally isolated, believed itself to be rather 'neglected' even by Italy.[14]

During the second Indo-Pakistani conflict, however, the official position of the government of Rome was fully aligned with the American lack of support for Pakistan, which was held responsible for provoking the Indian attack. But, as usual, in consultations with Pakistani diplomats, Italian foreign affairs representatives took great care to use non-hostile language, suggesting a peaceful resolution of the crisis within the United Nations.[15]

As far as concerns the Kashmir issue, although the general guidelines of international politics could certainly have pushed Italy towards greater support for Pakistani positions, efforts were made to remain as neutral as possible. Talks with Pakistani leaders often led them to claim that Italy was unable to support the plebiscite in Kashmir. A similar problem also lay at the centre of the South Tyrol matter, which threatened Italy from within its own borders and complicated its relations with Austria so that, in the opinion of Palazzo Chigi, adherence to the plebiscitary principle in the Kashmiri matter could have led to a series of retaliations in Italy. It is not to be excluded, however, that this argument was used as an excellent alibi for not excessively compromising relations with New Delhi.[16]

All in all, Italian–Pakistani relations remained friendly throughout the 1960s, and the huge share of public work entrusted to Italian companies in the 'Land of the Pure' was proof of this. In particular, Italy participated in the Indus plan, a project to build dams and canals for the use of river water from the main Pakistani river, launched in 1960 with international funding under the control of the International Bank for Reconstruction and Development (IBRD). Italy also entered the Aid-to-Pakistan Consortium in 1963.[17] A visit by Minister of Industry Giulio Andreotti in February 1967 was welcomed very positively by the Pakistani authorities, and the following year a contract for the construction of the Tarbala Dam, a colossal job, was assigned to an Italian–French consortium led by Italian companies (the most important being Impregilo SpA). This work was financed by the IBRD yet again and constituted one of the main interests of Italy in Pakistan in the following years. The construction of the dam required the collaboration of five thousand technicians from various companies, mostly Italian, and fifteen thousand indigenous workers and was completed in April 1976.[18]

Italy and Pakistan from 1971 to 1978

The Indo-Pakistani war of 1965 had marked the slow but inexorable political decline of Ayub Khan, whose attempts at reform and modernization imposed from above had dissatisfied almost all the Pakistani social classes as well as religious sectors, and had led to him being increasingly isolated and not well-tolerated.

Between 1966 and 1969, in various urban areas, protest demonstrations against the government occurred to which the authorities responded with mass arrests. The war had especially exacerbated the situation in East Pakistan: here, the autonomous demands of the Bengali population had always been at the centre of Pakistani internal debate and had also often been inappropriately suppressed. The main Bengali party, the Awami League, under the leadership of Mujibir Rahman, presented a six-point programme in 1966 to promote the autonomy of the eastern province.

The central government was now accused of carrying out a colonial policy against East Bengal, which was underrepresented at all levels even though for Islamabad (the newly founded capital completed in 1967) it constituted an important source of foreign currency and absorbed many of Pakistan's goods.[19] Rahman's programme and the Bengali claims were ignored by the ruling class of the Northwest, who persisted in interpreting them as an attempt by the Indian side to fragment Pakistan. When, two years later, Mujibur Rahman was accused of conspiring with India, Bengali resentment resulted in massive student demonstrations. In this context of increasing unrest, on 25 March 1969, Ayub Khan resigned.

General Agha Mohammed Yahya Khan, commander-in-chief of the army, imposed martial law again, dissolved the National Assembly and provincial assemblies, abrogated the Constitution of 1962 and, on 31 March 1969, proclaimed himself president. After re-establishing political activities, the general called for new elections, perhaps foreseeing, in light of the very high number of independent parties and candidates, that the vote would be fragmented, and that the armed forces could therefore continue to maintain control of the national political scene.[20]

Conversely, the general elections of 7 December 1970 caused a political earthquake: the Awami League won all the seats in the National Assembly reserved for East Pakistan except two, thus obtaining the right to form the central government. In the West, the Pakistan Peoples' Party (PPP) of former foreign minister Zulfikar Ali Bhutto won the majority of votes, which came from social classes that had been disadvantaged by Ayub Khan's reforms, especially the poorer classes in urban and rural areas of Punjab and Sind. The programmes of the Awami League demanded provincial autonomy for East Bengal while the PPP promised to restructure society in a more egalitarian sense.

In the face of the reluctance of the leaders of the armed forces and Bhutto to acknowledge the Awami League victory, the situation rapidly deteriorated. When the Awami League launched a campaign of civil disobedience in March 1971, Islamabad responded by arresting Mujibur Rahman and sending the army to quell the revolt with the collaboration of some religious parties such as the Jamaat-e-Islami, which considered the Bengali rebels 'enemies of Islam',[21] and paramilitary forces composed mainly of Bihari (an ethnic group which had fled en-masse from Bengal during the Partition).

The suppression of the protests in East Pakistan was fierce. The university and the headquarters of the unions and newspapers in Dhaka were destroyed, the army entered university campuses, killing male students and raping female ones, the Awami League's activists and sympathizers were systematically eliminated and the population, primarily the Hindu one, was terrorized. The atrocities committed by the Punjabi soldiers, of which the population in western Pakistan was kept in the dark by a press subject to strict censorship, fuelled the determination of the rebels but also induced several million Bengalis (ten million, according to various estimates) to leave the country and relocate to India.[22]

In the context of the international situation at that moment, which was marked by a strong international mobilization for the 'freedom of the people', and for the resistance of the Vietnamese revolutionary forces against US intervention, the battle of the Bengalis was seen by many in the Western world as a phenomenon similar to the struggles of Algeria or Vietnam against an oppressive external regime (with this being exactly how Pakistan's domination by the Punjabi military was viewed).

The Soviet leadership invited Yahya to end the violence in Bengal without interrupting economic and military assistance to India. Beijing, however, publicly supported the Pakistani government although, in private, Zhou Enlai, worried that the conflict could escalate and induce India and the USSR to intervene, invited the Pakistani government to make every effort to normalize relations with its eastern wing.[23] From the United States, there was no official statement against the suppression in East Bengal even though President Nixon was fully aware of the atrocities committed by Pakistani soldiers, as they were described in several telegrams sent by both the US consul in Dhaka, Archer Blood, who did not hesitate to describe what was happening under his eyes as 'genocide', and the US ambassador in New Delhi.[24]

Nixon and national security advisor, Henry Kissinger, went on to privately support Yahya Khan against the position of the State Department, which was more critical of the suppression. The government of Islamabad was, however, reassured that the United States would not interfere with 'Pakistani internal issues' and would not take any initiatives that might jeopardize the country.[25]

A phase of secret diplomacy was under way between Washington, Beijing and Islamabad, which culminated in Kissinger's secret visit to the Chinese capital in July 1971 and, a year later, in a meeting between Nixon and Zhou Enlai. This is why the US president did not want to take a stand in favour of the Bengali positions; in order not to compromise the Pakistani leadership, the essential vehicle for getting closer to China. Kissinger tried to justify the position of the Nixon administration with the following:

> We faced a dilemma. The United States could not condone a brutal military repression in which thousands of civilians were killed and from which millions fled to India for safety. There was no doubt about the strong-arm tactics of the Pakistani military. But Pakistan was our sole channel to China.[26]

The number of deaths ended up being much higher than was originally thought: hundreds of thousands or, according to other estimates, even a few million.[27]

The Italian government was aware of the brutality of the Pakistani suppression in East Bengal. A series of letters and petitions reached the Italian Ministry of Foreign Affairs and the Italian Head of State requesting interventions in order to stop the atrocities of Islamabad, to save the leader of the Awami League, Mujibur Rahman, and to recognize the independence of Bangladesh. Bangladesh also asked Italy, as a member of the Aid-to-Pakistan Consortium, to suspend all funding because, according to the Stop-Aid-to-Pakistan Campaign Committee, any economic aid would have been spent on carrying out massacres.[28]

In 1971, Italy was elected as a member of the UN Security Council. It took a stand similar to that of the United States on the civil war in East Bengal and was inspired by the principle of non-interference in the internal affairs of a sovereign state. This substantial orientation of Rome's government had already emerged in the first consultations with British diplomacy and within the Western European Union (WEU). The Foreign Office had been approached quite regularly and at various institutional levels by Italians, who wanted to obtain updated information on the Pakistani crisis, a sign of clear public interest in the situation in spite of Italy's limited involvement in that area.[29] In particular, concern for the Italian community present in Pakistan and especially in East Bengal, most of whom were Catholic missionaries, emerged. They were also worried about economic/financial issues linked to the construction of the Tarbala dam, for the realization of which Italy had granted loans to the Islamabad government. During the Italian-British talks in May 1971, London's diplomats made the dramatic gravity of the situation in Pakistan clear to the Italian interlocutors, stressing that this crisis was aggravated by financial bankruptcy and the winds of war with India, which made Whitehall fear the disintegration of the state created by Jinnah and Lord Mountbatten.

'This was why HMG was supporting West Pakistan; because otherwise it would disintegrated'.[30]

The Under-Secretary for Foreign Affairs, Angelo Salizzoni, spoke about Italian attempts to intervene between the Indian and Pakistani governments, urging them to contain the situation. Italian and British talks also addressed the likelihood of UN Security Council involvement. Indeed, a private meeting in London between UN Secretary-General U-Thant, the Secretary of State for Foreign Affairs and the British Commonwealth Alec Douglas-Home, and the US Secretary of State William Rogers had already taken place. The Director of Political Affairs in the Ministry of Foreign Affairs, Roberto Ducci, expressed some perplexity about the idea of the UN intervention since he judged the Pakistani crisis to be an internal one, agreeing with his British interlocutor, the Under-Secretary of the Foreign Office, Anthony Royle.[31]

In the WEU conferences, the Italian diplomat Pasquale Ricciulli supported more or less the same ideas as Ducci.[32]

According to the Italian government, therefore, the Pakistani crisis was essentially a crisis of an internal nature, which could be resolved by Pakistan autonomously through 'politics of wise farsightedness',[33] without their seeking external interventions or UN Security Council ones. The only desirable intervention would have been a humanitarian one, encouraging assistance to the Bengali refugees in order not to offload onto India the burden of what was turning into a real civil war.[34] But soon enough, East Bengal's drama could no longer be overlooked by the international community and the UN. In July 1971, Aldo Moro had a talk with the Pakistani ambassador, Nawaz Khan, in which he expressed his full solidarity with the Pakistani people and his belief that the government of Islamabad could favour the search for solutions that would bring an end to the crisis, employing a spirit of collaboration and detente with the Bengalis and India.[35] Moro said he would consider any initiative that would not further exacerbate the disagreements, renewing the hope that a formula could be found which, considering the interests of all parties, would encourage a return to an atmosphere of peace and active collaboration on the Indian subcontinent. To reach this goal, Moro no longer excluded UN intervention (contrary to the wishes of Pakistan) but he left the non-interference principle intact.[36]

On 3 August 1971, Secretary-General U-Thant sent a memorandum to the UN Security Council president, the Italian Piero Vinci, in which he was asked to do everything possible to ease the tension between India and Pakistan. Meanwhile, New Delhi strengthened its position by signing a treaty of peace, friendship and cooperation with the USSR.[37] This was the Indian response to the speech Nixon gave on 15 July, when the US president revealed that Kissinger's trip to China had taken place and announced his next visit would be in May 1972 at the latest. The Indian leadership feared that a dangerous Washington–Islamabad–Beijing axis was forming against New Delhi.[38]

The United States and its Western allies made every effort to prevent India from intervening in the East Bengal crisis. In addition to pressuring the Pakistani authorities not to condemn Mujibur Rahman to the death penalty, the Nixon presidency offered humanitarian assistance to the Bengali refugees who had sought refuge in India, thus hoping not to give New Delhi an excuse to start a war. However, there were profound contradictions in US policy regarding Indira Gandhi's state, if not a true leaning towards Pakistan.[39]

Partly because of the influence of Washington, Moro continued to support non-interference in the affairs of Pakistan, even when the refugee problem had become unsustainable. He felt it necessary to do something about this serious matter and worked to provide aid to the Bengali refugees, together with the United States and Britain. In particular, the Italian government and the Italian Red Cross provided them with medicines and basic necessities and participated in the United Nations High Commissioner for Refugees (UNHCR) and the European Economic Community (EEC) multilateral assistance programs.[40]

The Indo–Soviet treaty of friendship was considered alarming by the Italian government as it marked the definitive sliding of India into the area of Soviet influence, the end of non-alignment, and greater international polarization. All of this contributed greatly to inspiring Rome to adopt a general pro-Pakistani political line during the November–December 1971 crisis.[41] For instance, the former ambassador in Karachi, Luca Dainelli, wrote an article in *Rivista di Studi Politici Internazionali* entitled *Il dramma pakistano* ('The Pakistani drama'), in which he reminded Europe of the need to defend Islamabad and heal the wounds opened in East Bengal.[42]

On 21 November 1971, India, which already supported the Mukti Bahini (Bengali Freedom Fighters), began to amass its troops on the East Pakistan border. According to the Indian government, the maintenance of ten million Bengali refugees was an unbearable burden from a logistical and economic point of view. New Delhi also feared that a prolonged civil war could have dangerous repercussions on the north-eastern areas of India, including West Bengal, which were affected by profound social tension, and that the Awami League could be bypassed by more radical elements. But as Pakistani historiography has always said, it is not to be excluded that Indian leadership looked at the Bengal civil war as an opportunity to fragment and weaken Pakistan.[43]

On 22 November, Washington informed the Italian government of a meeting in Moscow which had been planned for 26 November and would involve Soviet and US officials using the United Nations to try and find a way to avoid the conflict escalating.[44] But on 3 December, the Pakistanis bombed the Indian positioning and then Indian troops invaded East Bengal, occupying vast territories within a few days. Nixon, who had been forced by the pressure of American public opinion to suspend military and then economic assistance to Pakistan, secretly invited his allies in the region to send weapons and equipment to Pakistan. Moreover, he sent a warship to the Bay of Bengal in order to convince the USSR not to intervene. China provided military aid to Pakistan in a very limited manner and just at the end of hostilities, refusing to intervene militarily even though a Chinese mobilization would have distracted the Indian troops in Aksai Chin or near the border with Sikkim or Arunachal Pradesh, slowing their advance in Bengal.[45]

The war between Pakistan and India lasted just two weeks and promoted India as a regional power. Despite the UN condemnation of human rights violations, the organization failed to find a political solution to the crisis before the outbreak of the war and was equally ineffective during the conflict. In the meetings that took place in the aftermath of the outbreak of hostilities, the People's Republic of China's attacks on the USSR stood out in particular. China had been recognized as a permanent member of the Security Council just a month earlier.

The USSR opposed the resolutions that were presented twice, allowing the Indian forces to carry on the *blitzkrieg* against Pakistani Bengal. On 7 December, a majority vote in the General Assembly called for an immediate ceasefire and withdrawal of the Indian troops, but it was in vain. The United States asked for a new Security Council summons on 12 December, but the war ended before appropriate measures could be taken.

Italy, in collaboration with other members of the Council, had tried to mediate as much as possible: starting from a general pro-Pakistan leaning, it had proposed the appointment of a smaller committee in the Council in order to facilitate the search for a solution. But it was merely an academic expedient, rendered pointless by the facts.[46] The UN's ineffectiveness during the crisis in Bengal was widely criticized. The conflict also demonstrated the slowness of the decisions, which was precisely the cause of the failure of any decisive action to stop the war. In any case, the Pakistani defeat was total. Islamabad lost half its fleet, a third of its army and a quarter of its air force, saw Indian troops penetrate deep into its territory and left about ninety-three thousand soldiers in the hands of the Indians. Yahya Khan handed in his resignation on 20 December 1971, after appointing Bhutto as the chief administrator of martial law. In January 1972, the Eastern Pakistani wing became formally independent and was named Bangladesh.

It was the end of the Pakistani nation created by Jinnah that marked a significant change in the Indian subcontinental framework[47] and, more generally, in the Asian geopolitical framework. But the third conflict between New Delhi and Islamabad had also made clear a new configuration of the international order; it was not founded on US–USSR bipolarity anymore and had instead assumed a tripolar appearance (US–USSR–People's Republic of China).[48]

In a meeting held in Rome in January 1972, several Italian ambassadors, including Fracassi, Straneo, Pietromarchi, Bova Scoppa, Ghigi, Capomazza, Colonna and others dealt with these problems in the context of a conference that focused on the Indo-Pakistani conflict and its aftermath. They emphasized, in particular, the impotence shown by the United States, Western powers and Maoist China in defending their common Pakistani ally, a kind of powerlessness that had benefited the USSR as well as India. The serious historical responsibilities of Great Britain were reported, together with the political ones of New Delhi and Islamabad, and a comparison with the Israeli-Palestinian situation was drawn. According to Italian diplomats, the Indian subcontinent had been the scene of a 'proxy war' between China and the USSR, a conflict that had also had the opportunity to take place even in the UN Security Council, with the exchange of a cross-fire of vetoes between Beijing and Moscow preventing any resolutions from being made. They started to fear that the entry into the Glass Palace of the new permanent Chinese member, who was in bitter disagreement with the Soviet State, could irreparably compromise the effectiveness and functioning of the UN itself. During the Indo-Pakistani conflict, Rome's diplomats saw various signs of shared intentions between China and the United States while, on the other hand, they observed that certain characteristics of India (i.e. a thousand-year-old culture, a huge population and remarkable self-esteem) made its total subjugation to the Kremlin unlikely.

Moreover, the focus of the public speakers was on the precarious economic and political situation in the new Bangladesh along with the particular concerns regarding the rise of 'Naxalism' from the more markedly Maoist and revolutionary faction of the CPI(M)-Communist Party of India (Marxist). Established in 1967, following the oubreak of a series of riots in West Bengal, the Naxalites had made an important contribution to the secessionist cause of Bangladesh, swelling the ranks of anti-Pakistani nationalist guerrillas. The situation in Pakistan was seen as equally precarious as the country was grappling with the immense problems caused by the war, not least of which was the resumption of clashes between the different ethnic groups of the Pakistani mosaic, which caused fear that other centrifugal forces would develop. Finally, Italy reflected on the marginal role assumed by Europe during the crisis and the fact that the European countries needed to undertake the delicate task of extricating themselves from the new tripolar balance, particularly as regards the matter of aid to poor Asian countries. Ambassador Colonna stated:

> Following American receptiveness to China, our countries in Europe risk having to make a choice between China and Russia and between the poor countries under Chinese influence and those under Russian influence. To realize how delicate this problem is, we need only consider Germany with its *Ostpolitik*, the implementation of which depends to a large extent on the will of Russia. In Italy, pro-Pakistan/pro-China sympathies are at odds with pro-India/pro-Russia ones as a consequence of the rift in the Italian communist and pro-communist forces. If we fail to avoid these choices, we risk finding ourselves in impossible situations. An Italian initiative to help Pakistan, Bangladesh or India would become a new reason for division or discord and the same goes for any such initiatives taken by the rest of Europe.
>
> The solution should consist in the development of an authentically European concept regarding the future Asian order, so as to allow us to exercise our mission in the Third World as Italians and Europeans, setting aside the competing ideologies of Russia and China and the hegemonic conflicts hiding behind them.

The Italian ambassadors demanded greater activism and greater unity in Europe and in the EU institutions in Asian politics, in a similar way to what was being done in the Middle East.[49]

The situation in the Indian subcontinent remained constantly on the agenda in high-level international discussions, with the war having left a whole series of important issues on the table that would require a long and complicated interlocutory phase. Key issues included the recognition of Bangladesh, the return of the prisoners of the Pakistani war, the fate of the Bengali leader Majbur Rahman, and the other Bengali political prisoners held by the Pakistanis, the normalization of relations between India and Pakistan, and every legal and economic problem that might derive from a secession. Thus, the Indian subcontinent's political developments were at the centre of the talks in the two meetings held in Rome between Aldo Moro and the new UN Secretary-General, Kurt Waldheim, in January and February 1972.[50]

During the WEU's Council of Ministers in Bonn on 3 March 1972, the Under-Secretary for Foreign Affairs, Salizzoni, argued it was in the interest of all Western European countries for a dialogue between India and Pakistan to take place soon. The European countries, therefore, would have to carry out harmonized interventions to facilitate the start of the Indian-Pakistani conversations aimed at creating a balance in the area, which clearly involved taking Bangladesh's existence into account.[51] The first states that recognized Bangladesh were India and Bhutan, of course, followed by the USSR, the Warsaw Pact countries and Yugoslavia. Then it was the UK's turn, which caused the withdrawal of Pakistan from the Commonwealth. Italy proceeded cautiously regarding the recognition of Bangladesh, acting in concert with the EEC countries. Specifically, Italy aligned itself with the position of France, which was in no hurry to recognize the new state, thus avoiding offending Pakistan and other Muslim countries which were particularly sympathetic towards Islamabad. Italian recognition took place on 12 February 1972, after Bhutto's return from a visit to China and following the Indian assurances that they would withdraw their troops from Bangladesh as soon as possible.[52]

An Italian diplomatic representation in Dhaka was established in September 1972. In Rome, a Bengali ambassador had already been present since April.[53] From that point onwards, the bilateral relations between Italy and the former Pakistani Eastern section, an area which had always been considered rich in raw materials, especially jute, naturally followed a completely different path.

Italy's actions during all the phases of the Pakistani crisis were well-received by Islamabad. Firstly, Italy was appreciated for having put effort into preventing the Indo-Pakistani conflict, then for having tried to bring it to an end quickly, and finally for having attempted to mitigate the harsh consequences suffered by Bhutto's new Pakistan, for example, by acting as a go-between for the handing over of prisoners of war taken by the Indians or Bengalis.[54] On the other hand, Italy's actions did not produce negative effects even in New Delhi, as affirmed by the following note:

> In the Indo-Pakistani crisis and in the subsequent conflict, even though Italian diplomatic action won the appreciation of Islamabad, it also managed to satisfy Indian needs, eliciting declarations of respect and gratitude from the aforementioned government for our impartial work.[55]

In June 1972, Aldo Moro and Indira Gandhi met each other in Rome and both expressed hopes that the imminent meetings between the Indian leader and the new Pakistani Prime Minister, Zulfikar Ali Bhutto, could lead to a successful outcome. Moro, in particular, hoped for a proper settlement in the subcontinent and a heightened sense of responsibility of the parties involved. During this talk, he showed goodwill towards Nehru's daughter.[56]

Oriana Fallaci's interviews with the two prime ministers, Gandhi and Bhutto, between February and April 1972, particularly stood out, with the one with Bhutto 'unleashing pandemonium. Not of a journalistic nature, as in the case of Kissinger, but of a diplomatic and even international one.'[57] Gandhi took great offence at the insults received from the Pakistani prime minister via the Florentine journalist's microphone and decided to cancel the meeting in which a peace treaty between India and Pakistan would have been signed. Therefore, there were many attempts by the Pakistani ambassador in Rome and other important Pakistani personalities to get Fallaci to deny the veracity of the interview and to even go as far as claiming that it had been completely made up. The impasse, along with the pressure on the Italian journalist, ended when Indira Gandhi decided to overlook Bhutto's rash declarations and sign the peace treaty.[58]

The Simla agreement of 2 August 1972 and the Delhi one of 28 August 1973 represented significant steps in trying to overcome the aftermath of rancour and tensions left by the Indo-Pakistani war. The Delhi agreement, in particular, regulated the exchange of the Bengali and Pakistani prisoners of war and internees who were still in Pakistan and Bangladesh, respectively. Moreover, it paved the way for the Pakistani recognition of the new Bengali state.[59] The Bihari issue was left open and remains so to this day: the Biharis are an ethnic group whose mostly Muslim members settled in Bengal after the Partition. During the civil war, they had largely cooperated with the Pakistani army's repression and as a result they remained disliked and discriminated against in Bangladesh. Nevertheless, Bhutto refused to accept them.[60]

Italy hailed the negotiations between India and Pakistan as a success, recognizing they might be useful in creating a new balance between the people of Asia; a balance which was also partly due to the reintegration of the People's Republic of China into the international political circle:

> All this – stated Andreotti when he presented the programmatic declarations of his first government – encourages an increase in exchanges between Italy and the East in every sector, given our cordial relations with all the nations of Asia.[61]

As far as Italian–Pakistani economic relations were concerned, the financial chaos produced by the Indo-Pakistani crisis and Bangladesh's secession had to be sorted out. Italy, which was a creditor to Islamabad, both individually and within the Aid-to-Pakistan Consortium, had suspended any authorization for its credit to be used during the crisis. Therefore, arrangements had to be made for the restructuring of Pakistani debt, both within the IBRD and bilaterally. On 6 December 1972, a financial agreement was signed in Rome for the restructuring of US$18 million worth of Pakistani debt, which sanctioned the normalization of Italian–Pakistani financial relations. The issue of the credit provided by IBRD was more complex, given that Islamabad had no intention of paying debts for projects or supplies that would benefit Bangladesh. Pakistan accepted a compromise formula pushed for by the United States and adhered to a memorandum of understanding with IBRD representatives, with the methods of credit recovery having to be regulated. This implied the need for an agreement on the pending debt issue with Dacca.[62]

Bhutto's foreign policy attempted to help Pakistan recover from the ill-fated outcomes of the 1971 conflict while also having to face a return of the Afghan antagonism after the 1973 coup of Mohammed Daud, which emerged clearly in the context of the claims of the Baluch autonomists (supported by Kabul). Furthermore, the Quaid-e-awam was very worried by the geopolitical and strategic/military strengthening of India, which officially reached the status of a nuclear power in May 1974,[63] pushing him to accelerate the time and provision of resources for the development of a Pakistani atomic arsenal, a project that he had supported since he was foreign minister in Ayub Khan's government.[64] Bhutto then aimed at strengthening ties with the Islamic countries and reactivating the non-aligned movement under his aegis, thus disavowing the political-expansionist use of it made by India. In 1974, he organized the summit of the Islamic Conference in Lahore. This gave him great prestige, foreshadowing the formation of a possible pan-Islamic bloc.[65]

The 1971 war caused Pakistan to leave SEATO and the Commonwealth, although Pakistan tended to maintain ties with the United States and China, possibly improving relations with the USSR and investing heavily in cooperation with the Arab Gulf countries. The experience of the previous years led Bhutto to consider the traditional allies (the United States in particular) from a more disenchanted and pragmatic perspective. He defined his 'bilateralist policy' as aimed at 'conducting and developing relations with each of the great powers, on a bilateral basis, identifying areas of cooperation with each of them without repudiating the alliance with the others'. This principle also needed to be applied to the relations with all the other countries.[66]

Italy did not fail to be friendly towards Bhutto, whose policies (especially the nuclear one) would cause a cooling of relations with the United States within a few years.[67] In July 1973, just before the signing of the Delhi agreement, the Quaid-e-awam arrived in Rome on a private visit and was welcomed by Mariano Rumor, who had just formed his fourth government; one which saw the return of the socialists to Palazzo Chigi after the centre-right experience of Andreotti Government II. Italy would host a conference of Pakistani ambassadors accredited to European capitals (including Moscow), to the United States, to Canada, and to Latin America, which would prepare the ground for Bhutto's official visit to Washington. Received by the President of the Republic, Giovanni Leone, in the presence of the highest authorities of the Farnesina, including Aldo Moro, the Pakistani prime minister thanked them for allowing Islamabad's diplomatic corps to gather in Rome and expressed his gratitude for the impartial role played by Italy during the Bengal crisis. The Italian–Pakistani friendship had, therefore, remained intact. After all, Leone himself repeated in the final toast to Bhutto that

> Italy, to the extent that it can, intends to continue contributing to the economic and social growth of Pakistan, as an element of stability in a particularly delicate sector.[68]

Bhutto made another visit to Italy in February 1975, which led to an agreement to supply food aid to Pakistan (the equivalent of ten thousand tonnes of wheat flour was granted), a financial agreement regarding debt consolidation and an agreement on technical and scientific collaboration with which Italy would offer Islamabad funds, equipment and facilities for the professional education of Pakistanis in Italy, as well as materials and equipment for development projects to be carried out in Pakistan itself.[69]

Meanwhile, the Political Committee of the EEC countries studied the possibilities for coordination and common European action in the Indian subcontinent. In the 9–10 September 1976 meeting of the *Asia Experts Working Group*, the Federal Republic of Germany's delegation suggested that this area shouldn't be neglected and that ECC action should start, given the considerable economic interests of the Nine here. It proposed that this huge Asian region be constantly monitored, that its problems be studied in depth (possibly with the help of diplomatic missions) and that shared points of view be formulated. The other delegates were in favour of these proposals and gave this working group the following mandate:

> The experts were requested to undertake political analysis of the countries of the Indian sub-continent in order to facilitate the co-ordination of the Nine's positions in respect of those countries.[70]

In February 1977, the *Asia Working Group* met to discuss the first political report on the Indian subcontinent, which had been prepared by the UK. In general, it was argued that the developments of the previous five years in South Asia had brought stability to the area, especially when compared to previous decades. The main stabilizing element was the political and military pre-eminence reached by India in the subcontinent, followed by the slowing down of the military competition between New Delhi and Islamabad, as evidenced by the lack of requests for military supplies on both sides since 1972. The process of 'normalizing' the area seemed to have been completed and, despite two military defeats, even Pakistan appeared to have gained respect from India, although some problems, like that of Kashmir, remained shelved. Improvements in relations between Pakistan and Afghanistan were also seen in 1976 thanks to the meetings between Daud and Bhutto, which were in part intermediated by the Iranian Shah. The conclusion of the British report stated:

> Our common interest in South Asia is that the region should remain stable, so that economic development can proceed; that it should not fall under the dominance of any hostile major power; and that it should not trouble each of us with international disputes towards whose solution we can make no real contribution – as over Kashmir. Conditions for such stability now effectively exist. They could be disturbed by any major change in the relations of one or more of the South Asian countries with one of the super-powers. They could also be disturbed by the emergence of India as a military nuclear power or, short of that, by nuclear rivalry between Pakistan and India. Both this issue and that of the relationship of India and her neighbours with the super-powers deserve further study. If there is at this stage a general conclusion to draw about policy it is probably that in our relations with the countries of the area we should be scrupulous to treat each of the lesser countries as simply subsidiary to our policy towards India.[71]

In the discussion that followed, the Italian delegate Cerulli informed the other eight delegations of Bhutto's intention to support the establishment of a Euro-Asia dialogue on the model of the one started with the Arab countries.[72]

Despite the apparent stability, the Asian-Southern framework was soon destined to deteriorate. The political crisis that followed the Pakistani elections of 1977 led to yet another military coup headed by General Zia-Al-Uq. The government of Rome was immediately notified by the ambassador in Islamabad, Gerardo Zampaglione, who assured them that the Italian community had not been hurt.[73]

Bhutto, who during the crisis had been accused by a growing number of opponents of electoral rigging, was removed and placed under house arrest. He was then freed but, convinced that he was able to return to power, he was arrested again in September 1977, charged with being the instigator of the murder of a political opponent and sentenced to death.

Requests for clemency in his favour came from all over the world. Even the President of the Republic Sandro Pertini intervened with an appeal to overturn the sentence imposed on the former Pakistani leader by the Supreme Court of Islamabad.[74] But all requests fell on deaf ears: the Quaid-e-azim was hanged on 4 April 1979,[75] provoking many expressions of international condemnation, including that of Foreign Minister Arnaldo Forlani.[76] The Asia expert Paolo Beonio Brocchieri considered Bhutto's execution 'a political assassination' and 'a regime crime' driven by an internal Islamic opinion that, on the whole, wanted Bhutto dead.[77]

Italy, Pakistan and the reignition of the Cold War in Central Asia (1979–91)

It was above all the Khomeinist revolution in Iran and the Afghan internal crisis that shook up the geopolitical order, creating the conditions for the acceleration of regional political dynamism. This dynamism was also crucial for the fate of the strategic balance of the Cold War, especially in the aftermath of the Soviet occupation of Afghanistan.[78] Before this military intervention, relations between the US and Pakistan had worsened considerably, mainly because of the atomic policy that Islamabad continued to pursue even after Bhutto's death, as well as due to the emphasis placed by the Carter Administration on the issue of human rights, for which Zia-Ul-Haq showed no regard with the constant arrests, torturing and repression of his opponents. All of this led Washington to a rapprochement with India,[79] where a new government run by the Janata Party (the largest party of Hindu nationalism) had been established and had temporarily put an end to the hegemony of the Congress Party. Indira Gandhi had often been accused by the Italian side of representing a danger to democracy in India due to her frequent recourse to authoritarian methods of government or to constitutional prerogatives typical of a 'state of emergency'.[80] It was precisely at the same time as the success of the Janata Party, as well as the United States exhibiting its best intentions towards New Delhi, that Italy took the opportunity to establish a closer link to India, as attested by a series of visits made by leading political figures including the Senate President, Fanfani, and the Foreign Minister, Forlani.[81]

Italian–Pakistani relations had appeared colder during Zia-Ul-Haq's first years in the Islamabad government, mainly due to the greater space that the news about the atrocities committed under its dictatorial regime had obtained in the Italian press and not least because of the effect Bhutto's execution had.[82] But despite the poor democratic attitude of the new Islamabad regime, and the enduring Pakistani willingness to carry on the nuclear programme, it was impossible not to continue to recognize the very high strategic value represented by the 'Land of the Pure' and the need to keep it tied to Western countries. Immediately after the Afghan coup d'état that brought the pro-Soviet People's Democratic Party to power (April 1978), Zia started to fund and protect Pashtun opponents, especially those connected to the radical Islamic party Jamaat-e-Islami, who later formed the main core of anti-Soviet military resistance.[83]

At the Asia Working Group meeting in Paris in May 1979, there was unanimous intention to support the Islamabad government in order 'to help Pakistan to continue to fulfill her strategic role' and 'to keep Pakistan's head above water, even while recognizing the risk that she would drown'.[84]

The conflict in Afghanistan, therefore, led Italy to reconsider bilateral relations with Pakistan and to reduce the coldness and circumspection with which Italy had treated it in the early days of Zia-Al-Huq's military dictatorship. This occurred naturally in accordance with the US attitude which, from the time of the Khomeinist Revolution, but even more so when it became clear that the USSR could be dragged 'into the Afghan trap', had begun to re-evaluate Pakistan's strategic role and to collaborate secretly to support Afghan insurgents.[85] The commitment to provide military help, food aid and other assistance to Islamabad was explicitly stated in Carter's speech following the Soviet occupation of Afghanistan and was also made by the European Economic Community (EEC) countries and Italy.[86] Therefore, many of the American qualms regarding the Pakistani attitude towards the Nuclear Non-Proliferation Treaty dissolved.[87]

In Pakistan, for the first time, there was 'strategic coordination' between the United States and the People's Republic of China as both were intent on containing the USSR in Asia. All this was going in the direction of a Sino–Japanese–American axis that from Moscow's point of view represented the most worrying prospect of encirclement.[88] Soviet isolation was completed by the UN condemnation of almost all non-aligned and Islamic states, and even India backed this condemnation promoted by the General Assembly by abstaining from voting.[89]

Once the difficulties of the Soviet occupation were perceived, the Islamabad government had no interest in finding a peaceful solution to the Afghan matter quickly. In particular, Pakistan saw in the fight against the Soviet presence in Afghanistan a tool to strengthen its international weight. The United States, Saudi Arabia, the People's Republic of China and the Arab Gulf States entrusted Pakistan with the organization of anti-Soviet resistance, providing it with enormous amounts of money and armaments. Islamabad was thus able to improve its economic position and return to being a protagonist of Afghan internal affairs. It could, moreover, continue to develop nuclear weapons undisturbed.[90] Italy made substantial contributions to the financing of Pakistan in order to help the Afghan refugees even though the Zia regime was not looked upon favourably by most of the Italian public. In Rome in January 1982, amidst considerable perplexity and not much cordiality, the 'soldier-statesman' was subjected to a tough press conference in which he was called to account for political detentions, torture and human rights violations.[91]

In the early 1980s, several visits by Italian ministers to Pakistan led to the signing of a whole series of economic and cooperation agreements, demonstrating how intact Italian solidarity had remained with a country that at that time represented the main anti-Soviet bulwark.[92] Several committees and solidarity groups in favour of the Afghan resistance were created, together with Pakistan investigation and assistance missions. Human rights commissions were set up (the Ungari Mission was very important in autumn 1985), and fund-raising and awareness campaigns regarding the issue of refugees were carried out.[93] The Italian government also tried to reassure India that it need not worry about the Pakistani military-political strengthening by starting new forms of collaboration with New Delhi in the defense sector.[94]

Italian actions during the Soviet occupation in Afghanistan were geared at restoring peace as quickly as possible, with Italy striving for a political solution to the crisis rather than a military one. In particular, in the discussions concerning the political-institutional reorganization of the Afghan post-war settlement, the Italian government's aim was to help put King Zahir, who had been in exile in Rome since 1973, back on the throne in Kabul. But it was with distrust that the Islamabad government, assisted by the Saudi one, looked on 'the group of Rome', that is, the elite of monarchists linked to Zahir and resident in Italy, preferring instead to strengthen the Islamic fundamentalist anti-Soviet groups. While the Red Army's withdrawal was being negotiated, the Pakistani government was working to set up an Afghan government closely linked to, and dependent on, Islamabad itself. From this point of view, Zahir and his supporters were instead seen as less malleable than mujaheddin or even pro-India.[95]

The Islamabad government's approach was accepted by the United States and other Western countries despite some surveys in the refugee camps in Pakistan indicating that the majority of Afghans preferred Zahir to any other Islamist leader.[96] As already mentioned, though, despite being amongst the protagonists of a negotiation for the withdrawal of Soviet troops since 1982, Pakistan was in no hurry to try to bring the conflict to an end immediately, given the huge amount of economic and military aid it was receiving.[97]

In April 1988, the day after the signing of the Geneva agreements governing the Soviet withdrawal from Afghanistan, the Italian representative in Islamabad, Arduino Fornara, analysed the official reaction of Pakistan to the agreements reached and the prospects that were opening up for the rulers of the 'Land of the Pure'.[98] Although they publicly avoided triumphalist tones, since the agreements simply contained a legal framework that would have allowed the Red Army to withdraw and not a political agreement or any Afghan resistance involvement, the Italian diplomats could not help but report their profound satisfaction with the conclusion of a phase that had engaged them enormously for nine years.

The positive Pakistani evaluation concerned the feasible consequences that the Geneva agreement might be able to produce both in the sphere of domestic politics and in that of foreign policy, with a view to creating a 'dynamization' of Islamabad's future foreign affairs. Given that, for Pakistan, Geneva's negotiation process had represented the 'first major international negotiation'[99] conducted independently for nine years (albeit with various ups and downs), it was in terms of awareness that the Pakistani leadership felt elevated in terms of international prestige. The Geneva negotiations would also allow a growth in expectations and actual democratic achievements in Pakistan, 'with international public opinion being unlikely to forgive this ruling class if it made demands for the restoration of minimum democratic conditions in Kabul when these were not simultaneously being abided by in Islamabad'.[100] Fornara saw a real 'singular harmony' between the Geneva process set in motion in 1982 and the restoration of democratic conditions in Pakistan:

> Even though in the same year, in 1979, Soviet intervention occurred in Afghanistan and General Zia seized power in Pakistan, this slowly led to the awareness of the importance of strengthening the democratic foundations, which resulted in the abolition of martial law in 1985, the holding of administrative elections in 1987 and the commitment to call political elections in 1990.[101]

It also seemed that the Afghan conflict had brought greater national cohesion, thwarting the initiatives of the internal opposition to the Zia regime.

In the international field, the Italian diplomat pointed out the various positive results obtained by Islamabad with the signing of the Geneva agreements. Among these were the rapid withdrawal of the Soviet Union, the non-recognition of the (pro-Soviet) government in Kabul, the non-renegotiation of the Afghan-Pakistani border, the exclusion of India from the negotiation process, the gratitude of Washington, Beijing and the Gulf countries, which was opportunely reciprocated in the hope that Pakistan would be able to continue to obtain economic aid. With the success achieved in opposing Soviet expansionism, Pakistan aimed at growing as a great regional power and a point of reference for non-aligned and Islamic states.[102]

One of the most important effects of Geneva, which subsequently had considerable repercussions, concerned the possibility for the over three million Afghan refugees who lived in Pakistan to return home. These refugees had established a very intense relationship with the Pakistani leadership.

> It is unlikely refugees will be able to forget ... that Pakistan has hosted them for nine years and has physically allowed their survival. The aid, at least in part, came from the Western countries of course. The Pakistanis, however, are convinced that the refugees will not forget the role played by Islamabad in the name of the 'Islamic brotherhood'.[103]

Having obtained all these advantages and having also developed the doctrine of 'strategic depth' in recent years, namely control over 'a manoeuvring space all of our own [as Zia called it] that goes far beyond our borders, ... which is available if the Indian invading armies cross the southern border and storm our territory',[104] Pakistan emerged greatly strengthened by the war in Afghanistan and secretly started to fan the flames of the Kashmir fire that had flared up again in the late 1980s[105]

After the collapse of the USSR and of the pro-Soviet Najibullah government in Kabul, Afghanistan was the scene of yet another civil war, this time among the former mujhaiddin who, after having proclaimed the existence of the Islamic State, fragmented into various rival factions. In 1996, the fundamentalist Sunni militias of the Taliban, young Pashtun students of the madrasas financed by Saudi Arabia and Pakistan, were victorious against all these factions. Islamabad thus secured a friendly Afghanistan which was closely bound to its army and its secret services while, from another point of view, it seemed that after the mysterious death of Zia-Ul-Haq and the elections of 1988, it had succeeded in re-establishing a democratic regime with civil governments.[106]

All of this was welcomed by Ambassador Fornara in a speech given at the Pakistan Institute of International Affairs in Karachi in May 1991, and by the President of the Senate, Giovanni Spadolini, in an article published in the *Dawn* in December of the same year. In the latter, the republican statesman also expressed his approval regarding the creation of the Pakistan Italy Friendship Association. Both saw the end of the USSR as the most favourable opportunity to bring Europe, and therefore Italy, closer to Pakistan, whose role within the Islamic community was considered to be becoming more prominent:

by the end of this decade [Spadolini said] Europe could stretch as far as the Urals and find the emerging Republics of Central Asia at its borders. This is an area where both Pakistan and Italy will be able to find new chances to play international constructive roles in the near future.[107]

The new world situation [Fornara declared] brought about by the economic collapse of the socialist system and the political liberation of the former so-called people's democracies will in fact provide, in my view, an ever larger space for manoeuvre for countries willing to promote their legitimate interests in a world which, contrary to popular belief, is becoming increasingly multipolar. Another example: now that the Afghan page is about to be turned (at least as regards its former characteristics of a heavily charged political confrontation with global repercussions), I am convinced that the ties between Pakistan and the West, and in particular with Europe and Italy, can be, as a consequence, more mature, strengthened and opened to a much wider range of areas of cooperation.[108]

According to Fornara, evidence of this had already been provided during the Gulf War, when the Pakistani government had vigorously defended the decision to assist the international coalition and the principle of non-aggression deliberately transgressed by Iraq's Saddam Hussein.[109]

The Italian diplomat also declared that it was the intention of the Italian government to continue to provide support in terms of finding a solution to the two major problems afflicting Pakistan, namely Afghanistan and Kashmir, and the nature of this support would, in both cases, be focused on the search for a dialogue between the parties involved in the conflict.[110] We can conclude this chapter with the last words pronounced by Fornara on the same occasion:

Our two countries also share certain common features: they are relatively young (Italy as an independent state only dates back to 1860), they have experienced the persistence of a trend of provincial autonomy within the country (which can be a factor of strength as well as of weakness), they have a business community that under appropriate circumstances can do well without the support of the state and, finally, they both have a sense of human understanding that prevails among the people and which I personally experienced during my stay in this country. In the years to come, we can build a better, closer and stronger relationship upon these similarities.[111]

Notes

1 For an initial historiographic profile on Italian-Pakistani relations from 1947 to 1973, see Giuseppe Spagnulo, 'Aldo Moro e le relazioni italo-pakistane', in Federico Imperato, Rosario Milano and Luciano Monzali (eds), *Fra diplomazia e petrolio: Aldo Moro e la politica italiana in Medio Oriente (1963–1978)* (Bari: Cacucci, 2018),

199–238. For the events concerning the appointment of an Italian representative in Karachi, see DDI, s. X, vol. VI, docs. 361, 801; DDI, s. X, vol. VII, docs. 114, 264, 497. Extensive documentation is also present in ASMAE, AP 1946–50, India, b., 1947, f. Rapporti politici; ASMAE, DGP, Ufficio I-II, b. 180, Karachi.

2   See ASMAE, DGP, Uff. I-II, b. 180, Karachi, Tel. del ministro plenipotenziario Assettati indirizzato al Ministero degli Affari Esteri su Presentazione credenziali, 9 September 1949; ASMAE, DGP, Uff. I-II, b. 180, Karachi, Lettera di Assettati al sottosegretario Brusasca, 23 December 1948; ASMAE, DGP, Uff. I-II, b. 180, Karachi, Tel. di Assettati a Ministero degli Affari Esteri, 21 December 1948. Regarding Italian economic interests in Pakistan, see ASMAE, AP 1946–50, India 1949–50, b. 6, f. 'Relazioni con l'Italia', Istituto Commercio Estero. Relazione sulla missione economica italiana in India e Pakistan, 1949.

3   On the Mediterranean and Middle Eastern politics of Italy, see Luca Riccardi, *Il 'problema Israele':. Diplomazia italiana e PCI di fronte allo Stato ebraico (1948–1973)* (Milan: Guerini, 2006); Matteo Pizzigallo (ed.), *L'Italia e il Mediterraneo Orientale 1946–1950* (Milan: Franco Angeli, 2004); Pizzigallo (ed.), *La diplomazia italiana e i paesi arabi del Mediterraneo (1946–1952)* (Milan: Franco Angeli, 2008); Pizzigallo (ed.), *Amicizie mediterranee e interessi nazionali 1946–1954* (Milan: Franco Angeli, 2006); Alessandro Brogi, *L'Italia e l'egemonia americana nel Mediterraneo* (Florence: La Nuova Italia, 1996); Luigi Vittorio Ferraris (ed.), *Manuale della politica estera italiana 1947–1993* (Rome: Laterza, 1996); Daniele Caviglia and Massimiliano Cricco, *La diplomazia italiana e gli equilibri mediterranei: La politica mediorientale dell'Italia dalla guerra dei Sei Giorni al conflitto dello Yom Kippur (1967–1973)* (Soveria Mannelli: Rubbettino, 2006); Ilaria Tremolada, *All'ombra degli arabi: Le relazioni italo-israeliane 1948–1956: dalla fondazione dello Stato ebraico alla crisi di Suez* (Milan: M & B, 2003); Mario Toscano, *La 'Porta di Sion': L'Italia e l'immigrazione clandestina ebraica in Palestina 1945–1948* (Bologna: Il Mulino, 1990); Elena Calandri, 'Europa e Mediterraneo tra giustapposizione e integrazione', in Massimo de Leonardis (ed.), *Il Mediterraneo nella politica estera italiana del secondo dopoguerra* (Bologna: Il Mulino, 2003), 47–60; Calandri, 'L'Italia e la questione dello sviluppo: una sfida fra anni sessanta e anni settanta', in Piero Craveri and Antonio Varsori (eds), *L'Italia nella costruzione europea. Un bilancio storico 1957–2007* (Milan: Franco Angeli, 2009), 109–34; Luciano Monzali, 'Aldo Moro, la politica estera italiana e il Corno d'Africa (1963-1968)', in Francesco Perfetti, Andrea Ungari, Daniele Caviglia and Daniele De Luca (eds), *Aldo Moro nell'Italia contemporanea* (Florence: Le Lettere, 2011), 641 et sqq.; Antonio Varsori, *L'Italia nelle relazioni internazionali dal 1943 al 1992* (Rome: Laterza, 1998), *passim*. On Islamic-Italian policy during the Fascist period, see Renzo De Felice, *Il fascismo e l'Oriente: Arabi, ebrei e indiani nella politica di Mussolini* (Bologna: Il Mulino, 1988); Nir Arielli, *Fascist Italy and Middle-East (1933–1940)* (Basingstoke: Palgrave Macmillan, 2013); Enrico Galoppini, *Il fascismo e l'Islam* (Parma: All'insegna del Veltro, 2001); Giovanni Armillotta, La politica islamica del fascismo, in 'Affari Esteri', no. 174, 2014, 404–7; Luciano Monzali, *Il colonialismo nella politica estera italiana. Momenti e protagonisti (1878–1949)* (Rome: Società Editrice Dante Alighieri, 2017), 223 et sqq. On the Italian role in the process of Pakistan's creation, see Vito Salierno, *Fascism and British India* (Lahore: Iqbal Academy Pakistan, 2017), 139 et sqq.

4   See Spagnulo, 'Aldo Moro e le relazioni italo-pakistane', 199 et sqq.

5 The words of the Foreign Minister Giuseppe Pella during a speech to the Camera dei Deputati in October 1953. See ASMAE, AP 1951–7, Estremo Oriente, 1954, b. 1482, f. 'Discorso Presidente del Consiglio Pella'.
6 See Gaetano Martino, *L'Italia e Paesi asiatici. Rapporti e prospettive. Discorso pronunciato a Milano, nella sede dell'ISPI*, il 21 gennaio 1956, in ASSR, GM, Attività politica, Ministero degli Affari Esteri, b. 7, 'L'Italia, i Paesi asiatici e l'ONU'. See also Ferraris, *Manuale della politica estera italiana 1947–1993*, 185–6; Angela Villani, *Un liberale sulla scena internazionale. Gaetano Martino e la politica estera italiana (1954–1967)* (Messina: Trisform, 2008).
7 See ASSR, GM, Attività politica, Ministero degli Affari Esteri, b. 6, *Traccia per una relazione di V.E. sul viaggio in Estremo Oriente*.
8 In order to get an idea of the international political climate at the time of Martino's trip to Asia, see Federico Niglia, 'Ginevra 1955. La diplomazia italiana e l'apogeo del disgelo', in Francesco Perfetti (ed.), *Feluche d'Italia: Diplomazia e identità nazionale* (Florence: Le Lettere, 2012), 131–60; Francesco Perfetti, 'L'ammissione dell'Italia alle Nazioni Unite. Il ruolo dell'Italia', in Perfetti (ed.), *Feluche d'Italia*, cit., 161–82. On the Not-Aligned Movement, see Giampaolo Calchi Novati, *Neutralismo e guerra fredda* (Milan: Edizioni di Comunità, 1963); Novati, *Decolonizzazione e Terzo Mondo* (Rome-Bari: Laterza, 1979); Novati, 'I paesi non allineati dalla Conferenza di Bandung a oggi', in Romain H. Rainero (ed.), *Storia dell'età presente: I problemi del mondo attuale dalla seconda guerra mondiale a oggi*, vol. I (Milan: Marzorati, 1985); Giampaolo Calchi Novati and Lia Quartapelle (eds), *Terzo Mondo addio: La Conferenza afro-asiatica di Bandung in una prospettiva storica* (Rome: Carocci, 2007); John Lewis Gaddis, *La guerra fredda: Rivelazioni e riflessioni* (Milan: Corbaccio, 1996); Federico Romero, *Storia della guerra fredda: L'ultimo conflitto per l'Europa* (Turin: Einaudi, 2009); Jawaharlal Nehru, *Independence and After* (New Delhi: Publications Division, Ministry of Information and Broadcasting, Government of India, 1949); Nehru, *India's Foreign Policy: Selected Speeches, September 1946–April 1961* (New Delhi: Publications Division, Ministry of Information and Broadcasting Government of India, 1961); G. Procacci, *Storia del XX secolo* (Milan: Mondadori, 2000); Marco Galeazzi, *Il PCI e il movimento dei paesi non allineati (1955–1975)* (Milan: Franco Angeli, 2011); Odd Arne Westad, *La Guerra fredda globale: Gli Stati Uniti, l'Unione Sovietica e il mondo. Le relazioni internazionali del XX secolo* (Milan: Il Saggiatore, 2015).
9 On Pakistani foreign policy, see Samuel Martin Burke, *Pakistan's Foreign Policy: An Historical Analysis* (London: Oxford University Press, 1973); Mehrunnisa Ali, 'Soviet-Pakistan: Ties since the Afghanistan Crisis', in *Asian Survey* 45, no. 4 (1984), 1025–42; Shahid M. Amin, *Pakistan's Foreign Policy: A Reappraisal* (Karachi: Oxford University Press, 2000); Dennis Kux, *The United States and Pakistan, 1947–2000: Disenchanted Allies* (Washington, DC: Woodrow Wilson Center Press, 2001); Shirin Tahir-Kheli, *The United States and Pakistan: The Evolution of an Influence Relationship* (New York: Praeger, 1982).
10 See Altaf Gauhar, *Ayub Khan: Pakistan's First Military Ruler* (Karachi: Oxford University Press, 1996); Lawrence Ziring, *The Ayub Khan Era: Politics in Pakistan, 1958–1969* (Syracuse: Syracuse University Press, 1971); Elisa Giunchi, *Pakistan. Islam, potere e democratizzazione* (Rome: Carocci, 2009), 71 et sqq.; Tariq Ali, *Pakistan dal 1947 al Bangla-Desh: Lotte popolari e crisi del regime militare* (Milan: Mazzotta, 1971), 80 et sqq. On the evolution of the process that led to the coup, see the American documentation contained in FRUS, 1958–60, v. XV, *South and Southeast Asia*, Pakistan, docs 292–337.

11 On Indian foreign policy, see Prem Arora *India's Foreign Policy* (Cosmos: Bookhive, 2000); Uma Shankar Bajpai (ed.), *India and Its Neighbourhood* (New Delhi: Lancers International, 1986); Chandra P. Bhambhri, *Foreign Policy of India* (New Delhi: Sterling, 1987); Jayantanuja Bandyopadhyaya, *The Making of India's Foreign Policy* (Bombay: Allied Pubox, 1970); Michael Brecher, *Vita di Nehru* (Milan: Il Saggiatore, 1965); Dennis Kux, *Estranged Democracies: India and the United States 1941–1991* (New Delhi: Sage, 1994).
12 See Spagnulo, 'Aldo Moro e le relazioni italo-pakistane', 210 et sqq.
13 Ibid. On the Sino-Indian crisis, see James Barnard Calvin, *The China-India Border War* (Quantico: Marine Corps Command and Staff College, 1984); Alastair Lamb, *The China-India Border: The Origins of the Disputed Boundaries* (London: Oxford University Press, 1964); Bertil Lintner, *Great Game East: India, China and the Struggle for Asia's Most Volatile Frontier* (New Delhi: HarperCollins, 2012).
14 See ACS, PCM, Cons.Dipl., 40, folder 'Pakistan', *Lettera dell'ambasciatore a Karachi di Gropello ad Ortona*, 24 October 1962. See also ACS, PCM, Cons.Dipl., b. 13, f. 'India', Aiuti all'India, *Appunto per S.E. il Ministro*, 27 October 1962.
15 See Spagnulo, 'Aldo Moro e le relazioni italo-pakistane', 217 et sqq. On the second Indo-Pakistani war, see Farooq Naseem Bajwa, *From Kutch to Tasksent: The Indo-Pakistan War of 1965* (London: Hust, 2013).
16 This was declared by the Italian Prime Minister Amintore Fanfani to the Secretary of the Foreign Affairs Ministry of Pakistan, Saidullah Kahn Delhavi. See ACS, PCM, Cons.Dipl., b. 40, f. 'Pakistan', *Appunto colloquio Fanfani-Dehlavi*, 5 January 1963.
17 See ACS, PCM, Cons.Dipl., b. 40, f. 'Pakistan', *Tel. 849/110 della Legazione italiana a Karachi. Attività italiane nel Pakistan. Relazione annuale*, 1 March 1963.
18 See ILS, GA, Scritti e discorsi, 'Concretezza', 1 marzo 1967: *L'Asia che programma: il Pakistan*; ACS, AM, PCM (1964–8), Cons.Dipl., Paesi esteri, f. 'Pakistan', *Lettera a Giulio Andreotti*, Rome, 9 March 1967; ACS, AM, PCM (1964–8), Cons.Dipl., Paesi esteri, f. 'Pakistan', *Tel. in partenza. Firma accordo di Tarbala*, 22 April 1968. In the same folder, other relevant records can be found. Andreotti's visit to Pakistan is described in: Spagnulo, 'Aldo Moro e le relazioni italo-pakistane', 225 et sqq.
19 See Ali, *Il duello*, 94.
20 See Henry Kissinger, *The White House Years* (Boston: Little, Brown, 1979), 850.
21 See Vali Reza Nasr, *The Vanguard of the Islamic Revolution: The Jamaat-i-Islami of Pakistan* (Los Angeles: University of California Press, 1994), 165–9.
22 See Sumit Ganguly, *Conflict Unending: India-Pakistan Tensions since 1947* (New Delhi: Oxford University Press, 2001), 61.
23 See Giunchi, *Pakistan*, 91.
24 See US Embassy New Delhi Cable, 29 March 1971; US Consulate Dacca Cable, 28 March 1971; US Consulate Dacca Cable, Killings at University, 30 March 1971; US Consulate Dacca Cable, Extent of Casualties in Dacca, 31 March 1971, in Sajit Gandhi (ed.), *The Tilt: The US and South Asian Crisis of 1971* (Washington, DC: National Security Archive, 2002). See also FRUS, 1969–76, v. XI, *South Asia Crisis, 1971*, docs 1–335.
25 See Memorandum of Conversation, Washington, 10 May 1971, in Gandhi (ed.), *The Tilt*.
26 See Kissinger, *The White House Years*, 854.
27 See Phillips Talbot, 'The Subcontinent: Ménage à trois', in *Foreign Affairs* 50, no. 4 (1972), 698–710.
28 See ASPR, b. 117 Documentazione Paesi, f. 'Bangladesh'.

29 See TNA, FCO 37/898 Attitudes of other countries to the political situation in East-Pakistan, 1971, 211–12.
30 See Record of conversation between Mr. Anthony Royle and Sr. Salizzoni, 5 May 1971, ibid., 224–5.
31 Ibid., 225.
32 See TNA, FCO 37/871 Report on the political situation in Pakistan, 1971, f. 2.
33 See ACS, AM, MAE (1969–72), Questioni nazionali ed internazionali, b. 147, f. Colloqui con ambasciatori e personalità straniere di lingua inglese, *Memorandum di conversazione*, 23 July 1971.
34 See TNA, FCO 37/885 Political crisis in East-Pakistan, 1971, f. 10, 60.
35 See ACS, AM, MAE (1969–72), Questioni nazionali ed internazionali, b. 147, f. Colloqui con ambasciatori e personalità straniere di lingua inglese, *Memorandum di conversazione*, 23 July 1971.
36 Ibid.
37 See Paolo Beonio-Brocchieri, 'Tra India e URSS una assicurazione contro terzi', *Relazioni Internazionali*, nos 34–5, 28 August 1971.
38 See Mariele Merlati, *Gli Stati Uniti tra India e Pakistan. Gli anni della presidenza Carter* (Rome: Carocci, 2009), 54–5; Henry Kissinger, *Cina* (Milan: Mondadori, 2011), 216 et sqq.
39 See ibid., 55–9; Giunchi, *Pakistan*, 92–5.
40 See ASPR, b. 136, Documentazione Paesi, Pakistan.
41 See Ferraris, *Manuale della politica estera italiana 1947–1993*, 307–8.
42 See Luca Dainelli, 'Il dramma pakistano', in *Rivista di Studi Politici Internazionali* 38, no. 4 (October–December 1971), 570–84.
43 See Qutubuddin Aziz, *Blood and Tears* (Karachi: Din Muhammadi Press, 1974).
44 See ASSR, FDM, 1, Attività Politica, s. 1 Incarichi istituzionali, f. 4 Governo Colombo: attività di vicepresidente del Consiglio, *Appunti del Consigliere diplomatico Aldo Marotta per il vicepresidente del Consiglio*, 23 November 1971.
45 See Giunchi, *Pakistan*, 92–5.
46 See Giampaolo Calchi Novati, 'I cerchi delle grandi influenze nel subcontinente', *Relazioni Internazionali* 58 (18 December 1971); 'La risoluzione italiana al consiglio di sicurezza', in *Il Popolo* (daily newspaper of the Christian Democracy's Party), 15 December 1971.
47 See Giunchi, *Pakistan*, 94.
48 See Robert S. Ross (ed.), *China, the United States and the Soviet Union: Tripolarity and Policy Making in the Cold War* (New York: M.E. Sharpe, 1993).
49 See 'Il conflitto indo-pakistano e le sue ripercussioni internazionali', in *Dialoghi diplomatici* 40, Circolo di Studi diplomatici, Rome, 1972.
50 See MAE-Servizio storico e documentazione, *1972. Testi e documenti sulla politica estera dell'Italia* (Rome: Istituto Poligrafico e Zecca dello Stato, 1972); *Colloqui a Roma del Segretario generale dell'ONU Waldheim*, 26 January 1972, 217 e *Il Segretario generale dell'ONU Waldheim e l'amb. Jarring a Roma*, 5 February 1972, 222.
51 See *Consiglio ministeriale dell'UEO*, Bonn, 3 March 1972, ibid., 232.
52 See ASPR, b. 117, Documentazione Paesi, Bangladesh, f. 'Riconoscimento del Bangladesh'.
53 See ASPR, b.746, Lettere Credenziali, Bangladesh, *Appunto sul Bangladesh*.
54 See ASPR, b. 699, Udienze (1965–78), f. 'Pakistan', *Appunto sul Pakistan*.

55 See ASPR, b. 749, Lettere credenziali - India, f. 'Ambasciatore Shri Apashaeb Balashaet Pant', *Appunto sull'India*, no date.
56 See MAE-Servizio storico e documentazione, *1972. Testi e documenti sulla politica estera dell'Italia* (Rome: Istituto Poligrafico e Zecca dello Stato, 1972), *Colloquio Moro-Indira Gandhi*, Roma, 13 June 1972, 300.
57 See Oriana Fallaci, *Intervista con la storia* (Milan: BUR, 1980), 219.
58 For the interviews, see ibid., 188–242.
59 See ISPI, *Annuario di politica internazionale 1972* (Milan: Dedalo, 1974), 273 et sqq.
60 See Howard S. Levie, 'The Indo-Pakistani Agreement of August 28, 1973', *American Journal of International Law* 68, no. 1 (January 1974), 95–7.
61 See MAE-Servizio storico e documentazione, *1972. Testi e documenti sulla politica estera dell'Italia* (Rome: Istituto Poligrafico e Zecca dello Stato, 1972), *Dalle dichiarazioni programmatiche del Presidente del Consiglio Andreotti*, Camera e Senato, 4 luglio 1972, 180. See also the intervention of the Minister of Foreign Affairs Giuseppe Medici at the UN's General Assembly: ibid., *Intervento del ministro Medici alle Nazioni Unite*, New York, 28 September 1972, 362.
62 See ASPR, b. 848, Visite in Italia di Capi di Stato e personalità estere, f. 'Visita privata di Bhutto', July 1973, *Appunto Pakistan*.
63 At the *India Aid Consortium* meeting, the Italian representative claimed that the government of Rome had accepted the assurances given by New Delhi regarding the peaceful use of nuclear technology, but the atomic tests of May 1974 had nevertheless had a negative impact on parliament as well as on the Italian people. This could have made Italian aid to the Consortium more difficult. At the meeting of the EEC Political Committee of 18 June 1974 the Italian representative declared that 'much of the reaction [to Indian atomic tests] had been emotional', although he accepted the idea that 'the cost must have been high and stability had been impaired'. However, he mentioned two useful results: 'Might not India be more self confident and thus prepared to come closer to China and at the same time become less reliant on the Soviet Union [?]'. See FCO 37/1470 Indian nuclear test, 18 May 1974, f. 2, 1974, 72 and 76.
64 See Shahid Javed Burki, *Pakistan under Bhutto, 1971–1977* (London: Macmillan, 1988); Ashok Kapur, *Pakistan's Nuclear Development* (London: Croom Held, 1987); Daniela Bredi, 'Il Pakistan e la bomba islamica: il retroterra storico', in *Giano* 29/30 (1998), 65–74.
65 For the final declarations of the Lahore Conference, see MAE-Servizio storico e documentazione, *1974: Testi e documenti sulla politica estera dell'Italia* (Rome: Istituto Poligrafico e Zecca dello Stato, 1974), 272–5.
66 See ASPR, b. 136 Documentazione Paesi - Pakistan, *Ambasciata d'Italia – Islamabad, Tel. n. 2401*, 5 November 1976.
67 See Giunchi, *Pakistan*, 98 et sqq.; Ali, 127 et sqq.
68 See ASPR, b. 848 Visite in Italia di Capi di Stato e personalità estere, f. 13, 'Visita privata di Zulfikar Bhutto', July 1973.
69 See MAE-Servizio storico e documentazione, *1975. Testi e documenti sulla politica estera dell'Italia* (Rome: Istituto Poligrafico e Zecca dello Stato, 1975) *Pakistan*, 289–90.
70 See TNA, FCO 37/1806 EEC Asian Experts Working Group, f. 2, 1977, *Extract from releve de conclusion of political committee 9th-10th September 1976*.
71 See TNA, FCO 37/1807 EEC Asian Experts Working Group, f. 3, 1977, *European Political Cooperation, Meeting of Asia Experts Working Group: 21st–22nd February*

1977, Annex B, *Relations between the Countries of the South Asian Region*, South Asian Department, Foreign and Commonwealth Office, February 1977, p. 118.
72 See *European Political Cooperation, Meeting of Asia Experts Working Group: 21st-22nd February 1977, Agenda Item 1: The Indian Subcontinent*, ibid., 109.
73 See ASPR, Documentazione Paesi, b. 136, Pakistan, *Appunto. Situazione in Pakistan*, Rome, 5 July 1977.
74 See MAE-Servizio storico e documentazione, *1979: Testi e documenti sulla politica estera dell'Italia* (Rome: Istituto Poligrafico e Zecca dello Stato, 1979), 18.
75 See Kamal Afzar, *Pakistan: Political and Constitutional Dilemmas* (Karachi: Pakistan Law House, 1987), 100-7.
76 See *L'Avanti*, 5 April 1979.
77 See 'Il Pakistan dopo l'impiccagione di Bhutto', in *Relazioni Internazionali*, n. 15-14 aprile 1979, p. 330.
78 See Luciano Monzali, 'La politica estera italiana e l'occupazione sovietica dell'Afghanistan (1979-89). Note e documenti', in Federico Imperato, Gianvito Galasso, Rosario Milano and Luciano Monzali (eds), *Europa e Medio Oriente (1973-1993)* (Bari: Cacucci, 2017), 285 et sqq.
79 See Merlati, 92 et sqq. Kux, 345 et sqq.
80 See Ferraris, *Manuale della politica estera italiana 1947-1993*, 308.
81 Ibid. See also MAE-Servizio storico e documentazione, *1977: Testi e documenti sulla politica estera dell'Italia* (Rome: Istituto Poligrafico e Zecca dello Stato, 1977), 17; MAE-Servizio storico e documentazione, *1978: Testi e documenti sulla politica estera dell'Italia* (Rome: Istituto Poligrafico e Zecca dello Stato, 1978), 206-7; Bela Butalia, 'Indo-Italian Relations since 1947', *International Studies* 23 (1986), 134-5.
82 See Ferraris, *Manuale della politica estera italiana 1947-1993*, 494.
83 See Monzali, *La politica estera italiana e l'occupazione sovietica dell'Afghanistan (1979-1989)*, 285 et sqq.
84 See TNA, FCO 37/2118 European Political Cooperation: Asia Working Group, 1979, *European Political Cooperation: Asia Working Group, Paris 17th-18th May 1979. Item 1: The India Sub-Continent*.
85 See Giunchi, *Pakistan*, 114 et sqq.
86 In order to analyse the US reaction to the Soviet invasion of Afghanistan, see Raymond L. Garthoff, *Détente and Confrontation. American-Soviet Relations from Nixon to Reagan* (Washington, DC: Brookings Institution, 1994); Zbigniew Brzezinski, *Power and Principle: Memoirs of the National Security Adviser 1977-1981* (London: Weidenfeld and Nicolson, 1983); Anatoly Dobrynin, *In Confidence: Moscow's Ambassador to America's Six Cold War Presidents (1962-1986)* (New York: Times Books-Random House, 1995), 443 et sqq.; Jimmy Carter, *Keeping Faith: Memoirs of a President* (Toronto: Bantam Books, 1982), 471 et sqq.; Carter, *White House Diary* (New York: Picador, 2011), 380 et sqq.; Cyrus Vance, *Hard Choices: Critical Years in America's Foreign Policy* (New York: Simon & Schuster, 1983), 387 et sqq.; Richard N. Gardner, *Mission Italy. Gli anni di piombo raccontati dall'ambasciatore americano a Roma 1977-1981* (Milan: Mondadori, 2004), 331 et sqq. See also: ILS, GA, b. Afghanistan, *Appunto per il Ministero degli Affari Esteri. Misure adottate dal Governo Italiano, nei confronti dell'URSS, in connessione con la crisi afghana*, 21 January 1980; ILS, GA, b. Afghanistan, *Tel. in arrivo da Italdipl Bruxelles. Conclusioni del Consiglio su misure CEE in relazione sviluppi Afghanistan*, 16 January 1980.

87 See Sitara Noor, 'L'arsenale pakistano è figlio della paura dell'India', in *A qualcuno piace atomica*, I quaderni speciali di *'Limes'*, no. 2 (2012), 135–46.
88 See ILS, GA, b. Afghanistan, *Tel. in arrivo da Italdipl Washington. Valutazioni americane sulle implicazioni geopolitiche dell'intervento sovietico in Afghanistan*, 10 January 1980.
89 On the Indian attitude during the Soviet occupation of Afghanistan, see John Fullerton, *The Soviet Occupation of Afghanistan* (Hong Kong: Far Eastern Economic Review, 1983), 39 et sqq.; David M. Malone, *Does the Elephant Dance? Contemporary Indian Foreign Policy* (Oxford: Oxford University Press, 2011), 114 et sqq.; Jayanta Kumar Ray, *India's Foreign Relations, 1947–2007* (New Delhi: Routledge, 2011), 533 et sqq.
90 See Noor, 'L'arsenale pakistano è figlio della paura dell'India', 139–41.
91 See Ferraris, *Manuale della politica estera italiana 1947–1993*, 494; 'Zia-ul-Haq in Italia', *Relazioni Internazionali*, nos 1–2, 30 January 1982.
92 See Ferraris, *Manuale della politica estera italiana 1947–1993*, 495.
93 See Monzali, *La politica estera italiana e l'occupazione sovietica dell'Afghanistan (1979–1989)*, 303–36.
94 Of course, the rearmament of Pakistan did not please Indira Gandhi, who returned to power in 1980. During a visit to Rome on 8–9 November 1981, the Indian prime minister claimed the right to self-defend and to arm against potential opponents and threats. Nevertheless, India abstained from voting on the condemnation of the Soviet invasion of Afghanistan promoted at the UN Assembly, contradicting, in part, its closeness to Moscow as enshrined in the Treaty of Indo-Soviet friendship and cooperation. See Ferraris, *Manuale della politica estera italiana 1947–1993*, 493; Butalia, 'Indo-Italian Relations since 1947', 135.
95 See Monzali, *La politica estera italiana e l'occupazione sovietica dell'Afghanistan (1979–1989)*, 303–36.
96 Ibid., 333–6.
97 Ibid., 319.
98 See ILS, GA, Afghanistan, b. 32, *Fornara a Ministero degli Affari Esteri*, 17 April 1988.
99 Ibid.
100 Ibid.
101 Ibid.
102 Ibid.
103 Ibid.
104 Quoted in Daniele Raineri's 'In Pakistan è 'come chiedere al Diavolo di prendere Dracula': Perché i generali di Musharraf hanno cominciato la loro guerra privata a fianco di Talebani e Al Qaida', *Il Foglio*, 30 September 2008.
105 See Victoria Schofield, *Kashmir. India, Pakistan e la guerra infinita* (Rome: Fazi, 2004), 142 et sqq.
106 See Monzali, *La politica estera italiana e l'occupazione sovietica dell'Afghanistan (1979–1989)*, 334–6.
107 See Fondazione Spadolini Nuova Antologia, GS, s. 12 Presidenza del Senato della Repubblica, f. 6 Articoli e interviste, *Inserto Italia su 'Dawn'*, 23 December 1991.
108 See Arduino Fornara, 'Pakistan-Italy Relations', *Pakistan Horizon* 44, no. 3 (1991), 20.
109 Ibid., 20–1.
110 Ibid., 23–4.
111 Ibid., 27.

Bibliography

André, Gianluca, *L'Italia e il Mediterraneo alla vigilia della prima guerra mondiale: I tentativi di intesa mediterranea (1911-1914)* (Milan: Giuffrè, 1967).
Arieli, Nir, *Fascist Italy and the Middle East, 1933-1940* (Basingstoke: Palgrave, 2010).
Bagnato, Bruna, *L'Italia e la guerra d'Algeria 1954-1962* (Soveria Mannelli: Rubbettino, 2012).
Bagnato, Bruna, *Petrolio e politica. Mattei in Marocco* (Florence: Polistampa, 2004).
Bosworth, Richard J., *Italy, the Least of the Great Powers: Italian Foreign Policy before the First World War* (Cambridge: Cambridge University Press, 1979).
Brogi, Alessandro, *L'Italia e l'egemonia americana nel Mediterraneo* (Florence: La Nuova Italia, 1996).
Buccianti, Giovanni, *Libia: Petrolio e indipendenza* (Milan: Giuffrè, 1999).
Calchi Novati, Gian Paolo, *Il canale della Discordia: Suez e la politica estera italiana* (Urbino: Quattro Venti, 1998).
Caviglia, Daniele, and Massimiliano Cricco, *La diplomazia italiana e gli equilibri mediterranei: La politica mediorientale dell'Italia dalla guerra dei sei giorni al conflitto dello Yom Kippur (1967-1973)* (Soveria Mannelli: Rubbettino, 2006).
Cricco, Massimiliano, and Federico Cresti, *Gheddafi: I volti del potere* (Roma: Carocci, 2011).
De Felice, Renzo, *Il fascismo e l'Oriente: Arabi, ebrei e indiani nella politica di Mussolini* (Bologna: Il Mulino, 1988).
De Leonardis, Massimo (ed.), *Il Mediterraneo nella politica estera italiana del secondo dopoguerra* (Bologna: Il Mulino, 2003).
Del Boca, Angelo, *Gli Italiani in Libia* (Milano: Mondadori, 2012, Vol. II).
Duggan, Christopher, *Francesco Crispi, 1818-1901: From Nation to Nationalism* (London: Oxford University Press, 2002).
Ferraioli, Gianpaolo, *Politica e Diplomazia in Italia tra XIX e XX secolo. Vita di Antonino di San Giuliano (1852-1914)* (Soveria Mannelli: Rubbettino, 2007).
Gaja, Roberto, *Console in Libia 1949-1952*, edited by Luciano Monzali (Rome: Società Dante Alighieri, 2020).
Galasso, Gianvito, Federico Imperato, Rosario Milano and Luciano Monzali (eds), *Europa e Medio Oriente (1973-1993)* (Bari: Cacucci, 2017).
Garzia, Italo, Luciano Monzali and Federico Imperato (eds), *Aldo Moro, l'Italia repubblicana e i Popoli del Mediterraneo* (Nardò: Besa, 2013).
Giovagnoli, Agostino, and Luciano Tosi (eds), *Amintore Fanfani e la politica estera italiana* (Venice: Marsilio, 2010).
Grange, Daniel J., *L'Italie et la Méditerranée (1896-1911)* (Rome: Ecole française de Rome, 1994).
Imperato, Federico, *Aldo Moro e la pace nella sicurezza: La politica estera del centro-sinistra 1963-1968* (Bari: Progedit, 2011).

Imperato, Federico, Rosario Milano and Luciano Monzali (eds), *Fra diplomazia e petrolio: Aldo Moro e la politica italiana in Medio Oriente (1963–1978)* (Bari: Cacucci, 2018).

La Fortezza, Roberta, *Cedri e ulivi nel giardino del Mediterraneo: Storia delle relazioni diplomatiche italo-libanesi tra il 1943 e il 1958* (Soveria Mannelli: Rubbettino, 2020).

Labanca, Nicola, *Oltremare: Storia dell'espansione coloniale italiana* (Bologna: Il Mulino, 2002).

Malgeri, Francesco, *La guerra libica 1911–1912* (Rome: Edizioni di Storia e Letteratura, 1970).

Martelli, Evelina, *L'altro atlantismo. Fanfani e la politica estera italiana (1958–1963)* (Milan: Guerini, 2008).

Micheletta, Luca, and Andrea Ungari (eds), *The Libyan War 1911–1912* (Newcastle upon Tyne: Cambridge Scholars, 2013).

Milano, Rosario, *L'ENI e l'Iran (1962–1970)* (Napoli: Giannini, 2013).

Minerbi, Sergio, *L'Italie et la Palestine 1914–1920* (Paris: Presses universitaires de France, 1970).

Monzali, Luciano, *Guerra e diplomazia in Africa orientale: Francesco Crispi, l'Italia liberale e la questione etiopica* (Rome: Società Dante Alighieri, 2017).

Monzali, Luciano, *Il colonialismo nella politica estera italiana 1878–1949: Momenti e protagonisti* (Rome: Società Dante Alighieri, 2017).

Monzali, Luciano, *Un Re afghano in esilio a Roma: Amanullah e l'Afghanistan nella politica estera italiana 1919–1943* (Florence: Le Lettere, 2012).

Petricioli, Marta, *L'Italia in Asia minore: Equilibrio mediterraneo e ambizioni imperialiste alla vigilia della prima guerra mondiale* (Florence: Sansoni, 1983).

Pizzigallo, Matteo, *Alle origini della politica petrolifera italiana (1920–1925)* (Milan: Giuffrè, 1981).

Pizzigallo, Matteo, *La diplomazia italiana e i paesi arabi del'Oriente mediterraneo (1946–1952)* (Milan: Franco Angeli, 2008).

Riccardi, Luca, *Il 'problema Israele': Diplomazia italiana e PCI di fronte allo Stato ebraico (1948–1973)* (Milan: Guerini, 2006).

Riccardi, Luca, *L'internazionalismo difficile: La 'diplomazia' del PCI e il Medio Oriente dalla crisi petrolifera alla caduta del muro di Berlino (1973–1989)* (Soveria Mannelli: Rubbettino, 2013).

Riccardi, Luca, *L'ultima politica estera: L'Italia e il Medio Oriente alla fine della prima Repubblica* (Soveria Mannelli: Rubbettino, 2014).

Serra, Enrico, *La questione tunisina da Crispi a Rudinì ed il 'colpo di timone' alla politica estera italiana* (Milan: Giuffrè, 1967).

Soave, Paolo, *Fezzan: Il deserto conteso (1842–1921)* (Milan: Giuffrè, 2001).

Soave, Paolo, *Fra Reagan e Gheddafi: La politica estera italiana e l'escalation libico-americana degli anni '80* (Soveria Mannelli: Rubbettino, 2017).

Soave, Paolo, *Una vittoria mutilata? L'Italia e la Conferenza di Pace di Parigi* (Soveria Mannelli: Rubbettino, 2020).

Spagnulo, Giuseppe, *Il Risorgimento dell'Asia: India e Pakistan nella politica estera dell'Italia repubblicana (1946–1980)* (Firenze: Le Monnier, 2020).

Toscano, Mario, *Gli accordi di San Giovanni di Moriana: Storia diplomatica dell'intervento italiano, II (1916–1917)* (Milano: Giuffré, 1936).

Toscano, Mario, *La 'Porta di Sion': L'Italia e l'immigrazione clandestina ebraica in Palestina 1945–1948* (Bologna: Il Mulino, 1990).

Tremolada, Ilaria, *All'ombra degli arabi: Le relazioni italo-israeliane 1948–1956: dalla fondazione dello Stato ebraico alla crisi di Suez* (Milan: M & B, 2003).

Varsori, Antonio, *L'Italia e la fine della guerra fredda: La politica estera dei governi Andreotti 1989–1992* (Bologna: Il Mulino, 2013).

Varvelli, Arturo, *L'Italia e l'ascesa di Gheddafi: La cacciata degli italiani, le armi e il petrolio (1969–1974)* (Milan: Baldini Castoldi Dalai, 2009).

Villani, Angela, *L'Italia e l'Onu negli anni della coesistenza competitiva (1955–1986)* (Padova: Cedam, 2007).

Webster, Richard, *Industrial Imperialism in Italy 1908–1915* (Berkeley: University of California Press, 1975).

Index

Abbas, Bandar 236
'Abd al-Majid, Wahid 32
Abdel-Shafi, Haidar 32, 38 n.57
Abdessalam, Belaid 227
Abdul Hadi, Mahdi 32–3
Abed, George T. 37 n.26
Abrahms, Max 30, 37 n.33
Abu Dhabi 131
Abu Nidal group 156
Abyssinian Empire xi
Achille Lauro hijacking 101, 158–60
Acquaviva, Gennaro 106 n.53, 167 n.51
Adalet Partisi (AP–Justice Party) 204
Adalia/Antalya 59
Adana 58–9
Addis Ababa 50
Adelman, Morris A. 229
Adriatic coast 43
Adriatic Sea xii
Afflerbach, Holger 74 n.13
Afghan Communist Party 250
Afghanistan and Italy 5, 10, 14
  Amanullah to Soviet invasion of 1979 250–3
  Zahir and Afghan after Gorbachev's rise to power 254–7
  Zahir and the Soviets, negotiations 256–9
Afghan refugees in Pakistan 251
Agrarian Revolution 1971 policy 188
Agusta helicopter issue 240
Ahmed, Mustafa 181 n.13
Aid-to-Pakistan Consortium in 1963 267
Aksai Chin 272
al-Assad, Hafiz 140
Albania 49, 195
Albertini, Luigi 57
Alenia G222 military transport aircraft 213
Alexandria 112

Algeria and Italy 2, 28, 110, 189, 195
  Algeria 1973–99 187–97
  assassination of foreigner workers by Islamist groups 191
  industrialization 188
  natural gas connection 193–5, 197
  political stabilization 5
  post-electoral case 3
  Sant'Egidio peace mediation 195–7
  war for Algerian independence 192–4
Algerian Civil War 115
Algerian revolution 238
Algerian society 187
Algeria-Sardinia Italy Gas Pipeline 194
Algiers 110
Al-Jaber, Sheikh Sabah 128
Allen, David 134 n.2
Alpine territories 43
al-Qaeda 179, 190
Amanullah in Afghanistan 249
American bombing of Libya 15, 178
American foreign policy 9
American hegemony in the Middle East 3
American presidential campaign, 1956 9
Amin, Hafizullah 250
Amir-Entezam, Abbas 235
Anatolia 59
Anatolian peninsula xii
Andoni, Lamis 37 n.25
Andreotti, Giulio 96, 99, 103, 106 n.46, 141, 153–4, 165 n.3, 213, 218 n.53, 263 n.51, 264 n.60, 267
Andrew, Gumbel 197 n.4
Angioni, Franco 146, 152 n.43
Anglo-American influence 169–70
Anglo-American military base 170
Anglo-French-Italian Treaty of 1906 63
Anglo-Italian rivalry 220
Anglo-Saxon company 220
Ankara 5, 73, 214

Ankara Agreement (1963) 209
antagonism 123
anti-British nationalist movements xii
anti-Chinese capacity 267
anti-French propaganda campaign 67
anti-German coalition Paris 65
anti-German nationalism 63
anti-Habsburg convention 62
anti-Iraq coalition 28–9
Anti-Komintern pact 67
anti-Pahlavi coalition 235
anti-Pakistani nationalist guerrillas 273
anti-Yugoslav Croatian nationalism 67
Arab Deterrent Force (ADF) 142
Arabian Peninsula 10
Arab–Israeli conflict 4, 11–12, 16, 19, 20 n.14, 26, 94, 97, 153, 206
Arab–Israeli peace process 153
Arab League meeting 27
Arab League Ministerial Council 37 n.18
Arab Summit Conference 28
Arafat, Yasser xiii, 13, 28, 32–3, 100, 149, 151 n.3–4, 157
Ardalan, Ali 235–6
Arieli, Nir xiv n.8
Armed Islamic Groups (GIA) 190
Armenian crisis 49
Arunachal Pradesh 272
Aryomand, Said Amir 245 n.1
Aswan Dam 16
Ataturk, Kemal xii, 61, 64
Atatürk, Mustafa Kemal 204
Atlantic Alliance, Middle East and 1, 212–13
  Achille Lauro hijacking 158–60
  Mediterranean and the Italian governments 155–6
  missiles, issue of 153–5
  Sigonella crisis 160–4
  terror and peace 156–8
  turning point 162–3
Atlantic bloc 265
Atlanticism 198 n.7
Austria-Hungary 44, 48
Austro-German diplomacy 45, 56
Austro-Hungarian policy 45
Austro-Russian rivalry 48
authoritarian dictatorship 63
autonomist 154

Avineri, Shlomo 26, 36 n.10
Awami League 268–9, 272
Axis policy 66
Aydin 58–9
Aydin, Mustafa 37 n.16
Ayoob, Mohammed 19 n.7
Azerbaijan 195

Badini, Antonio 106 n.54–106 n.55, 156–7, 166 n.26, 167 n.51
Badoglio, Pietro 70
Baghdad 20, 28, 110, 115
Baghdad Pact 11
Bagnato, Bruna 90 n.187, 117 n.9, 194, 198 n.6
Bailey, Thomas A. 19 n.9, 20 n.10
Baker, James 31
Bakhash, Shaul 245 n.3
Baldacci, Valentino 106 n.47
Baldinetti, Anna 182 n.19
Balkans 44, 47
  Austro-Russian rivalry 48
  crisis 44
Balkan War 56
Ballero, Pietro 255
Bamberg, James 234 n.82
Banco di Roma 64
Bandung Conference 266
Bangladesh 270
Bani Sadr, election of 239–43
Barak, Oren 35, 39 n.66
Barbary and Tripoli wars 11
Barnett, Michael N. 37 n.17
Basciani, Alberto 86 n.149
Battle of Algiers 193
Bazargan, Mehdi 235
Beilin, Yossi 33
Beirut 15, 26, 145, 147–8
Belgrade 62
Bella, Ahmed Ben 188
Bendjedid, Chadli 188–9
benevolent neutrality 46
Bengalis 269
Benso, Camillo of Cavour 43
Berlin 45, 48, 50
Berlinguer, Enrico 140, 145, 204, 251
Bevin-Sforza agreement 72, 169
BGM-109 G Gryphon missiles 154
Bhutto, Zulfikar Ali 270, 275–6

bilateral cultural diplomacy 110
Bini, Elisabetta 233 n.53
Blair, John M. 231 n.18
Blanc 49–50
Blanchard, Christopher 182 n.21
Bolshevik Russia 62
Bona, Enrica Costa 105 n.39, 216 n.10
Bongiorno, Joseph A. 4, 22 n.27
Bonomi, Ivanoe 58–9
border territories 13
Boselli, Paolo 58
Bosnia 53
Bosworth, Richard J. 78 n.65
Boumediene, Houari 188
Bozzo, Baget 216 n.12
BP 220
Brenner Pass 43
Breslauer, George W. 36 n.5
Brezhnev, Leonid 16
British colonial power 265
British Empire 26
Brogi, Alessandro 117 n.6
Brouille, Alain 151 n.34
Brown, George 220
Brzezinski, Zbigniew 22 n.26, 238
Bucarelli, Massimo 234 n.73
Bucharest 62
Bulgarian crisis 48
Bülow, Bernhard von 56
Buongiorno, Pino 165 n.17
Burke, Samuel Martin 285 n.9
Bush, George 26, 30, 257
Bush-Gorbachev News Conference 37 n.35

caesura 203
Caetani, Onorato 50
Çağlayangil 206
Cairo 13, 27, 132, 162
Cairoli, Benedetto 45
Cairoli-Corti government 74 n.11
Calandri, Elena xv n.13, 120 n.35
Cambodian crisis 256
Camp David Accords, 1978 14–15, 17, 97, 174
Camp David summit, 2000 34
Camp David Treaty of 1979 28
Canevaro, Felice 51
Caracas Resolution 122 of 1970 221, 228
Carrié, René Albrecht 82 n.109

Carter, Jimmy 13–14, 97, 153, 241
Casini, Fabio 185 n.92
Cassels, Alan 84 n.127
Catholic missionaries 270
Cattaro 43
Cavalchini, Luigi 160
Caviglia, Daniele xv n.15, 104 n.6, 151 n.5
Cavour's foreign policy 73 n.2
Central Treaty Organization (CENTO) 11
Chabod, Federico xiv n.1
Chamberlin, Paul T. 36 n.8
Chiala, Luigi 74 n.13
Chigi, Palazzo 267
Chinese mobilization 272
Christian Democracy (DC) 203
Christians 139, 150
Ciano, Galeazzo 66, 86 n.146
Claverie, Pierre 196
climat de confiance 124
Coen, Federico 253
Colarizi, Simona 165 n.18, 166 n.23
Cold War xii–xiii, 1, 5, 9–10, 18, 26, 29, 98, 109, 265–6
    Central Asia (1979–91) 279–83
    Israeli–Palestinian conflict (1989–93) 25–7
    Soviet Union 15–18
    United States 11–15
Colitti, Marcello 236
Colombo, Emilio 96, 99, 105 n.34, 143, 143
Colombo, Vittorino 205
colonial expansionism 46, 58, 93
colonial policies 187
conciliateurs 196
Condotte 240
confiscation 187
Contarini, Salvatore 63
controlled competition 26
Coordinating Committee on Multilateral Export Controls (COCOM) 252
Cordovez, Diego 255
Corti, Luigi 45
Cossiga, Francesco 97, 105 n.36, 154, 164, 242
Courten, Franco De 199 n.15
Coverdale, John F. xiv n.7
Crainz, Guido 103 n.1
Crankshaw, Edward 23 n.41
Craveri, Piero 104 n.10, 217 n.34

Craxi, Bettino 99–101, 146, 156, 158, 163, 185 n.84, 210
Craxi-Andreotti period 99–101
Cricco, Massimiliano xv n.15, 104 n.8, 183 n.10, 181 n.14, 232 n.41
Crispi, Francesco 48, 50, 74 n.10, 75 n.21–2
Cristofori, Carlo 253
crude oil exploration 227
Cuba 27
cultural cooperation 110
cultural diplomacy in the Middle East 5, 109–16
cultural sensitivity 5
Cumhuriyet Güven Partisi (CGP-Republican Reliance Party) 204
Cumhuriyet Halk Partisi (CHP–Republican People's Party) 204
Cypriot National Guard 205
Cyprus 205, 212
  crisis 207
Cyrenaica 51, 53–5, 72, 169
Czechoslovakia 62

Dalmatian Coast xii
Damascus Declaration of March 1991 27
Dannreuther, Roland 36 n.12
Dante Alighieri 110
Dark Decade 192, 195
Dayan, Moshe 35
Dayan, Yael 35
Declaration of Independence 28
Declaration of Principles of 13 September 1993 25, 32–5
Declaration of Venice and the Middle East 96–7
decolonization 72, 93, 265
De Felice, Renzo xiv n.9, 66, 155
De Gasperi, Alcide xii
De Gasperi centrism 170
De Gasperi's foreign policy 89 n.186
de-globalization of the Arab-Israeli conflict 26
de Leonardis, Massimo 117 n.8, 181 n.7
Demirel, Süleyman 204
De Mita, Ciriaco 103
democracy 169
Democratic Party (DP–Demokratik Parti) 204
Depretis, Agostino 45, 48

Depretis-Mancini government 47
Desert Storm 31
d'Estaing, Giscard 97
Deuxiè me Bureau for intelligence 147
Dietrich, Christopher R. W. 234 n.80
Dini, Lamberto 196
Diószegi, István 74 n.7
diplomatic activism, 1970 2
direct linkage 30
Directorate General of Cultural Relations (DGCR) 113
DİSK (Confederation of Progressive Trade Unions of Turkey–Türkiye Devrimci İşçi Sendikaları Konfederasyonu) 211
Dobbins, James F. 260 n.4
Dodecanese Islands xi, xii, 56, 55, 58, 64
Dodge, David 149
Donnini, Guido 78 n.59
D'Onofrio, Francesco 161
d'Orsay, Quai 133
'double-track' strategy 72
Douglas, Alec 270
Drake, Eric 223
dual anchorage 98
dual-track decision 155
Dublin formula 130–2
Ducci, Roberto 104 n.19, 126, 208

EAD see Euro-Arab dialogue (EAD)
Eastern Mediterranean 56
East Pakistan 268
Ecevit, Bülent 204
economic crisis 94, 203
economic growth xiii
EEC see European Economic Community (EEC)
Egypt 3, 14, 27, 44, 110, 113, 172
  and USA ties 22 n.27
Eisenhower, Dwight D. 9–10
election of Bani Sadr 239–43
El Suwaidi, Ahmed Khalifa 128
Emanuele III, Vittorio 52
Emiliani, Marcella 105 n.26
ENI (Ente Nazionale Idrocarburi, the National Hydrocarbons Authority) 219–20, 240
  Anglo-Italian talks on ENI and Middle East 222–5

Conference of Caracas 220–3
    Tehran Agreements, aftermath of 225–8
Enlai, Zhou 269
Ente Nazionale Idrocarburi (ENI) 236
equidistanza 93
Erbakan, Necmettin 208–9
Erim, Nihat 204
Eritrea xi
Esteri, Affari 118 n.11–21, 120 n.33–4, 121 n.43, 122 n.61–5, 122 n.67
Ethiopian war 109
Euro-Arab dialogue (EAD) 2, 123, 129, 131
    before 1973 oil crisis 123–5
    Euro-Arab cooperation 125–8
    Italy's role 128–33
Euro-Mediterranean power 66
Euromissiles 156–7, 210
European diplomacy 95
European Economic Community (EEC) 142, 239, 242, 251–2
European energy policy 134
European Political Cooperation (EPC) 127
Evron, Yair 26, 36 n.4
expansionism 93
    in African continent xii
    colonial 46–7
    German 66
    Italian aggressive 64
    Russian 48

Facta, Luigi 62
Fadlallah, Sheik Mohammed Hussein 157
Fahmi, Assad 132
fait accompli 56
Fanfani, Amintore 91 n.192, 93–4, 220
Farnesina 111
Fasci all'estero 64
fascism 65–6, 110
Fascist authoritarian regime 65
Fascist civilization 66
Fascist diplomacy 67
Fascist imperialism 66, 71
Fascist Italy's foreign policy (1940–43) 68–70
'fascistizzazione' of Italian society 65
Fascist movement 62
Fascist party 64
Ferdinand, Francis, assassination of 56
Ferdinand of Saxe-Coburg 48

Ferrari, Silvio 104 n.9
Ferraris, Luigi Vittorio 107 n.80, 197 n.3, 216 n.9, 218 n.55
Ferretti, Valdo 84 n.131
Fezzan 169
Fink, Carole K. 19 n.4
first treaty of alliance 50
First World War 10
Ford, Gerald 208
Foreign Affairs Commission 99
Forlani, Arnaldo 132, 141, 144, 279
Fortezza, Roberta La 5
Four Powers Pact 64
France 71
    Austro-German refusal to back the Italian initiative 46
    Morocco and Tripolitania 47
    political autonomy 2
Franco, Massimo 106 n.52
Franco-British rivalry 52
Franco-German war 52
Freedman, Robert O. 37 n.20
French-British-German war 67
French colonial policy 187
French–German cooperation 65
Frisch, Hillel 32, 38 n.48
Funke, Manfred 85 n.136

Gabriele, Mariano 80 n.90
Gaddafi, Muammar al- 172–79, 213, 218 n.54
Gaddafi and relations with Italy
    advent of Gaddafi 171–2
    after Second World War 169–71
    after the Cold War 179
    Moro's answer to Gaddafi 172–4
    Terrorism and global Cold War 175–9
Gaja, Robert 2, 71
Gallo, Giorgio 39 n.64
Galsi 194
Gandhi, Indira 275
Garavini, Giuliano 227, 233 n.66, 233 n.67
Gardner, Richard N. 261 n.18
Garibaldi, Giuseppe 48
Garthoff, Raymond L. 167 n.6, 264 n.42
Gauhar, Altaf 285 n.10
Gaza Strip 28, 31–2, 35
Gemayel, Benchir 146

Generalised Scheme of Preferences
    (GSP) 207
Geneva negotiations 281
Geneva peace agreements 256, 263
    n.44, 283–4
Geneva Peace Conference 14, 17
Geneva peace process 256
Genoa 43
Genoa Conference 62
Gentile, Giovanni 64
George, Lloyd 62
Georgia 195
Gera, Gideon 28, 32, 37 n.21, 38 n.46
Gerlini, Matteo 5, 165 n.4
German expansionism 66
German-Italian cooperation 65
German revisionism 65
Germany, alliance with xii
Gervasoni, Marco 166 n.23
Ghaddafi, Muammar 15
Ghadiri, Hassan 241
Gheddafi, Muammar 21–20
Ghotbzadeh, Sadegh 240–1
Giannini, Amedeo 64
Giarabub 61
Giolitti, Giovanni 52, 55, 60, 62
Giorgio, Massimiliano Di 198 n.11
Giovagnoli, Agostino 104 n.6
Girotti, Raffaele 223–4
Giuliano, San 54, 56–7
Giurato, Luca 165 n.11
globalization 2
Global Turn 4
Golan, Galia 30, 33–4, 37 n.34, 38 n.44,
    38 n.54
Gorbachev, Mikhail 15, 18, 23 n.45, 24
    n.46, 30, 256
Gorbachev–Reagan summit in
    Washington 256
Gorla 141
Gottsmann, Andreas 74 n.13
Gowers, Andrew 104 n.20
Greece 111, 195, 205
Greek civil war 11
'green helmets' of ADF 142
Green Stream 195
Group of Rome 249, 252
Guida, Francesco 74 n.24
Guido Quaranta 165 n.2

Gulf crisis 34
Gulf War 115
    and its consequences 27–30
    PLO relationship with Saudi Arabia and
        Kuwait 29
Gymnich formula 127–8

Habib, Philip 151 n.33
Habib Plan 144
Habsburg calculation 56
Habsburg diplomacy 52
Habsburg empire 56
Habsburg restoration 62
Hadi, Mahdi Abdul 38 n.49
Haifa 112
Halevi, Efraim 34
Haley, Edward 182 n.22
Halim, Ben 170, 181 n.13
Hamas 29, 33
Hantsch, Hugo 57
Hassan, Shamir 34, 38 n.56, 159
Healey, Denis 229
Herzegovina 44
Hinsley, Francis Harry 75 n.17
Hirschfeld, Yair 33
Hitler, Adolf 65
Holloway, David 165 n.9, 165 n.12,
    165 n.19
Holst, Johan Jorgen 33
Howarth, Stephen 23 n.36
human trafficking 197
Hussein, Saddam 28, 30
hydrocarbon production 235
Hydrocarbons Technology 198 n.10

Ilaria Tremolada's thesis 224
Imam' *(Khat-e Imam)* 238
Imperato, Federico 5
Imperial Japan 66
Impregilo 240
India Aid Consortium 288 n.63
Indian Congress Party 265
Indian foreign policy 286 n.11
Indian-Pakistani conversations 274
Indo-Pakistani crisis 275
Indo-Pakistani war
    1965 268
    1971 276–7
Indo–Soviet treaty of friendship 272

industrial take-off xi
Indyk, Martin 32, 37 n.36, 38 n.42
Insiders 32
intellectual property 214
International Bank for Reconstruction and Development (IBRD) 267
international peace conference for Middle East 31
international polarization 272
Intifada 28, 102–3
intra-religion conflict 139
Iran 2, 10, 110, 113, 172
Iran Crisis of 1946 16
Iranian revolution and Italy 5, 115, 235–7
 election of Bani Sadr 239–43
 production of hydrocarbons 238
 Revolutionary Council 240
 second phase of Iranian revolution 237–9
 Shatt al-Arab and Europe 243–5
Iranian Revolution Council (Shury-e-Enqelab-e-Eslami) 235
Iranian-Soviet exchange 242
Iran–Iraq War 115
Iraq 3, 27–8, 110
Iraq-Iran war xiii
Islamic Front of Salvation (FIS) 189
Islamic Holy places 58
Islamic Land of the Maghreb (AQIM) 190
Islamic Republican Party 237
Islamic revolution 96
Islamic Salvation Army (AIS) 190
Islamist violence 196
Israel 2, 93, 110–11
 deterrence measure against 140
 withdrawal from occupied Palestinian territories 28
Israel–Egypt peace process 96
Israeli–American relationship 29
Israeli–Arab conflict 4, 11–12, 15, 171
Israeli–Egyptian peace negotiations 13
Israeli–Egyptian Peace Treaty, 1979 17
Israeli Lebanon invasion 115
Israeli–Palestinian conflict (1989–93) 25, 100
 American economic assistance to 26
 Cold War and 25–7
 Declaration of Principles of 13 September 1993 32–5
 Gulf War and its consequences 27–30
 Madrid Conference 30–2
Israeli-Palestinian negotiation 141
Istituto per il Medio ed Estremo Oriente 64
Istituto per l'Oriente 64
Istria 62
Istrian peninsula xii
ITALCON contingent 145
Italian–Afghan relations 260 n.1
Italian aggressive expansionism 64
Italian–Austrian accords 56
Italian-British growing antagonism 86 n.143
Italian Catholicism 252
Italian colonialism in Libya 180 n.1
Italian Communist Party (PCI) 99, 140, 146, 251
Italian cultural diplomacy 111
Italian domestic terrorism 142
Italian-Ethiopian war 85 n.135
Italian foreign policy and the Middle East 1, 5, 43–7, 90 n.193
 colonial policy xiv n.2
 extra-European cultures 1
 Fascist Italy's foreign policy 68–70
 First World War and 'mutilated victory' 55–62
 Italian predominance in the Mediterranean Sea (1932–40) 65–8
 Liberal Left 44
 Mussolini's foreign policy 62–4
 partition of Ottoman Empire and conquest of Tripolitania and Cyrenaica 48–55
 post-colonial transition 1
 post-Fascist Italy 70–3
 social and economic differences 1
 south-eastern foreign policy 1
 Triple Alliance with Germany and Austria-Hungary 46
Italian *Lebensraum* 67–8
Italian–Ottoman peace preliminaries 55, 61
Italian–Pakistani economic relations 276
Italian-Pakistani relations 283 n.1
Italian predominance in Mediterranean Sea (1932–40) 65–8
Italian regionalism 170
Italian Republican Party (Partito Repubblicano Italiano, PRI) 253

Italian Socialist Party (PSI) 204
Italian–Turkish relations 86 n.140, 91 n.194
Italian–Yugoslav controversy 61
Italo-Austro-British alliance 48
Italo-Austro-German naval convention 56
Italo-British collaboration 45
Italo-Ethiopian war 50
Italo-Russian agreement at Racconigi 53
Italo-Russian collaboration 45
Italo-Turkish War 56
Italstrade 240
Italy and Turkey
   in 1980s 209–14
   convergence and crisis in
      Mediterranean 203–09
Italy–Pakistan bond of friendship 266
Italy's hegemony in Albania 63
Italy's policy in the Middle East
   Achille Lauro, hijacking 101–2
   anti-US course 96
   Craxi-Andreotti period 99–101
   Declaration of Venice 96–7
   intifada and its consequences 102–3
   origins of 93–4
   soldiers and diplomacy 97–9
   Yom Kippur War 94–6
Izmir, Turkey 59

Jabotinsky, Vladimir 66
Jamaat-e-Islami 269, 279
Jarabub 61
Jefferson, Thomas 11
Jerusalem 13, 29–31
Jibril, Ahmed 157
Jordan 28, 31, 110, 144–5
Jordanian delegation 32
Jubaland 61
Judaea 31

Kafi, Ali 191
Kamel, Lorenzo 36 n.3
Karamanlis, Konstantinos 208
Karmal, Babrak 250
Kashmir 278
Kennan, Geroge F. 20 n.12
Kennedy, John F. 12
Khalde 146
Khaleeli, Mirza 255
Khamenei, Ali 245

Khan, Aga 256–7
Khan, Agha Mohammed Yahya 268
Khan, Ayub 268
Khan, Mohammad Ayub 266
Khan, Nawaz 271
Khan, Yahya 273
Khomeini, Ayatollah Ruhollah 14, 96
Khomeini, Imam 235
Kiderlen-Waechter, Alfred von 56
King Umberto 48
Kissinger, Henry Alfred 10, 12, 19 n.8, 21
   n.20, 126, 230 n.7, 271, 286 n.20
Komer Incident 215 n.3
Konia 58–9
Korean War 266
Kurtzer, Daniel C. 38 n.37
Kuwait 29–30
   Iraqi troops invaded 27
   Iraq's withdrawal 28

Labbate, Silvio 119 n.25, 121 n.44, 231
   n.13, 232 n.32
Labour Party 30
LaFeber, Walter 20 n.7
Lagorio, Lelio 155, 166 n.40
Lahat, Shlomo 35
La Malfa, Ugo 96
Langer, William L. 73 n.7
Laqueur, Walter 181 n.16
Laurens, Franklin D. 85 n.135
Lausanne treaty of 1912 58
Laval-Mussolini agreements 65
Layachi, Azzedine 5
League of Arab States (LAS) 18, 125, 128
League of Nations' coalition 65
Lebanese 'civil' war and Italy 5, 15, 115,
   139, 150 n.1
   first phases 139–44
   Italian military involvement in
      Lebanon 144–9
Lebanese conflict 140
Lebanese crisis 145
Lebanese religious communities 149
Lebanon xiii, 26, 110, 113, 129
   invasion against territorial integrity 140
   Palestinian guerrilla fighters in 141
   peace-keeping multinational force in xiii
   political unity 140
   territorial integrity 140

Lebanon Crisis of 1958 11, 144
Lebedev, Nikolai 23 n.44
Lectura Dantis 110
Ledeen, Michael 155, 165 n.16
Levy, David 31, 38 n.40-1
Levy, W. J. 233 n.59
liberal and pluralist democracy 62-3
Liberal Left in Italy 44, 48
liberation of Palestine 159
Libya xi, 2, 28, 110-11, 113, 142, 195, 219-20
Libyan oil crude 220
linea della fermezza 209-10
liquefied natural gas (LNG) ships 194
Lissi, Giuseppe 105 n.44
L'Italia e la guerra d'Algeria (Bagnato) 192
Locarno treaties of 1925 63
lodo Moro 95
London Declaration of June 1977 132
London Treaty of 1915 xi, xii, 60
Lorenzini, Sara xv n.10

MacDonald, Robert W. 24 n.48
Madrid Conference 25, 26, 30-2
Maghreb 187
Mahan, Alfred Thayer 19 n.5
Malgeri, Francesco 78 n.61, 185 n.91
Mancini, Pasquale Stanislao 46, 48, 75 n.15
Mancini declaration 50
Manifestazioni antiamericane in Turchia 215 n.3
Mansour, Camille 38 n.50
Mare Nostrum 207
Marescotti, Luigi Aldrovandi 82 n.110
Maronite-Phalangist government 147
Martin, John Bartlow 19 n.1
Martin, Kevin W 20 n.13
Martino, Gaetano 266
Marzano, Arturo 4, 39 n.64, 166 n.21
Mascara 192
Mattei, Enrico 170
Mazzanti, Giorgio 236
Mazzini 44
McCloy, John J. 221
Medici, Lorenzo 5, 116 n.2-3, 117 n.4, 117 n.10, 122 n.56
Mediterranean and Middle Eastern politics of Italy 284 n.3
Melchionni, Maria Grazia 83 n.116

Melegari 44
Melen, Ferit 207
Menderes, Adnan 204
Meyer, Klaus 130
Mezzalama, Francesco 244
Micheletta, Luca xiv n4
Middle East 1
  crisis, 1973 2
  Fascist Italy's foreign policy (1940-43) 68-70
  regional identity 2
Middle East and the Cold War 9-10
  Soviet Union 15-18
  United States 11-15
Milano, Rosario 5, 231 n.16
Miller, Rory xv n.18
Milton-Edwards, Beverley 36 n.2
Ministero degli Affari Esteri (MAE) 124
MİSK (Confederation of Turkish Nationalist Workers Unions-Türkiye Milliyetçi İşçi Sendikaları Konfederasyonu) 211
mission ITALAIR 144
Mitterrand, François 17
Molotov-Ribbentrop agreements 67
Montedison 240
Montgomery, Hugh 164
Monticone, Alberto 57
Monzali, Luciano 4-5, 57, 82 n.111, 83 n.119, 84 n.129-30, 90 n.188
Moro, Aldo 93-4, 104 n.7, 109, 111, 116 n.1, 119 n.24, 119 n.24, 123, 126, 205, 209, 210, 224, 275
  assassination 96
  external and internal political strategy 214 n.1
Moro agreement 95
Morocco 110, 113
Moro's pro-Arab policy 125
Morris, Benny 36 n.1
Moscati, Ruggero 84 n.127
Mostaganem 192
Mourlane, Stéphane 198 n.8
Mozambique civil war 195
mujhaiddin 282
Mukti Bahini (Bengali Freedom Fighters) 272
multilateral cooperation 169
multilateralism 3

Multinational Force in Lebanon (MNF) 144
Multinational Force & Observers (MFO) 144
multinational peacekeeping force (MNF) 15
Munich agreements 67
Murphy, Emma 33, 37 n.23
Musallam, Musallam Ali 36 n.14
Muslims 139
Mussolini, Benito xii, 62, 65–8
Mussolini's dictatorship 109
Mussolini's foreign policy (1922–32) 62–4

Najibullah, Mohammed 258
Naples Council of Ministers 242
Napoleon III 46
Nasser, Gamal Abdel 11, 182
'National Concorde' law 192
National Hydrocarbons Authority *see* ENI (Ente Nazionale Idrocarburi, the National Hydrocarbons Authority)
nationalist revolution in Libya xiii
National Palestinian Council 102
national self-determination principle 250
national socialism in Germany 65
NATO Dual-Track Decision *(Euromissiles)* 210
NATO Sovmedron (Soviet Mediterranean Squadron) 155
natural gas 194
naval school of Civitavecchia 66
Nazi Germany 66
Nazih, Hassan 236
neo-Atlantism 93, 103 n.5
neoatlantismo 170
neocolonialism 173
Nerazzini, Cesare 51
'new' Cold War xiii
Nezzar, Khaled 190–1
Nirenstein, Fiamma 166 n.41
Nitti, Francesco Saverio 59–60
Nixon Doctrine of 1969 12, 21 n.18, 125, 175, 220, 269–70
Njølstad, Olav 105 n.40
non-aligned Libya 171
Non-Aligned Movement 266
North Africa 44
North Atlantic Treaty Organization (NATO) 11, 16, 154–5, 173, 213
Novati, Giampaolo Calchi 117 n.9, 246 n.11

Nuova formazione politica 215 n.4
Nuti, Leopoldo 165 n.10, 166 n.25

Occupied Territories 97
oil addiction 2
Oil Crisis, 1973 123–5
oil market 2
oil shock xiii
Olympics 252
Oman 110
OPEC Conference of Algiers 244
OPEC Conference of Caracas 221
OPEC Gulf countries 228
operation *Litani* 141
Oran 192
Organization of the Arab Petroleum Exporting Countries (OAPEC) 125
Orlando, Vittorio Emanuele 59–60
Orthodox in Jerusalem 15–16
Ortoli, François-Xavier 128
Oslo Accords of 1993 15, 33–4
Oslo treaty 4
Ottolenghi, Sandro 166 n.36
Ottoman Empire 43–4, 48
   Christian populations 44
   conflicts within 77 n.48
   in Northern Africa xi, xii
Ottoman-Italian war 55
Ottoman powerlessness 45
Ottoman vilayets of Tripolitania and Cyrenaica 47
Özal, Turgut 214

Pahlavi, Shah Reza 14, 170, 244
Pahlavi dynasty 240
Pakistan and Italy
   1948-70 265–8
   1971–78 268–79
   Cold War in Central Asia (1979–91) 279–83
   consolidation and development 265–8
   Islamic policy 265
Pakistani Bengal 272
Pakistani crisis 270–1
Pakistani foreign policy 285 n.9
Pakistan Peoples' Party (PPP) 268
Palazzo Chigi 159
Palestine 28
Palestinian Academic Society for the Study of International Affairs 32–3

Palestinian Arabs 31
Palestinian guerrilla fighters 144, 145
Palestinian Interim Self-Government Authority 32
Palestinian–Jordanian delegation 32
Palestine Liberation Organization (PLO) 5, 13, 25–7, 35, 95, 129, 144–5, 153, 160
  involvement in peace process 32
  Moscow support to 27
  relationship with Saudi Arabia and Kuwait 29
  to support Iraq 28
  Syrian-PLO tensions in Lebanon 27
Palestinian Movement 139
Palestinian refugees 94, 139–40
Palestinian right to self-determination 140
Palestinian territory 14
Palestinian terrorism xiii
Palmer, Michael A. 231 n.12
pan-Arab nationalist movements 66
pan-Arab security 27
parallel diplomacy 5
Parcham Group 250
Paris Peace conference 59–60
Paris' protectorate xi
Parra, Francisco R. 234 n.75
Partito Popolare Italiano 59
Pastorelli, Pietro xiv n.6, 57
Paterson, Thomas G. 19 n.2
peace agreement in 1979 30
peace camp 30
peace conferences Geneva, 1973 10
peaceful coexistence 169
'Peace in Galilee' operation 98, 144
peace treaty xii, 50
Pella, Giuseppe 285 n.5
Pellizzari, Valerio 217 n.24
Pelloux, Luigi 51
People's Democratic Party of Afghanistan (PDPA) 250
Peres, Shimon 33
Peretz, Don 37 n.28
Pershing II 154
Peteani, Luigi 77 n.47
Petricioli, Marta 77 n.57
Petrignani, Rinaldo 160–1, 166 n.44, 167 n.50, 167 n.66, 257–8
Petrini, Francesco 227, 231 n.27, 233 n.55, 233 n.58, 233 n.66

petrodollars 128
Piedmonts 43
Pierri, Bruno 5
Pijpers, Alfred 134
Pinto 141
Pisa 43
Pizzigallo, Matteo xv n.12, 117 n.9
politica di presenza 2
Political Committee 94
Political Consultations in Venice 131
political-diplomatic relations 115
political stability 2
political terror 3
Polsi, Alessandro 105 n.29, 120 n.36
Pontecorvo, Gillo 193
post-colonialism 180
Prague 62
Prague Spring 203
Presidency of the European Council (PEC) 127
Pribram, Alfred Francis 74 n.13
Prima Repubblica 3
Prinetti, Giulio Nicolò Marchese 51
pro-Arab engagement 4–5
pro-British foreign policy 63
pro Third World approach 169
Prunas, Renato 71
Puglia 195
Pundak, Ron 33
punishing taxation 187

Quaid-e-azim 278–9
Quandt, William B. 38 n.38
Quaroni, Pietro 71, 89 n.179, 169
quarta sponda 169

Rabat 112
Rabin, Yitzhak 30, 32–3, 35
Radio Bari xii
Raffaella, Brunozzi 121 n.48
Rahman, Mujibir 268, 274
Ramaioli, Massimo 105 n.44
Ranzoni, Alvaro 166 n.39
Rapallo agreements 83 n.118
Rapallo treaty 62
Ratz party 30
razzias 187
Reagan administration xiii, 15, 26, 29
realism 179
Rechberg 43

Reagan, Ronald 155, 175
regional credibility 3
regionalism 3–4
regional stability 3
Reich, Bernard 36 n.7
Resolution 242 of the UN Security
    Council 94
Rhodes 60
Riad, Mahmoud 128, 131–2
Riccardi, Luca xv n.16, 4, 91 n.193, 91
    n.195, 104 n.16, 104 n.22, 105 n.24,
    106 n.70, 107 n.72–3, 107 n.79, 117
    n.7, 118 n.22, 119 n.25, 180 n.2
Ricciu, Francesco 216 n.16
Ricciulli, Pasquale 271
Ridgway, Rozanne L. 163
right-wing parties 62
Risorgimento 58
Rivista di Studi Politici Internazionali
    entitled *Il dramma pakistano* 272
Robilant, Carlo di 44
Rome 48, 133
Rome document 198 n.14
Rome General Peace Accords of 1992 195
Rossi, Gianluigi 117 n.5, 181 n.3
Roy, Sara 38 n.58
Rubbi, Antonio 261 n.10
Rudinì's foreign policy 50
Ruggiero, Renato 162
Rumor, Mariano 94, 130
Russia 15, 44
    sequential linkage 30
Russian expansionism 48
Russian Federation 18
Riyadh 128

Sabra and Shatila massacres 146, 156
Sacco, Giuseppe 165 n.15
Sadat, Anwar 12–13
Sadr, Bani 239
Safety Net Agreement 221
Said, Edward 35, 38 n.59, 39 n.67
Saikal, Amin 260 n.3
Sant'Egidio community 5
Saint-Hilaire, Barthélemy 47
Saiu, Liliana 165 n.13
Salafist Group for Preaching and Combat
    (GSPC) 190
Salandra, Antonio xi, 57–8

Salizzoni, Angelo 270
Salvatorelli, Luigi 55
Samaria 31
Sampson, Anthony 231 n.20
sanjak of Novi Pazar 53
Sant'Egidio 195–6
    peace mediation 195–7
Saracco, Giuseppe 51
Saragat, Giuseppe 223
Sarchi, Carlo 236
Sarid, Yossi 30
Sarkis, Jean 146
Sartori, Nicolò 198 n.9
Saudi Arabia 2, 29–30, 110, 113, 128
Savoy kingdom 46
Savoy monarchy 43
Sayigh, Yezid 36 n.13, 37 n.24
Schanzer, Carlo 62
Schiff, Ze'ev 36 n.9, 37 n.32
Schindler, John R. 197 n.1
Schlesinger, James 154
Schmidt, Helmut 154
Schmitt, Bernadotte E. 78 n.58, 78 n.61
Schwartz, Guri 166 n.21
Sechi, Salvatore 104 n.21
Seconda Repubblica 179
Second Cold War 3, 5, 153, 176
Second World War xii, 1, 109
    Italy and Libya after 169
    political instability after 1
self-determination 14
sentimentalism 95
sequential linkage 30
Serra, Enrico 78 n.65
Seven Sisters 170, 221
Sèvres Treaty 61
Seymour, Ian 230 n.9
Sforza, Count Carlo xii, 61, 83 n.116
Shalim, Avi 33
Shamir, Israel 31
Shamir, Yitzhak 27, 31–2, 35
Shatt al-Arab 244
Shell 226–7
Shevardnadze, Eduard 258
Shiite 235
Shiite and Sunnis 149
Shlaim, Avi 29, 37 n.29, 38 n.53, 107 n.81
Shultz, George 159, 175
shuttle diplomacy 12, 127

Sicily 155
Sidi Bel Abbes 192
Sidra Crisis of 1986 15
Sigonella 159
  Hub of the Med 155
Sigonella crisis 115, 160–4
Sikkim 272
Silj, Alessandro 167 n.49
Simla agreement 275
Simons, Geoff 182 n.30
Sinai Agreement 131
Sinai peninsula 98
Six-Day War crisis xiii, 94, 171
Soave, Paolo 5, 217 n.26
Socialist Party 102
social transformation xi
Somaliland xi, xii
Sonnino, Sidney 57, 81 n.96
Sormani, Pietro 218 n.41–2
Souaidia, Habib 197 n.2
South Tyrol xii
Soviet cooperation 4
Soviet–Egyptian Friendship Treaty 17
Soviet intervention in Afghanistan 115
Soviet invasion of Afghanistan 5, 155
Soviet Union 10, 27, 71
Spadolini, Giovanni 77 n.55, 99–100, 155
Spagnulo, Giuseppe 5
Spanish Civil War in 1936 66
Spencer, John H. 89 n.178
Spriano, Paolo 88 n.176
Stanik, Joseph 185 n.82
status of Jerusalem 97
Sant'Egidio Community of Rome 195
Stethem, Robert. D. 157
Stevenson, Adlai E. 9
St. Jean de Maurienne agreements 60
Stop-aid-to-Pakistan Campaign Committee 270
Stork, Joe 229, 233 n.68, 234 n.81
Strait of Hormuz 243–4
strategia della tensione 203
Strategic Defence Initiative (SDI) 210
Sudan 144–5
Suez Canal crisis 9–10, 123
Suez crisis xiii
superpowers' interferences 2
Syria 30–1, 110, 113
  sequential linkage 30

Syrian interference in Lebanese affairs 142
Syrian-PLO tensions in Lebanon 27

Taché, Stefano Gay 156
Taiana, Franco 217 n.21
Tali, Pietro 197
Tamagnini, Giulio 235–6, 239, 242–3
Tana, Fabio 152 n.35
Taraki, Nur Mohammad 250
Tarbala Dam 267, 270
Tareq, Baconi 37 n.27
Tehran 110, 238
Tehran agreement of 1971 5, 219, 225–8
Tel Aviv 35, 110, 132
terrorism 153, 193
  activities 13
  and the global Cold War 175–9
  threat xiv
Testoni, Piero 105 n.36
Thornton, Richard C. 166 n.33, 232 n.46
Tittoni-Venizelos agreement 60
Tonini, Alberto 117 n.9
Tornielli 44
Torretta, Pietro Tomasi Della 62
Toscano, Mario 57, 86 n.145, 88 n.175
Tosi, Luciano 104 n.6, 105 n.39
Trans Adriatic Pipeline (TAP) 194–5
trans-Atlanticism 198 n.7
trans-mediterranean Pipeline
    (Transmed) 195
Treaty of Addis Ababa 50
treaty of alliance 56
Treaty of Berlin 45
treaty of the Triple Alliance 46–7
Treaty of Washington 96
Tremolada, Ilaria 181 n.11, 224, 233 n.69
Trentino xii, 45
Trieste 62
Triple Alliance xi, 48–51, 56, 74 n.13
Triple Alliance Robilant 47
Tripoli regime xiii, 220
Tripolitania 49, 51, 53–5, 169
Truman, Harry S. 11
Tsana Lake region 63
Tucci, Giuseppe 64
Tunisia xi, 28, 50, 110, 113, 144, 171
Turkey 5, 27, 110–11, 195
  history 217 n.2
  and Iran 73

Turkish 44
Turkish-American agreement 208
Turkish crisis 205
Turkish-Cypriot community 212
Turkish-Italian treaty of friendship, 1928 64
Turkish nationalism xii
Turner, Louis 234 n.74

Ugolini, Romano 74 n.13
ul-Haq, Zia 259
UN 'blue helmets' 142
UNESCO 110, 113–14
Ungari, Andrea xiv n.4
UNIFIL (United Nations Interim Force in Lebanon) mission 142, 144
United Kingdom Western alliance 2
United Nations Organization 18, 112–13
United States 26, 30
UN Security Council Resolution
    242 (1967) 12, 21 n.17, 24 n.47, 94, 206
    367 (1975) 205
    425 (1978) 142
    n. 541/1983 212
US bombing of Tripoli 115
US–Italy Cold War 5
US pro-Israeli policy 124
USSR 26
U-Thant 270–1

Valderrama, Fernando 120 n.37
Valiani, Leo 57
Vance, Cyrus 13
Varsori, Antonio xiv n.5, xv n.11, xv n.17, 2, 103 n.2, 104 n.17, 107 n.74, 107 n.82
Varvelli, Arturo xv n.14
velayat-e faqih 237–8
Venice 43
Venice Declaration 132–3, 243
Venice resolution 102
Venn, Fiona 234 n.77
Venosta, Barrère-Visconti 51
Venosta, Emilio Visconti 44, 50, 73 n.6
Veronese, Vittorino 113
Vienna 45, 50
Vigezzi, Brunello 57
Villani, Angela 91 n.191

Visconti, Emilio 44
Viti, Donatella 215 n.5–6, 217 n.28, 218 n.37, 218 n.48–9
von Bülow, Bernhard 80 n.92
Vorontsov, Yulii Michailovič 257

Wall, Bennet H. 234 n.82
war against
    Austria-Hungary xi–xii
    Germany xi–xii
war for Algerian independence 192–3
Warsaw Pact SS-20 154, 274
Webster, Richard xiv n.3
Weizman, Ezer 142
Westad, Odd Arne 36 n.11
West Bank 32, 35
Western alliance xiii
Western European Union (WEU) 270
Whitehead, John C. 163
Wills, David C 166 n.34

Ya'ari, Ehud 36 n.9
Yaqub, Salim 26, 36 n.6
Yavuztürk, Zeki 213
Yemen 28, 110, 142
Yesh Gvul 30
Yom Kippur War xiii, 2–3, 104 n.11, 114, 123, 157, 171
Yorke, Valerie 39 n.65
Yo-Yo Express 12
Yugoslavia 62

Zaccaria, Giuseppe 166 n.22
Zadar/Zara 62
Zagari, Mario 205
Zaghi, Carlo 74 n.14
Zahir, King of Afghanistan 249, 254–9
Zanardelli, Giuseppe 51
Zanardelli-Prinetti government 51
Zanotti, James 182 n.21
Zecchino, Ortensio 74 n.14
Zeroual, Lamine 191, 196
Zia-Ul-Haq, Muhammad 279
Zionist movement in Palestine 66, 86 n.141
Zoppi 90 n.189
Zouk Mikhael 115
Zucker, Dedi 30
Zürcher, Erik 218 n.36, 218 n.38, 218 n.51

www.ingramcontent.com/pod-product-compliance
Lightning Source LLC
Chambersburg PA
CBHW072122290426
44111CB00012B/1742